To the
POINT

To the POINT

Reading and Writing Short Arguments

GILBERT H. MULLER
The City University of New York
LaGuardia

HARVEY S. WIENER
The City University of New York
LaGuardia

PEARSON
Longman

New York   San Francisco   Boston
London   Toronto   Sydney   Tokyo   Singapore   Madrid
Mexico City   Munich   Paris   Cape Town   Hong Kong   Montreal

Vice President and Publisher: Eben W. Ludlow
Marketing Manager: Deborah Murphy
Senior Supplements Editor: Donna Campion
Managing Editor: Valerie Zaborski
Production Manager: Denise Phillip
Project Coordination, Text Design, and Electronic Page Makeup: Shepherd Incorporated
Cover Design Manager: John Callahan
Cover Designer: Kay Petronio
Cover Image: Arrow and Target (digital) by Dean C. Kalmantis. Courtesy of The Stock
     Illustration Source, Inc.
Senior Manufacturing Buyer: Dennis J. Para
Printer and Binder: R.R. Donnelley & Sons, Crawfordsville
Cover Printer: Coral Graphic Services

For permission to use copyrighted material, grateful acknowledgment is made to the
copyright holders on pp. 517–519, which are hereby made part of this copyright page.

Library of Congress Cataloging-in-Publication Data
Muller, Gilbert H., 1941–
     To the point : reading and writing short arguments / Gilbert H. Muller, Harvey S. Wiener.
     p. cm.
     ISBN 0-321-20786-6
     1. English language—Rhetoric—Problems, exercises, etc. 2. Persuasion (Rhetoric)—
Problems, exercises, etc. 3. Report writing—Problems, exercises, etc. 4. College readers.
I. Wiener, Harvey S. II. Title.

PE1431.M845 2004
808'.0427—dc22   2004053446

Please visit our website at http://www.ablongman.com

ISBN 0-321-20786-6

2 3 4 5 6 7 8 9 10—DOC—07 06

Brief Contents

Detailed Contents

2 ▶ Writing Arguments   45

Preface

In our long history of teaching composition courses, we have come to believe that short is good—and that getting to the point in an essay without fluff and with clear propositions and well-supported arguments is a major objective of academic writing. Hence, this composition textbook wears its heart on its sleeve, so to speak, as it makes its main assertion in its title, *To the Point: Reading and Writing Short Arguments.* In it, we aim to provide essential instruction for college students in composition courses. By choosing short readings and providing an extensive apparatus, we offer a multitude of selections that cut a wide swath in major contemporary issues. From cell phones to environmentalism, from human rights to love and marriage, from immigration to terrorism—and these are just a few of the explosive issues we address here—we have gathered essays and other short pieces that cut to the chase and provide invaluable models for writing arguments as well as dynamic issues for class discussion.

We realize that "short" is a matter of opinion: what's short to one reader might be too long to another. Most of our selections are three pages or under, and we have tried to keep the essays generally to fewer than seven pages. Occasionally, because of its powerful argument, historical relevance, or in our opinion, high interest, the essays we have chosen run somewhat longer. (See Nathan Glazer's piece on affirmative action, "In Defense of Preference," pages 207–219.)

FEATURES

To the Point starts with three introductory chapters that present an overview of reading and writing in general and reading and writing arguments in particular. These chapters introduce (to the point, without question) the basic argumentative paradigms—Aristotelian logic, the Toulmin system, syllogisms, deduction, and logical fallacies, for example—as well as the key elements in the writing process and needed to develop a strong argument. We have aimed in these chapters for clarity, accessibility, and contemporary flavor in order to set the tone for the whole textbook and its apparatus. We are passionate about clear instructional language and are certain that we have turned the often-complex explanations of argumentative strategies into unclouded and comprehensible prose. Also, we are keenly aware of the value of visual representations: word charts, columns, boxed information, screen shots, icons, artwork, cartoons, photographs, advertisements, and images of Web pages, for instance. These features are integrated into many sections of the text and provide an important nonverbal dimension to students of argumentation and their teachers.

We highlight critical thinking throughout in our chapter questions and discussions. Chapters 1 and 2 introduce the reading and writing process within the context of learning approaches to argumentation. Chapter 3 provides a natural link to composition instruction that may precede the course in argument, showing the ways in which key rhetorical patterns can help produce clear arguments. Argument readers rarely make this link: we demonstrate how the familiar rhetorical modes—description, narration, comparison and contrast, mixed patterns, and so forth—advance argumentation. Part 1 sets the framework for the chapters of argumentative essays that follow. Again, short prose essays included in Part 1 demonstrate the various strategies that we introduce to readers in later parts of the book.

In Part 2, we offer a series of paired essays (six chapters in all), pro-con takes on contemporary issues such as rap culture, equal rights in college sports, animal rights, immigration, affirmative action, and capital punishment. Although some current argument theory shies away from stark pro-con debates in favor of a "positional" approach, we acknowledge that much of argumentation and persuasion in the public arena, in the media, and not least of all in classrooms and student dorms adheres to the sharp tone inherent in opposing viewpoints.

With Part 3, however, where we offer seven chapters of several short essays each, we develop a more subtle approach, suggesting that argument and persuasion can serve as mediating strategies when individuals debate issues of significant concern. We organize these chapters around key world perspectives. These are not pro-con selections, but multiple views on major concerns facing citizens today—the prospects of the Internet; work, money, and class; and media control, to name just three.

Part 4 presents five longer classic prose arguments by Plato, Swift, Woolf, Carson, and King. This part addresses the needs of instructors who like to challenge students with more demanding material, thereby preparing them for the more extended modes of argumentation that they might encounter in later courses.

Designed to permit a deep and broad examination of an issue of continuing popular interest, Part 5 offers a casebook of varied pieces—including essays, Web sites, and advertisements—on the issue of weight gain and weight control, now so much a part of the American identity. Part 6 shows students how to construct a brief argumentative research paper and provides a model of successful academic research within the reach of today's student.

APPARATUS

In Parts 1 through 3 we have divided our questioning strategies after each selection into four major groups, using a variety of subheads that target specific skills.

PREREADING

Thinking About the Essay in Advance—The reader considers some of the underlying issues, tapping into prior knowledge and concerns reflected in the piece.

Words to Watch—We highlight and define difficult words, once again *before* the student reads the essay, so as to forestall vocabulary issues that might prevent access to the selection.

BUILDING VOCABULARY

After students read the argumentative selection at hand, we provide vocabulary activities that help students expand their linguistic resources and understand words in context.

THINKING CRITICALLY ABOUT THE ARGUMENT

Understanding the Writer's Argument—These questions focus on content issues: Does the student understand the basic elements of the writer's discussion?

Understanding the Writer's Techniques—This category of questions highlights the various rhetorical strategies that define and advance the argument.

Exploring the Writer's Argument—With these questions, readers react to the ideas advanced by the writer. Students consider the terms of the argument within their own worldview.

IDEAS FOR WRITING ARGUMENTS

Prewriting—Following the principles of the writing process that we have laid out in Chapter 2, we engage students in thinking about and planning an essay before actually writing it. This section leads naturally into the next.

Writing a Guided Argument—A key feature of *To the Point: Reading and Writing Short Arguments*, here we steer students through the writing of an argumentative essay inspired by the reading and the rhetorical strategies used by the writer. Students follow a series of suggested steps to produce an appropriate original essay of their own.

Thinking, Arguing, and Writing Collaboratively—Students work in groups to respond to a major issue that the essay addresses.

Writing About the Text—In this group of questions, we ask students to think about and write a brief critique about features in the text itself.

More Writing Ideas—Here we offer further writing activities that include journal entries, single-paragraph responses, letters, and brief essays.

In short (one of our favorite phrases), with approximately 65 brief, thoughtful essays, fresh but significant topics, integrated visuals and Internet resources, and comprehensive questions and writing assignments, *To the Point* presents concisely and clearly the contemporary world of controversy and persuasion for today's students of argumentative writing.

ACKNOWLEDGMENTS

We want to thank Eben Ludlow, vice president at Longman, for his support of *To the Point*. Calm and collected, droll and experienced, he is the perfect guide for any author embarking on a textbook project. To our friend and agent, John Wright, we offer our gratitude once again for his assistance. Our assistant Scott Smith has been invaluable in helping us to design apparatus, while Meg Botteon brought her expertise to the development of the research section. And thanks to Igor Webb for his preparation of the instructor's manual. Several reviewers have been most supportive and helpful: Peggy Jolly, University of Alabama at Birmingham; Kathleen Lay, Indiana State University; Janice Neuleib, Illinois State University; William Rivers, University of South Carolina; and Donnalee Rubin, Salem State College.

Gilbert H. Muller
Harvey S. Wiener

Part One

An Overview:
Critical Thinking
and Argumentation

1 Reading Arguments

Contemporary American culture often seems dominated by argument. Television talk show hosts and radio shock jocks battle over countless issues. Hip-hop artists contrive elaborate "beefs" to get under the skin of their rivals. Politicians are in constant attack mode. Advertisements and commercials seduce us into crazed consumption. Internet chat rooms flame with aggressive language. Deborah Tannen, in *The Argument Culture* (1998), terms this phenomenon the "ethic of aggression." Indeed, the world is awash in what passes for argument, but frequently in its most irritating, insulting, ill-conceived, and illogical forms.

Forget about argument as a quarrel or a beef. Instead, think of argument as *any text—in written, spoken, or visual form—that presents a debatable point of view*. Closely related to argument (and in practice often indistinguishable from it) is *persuasion*, the attempt to get others to act in a way that will advance a cause or position. The kind of argument we deal with in this text involves a carefully reasoned attempt to get people to believe or act according to our own beliefs or points of view. Typically this type of argument requires you to deal with significant issues about which individuals might justifiably disagree. It also requires you to respectfully consider the positions and perspectives of others in an effort to promote civil discourse.

WHY ARGUE?

You argue in order to influence others to think or believe as you do about an idea or issue, or to act as you would act. Stated differently, you argue to *convince* an audience about your point of view or to *persuade* this audience to adopt a desired course of action or behavior. When you read and write arguments, you enter into a dialogue with this audience. This dialogue or conversation is typically dramatic because your point of view must be defended and usually is open to dispute or debate. Admittedly, much argument—and courtroom dramas in real life or on television provide excellent examples—results in winners and losers.

Argumentation, however, is not always about winning and losing. You can argue for other reasons as well. Sometimes you argue *to explore*

3

why you think or act in a certain way. Exploration enables you *to make decisions*: Should you vote for one candidate or another, attend a private or public college, date a certain person, support abortion, oppose the death penalty, believe in God? You engage constantly in these forms of argument, either on your own or with others, in matters both large and small. You develop options and make decisions through a complex process of internal thinking and even meditation. To be able to arrive at a valid conclusion about an issue or course of action is a powerful aspect of argumentation that involves critical thinking and self-discovery.

Even as you use argument to clarify opinions and beliefs, you can employ argument *to form a consensus* with others about ideas that otherwise might divide or polarize individuals. Rather than constantly battling people and groups, you can advance an argument in order to engage others in a conversation that might produce common ground concerning ideas, policies, and programs. With this approach to argument, you seek a win/win outcome. Looked at this way, argument is integral to free speech and open inquiry and is vital to civil society. Honest and truthful argument (which admittedly is difficult to achieve) is essential to the health of democracy and of nations around the world.

Argument, as you will see, is as old as Aristotle and as new as questions on a standardized writing test that you might have taken when applying for college. Valid argument can produce toleration, consensus, and understanding among people holding diverse points of view. It can be subtle and liberating, encouraging you to examine and perhaps even change what you think or believe about critical ideas and issues.

THE VOCABULARY OF ARGUMENT

Before reading or writing arguments, you need to know the basic vocabulary of the argumentative process. Think of the vocabulary of argument as the rules that create the outlines of a special type of game. Just as in any game—whether basketball or chess or poker—the vocabulary of argumentation establishes and governs the playing field. This vocabulary helps you to understand both the uniqueness and the utility of argumentation as a form of discourse.

At the outset, it is important to understand that argument relies on *logic*—on an appeal to reason—more than other kinds of writing. This does not mean that arguments lack emotion. In fact, as you will see later in this chapter, a carefully constructed argument often blends rational, emotional, and ethical elements. Moreover, other forms of writing—narration, description, and varieties of exposition like analysis and definition—often are used to advance arguments, as we illustrate in Chapter 3. Some teachers maintain that all writing, to the extent that it tries to make a point, is inherently argumentative. Nevertheless, the starting point of any effective argument is the application of certain standards of reason—a logical train of thought—to a topic that normally can be debated. Argumentation creates a "court of standards" in which the rules of reason and evidence apply.

Here, then, are some of the critical terms that will help you to read and ultimately write arguments effectively:

1. *Argument* is a process of reasoning that presents reasons or proofs to support a position, belief, or conclusion.

2. A *claim* is the main idea or conclusion in an argument. It is the statement that needs to be justified or proved. A claim is like a *thesis* or main idea that can be debated, argued, or proved.

3. A *proposition* is another term for a claim. The *major proposition* is the main point of the argument. It is what you are trying to prove based on what there is in common in a certain number of acts of knowing, asserting, believing, or doubting. *Minor propositions* are the reasons offered to support the major proposition.

4. *Grounds* are like minor propositions. They are the reasons, support, and evidence offered to support a claim. Grounds are any material that serves to prove a claim.

5. *Evidence* supports the claim and the minor propositions of an argument. Evidence can be facts, statistics, accepted opinions, expert testimony, examples, or personal experience. Valid evidence will be accurate and true.

6. A *fact* is information that can be taken as verifiable. Stated differently, a fact is something believed to have objective reality. Facts differ from *opinions*, which are judgments based on the facts and, if valid, careful reasoning.

7. A *warrant* is the connection, typically assumed and unstated, between a claim and the supporting reasons. It is the rule, belief, or principle underlying the argument, the assumption that makes the claim appear to be acceptable. A *backing* is an even larger principle that serves as the foundation for a warrant.

8. *Deduction* is a process of reasoning that seeks valid conclusions. Deduction establishes that a conclusion must be true because the *premises*, or statements on which it is based, are also true. As a way of reasoning, deduction proceeds from the general to the particular. By contrast, *induction* is a way of reasoning in which a general statement is reached on the basis of specific examples. As such, induction moves from the particular to the general.

9. A *fallacy* is an error of reasoning based on faulty use of evidence or incorrect reasoning from premises or assumptions.

10. *Refutation* is the attempt to rebut, weaken, or invalidate the viewpoints of the opposition.

JUSTIFYING AN ARGUMENT

Argument involves a complex pattern of thought that does not appear in every statement. It is inaccurate to claim that "everything is an argument" because, when thought about carefully, every statement is *not* an argument. You need to determine through a basic *test of justification* whether or not a statement qualifies as an argument.

Imagine what you were thinking about when you woke up this morning. Here are some possibilities:

1. *What a beautiful day—so clear and sunny!*
2. *Did I complete my homework assignment for English composition?*
3. *I'm looking forward to seeing that good-looking classmate in my first-period class.*
4. *I'll wear something light because it is warm outside.*
5. *I need to change my major and get another advisor because I'm not satisfied with either.*

All of these sentences involve varieties of thinking, but not all of them express an argument. Sentence 1 is a simple statement of fact: if indeed the day *is* clear and sunny, who would want to argue with you about its beauty? Sentence 2 is an effort at recall, framed as a question, and generally interrogative and imperative (involving commands or prayers) statements do not express claims or propositions. Sentence 3 suggests a bit of pleasant daydreaming; it does not rise to the level of argumentation. Sentence 4 reflects a mental activity that could qualify as an argument if stated differently, but in this form it simply reflects a decision—not essentially debatable—deriving from an observation. The first four sentences suggest a range of thinking largely devoid of argumentation.

Now read again sentence 5, which contains an argument and therefore passes the test of justification. To begin, you see clearly that there is an "argumentative edge" to this statement. Sentence 5 reflects a traditional approach to argument in which a combative or debatable point of view appears. (Greek theorists called this the "agonistic" theory of argument.) This statement, reflecting dissatisfaction with both a major and an advisor, actually has several argumentative and persuasive purposes embedded in it. Reading this statement critically, you sense that the speaker will have to *explore options, inform, convince,* and *make decisions*—four common goals in the construction of an argument. Sentence 5 reflects a process of reasoning and the implicit need to advance reasons or proofs in order *to justify* how an individual thinks and acts, which form the core of argument.

ARISTOTLE AND THE APPEAL TO REASON

Arguments must be read critically, based in part on your understanding of concepts, methods, and conventions that follow a long tradition starting with Aristotle (384–322 B.C.). According to Aristotle in his *Rhetoric*, the best arguments contain logical, emotional, and ethical appeals. In other words, reason (which classical commentators termed *logos*), emotion (*pathos*), and moral authority (*ethos*) appear in varying degrees in arguments, working together to change opinions and prompt action. When you read argumentative essays, you see that these three appeals can support a point of view, change attitudes, elicit desired responses, and meet various needs. For now, we will focus on logical appeals—the process of reasoning—and the ways they appear when you read texts.

The ancients emphasized that an argument presupposes a topic, what the Greeks called *topos*. The essays you will read in this book contain a central topic that you should be able to identify. Aristotle claimed that every argument contains this statement of a central topic and proof to support it. For example, Martin Luther King Jr.'s famous speech, "I Have a Dream," which appears in Part 4 of this book, takes as its topic the need for an American society reflecting equality for everyone. His speech contains echoes of many classic documents, among them the Declaration of Independence, which also appears in this book. It is useful to examine the key idea—or topic—that is the essence of the classic document written by Thomas Jefferson and his collaborators and that influenced King as he prepared his speech.

> We hold these truths to be self-evident, that all men are created equal:
> that they are endowed by their Creator with certain inalienable rights;
> and that among these rights are life, liberty, and the pursuit of happiness.

You will have the opportunity to read, discuss critically, and respond in writing to the texts by Jefferson and King, but for now it is only necessary to understand that the topic at the center of these texts is controversial and open to challenge. For example, do you believe that everyone is created equal? Do you think that a Creator endows us with inalienable rights? Do you anticipate, as Martin Luther King Jr. does, that some day all God's children will be free at last? Where is the *proof*? The topics you will be reading about in this book require judgment, evaluation, and confirmation. In essence, you have to test the *assumptions*, or underlying beliefs governing certain statements. Your critical response to these essays will benefit from your understanding of the reasoning or logic supporting the assumptions that are made.

A stated assumption is called a *premise*, and premises are the first elements you must uncover when reading an argumentative essay. You probably have heard about syllogistic reasoning, that type of logic in which a major premise, followed by a minor premise, produces a conclusion. This is the method of *deduction*, the process of reasoning where a conclusion is taken to be true because the statements on which it is based are true. The most famous syllogism, of course, is the one using Socrates as an example.

> *Major premise*: All human beings are mortal.
> *Minor premise*: Socrates is a human being.
> *Conclusion*: Therefore, Socrates is mortal.

This example demonstrates that the validity of any syllogism rests on the "truth" of the premises. In other words, if you accept the truth of the major and minor premises, then you must accept the conclusion.

Of course, there can be false and misleading applications of syllogistic reasoning. For the purposes of this book, we need not go into these errors in syllogistic reasoning in depth, but instead we illustrate the problem with two examples. Here is the first:

> *Major premise:* All cats die.
> *Minor premise:* Socrates died.
> *Conclusion:* Socrates was a cat.

Here the premises are true but the conclusion clearly is false, and thus the argument is not valid.

Consider a second, more subtle (some might say devious) example of syllogistic reasoning:

> *Major premise:* Unwantedness leads to high crime.
> *Minor premise:* Abortion leads to less unwantedness.
> *Conclusion:* Abortion leads to less crime.

Two noted scholars—an economist at the University of Chicago and a professor of law at Stanford—have provoked debate by publishing a paper that can be reduced to this syllogism. They maintain that because of *Roe* v. *Wade*, precisely those women—poor, single, black, or teenage—who might have given birth to unwanted children opted for abortions instead. Thus, the unwanted children who would have committed crimes were never born, and consequently overall crime has declined in the United States. Do you think that the two premises are true? If so, then you must accept the conclusion. If not, you can reject the conclusion because it does not follow from the premises.

The two contemporary professors who base their paper on the relationship between abortion and crime used deduction—what Aristotle termed *artistic appeal*—to construct their argument. In practice, however, as Aristotle asserts, few individuals rigorously apply "artistic" or deductive reasoning to the development of their compositions. More often than not, they use what Aristotle labeled *inartistic appeals*—varieties of *inductive* logic where evidence (in the form of facts, statistics, reports, testimonies, interviews, and other evidentiary modes) support a claim or proposition. When inductive thinking appears in an argumentative essay, the writer gathers and applies evidence in order to make *empirical* (based on observation and experiment) claims. Inductive thinking appears most rigorously in scientific and technical reports, where claims require unassailable evidence or, in Aristotle's words, where statements require proof. But inductive logic is also at the heart of most personal, expository, and argumentative writing. In fact, most of the writing you do in response to the essays in this book will require you to martial evidence to support the propositions or claims that you establish.

You can best appreciate the importance of inductive logic by considering Aristotle's observation that every argument can be reduced to two basic parts: **Statement + Proof**. To use contemporary terms, we would say that an argument requires a claim that is supported by evidence. If you become familiar with this approach to argumentation, you will find it much easier to read and write arguments with a critical eye. Remember that any debatable thesis, claim, or proposition (to get you comfortable with these interchangeable terms) requires evidence to back it up. The varieties of evidence will be considered later in this chapter. For now, examine the way in which evidence supports the claim in the following paragraph by Marian Wright Edelman, a noted attorney, activist, and founding president of the Children's Defense Fund:

> The legacies that parents and church and teachers left to my generation of Black children were priceless and not material: a living faith reflected in daily service, the discipline of hard work and stick-to-it-ness, and a capacity to struggle in the face of adversity. Giving up and "burnout" were not part of the language of my elders—you got up every morning and you did what you had to do and you got up every time you fell down and tried as many times as you had to get it done right. They had grit. They valued family life, family rituals, and tried to be and to expose us to good role models. Role models were of two kinds: those who achieved in the outside world (like Marian Anderson, my namesake) and those who didn't have a whole lot of education or fancy clothes but who taught us by the special grace of their lives the message of Christ and Tolstoy and Gandhi and Heschel and Dorothy Day and Romero and King that the Kingdom of God was within—in what you are, not what you have. I still hope I can be half as good as Black church and community elders like Miz Lucy McQueen, Miz Tee Kelly, and Miz Kate Winston, extraordinary women who were kind and patient and loving with children and others and who, when I went to Spellman College, sent me shoeboxes with chicken and biscuits and greasy dollar bills.
>
> —*The Measure of Our Success: A Letter to My Children and Yours*

Edelman shapes her message (which is another way to say that she presents a claim or proposition) around evidence drawn from personal experience. She supports her claim—that she grew up in a community where children were valued and where beliefs were transmitted from one generation to the next—with references to numerous role models that molded her values and beliefs. Here we have clear "proof" of the validity of the basic Aristotelian equation: **Argument = Statement + Proof**. Essays based on personal experience offer real intellectual pleasure as well as an accessible way of understanding the arguments they can frame. When you examine the paragraph by Edelman, for example, you see that it is not about "winning" but rather about the strengths of individuals and communities, as well as Edelman's desire to enter into a dialogue with you—the reader—about her complex but nurturing world.

EMOTIONAL AND ETHICAL APPEALS

An argumentative essay has to be rational, reflecting a process of logical thinking. When reading an argumentative essay for its logical or rational appeal, we have to ask these questions:

- *Is the claim or proposition presented in a logical way?*
- *Is the claim presented accurately and fairly?*
- *What reasons or minor propositions support the claim?*
- *What evidence supports the minor proposition?*
- *Is the entire argument logically convincing?*

However, we do not read arguments purely for their logical content. The rational basis of an argument typically contains other essential qualities, appealing also to emotion and ethics. Remember that the best arguments, as Aristotle maintained, contain these emotional and ethical appeals.

Many issues—race and ethnicity, sexuality and gender, crime and punishment, to name just three—are complex, emotional, and touch on personal sensitivities. Consequently, it is not surprising that writers would approach such topics not from a strictly logical perspective but also from perspectives touching on emotion and ethics. For example, topics relating to race—as you saw in the paragraph by Marian Wright Edelman—provoke complex meanings, emotions, and beliefs. Reread Edelman's paragraph to see how emotional and ethical appeals support her argument. Use the following questions, which can be applied to all essays you read, to determine the nature of her emotional appeal.

- Does the writer appeal to basic human emotions such as love, caring, sympathy, rejection, pity, fear?
- Does the writer appeal to the basic senses of sight, smell, hearing, taste, and touch?
- Does the writer appeal to essential physical needs or desires?

- Does the writer appeal to such "higher" emotions or universal truths as patriotism, loyalty, belief in various gods, freedom, and democracy?

Although using claims and evidence to arrive at certain truths is the primary goal of argumentative writing, the appeal to emotion is complementary and perhaps even more powerful than logic in its effect on an audience. Logicians often warn us against the use of emotion in argument, and in fact certain false emotional appeals will be considered in the next chapter. Nevertheless, emotional appeals—especially when they involve the use of humor, satire, and irony—can work effectively in the effort to persuade a reader to accept the writer's point of view.

Consider the emotional impact of these representative paragraphs from an essay titled "Women Are Just Better" by the columnist Anna Quindlen:

> The inherent superiority of women came to mind just the other day when I was reading about sanitation workers. New York City has finally hired women to pick up the garbage, which makes sense to me, since, as I discovered, a good bit of being a woman consists of picking up garbage. There was a story about the hiring of these female sanitation workers, and I was struck by the fact that I could have written that story without ever leaving my living room—a reflection not on the quality of the reporting but the predictability of the male sanitation worker's response. . . .
>
> As a woman who has done dishes, yard work, and tossed a fair number of Hefty bags, I was peeved—more so because I would fight for the right of any laid-off sanitation man to work, for example, at the gift-wrap counter at Macy's, even though any woman knows that men are hormonally incapable of wrapping packages and tying bows.

The emotional *tone* (the writer's attitude toward the topic, self, and audience) of these two paragraphs is evident. The writer, a woman, is angry, provocative, and downright savage in her humor. But the emotional edge is part of the writer's effort to persuade. Of course, her emotional tone might provoke readers—especially those men who know how to wrap packages and tie bows, and even those who don't but believe that those skills have nothing to do with superiority of gender. Nevertheless, Quindlen does have a point or claim that is suggested by the very title of the essay, and she attempts to stir the reader's feelings as well as opinions through the evocation of emotion. Here, emotion sustains what the writer presents as a debatable proposition: that women are better than men.

Another paragraph, this time by Lorenzo Albacete, a Roman Catholic priest and theologian writing in "The Struggle with Celibacy," raises the role of ethical appeals when considering the overall effectiveness of an argument.

> In the future, the church may decide that particular pastoral situations require a change in the requirement of priestly celibacy. Still, I believe

that even if priests marry, they are called to be witnesses of that "celibacy of the heart" that human love requires—namely, the absolute respect for the loved one's freedom. It's time for those of us who treasure priestly celibacy to live in accordance with its intended message or else give it up as an obstacle to what we wish to say.

This paragraph shows the quality of *ethos* that Aristotle mentioned—the presence of the writer offering himself to the reader or audience as an ethical authority worthy of trust and acceptance. Good sense, goodwill, high moral character—these are the three qualities of the writer discussed by Aristotle and the ancients that make the rhetorical situation of any argument complete. Alcabete *claims authority* about his subject based on his personal knowledge and experience of the subject, as well as his background, position, and reputation as a scholar. You thus have to pay attention to this writer, even as his bold and provocative argument in the essay—that celibacy should not be a casualty of the recent scandals involving the priesthood—might raise objections or rebuttals. In fact, when a topic is controversial, readers might understandably be skeptical about the writer's claim to authority. Nevertheless, the sort of thoughtfulness and candor shown in Alcabete's remarks is an excellent way to establish *ethos*, which involves a willingness by the audience to trust the writer's viewpoint. When you read the entire essay in Chapter 3, you will see that Alcabete also adds logical and emotional appeals to his ethical stance.

When considering the impact of ethical appeal in an argumentative essay, pose the following questions:

- What is the tone or *voice* of the writer, and does this tone enhance the logic of the argument?
- What is the writer's training or expertise, and how does this knowledge establish credibility?
- Does the writer have the goodwill of the audience in mind? Why or why not?
- Does the writer have a strong sense of right and wrong in approaching the subject? How strong is this moral sense?
- Does the writer seem honest and trustworthy? How are these qualities revealed?

Building credibility—creating a relationship of trust—is essential to good argument. A writer speaks to readers in many voices, and it is up to you as an active reader to determine if the voice selected is appropriate for the argument the writer presents.

TOULMIN ARGUMENTS

A currently popular way of reading arguments derives from the ideas of British philosopher Steven Toulmin, who in *The Uses of Argument* (1958) offers a method that updates the argumentative systems of the ancients.

According to Toulmin and teachers of writing who have modified his ideas, you do not read or write argumentative essays that follow the demands of formal logic. Instead, writers compose arguments according to the ways they actually think carefully and critically through an issue or debate. As such, Toulmin offers an easy way to understand the dynamics of argumentative and persuasive prose.

Toulmin asserts that all arguments begin with a *claim*—a word that you already are familiar with. Claims, you will recall, are statements of belief or truth that involve positions that others might find controversial or debatable. In other words, a writer's audience must perceive that a statement is open to controversy. There is no sense in arguing that it is not a beautiful day if indeed the sun is out, the temperature is perfect, and the sky is clear. No one would declare that this statement about the weather conditions is ripe for argument.

An essay that contains a claim tends to address readers by taking a stand or arguing a case. Here are some statements that clearly contain claims:

> *The September 11, 2001, terrorist attacks could have been prevented.*
>
> *The SATs should be abolished.*
>
> *There is no such thing as global warming.*
>
> *Eminem is the greatest rap artist today.*

These are debatable points. In themselves, however, they prove nothing. They assuredly do not prove a case. According to Toulmin, a claim is just the first logical and necessary step in a process of reasoning designed to make or prove a case.

Any claim needs *reasons* to support it. Again, you already have learned about the need for reasons drawn from personal experience, facts, authorities, and other sources to create the framework for an argument. Writers often provide readers with *arguments in brief*—a claim appearing early in an essay, perhaps in an introductory or concluding paragraph, and followed by a few reasons. Aristotle called these compressed arguments *enthymemes*. Here is an enthymeme drawn from one of the previous examples:

> The SATs should be abolished because they place undue emphasis on certain learning styles, create false impressions of a student's real talents and abilities, and are culturally biased.

Here you see how both the terms and the framework for an argument develop from the enthymeme. Toulmin, however, would say that these reasons are assumptions that need to be tested and supported further. The need for *connections* between the claim and the reasons takes us to the next step in Toulmin argument.

Toulmin calls the connection between the claim and the supporting reasons in an argument the *warrant*. (This word appears in the "Vocabulary of Argument" section presented earlier in this chapter, but it requires further explanation.) Often unstated or implied, a warrant establishes the authority underlying a particular claim and its supporting reasons. If the warrant is sound, the evidence assembled to support the claim appears to be justified. On the other hand, if the warrant itself can be challenged or is debatable, then you would expect the writer to defend it.

Based on Toulmin's method, we can diagram the connections among claim, reason(s), and warrant.

This diagram suggests that a warrant is the glue that holds a claim and the reasons supporting the claim together. It is the general principle or underlying assumption that makes the claim plausible or fundamentally acceptable.

Look now at a simple application of the Toulmin diagram to a common situation.

Don't go swimming—there is a strong undertow.

The reason ("there is a strong undertow") is connected to the claim ("Don't go swimming") by the following warrant:

If there is a strong undertow, it is dangerous to go swimming.

Do you see how the warrant is the principle underlying the entire statement consisting of the claim and the reason? Although we could state it in different ways, the warrant for this statement is obvious: you do not want to go swimming in dangerous waters. Diagrammed, the example would look like this:

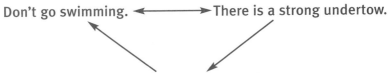

A warrant implying we should avoid a specific dangerous—indeed, life-threatening—situation when deciding whether or not to swim is commonsensical. Such a plausible warrant makes the claim and reason supporting it seem reasonable.

The Use of Evidence

Claims, warrants, and reasons are the framework of a Toulmin argument, or any argument for that matter, but *evidence* is what makes the case. Evidence—various items of information that support a claim as well as the reasons supporting a claim—is what you look for in any pattern of argument. Toulmin reduces this need for evidence to a question: "What have you got to go on?" Only evidence, carefully selected and clearly presented, permits a writer to present an argument fully and convincingly. If the evidence in an argument is too sparse, it will not convince an audience. If it is too flimsy—based on mere opinion, hearsay, or colorful comparisons or analogies—it will not support an otherwise valid claim or generalization.

You already know that evidence can consist of facts and examples, specific cases and events, statistics and other forms of data, expert opinion, and, if used judiciously and in a representative rather than idiosyncratic way, personal experience. Evidence also can derive from scientific observation, field research, and controlled experimentation—forms of evidence common to technical writing and often appearing in tables, graphs, and other visual documents. In all instances, the most distinctive feature of evidence is that it supports a relevant generalization.

An example from an essay by Ronald Takaki, "The Harmful Myth of Asian Superiority," which appears in Chapter 3 of this book, illustrates the way in which evidence provides a degree of authority for any proposition or generalization:

> The "model minority" image homogenizes Asian Americans and hides their differences. For example, while thousands of Vietnamese American young people attend universities, others are on the streets. They live in motels and hang out in pool halls in places like East Los Angeles; some join gangs.
>
> Twenty-five percent of the people in New York City's Chinatown lived below the poverty level in 1980, compared with 17 percent of the city's population. Some 60 percent of the workers in the Chinatowns of Los Angeles and San Francisco are crowded into low-paying jobs in garment factories and restaurants.
>
> "Most immigrants coming into Chinatown with a language barrier cannot go outside the confined area into the mainstream of American industry," a Chinese immigrant said. "Before, I was a painter in Hong Kong, but I can't do it here. I got no license, no education. I want a living; so it's dishwasher, janitor, or cook."

Takaki, who is an authority on ethnicity in American life, makes his case by fleshing out the claim or generalization that appears in the first sentence with examples, statistics, and interviews. Evidence supports his claim.

The chain of argument is never complete without authoritative and compelling evidence. When you read an essay, ask the following questions about the nature of the evidence that a writer presents:

- Are the examples relevant and convincing? Are they sufficient to make the case?
- Is the evidence presented clearly?
- Is the evidence used to support a warrant (we call such evidence *backing*), a claim, or minor propositions, and in each case is it sufficient?
- If statistics appear, are they relevant, accurate, current, complete, and from a reliable source?
- If the writer offers quotations or expert testimony, is it from a knowledgeable, trustworthy, and authoritative source?

Not all evidence is of the same quality or validity. When reading an argumentative essay, you have to be prepared to think critically about the evidence and even enter into a conversation with the writer in which you ask if the factual information is convincing.

READING VISUAL ARGUMENTS

Visual images are as old as the cave paintings of your Neolithic ancestors and as new as the latest streaming advertisements on your computer screen. In fact, some commentators argue that we are in the process of moving from a print-oriented society toward new forms of literacy in which visual images predominate over written texts. It is probably more useful to appreciate the ways in which visual materials—photographs, cartoons, posters, computer graphics, tables and graphs, various forms of type and other design elements, and more—contribute to written texts. If, as Marshall McLuhan declared more than forty years ago, "the medium is the message," then you should pay attention to the ways in which visual texts mold your response to ideas, information, and arguments.

Visual texts can convey powerful cultural messages and arguments. Figure 1.1 shows firefighters at the site of the World Trade Center erecting an American flag over the rubble that was once the Twin Towers. How do you "read" this photograph? What does the symbolism of the heap of twisted metal and of the flag convey? In what way does a similar image (see Figure 1.2) of soldiers raising the American flag at Iwo Jima during World War II deepen your interpretation of the message? A photograph is a representation of reality, and here we sense that the photographer has framed a scene in order to convey both the horror of the attack against the heart of America and the heroic resilience of its citizens to respond.

When reading and interpreting visual texts that contain explicit or implicit arguments, you have to be aware of the ways in which the creators or designers "massage" their message in order to influence (and sometimes control) your response. When, for instance, you see a

Figure 1.1   Firefighters at the World Trade Center.

30-second television commercial for a particular brand of beer in which attractive young people are having a great time, you readily sense the massage and the message. When the blurred, decidedly unappealing image of a political candidate appears in a negative campaign ad, you also know the creators' purpose. Or when great graphics pop up on your screen extolling the virtues of a new snowboard, you know you have been targeted. (How did they know you were a boarder?)

Of course, not all visual arguments sell a product or a person. Ideas—as you see in the photographs from Iwo Jima and the Twin Towers—also can be presented; or complex data can be made manageable while advancing a writer's technical or scientific argument. Again, you might use a Power Point presentation to highlight the outlines of a speech you have to give to the class advocating free downloading of music on the Internet. In all of these cases, you see that visual texts present a dialogue or conversation, a struggle of sorts, for your time, money, allegiance, attention, or action.

Figure 1.2   Iwo Jima.

Visual literacy involves an ability to analyze simple and complex images in terms of their design and content. Here are the key questions that
you should consider when attempting to decipher a visual argument:

- What specific images or details draw your attention immediately?
  What sorts of design elements (print, media, photographs, video
  clips, etc.) come into play? How are color and light used? If there
  is printed text, what does the visual contribute to it?
- What is the argumentative purpose of the visual? What is the
  claim or message? What is its intended effect? Do you respond
  positively or negatively to the visual, and why?
- What is the overall design of the visual? From what perspective
  (for example, left to right, top to bottom, foreground to background) do various elements appear? What emphases and relationships do you see among these details? What is the effect of
  this design on the argumentative message?
- Who is the audience for this visual, and what cultural assumptions
  about this audience's values does it suggest?
- What is the nature of the evidence presented in the visual, and
  how can it be verified?

As with written arguments, you should take nothing for granted when
considering visual texts containing arguments, especially when they promote products, personalities, and ideas. When examining visual texts,
think critically about their validity and whether or not they are grounded
in sound logical, emotional, and ethical appeals.

In the final analysis, reading argumentative texts cannot be reduced to any single system, whether it is Aristotelian, Toulmin, or any other. But you know a good argument when you see that claims are clear, support is good, and evidence is solid. (A sound argumentative essay also typically deals with the opposition and anticipates the possible objections of readers—what Toulmin calls "the conditions of rebuttal.") As you read the five essays appearing next in this chapter, begin to develop a critical perspective on the terms and conditions of argumentation and the various rhetorical and stylistic strategies writers use to bring you around to their point of view.

READING AND WRITING ABOUT FIVE CURRENT ISSUES

BARBARA EHRENREICH
From Stone Age to Phone Age

Biologist Barbara Ehrenreich (she got her Ph.D. from Rockefeller University in 1968) became involved in political activism during the Vietnam War and began writing on topics such as feminism, class in America, and health care. Her books include The American Health Empire: Power, Profits, and Politics *(1970) and* The Hearts of Men: American Dreams and the Flight from Commitment *(1983). She has written for the* Progressive, In These Times, *the* Nation, Time, *and many other magazines. Her book* Nickel and Dimed: On (Not) Getting by in America *(2001), recounting her experience working in low-class jobs, was a best-seller. In this selection, which appeared in 1999, Ehrenreich takes a whimsical look at the ubiquitous phenomenon of cell phones.*

▶ Prereading: Thinking About the Essay in Advance

If you use a cell phone, how is it useful? Why did you want one in the first place? Could you live without it? Why or why not? If you don't own a cell phone, do you want one? Explain.

▶ Words to Watch

primal (par. 1) old, instinctive
savanna (par. 2) area of tropical grasslands
hordes (par. 3) large groups
eons (par. 4) millions of years
convivial (par. 12) friendly, social
atomized (par. 12) broken up into small units

I was struck by the primal force of my craving for a cell phone. Obvi- 1
ously, others must have felt this, too, since there are now an estimated 100 million people worldwide running around and talking into

the air, with only a small black object nestling against one ear to distinguish them from the deinstitutionalized psychotics. It had become impossible to go anywhere—out on the street, to a shopping mall, or to an airport—without noticing that every other person in earshot was engaged in a vast and urgent ongoing conversation which excluded only myself.

2   For a stylish explanation of primal urges and even ordinary whims, we turn to evolutionary psychology, which claims that we do what we do because our apelike ancestors once did the same thing. It doesn't matter that our ape-like ancestors did not possess cell phones; they no doubt had cell-phone-related urges. Like most of our primate cousins, humans are social animals. Paleo-anthropologists think we got this way when we left the safety of the forests for the wide open savanna, where we had to band together for defense against a slew of nasty predators. Hence, we are hardwired for wireless telecommunications, or at least for the need to be verbally connected to others of our kind—in case a leopard is lurking nearby. The explosion of cell phone use is simply a reflection of the genetically scripted human inclination to huddle in groups.

3   There is another interpretation of the evolutionary psychology of cell phones, according to which the cell phone users are seeking not fellowship but isolation from the hordes of fellow humans around them. To a non-cell-phone user, the cell phoners marching through supermarkets and malls project an aura of total inaccessibility. Maybe they are really having meaningful and satisfying conversations. And maybe they are simply trying to repel the advances of any phone-less fellow humans who happen to be physically present.

4   In their 1992 book, *The Social Cage: Human Nature and the Evolution of Society* (Stanford University Press), Alexandra Maryanski and Jonathan H. Turner argue that for eons before our ancestors were forced to band together in the savanna, they lived contented solitary lives in the trees, much like orangutans today. Our arboreal ancestors were probably pleased to run into others of their own kind only at mating time; otherwise, they regarded each other as competitors for the nicest berries and comfiest nesting spots. If these orangutan-type pre-humans had cell phones, they would have used them to signal each other: "Bug off. Can't you see I have an important call right now?"

5   Yet another evolutionary-psychological factor probably contributed to cell phone mania. Since the advent of agriculture about 10,000 years ago, and possibly well before then, humans have lived in hierarchical societies where we have been eager to signal our status with accessories such as feather-tufted spears and shrunken-head pendants.

6   Cell phones serve much the same function, and will continue to do so until they become as common as Walkmen. Thus, the point is not to communicate with distant kin and colleagues, but with all the anonymous others who are around at the moment.

If you doubt this, consider when you last heard someone say into a   7
cell phone: "Yes, I am a worthless turd, and if I screw up again, please
hasten to fire me." What the person is saying, instead, is invariably, "God
damn it, Craig, I told you we need that order by Thursday and no later,"
or something very similar. It was the opportunity to speak command-
ingly in public places that tempted me, for several years, to find a fake
cell phone designed for playpen use so that I, too, could stride along the
sidewalk barking at imaginary brokers and underlings.

As soon as I got my own cell phone, I was disappointed to find   8
that, although we may have evolved to be psychologically cell-phone-
dependent, our anatomy is still stuck in the era when technology con-
sisted of a sharpened stone.

For one thing, our fingertips are too fat for the keypad, so that it takes   9
several tries to dial even "911" with any degree of accuracy.

Then there's the tiny size of the phones themselves—more appropri-   10
ate to a lemur or some other remote primate ancestor than to full-grown
Homo sapiens. My own phone's total length is about four-and-a-half
inches, so that if I wish to speak and listen at the same time, I have to reduce the distance between mouth and ear by screwing my mouth way
over into my right cheek, as if suffering an attack of extreme insecurity.
The only hope is that the process of natural selection will soon lead to humans with antenna-like fingers and mouths situated at temple level.

Another problem is that my relationships with other humans have   11
not yet evolved to the point that would be truly helpful in the cell phone
era. I have the usual quota of friends, relatives, and so-called business associates, but none of them is so underemployed that I can call and ask:
"Hey there, you got a few minutes to walk me over to the bank so that I
don't look like I, uh, don't have anyone to talk to?" Sometimes there is no
alternative but to dial up 1-900-WEATHER and pretend to converse with
it, and I suspect that many other cell phone users are doing the same.

So here's what I conclude about the evolutionary psychology of cell   12
phones: We are social animals, no question about it, better suited to traveling in convivial bands, hooting and chattering, than to wandering alone
in crowds. But few such convivial bands exist within our famously atomized and individualistic capitalist society, where most human relationships now take the sinister form of "deals." So we have regressed to a
modified orangutan state: Despairing of true sociality, we settle for faking
it. The satisfaction, such as it is, lies in making our equally lonely fellow
humans feel jealous.

I do have one new friend, though. Everywhere I go now, it comes   13
along, tucked neatly in my pocket or purse. At night I plug it into the wall
to recharge, and hear its happy little beep as the nurturing current flows
in. Sometimes I take it out during the day, play with its keypad, and con-
fide into its mouthpiece for a moment. Pathetic? Perhaps, but it's not easy
striding out into that savanna alone.

▶ Building Vocabulary

Define the following terms from the professional vocabulary of the social sciences:

1. psychotics (par. 1)
2. evolutionary psychology (par. 2)
3. primate cousins (par. 2)
4. paleo-anthropologists (par. 2)
5. hierarchical societies (par. 5)
6. Homo sapiens (par. 10)
7. natural selection (par. 10)
8. capitalist (par. 12)

▶ Thinking Critically About the Argument

Understanding the Writer's Argument

1. What does the writer mean by the "primal force" of her "craving for a cell phone"? (par. 1)
2. What scientific discipline does the writer use to explain her urge for a cell phone? Why does she choose that discipline?
3. What is the paleo-anthropologists' explanation for why humans are "social animals"?
4. What are two other interpretations, from the world of evolutionary psychology, for why people like to talk on cell phones?
5. Why, according to the writer, would people pretend to be on a cell phone?

Understanding the Writer's Techniques

1. Why does the writer admit at the start of her essay that she craved a cell phone? What argumentative purpose does that serve?
2. What are Ehrenreich's implied warrant or warrants in this essay?
3. How does she move from discussing herself and her personal relation to cell phones to discussing humanity as a whole? Why does she do this?
4. Where is the writer's central claim? Write the sentence that best expresses it.
5. Ehrenreich offers several variations on the theme of her claim. List those variations and paraphrase each one.
6. What is the writer's tone? How do you know? Use quotes from the essay to demonstrate your answer.
7. How does the writer's argument change after she says, in paragraph 8, that she got her own cell phone?
8. Near the end of her essay, the writer attempts to reconcile the variations on the theme of her claim and make one central argument. What is that argument, and is her closing effective?

Exploring the Writer's Argument

1. There are two types of arguments here: serious attempts at a critique of cell phone use and flip, jokey attempts at humor. Give an example of each, and analyze the writer's use of humor.
2. After answering question 1, discuss whether you think the jokey quality of the essay is effective or not, and explain your answer.
3. One of the points is that cell phones are status symbols. Explain why you think that is either true or not true.

▶ Ideas for Writing Arguments

Prewriting

Jot down recollections of incidents when you have seen and heard someone talk on a cell phone in an inappropriate place or in an inappropriate way.

Writing a Guided Argument

Write an essay in which you argue that there are some places where cell phones should not be allowed. Before writing, make sure that you build evidence, coming up with good examples to back up your minor propositions.

1. Begin by establishing rapport with the reader by making it clear that you too use a cell phone or that you are not against cell phones as a rule.
2. Explain the fact that people can often be rude.
3. Make your claim in a clear, declarative sentence.
4. Offer several examples for cell-phone-free zones, using examples to back up your claims.
5. Anticipate one objection for each of your points.
6. It is important to conclude with a statement of solidarity with cell phone users, except for the rude ones.

Thinking, Arguing, and Writing Collaboratively

Form into groups of three or four. In these groups, discuss modern technological devices other than cell phones that are used widely or becoming increasingly popular. Each group should choose one device and apply Ehrenreich's method to that device. Come up with at least two or three explanations based in paleo-anthropology. Then each student should write a paragraph on the topic chosen by the group. Exchange paragraphs and peer-critique them.

Writing About the Text

Ehrenreich published this article in 1999, when cell phones were just starting to become popular. Cell phones are much more common now. How is Ehrenreich's essay out of date? How could you update it and still keep her central claim? Is it possible to write an essay such as this without the risk of being out of date several years later? Write an essay responding to one or more of these questions.

More Writing Ideas

1. Many states are passing laws that ban drivers from talking on hand-held cell phones. Many drivers disagree with these laws. In your journal, come up with reasons for both sides of the argument.
2. Write a paragraph or two about the benefits cell phones have brought to humankind.
3. Find a magazine ad for cell phone service or for a kind of cell phone with special features and analyze the images and text in the advertisement. Write an essay comparing the promises the ad makes to the consumer—both stated and implied—with the realities of owning and using a cell phone.

WOODY HOCHSWENDER
Did My Car Join Al Qaeda?

A former reporter and fashion columnist for The New York Times, *Woody Hochswender has also edited for* Esquire *magazine. He is the coauthor of* The Buddha in Your Mirror, *a book that attempts to apply the lessons of Buddhism to everyday life. In this selection Hochswender, who lives in Connecticut, defends his use of the small truck known as the SUV, or sport utility vehicle.*

▶ Prereading: Thinking About the Essay in Advance

The SUV famously gets very low gas mileage, and thus conservationists accuse drivers of SUVs of being wasteful. What do you think about drivers of SUVs? If a friend or someone in your family has an SUV, do you agree with the purchase? Why or why not?

▶ Words to Watch

petrodollars (par. 2) money from oil and gasoline
transmigrate (par. 2) move
implicate (par. 3) accuse of guilt
insidious (par. 4) sinister, dangerous

propensity (par. 6) tendency
harrowing (par. 6) terrifying
voracious (par. 8) hungry

I drive a large, four-wheel-drive vehicle. Does that mean I'm a bad 1
person?

You might think so, from all the sturm und drang we've heard lately 2
from the Virtuous Ones who insist that America's fuel consumption—
indeed, our very style of life—is somehow responsible for the enmity toward us in the Middle East, not to mention the rest of the world. A series
of TV commercials put together by the columnist Arianna Huffington and
Lawrence Bender, the Hollywood producer behind "Pulp Fiction," have
even linked S.U.V.'s with Mideast terrorism. The idea is that the petrodollars transmigrate from the Gas 'n' Go to the oil sheiks to the hands of ma-
niacs wielding AK-47's.

Leaving aside for the moment that this is trendy, illogical thinking— 3
and leaving aside also the odd sensation of being lectured on socially responsible behavior by the producer of "Pulp Fiction"—isn't this really a
backdoor way of blaming America for Sept. 11 and other crimes like it?
Those who implicate Americans—particularly our adventurous habits,
offbeat choices and breathtaking freedoms, including the freedom to
drive to a poetry reading followed by dinner at a French restaurant in the
midst of a raging snowstorm—validate the terrorists as essentially right.

Where I live, about 100 miles north of New York City, at least half of 4
all the vehicles you see on the road are S.U.V.'s or other light trucks. They
make a great deal of sense. This is not just because we have plenty of long
steep driveways and miles and miles of dirt roads. We also have had
more than 70 inches of snow this winter. When the sun goes down and
the melted snow re-freezes, the roads are covered with insidious stretches
of black ice.

Four-wheel-drive vehicles allow workers to get to and from their 5
jobs, and parents to transport their children safely to school, sporting
events, ballet classes and the rest. Yes, there is something vaguely obscene
about driving solo to the supermarket in Beverly Hills to pick up a carton
of milk in your two-ton Navigator. But not so much in Portland or Green
Bay or Chicago.

The well-publicized notion that S.U.V.'s are actually unsafe, based 6
on their propensity to roll over, does not take into account personal
responsibility. Rollover accidents tend to be something the driver has a
substantial degree of control over. I choose not to whip around corners or
to follow others so closely and at such high speeds that I have to make
harrowing emergency stops. I drive so as not to roll over.

However, if some drunken driver veers across the center divider—a 7
situation I have no control over—I would prefer that my 9-year-old and I

not be inside a Corolla. From the standpoint of a reasoned individualism, S.U.V.'s are safer in many situations than cars. I think a lot of intelligent people realize that.

8   Of course, S.U.V.'s use a lot of gas. This goes for my wife's all-wheel-drive Volvo as well as for my voracious mistress, my 1989 GMC. But a car's miles-per-gallon rating is only one measure of fuel efficiency. Miles driven is another. People who drive light trucks quickly learn not to drive around aimlessly. We tend to combine trips and to keep engines finely tuned and tires properly inflated. It all comes down to home economics.

9   What are we supposed to do now, turn our S.U.V.'s in? En masse? Only the independently wealthy can treat their cars purely as fashion items.

10   The S.U.V.-bashers' argument also falls apart on macro-economic grounds. Were we to somehow cut our national fuel consumption by 20 percent, would that deprive the terrorism sponsors of cash? Unfortunately, the world oil market is, well, a market. Even if America were energy independent, there is no guarantee that Exxon, Texaco, and Getty—or, for that matter, France, the Netherlands, and Japan—would cease buying oil from Middle Eastern states.

11   My guess is that this campaign has less to do with politics and economics than with an American tendency to mind everybody else's business. So busybodies, let me ask you a question. How big is your house? Ms. Huffington's is reported to be 9,000 square feet. We all know what it costs to heat and air-condition a joint like that. A couple of years ago I replaced the aging oil furnace in my 3,000-square-foot house with a new fuel-injected system. It saves me about 800 gallons of oil a year. Hey, that's almost precisely the yearly fuel consumption of my GMC. I think of that as progress for me, as a world citizen. Maybe I'm not such a bad person after all.

▶ Building Vocabulary

Hochswender uses some common phrases and idioms to enrich his essay. Below are some that he uses. Explain what each phrase or idiom means, and use each in a sentence:

1. sturm und drang (par. 2)
2. whip around corners (par. 6)
3. home economics (par. 8)
4. en masse (par. 9)
5. macro-economic (par. 10)
6. energy independent (par. 10)
7. busybodies (par. 11)
8. a joint (par. 11)

▶Thinking Critically About the Argument

Understanding the Writer's Argument

1. What is the major objection against driving SUVs, according to the writer? What is he being accused of?
2. What does the writer mean when he says, "Those who implicate Americans . . . validate the terrorists as essentially right"? (par. 3)
3. How does the SUV make life easier for the writer?
4. Why is the SUV safer than a smaller car?
5. The writer admits in paragraph 8 that the SUV uses a great deal of gasoline. How does he defend himself against the accusation of being wasteful?
6. The writer says that "the SUV-bashers' argument also falls apart on macro-economic grounds." (par. 10) What does he mean by this? How does the argument fall apart, according to him?

Understanding the Writer's Techniques

1. What do you think about the opening? Is it effective?
2. Who is the audience? How does that affect the tone of this essay?
3. Where does the writer express his major proposition most clearly and fully?
4. Hochswender has several minor propositions, and they are essentially of two kinds: propositions that are positive reasons to own SUVs and propositions that are rebuttals to perceived oppositions. Make an outline of the propositions offered in the body of his essay.
5. In paragraph 7, the writer mentions his 9-year-old child. Why does he do that? What is the effect of bringing a child into the argument?
6. In paragraph 7, the writer states, "I think a lot of intelligent people realize that." To what is he referring, and what argumentative purpose does this serve?
7. Which minor proposition do you find most effective? Why?
8. What do you think of the conclusion?
9. Why does the writer echo his statement from the beginning of the essay?

Exploring the Writer's Argument

1. One of the writer's arguments is that he drives "so as not to roll over." (par. 6) Why is this proposition weak? Could you strengthen his argument in this section?
2. One objection that some people have to SUVs that the writer doesn't mention is that although they might be safer for those driving them, they can be dangerous to those in smaller cars in the event of an accident. What might the author say to defend against this charge?
3. Paragraph 9 is short, but it includes an interesting idea. Paraphrase the idea, and think of a rebuttal to the point.

▶ Ideas for Writing Arguments

Prewriting

Make a list of lifestyle choices that you have made, actions that you perform often, or decisions that still have an impact on your life now (smoking, piercing), that people might have objections to, and try to come up with answers to objections.

Writing a Guided Argument

Woody Hochswender saw an aspect of his lifestyle that the media and people around him were attacking, and he wrote an essay defending himself. Write an essay in which you identify an aspect of *your* lifestyle that someone conceivably could object to on moral grounds, and defend yourself against the charges. For example, you might smoke cigarettes or cigars; you might consume alcohol; you might like loud music.

1. Begin by explaining your lifestyle choice to your reader, appealing to the reader's compassion.
2. Continue by describing the person or people who accuse you of acting poorly because of your lifestyle choice.
3. Next, offer a minor proposition that explains a positive side of your choice.
4. Then explain one of the objections to your choice, and give your rebuttal.
5. Repeat the process in order, alternating a positive idea with a rebuttal.
6. Emphasize an emotional appeal to the reader.
7. Conclude the essay with a reiteration of the beginning appeal.

Thinking, Arguing, and Writing Collaboratively

In small groups, compare the lists you made for the Prewriting exercise. Allow your fellow students to help you choose a lifestyle choice that would be best for the Guided Argument assignment, and then ask them for objections to your choice. Collect their answers and use them in your rebuttals.

Writing About the Text

In an essay, answer Hochswender's question to his audience in the negative—that no, he is not a bad person, but argue that he has a bad argument. Analyze his argument for him, focusing on how successful his individual points are. Address each minor proposition in his essay, and offer some suggestions for revisions.

More Writing Ideas

1. In your journal, freewrite about this topic: freedoms you enjoy that might hurt other people. Write for 15 minutes without editing your writing. Then exchange your writing with a partner and discuss your ideas as a possible basis for an essay.
2. Write a paragraph in which you critique the argumentative basis for this statement: "Everyone does it, so I should be allowed to also." Is there anything valid about that reasoning? Explain your answer fully.
3. Terrorism, of course, is the reason Hochswender wrote this essay in the first place. He was upset that people accused him and other SUV drivers of supporting terrorism. Write an essay about other day-to-day activities that you think unintentionally might support terrorism.

JAMES TRAUB
All Go Down Together

James Traub is a freelance writer and the author of Too Good to Be True *(1990), a book about a corporate corruption and fraud case in New York in the 1980s, and* City on a Hill *(1994), a history of City College of New York, a public institution in Harlem. He has also written a book about Times Square in New York,* The Devil's Playground *(2004). In this selection, Traub addresses the pitfalls of the country's all-volunteer military and a possible alternative.*

▶ Prereading: Thinking About the Essay in Advance

France and Israel, among other countries, require all citizens of a certain age to serve in the military for a fixed term. Do you think this is a good idea? Why or why not?

▶ Words to Watch

beneficiaries (par. 1) those benefiting
deferment (par. 1) putting off until later
conscription (par. 2) military draft
equitable (par. 2) fair
imperative (par. 5) necessity
calculus (par. 6) method of figuring out

When Richard Nixon abolished the draft in 1973, I was one of the beneficiaries. I had just become eligible, and in the normal course of things I would have been assigned a lottery number. Of course, it's unlikely that I would have donned a uniform even if I had come up No. 1; there was always a way out if you had access to the right lawyers and doctors. At the   1

time, I knew literally no one who served—no one. Thanks to college deferment, during the Vietnam War, college students served at only half the rate
of high-school graduates, and the higher up you went in the socioeconomic
scale, the likelier it was that you would keep out of harm's way.

2   But what if conscription were equitable and were used to fill a military
that was widely respected rather than scorned? This was the case, after all,
in the period between the Korean and Vietnam Wars, when military service was widely accepted as the price of citizenship. Why wouldn't that be
true today? Why wouldn't it be just the kind of sacrifice young Americans
would agree to make at a time of heightened patriotism? The idea has
been in the air since earlier this year, when Representative Charles Rangel
of New York introduced a bill to restore conscription. Since Rangel got a
grand total of 11 co-sponsors, it is safe to say that conscription is an idea
whose time has not come, but it's still one worth thinking seriously about.

3   The most obvious objection to a restoration of the draft is that the all-
volunteer force, as it is known, is one of the most successful institutions in
the country. The A.V. F. is both the world's most powerful fighting force
and a shining example of harmonious race relations and affirmative action. When asked about the draft, Secretary of Defense Donald H. Rums-
feld has essentially said, Why fix what isn't broken? There are several answers to this question. First of all, the war on terrorism is already straining
the military and imposing terrible burdens on reservists. Second, we may
soon be redefining such civilian tasks as border patrol and airport security
as military ones, thus requiring a much larger uniformed force. Charles
Moskos, a professor of sociology at Northwestern and an expert on military affairs, has proposed a three-tier draft involving a military, a homeland defense and a civilian component, the last essentially a form of "national service." So a draft would satisfy manpower needs that an
all-volunteer force might not. It would also almost certainly be cheaper.

4   But the ultimate justification for conscription must be moral. Both
Rangel and Moskos argue that the A.V. F. recruits working-class young
men and women with bleak job prospects and pays them to put their
lives on the line. "These people should not have to die merely because
they were born to a class of people that lacked the advantages of other
people," as Rangel says. There is also an important issue of political philosophy. Conscription assumes a relationship between citizen and state
that makes most conservatives, and many liberals, uncomfortable. Libertarian conservatives like Milton Friedman object vehemently to any form
of compulsion on the part of the state that's not absolutely unavoidable.
Liberals have traditionally feared the use to which the state puts its soldiers. In 1970, at the height of the Vietnam War, the political philosopher
Michael Walzer wrote that since many citizens are bound to find almost
any use of military power unjust, conscription may be justified only

when the state's very existence is threatened. We owe the state no more than that.

But is that so? In the age of terrorism, doesn't the imperative of self-defense go well beyond acts of direct territorial threat? What's more, is the draft really a form of tyranny? We live in a culture in which everyone has rights and no one has obligations; the social contract has never been so wan. Perhaps now that our collective safety is jeopardized, the time has come to rethink that contract. Moskos says that in the Princeton class of 1956, from which he graduated, 450 of 750 men served in the military. Last year, Moskos says, 3 of Princeton's approximately 1,000 graduates served. That can't be a good thing for the country.

Of course, the country was at peace in 1956. A young man or woman drafted today might very well face combat—and might even have to serve in a war, like Iraq, that he or she considered wrongheaded—the Walzer problem. Perhaps draftees could be permitted to elect other forms of national service. But a truly democratic draft might also, as Rangel suggests, alter the strategic calculus: if the children of journalists, legislators and policy experts were called to military service, we might do a more thorough, and a more honest, job of deciding exactly what it is that's worth fighting for.

I have a 12-year-old son. The idea that in six or seven years Alex might be drafted is a little bit comical, but mostly appalling. My wife thinks I'm crazy even to suggest the idea. Nevertheless, it's true that we live in a genuinely threatening world; that is, alas, the very reason that military service, or at least some kind of service, should be mandatory, rather than a matter of individual conscience or marketplace choice.

▶ Building Vocabulary

1. Traub uses some words that refer to political ideologies and situations. Identify the following and offer examples from history or the present day:
   a. conservatives (par. 4)
   b. liberals (par. 4)
   c. libertarian (par. 4)
   d. tyranny (par. 5)
2. A number of words in this essay refer to social service concepts. Identify the following and use them in a sentence of your own:
   a. socioeconomic scale (par. 1)
   b. bill (par. 2)
   c. co-sponsors (par. 2)
   d. affirmative action (par. 3)
   e. social contract (par. 5)

▶ Thinking Critically About the Argument

Understanding the Writer's Argument

1. Why does the writer start his essay with his experience?
2. Why did Richard Nixon abolish the draft in 1973?
3. During the Vietnam War, why were wealthier young men able to "keep out of harm's way"? (par. 1)
4. Why do Charlie Rangel and other members of Congress want to restore conscription?
5. What is the writer's answer to the objection that the all-volunteer military is working well as it is?
6. The writer gives statistics in paragraph 5 for the number of students in two classes at Princeton who served in the military. Why does he do this?
7. Why does the writer mention his son at the end of his essay?

Understanding the Writer's Techniques

1. What is the tone in this essay? Who is the audience, and how does this affect the tone?
2. Where does his claim appear most clearly? If you don't see the claim, how does the essay succeed without it?
3. What is the argumentative effect of opening this essay with a personal recollection?
4. What, according to the writer, is the main ground for his claim? Where does he express it most clearly?
5. In paragraphs 3 and 5, the writer asks rhetorical questions. Why does he do this, and how effective are they? In the conclusion, what is the rhetorical effect of the writer's mentioning his son and his wife? How effective is the technique?
6. In addition to responding to arguments by the opposition, the writer puts forward his own arguments. What are these, and why are they presented in the order in which they are presented?
7. What is the meaning of the title? How does it reflect Traub's claim?

Exploring the Writer's Argument

1. Traub says in paragraph 2 that the lack of congressional support for the Rangel bill shows that "conscription is an idea whose time has not come, but it's still one worth thinking seriously about." Does this admission weaken the argument or strengthen it? Why?
2. In this essay, the writer is never absolutely specific about what a draft would entail. Is this a problem with the argument? Why or why not? What do you think would be the writer's answer if you asked him what form he preferred the draft came in?

3. Paraphrase the writer's argument in paragraph 6. What is "the Walzer problem"? Are you convinced by the argument in this paragraph? Explain your answer fully.

▶ Ideas for Writing Arguments

Prewriting

Do a focused 10 to 15 minute freewrite about what you think your reaction would be if you were drafted to be in the United States military right now.

Writing a Guided Argument

Pretend that the United States has reinstated the draft, and both men and women are eligible. Write a letter to the draft board either telling them that you will appear as requested, or that you refuse to serve, knowing that the former decision could put you in harm's way and that the latter decision could mean jail time. For either choice, explain yourself fully.

1. Begin, "Dear Draft Board:"
2. Indicate your own particular socioeconomic level, and explain why this has influenced your choice and why it is relevant to your argument.
3. Give at least two grounds for your choice, referring at least once to the arguments over the obligation of the citizen to the state as introduced in paragraph 4 of Traub's essay.
4. Write a rebuttal to a perceived objection to your choice.
5. Include evidence in the form of examples or cause-and-effect analysis for each of your points.
6. Conclude your letter by saying that your choice is one that all young people should make, and reiterate the grounds for your decision.
7. Sign your name (don't worry—it's not official).

Thinking, Arguing, and Writing Collaboratively

Exchange a draft of your Guided Argument assignment with a classmate. Review your partner's essay for its success in following the steps. Is the major proposition expressed as a choice? Is the major proposition reflected in the minor propositions? Is there sufficient evidence to back up the minor propositions? Write a paragraph evaluating the essay and suggesting revisions.

Writing About the Text

Traub writes several statements in this selection that point to the political spectrum, from conservative to liberal, but he never identifies his own politics. In fact, he seems to avoid the subject explicitly. Try to identify Traub's political bent or ideology and write an argumentative essay to defend your claim.

More Writing Ideas

1. What does a citizen owe his or her country? What is "the price of citizenship"? Write about this in your journal.
2. Write a paragraph in which you argue in favor of or against Charles Moskos's proposed three-tier draft.
3. In an essay, argue that the situation in the United States today falls under Michael Walzer's criterion for conscription, that "the state's very existence is threatened."

Paul Krugman
A Failed Mission

Paul Krugman went to college at Yale University and received his doctorate from MIT in 1977. Since then he has taught at Yale, Stanford, and MIT, and he now holds a position at Princeton University. Krugman's work on economics, especially in the field of international trade, has been significant; he received the prestigious John Bates Clark medal for economics in 1991. Krugman has written extensively on many topics. In this article he presents an unpopular argument about the space shuttle. The piece appeared in The New York Times *soon after the* Columbia *shuttle exploded in the atmosphere in early 2003.*

▶ Prereading: Thinking About the Essay in Advance

Do you remember the space shuttle *Columbia* disaster? What were your feelings at the time, or now, reflecting on it? More specifically, what does the accident say about humanity's desire to explore space? Why is the endeavor important?

▶ Words to Watch

boon (par. 3) benefit
prohibitively (par. 6) not allowing
epiphany (par. 8) sudden realization
dubious (par. 9) questionable

Some commentators have suggested that the Columbia disaster is 1
more than a setback—that it marks the end of the whole space shuttle
program. Let's hope they're right.

I say this with regret. Like millions of other Americans, I dream of a 2
day when humanity expands beyond Earth, and I'm still a sucker for
well-told space travel stories—I was furious when Fox canceled "Firefly."
I also understand that many people feel we shouldn't retreat in the face
of adversity. But the shuttle program didn't suddenly go wrong last
weekend; in terms of its original mission, it was a failure from the get-go.
Indeed, manned space flight in general has turned out to be a bust.

The key word here is "manned." Space flight has been a huge boon to 3
mankind. It has advanced the cause of science: for example, cosmology,
and with it our understanding of basic physics, has made huge strides
through space-based observation. Space flight has also done a lot to improve life here on Earth, as space-based systems help us track storms,
communicate with one another, even find out where we are. This column
traveled 45,000 miles on its way to *The New York Times:* I access the Internet via satellite.

Yet almost all the payoff from space travel, scientific and practical, 4
has come from unmanned vehicles and satellites. Yes, astronauts fitted
the Hubble telescope with new eye glasses; but that aside, we have basically sent people into space to show that we can. In the 1960's, manned
space travel was an extension of the cold war. After the Soviet Union
dropped out of the space race, we stopped visiting the moon. But why do
we still send people into orbit?

In space, you see, people are a nuisance. They're heavy; they need 5
to breathe; trickiest of all, as we have so tragically learned, they need to
get back to Earth.

One result is that manned space travel is extremely expensive. The 6
space shuttle was supposed to bring those costs down, by making the vehicles reusable—hence the deliberately unglamorous name, suggesting a
utilitarian bus that takes astronauts back and forth. But the shuttle never
delivered significant cost savings—nor could it really have been expected
to. Manned space travel will remain prohibitively expensive until there is
a breakthrough in propulsion—until chemical rockets are replaced with
something better.

And even then, will there be any reason to send people, rather than 7
our ever more sophisticated machines, into space?

I had an epiphany a few months ago while reading George Dyson's 8
"Project Orion," which tells the true story of America's efforts to build a
nuclear-powered spacecraft. The project was eventually canceled, in
part because the proposed propulsion system—a series of small nuclear
explosions—would have run afoul of the test-ban treaty. But if the
project had proceeded, manned spacecraft might have visited much of
the solar system by now.

9   Faced with the thought that manned space travel—the real thing, not the show NASA puts on to keep the public entertained—could already have happened if history had played out a bit differently. I was forced to confront my youthful dreams of space flight with the question, So what? I found myself trying to think of wonderful things people might have done in space these past 30 years—and came up blank. Scientific observation? Machines can do that. Mining the asteroids? A dubious idea—but even if it makes sense, machines can do that too. (A parallel: Remember all those predictions of undersea cities? Sure enough, we now extract lots of valuable resources from the ocean floor—but nobody wants to live there, or even visit in person.)

10   The sad truth is that for many years NASA has struggled to invent reasons to put people into space—sort of the way the Bush administration struggles to invent reasons to . . . but let's not get into that today. It's an open secret that the only real purpose of the International Space Station is to give us a reason to keep flying space shuttles.

11   Does that mean people should never again go into space? Of course not. Technology marches on: someday we will have a cost-effective way to get people into orbit and back again. At that point it will be worth rethinking the uses of space. I'm not giving up on the dream of space colonization. But our current approach—using hugely expensive rockets to launch a handful of people into space, where they have nothing much to do—is a dead end.

▶ Building Vocabulary

The following are concepts and terms of which the author of this selection assumes knowledge. Identify and define:

1. cosmology (par. 3)
2. Hubble telescope (par. 4)
3. cold war (par. 4)
4. space race (par. 4)
5. NASA (par. 9)
6. asteroids (par. 9)
7. International Space Station (par. 10)

▶ Thinking Critically About the Argument

Understanding the Writer's Argument

1. Why has space flight been a "huge boon to mankind"? (par. 3)
2. Why, according to the writer, did we pursue manned space travel starting in the 1950s?

3. Why is manned space flight a "nuisance"?
4. How has the space shuttle not fulfilled its promise?
5. What is the writer's reaction to his realization that manned space travel to the entire solar system is possible?
6. How does the writer compare the ocean floor to space?
7. In paragraph 10, the author writes that "NASA has struggled to invent reasons to put people into space—sort of the way the Bush administration struggles to invent reasons to . . . but let's not get into that today." To what is he referring, and why does he include this reference?

Understanding the Writer's Techniques

1. What is the writer's claim in this essay? Where does he best express it?
2. Why does he start out by saying that he hopes the *Columbia* disaster would spell the end of the space shuttle program? What rhetorical effect is he going for? Is it effective? Explain your answer.
3. What is the writer's tone in this essay? Is the chosen tone effective? Why or why not? Rewrite paragraph 5 to make the tone more serious.
4. Why does Krugman place the word *manned* in quotation marks?
5. What is the rhetorical effect of the writer's question in paragraph 7?
6. How many minor propositions does the writer have? List them.
7. Is the closing effective? Why or why not?

Exploring the Writer's Argument

1. Why does Krugman argue that we should end the space shuttle program without suggesting an alternative? Do you think he has an alternative in mind? What might that be?
2. Has space flight been, as Krugman says, a "boon for mankind," or have there been negative effects in our forays into space? Explain your answer.
3. At the end of his essay, the writer uses the phrase "dead end." Remember that this was written a short time after the *Columbia* exploded. Do you think the writer's language is insensitive or inappropriate? Why or why not? Where else could his language be considered insensitive?

▶ Ideas for Writing Arguments

Prewriting

Think about how popular culture images of space have influenced our desire to explore the solar system and beyond. Freewrite for at least 10 minutes about which TV shows, movies, or images you think have influenced space travel.

Writing a Guided Argument

Pretend you are an official at NASA, and you have read Paul Krugman's column. Form a rebuttal to his arguments and write your own argument in an essay, explaining why the space shuttle program must go on. Do some research online, if necessary, to build evidence. Examine NASA's Web site for information about the shuttle.

1. Begin with a reference to Krugman's essay and an explanation that he is not the only one who feels this way.
2. Gain sympathy for NASA and the space shuttle program by casting the agency as having the minority opinion.
3. State your major proposition clearly.
4. Offer your central ground for the survival of the space shuttle program clearly, with evidence to support your idea.
5. Rebut at least one of Krugman's points, quoting from his essay and critiquing the quote.
6. Link paragraphs between rebuttals with appropriate transitions.
7. In your conclusion, appeal once more to the reader's emotions and sense of hope.

Thinking, Arguing, and Writing Collaboratively

In small groups, discuss the freewriting you did for the Prewriting exercise. Attempt to develop a claim about how popular culture about space and the real-life space program affect each other. In your group, work together to make an outline for an essay on the topic.

Writing About the Text

Write an essay on Krugman's style. Examine his use of idiom and vocabulary. What does the fact that Krugman wrote this as a newspaper column suggest about why he chose his style? Does it make a difference that the column appeared in *The New York Times*?

More Writing Ideas

1. In your journal, make a list of everything that comes to mind about the phrase "space shuttle." Share your list with your fellow students. Are their lists similar? Different? How so?

2. In a paragraph, speculate on how the history of the space shuttle could have been a success. What would have made it a success, especially in Krugman's eyes?

3. Some experts think that the future of manned space travel is not astronauts doing science experiments but rather commercial travel—tourism. Write
   an essay arguing either that space tourism is a good idea or that it is a bad one.

ANNA QUINDLEN
One Nation, Indivisible? Wanna Bet?

Anna Quindlen has written extensively, but most visibly as a columnist for The New York Times *from 1981 to 1994. In 1992 she won a Pulitzer Prize for her commentary. A collection of columns,* Thinking Out Loud, *was published in 1993. She is also a novelist.* One True Thing *(1994) was adapted into a movie in 1998. She is now a columnist for* Newsweek *magazine's "Last Word" back-page feature. Her position as an observer of American life serves her well in this selection from* Newsweek, *which examines the controversy over the words "under God" in the Pledge of Allegiance.*

▶ Prereading: Thinking About the Essay in Advance

The Constitution of the United States calls for a separation of religion and government, more commonly known as "church and state." Do you think this is a good idea? Why or why not? When have you seen a blending of church and state in the United States?

▶ Words to Watch

impermissible (par. 2) not allowed
jingoism (par. 2) excessive patriotism
deplorable (par. 4) morally wrong
machinations (par. 4) workings
spate (par. 6) outburst
eschew (par. 6) avoid

1   Every year somebody or other finds a way to show that American kids are ignorant of history. The complaint isn't that they don't know the broad strokes, the rationale the South gave for keeping slaves, the ideas behind the New Deal. It's always dates and names, the game-show questions that ask what year the Civil War began and who ordered the bombing of Hiroshima, the stuff of the stand-up history bee. But if American adults want to give American kids a hard time about their dim knowledge of the past and how it's reflected in the present, they might first become reasonable role models on the subject. And the modeling could begin with the members of Congress, who with few exceptions went a little nuts when an appeals court in California ruled that the phrase "under God" in the Pledge of Allegiance was unconstitutional.

2   I don't really know whether that is an impermissible breach of the firewall between church and state. The proper boundaries 'twixt secular and sacred have been argued long and hard by legal minds more steeped in the specific intricacies than my own. But I do know this: attempts to make the pledge sound like a cross between the Ten Commandments and the Constitution are laughable, foolish and evidence of the basest sort of political jingoism.

3   So let's go to the history books, as citizens of this country so seldom do. The Pledge of Allegiance started in 1892 as a set piece in a magazine, nothing more, nothing less. It was written by a man named Francis Bellamy in honor of Columbus Day, a holiday that scarcely exists anymore except in terms of department-store sales and parades. The words "under God" were nowhere in it, hardly surprising since Bellamy had been squeezed out of his own church the year before because of his socialist leanings. His granddaughter said he would have hated the addition of the words "under God" to a statement he envisioned uniting a country divided by race, class and, of course, religion.

4   Those two words went into the pledge nearly 50 years ago, and for the most deplorable reason. It was the height of the Red scare in America, when the lives of those aligned or merely flirting with the Communist Party were destroyed by paranoia, a twisted strain of uber-patriotism and the machinations of Sen. Joseph McCarthy, after whom an entire vein of baseless persecution is now named. Contrary to the current political argument that "under God" is not specifically devout, the push to put it in the pledge was mounted by the Knights of Columbus, a Roman Catholic men's organization, as an attempt to counter "godless communism." President Dwight D. Eisenhower signed a bill making this law, saying that the words would help us to "remain humble."

5   Humility had nothing to do with it. Americans are not a humble people. Instead the pledge had become yet another cold-war litmus test. The words "under God" were a way to indicate that America was better than other nations—we were, after all, under the direct protection of the

deity—and adding them to the pledge was another way of excluding, of saying that believers were real Americans and skeptics were not. Would any member of Congress have been brave enough at that moment to say that a Pledge of Allegiance that had been good enough for decades was good enough as it stood?

Would any member of Congress, in the face of the current spate of unquestioning flag-waving, have been strong enough to eschew leaping to his feet and pressing his hand over his heart, especially knowing that the percentage of atheist voters is in the low single digits? Well, there were a few, a few who said the decision was likely to be overturned anyhow, a few who said there were surely more pressing matters before the nation, a few who were even willing to agree with the appeals court that "under God" probably did not belong in the pledge in a country founded on a righteous division between government and religion.   6

But most of the rest went wild. Even Sen. Hillary Clinton invoked "divine providence," even Sen. Dianne Feinstein called the court decision "embarrassing." What was embarrassing was watching all those people—Republicans, Democrats, liberals, conservatives—shout "under God" on the Senate floor, as though government were a pep rally and they were on the sanctified squad. Sen. Bob Smith of New Hampshire had this to say: "If you don't believe there's a God, that's your privilege, but it is still a nation under God." Huh?   7

I have a warm personal relationship with God; I often picture her smiling wryly and saying, in the words of Shakespeare's Puck, "Lord, what fools these mortals be!" Or perhaps something less fond. Now, as almost 50 years ago, a nation besieged by ideological enemies requires nuanced and judicious statecraft and instead settles for sloganeering, demonizing and politicking. One senator said after the court decision was handed down that the Founding Fathers must be spinning in their graves. The person who must be spinning is poor Francis Bellamy, who wanted to believe in an inclusive utopia and instead became in our time the father of convenient rhetoric.   8

▶ Building Vocabulary

This selection requires knowledge of some concepts, issues, and people relating to U.S. politics. Check with a dictionary or other reference work and define, identify, and explain the relevance of the following:

1. the New Deal (par. 1)
2. the Red scare (par. 4)
3. Joseph McCarthy (par. 4)
4. cold war (par. 5)
5. litmus test (par. 5)
6. Sen. Hillary Clinton (par. 7)

7. Sen. Dianne Feinstein (par. 7)
8. Sen. Bob Smith (par. 7)

Understanding the Writer's Argument

1. Why does Quindlen compare the members of Congress to ignorant schoolchildren? What point is she making?
2. What is the "firewall" between church and state? To what is she referring?
3. What are the origins of the Pledge of Allegiance?
4. What would the writer of the Pledge have thought of the addition of the words "under God" inserted in his work? How do you know?
5. Why were the words "under God" finally inserted into the Pledge?
6. Why were members of Congress so against taking out those words? Did any think taking them out was a good idea?

Understanding the Writer's Techniques

1. What tone is set by the title of the essay?
2. The body of the essay includes some strong and combative language that sets a certain tone reflecting how Quindlen feels about the issue. How would you describe that tone, and why? Do you think it is consistent with the title? Why?
3. Where does the major proposition appear most clearly and fully?
4. What argumentative function does the opening serve?
5. Paraphrase the minor proposition in paragraph 2.
6. The writer uses the facts of history to help argue her case. Where in the essay does she do this? Explain why the technique is effective.
7. How do paragraphs 6 and 7 support her position?
8. What is your view of the conclusion? Do you think it is effective? Why or why not?

Exploring the Writer's Argument

1. Quindlen accuses members of Congress of being extreme in their politics. Do you think she is being extreme as well? Why or why not?
2. To help make her case, the author writes in paragraph 5 that "Americans are not a humble people." Do you think this is true? Why or why not?
3. The author says that the Pledge didn't have the words "under God" in it for more than 50 years, so why shouldn't we change it back to how it was? But now the phrase has been in there for almost 50 years. Which tradition should take precedence? Explain your answer fully.

▶ Ideas for Writing Arguments

Prewriting

Read the words to "America the Beautiful," a song that is now sung during the seventh-inning stretch at baseball games in place of "Take Me Out to the Ballgame." What is your reaction to the lyrics of "America the Beautiful" in light of this essay? Why is this a different case?

Writing a Guided Argument

Write an essay arguing that we don't need a Pledge of Allegiance at all.

1. Open your essay with a recollection of reciting or learning the Pledge and of the first time you thought about the words.
2. Refer to the controversy that Quindlen discusses, using a quote from her essay and commenting on it.
3. Use a tone similar to Quindlen's.
4. Clearly state your position and the main ground for your position.
5. Anticipate the main objection to dropping the Pledge in one paragraph, and in a separate paragraph, using proper transitions, rebut the objection.
6. Close the body of your essay with an appeal to the true meaning of America.
7. Conclude by restating your position in light of your supporting points and your rebuttal.

Thinking, Arguing, and Writing Collaboratively

In small groups, examine the concept of jingoism. Where do you see jingoism in your neighborhood? In the media? Write individually on this topic for 10 minutes, and then come together and share your thoughts with your group. Then, as a class, discuss the dangers of jingoism and why it is so tempting.

Writing About the Text

Quindlen uses a sarcastic tone in this selection. Write an essay in which you argue that this tone and use of language is effective here, and explain why. In your essay, be sure to explain exactly which passages you find sarcastic, and explore why you think she uses that language.

More Writing Ideas

1. Do some research on the history of the division between church and state. Quindlen writes that the United States was "founded on a righteous division between government and religion." In which founding document is this division guaranteed, and where? What

exactly does the document say? Write a journal entry exploring the quote you find.

2. Use your work on question 1 to add to Quindlen's argument. Write a paragraph in which you develop a minor proposition using the evidence you have gathered.

3. What other rights, privileges, or guarantees from the Constitution do you think are eroding in our times? Write an essay on this question, explaining your answer fully.

2 Writing Arguments

As you attend the various courses in your college program, you probably have already noticed that your instructors across the spectrum of study are asking you to take a stand on a topic and support it with thoughtful, well-reasoned detail. In the previous chapter we suggested that the world of academic writing has its roots in argumentation. In history, biology, psychology, sociology, computer applications, education, in midterms and finals and research papers, you have to state a position on an issue, propose (or imply) that position in a thesis, and defend that position logically. An important part of argumentation in the disciplines is *persuasion*, that is, effecting some action on the part of your reader—from doing something tangible like buying a battery-driven car or joining a political action group to adopting a point of view, such as acknowledging that global warming is a serious threat to the world. As a writer, you need to persuade readers as a result of your appeals to their intelligence, emotions, and beliefs.

You've already seen that it's important to distinguish written arguments from the heated verbal interchange you have with roommates, friends, or family members. In such an exchange, your position on an issue can stimulate strong emotions on either side of a topic and arouse passionate feelings (and loud voices). We rarely plan our verbal arguments; mostly they just burst open in the course of conversation, and we just as rarely have the luxury to think them out clearly or to marshal convincing support in our own behalf.

Strong written argument, on the other hand, prides itself on its cool logic and substantive details to back up a position. Its purpose is clear. It takes into account its audience. It follows a lucid plan based on careful organization. It builds on appropriate rhetorical strategies—description, narration, comparison and contrast, classification, and definition, to name a few. It draws on reflective research. And through drafting and revision, it develops its thesis through suitable language and style.

THE WRITING PROCESS

As you saw in Chapter 1, we can identify the qualities of well-written arguments when an end product is at hand. As a writer, you need to know how to get to such a place yourself—the production of an effective argumentative paper that is to the point and fulfills the requirements of your assignment. You have to think of writing your argument as the culmination of a process, not simply a one-shot effort but a series of interrelated activities that can help you construct a successful paper.

Within the writing process, most writers identify various stages and activities in creating a piece of writing. Although we can name, more or less, the major elements in this process and encourage you to rely on them as you write, we don't want you to think of them as lock-step procedures where all efforts follow sequentially and require mindless adherence. Many of the steps overlap, some you can take simultaneously, and you may have good reason to skip some steps along the way.

The strategies that follow are essential elements in the writing process. We'll have more to say about many of them later in this chapter as we explore the writing of an argumentative paper.

Stages in the Writing Process

- Discuss your ideas with reliable people who can provide an initial reaction to your proposal.
- Do preliminary research online and in your library.
- Do *prewriting*—warmup activities before you start to draft your paper.
- Limit your topic.
- Identify your purpose and audience.
- State your claim in a thesis.
- Identify supporting details and evidence.
- Organize your ideas.
- Prepare a first draft.
- Share your draft.
- Revise your draft based on readers' comments and suggestions.
- Produce and edit your final copy.
- Proofread your final draft.

FIRST STEPS

After initial thought and preliminary research, the stages of the writing process usually begin with *prewriting*, a convenient term to identify the limbering-up activities writers produce on paper *before* they start creating a draft. (You know that the prefix *pre* means "prior to" or "before.") This is a very important stage in writing your paper: prewriting helps you thrash out ideas and circle your topic until you can identify clearly what you want to write about. If you begin a draft too soon, you may find that you have to start over and over again, wasting your valuable time and increasing your frustrations as a writer.

Prewriting Options

- *Make a list of ideas that your topic stimulates in your mind.* You can use this list to expand ideas and eliminate others.
- *Keep a journal of thoughts and ideas.* Jot down anything that comes to mind about any topic in an informal notebook that you can return to regularly to help identify a subject that you could develop into an argumentative paper.
- *Freewrite.* Write nonstop for 15 minutes or so. Do not stop to edit or revise. Just let your thoughts fill the page, no matter how disjointed or even silly they seem to you as you write. Free association gets words on the page; if you suffer from writer's block, you know how important it is simply to have something concrete to look at. You can use these words and sentences to zero in on a topic or to eliminate those topics that don't fit your intended task.
- *Use a visual aid.* With a subject map or subject tree, you can write a key word on a blank page and, using lines to indicate roads or branches, follow different elements of the topic by connecting them to lines or shapes that help you track different possibilities.
- *Brainstorm.* Raise unedited questions about the topic. Questions can dislodge answers that might set you on the right track to a strong essay. On a sheet of paper, write the reporter's essential questions, the five W's—*who, what, where, when, why*—and also *how.* Use these to start your own list of questions about your topic.
- *Make a scratch outline.* As ideas take shape in your mind, they can suggest linkages and interrelations, and you can capture them in a scratch outline. Write down an aspect of your topic, and underneath it list the various subtopics that come to mind. A scratch outline is an informal first step in organizing your ideas and can help you later on as you aim for a coherent, unified paper.

Of course, you'll need to pick and choose among these steps. Nobody takes all of them all the time. But if you're attentive to prewriting efforts, you'll discover many possibilities for developing a fruitful topic. As we point out later, once you have a topic, you can proceed to writing a thesis around a debatable issue, finding supporting detail to back up your assertions, organizing your information into a coherent entity, and writing an initial draft and any subsequent drafts that advanced thinking on your topic might require. Editing your manuscript and submitting it for review are important culminating acts in the writing process.

IDENTIFYING ISSUES

A manageable topic is the best way to assure that your essay won't derail as you move through the various stages of the writing process. Where do you begin your efforts to find a topic that you can develop into a thoughtful argument?

If your instructor has made an assignment—the extinction of the dinosaurs, let's say, or the causes of the Boer War, or the psychological manifestations of Alzheimer's disease—some of your work is done for you. (You'll still have to limit the topic, no doubt, in ways that we explain later on.) With an open-ended topic, however, you should let your interests and concerns lead you. Are you worried about global warming? Does the death penalty trouble you? Do the potentials of cyberspace stimulate your thoughts? (*To the Point* presents controversial essays on these topics; if you've read and discussed a selection in class, one of the ideas emerging from the essay may generate a good topic starting point.)

"We're not certain why they disappeared, but archeologists speculate that it may have had something to do with their size."

© The New Yorker Collection 2000 Harry Bliss from cartoonbank.com. All Rights Reserved.

The best papers always emerge from a writer's lively interests, and you want to honor your own curiosity and awareness of the world around you. Some global issue may pique your interest—the American military, taxes, famine in Africa—and you'll be able to form an opinion about them. Because of their complexity, you'd have to provide convincing reasons and evidence to support your claim. But topics of more personal and immediate concern also have rich potential as argumentative papers, and you should consider them. Should a strip mall open adjacent to the campus? Is the ban of religious symbols in the town square appropriate? Is the nutritional content of Burger King meals open to serious criticism? Should parents of very young girls allow them to participate in beauty contests?

On reflection, you may find that a topic that interests you is just not arguable or is not worth arguing about. If you believe that children should never be allowed to sample alcohol, for example, who would disagree with you? Almost everyone concurs that alcohol and children are a dangerous mix, and you'd be shouting in the wind—who would listen?—no matter how strongly you made your case.

LIMITING YOUR TOPIC

When you have the germ of a topic in mind, you have to limit it. The best way to begin to limit your topic is, as we've suggested, thinking carefully in advance about it through some of the prewriting strategies presented in the previous section, including, of course, browsing on the Web and in the library. You want to narrow down your topic so that you can accomplish your assigned writing task in a reasonable time. Often, you can narrow your topic in stages so that you can reach a desired level of specificity.

In the following table, look at the way writers have limited the broad topics in the first column into more productive argumentative essay topics. Items in the last column stand the best chance of developing into powerful argumentative essays.

Broad Topic	Limted Topic	Even More Limited
Cell phones	Dangers in using cell phones	The dangers of using cell phones while driving automobiles
Home instruction for children	Teaching children basic skills at home	Teaching reading skills to preschoolers in a home setting
Terrorists	Home-grown terrorists	Conditions in homes and schools that can create terrorists among American teenagers

Writers using the limited topics will have an easier time than those approaching the issues with too broad a scope. For the topic on cell phones, for instance, the writer can rule out any ideas about their use in public places like restaurants and movie theaters. The writer can rule out skyrocketing costs for cell phones and for required monthly service. Though these topics also might make effective papers, for this writer the issue is the dangers of cell phone use while driving automobiles. Any research efforts would concentrate on that dimension of the topic.

KNOWING YOUR PURPOSE AND AUDIENCE

Once you have limited your topic, you have to consider your *purpose* and *audience*. Purpose relates to what you hope to accomplish in your essay. Will your argument about the dangers of cell phones center on a narrative of some dangerous uses you witnessed or read about? Will you explain how to avoid the dangers? Will you show the causes and effects of dangerous use? Will you compare and contrast safe and hazardous cell phone uses? Your argumentative essay will allow you great latitude in addressing your topic through proven rhetorical strategies, and you have to determine which will enhance your topic development. In writing your argument, your purpose might be to propose that some belief or activity is good or bad, moral or immoral, harmful or beneficial. You might wish to push your readers to take some course of action that you deem essential or merely to have them consider a familiar issue in a new light. Being certain of your purpose will help you state your claim forcefully as you continue to think about your essay.

When your purpose is clearly in mind, you need to focus on your intended audience. Just what kind of reader are you aiming for? The glib response here, of course, is "I'm writing for my teacher so I can get a good grade." That's true, certainly, but not to the exclusion of other possible audiences: your classmates, perhaps, or the editor of the school newspaper, or the CEO of some company that treated you badly. When writing, it's always best to imagine specific audiences other than your English professor. In general, your teacher can adapt easily and can assume the personality and characteristics of varied reader audiences. Define a reader, and approach that reader with strategies targeted to her interests.

To take one example, with your cell phone topic, just think about how your approach would differ if your were writing your essay for teachers of driver education in urban high schools or for applicants for drivers' licenses at the Department of Motor Vehicles or for high-level executives at AT&T, whose corporate growth over the past several years hinged on increased sales of cellular telephones. Similarly, if you wrote about home teaching, your methods would vary significantly if you wrote for future mothers as opposed to booksellers at a national convention or teachers in your local elementary school. Vocabulary, style, sentence structure, and diction—audience and purpose markedly influence these fundamental elements of writing.

MAKING A CLAIM IN YOUR THESIS

Among the many important steps in the writing process, creating a thesis is high on the ladder of developing an argument. In an argumentative essay, you have to take a position on—that is, make a claim about—a topic. Your thesis must present an arguable topic. So even with a limited subject, you need to restrict your paper's concerns even further: you need to take a position on the topic, and the position on the topic must be debatable.

Note how writers have developed theses from the limited topics you looked at before.

Limited Topic	Possible Thesis
The dangers in using a cell phone while driving an automobile	The dangers to people who use cell phones while operating an automobile are serious, and current laws requiring "hands-free" technology do not adequately address the problems.
Teaching reading skills to preschoolers in a home setting	Teaching reading to preschoolers at home subverts the teacher's role, and parents should avoid the trap of becoming their children's teachers.
Conditions in homes and schools that can create terrorists among American teenagers	Home environments with remote, self-absorbed parents and ready access to weaponry—no matter what the social and financial conditions of the household or the psychological makeup of the child—contribute more than any other factor to developing teenage school terrorists.

Note how one could argue easily *against* any of these claims, which is the best assurance that each has the potential for becoming a successful paper. The topics are arguable; people stand on both sides of the issues. Many writers will produce an antithesis—that is, a thesis sentence opposite to the one they propose—to assure that their own position is arguable.

Possible Thesis	Antithesis
The dangers to people who use cell phones while operating an automobile are serious, and current laws requiring "hands-free" technology do not adequately address the problems.	"Hands-free" technology has reduced dramatically the dangers of cell-phone use by drivers on the road.

Once again, we put in a few words about flexibility here. Your thesis must be flexible. As you write your first and subsequent drafts, you may have to change your thesis as your topic takes shape and your claim undergoes refinement. Don't adhere blindly to the thesis you first developed, no matter how good it seems to you. As you marshal evidence, change your thinking, and delve deeply into evidence from many sources, your thesis may change considerably, usually for the good. Just be sure that you state your topic clearly, that you have identified your position on the topic, and that you make a claim that is debatable.

SUPPORTING YOUR CLAIM

After you have decided on your position and stated it as your claim in a thesis sentence, you have some important work ahead. Because your objective is to convince readers that your claim is valid and worth considering, only strong supporting detail drawn from personal experience or reliable sources will help you win over your audience. As you'll see later on, refutation—that is, acknowledging (and also challenging) viewpoints that oppose your own—is a key element in successful argumentation; not only must you discover information that supports your position, but you must also seek information that tells you what the other side is arguing. As you sift through the potential sources of supporting details, pay close attention to what those who disagree with you say. You'll need to give them due consideration when you write. (We'll say more about refutation later in this chapter.)

If you want to convince readers to accept your claim based on your own observations, you'll need to draw on concrete sensory detail to evoke the moment you are highlighting. Color, sound, and images of smell and touch all can set your reader in the scene as you see it and help make your points. Drawing on personal experience to support an argument doesn't *prove* anything easily, but it can convince readers if the illustration is apt. If you choose to draw on testimony from others—providing proof or evidence—you need to seek out the best possible information to back up your claim about the topic.

For example, arguing that global warming is a serious threat based only on days of high heat and humidity in your hometown during a winter season would not easily convince your readers. Similarly, arguing that your state should lower the driving age to 15 based on your own excellent (if illegal) tractor driving on your aunt's farm would not *prove* anything really, other than that in a single instance a teenager showed responsibility and skill in manipulating a gas-driven vehicle. You'd need to supplement these moments in your personal life with other convincing examples drawn from personal experience or with expert testimony from reliable sources in books and articles and on Web sites.

To prod readers to accept your claim, you often must draw on material that is solid and plentiful, evidence that is plausible, and reasoning that is not faulty. Here, the Internet and library catalogs can point you in the right direction. The World Wide Web has evolved into an invaluable research tool for writers, and you can find list serves and links from which to download abstracts, chapters, articles, and even full books. You already know, no doubt, that amid its many riches, the Web also can lead you on a path to disaster. Misinformation abounds; unreliable sources making wild claims may appear as regular popup windows on your computer or as unsolicited spam e-mail messages. Many chat rooms are notorious hotbeds of hysterical proclamations and assertions that defy logic even on superficial inspection. Also, some assessments on the Web are not current or reliable, or the site may not be open about its biases and objectives.

Therefore, we recommend some serious work at your college or local library, where research librarians can help you appraise Web sites and refer you to appropriate electronic sources. Your librarians, of course, also can put you on the trail to books and periodicals that will supplement your cyberspace ventures with solid resources on the library shelves or on microfilm or microfiche.

Your initial browsing in the library and on the Web helped you find a topic; now, as we have indicated, you need to amass supporting details to back up the topic you've chosen. Read as widely as you can; visit valid Web sites; watch television programs and films; talk with anyone who will listen. Take notes on what you've read and seen and be prepared to present some of your materials as evidence to your argument. Use the three C's as you evaluate your evidence: *currency*, *completeness*, and *credibility*.

Don't be surprised if you find yourself changing the terms of your argument dramatically. The more deeply you explore the topic, the more potential information you have to solidify your position or to alter it dramatically or subtly. With a great deal of resources at hand, you can select those details that seem best to bolster your position.

ORGANIZING YOUR ARGUMENT

The supporting details—the reasons and evidence you garner—make up the *grounds* of your argument, the key elements that establish the validity of your claim. Your claim, stated in your thesis, establishes your general point of view; the grounds provide the reasons and evidence. As you gather information, you should be thinking of how to organize your materials once you're ready to begin. You need to keep in mind the way your grounds will devolve to minor propositions and how you actually will use your evidence to support your claim or to refute an opposing claim.

You might find it helpful even at this stage to consider using one of the following patterns as a guide when writing your essay.

Pattern 1: Refutation First	Pattern 2: Refutation Last	Pattern 3: Refutation Point by Point
Introduce your claim.	Introduce your claim.	Introduce your claim.
State opposing arguments and refute them.	State first minor proposition and supporting information.	State first minor proposition and supporting information and refute opposing arguments.
State first minor proposition and supporting information.	State second minor proposition and supporting information.	State second minor proposition and supporting information and refute opposing arguments.
State second minor proposition and supporting information.	State third minor proposition and supporting information.	State third minor proposition and supporting information and refute opposing arguments.
State third minor proposition and supporting information.	State opposing arguments and refute them.	Conclude the essay.
Conclude the essay.	Conclude the essay.	

We don't propose these patterns as absolutes, and it's probably a bit too early in the writing process for you to map out the full approach your essay will take. Nevertheless, keeping in mind the possibilities for organizing your information and conveying it logically will help you over the hurdles when it comes to drafting your paper.

CHECKING YOUR ASSUMPTIONS (OR WARRANTS)

As you learned in Chapter 1, a warrant is the essential underpinning for your assertion. It establishes the certainty underlying a particular claim and its supporting reasons. A firm warrant justifies the supporting information that you assemble to support your contention. However, if your readers can challenge your warrant, you'll have to defend it.

Why do you have to think about warrants when you write your essays? In many of your argumentative assignments, you can assume that your readers—generally your instructor, other students, family members, or the particular readers that you have defined—are friendly and won't question the warrants supporting your claim. Yet warrants based on certain cultural assumptions, systems of belief, or core values often require their own defense because they too are debatable. When your warrant is controversial, you need to explain or qualify it.

Consider the ongoing debate over abortion rights. Some would use as a warrant the belief that all life from conception is sacred and would build a case from there against all forms of abortion. Others would establish as a warrant that idea that freedom of choice is the principle upon which a woman makes a decision involving abortion. There are numerous additional warrants underlying the abortion debate that often serve as "universal" values that in themselves are controversial. Defending the warrant is as important as providing points to support your assertion. Differing warrants or assumptions underlying debates over abortion, gun control, the death penalty, and other hot-button issues require writers to subject these warrants to the same scrutiny that they bring to their claims and supporting evidence.

REFUTATION: MEETING THE OPPOSITION

Particularly with assertions that you know many people would disagree with, effective arguments always consider the opposition's point of view. As we pointed out briefly before, you have to be aware of what contrasting arguments suggest, and you have to treat them fairly in your essay.

You have some options here. One strategy is to indicate the views that run counter to your own and simply to admit that some parts of these arguments are legitimate—but that your point is more substantial and worthy of greater support. Conceding arguments is an attractive option: this tactic shows your lack of prejudice and your ethical approach to the issue. Essentially, you are saying here "I know that others disagree with me—and here are some of their reasons, which have some validity. Nevertheless, the points I will make are much more convincing."

Another strategy is to identify opposing arguments and then refute them as part of your own presentation. How can you refute an opposing argument?

- Question the evidence proposed by the opposing camp. Is it valid? Up to date? Sufficient? Accurate?
- Probe the warrants of an opposing argument. What are the underlying assumptions and beliefs for the writer's claim? Has the writer offered a substantive rationale for the warrants on which he builds his argument?

- Identify evidence that challenges the specific elements in the opposing arguments. Thus, you can extract fundamental points and
  rebut them one at a time rather than making a sweeping refutation.

With either strategy, concession or refutation, you must treat the opposing arguments justly and respectfully. True, satirists and ironists often
mock opposing views, but in your papers you want to aim for fairness
that will establish your credibility and lack of bias as a writer and win
over your readers.

AVOIDING TRAPS IN APPEALS AND LOGIC

Argumentative essays often deal with heated topics, but as a fair and
thoughtful writer, you want to be aware of excessive appeals to emotion
and to a wide range of logic traps that can show fault lines in your thinking. Be alert to these logic traps and wrongheaded emotional appeals as
you write your papers.

- *Ad hominem ("to the man") arguments.* These discredit the person
  rather than the argument: "Gloria Lee never married. How can she
  talk about the sacredness of marriage between men and women?"
  Here, the attack is against the person, not the issue. Avoid *ad
  hominem* arguments—but do not shrink from challenging someone
  if the person lacks appropriate credentials to make the claim. You
  would be right to contest the author of a pro-death penalty Web
  site put up by a dentist who has no authority in the debate other
  than his passionate commitment to the issue.
- *Arguments based on longevity.* Avoid proving a point by stating that
  people always believed it, so why should we change it now?
  "Women have never competed in professional football in the past,
  and there's no need to alter common practice." We'd still be talking about an earth-centered universe if we adhered to beliefs
  based only on their standing through time.
- *Arguments based on transfer.* Here the argument connects the
  point to a famous person in order to win support. This is an example of *positive* transfer: "President Bill Clinton is a brilliant
  scholar and his recent support of the newly nominated federal
  judge should not be questioned." This is an example of *negative*
  transfer (or name calling): "President Bill Clinton's personal behavior challenged family values. Why should we consider as relevant his defense of the family support bill?" Neither example
  makes any logical connection between the person and the issue
  and, in fact, the transfer distracts the reader from the point to
  the person.
- *Hasty generalizations.* In this logic trap, you leap to false conclusions based on insufficient, untrue, or unrepresentative evidence.

"Cats are disloyal pets. Our cat Phoebe, whom we had for five years, ran off one day and never returned." One example cannot support the generalization. Hasty generalizations at their most pernicious lead to stereotyping, when you use reductive generalizations to characterize an individual or group. "Our South American gardener is sluggish and has no resolve. Newly arrived immigrants in our country are lazy and unambitious."

- *Broad generalizations.* By using words like *never, always,* and *all* in an argument, you leave yourself open to accusations of overstatement. "George Washington always knew how to lead a battle"; "All Germans supported the Nazi purge of Jews during World War II"—sweeping statements like these are open easily to challenge. It's best to qualify them: "George Washington almost always knew how to lead a battle"; "Large numbers of Germans supported the Nazi purge of Jews during World War II."

- *Post hoc, ergo propter hoc ("after this, therefore because of this").* This is a logical fallacy built on false cause-and-effect relationships. "The boys ran out of the department store quickly. They must have stolen the woman's purse." Just because their departure was hasty and might seem suspicious, there is no necessary cause and effect relationship between the boys' rapid disappearance and the purse snatching. Our most ingrained superstitions—bad luck following a black cat's crossing our path, for example—assume that one event in time causes another soon after. Be sure that any cause-and-effect relationships that you establish are valid.

- *Argumentum ad populum ("to the people").* Arguments that draw on highly charged language can manipulate readers' responses by arousing strong emotions. Words that appeal to virtuous elements, such as patriotism, motherhood, and America, can produce "glittering generalities" that distort meaning so that readers must accept a premise through illogical association. Negative words similarly can make illogical connections: "The dictatorial president of the Student Association has made another bad choice."

- *Bandwagon arguments.* In these arguments the writer falsely generalizes that the voice of the people is always right. "The citizens of this city are voting to renew Proposition 13, and you should too." Just because everyone's doing it doesn't make it desirable.

- *Begging the question.* Here, the writer takes a conclusion for granted before she proves it. "Teenagers are by nature reckless and will benefit greatly from required counseling prior to any voluntary abortion." The writer can go on to indicate the benefits of this counseling; but she has not offered any proof for her conclusion that teenagers are irresponsible. Another dimension of begging the question is assuming in your premise what your conclusion should prove. Thus, if you argue that elected officials' greed is unavoidable because they put personal gain above service to constituents, you are not proving your premise and hence are begging the question.

- *Oversimplified arguments.* Oversimplification is a major impediment to logical argumentation and can take many forms.
  - *One solution.* Complicated issues usually have more than one resolution, and you don't want to argue for just one solution to a sticky problem. "Censoring violence on television will reduce violence in our communities." Surely other possible solutions warrant consideration in the serious issue of violent behavior.
  - *Either-or reasoning.* You shouldn't assume that only two sides exist on an issue—yes or no, good or bad, right or wrong. "He failed so many courses because he works after school and on weekends. Either you work or go to school; you can't do both."
  - *No cost or harm.* If you project a benefit for some course of action, don't assume automatically that no problems, costs, or penalties will follow. "Prohibit all pagers and cell phone use in public places." The benefits are clear: no interruptions, annoying rings or music, or loud talking in indoor spaces. But what about consequences: preventable emergencies, parents needing to be in touch with children, doctors on call. No-harm generalizations often overlook precarious repercussions.
- *Non sequitur ("It does not follow").* This logical fallacy draws conclusions when no logical connection exists between ideas. "Arnold Schwarzenegger will be a good governor for California because he is a very popular actor." He may be popular, and people might have voted for him because he's popular, but that doesn't guarantee that he will be a good governor. The argument's conclusions do not stem from its premise. The writer might see a logical connection between popularity and leadership, but he should make it explicit. Otherwise, he has generated a non sequitur—that is, disconnected ideas.
- *Weak or untrue analogies.* A familiar tool of argument is the analogy, a type of comparison that relates one object or idea to a basically dissimilar idea so that readers can see the point in a new light. Alfred Posamentier, a professor of education, made this comment about the anxiety at the start of a new school year awash with new policies and procedures: "It's akin to an engineering firm that develops this new machine and doesn't know if all the parts are going to behave the way they are supposed to behave when they flip the switch on a certain day." Analogies enliven writing and help illustrate a point but never serve as evidence. Posamentier, after all, hasn't proved that the system is untested and risks uncoordination. But his analogy helps us see how he views the problem.

- *The straw man.* An argument sets up a straw man when it asserts a weak or invented argument attributed to an opponent for the exclusive purpose of disproving it. "The television commentator would no doubt approve of music that glorifies drugs and indifferent sex. Only an extremist libertine who doesn't believe in family values would question the censorship of any material aimed at teenagers." The statement asserts that the commentator would endorse music that praises drugs and sex—but the operative words here are "no doubt." The phrase suggests an invented argument, one that the writer can attack along with the person who made the argument.

Strong written arguments reflect logical thinking, and we've tried to point out ways in which you can produce thoughtful topics; carefully stated assertions; well-defined claims, grounds, and evidence; and objective data and testimony. These elements in your writing will mark you as a fair analyst with a lively, inquiring mind, and they will help you to produce strong argumentative papers.

PERSPECTIVES ON LOVE AND MARRIAGE: READING AND WRITING ABOUT A CRITICAL ISSUE

JUDY BRADY
I Want a Wife

Judy Brady was born in 1937 and went to college at the University of Iowa. A breast cancer survivor, she is an activist with the Women's Cancer Resource Center and a cofounder of the Toxic Links Coalition, which works to prevent cancer by reducing pollution. In this funny but bitter satire, which appeared in Ms. *magazine in 1971, Brady, a wife and mother, argues that she, too, would like someone to take care of her.*

▶ Prereading: Thinking About the Essay in Advance

Think about the traditional roles that men and women have played in their relationships. What is expected of a husband? Of a wife? Do you think things are the same now as in 1971 when Brady wrote the piece? Why or why not?

▶ Words to Watch

nuturant (par. 3) giving attention and affection
hors d'oeuvres (par. 6) appetizers
adherence (par. 8) faithful attachment

1   I belong to that classification of people known as wives. I am A Wife. And, not altogether incidentally, I am a mother.

2   Not too long ago a male friend of mine appeared on the scene fresh from a recent divorce. He had one child, who is, of course, with his ex-wife. He is obviously looking for another wife. As I thought about him while I was ironing one evening, it suddenly occurred to me that I, too, would like to have a wife. Why do I want a wife?

3   I would like to go back to school so that I can become economically independent, support myself, and, if need be, support those dependent upon me. I want a wife who will work and send me to school. And while I am going to school, I want a wife to keep track of the children's doctor and dentist appointments. And to keep track of mine, too. I want a wife to make sure my children eat properly and are kept clean. I want a wife who will wash the children's clothes and keep them mended. I want a wife who is a good nurturant attendant to my children, who arranges for their schooling, makes sure that they have an adequate social life with their peers, takes them to the park, the zoo, etc. I want a wife who takes care of the children when they are sick, a wife who arranges to be around when the children need special care, because, of course, I cannot miss classes at school. My wife must arrange to lose time at work and not lose the job. It may mean a small cut in my wife's income from time to time, but I guess I can tolerate that. Needless to say, my wife will arrange and pay for the care of the children while my wife is working.

Surfing Couples (© Peter M. Fisher/CORBIS)

I want a wife who will take care of *my* physical needs. I want a wife   4
who will keep my house clean. A wife who will pick up after me. I
want a wife who will keep my clothes clean, ironed, mended, replaced
when need be, and who will see to it that my personal things are kept
in their proper place so that I can find what I need the minute I need it.
I want a wife who cooks the meals, a wife who is a *good* cook. I want a
wife who will plan the menus, do the necessary grocery shopping, prepare the meals, serve them pleasantly, and then do the cleaning up
while I do my studying. I want a wife who will care for me when I am
sick and sympathize with my pain and loss of time from school. I want
a wife to go along when our family takes a vacation so that someone
can continue to care for me and my children when I need a rest and
change of scene.

I want a wife who will not bother me with rambling complaints   5
about a wife's duties. But I want a wife who will listen to me when I feel
the need to explain a rather difficult point I have come across in my
course of studies. And I want a wife who will type my papers for me
when I have written them.

I want a wife who will take care of the details of my social life. When my   6
wife and I are invited out by my friends, I want a wife who will take care of
the babysitting arrangements. When I meet people at school that I like and
want to entertain, I want a wife who will have the house clean, will prepare
a special meal, serve it to me and my friends, and not interrupt when I talk
about the things that interest me and my friends. I want a wife who will
have arranged that the children are fed and ready for bed before my guests
arrive so that the children do not bother us. I want a wife who takes care of
the needs of my guests so that they feel comfortable, who makes sure that
they have an ashtray, that they are passed the hors d'oeuvres, that they are
offered a second helping of the food, that their wine glasses are replenished
when necessary, that their coffee is served to them as they like it.

And I want a wife who knows that sometimes I need a night out by   7
myself.

I want a wife who is sensitive to my sexual needs, a wife who makes   8
love passionately and eagerly when I feel like it, a wife who makes sure that
I am satisfied. And, of course, I want a wife who will not demand sexual attention when I am not in the mood for it. I want a wife who assumes the
complete responsibility for birth control, because I do not want more children. I want a wife who will remain sexually faithful to me so that I do not
have to clutter up my intellectual life with jealousies. And I want a wife who
understands that *my* sexual needs may entail more than strict adherence to
monogamy. I must, after all, be able to relate to people as fully as possible.

If, by chance. I find another person more suitable as a wife than the   9
wife I already have, I want the liberty to replace my present wife with another one. Naturally, I will expect a fresh, new life; my wife will take the
children and be solely-responsible for them so that I am left free.

10   When I am through with school and have a job, I want my wife to quit working and remain at home so that my wife can more fully and completely take care of a wife's duties.

11   My God, who *wouldn't* want a wife?

▶ Building Vocabulary

1. After checking a dictionary for Brady's specific use of each of the following words, write out their definitions:
   a. attendant (par. 3)
   b. adequate (par. 3)
   c. peers (par. 3)
   d. tolerate (par. 3)
   e. rambling (par. 5)
   f. replenished (par. 6)
   g. monogamy (par. 8)
2. Write an original sentence for each word.

▶ Thinking Critically About the Argument

Understanding the Writer's Argument

1. What made Brady think about wanting a wife for herself?
2. How would a wife help the writer continue her education?
3. In what way would a wife help the writer around the house?
4. Why does the writer want someone to help her take care of the children?
5. How would a wife change the writer's sex life?
6. What kind of freedom does the writer want, finally?

Understanding the Writer's Techniques

1. What is Brady's major claim in this essay? Consider the ironic meaning of her essay, and decide if she ever truly expresses her claim. Explain your answer.
2. What are the implied warrants in this essay? How do you know?
3. What minor propositions does Brady give to show that she wants a wife?
4. Do you detect a pattern of coherence among the minor propositions? Why does she include them in the order she does? Would you change the order at all?
5. What is the effect of Brady's use of the word "I"? Do you find it effective? Why or why not?
6. What is Brady's tone in this essay? Explain your answer.

7. Why does the writer separate the idea that "sometimes I need a night out by myself" in paragraph 7? What rhetorical purpose does this serve?

8. What is the effect of the rhetorical question at the end of the essay and of the use of the phrase "My God" and the word "wouldn't" in italics?

Exploring the Writer's Argument

1. Brady wrote this essay two years before she and her husband separated. How does this knowledge change your opinion of the essay?

2. This essay was published in 1971. Do you think that this essay could be published in a major magazine today? Why or why not? Do husbands still expect their wives to perform all of these duties without help? Explain what has changed.

3. Brady lists many domestic duties traditionally assigned to the homemaker. What "wifely responsibilities" exist today that she doesn't mention?

4. In what ways are Brady's arguments old fashioned? In what ways are they relevant to today's men and women?

▶ Ideas for Writing Arguments

Prewriting

What kind of help do you need in life? What kind of person would you need? If you are living at home, would it be helpful to have a student of your own?

Writing a Guided Argument

Write an essay titled "I Want a Student."

1. Begin your essay by identifying yourself as a student. You will argue that you want a student to help you with your life as a student.

2. Offer a brief personal story (as Brady does in par. 2) to explain why you decided you wanted your own student.

3. Using Brady as a guide, support your main idea with supporting points, explaining the various activities your very own student could help you with in your life as a student.

4. Organize your points in an effective order, using transition words and phrases to improve the flow from paragraph to paragraph.

5. Use repetition in your language for rhetorical effect.

6. End your essay with a question, making that question as effective and dramatic as possible.

Thinking, Arguing, and Writing Collaboratively

Help to divide the class into two groups: one consisting of all the men in the class and the other consisting of all the women. Working in these groups, have the men come up with reasons why husbands (and boyfriends) need extra help, and have the women list reasons why wives (and girlfriends) need help. Each group should assign a representative to put the reasons on the board. The class should discuss the effectiveness of each reason.

Writing About the Text

Write an essay about the use of irony in this essay. What is the effect of writing such an emotional essay in such a straightforward style? Discuss Brady's use of humor.

More Writing Ideas

1. In your journal, explain which of Brady's complaints you find most effective and which you find most whiny or weak.
2. In a paragraph, argue for or against this statement: "Men should stay home while women go out and earn a living."
3. Write an essay arguing that it is more difficult to be a man in today's society than it is to be a woman.

NICOLAS KRISTOF
Love and Race

Born in 1959, Nicolas Kristof was raised in Oregon, educated at Harvard, and won a Rhodes scholarship to Oxford University in England. He and his wife, also a journalist, won a Pulitzer Prize for their work in China during the Tiananmen Square uprising. In this selection, Kristof sings the praises of the current rise in marriage between the races.

▶ Prereading: Thinking About the Essay in Advance

Do you know any interracial couples? If so, what problems do they face, if any, and why? If you do not know any, what problems do you think they might face in society today?

▶Words to Watch

genome (par. 6) entire code for DNA in a cell
superficial (par. 7) unimportant, only on the surface
miscegenation (par. 10) mixing of races
guru (par. 13) leader and guide
surge (par. 14) sharp rise

I n a world brimming with bad news, here's one of the happiest trends: 1
Instead of preying on people of different races, young Americans are
falling in love with them.

Whites and blacks can be found strolling together as couples   2
even at the University of Mississippi, once the symbol of racial
confrontation.

"I will say that they are always given a second glance," acknowledges   3
C. J. Rhodes, a black student at Ole Miss. He adds that there are still misgivings about interracial dating, particularly among black women and a
formidable number of "white Southerners who view this race-mixing as
abnormal, frozen by fear to see Sara Beth bring home a brotha."

Mixed-race marriages in the U.S. now number 1.5 million and are   4
roughly doubling each decade. About 40 percent of Asian-Americans and
6 percent of blacks have married whites in recent years.

Still more striking, one survey found that 40 percent of Americans   5
had dated someone of another race.

In a country where racial divisions remain deep, all this love is an enor-   6
mously hopeful sign of progress in bridging barriers. Scientists who study
the human genome say that race is mostly a bogus distinction reflecting very
little genetic difference, perhaps one-hundredth of 1 percent of our DNA.

Skin color differences are recent, arising over only the last 100,000   7
years or so, a twinkling of an evolutionary eye. That's too short a period
for substantial genetic differences to emerge, and so there is perhaps 10
times more genetic difference within a race than there is between races.
Thus we should welcome any trend that makes a superficial issue like
color less central to how we categorize each other.

The rise in interracial marriage reflects a revolution in attitudes. As   8
recently as 1958 a white mother in Monroe, N.C., called the police after
her little girl kissed a black playmate on the cheek; the boy, Hanover
Thompson, 9, was then sentenced to 14 years in prison for attempted
rape. (His appeals failed, but he was released later after an outcry.)

In 1963, 59 percent of Americans believed that marriage between   9
blacks and whites should be illegal. At one time or another 42 states
banned intermarriage, although the Supreme Court finally invalidated
these laws in 1967.

10   Typically, the miscegenation laws voided any interracial marriages, making the children illegitimate, and some states included penalties such as enslavement, life imprisonment, and whippings. My wife is Chinese-American, and our relationship would once have been felonious.

11   At every juncture from the 19th century on, the segregationists warned that granting rights to blacks would mean the start of a slippery slope, ending up with black men marrying white women. The racists were prophetic.

12   "They were absolutely right," notes Randall Kennedy, the Harvard Law School professor and author of a dazzling new book, "Interracial Intimacies," to be published next month. "I do think [interracial marriage] is a good thing. It's a welcome sign of thoroughgoing desegregation. We talk about desegregation in the public sphere; here's desegregation in the most intimate sphere."

13   These days, interracial romance can be seen on the big screen, on TV shows, and in the lives of some prominent Americans. Former Defense Secretary William Cohen has a black wife, as does Peter Norton, the software guru. The Supreme Court justice Clarence Thomas has a white wife.

14   I find the surge in intermarriage to be one of the most positive fronts in American race relations today, building bridges and empathy. But it's still in its infancy.

15   I was excited to track down interracial couples at Ole Miss, thinking they would be perfect to make my point about this hopeful trend. But none were willing to talk about the issue on the record.

16   "Even if people wanted to marry [interracially], I think they'd keep it kind of quiet," explained a minister on campus.

17   For centuries, racists warned that racial equality would lead to the "mongrelization" of America. Perhaps they were right in a sense, for we're increasingly going to see a blurring of racial distinctions. But these distinctions acquired enormous social resonance without ever having much basis in biology.

▶ Building Vocabulary

Explain the meaning of the following examples of figurative language. Rewrite the sentences by putting the figure of speech in your own words:

1. "all this love is an enormously hopeful sign of progress in *bridging barriers.*" (par. 6)
2. "Skin color differences are recent, arising over only the last 100,000 years or so, a *twinkling of an evolutionary eye.*" (par. 7)
3. "the segregationists warned that granting rights to blacks would mean the start of a *slippery slope.*" (par. 11)
4. "these distinctions acquired enormous social *resonance.*" (par. 17)

▶ Thinking Critically About the Argument

Understanding the Writer's Argument

1. Why is it significant that interracial couples exist at the University of Mississippi?
2. What lessons do the writer suggest we learn from the statistic that skin color differences are a relatively recent development evolutionarily?
3. What were segregationists afraid of in the 19th century?
4. Explain Randall Kennedy's quote, "We talk about desegregation in the public sphere; here's desegregation in the most intimate sphere." Paraphrase his quote.
5. What evidence does the writer give that interracial marriages are becoming more mainstream?
6. Why wouldn't students at Ole Miss discuss intermarriage with Kristof?

Understanding the Writer's Techniques

1. What is the writer's major proposition? Where is it best stated?
2. What minor propositions does the writer use to support his major proposition?
3. What evidence does the writer use to support his minor propositions? Make a rough outline of the essay's argument.
4. How effective is Kristof's use of statistics in paragraphs 4 through 7?
5. Does the writer only rely on rational arguments? What other kinds of appeals can you find? Explain your answer.
6. What is the persuasive effect of the writer explaining in paragraph 10 that he is in an interracial marriage?
7. How effective is the last paragraph?

Exploring the Writer's Argument

1. Do you find paragraphs 2 and 3 in Kristof's essay contradictory? Why or why not?
2. If racial differences are not that important and have little basis in biology, why does Kristof repeat his argument about racial distinctions in paragraph 17? Does he have a rhetorical reason? Could you strengthen his point here?
3. Do you think the structure of Kristof's essay is effective? Why or why not? Could you suggest a better structure? How would you structure the essay if you were assigned to write a column on the same issue?
4. Why does Kristof use the example of Hanover Thompson in paragraph 8? Why that example? He could have found a much more

tragic example from the early part of the 20th century. There were many lynchings of African Americans who merely looked at a white woman in a way she didn't like. Why, then, does he offer an example from 1958?

▶ Ideas for Writing Arguments

Prewriting

How common is interracial marriage where you live? Why do you think that is? Write about whether you think it is getting more common, and explain why it is or why it is not.

Writing a Guided Argument

Write an essay about a lifestyle that still is not accepted fully in society (for example, openly gay couples or unmarried couples living together). Argue that you see an improvement in the level of tolerance toward that lifestyle.

1. Begin your essay with a declaration that things are getting better.
2. Continue by offering examples or statistics to bolster your claim. Do some research, if you must, to gather evidence and, preferably, quotes. Save at least two pieces of evidence for later in your essay, under step 6.
3. While keeping an impartial distance to your writing, establish an optimistic tone.
4. In the next section, discuss the history of your chosen subject.
5. Develop and discuss the idea of opposing views to your subject.
6. Provide evidence to show how tolerance is increasing by offering evidence.
7. Link your ideas with well-developed transitions.
8. In your conclusion, link the fears opponents have about your subject with the reality or the coming reality in society.

Thinking, Arguing, and Writing Collaboratively

In small groups, share your papers that grew out of the Writing a Guided Argument assignment. Discuss suggestions for improvements in tone and word choice. Also, help your classmates to develop evidence for their essays by paying close attention to any pieces of evidence that are irrelevant and by helping with any awkward phrasing.

Writing About the Text

Write an essay in which you evaluate Kristof's use of statistics in this essay. Which do you find most impressive or effective for helping his claim? Which are less effective? What other statistics would you have liked to see?

More Writing Ideas

1. Are there any negative effects of interracial relationships on the children of those unions? Write in your journal about this topic.
2. Write a paragraph about why you think someone would be opposed to interracial marriage? What are people afraid of? Is there anything you could say to alleviate their fears?
3. In an essay, write about Kristof's statement in his conclusion that "we're increasingly going to see a blurring of racial distinctions." How would life in the United States change if he is correct? How is it already heading in that direction?

ANN PATCHETT
Kissing Cousins

Ann Patchett was born in Los Angeles in 1963 and moved to Nashville, Tennessee, with her family at the age of six. She was educated at Sarah Lawrence College and at the prestigious Writer's Workshop at the University of Iowa. She is the author of four novels: The Patron Saint of Liars *(1992),* Taft *(1994),* The Magician's Assistant *(1997), and* Bel Canto *(2001), which won the PEN/Faulkner award for fiction. She also has written for many publications, including the* Chicago Tribune, The Village Voice, GQ, Elle, Gourmet, Vogue, *and* The New York Times Magazine. *This selection appeared in 2002.*

▶ **Prereading: Thinking About the Essay in Advance**

What do you think of first cousins becoming romantically involved? Can you imagine falling in love with your first cousin? Why do you think there is a stigma on first cousins marrying?

▶ **Words to Watch**

star-crossed (par. 1) ill-fated
nominal (par. 3) almost nothing
lethal (par. 3) deadly
stigma (par. 5) part of someone's identity that causes shame
taboos (par. 5) things banned because of morality or social custom
pyromaniac (par. 8) one who enjoys lighting fires

1   Thanks to 12 years of Catholic single-sex education, a lack of brothers, and an over developed interest in reading as a child, I grew up in a world almost completely devoid of boys. Except, of course, for those boys I was related to. I had 25 first cousins, and I remember many summer family reunions eating sand-infused slices of sheet cake on the beaches of Southern California, so lost in the cousin crush of the moment that I could hardly swallow. These feelings were for the most part unexpressed and interchangeable (I liked cousin Lenny as much his brother Greg). One crush, however, started when I was 8 and proved hearty enough to follow me into adulthood. Whenever this cousin and I were on the same side of the country there were dinners, hand-holding, and a certain amount of sighing. Alas, we would be perfect for each other if only we weren't cousins. But we were, and so, feeling genetically star-crossed we always said good night and went our separate ways.

2   It turns out we didn't have to.

3   Popular mythology often takes the place of science. Lemmings do not, in fact, hurl themselves into the sea by the thousands to drown, and the country folk in the film "Deliverance" were not the product of parents who failed to take the initiative to go any farther than their aunt and uncles' houses to look for a spouse. An article published recently in *The Journal of Genetic Counseling* says that the increased risk of birth defects to children born of first cousins is nominal. This isn't exactly breaking news, either; research has been in for some time. Could it be that we are so unnerved by the idea of the union of cousins that we didn't even want to hear about it? The fact that marriage between first cousins is illegal in 24 states will probably go the way of laws that banned interracial marriage. The norm is capable of change. After all, my grandmother was forbidden to serve apple pie with cheddar cheese when she was a young waitress in Kansas. (The combination was once believed to be as lethal as cousin love.)

4   Certainly in just about every other place in the world, marrying your first cousin is an unremarkable event. For centuries royalty has had to look in the bank of immediate relatives to find suitable mates. Who would be good enough for a Hapsburg but another Hapsburg? The notion that there was something genetically weakening, if not downright creepy, about intermarriage is one that is distinctly American. Perhaps it is born from a distaste of what our ancestors left behind when they boarded their ships to the New World. What is thought of as essential in the highest social classes of other countries is seen as a mark of the most backward and impoverished factions of our own. Now we find out that all of those jokes about Appalachian families are utterly baseless.

5   Still, to think that the laws against close family marriages are entirely based in a concern over the medical well-being for the child that might come of that union seems to miss a large part of the point: marrying a cousin at 60 carries almost the same burden of stigma as marrying a cousin at 16. It's one those things we're not supposed to do, and these

days sexually active Americans have precious few limitations. For better or worse, we cling to the few taboos we have left. If the *Journal of Genetic Counseling* told us that there would be no major medical repercussions from reproduction with your brother or aunt, I don't think we would heave a national sigh of relief and say, well, as long as there are no medical issues. . . . Remember Oedipus and Jocasta? The story didn't turn out too well for them.

If you had to mark out the boundaries of incest, some of us are go- 6 ing to put first cousins on one side of the line and some are going to put them on the other. A friend of mine from Los Angeles recently met a first cousin once removed from Israel who she never knew existed. They fell madly in love at a family reunion in Spain. While they are working through cultural differences, a language barrier, and a long commute, the only thing that gives her a moment's pause is the blood tie, even though they have no plans to have children. Yet it seems impossible that a little thing like a common relative should ruin her chances for happiness.

Other cousins, the ones who were more like the pseudo-siblings of 7 your entire youth, may take more consideration. But true love is a rare and wonderful thing, and if you happen to find it with a first cousin in one of the 24 states of the union that will still put you in jail for your marriage, the wisest choice may simply be moving. There are enough of those couples in America now to merit an extensive and thoughtful Web site, cousincouples.com. They supply not only support and inspirational stories but also a very helpful map to show you just what your state thinks of your love life.

I, for one, am glad to have grown up in an era that made me feel that 8 following through on any of my earlier crushes would have been akin to my being pyromaniac. For me, cousin love was like a set of romantic training wheels: safe, steady little things that screwed onto the real wheels of the bike I wasn't actually big enough to ride. Watching the boys swim out into the ocean at those sunburned family reunions, I got to have all the fun without the chance of actually getting hurt. As for the cousin I thought I was in love with, after a few years we turned out not to get along at all. That had nothing to do with our being related but I thank my lucky gene pool that it kept me from marrying him.

▶ Building Vocabulary

This selection requires knowledge of some history and art. Identify the following terms and explain their significance for this article:

1. the film "Deliverance" (par. 3)
2. Hapsburg (par. 4)
3. Appalachian (par. 4)
4. Oedipus and Jocasta (par. 5)

▶Thinking Critically About the Argument

Understanding the Writer's Argument

1. What does Patchett mean when she writes that she was "so lost in the cousin crush of the moment that I could hardly swallow"? (par. 1)
2. What are some myths about cousin marriage?
3. How does the writer describe these myths?
4. What does Patchett mean when she says that "the notion that there was something genetically weakening, if not downright creepy, about intermarriage is one that is distinctly American"? (par. 4)
5. Why is the first cousin relationship on the borderline between acceptability and disgust, according to the writer?
6. How many states in the United States allow first cousins to marry?
7. What was the most positive thing for the writer about having crushes on her cousins?

Understanding the Writer's Techniques

1. What is the writer's major proposition? Where is it best expressed? If you can't find it, why do you think that is? If you can't find it, put her claim into your own words.
2. Why does the writer begin her essay with a recollection of her experiences with her many cousins? What argumentative purpose does this serve?
3. Outline the essay to highlight the minor propositions.
4. What evidence or support does the writer present for her minor propositions?
5. Which evidence in the essay do you think is the most effective? Why?
6. How effective is the writer's insistence in paragraph 7 that "true love" is the most important thing here?
7. In her closing, the writer moves away from saying that "cousin love" is a positive thing and says that it was only a good thing as "romantic training wheels." Why does she shy away from completely endorsing cousin love?

Exploring the Writer's Argument

1. Does Patchett's last sentence contradict the rest of her essay and its message of tolerance? Why or why not? Explain.
2. Many anthropologists believe that the taboo against incest is ingrained in humans as a survival instinct; the species would get stronger, evolutionarily, if people ventured out to other families rather than taking mates from their own families. They say the taboo exists for good reason. Do you agree or not, and why? What would Patchett say to that?

3. Do you think that Patchett's conclusion helps or hurts her argument? Explain your answer. Refer to question 7 in the "Understanding the Writer's Techniques" assignment.

▶ Ideas for Writing Arguments

Prewriting

What were some beliefs you had when you were a child that you now know were false, were myths? Where did those myths come from? How did they come to be dispelled? Did you learn the truth from books? From friends? From parents? From siblings? How did you feel when you learned the truth?

Writing a Guided Argument

Write an essay in which you examine a popular myth you grew up with (for example, that your father was the strongest man in the world or that there was a tooth fairy or Santa Claus). Argue that those mythologies were wrong, and dispel them for your reader.

1. Begin your essay with a recollection of growing up with a myth, and explain the myth's origins.
2. Write about your good or bad memories of the myth.
3. Note how the myth from your childhood affects your life today.
4. Write your major proposition, dispelling the myth.
5. In the next few paragraphs, write minor propositions in which you support the idea in your major proposition.
6. Offer specific examples or anecdotes to support each of your minor propositions.
7. Attempt to use a poetic or nostalgic tone.
8. Close by discussing whether or not you are glad that you believed the myth when you were younger.

Thinking, Arguing, and Writing Collaboratively

Assist in dividing the class into three parts. Each group should prepare for a debate on "cousin love," doing research on the Web (you may visit the Web site Patchett suggests, cousincouples.com) and in the library. Each group should develop some familiarity with the history and practice of cousin marriage around the world. The aim of the debate is to win based on persuasive illustration. Stage the debate, with one group arguing in favor of cousin marriage and the other arguing against it. The third group will act as a jury. The jury should deliberate, vote on the winner, and make a presentation explaining in a written statement the results of the vote.

Writing About the Text

Patchett is a novelist and is known for her prose style. Write an essay in which you examine how Patchett adapts techniques from writing fiction to the essay form. Look especially at how she sets a scene. Does she have any characters? How is her word choice and tone affected?

More Writing Ideas

1. Visit the Web site cousincouples.com, which Patchett mentions in paragraph 7. Record your impressions of the Web site's content in your journal.
2. Research one of the terms in the "Building Vocabulary" exercise, and write a paragraph explaining how it relates to the idea of incest.
3. In paragraph 5, Patchett writes, "For better or worse, we cling to the few taboos we have left." Besides incest, what other taboos do we have? Write an essay in which you answer this question, offering an explanation of each one as well as a judgment about whether we should still hold on to that taboo.

ANDREW SULLIVAN
Let Gays Marry

Andrew Sullivan was born in 1963 in a small town in England. He went to Oxford University and Harvard University, where he earned his Ph.D. in 1989. He was editor at The New Republic *magazine at the age of 27. Sullivan, who is openly homosexual, wrote* Virtually Normal: An Argument About Homosexuality *(1995), a book about gay rights. He resigned from* The New Republic *in 1996 and continues to write widely for many publications. In this selection, Sullivan makes the case for allowing homosexual couples to marry in civil ceremonies.*

▶ Prereading: Thinking About the Essay in Advance

Do you agree with the title of this essay? Should homosexuals be able to marry? Why or why not? If you agree that gays should marry, what do you think would be some common arguments against it?

▶ Words to Watch

subvert (par. 2) overturn
sanction (par. 6) officially approve of
fidelity (par. 7) faithfulness

"A state cannot deem a class of persons a stranger to its laws," de- 1
clared the Supreme Court last week. It was a monumental statement. Gay men and lesbians, the conservative court said, are no longer
strangers in America. They are citizens, entitled, like everyone else, to
equal protection—no special rights, but simple equality.

For the first time in Supreme Court history, gay men and women 2
were seen not as some powerful lobby trying to subvert America, but as
the people we truly are—the sons and daughters of countless mothers
and fathers, with all the weaknesses and strengths and hopes of everybody else. And what we seek is not some special place in America but
merely to be a full and equal part of America, to give back to our society
without being forced to lie or hide or live as second-class citizens.

That is why marriage is so central to our hopes. People ask us why 3
we want the right to marry, but the answer is obvious. It's the same reason anyone wants the right to marry. At some point in our lives, some of
us are lucky enough to meet the person we truly love. And we want to
commit to that person in front of our family and country for the rest of
our lives. It's the most simple, the most natural, the most human instinct
in the world. How could anyone seek to oppose that?

Yes, at first blush, it seems like a radical proposal, but, when you think 4
about it some more, it's actually the opposite. Throughout American history, to be sure, marriage has been between a man and a woman, and in
many ways our society is built upon that institution. But none of that need
change in the slightest. After all, no one is seeking to take away anybody's
right to marry, and no one is seeking to force any church to change any
doctrine in any way. Particular religious arguments against same-sex marriage are rightly debated within the churches and faiths themselves. That
is not the issue here: there is a separation between church and state in this
country. We are only asking that when the government gives out *civil* marriage licenses, those of us who are gay should be treated like anybody else.

Of course, some argue that marriage is *by definition* between a man 5
and a woman. But for centuries, marriage was *by definition* a contract in
which the wife was her husband's legal property. And we changed that.
For centuries, marriage was *by definition* between two people of the same
race. And we changed that. We changed these things because we recognized that human dignity is the same whether you are a man or a woman,
black or white. And no one has any more of a choice to be gay than to be
black or white or male or female.

Some say that marriage is only about raising children, but we let 6
childless heterosexual couples be married (Bob and Elizabeth Dole, Pat
and Shelley Buchanan, for instance). Why should gay couples be
treated differently? Others fear that there is no logical difference between allowing same-sex marriage and sanctioning polygamy and
other horrors. But the issue of whether to sanction multiple spouses
(gay or straight) is completely separate from whether, in the existing

institution between two unrelated adults, the government should discriminate between its citizens.

7   This is, in fact, if only Bill Bennett could see it, a deeply conservative cause. It seeks to change no one else's rights or marriages in any way. It seeks merely to promote monogamy, fidelity, and the disciplines of family life among people who have long been cast to the margins of society. And what could be a more conservative project than that? Why indeed would any conservative seek to oppose those very family values for gay people that he or she supports for everybody else? Except, of course, to make gay men and lesbians strangers in their own country, to forbid them ever to come home.

▶ Building Vocabulary

This essay is making a strong point, and thus it is trying to undermine the opposition's position. List five words or phrases in this essay that aim to strengthen the writer's position and weaken the opposition's. Explain how each word does this.

▶ Thinking Critically About the Argument

Understanding the Writer's Argument

1. Explain in your own words what the Supreme Court means by "A state cannot deem a class of persons a stranger to its laws."
2. Why is marriage so important to gays and lesbians, according to Sullivan?
3. According to Sullivan, what is the difference in the debate between the civil and religious worlds?
4. What is Sullivan's answer to those who say that marriage is by definition between a man and a woman?
5. How does he respond to those who say marriage is only for procreation?
6. Why is gay marriage actually a "conservative project"? Explain what this means.

Understanding the Writer's Techniques

1. Is the writer's major proposition the same as the title? If so, show where it appears in the essay. If not, what is the major proposition?
2. Analyze paragraph 2 and explain why it is effective.
3. What are the writers' minor propositions? Outline the body of the essay.
4. For what argumentative purpose does the writer make the distinction between marriage within a religion and civil marriage?

5. How would you characterize the writer's tone? Why do you think he wrote the essay in this tone? Do you think the fact that this appeared in *Newsweek*, a magazine read by a wide audience, made a difference? Why or why not?
6. Paraphrase the writer's argument in paragraph 5. Is it effective? Why or why not?
7. What minor proposition do you think is the writer's most effective?
8. Analyze the writer's use of the word "home" in paragraph 7.

Exploring the Writer's Argument

1. Sullivan is both openly gay and openly conservative. What is conservatism? How might Sullivan's two identities clash? Do you see evidence of the clash in his essay? Does he reconcile them persuasively?
2. Answer Sullivan's question in paragraph 3.
3. Sullivan says in paragraph 4 that "there is a separation of church and state in this country." Do you think that is absolutely true? How does the religious faith of our leaders affect policy, more specifically, policy toward homosexuality and gay marriage? Examine recent statements made by the president of the United States and members of Congress about the issue and compare them to Sullivan's assertions. Do you think he might persuade them? Explain your answer.

▶ Ideas for Writing Arguments

Prewriting

Will gay marriage inevitably be legalized? Write down some of your thoughts about how that might come about or why it would not come about.

Writing a Guided Argument

Many people think that the legalization of gay marriage is only a matter of time. What does that mean? Argue in an essay that gay marriage will or will not be legal nationally within the next 10 years.

1. Begin your essay with a quote from Sullivan's essay that asserts the moral right of gays to marry.
2. Continue with an analysis of how other social progress has been made.
3. Compare that progress with the advent of gay marriage and make your claim in the form of a prediction.
4. Give at least two minor propositions for why you think gay marriage will or will not soon be legal nationally.

5. Support your ideas with further evidence from other areas of civil rights.
6. Imagine a point the opposition might make; rebut the opposition's point.
7. Conclude your essay with an appeal to the reader's emotions and sense of morality.

Thinking, Arguing, and Writing Collaboratively

Exchange papers from your Writing a Guided Argument assignment with a classmate. Read the student's paper for the success of the argument. Outline the student's essay, listing his or her major proposition and minor propositions, with an indication of the support the student gives. Write a couple of paragraphs to the student, one praising the positive aspects of the paper and the other explaining what is weak and could be improved. Return the paper and your outline and notes.

Writing About the Text

In an essay, compare Sullivan's argument about gay marriage with Ann Patchett's argument about marriage between first cousins in "Kissing Cousins." How are their arguments similar, and how are they different?

More Writing Ideas

1. Gay marriage issues have filled the news recently with officials in some cities and states issuing marriage licenses and performing ceremonies for gay couples. Check newspaper and magazine articles and write a journal entry about your reactions to these official acts.
2. In 2003 the Supreme Court handed down a landmark decision in *Lawrence v. Texas* that has a bearing on gay marriage. The Court struck down sodomy laws in Texas and other states that made homosexual sex a crime. Write a paragraph summarizing either the Court's majority opinion (striking down the sodomy laws), or the dissent (which was written by the justices who wanted to uphold them). What were their claims?
3. In an essay, defend either the majority decision or the dissenting opinion. Use evidence from the texts to make your case.

BARBARA KANTROWITZ
Unmarried, with Children

Barbara Kantrowitz was educated at Cornell University and Columbia University. She is married with two children and lives in New York City. She has written for many magazines and newspapers, including The New York Times, The Philadelphia Inquirer, Newsday, Martha Stewart Living, *and* Newsweek, *where this article appeared in 2001 and where she is now senior editor. In this essay, Kantrowitz discusses the ever-shifting face of the American family, especially the mainstream acceptance of single-parent families.*

▶ Prereading: Thinking About the Essay in Advance

How has the American family changed in the past 20 years? 10 years? 5 years? What was a "traditional" family years ago, and what is a "traditional" family today?

▶ Words to Watch

negotiating (par. 1) dealing with
postmodern (par. 2) contemporary
demographers (par. 3) scientists who study patterns of human populations
stigma (par. 4) part of one's identity that seems shameful
watershed (par. 4) significant
serendipitous (par. 9) chance
futile (par. 14) without effect

Just imagine what would happen if June and Ward Cleaver were negotiat- 1
ing family life these days. The scenario might go something like this: they meet at the office (she's in marketing; he's in sales) and move in together after dating for a couple of months. A year later June gets pregnant. What to do? Neither feels quite ready to make it legal and there's no pressure from their parents, all of whom are divorced and remarried themselves. So little Wally is welcomed into the world with June's last name on the birth certificate. A few years later June gets pregnant again with the Beav. Ward's ambivalent about second-time fatherhood and moves out, but June decides to go ahead on her own. In her neighborhood, after all, single motherhood is no big deal; the lesbians down the street adopted kids from South America, and the soccer mom next door is divorced with a live-in boyfriend.

Figures released last week from the 2000 Census show that this post- 2
modern June would be almost as mainstream as the 1950s version. The number of families headed by single mothers has increased 25 percent since 1990, to more than 7.5 million households. Contributing to the numbers are a high rate of divorce and out-of-wedlock births. For most of the

past decade, about a third of all babies were born to unmarried women, compared with 3.8 percent in 1940. Demographers now predict that more than half of the youngsters born in the 1990s will spend at least part of their childhood in a single-parent home. The number of single fathers raising kids on their own is also up; they now head just over 2 million families. In contrast, married couples raising children—the "Leave It to Beaver" models—account for less than a quarter of all households.

3   Demographers and politicians will likely spend years arguing about all this and whether the shifts are real or just numerical flukes. But one thing everyone does agree on is that single mothers are now a permanent and significant page in America's diverse family album. "We can encourage, pressure, preach, and give incentives to get people to marry," says Stephanie Coontz, author of "The Way We Never Were" and a family historian at the Evergreen State College in Olympia, Wash. "But we still have to deal with the reality that kids are going to be raised in a variety of ways, and we have to support all kinds of families with kids."

4   This new breed of single mother doesn't fit the old stereotype of an unwed teen on welfare. She's still likely to be financially insecure, but she could be any age and any race. The median age for unmarried mothers is the late 20s, and the fastest-growing category is white women. She may be divorced or never-married. Forty percent are living with men who may be the fathers of one or more of their children; as the Census numbers also showed, there's been nearly a 72 percent increase in the number of cohabiting couples, many of whom bring along children from previous relationships. She may also be a single mother by choice. Unwed motherhood has lost much of its stigma and has even been glamorized by celebrity role models like Rosie O'Donnell and Calista Flockhart. "Twenty years ago middle-class women believed it took a man to have a child, but that's no longer true," says Rosanna Hertz, chair of the women's studies department at Wellesley College. "We've reached a watershed moment."

5   More women are better educated and better able to support themselves—so a husband is no longer a financial prerequisite to motherhood. That's a huge social change from the past few decades. Carolyn Feuer, 30, a registered nurse from New York, decided not to marry her boyfriend when she became pregnant with Ryan, now 6. "It wouldn't have been a good marriage," she says. "It's better for both of us this way, especially my son." Her steady salary meant she had choices. "I had an apartment," she says. "I had a car. I felt there was no reason why I shouldn't have the baby. I felt I could give it whatever it needed as far as love and support and I haven't regretted it for even a minute since."

6   For many women, the barrier to marriage may be that they care too much about it, not too little, and they want to get it right. If they can't find the perfect soulmate of their dreams, they'd rather stay single. So they're postponing that walk down the aisle until after college, grad school, or starting a career and putting a little money in the bank. "Para-

doxically, more people today value marriage," says Frank Furstenberg, professor of sociology at the University of Pennsylvania. "They take it seriously. That's why they're more likely to cohabit. They want to be sure before they take the ultimate step." The average age of first marriage is now 25 for women and 27 for men—up from 20 and 23 in 1960. That's the highest ever, which leaves plenty of time for a live-in relationship to test a potential partner's compatibility. "Today it's unusual if you don't live with someone before you marry them," says Andrew Cherlin, a sociologist at Johns Hopkins University. "Before 1970, it wasn't respectable among anyone but the poor."

Some of these women are adult children of divorce who don't want to   7
make their own offspring suffer the pain of watching a parent leave. They see living together as a kind of trial marriage without the legal entanglements that make breaking up so hard to do—although research indicates that cohabiting couples don't have a much better track record. "They're trying to give their marriages a better chance," says Diane Sollee, founder of the Coalition for Marriage, Family, and Couples Education. "They're not trying to be immoral and get away with something."

And if the first (or the second) relationship doesn't work out, many   8
women think there's no reason to forgo motherhood. Wellesley researcher Hertz has been studying middle-class single mothers older than 35. Most of the 60 women she has interviewed in-depth became pregnant "accidentally." While their babies may have been unplanned, they were not unwanted. Hertz says that for many of these women, the decision to become a mother was all about the modern version of "settling." In the old days a woman did that by marrying Mr. Almost Right. Now settling means having the baby even if you can't get the husband. "When I started this project in the mid-'90s," Hertz says, "these women were tough to find. Now they're all over—next door, at the playground, in your kid's classroom. They've become a normal part of the terrain."

Not all single mothers by choice wait for a serendipitous pregnancy.   9
There are so many options: sperm banks, adoption. New Yorker Gail Janowitz, a market researcher in her mid-40s, decided to adopt two years ago. She always wanted to be a mother, but never married. "As I got older," she says, "I didn't know if the timing of meeting a man was going to work out. I thought, well, I'll do the child part first." A year ago she adopted Rose, now 18 months old, in Kazakhstan. Although there have been difficult moments, Janowitz says she has no regrets. "I've never stopped knowing it was the right thing to do," she says. "I think I will still have the opportunity or the option, hopefully, to get married. But right now, I have a family."

Even under the very best of conditions, single motherhood is a long,   10
hard journey for both mother and children. No one really knows the long-term consequences for youngsters who grow up in these new varieties of single-parent and cohabiting homes. Much of the research in the past on

alternative living arrangements has concentrated on children of divorce, who face very different issues than youngsters whose mothers have chosen to be single from the start or are cohabiting with their children's fathers or other partners. "We need to start paying attention to how these kids" living in cohabiting homes are doing, says Susan Brown, a sociologist at Bowling Green State University in Ohio. "All the evidence we have suggests that they are not doing too well."

11   Single mothers in general have less time for each individual child than two parents, and cohabiting relationships are less stable than marriages. That means that children living in these families are more likely to grow up with a revolving set of adults in their lives. And the offspring of single parents are more likely to skip the altar themselves, thus perpetuating the pattern of their childhood. "Children living outside marriage are seven times more likely to experience poverty and are 17 times more likely to end up on welfare and to have a propensity for emotional problems, discipline problems, early pregnancy, and abuse," says Robert Rector, a senior research fellow at the Heritage Foundation, a conservative think tank. "It can be a recipe for disaster."

12   The average kid in a single-parent family looks much the same emotionally as children who grow up in the most conflicted two-parent homes, says Larry Bumpass, a sociologist at the University of Wisconsin. But, he adds, "the average is not the script written for every child. The outcomes are not all negative; it's just a matter of relative probability . . . the majority will do just fine." Lyn Freundlich, who is raising two boys in Boston with their father, Billy Brittingham, says her home is as stable as any on the block. Freundlich and Brittingham have no plans to marry even though they've been living together for 13 years. "It's not important to me," says Freundlich, 36, who works for the Boston AIDS Action Committee. "Marriage feels like a really unfair institution where the government validates some relationships and not others. I can't think of any reason compelling enough to become part of an institution I'm uncomfortable with." When she was pregnant with their first son, Jordan, now 6, Brittingham's parents "waged a campaign for us to get married," she says. His father was relieved when they decided to draft a will and sign a medical proxy. These days, the possibility of marriage hardly crosses her mind. "I'm so busy juggling all the details of having a two-career family, taking care of my kids, seeing my friends, and having a role in the community that it's just not something I think about," she says.

13   If Freundlich isn't thinking about marriage, a lot of politicians are—from the White House on down. In a commencement address at Notre Dame on Sunday, President George W. Bush planned to stress the need to strengthen families and assert that "poverty has more to do with troubled lives than a troubled economy," according to an aide. Bush believes funding religious initiatives is one way Washington can foster family stability. Policies to encourage marriage are either in place or under discussion around the country. Some states, such as Arizona and Louisiana, have es-

tablished "covenant" marriages in which engaged couples are required to get premarital counseling. It's harder to get divorced in these marriages. Utah allows counties to require counseling before issuing marriage licenses to minors and people who have been divorced. Florida now requires high-school students to take marriage-education classes that stress that married people are statistically healthier and wealthier.

Some researchers who study the history of marriage say that such efforts may be futile or even destructive. "Giving incentives or creating pressures for unstable couples to wed can be a huge mistake," says family historian Coontz. "It may create families with high conflict and instability—the worst-case scenario for kids." Other scientists say that lifelong marriage may be an unrealistic goal when humans have life expectancies of 80 or older. In their new book, "The Myth of Monogamy," David Barash and Judith Lipton say that in the natural world, monogamy is rare. And even among humans, it was probably the exception throughout much of human history. In "Georgiana: Duchess of Devonshire," biographer Amanda Foreman details bed-hopping among the 18th-century British aristocracy that would make even a randy Hollywood icon blush.   14

If a long and happy marriage is an elusive goal for couples in any century, most women—even those scarred by divorce—say it's still worth pursuing. When Roberta Lanning, 37, of Woodland Hills, Calif., became pregnant with her fifth child after a bitter divorce, she decided not to marry her boyfriend and raise Christian, now 9, on her own. As a child of divorce herself, she never wanted to raise a family on her own. "Single motherhood is not a good thing," she says. "It's definitely one hurdle after another." And despite everything, she hasn't given up. "It's been my heart's desire to have a father and mother in a structured home situation" for Christian, she says. "It just hasn't happened for me. Believe me, I've certainly been looking." If she finds the right man, chances are he'll probably have a couple of kids of his own by now, too.   15

▶ Building Vocabulary

Explain in your own words the meanings of the following phrases and words. Use clues from the surrounding text to help you understand or use reference texts:

1. soccer mom (par. 1)
2. out-of-wedlock births (par. 2)
3. median age (par. 4)
4. cohabitating couples (par. 4)
5. legal entanglements (par. 7)
6. Mr. Almost Right (par. 8)
7. think tank (par. 11)

8. religious initiatives (par. 13)
9. bed-hopping (par. 14)
10. aristocracy (par. 14)

▶Thinking Critically About the Argument

Understanding the Writer's Argument

1. June and Ward Cleaver were the parents in the TV series *Leave It to Beaver*, which showed an extremely traditional family in the 1950s. Why would the writer's hypothetical June Cleaver in paragraph 1 be mainstream today?
2. Why are so many families today headed by single moms?
3. Why does Stephanie Coontz say that people need to accept all kinds of families?
4. Who is today's single mother, and how has the profile changed?
5. Why are more and more women choosing to adopt or get artificially inseminated?
6. What are the different opinions the writer presents about the effect of single parenthood on children?
7. Why would conservatives' religious initiatives to foster traditional marriages "be futile or even destructive"? (par. 14)

Understanding the Writer's Techniques

1. What is the writer's claim? Does she place it effectively? If so, explain. If not, where would you put it?
2. What is the argumentative effect of the scenario outlined in paragraph 1?
3. In paragraph 5, the argument shifts. How would you characterize this shift?
4. Outline the minor propositions the writer gives for her claim. Which proposition is most interesting? Is that also the most effective? What is the weakest? What kind of evidence does the writer use to support her minor propositions?
5. What is the effect of the sentences at the beginning of paragraphs 13, 14, and 15 that act as transitions?
6. How effective is the writer's discussion in paragraphs 10 through 12 about how single-parent families affect the lives of children?
7. How does the writer rebut Robert Rector's quote in paragraph 11? Is her technique effective? Explain the effect the final example of Roberta Lanning has on the writer's argument.

Exploring the Writer's Argument

1. The writer of this essay has obviously done a great deal of reporting. She uses several single mothers as examples. Do you find this excessive? Are some of the examples more persuasive than others, and, more important, are they *meant* to be persuasive? If not, what is their purpose? If so, how are they persuasive?

2. Do you find this essay completely coherent? The concept of single motherhood is a wide topic, and the writer does a lot of work to tie everything together, exploring all the different reasons why women would be single parents or would choose that lifestyle. Where in the essay do you think the discussion becomes too broad?

3. The writer uses many quotes and opinions of other writers and thinkers, but rarely comes out and expresses her own opinions. Examine where in the essay the writer's own ideas stand out. Does she hide behind her research? Explain your answer.

▶ Ideas for Writing Arguments

Prewriting

Are there any examples in your life, or in the lives of your family members or friends, that show that children suffer from divorce? Write a few notes about some of the negative effects of divorce on children.

Writing a Guided Argument

Kantrowitz seems to think that "a long and happy marriage is an elusive goal," but she also says that divorce is usually difficult for everyone involved. Write an essay about how people give up on marriages too readily and why they should seek counseling if they are considering divorce.

1. Open with an example of how divorce can be harmful to everyone involved in a marriage.
2. Indicate that perhaps married couples need to be less hasty in getting divorces.
3. Give at least two grounds for your claim.
4. Use a tone of concerned detachment in your essay.
5. Support your ideas with statistics from Kantrowitz's essay.
6. Give an example of a success story by describing a couple at risk of divorce who sought counseling.
7. Conclude your essay by referring to the divorce rate and explaining why the rate is alarming.

Thinking, Arguing, and Writing Collaboratively

In small groups of three or four, choose two different quotes from single mothers in Kantrowitz's essay. Compare couples the women's approaches to the situation and discuss which you think is the more positive attitude. Present your opinions to the class.

Writing About the Text

Andrew Sullivan's "Let Gays Marry" states that most gay people want the opportunity to marry. Many observers think that gay marriage will soon be a reality: it already is in Canada, and some American cities have provided marriage licenses to gay couples. Write an essay explaining what lessons homosexuals could learn about marriage from Kantrowitz's essay. Argue that gays should still want to get married or that they should avoid the institution.

More Writing Ideas

1. In your journal, freewrite about the topic of adoption. Do not edit your writing. Write nonstop for at least 15 minutes. When you finish, exchange your journal with another student. Do you see any potential major propositions in your classmate's freewriting?
2. Do you think men—or women—are to blame for the high rate of divorce in this country? Write a paragraph defending your position.
3. Write an essay in the form of a letter to one of the experts quoted in Kantrowitz's essay, arguing against their position. Do research on the Web or in the library if necessary to build evidence for your claim.

3 Patterns of Argument

Why do we write essays? We might write to amuse, to excite, to educate, to clarify, to direct, and, of course, we might write to persuade or defend a reasoned position. We might even write because our teachers told us to. No matter what the reason, we write for an audience. Because we will always write for an audience, we have to understand which of these reasons motivate our writing. Once you understand your goals, you can understand how to achieve them.

Each piece of writing requires a different approach, and luckily you have many tools at your disposal. In the Socratic dialogue *Gorgias*, by Plato (an ancient Greek writer whose work appears in Part 4 of *To the Point*), philosophers debate the meaning of the art of rhetoric—the art of using language effectively. One of the definitions that they uncover is that rhetoric is the art of "manufacturing persuasion." This is an important definition, because it underlines the fact that no matter what kind of writing you do, you are, in some way, making a point. There will always be an aspect of argumentation in every essay you write.

Since Plato's time, writing teachers have studied rhetoric extensively and discovered that there are a number of techniques that all writers of essays use to make their points. These techniques are called rhetorical modes. A writer might recount an experience, explore the meaning of a term or concept, or compare two ideas to underline their similarities or differences. Each of these goals can advance an idea and make a point. These are, again, tools, means for supporting a claim, and not ends in themselves. This chapter shows how various rhetorical modes can help you advance a major proposition and make it persuasive to a reader.

One of the most vivid of the rhetorical modes is narration, or telling a story. The advantages of using narration are fairly obvious: The reader is interested and drawn into the events that are narrated. Also, we usually tell stories in chronological order, so that they are easy to follow. Remember that narration, as with all the rhetorical modes, is not an end in itself. It must support a claim. If you want to persuade your mother that you should go on a trip to Europe, you might tell her the story of a friend who recently went to Europe. In your story, you would highlight the positive aspects about his trip and leave out the fact that he really only partied or that he was mugged in Amsterdam. You are in control of the story, so the details you choose can be persuasive. Fae Myenne Ng, in her narrative essay "False Gold," tells the story of her father's emigration from China to the United States. She fills her essay with vivid details of her father's miserable experience, making her point about the unearned reputation of America as a promised land for Chinese immigrants. She uses her anecdotes to make a powerful point.

Another useful rhetorical mode is description. Think about how you experience the world. The human body takes in sensations through the eyes, nose, ears, skin, and tongue. Because writing is a way to communicate ideas and feelings to a reader, and because you as a writer want to influence your reader as much as possible, you want to make your reader experience what you want her to experience. (Writers frequently use description when writing narrative. As we will see, the rhetorical modes often are used together.) Joan Didion, in her essay "Marrying Absurd," uses the five senses to comment on the kitchy world of Las Vegas nuptuals. The well-placed sensory detail can say more than much abstract writing.

Imagine a friend is telling you about a recent movie that she hated. She is arguing for the poor quality of the film. If she told you simply that the movie was terrible, you would not be convinced. You would demand specific examples of why she didn't like the movie: the lighting was bad, or the acting was weak, or—better yet and more specifically—the lead actor's performance lacked energy. When you are making your case, offering examples—detailed, specific examples—can often mean the difference between a successful argument and an unsuccessful one. Illustration—that is, providing examples—can help bring abstract ideas to life. For instance, Manning Marable offers many examples of injustice against African Americans to make his argument for reparations for slavery stronger. Once again, you will notice some overlapping here: narrative, examples, and description all can interweave to hold the reader's attention.

Comparing or contrasting two points of view or two subjects in an essay can also help support your claim. You can strengthen an argument about proper behavior by standing an exemplar of properness next to someone poorly behaved. In "And Rarely the Twain Shall Meet," Deborah Tannen writes about the differences between how girls and boys approach competition in sports and playtime, and how that difference continues into adulthood. Her juxtaposing of examples and anecdotes of each sex (girls negotiate, boys fight) help make her powerful point.

A writer might choose to make a point by exploring the various facets of a term or phrase. An extended definition of marriage as, say, a prison, can be the basis for examples of henpecked husbands or dissatisfied housewives. As the writer of an essay, it is up to you to define your terms and lead your reader down the path you have set out, especially when readers might misconstrue your chosen concept or if you think it has been misinterpreted. Lorenzo Albacete, in "The Struggle with Celibacy," attempts to clarify the concept of priestly celibacy in the Catholic Church by limning its boundaries. His essay adds up to an extended definition of celibacy that is in service of his central point about the usefulness and significance of the practice.

Process, or writing instructions for an activity, carries with it an implicit argument as well. In "How to Duck Out of Teaching," Douglas Stalker's amusing instructions to professors on how to waste time in the classroom has a pointed message and a claim: Classroom time is something to be wasted, if possible. Stalker's essay, of course, aims for humor, but writers can make serious claims using process. For example, a writer might offer simple instructions on how to keep a bicycle in a city in order to support a proposition that more people in cities *should* travel by bicycle instead of by car.

If a writer explains to her readers the various reasons that she arrived at her point, she is using causal analysis to influence her readers. A writer arguing against the death penalty might explain the events or reasoning that led to her position. In perhaps the most famous causal argument in American history, Thomas Jefferson wrote in the Declaration of Independence the many reasons why the colonies were breaking off from Great Britain. The best feature of causal analysis is that we do it all the time instinctively. Why didn't you do your homework? "The dog ate it" is a causal analysis in service of your claim that your lack of homework wasn't your fault. We live in a causal world, and analyzing the world from that point of view can enrich your arguments.

Readers of essays don't appreciate confusion. They want clear transitions, clear divisions between ideas. Classification, or breaking down an issue or subject into its constituent parts, can help your readers orient themselves conceptually, and therefore classification is a powerful tool rhetorically. An argument that only movie comedies made before 1940 are any good would benefit from a classification of the different types of comedies made before and since, so that your reader understands the topic. Amartya Sen argues in "A World Not Neatly Divided" that we should not classify people and societies. Categories diminish them, he believes. But he has a difficult task in his argument because classification helps people understand their world. It can help them understand your argument better, as well.

Of course, as suggested earlier, these rhetorical modes are not mutually exclusive. Writers often use them in conjunction to make a strong case. Ronald Takaki, in "The Harmful Myth of Asian Superiority," uses illustration to make his point against seeing Asians as a model minority. He breaks down the large group, Asians, into various nationalities, thus using classification. He also engages causal analysis and extended definition. In your reading and in your writing, pay attention to the use of these various tools and how they can work together effectively.

In truth, in almost every essay you write you are making an argument, whether you want to or not. If you are mindful of the techniques available to you, your arguments will be stronger and your language more effective. You will be, as Plato says, "manufacturing persuasion."

ARGUMENT THROUGH NARRATIVE

FAE MYENNE NG
False Gold

Fae Myenne Ng, a first-generation Chinese-American, was born in 1957 and grew up in San Francisco's Chinatown. Her father was a cook for a University of California at Berkeley fraternity house, her mother a seamstress. After graduating from Berkeley, Ng went East and received a Master's degree from Columbia University in 1984. Not long after, she moved to Brooklyn, where she continued to work on her first novel, Bone. *The book is the story of a first-generation Chinese-American family and their trials and tribulations.* Bone *earned Ng many awards and honors. Much of Ng's work is autobiographical, and she uses narrative techniques to advance her main ideas and claims. She says that her primary goal is to "write about true life."*

▶ Prereading: Thinking About the Essay in Advance

Where were your ancestors born? Have you heard their stories, either directly or through stories others have told? What lessons can you learn from their experiences? Think about whether the people who told you their stories were trying to teach you a lesson.

▶ Words to Watch

ancestor (par. 1) forefather
duped (par. 1) fooled
communal (par. 4) shared
brothel (par. 7) where prostitutes work
indentured (par. 8) forced to work

1   It's that same old, same old story. We all have an immigrant ancestor, one who believed in America; one who, daring or duped, took sail. The Golden Venture emigrants have begun the American journey, suffering and sacrificing, searching for the richer, easier life. I know them; I could be one of their daughters. Like them, my father took the sacrificial role of being the first to venture. Now, at the end of his life, he calls it a bitter, no-luck life. I have always lived with his question, Was it worth it? As a child, I saw the bill-by-bill payback and I felt my own unpayable emotional debt. Obedience and Obligation: the Confucian curse.

For $4,000 my father became the fourth son of a legal Chinese immi-   2
grant living in San Francisco. His paper-father sent him a coaching book,
detailing complicated family history. It was 1940; my father paid ninety
more dollars for passage on the SS *Coolidge*. He had little hand luggage, a
change of clothes, herbs and seeds and a powder for soup. To soothe his
pounding heart during the fifteen-day voyage he recited the coaching
book over and over again. It was not a floating hell. "The food was Chinese. We traveled third-class. A bunk was good enough space." He was
prepared for worse. He'd heard about the Peruvian ships that transported
Chinese coolies for plantation labor in the 1850s. (Every generation has its
model.) One hundred and twenty days. Two feet by six for each man.
Were these the first ships to be called floating hells?

Gold Mountain was the name of my father's America. In February,   3
when the Golden Venture immigrants sailed from Bangkok, they were
shouting, Mei Guo! Mei Guo! "Beautiful Country" was the translation
they preferred. America is the land of light and hope. But landing here is
only the beginning of a long tale. When I saw the photos of the ship-
wrecked Chinese on the beach, I was reminded of the men kept on Angel
Island, the detention center in the middle of San Francisco Bay. A sea of
hats on the deck of the ship. Triple-decked bunkers. Men in loose pants
playing volleyball. "Was volleyball fun?" I wanted to know. My father
shrugged, "Nothing else to do. It helped pass the day." Our fathers spent
months detained on Angel Island. Their name for it was Wooden House.
What, I wonder, are the Chinese calling the detention center in Bethlehem, Pennsylvania?

After his release from Angel Island, my father lived at a bachelor hotel   4
on Waverly Place with a dozen other bachelors in one room, communal toilets, no kitchen. He had breakfast at Uncle's Cafe, dinners at the Jackson
Cafe, midnight noodles at Sam Wo's. Drinks at the Li Po Bar or Red's Place,
where fat burlesque queens sat on his lap. Marriage for duty. Sons for tradition. My father left the hotel but kept the habits. He still eats like a mouse, in
the middle of the night, cooking on a hot plate in his room. (I do my version
of the same.) He keeps his money under the floorboard. When I have it, I
like to have a grip, bill by bill. Like everyone, too little money upsets me; but
more money than I can hold upsets me too. I feel obliged to give it away. Is it
a wonder that money has a dirty feel? Get it and get it fast. Then get rid of it.

I remember this Angel Island photograph. Thirty bare-chested Chi-   5
nese men are waiting for a medical examination. The doctor, a hunching
man with a scraping stare, sits at a small desk, elbows and thick hands
over a black book. At his side, a guard in knee-high boots measures a
boy's forehead. Arranged by height, baby-eyed boys stand stoop-
shouldered on the outer edge. The men, at least a head taller, stand toward the center of the room, staring at the examiner. Those eyes scare me.
Bold and angry and revengeful. Eyes that owe. Eyes that will make you
pay. Humiliation with a vengeance.

6   As boldly, the Golden Venture men have looked into American cameras. (If they believed a foot on soil would make them legal, a photo in an American newspaper would be as good as a passport.) There was a "See me!" bounce in their faces. They'd arrived, and now they wanted to send their news back home. And back home, a grateful father jumped when he picked out his son as one of the survivors, "He's alive! My son made it."

7   Another photo. A Golden Venture man looks out from a locked door, his face framed by a tight window. He has a jail-view of the Beautiful Country. How would he describe his new world? I imagine he'd use his own body as a measure. "Window, two head high. Sun on both ears." Can we forget the other "face" photograph taken earlier this century? The sold and smuggled prostitute, demoted from brothel to a crib, a wooden shack with barred windows that barely fits a cot. Looking out from her fenced window, she has the same downcast eyes, the same bitter-strange lips that seem to be smiling as well as trembling. The caption quotes her price: "Lookee two bits, feelee floor bits, doee six bits."

8   Life was and still is weighed in gold. People buy people. Sons and wives and slaves. There was the imperial edict that forbade Chinese to leave China; there was China's contribution to France during World War I, in which tens of thousands of Chinese lived horrible lives as indentured slaves. I've heard parents threaten to sell children who misbehave. (Mine threatened to throw me into the garbage can where they claimed they found me.) There's the story of Old Man Jeong, the one on Beckett Alley. Lonely after his wife died, fearful no one would care for him in his senile retirement, he went back to his home village and bought himself a wife. A woman born in 1956.

9   Listen to the animal names. Snakes sneak into America. The Golden Venture was a snake ship. The emigrants are snake cargo; the middleman, a snakehead. In my father's time, a pig was sold to America. A pig gets caught, a pig gets cheated. My father feels cheated, sold, on an easy story.

10   On a recent visit to my father's house in Guangzhou, I found his original coaching book. I knew it had been untouched since he last held it. In my hand, the loosely bound papers felt like ashes. I thought about how when he committed everything to memory, he became another man's son. There's an elaborate map of the family compound; each page is lined with questions and answers, some marked with red circles. Tedious questions and absurd details. How much money did Second Brother send to Mother? How much farmland did Mother have and what vegetables were harvested? Third Brother's wife's feet, were they big or bound? The book has a musty smell that reaches into my throat.

11   One out of every four relations let me know they wanted to come to America. At the end of my visit, a distant relation and her 13-year-old daughter followed me into the rice paddies. "I'm selling her," the mother told me.

12   "What did you say? Say again?" I replied.

She held a palm over her (golden) lower teeth, and said it again,   13
"Don't know what I'm saying? Sell. We sell her."

I stared at her. She laughed some more and then just walked away,   14
back toward the village. The girl followed me, quiet till we got to the
river, where she posed for some pictures and then asked for my address. I
wrote it on the back of a business card. (I considered giving her my post
office box.) I hope never to be surprised. I hope never to see this child at
my door holding the card like a legal document.

"Don't add and don't take away" was the advice of an uncle who   15
heard that I wrote things. Stay safe. Keep us safe. How right that "China"
is written with the character "middle." Obedience is a safe position. The
Golden Venture men trusted the stories they heard. Their clansmen en-
trusted their dreams to them. The question is not how bad it is in China.
The question is how good it can be in America. My father believes the
Golden Venturers have only passed through the first hell. In coming to
America, he laments (there is no other word) that he trusted too much.
Ironic that in Chinese he bought a name that reads, To Have Trust.

▶ Building Vocabulary

Ng's essay contains words about the Asian immigrant experience you
might not be familiar with. Identify the following, consulting reference
works if necessary:

1. Confucian (par. 1)
2. coolies (par. 2)
3. Bangkok (par. 3)
4. burlesque (par. 4)
5. Guangzhou (par. 10)
6. rice paddies (par. 11)

▶ Thinking Critically About the Argument

Understanding the Writer's Argument

1. Why does Ng call the selection "False Gold"?
2. Why did Ng's father leave China? Why did he come to the United
   States?
3. In paragraph 1, what is the "bill-by-bill payback" Ng refers to? What
   does she mean by an "unpayable emotional debt"?
4. How is "Obedience and Obligation" the "Confucian curse"? What
   does that phrase mean?
5. What is the Golden Venture? What prompts Ng's trip back to China?
   Why would she make the opposite trip her father made years before?
6. In paragraph 2, what is the "coaching book" her father received?

7. Why does Ng give the 13-year-old girl her address on the back of a business card if she hopes she is never surprised by her presence?
8. What did Ng's father mean that "he trusted too much"? (par. 15)

Understanding the Writer's Techniques

1. What is the essay's claim? If there isn't one, what paragraph tells the reader what Ng's main idea is most clearly? Which sentence in that paragraph best states the main proposition?
2. Ng begins her essay by claiming that the story of her father's experience is typical, that it is "that same old, same old story." Why does she do this, and do you think she is right?
3. A narrative essay uses description to bring to life certain events. What images in Ng's essay do you find most effective?
4. Why does Ng include, in paragraphs 5 and 7, descriptions of photographs that she has seen?
5. What is your opinion of the conclusion of Ng's essay? What does it say about Ng as a writer? As a daughter? As an Asian American? As an American?

Exploring the Writer's Argument

1. Ng never tells us the conditions of the Golden Venture immigrants back in China. She writes, "The question is not how bad it is in China. The question is how good it can be in America." Why doesn't she explore the problems back in China?
2. Ng seems to suggest that the promises given to her father and other Golden Venture immigrants like him were wrong. Do you think they were? Why or why not?
3. Do you find Ng's essay too bitter about her father's experience? Do you think her bitterness is warranted? Why or why not?
4. In paragraph 15, Ng writes that "the Golden Venture men trusted the stories they heard." She seems to suggest that they believed in those stories because they were Chinese. What do you think it is about your ethnic background that made your ancestors come to the United States?

▶ Ideas for Writing Arguments

Prewriting

What prompts people to leave their country? What would force you to leave your country and go elsewhere? How would you choose where to go?

Writing a Guided Argument

Write a narrative essay in which you imagine the experience of your ancestors or family members who came to the United States. What prompted them to come, and what was their experience? Make sure that you, like Ng, have a claim, positive or negative, about the United States.

1. Begin your essay by giving some background about your ancestors. Who were they, and where did they come from? Why did they want to leave? Write your thesis statement at the end of the first paragraph.
2. First, tell the story of your ancestor's trip to this country.
3. Try to use vivid description to bring the story to life, even if it means inventing details to make it more dramatic.
4. Then write a narrative about how your ancestor came to the decision to leave.
5. Finally, write about the ancestor's experience in this country.
6. End your essay by commenting on the stories you presented. What is your opinion? Restate the claim in new words, and then bring the discussion around to you and your experience of the United States.

Thinking, Arguing, and Writing Collaboratively

Exchange drafts of your Writing a Guided Argument essay with another student in the class. Analyze your fellow student's essay for effective use of detail and description. Does the narrative serve the purpose of a main idea or proposition, or is it there merely as a narrative? If there is no claim, suggest one, and work together to come up with an acceptable one. If there is a claim, try to improve it together. Also, take out unnecessary details and events that do not serve the main idea.

Writing About the Text

Ng's style in this essay is distinctive. How would you characterize her style of writing? How does she use language to express the main idea of the essay? Write an essay about Ng's use of language, including her use of fragments and choppy sentences.

More Writing Ideas

1. We are not today immigrating to the United States, but all of us have a dream that can count as "false gold." Write a journal entry about what your personal "false gold" is.
2. In a paragraph, analyze a photograph of older family members. What does the photograph tell you about the people in it. Only say what you can figure out from what you see.
3. Ng is writing about a phenomenon that many others have written about: the United States being perceived as the promised land by immigrants. Write an essay in which you argue that the United States does or does not live up to these expectations.

ARGUMENT THROUGH DESCRIPTION

JOAN DIDION
Marrying Absurd

Joan Didion was born in 1934 in Sacramento, California. Her family has been in California for five generations, and she often writes about the state. She began her writing career when she won an essay contest sponsored by Vogue *magazine, which then hired her. Her first book, a novel called* Run River, *was published in 1963. She has written a number of other novels, but she is best known for her books of collected essays including* Slouching Toward Bethlehem *(1968) and* The White Album *(1979). Her writing is distinguished by her vividness of description and accurate dialogue.*

▶ Prereading: Thinking About the Essay in Advance

What does "absurd" mean? Under what circumstances might marrying be considered "absurd"? This essay is about marriage in Las Vegas. How does that change your answer?

▶ Words to Watch

moonscape (par. 1) a landscape marked by terrain that looks like the surface of the moon
mesquite (par. 1) a tree that grows in the desert
en masse (par. 1) as a whole, all together
allegorical (par. 2) symbolical
implausibility (par. 2) unbelievability
nosegay (par. 4) bouquet of flowers
Panglossian (par. 5) excessively optimistic

1   To be married in Las Vegas, Clark County, Nevada, a bride must swear that she is eighteen or has parental permission and a bridegroom that he is twenty-one or has parental permission. Someone must put up five dollars for the license. (On Sundays and holidays, fifteen dollars. The Clark County Courthouse issues marriage licenses at any time of the day or night except between noon and one in the afternoon, between eight and nine in the evening, and between four and five in the morning.) Nothing else is required. The State of Nevada, alone among these United States, demands neither a premarital blood test nor a waiting period before or after the issuance of a marriage license. Driving in across the Mojave from Los Angeles, one sees the signs way out on the desert, looming up from that moonscape of rattle-snakes and mesquite, even before the Las Vegas lights appear like a mirage on the horizon: "GETTING MARRIED?

Free License Information First Strip Exit." Perhaps the Las Vegas wedding industry achieved its peak operational efficiency between 9:00 p.m. and midnight of August 26, 1965, an otherwise unremarkable Thursday which happened to be, by Presidential order, the last day on which anyone could improve his draft status merely by getting married. One hundred and seventy-one couples were pronounced man and wife in the name of Clark County and the State of Nevada that night, sixty-seven of them by a single justice of the peace, Mr. James A. Brennan. Mr. Brennan did one wedding at the Dunes and the other sixty-six in his office, and charged each couple eight dollars. One bride lent her veil to six others. "I got it down from five to three minutes," Mr. Brennan said later of his feat. "I could've married them *en masse*, but they're people, not cattle. People expect more when they get married."

What people who get married in Las Vegas actually do expect—what,   2
in the largest sense, their "expectations" are—strikes one as a curious and self-contradictory business. Las Vegas is the most extreme and allegorical of American settlements, bizarre and beautiful in its venality and in its devotion to immediate gratification, a place the tone of which is set by mobsters and call girls and ladies' room attendants with amyl nitrite poppers in their uniform pockets. Almost everyone notes that there is no "time" in Las Vegas, no night and no day and no past and no future (no Las Vegas casino, however, has taken the obliteration of the ordinary time sense quite so far as Harold's Club in Reno, which for a while issued, at odd intervals in the day and night, mimeographed "bulletins" carrying news from the world outside); neither is there any logical sense of where one is. One is standing on a highway in the middle of a vast hostile desert looking at an eighty-foot sign which blinks "STARDUST" or "CAESAR'S PALACE." Yes, but what does that explain? This geographical implausibility reinforces the sense that what happens there has no connection with "real" life; Nevada cities like Reno and Carson are ranch towns, Western towns, places behind which there is some historical imperative. But Las Vegas seems to exist only in the eye of the beholder. All of which makes it an extraordinarily stimulating and interesting place, but an odd one in which to want to wear a candlelight satin Priscilla of Boston wedding dress with Chantilly lace insets, tapered sleeves and a detachable modified train.

And yet the Las Vegas wedding business seems to appeal to precisely   3
that impulse. "Sincere and Dignified Since 1954," one wedding chapel advertises. There are nineteen such wedding chapels in Las Vegas, intensely competitive, each offering better, faster, and, by implication, more sincere services than the next: Our Photos Best Anywhere, Your Wedding on A Phonograph Record, Candlelight with Your Ceremony, Honeymoon Accommodations, Free Transportation from Your Motel to Courthouse to Chapel and Return to Motel, Religious or Civil Ceremonies, Dressing Rooms, Flowers, Rings, Announcements, Witnesses Available, and Ample Parking. All of these services, like most others in Las Vegas (sauna baths,

payroll-check cashing, chinchilla coats for sale or rent) are offered twenty-four hours a day, seven days a week, presumably on the premise that marriage, like craps, is a game to be played when the table seems hot.

4   But what strikes one most about the Strip chapels, with their wishing wells and stained-glass paper windows and their artificial bouvardia, is that so much of their business is by no means a matter of simple convenience, of late-night liaisons between show girls and baby Crosbys. Of course there is some of that. (One night about eleven o'clock in Las Vegas I watched a bride in an orange minidress and masses of flame-colored hair stumble from a Strip chapel on the arm of her bridegroom, who looked the part of the expendable nephew in movies like *Miami Syndicate*. "I gotta get the kids," the bride whimpered. "I gotta pick up the sitter, I gotta get to the midnight show." "What you gotta get," the bridegroom said, opening the door of a Cadillac Coupe de Ville and watching her crumple on the seat, "is sober.") But Las Vegas seems to offer something other than "convenience"; it is merchandising "niceness," the facsimile of proper ritual, to children who do not know how else to find it, how to make the arrangements, how to do it "right." All day and evening long on the Strip, one sees actual wedding parties, waiting under the harsh lights at a crosswalk, standing uneasily in the parking lot of the Frontier while the photographer hired by The Little Church of the West ("Wedding Place of the Stars") certifies the occasion, takes the picture: the bride in a veil and white satin pumps, the bridegroom usually in a white dinner jacket, and even an attendant or two, a sister or a best friend in hot-pink *peau de soie*, a flirtation veil, a carnation nosegay. "When I Fall in Love It Will Be Forever," the organist plays, and then a few bars of Lohengrin. The mother cries; the stepfather, awkward in his role, invites the chapel hostess to join them for a drink at the Sands. The hostess declines with a professional smile; she has already transferred her interest to the group waiting outside. One bride out, another in, and again the sign goes up on the chapel door: "One moment please—Wedding."

5   I sat next to one such wedding party in a Strip restaurant the last time I was in Las Vegas. The marriage had just taken place; the bride still wore her dress, the mother her corsage. A bored waiter poured out a few swallows of pink champagne ("on the house") for everyone but the bride, who was too young to be served. "You'll need something with more kick than that," the bride's father said with heavy jocularity to his new son-in-law; the ritual jokes about the wedding night had a certain Panglossian character, since the bride was clearly several months pregnant. Another round of pink champagne, this time not on the house, and the bride began to cry. "It was just as nice," she sobbed, "as I hoped and dreamed it would be."

▶ Building Vocabulary

1. Define the following words and use each in a sentence of your own:
   a. mirage (par. 1)
   b. liaisons (par. 4)
   c. expendable (par. 4)
   d. crumple (par. 4)
   e. corsage (par. 5)
2. Didion makes several references that might be unfamiliar, some because they are obsolete. Identify the following:
   a. justice of the peace (par. 1)
   b. amyl nitrate poppers (par. 2)
   c. mimeographed (par. 2)
   d. phonograph (par. 3)
   e. chinchilla coats (par. 3)
   f. craps (par. 3)
   g. dinner jacket (par. 4)

▶ Thinking Critically About the Argument

Understanding the Writer's Argument

1. Nevada doesn't require a blood test for marriage. Why would other states require one?
2. In paragraph 1, Didion refers to a draft and states that 171 couples were married the last day that marriage would improve one's draft status. What draft is she referring to, and why does she include this information?
3. What is Didion's characterization of Las Vegas? What words does she use that help build that image?
4. How is Las Vegas different from other places, according to Didion?
5. Why are people who want to get married attracted to Las Vegas, besides the lack of a blood-test requirement?
6. What kinds of people typically get married in Las Vegas, according to Didion?
7. In what ways is Las Vegas "odd" (par. 2)? What examples does she give?

Understanding the Writer's Techniques

1. Didion places her claim, or main proposition, about halfway through the essay. What is the claim, and is the entire meaning of the essay expressed in only one sentence?
2. Why does Didion begin her essay with a rundown of the rules for getting married in Las Vegas?

3. What warrants are implied here? How does the reader "learn" to read this essay as he or she moves through it?
4. What points does Didion make to support her central proposition?
5. Who is Didion's ideal audience? What is Didion's tone, and how does she tailor it for her audience?
6. Didion relies on vivid description to help make her points. Why, for example, does she include the description of the bride in the "orange minidress" in paragraph 4? What effect does the description have on the reader?
7. What other images or descriptions are most effective in Didion's argument?
8. Why does Didion end the essay with the pregnant bride crying for joy?

Exploring the Writer's Argument

1. Didion's writing is often considered ironic. Do you think there is too much irony here? Why or why not?
2. Didion's extensive use of description can be quite effective, but sometimes it is possible to push her point too far. Are they any moments where you think Didion's description goes too far?
3. Are there moments when Didion does not use enough description? What would you add?
4. Didion has an argument here, but she only overtly judges her subject in the title by calling the things she is describing "absurd." Where in the essay does Didion stray from subtlety into open judgment?

▶Ideas for Writing Arguments

Prewriting

Take a good look at the place where you live. What is it about your town or city that might seem odd to an outsider? Do a guided freewrite on the topic, traveling in your mind through your city as a tourist.

Writing a Guided Argument

Write an essay called ". . . Absurd" and choose some aspect about where you live that seems strange when you look at it too closely, such as commuting, exercising, or living in small apartments or in large mansions.

1. Begin your essay by describing people in the process of performing your subject, and show—don't tell—how it is absurd.
2. Finish your introduction by explaining to your reader what your major proposition is.

3. Explain and then describe what people expect from performing your subject.
4. Describe what it is about your town that makes people do your subject.
5. Explain one aspect of your subject that is absurd.
6. Describe the first aspect by giving details based on images, sounds, smells, and your other senses.
7. Explain another aspect of your subject that is absurd, and bring the explanation to life with a strong description.
8. Finish your essay by highlighting the most absurd quality of your subject, and describe people in the process of going about their lives doing that action without realizing that they are being absurd.

Thinking, Arguing, and Writing Collaboratively

In groups of four or five, discuss ways to defend the subjects of Didion's essay from her charges of absurdity. How are the people she describes and quotes just being themselves and enjoying themselves? Come up with a rebuttal to Didion's strong argument.

Writing About the Text

Didion seems to be intensely dissatisfied and judgmental about how people come together in Las Vegas. She allows people like the justice of the peace, James Brennan, to say things she obviously thinks are silly, as in paragraph 1, when she quotes him as saying, "I could've married them *en masse*, but they're people, not cattle." She is obviously speaking ironically. How could you satisfy Didion? What does she want? What would she like to see change in Las Vegas? Write an essay in which you explore ways of reforming the marriage industry in Las Vegas, explaining what you think Didion's objections are and addressing them one by one.

More Writing Ideas

1. Write a journal entry about a place you've been that has seemed absurd to you. Why did it seem so absurd?
2. Write a paragraph describing a wedding or other ceremony you have been to. Describe the food, the sights, the sounds.
3. Some people now question the notion of marriage as an antiquated idea. Almost half of all marriages end in divorce. Write an essay in which you argue for or against marriage. Use strong descriptive passages to show marital bliss or discord.

ARGUMENT THROUGH ILLUSTRATION

MANNING MARABLE
An Idea Whose Time Has Come

Manning Marable is a professor of history and political science at Columbia University, where he is also the director of both the Institute for Research in African-American Studies and the Center for Contemporary Black History. Among his works are The Crisis of Color and Democracy *(1992),* Beyond Black and White *(1995), and* Black Leadership *(1998). He is also the editor of the anthology* Freedom on My Mind *(2003). This essay was published in* Newsweek *in 2001.*

▶ Prereading: Thinking About the Essay in Advance

What is your responsibility for the crimes committed by or against your ancestors? Do you have any responsibility? If so, what is that responsibility, and if not, why not?

▶ Words to Watch

fundamental (par. 2) basic
coded (par. 2) deeply ingrained
paradoxically (par. 4) in a way that is self-contradictory
disproportionate (par. 5) vastly unequal
reparations (par. 6) payments for damages

1   In 1854 my great-grandfather, Morris Marable, was sold on an auction block in Georgia for $500. For his white slave master, the sale was just "business as usual." But to Morris Marable and his heirs, slavery was a crime against our humanity. This pattern of human-rights violations against enslaved African-Americans continued under Jim Crow segregation for nearly another century.

2   The fundamental problem of American democracy in the 21st century is the problem of "structural racism": the deep patterns of socioeconomic inequality and accumulated disadvantage that are coded by race, and constantly justified in public discourse by both racist stereotypes and white indifference. Do Americans have the capacity and vision to dismantle these structural barriers that deny democratic rights and opportunities to millions of their fellow citizens?

3   This country has previously witnessed two great struggles to achieve a truly multicultural democracy. The First Reconstruction (1865–1877) ended slavery and briefly gave black men voting rights, but gave no

meaningful compensation for two centuries of unpaid labor. The promise of "40 acres and a mule" was for most blacks a dream deferred.

The Second Reconstruction (1954–1968), or the modern civil-rights   4
movement, outlawed legal segregation in public accommodations and gave blacks voting rights. But these successes paradoxically obscure the tremendous human costs of historically accumulated disadvantage that remain central to black Americans' lives.

The disproportionate wealth that most whites enjoy today was first   5
constructed from centuries of unpaid black labor. Many white institutions, including Ivy League universities, insurance companies, and banks, profited from slavery. This pattern of white privilege and black inequality continues today.

Demanding reparations is not just about compensation for slavery   6
and segregation. It is, more important, an educational campaign to highlight the contemporary reality of "racial deficits" of all kinds, the unequal conditions that impact blacks regardless of class. Structural racism's barriers include "equity inequity," the absence of black capital formation that is a direct consequence of America's history. One third of all black households actually have negative net wealth. In 1998 the typical black family's net wealth was $16,400, less than one fifth that of white families. Black families are denied home loans at twice the rate of whites.

Blacks remain the last hired and first fired during recessions. During   7
the 1990–1991 recession, African-Americans suffered disproportionately. At Coca-Cola, 42 percent of employees who lost their jobs were black. At Sears, 54 percent were black. Blacks have significantly shorter life expectancies, in part due to racism in the health establishment. Blacks are statistically less likely than whites to be referred for kidney transplants or early-stage cancer surgery.

In criminal justice, African-Americans constitute only one seventh of   8
all drug users. Yet we account for 35 percent of all drug arrests, 55 percent of drug convictions and 75 percent of prison admissions for drug offenses.

White Americans today aren't guilty of carrying out slavery and seg-   9
regation. But whites have a moral and political responsibility to acknowledge the continuing burden of history's structural racism.

A reparations trust fund could be established, with the goal of closing   10
the socioeconomic gaps between blacks and whites. Funds would be targeted specifically toward poor, disadvantaged communities with the greatest need, not to individuals.

Let's eliminate the racial unfairness in capital markets that perpetu-   11
ates black poverty. A national commitment to expand black homeownership, full employment, and quality health care would benefit all Americans, regardless of race.

Reparations could begin America's Third Reconstruction, the final   12
chapter in the 400-year struggle to abolish slavery and its destructive consequences. As Malcolm X said in 1961, hundreds of years of racism and

labor exploitation are "worth more than a cup of coffee at a white cafe. We are here to collect back wages."

▶Building Vocabulary

Identify the following terms and references related to the history of slavery in America. (*Hint:* Item 4 comes from a famous poem):

1. auction block (par. 1)
2. Jim Crow (par. 1)
3. 40 acres and a mule (par. 3)
4. a dream deferred (par. 3)
5. voting rights (par. 4)
6. Malcolm X (par. 12)

▶Thinking Critically About the Argument

Understanding the Writer's Argument

1. Why does Marable begin with his great-grandfather being sold as a slave?
2. Marable says in paragraphs 1 and 2 that the sale of his great-grandfather was part of a pattern. What does this pattern consist of?
3. What, in your own words, is "structural racism"? (par. 2)
4. According to Marable, what did the first reconstruction achieve? What did the second achieve?
5. What did both reconstructions fail to achieve?
6. Why, according to Marable, do white people have more wealth than black people, on average?
7. In what form does Marable expect reparations to come?
8. What are the major problems in the black community?
9. Why does Marable quote Malcolm X at the end of his essay?

Understanding the Writer's Techniques

1. What is the main proposition in this essay? Is it in an effective place? Explain.
2. Who is Marable's audience? How would you characterize his tone?
3. Why does Marable include the history lesson in the first part of his essay? Is it effective? Why or why not?
4. How does Marable support his argument?
5. What examples does Marable use to support his claim?
6. What kinds of support does he use? Is it effective? Why or why not?
7. How does Marable develop his conclusion?

Exploring the Writer's Argument

1. Why, according to Marable, has progress been so slow toward getting rid of "equity inequality"? Is his explanation satisfying? Why or why not?
2. Does Marable do a good job of connecting the statistics in paragraphs 6 through 8 to the history of "structural racism"? Why or why not?
3. In paragraph 9, Marable writes that "whites have a moral and political responsibility to acknowledge the continuing burden of history's structural racism." Do you agree? Why or why not?
4. If, as Marable says, "white Americans today aren't guilty of carrying out slavery and segregation," why are whites responsible for granting reparations?
5. Marable calls for funds "targeted specifically toward poor, disadvantaged communities with the greatest need, not to individuals." Does the United States have anything like this today? Why doesn't Marable talk about existing programs?
6. Marable writes in paragraph 11 that "a national commitment to expand black homeownership, full employment, and quality health care would benefit all Americans, regardless of race." What does he mean? How do you think that could happen?

▶ Ideas for Writing Arguments

Prewriting

Black slavery was a terrible crime and a monumental event of the early history of our country. There's a museum for the Holocaust in Washington, D.C., and memorials for the Vietnam, Korean, and World Wars, but there is neither a museum nor a memorial to the victims of slavery. Why do you think this is so?

Writing a Guided Argument

Write an essay arguing for a museum, in Washington, D.C., or some other city in the United States, which focuses on the history of slavery. Refer to Marable's essay at least twice in your essay.

1. Begin by illustrating the horror of American slavery with a striking story or fact.
2. Make your central claim in your introduction.
3. Offer examples of how tragedies and events have their own museums and question why slavery does not.
4. Give examples of what those museums do to educate the public.
5. Point out at least three things a museum could accomplish for the history of slavery and offer vivid examples of how you envision that happening.

6. Use at least one statistic in your essay.
7. Explain how a museum might accomplish some of what Marable wants to accomplish with reparations.

Thinking, Arguing, and Writing Collaboratively

Break into small groups and exchange drafts of your Writing a Guided Argument essay. Write comments on each other's papers, focusing specifically on the success of the use of examples in the essays. How can the writer's examples be more effective?

Writing About the Text

Often, for effect, a writer will use phrases and words that he or she knows the reader will recognize. Marable uses allusions or references to a number of people and phrases important in black history. Research these allusions and write an essay explaining them.

More Writing Ideas

1. If you were responsible for distributing reparations, how would you go about it? Write a journal entry addressing this problem.
2. At the end of his essay, Marable quotes Malcolm X on the subject of reparations. Malcolm X often differed with Martin Luther King Jr. on issues of civil rights. Do some research and write a paragraph or two on what Dr. King said or would say about reparations.
3. Write an essay exploring Marable's idea in paragraph 6 that a reparations program could be an "educational campaign." What does he mean? Explore how you think this might work or not work.

ARGUMENT THROUGH COMPARISON AND CONTRAST

DEBORAH TANNEN
And Rarely the Twain Shall Meet

Deborah Tannen is a professor of linguistics at Georgetown University. She has also taught at Princeton University. Her work specializes in linguistic differences between genders. She has written many books on the subject, including You Just Don't Understand: Women and Men in Conversation *(1991) and* Gender and Discourse *(1994). She has also published poetry, short stories, and essays, and has written plays. In this selection, Tannen displays her expertise in analyzing the differences between how boys and girls play sports and how those differences extend into adulthood.*

▶ Prereading: Thinking About the Essay in Advance

What do you think are the differences between how men and women approach competition? Do they approach work differently? How?

▶ Words to Watch

authoritarian (par. 6) overbearing
linguist (par. 6) one who studies language
compromising (par. 15) giving up something for something else
beseeching (par. 16) pleading
adamant (par. 18) firm, unmoving
trump card (par. 23) winning hand in many card games
perspective (par. 24) point of view

B ob Hoover of the Pittsburgh Post-Gazette was interviewing me when   1
he remarked that after years of coaching boys' softball teams, he was
now coaching girls and they were very different. I immediately whipped
out my yellow pad and began interviewing him—and discovered that his
observations about how girls and boys play softball parallel mine about
how women and men talk at work.

Hoover told me that boys' teams always had one or two stars   2
whom the other boys treated with deference. So when he started
coaching a girl's team, he began by looking for the leader. He couldn't
find one. "The girls who are better athletes don't lord it over the others," he says. "You get the feeling that everyone's the same." When a
girl gets the ball, she doesn't try to throw it all the way home as a
strong-armed boy would; instead, she throws it to another team member, so they all become better catchers and throwers. He goes on, "If a
girl makes an error, she's not in the doghouse for a long time, as a boy
would be."

"But wait," I interrupt. "I've heard that when girls make a mistake at   3
sports, they often say 'I'm sorry,' whereas boys don't."

That's true, he says, but then the girl forgets it—and so do her team-   4
mates. "For boys, sports is a performance art. They're concerned with how
they look." When they make an error, they sulk because they've let their
teammates down. Girls want to win, but if they lose, they're still all in it
together—so the mistake isn't as dreadful for the individual or the team.

What Hoover describes in these youngsters are the seeds of behavior   5
I have observed among women and men at work.

The girls who are the best athletes don't "lord it over" the others—   6
just the ethic I have found among women in positions of authority.
Women managers frequently tell me they are good managers because

they do not act in an authoritarian manner. They say they do not flaunt their power, or behave as though they are better than their subordinates. Similarly, linguist Elisabeth Kuhn has found that women professors in her study inform students of course requirements as if they had magically appeared on the syllabus ("There are two papers. The first paper, ah, let's see, is due . . . It's back here [referring to the syllabus] at the beginning"), whereas the men professors make it clear that they set the requirements ("I have two midterms and a final"). A woman manager might say to her secretary, "Could you do me a favor and type this letter right away?" knowing that her secretary is going to type the letter. But her male boss, on hearing this, might conclude she doesn't feel she deserves the authority she has, just as a boys' coach might think the star athlete doesn't realize how good he is if he doesn't expect his teammates to treat him with deference.

7   I was especially delighted by Hoover's observation that, although girls are more likely to say, "I'm sorry," they are actually far less sorry when they make a mistake than boys who don't say it, but are "in the doghouse" for a long time. This dramatizes the ritual nature of many women's apologies. How often is a woman who is "always apologizing" seen as weak and lacking in confidence? In fact, for many women, saying "I'm sorry" often doesn't mean "I apologize." It means "I'm sorry that happened." Like many of the rituals common among women, it's a way of speaking that takes into account the other person's point of view. It can even be an automatic conversational smoother. For example, you leave your pad in someone's office; you knock on the door and say, "Excuse me, I left my pad on your desk," and the person whose office it is might reply, "Oh, I'm sorry. Here it is." She knows it is not her fault that you left your pad on her desk; she's just letting you know it's okay.

8   Finally, I was intrigued by Hoover's remark that boys regard sports as "a performance art" and worry about "how they look." There, perhaps, is the rub, the key to why so many women feel they don't get credit for what they do. From childhood, many boys learn something that is very adaptive to the workplace: Raises and promotions are based on "performance" evaluations and these depend, in large measure, on how you appear in other people's eyes. In other words, you have to worry not only about getting your job done but also about getting credit for what you do.

9   Getting credit often depends on the way you talk. For example, a women tells me she has been given a poor evaluation because her supervisor feels she knows less than her male peers. Her boss, it turns out, reached this conclusion because the woman asks more questions: She is seeking information without regard to how her queries will make her look.

10   The same principle applies to apologizing. Whereas some women seem to be taking undeserved blame by saying "I'm sorry," some men seem to evade deserved blame. I observed this when a man disconnected

a conference call by accidentally elbowing the speaker-phone. When his secretary reconnects the call, I expect him to say, "I'm sorry; I knocked the phone by mistake." Instead he says, "Hey, what happened?! One minute you were there, the next minute you were gone!" Annoying as this may be, there are certainly instances in which people improve their fortunes by covering up mistakes.

If Hoover's observations about girls' and boys' athletic styles are fas-   11
cinating, it is even more revealing to see actual transcripts of children at play and how they mirror the adult workplace. Amy Sheldon, a linguist at the University of Minnesota who studies children talking at play in a day care center, has compared the conflicts of pre-school girls and boys. She finds that boys who fight with one another tend to pursue their own goals. Girls tend to balance their own interests with those of the other girls through complex verbal negotiations.

Look at how different the negotiations are: 12

Two boys fight over a toy telephone: Tony has it; Charlie wants it.   13
Tony is sitting on a foam chair with the base of the phone in his lap and the receiver lying beside him. Charlie picks up the receiver, and Tony protests, "No, that's my phone!" He grabs the telephone cord and tries to pull the receiver away from Charlie, saying, "No, that—uh, it's on MY couch. It's on MY couch. Charlie. It's on MY couch. It's on MY couch." It seems he has only one point to make, so he makes it repeatedly as he uses physical force to get the phone back.

Charlie ignores Tony and holds onto the receiver. Tony then gets off   14
the couch, sets the phone base on the floor and tries to keep possession of it by overturning the chair on top of it. Charlie manages to push the chair off, gets the telephone, and wins the fight.

This might seem like a typical kids' fight until you compare it with a   15
fight Sheldon videotaped among girls. Here the contested objects are toy medical instruments: Elaine has them; Arlene wants them. But she doesn't just grab for them; she argues her case. Elaine, in turn, balances her own desire to keep them with Arlene's desire to get them. Elaine loses ground gradually by compromising.

Arlene begins not by grabbing but by asking and giving a reason: 16
"Can I have that, that thing? I'm going to take my baby's temperature." Elaine is agreeable, but cautious: "You can use it—you can use my temperature. Just make sure you can't use anything else unless you can ask." Arlene does just that; she asks for the toy syringe: "May I?" Elaine at first resists, but gives a reason: "No. I'm gonna need to use the shot in a couple of minutes." Arlene reaches for the syringe anyway, explaining in a "beseeching" tone, "But I—I need this though."

Elaine capitulates, but again tries to set limits: "Okay, just use it   17
once." She even gives Arlene permission to give "just a couple of shots." Arlene then presses her advantage, and became possessive of her property: "Now don't touch the baby until I get back, because it IS MY BABY!

I'll check her ears, okay?" (Even when being demanding, she asks for agreement: "okay?")

18   Elaine tries to regain some rights through compromise: "Well, let's pretend it's another day, that we have to look in her ears together." Elaine also tries another approach that will give Arlene something she wants: "I'll have to shot her after, after, after you listen—after you look in her ears," suggests Elaine. Arlene, however, is adamant: "Now don't shot her at all!"

19   What happens next will sound familiar to anyone who has ever been a little girl or overheard one. Elaine can no longer abide Arlene's selfish behavior and applies the ultimate sanction: "Well, then, you can't come to my birthday!" Arlene utters the predictable retort: "I don't want to come to your birthday!"

20   The boys and girls have followed different rituals for fighting. Each boy goes after what he wants; they slug it out; one wins. But the girls enact a complex negotiation, trying to get what they want while taking into account what the other wants.

21   Here is an example of how women and men at work use comparable strategies.

22   Maureen and Harold, two managers at a medium-size company, are assigned to hire a human-resources coordinator for their division. Each favors a different candidate, and both feel strongly about their preferences. They trade arguments for some time, neither convincing the other. Then Harold says that hiring the candidate Maureen wants would make him so uncomfortable that he would have to consider resigning. Maureen respects Harold. What's more, she likes him and considers him a friend. So she says what seems to her the only thing she can say under the circumstances: "Well, I certainly don't want you to feel uncomfortable here. You're one of the pillars of the place." Harold's choice is hired.

23   What is crucial is not Maureen's and Harold's individual styles in isolation but how they play in concert with each other's style. Harold's threat to quit ensures his triumph—when used with someone for whom it is a trump card. If he had been arguing with someone who regards his threat as simply another move in the negotiation rather than a nonnegotiable expression of deep feelings, the result might have been different. For example, had she said, "That's ridiculous; of course you're not going to quit!" or matched it ("Well, I'd be tempted to quit if we hired your guy"), the decision might well have gone the other way.

24   Like the girls at play, Maureen balances her perspective with those of her colleague and expects him to do the same. Harold is simply going for what he wants and trusts Maureen to do likewise.

25   This is not to say that all women and all men, or all boys and girls, behave any one way. Many factors influence our styles, including regional and ethnic backgrounds, family experience, and individual personality.

But gender is a key factor, and understanding its influence can help clarify what happens when we talk.

▶Building Vocabulary

For each of the following words, write a definition and a sentence of your own making:

1. flaunt (par. 6)
2. deference (par. 6)
3. agreeable (par. 16)
4. syringe (par. 16)
5. capitulates (par. 17)
6. abide (par. 19)
7. sanction (par. 19)
8. retort (par. 19)

▶Thinking Critically About The Argument

Understanding the Writer's Argument

1. When Bob Hoover tells Tannen that he is coaching girls and they are different from boys, she immediately stops his interview of her and starts interviewing him. Why do you think she reacts like this?
2. According to Hoover, what are the differences between boys' teams and girls' teams, in your own words?
3. According to Tannen, what is the difference between how men and women view getting credit in the workplace?
4. What do the University of Minnesota studies show about how girls negotiate?
5. What do they reveal about how boys negotiate?
6. The last two paragraphs are set apart after a line break. Why?

Understanding the Writer's Techniques

1. Why does Tannen describe the difference between boys and girls in sports at the start of her essay?
2. What is Tannen's main proposition? Where does she express it most clearly?
3. Where does Tannen contrast the behaviors of boys/men and girls/women? Write an outline of the essay, showing the various areas of contrast.
4. Which technique does Tannen use to contrast, ABAB or AABB? Why, do you think?
5. Choose one area of contrast that Tannen uses. What examples does she use to illustrate that area?

6. Who is Tannen's audience? How does that affect the tone of her essay?
7. Which of Tannen's illustrations most effectively supports her main idea?

Exploring the Writer's Argument

1. Which gender is Tannen most interested in? Why? How do you know that?
2. Why does Tannen point out that there are gender differences? Isn't that obvious? What do you think is her unstated reason for writing this essay?
3. What other conclusions can you draw from the University of Minnesota studies?
4. Why is it so important to understand the differences in how the genders behave?
5. Tannen seems to assume that the differences between girls and boys are always played out between women and men. Do you agree? Why or why not?

▶ Ideas for Writing Arguments

Prewriting

Make two columns, one labeled "Men" and the other labeled "Women." Think of a different area of contrast than the one Tannen focuses on— attitudes toward love or sex, for example—and list points of contrast between the two columns.

Writing a Guided Argument

Write an essay that contrasts the ways in which men and women approach some aspect of life besides the one Tannen explores.

1. Begin your essay with an anecdote in which you are watching a man and woman or boy and girl interact. Explain why this experience led you to think about the differences between the sexes in the area you are exploring.
2. Make sure your claim reflects the comparison your essay will make between men and women.
3. Give a few examples of how women demonstrate how they react to your subject.
4. Wrap up your discussion of women with a conclusion about them.
5. Give a few examples of how men demonstrate how they react to your subject.
6. Wrap up your discussion of men with a conclusion about them.

7. End your essay by evaluating which you think is the proper attitude to the subject you chose. Attempt to choose the opposite sex's attitude.

Thinking, Arguing, and Writing Collaboratively

Exchange drafts of your Writing a Guided Argument essay with another student in the class. After making some general comments on the essay, write a paragraph or two on how successfully your partner achieved the goal of contrasting. Does the essay maintain coherence? Discuss your comments with your partner.

Writing About the Text

Write an essay based on questions 2 or 4 in Exploring the Writer's Argument.

More Writing Ideas

1. In your journal, write an entry about an experience you had that highlighted a difference between the sexes.
2. Write a paragraph comparing how you act at home with how you act at work.
3. Which method of negotiating—a man's or a woman's—is more effective? Write an essay explaining your choice.

ARGUMENT THROUGH DEFINITION

LORENZO ALBACETE
The Struggle with Celibacy

Lorenzo Albacete is a Catholic priest and writer. He is a professor of theology at St. Joseph's Seminary in New York and previously served as an associate professor of theology at the John Paul II Institute for Studies in Marriage and Family. In this selection, which appeared in The New York Times Magazine *on March 31, 2002, Albacete comments on the effect the priest molestation scandals have on an age-old priestly tradition—celibacy.*

▶ Prereading: Thinking About the Essay in Advance

In this article, Albacete attempts a definition of the Catholic priestly vow of celibacy. Why might celibacy need to be defined? In what ways could it be misinterpreted?

▶Words to Watch

pedophilia (par. 5) sexual attraction toward children
implicated (par. 5) guilty by association
garb (par. 5) clothes
scandalized (par. 7) shocked
caste (par. 8) rank or class in a hierarchy
trepidation (par. 9) hesitation

1   When I was in fifth grade and was invited to become an altar boy, my father would not allow it. He had made a promise to safeguard my faith, he explained, and if I got too close to priests, I might lose that faith, or—what seemed worse for him—I might become one of them. My father was born in Spain, and Spanish anticlericalism flowed through his veins.

2   His main objection was to priestly celibacy. He thought it divided priests into three kinds: saints who lived by it, rascals who took advantage of it to hide sexual desires of which they were ashamed, like homosexuality, and those who cheated. Since I gave no evidence of being saintly, I think he feared I might end up in one of the other categories.

3   I was angry and hurt by this response. I felt accused of something, though I wasn't sure exactly of what.

4   Eventually my father relented, and I became an altar boy. I tried hard to prove him wrong, and I resisted every indication of a priestly vocation. Many years later, though, having already begun my life as a secular adult, and on the verge of choosing a wedding date with my girlfriend, I found I could not resist anymore. My second Mass after ordination was at my father's grave. I hoped he would understand.

5   Now, with each new revelation of priestly pedophilia, in addition to shock and anger, I feel accused again. I worry that my altar boys and girls—not to mention their parents—are looking at me as a dirty old man, as a possible threat. When a case of abuse is exposed involving a married man, I doubt that most other married men feel implicated, embarrassed in front of their friends and relatives. They don't worry that the parents of their children's friends suspect them of horrible crimes. But because of my vow, even wearing my priestly garb has made me want to scream, "I'm not one of those!"

6   Like my father back then, an increasing number of people today think that celibacy must be blamed for this shameful situation. With none of the usual outlets, the theory goes, sexual energy inevitably explodes in manipulative forms based on the abuse of power.

7   This has not been my experience of celibacy. Still, I cannot help believing that there is some truth in the suspicion that celibacy is somehow related to the present crisis. There are those who use priestly celibacy to hide sexual desires. But I know a good many priests—in line, I believe,

with the vast majority—who struggle to be faithful to a vow they hold dear and are appalled to see it abused by others. They wonder how the requirement can be maintained without facing these issues. We priests owe an answer to our scandalized people.

My opinion is that the problem lies not with celibacy as such, but with the way it is understood and lived. One standard defense of celibacy is that it frees priests from the obligations of marriage and thereby allows them to respond to the needs of the faithful without reservations. I believe this to be completely false. I think it is an insult to the countless married doctors, social activists, non-Catholic clergy and counselors whose dedication to others is second to none. In fact, there is the danger that celibacy will give priests a feeling of being separated from others, forming a caste removed from ordinary men and women. I think it is precisely because priests evoke this mysterious world of the sacred that pedophilia among them seems more despicable—and more compelling—than the same behavior among nonclerical men.   8

When I decided to go into the seminary at the age of 28, I broke up with my girlfriend—not because I was suddenly opposed to marriage, but because church law requires it. Asked whether I would have chosen a life of celibacy had it not been required, I have to admit that I would not have. But I experienced a profound call to follow without reservations or conditions, and in that spirit, I accepted the celibacy requirement with trepidation, but with the faith that I would be sustained in doing whatever it took to conform to it. Throughout the years, though, I have come to value the vow of celibacy highly.   9

I began to understand the meaning of celibacy, oddly, during a time when I was seriously questioning it. A dear friend of mine in Europe had sent his only son to study in the United States and asked me to watch over him. This friend told me how much he was suffering from this separation. I told him that at least he had a son, whereas I would never experience being a father. This aspect of celibacy, I said to him, was much more difficult than the lack of a sexual companion.   10

"But you have many sons and daughters," he said. "Look at the way young people follow you. You are a true father to them."   11

"Yes," I replied, "but let's be honest. They are not really my sons and daughters. Each one of them would have existed even if I had not. They are not mine as J. is *your* son."   12

"But Lorenzo," he said, "that is the point. J. is not *my* son. I do not own him. I must respect his freedom. And I thought that's why priests took a vow of celibacy, to help spouses and parents understand that to love is not to own, but to affirm, to help, to let go. I need this help now that J. has left home."   13

I understood then that celibacy has more to do with poverty than with sex. It is the radical, outward expression of the poverty of the human   14 heart, the poverty that makes true love possible by preventing it from corrupting into possession or manipulation. That is why child abuse by priests is so shocking, so horrible, so destructive. It places celibacy at the service of power and lust, not of love.

15   In the future, the church may decide that particular pastoral situations require a change in the requirement of priestly celibacy. Still, I believe that even if priests marry, they are called to be witnesses of that "celibacy in the heart" that human love requires—namely, the absolute respect for the loved one's freedom. It's time for those of us who treasure priestly celibacy to live it in accordance with its intended message or else give it up as an obstacle to what we wish to say.

▶ Building Vocabulary

Albacete uses several terms used in religion in general and the Catholic Church in particular. Identify the following terms, and explain how each is used in Catholicism:

1. faith (par. 1)
2. anticlericalism (par. 1)
3. vocation (par. 4)
4. Mass (par. 4)
5. ordination (par. 4)
6. pastoral (par. 15)

▶ Thinking Critically About the Argument

Understanding the Writer's Argument

1. What is Albacete's father's main reason for not wanting his son to get "too close" to priests? Albacete's father divided priests into three kinds. What are they, and what effect did this division have on Albacete?
2. What does Albacete mean by his "priestly vocation," and why did he resist it?
3. Albacete mentions recent scandals in the Catholic Church over pedophilia. To what is he referring? What effect have the scandals had on Albacete and his fellow priests? Does Albacete think that priestly celibacy is related to the pedophilia scandals? Why or why not?
4. What is one of the ways to defend celibacy against its critics? In his own life, did Albacete choose celibacy enthusiastically? Why or why not?
5. Why would pedophilia among priests seem "more despicable"? (paragraph 8)
6. How does Albacete's experience with his friend, described in paragraphs 10 to 13, change his view of celibacy?

7. What does Albacete think is the future of the Catholic Church's views of celibacy?
8. Does Albacete think there should be priestly celibacy or does he give another answer? If the latter, what is that answer?

Understanding the Writer's Techniques

1. What is the major proposition in Albacete's essay? How do you know?
2. Why does Albacete begin his essay with a discussion of his father's opinion of priests?
3. How does Albacete's title work? Who is struggling with celibacy?
4. For whom has Albacete written this essay? How do you know? What is his tone? Give examples that led to your answer.
5. Albacete is writing as a priest and a man. What gives his essay authority? Why is he a good person to define celibacy? How, precisely, does he develop his extended definition?
6. What examples of transition words and phrases can you find in this essay? Why are they effective?
7. The essay shifts tone at the beginning of paragraph 8. How does it shift, and why?
8. After paragraph 8, Albacete makes a number of claims about celibacy. What are they, and what examples does he give to prove those claims?
9. Why does Albacete move away from explication and tell the story of his friend in paragraphs 10 to 13? How does this help his thesis?
10. The end of Albacete's essay is a little ambiguous in its conclusions. Why do you think that is, and is it an effective closing?

Exploring the Writer's Argument

1. Do you think Albacete's father was right to argue with his son against priests? Why or why not? What does Albacete think?
2. Do you think all priests should feel "implicated," as Albacete says in paragraph 5, for the crimes of their fellow priests who are caught molesting children? Why?
3. Albacete says that "priests owe an answer to our scandalized people." Do you think he's right? Why or why not?
4. One of Albacete's points about celibacy is that it gives "priests a feeling of being separated from others, forming a caste removed from ordinary men and women." Do you think this feeling of separation, of forming an exclusive club, is positive or negative? Justify your position.
5. Do you agree with Albacete's friend that priests are more like parents than one's biological parents? Explain.

▶ Ideas for Writing Arguments

Prewriting

Freewrite about a lifestyle choice that you have made, such as getting married, living alone, or living with a dog or other pet. Consider any criticisms of your lifestyle and your answer to those critics.

Writing a Guided Argument

Write an extended definition of a lifestyle choice that you have made. What does that choice mean to you? Defend your choice against any criticisms that you might imagine someone making. Address how important to your identity your choice has become.

1. Begin with an anecdote that introduces to the reader your subject, and end with a definition of your lifestyle choice.
2. Write a paragraph about the way the wider population has also made your choice.
3. Mention at least two objections someone might have to your lifestyle choice, and for each objection, defend your choice.
4. Give an example for each defense showing that your choice has been right for you.
5. Explain how you came to make your lifestyle choice.
6. Give an example or write a short narrative that shows a time in your life when your conception of your choice changed and you had a deeper understanding of it.
7. Explain what your altered definition of your choice is.
8. Conclude with a projection of the future of your lifestyle choice.

Thinking, Arguing, and Writing Collaboratively

In groups of three, read each other's Writing a Guided Argument essays and write a critique of each of the two essays you have read. Focus on how effective and convincing the writer's definition is. Are the examples detailed enough? Then read the critiques of your essay and think about how you can revise it to make it more accurate and convincing.

Writing About the Text

Focusing on Albacete's assertion that "celibacy has more to do with poverty than with sex," write an essay that disagrees with him and argues that celibacy is only about sex. Fully explain in your essay what Albacete's opinion is and why he thinks that.

More Writing Ideas

1. In your journal, write about an experience you have had with a priest, imam, rabbi, or other clerical figure who changed your mind about their religion.
2. In a paragraph, attempt a definition of pedophilia. Is pedophilia the act or is it thinking about the act? Be accurate.
3. Write an essay about some aspect of your religion or the religion that you grew up with that you either disagree with or have disagreed with in the past. Attempt an accurate definition of that aspect.

ARGUMENT THROUGH PROCESS ANALYSIS

DOUGLAS STALKER
How to Duck Out of Teaching

Douglas Stalker is a professor of philosophy at the University of Delaware. He writes on medical, aesthetic, and logic topics, and is the editor of Grue! A New Riddle of Induction *(1994) and coeditor of* Examining Holistic Medicine *(1986). In this selection from,* The Chronicle of Higher Education, *Stalker advises teachers (including yours) about how to reduce their work burdens.*

▶ Prereading: Thinking About the Essay in Advance

What do you think your professors consider to be their most unpleasant duties? Put yourself in their shoes. What would you like to avoid?

▶ Words to Watch

tenured (par. 1) protected from dismissal
isometric (par. 7) with muscular contraction
mea culpa (par. 8) Latin for "it's my fault"
cognitive (par. 13) relating to thought
paradigms (par. 16) models
hermeneuticist (par. 22) one who studies theories of interpretation
ergo (par. 23) Latin for "therefore"

What's new on campus? Duping! It's all the rage with professors who   1
are tired of giving lectures to the drifting youth of America. Duping is, quite simply, not doing. It is avoiding, evading, eluding, abstaining, dodging, and good old ducking. And it is now on display on almost every campus in the United States. Here are eight duping techniques that will work for any professor, tenured or untenured, in the time it takes to erase a moderate-size blackboard:

The Title Trick

2 Give the students honorary titles to make them feel special—and willing to take on new duties. It is easy to think of titles that sound great. For example, call everyone in class a peer editor. Then you can have the students pair up and take turns going over each other's term papers. Tell the students that you are going to selflessly give up some of your professorial power in order to empower them. When all is said and done, you won't have to raise your red pen even once.

3   You can also get students to record all the grades and sign the grade roster for you. Have a drawing (that is the democratic way, of course) to see who gets to have the title of peer executive officer for the day. Tell the students that this is an exercise in leadership and management ability. Remember to make a solemn display of handing over the official pen, grade book, and grade roster to the peer executive officer.

The Computer Razzle-Dazzle

4 If something is done with a computer, it must be educationally great. So set up a computer dupe: a computer-based course in which students have to send e-mail messages to each other a minimum of 10 times per day. To get them going, tell them psychological research has shown that first thoughts are always best thoughts, and that contact with your peers is essential to building and maintaining academic self-esteem. They will spend so much time on e-mail that they won't notice you haven't logged on for days.

5   You can add a personal touch by sending randomly generated e-mail messages to each student. Any high-school kid who likes computers can set the system up for you. You can easily create the messages by modifying the horoscopes in your daily newspaper. For example, one message might say: "You are doing well but have doubts about future endeavors like reading the next chapter. I know you have what it takes to overcome obstacles! Turn the pages of the textbook for yourself! Take responsibility for sharpening your own pencils! Your last fill-in-the-blank test showed great promise of things to come. Do not be surprised if I repeat this message to reinforce its meaning for you."

The Great Group Dupe

6 Tell the students that yours is a problem-based course with group learning, and have them divide up into groups. It doesn't matter whether any group actually solves the problems, what the problems are, or even if there are any problems at all. Everyone will be happy about working in a group because they will believe that things are getting done—even if nothing really happens. Like most people who can

program a VCR, today's students are perfectly happy to confuse the process with the product.

It might be good to walk among them every few weeks, reminding   7
everyone that the whole is greater than the sum of its parts, to discourage individual effort. You might want to walk around the room saying "Cohesion, think cohesion!" as you do some isometric push-pull exercises with your hands to make the point more vivid.

The Mea-Culpa Escape

Stand in front of your students and confess everything. Tell them that   8
higher education has become an institutionalized fraud because it keeps the students passive, subjects them to lectures, coerces them to take notes, and makes them endure tests. All that is miles away from real, multi-dimensional learning that lasts a lifetime. You need to pull out all the stops as you wail about the sins of academic America. Draw a circle on the board and keep pointing to it—try pounding your fist on the board— as you mention the cycle of passivity and the economic consequences associated with stunted growth and sheltered lives.

Then, with a selfless gesture toward the exits, send the students out   9
into the world to do experiential projects of their own devising, like running a lawn-care business for the semester. Make sure that they do your lawn on their rounds so that you can turn in some grades, and tell them not to come by too early in the morning. Word that instruction in terms of their being sensitive to the needs of others.

The Ticktock of Pointless Talk

You have about 2,000 minutes to fill during a 14-week semester. Why not   10
fill them with chitchat? Anyone who watches daytime TV simply loves pointless talk and, sooner or later, comes to believe that it has a point. If you have 2.5 hours of class time to fill per week and a class of 30 students, you have to get each student to speak for only five minutes a week. Following the three principles of chat satisfaction can make that relatively simple task a breeze.

Principle 1 is essential: There is no topic like no particular topic. Your   11
students can have a good chat bouncing from the last episode of *Friends* to anything else they care to discuss—the popularity of sport-utility vehicles, the history of pizza, the price of body piercing, you name it.

Principle 2 follows directly from Principle 1: Sticking to the topic is   12
for dorks. Coherence is irrelevant; indeed, relevance is irrelevant. Mental drift is in fashion, and it is fine to have a remark like "Burping should be a collegiate sport" followed by the statement "Cancún could be the 51st state."

13 Principle 3 is the basis of cognitive democracy: No one has to know what he or she is talking about. In the true marketplace of ideas, a marginal student can speak at length on everything from Sumerian poetry to soggy French fries.

The Yo-Yo Presentation

14 Why do professors have to stand in the front of the classroom—like truly alienated workers—trying to explain things? Why do they have to carry the load, day after day? You can redress that injustice with the best role reversal around: class presentations. You go from active to passive; your students go from passive to active.

15 The best topics, you should emphasize, are those with personal meaning to the presenter. Remind your students, in addition, that information is not learning. That is code for: No time in the library is required. Then just hand the students the formula: what _____ means to me. In class, they can say their talk is titled "A Personal Perspective on _____" Anything can go in the blank—the Yalta conference, the supply curve, Kant's categorical imperative, angular momentum.

16 Recitations are a dandy variation. They have another benefit: You can dispense with assigned readings because you have students read the books out loud in class. Plays are the paradigms here. You can have someone be Hamlet, someone else be Claudius, and so on. The students stand in front of the room and read their parts out loud to the rest of the class—no need for them to memorize anything beforehand. Other natural subjects for recitations are Plato's dialogues, Blake's poetry, and Faulkner's novels. Heck, it can work with anything that has sentences.

17 When reading paragraphs gets old, you might want to suggest that your students act out a page or two of text. Suppose, for instance, you are teaching an introductory biology course. Think about the improvisational possibilities inherent in the parts of the cell. Some students can play the cell wall; others can be structures in the cytoplasm. If they are honors students, they might even put together a little dance of cell division. (As for grading presentations, see my article titled "A Classroom Application of the Radio Shack Digital Sound-Level Meter.")

The Furniture Flimflam

18 Some of the best ideas are right under your nose—or your posterior. Rearrange the classroom each day. Have the students put the chairs in a different configuration—a circle, a triangle, a trapezoid. Any polygon or closed curve will do, but the best arrangements are those that take up to 10 minutes to complete. If you spend 10 minutes per class moving chairs, in two and a half years you will duck out of teaching the equivalent of an

entire three-credit course. Over a 30-year career, that becomes a dozen courses. The furniture flimflam is actually a course-reduction measure.

Today's students are used to putting chairs in a circle, so most of them won't ask any dumb questions about why they are moving the furniture. If a few of them cop an attitude, just mumble something about the difference between confronting and communicating, or how a classroom should facilitate their transformation into a community of learners.   19

You can get students really motivated by mentioning scientific studies. Tell them about the research comparing people in hospital rooms with and without a view of the outside, which showed that the people with a view were discharged earlier and used fewer pain pills during their hospitalization. Who, then, would hesitate to arrange the chairs so that they face the windows? If you don't know of any relevant research, make some up.   20

Or you could go metaphysical and download for your class some New Age hooey from the Web, or material from the dozen or more sites devoted to feng shui. With a few Chinese terms, you can energize students to lay out the chairs in a hexagon contiguous with a rhomboid.   21

The Heavenly Remote

Any hermeneuticist knows that the medium is the message. And what is the medium for today's professor? Every plugged-in classroom in America has it: a VCR. Bring in a video for class, dim the lights, push the play button on the remote, and you've done your academic work for the day.   22

You can use any video in any course. For openers, you have the presumption of relevance on your side: Everything that happens during class has something to do with the course. You can also rely on the dominant mental activity in higher-education circles, free association. With a little free association, your students will begin to believe that any video has something to do with the course. That is a logical point—everything freely associates with everything else; *ergo,* you're home free.   23

If rewinding and returning videos gets to be too much, start taping TV programs. You can spend class after class watching your homemade tapes of, say, daytime talk shows, reruns of sitcoms, detective shows, even the Weather Channel from time to time. For example, if you teach logic, tape Regis and that Kathie Lee impostor. When you show the tape in class, tell the students that you want them to spot the fallacious arguments that Regis tries to foist off on surrogate Kathie. If you teach ethics, tape Jerry Springer. For aesthetics, tape music videos from MTV. Marketing? Those Budweiser frogs are worth two or three upper-level courses. Physics? Professional beach volleyball on ESPN2. Criminal justice? Reruns of *Hawaii Five-O.*   24

It's a great time for a professor to be alive, isn't it? Unfortunately, it still takes some effort to record TV shows at home and bring the tapes to   25 your campus. Why can't each classroom be hooked up to cable TV? Surely your college or university can get group rates from a cable company and find a TV manufacturer to donate the sets. Very few administrators seem to realize how much that could mean to the educational process, especially insofar as it would allow them to say things like "We've got cable in all the classrooms, but Harvard and Yale don't." Perhaps faculty members will have to get the ball rolling by contacting their AAUP representatives so that cable service can get on the table at the next contract negotiation, right there alongside the dental plan and the early-retirement options.

▶ Building Vocabulary

1. In his essay, Stalker makes many cultural references that might seem obscure to you. Choose at least ten and identify them.
2. Define the following and write a sentence for each:
    a. empower (par. 2)
    b. solemn (par. 3)
    c. passivity (par. 8)
    d. stunted (par. 8)
    e. marginal (par. 13)
    f. alienated (par. 14)
    g. paradigms (par. 16)
    h. surrogate (par. 24)

▶ Thinking Critically About the Argument

Understanding the Writer's Argument

1. What is "duping," and why, according to Stalker, do teachers do it?
2. What is the advantage, according to Stalker, of working with a computer in the classroom?
3. What does Stalker mean by a "mea-culpa escape"? (paragraph 8)
4. Why are the best topics "those with personal meaning to the presenter"?
5. What is the "presumption of relevance"? (paragraph 23)
6. What does Stalker say are the benefits of showing movies in class?
7. What suggestions does Stalker make at the end of his essay for further reducing the workload for teachers?

Understanding the Writer's Techniques

1. What is the writer's claim?
2. Why does Stalker put his eight duping techniques in this order?
3. Explain Stalker's use of process analysis to make his argument.

4. Why does Stalker offer detailed examples, such as in paragraph 24, in which he suggests that showing Budweiser commercials could work in a marketing class?
5. Explain how Stalker moves from reasonable suggestions to over-the-top ideas. Where does he do this, and why?

Exploring the Writer's Argument

1. What is Stalker's unstated purpose for writing this essay? Can you determine a subtext?
2. This essay is obviously humorous, but can any of his suggestions be considered serious? Which ones, and why?
3. How has reading this essay changed your view of your professors?
4. Do you think that Stalker imagined his students reading this essay? What might be the downside to students like you reading it?
5. Stalker's essay is funny, but are there any times when the humor fails him? Does he ever try too hard? Where, and why do you say that?

▶ Ideas for Writing Arguments

Prewriting

Freewrite on ways that students can fill word requirements in paper assignments without really saying anything.

Writing a Guided Argument

Write an essay called "How to Fake Your Way Through Writing an Essay." Come up with a number of suggestions for your fellow students for how to complete a particularly odious writing assignment with a minimum of ideas.

1. Write an opening in the spirit of Stalker's essay, explaining the purpose of your essay and how many suggestions you will give.
2. Offer your reader at least four ideas for how they can pad their essays with the least amount of work.
3. Give the benefits of each idea.
4. Explain to your reader how versatile your ideas will be, not only in college but after college as well.
5. Write a conclusion that outlines the success you have had with your ideas.

Thinking, Arguing, and Writing Collaboratively

Working with your fellow students in small groups, figure out how many minutes of class time are left in your semester. Write a list of suggestions of ways you as students can dupe your professor by wasting class time.

Fill up the total number of minutes left, offering specific suggestions for how to fill the time. Share your plan with the rest of the class.

Writing About the Text

Stalker is a professor at a university, and this essay appeared in a journal of university affairs, yet the language he uses is not always formal. How does he use a combination of formal words and slang? Write an essay explaining why he uses the words he does, focusing particularly on his use of slang. Give examples, and show how the use of slang helps to achieve his thesis.

More Writing Ideas

1. In your journal, write an entry about times when your teachers have done what Stalker suggests.
2. Write a paragraph or two about which duping technique you wish your teachers would take most advantage of.
3. Write an essay in which you argue that Stalker's techniques, if altered slightly, can be extended to any profession.

ARGUMENT THROUGH CAUSAL ANALYSIS

THOMAS JEFFERSON
The Declaration of Independence

Thomas Jefferson (1743–1826) was the first secretary of state and the third president of the United States of America. During the Revolutionary War, he was the governor of Virginia. He was one of the members of the Continental Congress in Philadelphia in 1775. In addition to being a politician, Jefferson was an architect (he designed, among other things, his estate, Monticello) and an educator (he founded the University of Virginia). Jefferson was one of only a few men who designed the political and legal basis for the colonies' break from Great Britain, but he was the main author of the Declaration of Independence, which laid out, in forceful phrases, the colonies' case against the king, George III.

▶ Prereading: Thinking About the Essay in Advance

What do you know about the reasons the United States seceded from Great Britain? Make a list of the reasons.

▶ Words to Watch

dissolve (par. 1) break apart
unalienable (par. 2) not able to be denied
usurpations (par. 2) takeovers of power
despotism (par. 2) tyranny
sufferance (par. 2) suffering
inestimable (par. 5) valuable
abdicated (par. 16) given up
magnanimity (par. 22) generosity

When in the Course of human events it becomes necessary for one 1 people to dissolve the political bands which have connected them with another, and to assume among the powers of the earth, the separate and equal station to which the Laws of Nature and of Nature's God entitle them, a decent respect to the opinions of mankind requires that they should declare the causes which impel them to the separation.

We hold these truths to be self-evident, that all men are created equal, 2 that they are endowed by their Creator with certain unalienable Rights, that among these are Life, Liberty and the pursuit of Happiness.—That to secure these rights, Governments are instituted among Men, deriving their just powers from the consent of the governed.—That whenever any Form of Government becomes destructive of these ends, it is the Right of the People to alter or to abolish it, and to institute new Government, laying its foundation on such principles and organizing its powers in such form, as to them shall seem most likely to effect their Safety and Happiness. Prudence, indeed, will dictate that Governments long established should not be changed for light and transient causes; and accordingly all experience hath shewn that mankind are more disposed to suffer, while evils are sufferable, than to right themselves by abolishing the forms to which they are accustomed. But when a long train of abuses and usurpations, pursuing invariably the same Object evinces a design to reduce them under absolute Despotism, it is their right, it is their duty, to throw off such Government, and to provide new Guards for their future security.—Such has been the patient sufferance of these Colonies; and such is now the necessity which constrains them to alter their former Systems of Government. The history of the present King of Great Britain is a history of repeated injuries and usurpations, all having in direct object the establishment of an absolute Tyranny over these States. To prove this, let Facts be submitted to a candid world.

He has refused his Assent to Laws, the most wholesome and neces- 3 sary for the public good.

He has forbidden his Governors to pass Laws of immediate and 4 pressing importance, unless suspended in their operation till his Assent should be obtained; and when so suspended, he has utterly neglected to attend to them.

5   He has refused to pass other Laws for the accommodation of large districts of people, unless those people would relinquish the right of Representation in the Legislature, a right inestimable to them and formidable to tyrants only.

6   He has called together legislative bodies at places unusual, uncomfortable, and distant from the depository of their public Records, for the sole purpose of fatiguing them into compliance with his measures.

7   He has dissolved Representative Houses repeatedly, for opposing with manly firmness his invasions on the rights of the people.

8   He has refused for a long time, after such dissolutions, to cause others to be elected; whereby the Legislative powers, incapable of Annihilation, have returned to the People at large for their exercise; the State remaining in the mean time exposed to all the dangers of invasion from without, and convulsions within.

9   He has endeavoured to prevent the population of these States; for that purpose obstructing the Laws for Naturalization of Foreigners; refusing to pass others to encourage their migrations hither, and raising the conditions of new Appropriations of Lands.

10   He has obstructed the Administration of Justice, by refusing his Assent to Laws for establishing Judiciary powers.

11   He has made Judges dependent on his Will alone, for the tenure of their offices, and the amount and payment of their salaries.

12   He has erected a multitude of New Offices, and sent hither swarms of Officers to harass our people, and eat out their substance.

13   He has kept among us, in times of peace, Standing Armies without the Consent of our legislatures.

14   He has affected to render the Military independent of and superior to the Civil power.

15   He has combined with others to subject us to a jurisdiction foreign to our constitution, and unacknowledged by our laws; giving his Assent to their Acts of pretended Legislation:

For quartering large bodies of armed troops among us:

For protecting them, by a mock Trial, from punishment for any Murders which they should commit on the Inhabitants of these States:

For cutting off our Trade with all parts of the world:

For imposing Taxes on us without our Consent:

For depriving us in many cases, of the benefits of Trial by jury:

For transporting us beyond Seas to be tried for pretended offences:

For abolishing the free System of English Laws in a neighboring Province, establishing therein an Arbitrary government, and enlarging its Boundaries so as to render it at once an example and fit instrument for introducing the same absolute rule into these Colonies:

For taking away our Charters, abolishing our most valuable Laws and altering fundamentally the Forms of our Governments:

For suspending our own Legislatures, and declaring themselves invested with power to legislate for us in all cases whatsoever.

He has abdicated Government here, by declaring us out of his Protection and waging War against us.   16

He has plundered our seas, ravaged our Coasts, burnt our towns, and destroyed the lives of our people.   17

He is at this time transporting large Armies of foreign Mercenaries to complete the works of death, desolation and tyranny, already begun with circumstances of Cruelty & Perfidy scarcely paralleled in the most barbarous ages, and totally unworthy the Head of a civilized nation.   18

He has constrained our fellow Citizens taken Captive on the high Seas to bear Arms against their Country, to become the executioners of their friends and Brethren, or to fall themselves by their Hands.   19

He has excited domestic insurrections amongst us, and has endeavoured to bring on the inhabitants of our frontiers, the merciless Indian Savages, whose known rule of warfare, is an undistinguished destruction of all ages, sexes and conditions.   20

In every stage of these Oppressions We have Petitioned for Redress in the most humble terms: Our repeated Petitions have been answered only by repeated injury. A Prince, whose character is thus marked by every act which may define a Tyrant, is unfit to be the ruler of a free people.   21

Nor have We been wanting in attentions to our British brethren. We have warned them from time to time of attempts by their legislature to extend an unwarrantable jurisdiction over us. We have reminded them of the circumstances of our emigration and settlement here. We have appealed to their native justice and magnanimity, and we have conjured them by the ties of our common kindred to disavow these usurpations, which would inevitably interrupt our connections and correspondence. They too have been deaf to the voice of justice and of consanguinity. We must, therefore, acquiesce in the necessity, which denounces our Separation, and hold them, as we hold the rest of mankind, Enemies in War, in Peace Friends.   22

We, therefore, the Representatives of the United States of America, in General Congress, Assembled, appealing to the Supreme Judge of the world for the rectitude of our intentions, do, in the Name, and by Authority of the good People of these Colonies, solemnly publish and declare, That these United Colonies are, and of Right ought to be Free and Independent States; that they are Absolved from all Allegiance to the British Crown, and that all political connection between them and the State of Great Britain, is and ought to be totally dissolved; and that as Free and Independent States, they have full Power to levy War, conclude Peace, contract Alliances, establish Commerce, and to do all other Acts and Things which Independent   23

States may of right do. And for the support of this Declaration, with a firm reliance on the protection of divine Providence, we mutually pledge to each other our Lives, our Fortunes and our sacred Honor.

▶ Building Vocabulary

Connotation refers to the shades of meaning or emotional associations a word or phrase provokes in readers. Explain the connotations raised by the following and why you think Jefferson selected them.

1. Nature's God (par. 1)
2. unalienable rights (par. 2)
3. Life, Liberty, and the pursuit of Happiness (par. 2)
4. absolute Tyranny (par. 2)
5. plundered . . . ravaged . . . burnt . . . destroyed (par. 17)
6. our British brethren (par. 22)

▶ Thinking Critically About the Argument

Understanding the Writer's Argument

1. Paraphrase Jefferson's first paragraph.
2. Why, according to Jefferson, are governments formed?
3. Why, in a few words, are the colonies determined to "throw off" the British government?
4. Why is Jefferson's objection in paragraph 13 important?
5. According to Jefferson, what actions did the colonies take before writing this declaration?
6. What, in the last paragraph, does Jefferson list as the powers of the United States?

Understanding the Writer's Techniques

1. What is the main proposition of the Declaration of Independence? Where does Jefferson most forcefully express it?
2. Why does Jefferson place the claim where he does?
3. What is Jefferson's central reason for his main proposition?
4. What are Jefferson's best three supports for his reason? Are there other reasons? What are they?
5. In paragraph 2, Jefferson sets up his warrant. Paraphrase the warrant.
6. What effects does Jefferson predict will come as a result of the declaration?
7. What purpose does the conclusion serve? What does Jefferson hope to accomplish with this conclusion?

Exploring the Writer's Argument

1. What information would you like to have to understand the declaration better?
2. Why in paragraph 2, does Jefferson explain that "Governments long established should not be changed for light and transient causes"?
3. Jefferson's warrants, as listed in paragraph 2, are described as self-evident. Why does he find them to be self-evident?
4. Why does Jefferson describe the world as "candid" in paragraph 2?
5. Unconsented taxes were a large part of why the colonies went to war. Why does Jefferson place that as a reason in paragraph 15?
6. This is a political document, but it is also a call to arms. Is it effective in this way? If so, how?

▶ Ideas for Writing Arguments

Prewriting

Freewrite for 10 minutes, making a list of grievances you have against your boss, a parent, or a teacher.

Writing a Guided Argument

Write a declaration of independence of your own that shows the causes for your dissatisfaction with a figure in authority—a parent, an elder, a boss, a teacher—giving examples throughout. What are the worst offenses? In what order will you list them? What form of satisfaction do you demand? Do not write directly to the person but rather to a third person to whom you are making your case.

1. Start with an opening that uses ceremonial speech, in much the same way the Declaration of Independence does. Write in such a way that your reader knows that you are being serious.
2. Begin laying out your list of grievances, your causes for desiring your independence, by offering examples for each cause. Make sure you have at least three and that your examples are detailed.
3. Explain that you have attempted to express your unhappiness but that your pleas have not been answered.
4. Conclude by declaring your independence again, in formal language.

Thinking, Arguing, and Writing Collaboratively

In small groups, exchange your Writing a Guided Argument papers with members of your class. Circle any grievances that you think are not backed up with enough evidence. Try to strengthen your classmates' cases against their chosen authority figure.

Writing About the Text

Jefferson wrote a document that was meant to incite the population of the colonies to rise up against the King of England. Examine his language and choice of words. How does he choose carefully in order to raise the emotional level of this very legalistic essay? Write an essay of your own that explores Jefferson's word and phrase choices, and explain how he achieves his goals in this way.

More Writing Ideas

1. Pretend that you are George III. Write a journal entry in the form of a letter to Thomas Jefferson and the colonists arguing why the colonies are the property of Great Britain and should not be independent.
2. Write a paragraph about the power of the opening of the Declaration of Independence. Those words have been quoted often. What makes them so powerful?
3. For many Americans who are not familiar with the founding documents of the United States, reading the Declaration of Independence for the first time, or for the first time in a while, can be an interesting experience and full of surprises. Write an essay outlining the reasons you were surprised upon this reading of the declaration.

ARGUMENT THROUGH CLASSIFICATION

AMARTYA SEN
A World Not Neatly Divided

Amartya Sen was born in Santiniketan, India, in 1933 and received a B.A. in economics from Presidency College in Calcutta, India, in 1953. He went on to earn a second B.A. from Trinity College in Cambridge, England, in 1955, and his Ph.D. from that school in 1959. Sen has taught at Harvard University, the London School of Economics, and Oxford, and he is currently a professor at Trinity College in Cambridge. His books Collective Choice and Social Welfare *(1970),* On Economic Inequality *(1973), and* Commodities and Capabilities *(1985) examine the role of poverty in the world. Sen won the Nobel Prize for economics in 1998. At the time, the Nobel committee wrote that Dr. Sen's work has "enhanced our understanding of the economic mechanisms underlying famines."*

▶ Prereading: Thinking About the Essay in Advance

How can the world be "neatly divided"? How does the world resist division? What kinds of division exist?

▶ Words to Watch

befuddling (par. 2) confusing
impoverished (par. 2) not detailed enough
futile (par. 2) useless
pluralist (par. 3) consisting of many
homogeneous (par. 4) containing parts that are the same
excommunicating (par. 4) expelling from a group
heresy (par. 4) unorthodox ideas about religion
imperious (par. 5) overbearing
flammable (par. 7) dangerous

When people talk about clashing civilizations, as so many politicians   1
and academics do now, they can sometimes miss the central issue.
The inadequacy of this thesis begins well before we get to the question of
whether civilizations must clash. The basic weakness of the theory lies in
its program of categorizing people of the world according to a unique, allegedly commanding system of classification. This is problematic because
civilizational categories are crude and inconsistent and also because there
are other ways of seeing people (linked to politics, language, literature,
class, occupation, or other affiliations).

The befuddling influence of a singular classification also traps those   2
who dispute the thesis of a clash: To talk about "the Islamic world" or "the
Western world" is already to adopt an impoverished vision of humanity as
unalterably divided. In fact, civilizations are hard to partition in this way,
given the diversities within each society as well as the linkages among different countries and cultures. For example, describing India as a "Hindu civilization" misses the fact that India has more Muslims than any other country except Indonesia and possibly Pakistan. It is futile to try to understand
Indian art, literature, music, food, or politics without seeing the extensive in-
teractions across barriers of religious communities. These include Hindus
and Muslims, Buddhists, Jains, Sikhs, Parsees, Christians (who have been in
India since at least the fourth century, well before England's conversion to
Christianity), Jews (present since the fall of Jerusalem), and even atheists
and agnostics. Sanskrit has a larger atheistic literature than exists in any
other classical language. Speaking of India as a Hindu civilization may be
comforting to the Hindu fundamentalist, but it is an odd reading of India.

A similar coarseness can be seen in the other categories invoked, like   3
"the Islamic world." Consider Akbar and Aurangzeb, two Muslim emperors of the Mogul dynasty in India. Aurangzeb tried hard to convert Hindus
into Muslims and instituted various policies in that direction, of which taxing the non-Muslims was only one example. In contrast, Akbar reveled in
his multiethnic court and pluralist laws, and issued official proclamations
insisting that no one "should be interfered with on account of religion" and
that "anyone is to be allowed to go over to a religion that pleases him."

4   If a homogeneous view of Islam were to be taken, then only one of these emperors could count as a true Muslim. The Islamic fundamentalist would have no time for Akbar; Prime Minister Tony Blair, given his insistence that tolerance is a defining characteristic of Islam, would have to consider excommunicating Aurangzeb. I expect both Akbar and Aurangzeb would protest, and so would I. A similar crudity is present in the characterization of what is called "Western civilization." Tolerance and individual freedom have certainly been present in European history. But there is no dearth of diversity here, either. When Akbar was making his pronouncements on religious tolerance in Agra, in the 1590's, the Inquisitions were still going on; in 1600, Giordano Bruno was burned at the stake, for heresy, in Campo dei Fiori in Rome.

5   Dividing the world into discrete civilizations is not just crude. It propels us into the absurd belief that this partitioning is natural and necessary and must overwhelm all other ways of identifying people. That imperious view goes not only against the sentiment that "we human beings are all much the same," but also against the more plausible understanding that we are diversely different. For example, Bangladesh's split from Pakistan was not connected with religion, but with language and politics.

6   Each of us has many features in our self-conception. Our religion, important as it may be, cannot be an all-engulfing identity. Even a shared poverty can be a source of solidarity across the borders. The kind of division highlighted by, say, the so-called "antiglobalization" protesters—whose movement is, incidentally, one of the most globalized in the world—tries to unite the underdogs of the world economy and goes firmly against religious, national, or "civilizational" lines of division.

7   The main hope of harmony lies not in any imagined uniformity, but in the plurality of our identities, which cut across each other and work against sharp divisions into impenetrable civilizational camps. Political leaders who think and act in terms of sectioning off humanity into various "worlds" stand to make the world more flammable—even when their intentions are very different. They also end up, in the case of civilizations defined by religion, lending authority to religious leaders seen as spokesmen for their "worlds." In the process, other voices are muffled and other concerns silenced. The robbing of our plural identities not only reduces us; it impoverishes the world.

▶ Building Vocabulary

The writer lists several religions in paragraph 2. Provide definitions for these words:

1. Hindus
2. Muslims
3. Buddhists
4. Jains

5. Sikhs
6. Parsees
7. Christians

▶ Thinking Critically About the Argument

Understanding the Writer's Argument

1. What, in Sen's opinion, is the "basic weakness" of the thesis of clashing civilizations?
2. Why is classifying people in terms of their civilization "crude and inconsistent"?
3. What is the weakness in the argument that India is a "Hindu civilization"?
4. What does "singular classification" mean?
5. How does Sen demonstrate that a "homogeneous view of Islam" is wrong?
6. Paraphrase Sen's argument in paragraph 5.
7. Where does the "main hope for harmony" lie, according to Sen?

Understanding the Writer's Techniques

1. What technique does Sen use in his introduction?
2. In this classification essay, Sen argues against classification, yet he does have a structure. What is that structure? How does he classify?
3. Sen relies on many examples to make his point. Mention two examples he gives, and explain what purpose they serve in the essay.
4. Much of this essay is used to work against a popular viewpoint. How does Sen work to refute this idea?
5. Near the end of the essay, Sen stops giving examples. Why does he do this, and is this effective?
6. Paraphrase Sen's argument in his conclusion. Is the closing effective? Why?

Exploring the Writer's Argument

1. Do singular classifications always have a negative effect on public discourse? Can you think of any examples of how they can have a positive effect? What are they?
2. Sometimes, it seems, classifying a group of people by a single concept is unavoidable. What would Sen say to this objection, in your opinion?
3. Sen is particularly worried about the use of singular classification by political leaders. Are they the people we need to worry about? Argue for or against this idea.

▶ Ideas for Writing Arguments

Prewriting

Make a list of singular classifications that you come across every day—for example, New Yorkers, bald people, dog lovers. How are those classifications useful? Why do we persist in employing them in everyday speech? Are they harmless, beneficial, or neutral?

Writing a Guided Argument

Many singular classifications not related to charged topics such as religion or race do not have the same emotion attached to them, and they cannot be seen as quite as dangerous. Nevertheless, these singular classifications can have their harmful effects on both the subject and the speaker of the terms. Write a humorous essay in which you choose three classifications and offer examples of how "harmful" they can be.

1. Begin with a declaration of mock alarm, explaining that there is a serious problem.
2. Discuss the "dangers" of speaking in generalizations about groups of people.
3. Offer your first example, and show how people might "suffer" from being classified. For example, New Yorkers might begin to see themselves as rude if defined that way, and begin to act rudely.
4. Give examples of how the negative effects take hold.
5. Repeat the process for the other two classifications.
6. Conclude by proposing alternate ways of referring to people. Instead of Californians, for example, people from San Francisco. Explain why this would help.

Thinking, Arguing, and Writing Collaboratively

In small groups, discuss the stereotypes associated with your ethnic groups, and offer examples of why that stereotype is often not true. One person in the group should create a list of the group's members' ethnic groups and the debunking examples. Offer the evidence to the rest of the class.

Writing About the Text

Sen mentions a number of different religions in paragraph 2, including Hindi, Islam, Judaism, Christianity, Buddhism, and the Jain and Sikh religions. Choose one of these religions, and write an essay of classification. Look up the traditional divisions within the religion you choose, and explain the differences and similarities. Explain which form of the religion has been most tolerant over history.

More Writing Ideas

1. Do some research to find an example of a political leader who thought in terms of singular classification even though, as Sen mentions in his conclusion, his or her "intentions [were] very different." Write in your journal about what happened.
2. In a paragraph, define what is meant by "globalization" and why someone would be against it.
3. What particular prejudices are present in your community? Write an essay about the problems of singular classification in your neighborhood. Offer examples of intolerance, and propose a solution at the end.

MIXING PATTERNS

RONALD TAKAKI
The Harmful Myth of Asian Superiority

Ronald Takaki is Professor of Ethnic Studies at the University of California, Berkeley, from which he received his Ph.D. in 1967. His books include Pau Hana: Plantation Life and Labor in Hawaii *(1983),* Strangers from a Different Shore: A History of Asian Americans *(1989), and* Hiroshima *(2001). In this selection, Takaki writes about the way even positive stereotypes can have unexpected negative effects.*

▶ Prereading: Thinking About the Essay in Advance

What are the positive stereotypes of various immigrant groups? Why might those stereotypes be "harmful"?

▶ Words to Watch

provocatively (par. 2) designed to get a reaction
ubiquity (par. 2) state of being everywhere
entrepreneurial (par. 2) individually business-minded
plight (par. 3) serious problem
homogenizes (par. 7) makes the same
median (par. 12) a kind of statistical average
paragons (par. 12) perfect examples
exacerbates (par. 15) makes worse

1   Asian Americans have increasingly come to be viewed as a "model minority." But are they as successful as claimed? And for whom are they supposed to be a model?

2   Asian Americans have been described in the media as "excessively, even provocatively" successful in gaining admission to universities. Asian American shopkeepers have been congratulated as well as criticized, for their ubiquity and entrepreneurial effectiveness.

3   If Asian Americans can make it, many politicians and pundits ask why can't African Americans? Such comparisons pit minorites against each other and generate African American resentment toward Asian Americans. The victims are blamed for their plight, rather than racism and an economy that has made many young African American workers superfluous.

4   The celebration of Asian Americans has obscured reality. For example, figures on the high earnings of Asian Americans relative to Caucasians are misleading. Most Asian Americans live in California, Hawaii, and New York—states with higher incomes and higher costs of living than the national average.

5   Even Japanese Americans, often touted for their upward mobility, have not reached equality. While Japanese American men in California earned an average income comparable to Caucasian men in 1980, they did so only by acquiring more education and working more hours.

6   Comparing family incomes is even more deceptive. Some Asian American groups do have higher family incomes than Caucasians. But they have more workers per family.

7   The "model minority" image homogenizes Asian Americans and hides their differences. For example, while thousands of Vietnamese American young people attend universities, others are on the streets. They live in motels and hang out in pool halls in places like East Los Angels; some join gangs.

8   Twenty-five percent of the people in New York City's Chinatown lived below the poverty level in 1980, compared with 17 percent of the city's population. Some 60 percent of the workers in the Chinatowns of Los Angeles and San Francisco are crowded into low-paying jobs in garment factories and restaurants.

9   "Most immigrants coming into Chinatown with a language barrier cannot go outside this confined area into the mainstream of American industry," a Chinese immigrant said, "Before, I was a painter in Hong Kong, but I can't do it here. I got no license, no education. I want a living; so it's dishwasher, janitor, or cook."

10   Hmong and Mien refugees from Laos have unemployment rates that reach as high as 80 percent. A 1987 California study showed that three out of ten Southeast Asian refugee families had been on welfare for four to ten years.

11   Although college-educated Asian Americans are entering the professions and earning good salaries, many hit the "glass ceiling"—the barrier

through which high management positions can be seen but not reached. In 1988, only 8 percent of Asian Americans were "officials" and "managers," compared with 12 percent for all groups.

Finally, the triumph of Korean immigrants has been exaggerated. In   12
1988, Koreans in the New York metropolitan area earned only 68 percent of the median income of non-Asians. More than three-quarters of Korean greengrocers, those so-called paragons of bootstrap entrepreneurialism came to America with a college education. Engineers, teachers, or administrators while in Korea, they became shopkeepers after their arrival. For many of them, the greengrocery represents dashed dreams, a step downward in status.

For all their hard work and long hours, most Korean shopkeepers do   13
not actually earn very much: $17,000 to $35,000 a year, usually representing the income from the labor of an entire family.

But most Korean immigrants do not become shopkeepers. Instead,   14
many find themselves trapped as clerks in grocery stores, service workers in restaurants, seamstresses in garment factories, and janitors in hotels.

Most Asian Americans know their "success" is largely a myth. They   15
also see how the celebration of Asian Americans as a "model minority" perpetuates their inequality and exacerbates relations between them and African Americans.

▶ Building Vocabulary

Takaki uses terms and concepts drawn from the social sciences, especially sociology and economics. Define the following terms:

1. "model minority" (par. 1)
2. racism (par. 3)
3. upward mobility (par. 5)
4. poverty level (par. 8)
5. "glass ceiling" (par. 11)
6. median income (par. 12)

▶ Thinking Critically About the Argument

Understanding the Writer's Argument

1. Why are Asian Americans considered a "model minority"?
2. How is the supposed business success of Asian Americans misinterpreted?
3. How does the image of Asian Americans as a "model minority" affect African Americans, according to Takaki?
4. How does the idea of the model minority "homogenize" Asian Americans?

5. What problems do college-educated Asian Americans face?
6. Why is the success of Korean shopkeepers not considered a success for many of the shopkeepers themselves?

Understanding the Writer's Techniques

1. What is Takaki's claim?
2. The writer uses a number of different rhetorical modes in this essay. What are they? Give examples.
3. Takaki writes two questions in the first paragraph. Why does he do that? Does he answer his own questions? Where, and if not, why not?
4. Takaki makes a number of points to back up his claim. What are the arguments he outlines?
5. There are a number of examples in this essay. Make a list of the examples and the point each one makes.

Exploring the Writer's Argument

1. If the term "Asian American" is too broad, what do you think Takaki would say about the term "Chinese" or "Korean"? Are those terms too broad? Why or why not?
2. Takaki mentions many ways in which the idea of the Asian American as a model minority can be a negative thing, but can it be positive? Can it work for Asian Americans?
3. Takaki states that many Korean immigrants consider their position as shopkeepers to be a step down. If this is true, why did they come to the United States? Does your answer change your view of Takaki's argument?

▶ Ideas for Writing Arguments

Prewriting

Do you know someone who people consider successful but who does not consider himself or herself successful? What are the reasons for the difference of opinion? Write down examples of the person's self-perception and those of his or her friends and neighbors.

Writing a Guided Argument

Write an essay called "The Myth of Success" about an acquaintance, family member, friend, or yourself. Make the myth an idea that people have about the success of that person, and explore the difference between the person's public persona and how the person feels about himself or herself. Perhaps the person is a successful teacher who feels like a failure or a good mother who thinks she could do better.

1. Begin by stating the myth. Question the myth's truth, or raise the idea of it being an idea or point of view.
2. Explain the difference between the myth and the person's perception of himself or herself.
3. Use at least three examples of how the external view of the person and the person's view of himself or herself differs.
4. Use techniques of comparison and contrast, illustration, definition, and narration to advance the claim of what you think is the proper view of the person.
5. Conclude by restating your belief about the success of the person, and give an example of why you think this is so.

Thinking, Arguing, and Writing Collaboratively

Exchange Writing a Guided Argument essays with another member of the class. Has your partner written an effective paper? Is the myth well defined? Is the difference between points of view clear? Is there a thesis, and is it backed up by good examples? Write a note to your partner explaining how his or her paper can be improved.

Writing About the Text

In an essay, compare Takaki's argument with Amartya Sen's. Can you find any differences? What are the similarities? What is your personal opinion about stereotypes, both positive and negative?

More Writing Ideas

1. Write a journal entry about the struggles of your ancestors who were immigrants. How do you think society perceived them?
2. What myths are attached to your ethnic group? Write a paragraph in which you outline the harmful myths attached to your ethnic group.
3. Many immigrant groups struggle when they come to the United States. Read "False Gold" by Fae Myenne Ng and write an essay about the harmful myth of American success to Asian immigrants, offering examples from both Ng's and Takaki's essays.

Part Two

Contemporary Debates

Arguments Pro and Con

4 Rap Culture: Is It Too Negative?

R ap started in the cities, in poor, largely African-American neighborhoods. At parties, disc jockeys, or DJs, played records—the then-
current music technology—and some began to experiment with moving
the record back and forth under the needle, manipulating the beats on the
record. Rap's basic paradigm was solidified when masters of ceremony,
called MCs, picked up a microphone at those parties and began reciting
rhyming poems. This spoken-word performance gave the new music the
name of *rap*. Rap was a revolutionary music, and early performers such as
Grandmaster Flash were interested in its power to reach black youth and
expose the conditions in the inner cities. In the early 1990s, a form of rap
called "gangsta rap" emerged out of Los Angeles and expressed the frustration evident in the inner cities. The stance of gangsta rappers included
threatening the police (whom they saw as their enemies), dealing drugs,
carrying guns, taking advantage of women, and expressing a callous attitude toward everything except money.

A controversy emerged: One side claimed that the violence and crime
depicted in rap music is a realistic reflection of poor urban neighborhoods
and that rappers, like all artists, aim to transform what they see into art.
Those on the other side of the debate—especially but not exclusively media observers and politicians—see rap music as overly and unnecessarily
negative and maintain that rap artists do more harm than good. These
critics charge that rap glorifies violence and crime and alienates and provokes neighborhood police. The debate has raged for years and still rages.

In the first selection that follows, a college student argues that rap is
moving the black community in the wrong direction. In the second selection, a magazine columnist insists that we should not call upon artists to
censor themselves.

GREG JONES
Rap Fans Desire a More Positive Product

This selection appeared in the Daily Cougar, *the student newspaper for the University of Houston, in the summer of 2002. The writer, Greg Jones, was a communications major at the school. In this selection, Jones makes a distinction between "old school," conscience-raising hip-hop and what he perceives as the more negative message appearing in rap music today.*

▶ Prereading: Thinking About the Essay in Advance

Do you listen to rap music? Why or why not? What associations does rap music have for you? Do you agree with the title of this essay?

▶ Words to Watch

materialism (par. 2) concern with money and possessions
disenfranchisement (par. 2) exclusion from power
ideology (par. 4) belief system
entrepreneurship (par. 6) position as owner of a business
reparations (par. 6) money as payment for suffering, as in slavery

1   In the early stage of rap music before the bling bling era, rap music was the CNN for poor and working-class blacks in America. Songs such as "The Message" and "Fight the Power" raised the conscience levels of people and the need for social change in America.

2   Then, in the early 1990s, greedy, out-of-touch record executives took control of the art form and made materialism the main priority, over the continued disenfranchisement of blacks, latinos, and poor whites.

3   I believe the billion-dollar rap industry, which has a great influence on American culture, needs to take a turn for the better by going back to its roots. Record executives use rap artists for major profits at the expense of the African-American poor and working-class people that actually experience what these rappers are rapping about.

4   Many people wonder why anyone should make a big deal out of negative rap music, because they believe it is only entertainment. Most fans know many of the artists such as Dr. Dre and Jay Z actually don't perform many of the activities they claim. This ideology is wrong and lacks serious thought. The reason we listen to music is because it makes us feel emotions such as joy, sadness, motivation, or even relaxation.

5   In other words, it affects the soul of an individual. The imbalance in rap music is consistently reflected on the radio and shown on the video programs such as "Rap City." The images presented are not an actual account of how blacks are living as a whole.

As a kid growing up on the West side of Chicago I saw many im-   6
ages I thought were good because I saw them over and over again. For
example, I thought gang banging was good because it was around me.
The same concept applies to music. Blacks in America have many concerns such as police brutality, entrepreneurship, reparations, election
reform, employment, quality health care, and quality education. This is
what the art form needs to reflect instead of promoting materialism
and violence.

Black music has historically always voiced the concerns of issues in   7
America that effect their way of living. Instead, rappers and even some
R&B and rock artists admit to committing crimes consistently on
records, thus promoting some of the worst elements our society has to
offer. Songs such as "Hood Rich" or "My Neck/My Back" have become the norm.

Record executives such as Jimmy Iovine, L.A. Reid, Tommy Mottola,   8
Andrew Herrera, Bryan Turner, Russell Simmons, Tony Brown, and Ted
Fields don't want positive images seen or heard, because it will interfere
with the millions they make off young, uneducated, and misled black
rappers from the inner cities of America.

Female rapper Foxy Brown and former rapper Mase both have   9
gone on record saying they portrayed negative images on albums and
videos because the record executives forced them to do so in order to
sell more records. This is the norm also for the entire music industry.
Just look at Britney Spears.

What can cure the problems of negative images of Black America pre-   10
sented in rap and other forms of music?

Music fans of all backgrounds must e-mail and write letters to the   11
major record company executives and voice their concerns. Also don't
buy the music when you hear songs such as "Big Pimpin'."

Music fans can turn off the television and the radio when these im-   12
ages are displayed. Music listeners must e-mail and write the executives
of the products that pay for advertising space on rap shows and in magazines such as *Vibe* and *The Source.* If companies such as the Coca-Cola
Corporation do not take the concerns seriously, then music fans must stop
buying their products.

Positive artists such as Common, Black Star, Dead Pres., KRS1, Mos   13
Def, Gang Star, Goodie Mob, Pharoahe Monch, and The Roots must get
more requests on the radio and rap video programs.

The most important aspect is to shift the focus from the rap artist and   14
put the heat on the record executives who run the major distributors such
as Universal and AOL/Time Warner.

The executives are responsible for what is seen and heard, not the   15
artist. So the next time you have issues with a song such as "Money, Cash,
Hoes," send Russell Simmons an e-mail, or just don't buy the album.

▶ Building Vocabulary

The writer of this essay assumes knowledge of a few topical phrases relating to the world of music and rap music in particular. Identify the following terms, and explain their relevance to rap music:

1. bling bling (par. 1)
2. gang-banging (par. 6)
3. R&B (par. 7)

▶ Thinking Critically About the Argument

Understanding the Writer's Argument

1. What does Jones mean in paragraph 1 when he writes that "rap music was the CNN for poor and working-class blacks in America"?
2. What change came over rap music in the early 1990s, according to Jones?
3. Why does Jones put so much emphasis on the financial situations of the record executives and the fans of rap music?
4. What are some of the issues facing blacks in America, according to Jones? Do you think rap music addresses some of these? How?
5. Why don't record executives want positive images in rap music, according to Jones? Why are the record executives responsible for the negative images in rap, as opposed to the artists, as Jones says in paragraph 15?
6. Which rap musicians does Jones cite for presenting a positive message? Whom does he cite as being negative?

Understanding the Writer's Techniques

1. Why does Jones start his essay with a short history of rap music?
2. What is Jones's major proposition? Is it simply his statement in paragraph 3, or is there another aspect to his argument? What minor proposition does Jones present to show that rap needs to "take a turn for the better"? What evidence does Jones give to support the minor proposition?
3. What is the writer's tone in this essay? Who is his audience, and how does that affect the tone? Explain your answer. This is an emotional issue for Jones, but do you sense emotion? Where? If not, why?
4. How effective is Jones's mini-recollection in paragraph 6? What purpose does it serve in his argument?
5. Jones's essay shifts strategy with his question in paragraph 10. What is the shift, and is his rhetorical question effective? Does his essay maintain coherence despite the shift?

6. In his conclusion, Jones returns to his major proposition, but there has been a change. What is that change, and is his conclusion effective?
7. What is your view of the title? If you could change it, would you? What would you call the essay?

Exploring the Writer's Argument

1. Jones implies in his first paragraph that "poor and working-class blacks in America" only get their identity and news from rap music and that music in general is the biggest influence on Americans. Do you think this is true? Why or why not?
2. This essay was written by a college student. Do you expect him to have these views? How does this fact alter your reception of his argument?
3. Are you convinced by Jones's argument in paragraph 7 regarding his opinion that rappers who admit to committing crimes promote "the worst elements our society has to offer"? Why or why not?
4. In paragraph 7, Jones cites the song "My Neck/My Back" as being one of the "worst elements" in society that rap glorifies. This song, however, is about two consenting adults having sex. Knowing this, do you accept or reject Jones's argument? Why?
5. Do you agree that record executives are responsible for the content of rap records but that the artists are not? Why or why not?
6. What in this essay's argument do you think is effective? Too simple or generalized? Which of Jones's points do you think are well reasoned? Open to question or serious disagreement?

▶ Ideas for Writing Arguments

Prewriting

Jot down notes on what images you see on TV or in the movies and how they affect you negatively.

Writing a Guided Argument

A *genre* is a kind of artistic form. Write an essay in which you argue that some genre other than rap music is responsible for negative effects on children. Be specific. Don't just write about movies—write about action movies or horror films. Don't just write about TV shows—write about *South Park, The Simpsons,* or reality programming.

1. Begin your essay by explaining a little about the history of the particular medium.
2. Write your major proposition clearly and place it prominently in your essay.

3. Give at least two minor propositions for why you think your medium has negative effects on children.
4. Offer ample evidence for your minor propositions in the form of anecdotes or examples.
5. Decide who is mostly responsible for the continuing popularity of that genre.
6. Make sure to use proper transitions in your essay to ensure coherence.
7. In the conclusion of your essay, offer solutions that will minimize the damage done by your chosen offending genre.

Thinking, Arguing, and Writing Collaboratively

Play a song from the gangsta rap era in class, and in small groups analyze the music and lyrics for what you consider positive or helpful to society. Present your findings to the class and solicit their objections. Rebut their objections as a group.

Writing About the Text

Jones states in paragraph 5 that music "affects the soul of an individual." How well has he developed that idea? Do you think music has that much influence on people? Has the essay convinced you of that? Does Jones's argument depend on that statement being true? If so, and if it is not true, does the essay still work? Address these questions in an essay that analyzes "Rap Fans Desire a More Positive Product."

More Writing Ideas

1. In your journal, outline an essay about how you are personally affected by music.
2. Find the lyrics to one of the songs cited by Jones, and analyze it in a paragraph based on his ideas.
3. When novels were first becoming popular in the late 1700s, people accused the form of having a terrible effect on young people. When jazz became popular in the 1920s, critics leveled the same accusation at that music. In the 1950s, when rock and roll was becoming popular, the same thing happened. Research the history of the popular reception of one of these art forms. In an essay, compare the reaction against rap music with the reaction of those who thought novels, jazz, or rock and roll were going to have a negative effect on youth. How are the two situations similar? How are they different?

BARBARA EHRENREICH
Ice-T: The Issue Is Creative Freedom

Biologist Barbara Ehrenreich (who earned her Ph.D. from Rockefeller University in 1968) became involved in political activism during the Vietnam War and began writing on topics such as feminism, class in America, and health care. Her books include The American Health Empire: Power, Profits, and Politics *(1970),* The Hearts of Men: American Dreams and the Flight from Commitment *(1983) and* Blood Rites: Origins and History of the Passions of War *(2001). She has written for the* Progressive, In These Times, *the* Nation, Time, *and many other publications. In 1992, rap artist Ice-T released a rock song called "Cop Killer." The reaction among the public and politicians was swift and angry. As Ehrenreich mentions in this selection, even the president at the time, George H. Bush, offered his opinion that Ice-T was "sick." Ehrenreich's essay, which appeared in* Time *magazine that year, argues that everyone was overreacting.*

▶ Prereading: Thinking About the Essay in Advance

What is the first emotion that comes to mind when you think of a song titled "Cop Killer"? What do you think Ehrenreich means by "the issue is creative freedom"?

▶ Words to Watch

taboo (par. 1) against social customs
paroxysm (par. 2) attack of violent emotion
boycott (par. 2) protest that takes the form of refusing to take part in
sedition (par. 2) act of trying to overthrow those in power
hyperbole (par. 4) exaggeration
decorum (par. 5) the social norm
demagogues (par. 5) dangerously charismatic speakers
miscreants (par. 6) delinquents

Ice-T's song "Cop Killer" is as bad as they come. This is black anger— 1
raw, rude, and cruel—and one reason the song's so shocking is that in postliberal America, black anger is virtually taboo. You won't find it on TV, not on the *McLaughlin Group* or *Crossfire,* and certainly not in the placid features of Arsenio Hall or Bernard Shaw. It's been beaten back into the outlaw subcultures of rap and rock, where, precisely because it is taboo, it sells. And the nastier it is, the faster it moves off the shelves. As Ice-T asks in another song on the same album, "Goddamn what a brotha gotta do / To get a message through / To the red, white, and blue?"

2   But there's a gross overreaction going on, building to a veritable paroxysm of white denial. A national boycott has been called, not just of the song or Ice-T, but of all Time Warner products. The president himself has denounced Time Warner as "wrong" and Ice-T as "sick." Ollie North's Freedom Alliance has started a petition drive aimed at bringing Time Warner executives to trial for "sedition and anarchy."

3   Much of this is posturing and requires no more courage than it takes to stand up in a VFW hall and condemn communism or crack. Yes, "Cop Killer" is irresponsible and vile. But Ice-T is as right about some things as he is righteous about the rest. And ultimately, he's not even dangerous— least of all to the white power structure his songs condemn.

4   The "danger" implicit in all the uproar is of empty-headed, suggestible black kids, crouching by their boom boxes, waiting for the word. But what Ice-T's fans know and his detractors obviously don't is that "Cop Killer" is just one more entry in pop music's long history of macho hyperbole and violent boast. Flip to the classic-rock station, and you might catch the Rolling Stones announcing "the time is right for violent revoloo-shun!" from their 1968 hit "Street Fighting Man." And where were the defenders of our law-enforcement officers when a white British group, the Clash, taunted its fans with the lyrics: "When they kick open your front door / How you gonna come / With your hands on your head / Or on the trigger of your gun?"

5   "Die, Die, Die Pig" is strong speech, but the Constitution protects strong speech, and it's doing so this year more aggressively than ever. The Supreme Court has just downgraded cross burnings to the level of bonfires and ruled that it's no crime to throw around verbal grenades like "nigger" and "kike." Where are the defenders of decorum and social stability when prime-time demagogues like Howard Stern deride African Americans as "spear chuckers"?

6   More to the point, young African Americans are not so naive and suggestible that they have to depend on a compact disc for their sociology lessons. To paraphrase another song from another era, you don't need a rap song to tell which way the wind is blowing. Black youths know that the police are likely to see them through a filter of stereotypes as miscreants and potential "cop killers." They are aware that a black youth is seven times as likely to be charged with a felony as a white youth who has committed the same offense, and is much more likely to be imprisoned.

7   They know, too, that in a shameful number of cases, it is the police themselves who indulge in "anarchy" and violence. The U.S. Justice Department has received 47,000 complaints of police brutality in the past six years, and Amnesty International has just issued a report on police brutality in Los Angeles, documenting forty cases of "torture or cruel, inhuman, or degrading treatment."

Musician Ice-T explains to reporters his reasons for pulling "Cop Killer" from his "Body Count" album in Los Angeles, Calif., on July 28, 1992. Ice-T pulled "Cop Killer" from the album because of threats against Times Warner and Warner Bros.(Associated Press/Bob Galbraith)

Menacing as it sounds, the fantasy in "Cop Killer" is the fantasy of the powerless and beaten down—the black man who's been hassled once too often ("A pig stopped me for nothin'!"), spread-eagled against a police car, pushed around. It's not a "responsible" fantasy (fantasies seldom are). It's not even a very creative one. In fact, the sad thing about "Cop Killer" is that it falls for the cheapest, most conventional image of rebellion that our culture offers: the lone gunman spraying fire from his AK-47. This is not "sedition"; it's the familiar, all-American, Hollywood-style pornography of violence.   8

Which is why Ice-T is right to say he's no more dangerous than George Bush's pal Arnold Schwarzenegger, who wasted an army of cops in *Terminator 2*. Images of extraordinary cruelty and violence are marketed every day, many of far less artistic merit than "Cop Killer." This is our free market of ideas and images, and it shouldn't be any less free for a   9 black man than for other purveyors of "irresponsible" sentiments, from David Duke to Andrew Dice Clay.

10   Just, please, don't dignify Ice-T's contribution with the word *sedition.* The past masters of sedition—men like George Washington, Toussaint L'Ouverture, Fidel Castro, or Mao Zedong, all of whom led and won armed insurrections—would be unimpressed by "Cop Killer" and probably saddened. They would shake their heads and mutter words like "infantile" and "adventurism." They might point out that the cops are hardly a noble target, being, for the most part, honest working stiffs who've got stuck with the job of patrolling ghettos ravaged by economic decline and official neglect.

11   There is a difference, the true seditionist would argue, between a revolution and a gesture of macho defiance. Gestures are cheap. They feel good, they blow off some rage. But revolutions, violent or otherwise, are made by people who have learned how to count very slowly to ten.

▶ Building Vocabulary

1. For the following words, write definitions (attempt to understand their meanings from the context of the essay, or look them up in a dictionary), and write a sentence of your own using each word:
   a. placid (par. 1)
   b. subcultures (par. 1)
   c. veritable (par. 2)
   d. denounced (par. 2)
   e. posturing (par. 3)
   f. detractors (par. 4)
   g. indulge (par. 7)
   h. ghettos (par. 10)
   i. adventurism (par. 10)
   j. defiance (par. 11)
2. Ehrenreich mentions a number of people and institutions from recent and distant history. Identify these people, and explain how they are relevant to Ehrenreich's argument:
   a. Arsenio Hall (par. 1)
   b. Bernard Shaw (par. 1)
   c. Time Warner (par. 2)
   d. Ollie (Oliver) North (par. 2)
   e. VFW (par. 3)
   f. Rolling Stones (par. 4)
   g. Howard Stern (par. 5)
   h. Amnesty International (par. 7)
   i. Arnold Schwarzenegger (par. 9)
   j. David Duke (par. 9)
   k. Andrew Dice Clay (par. 9)

l. George Washington (par. 10)

m. Toussaint L'Ouverture (par. 10)

n. Fidel Castro (par. 10)

o. Mao Zedong (par. 10)

▶ Thinking Critically About the Argument

Understanding the Writer's Argument

1. Paraphrase the writer's first two sentences.
2. According to the writer, why does "angry" rap sell?
3. What is the writer's opinion of Ice-T's song "Cop Killer"? What is her opinion of the song's most outspoken critics?
4. How does the writer place Ice-T's song in the perspective of music history?
5. How does "Cop Killer" relate to the harsh realities of the criminal justice system and police brutality, according to the writer?
6. What is the writer's main criticism of "Cop Killer"?
7. What, according to the writer, is the difference between "revolution and a gesture of macho defiance"? Why is one more impressive than the other?

Understanding the Writer's Techniques

1. What is the intended argumentative effect of Ehrenreich's confrontational opening?
2. Where does Ehrenreich's introduction end? Where is her claim? Is it placed in her introduction? Explain.
3. What are the writer's minor propositions? Which makes her point most effectively? Which is weakest?
4. Compare and contrast the kinds of support Jones and Ehrenreich use to make their arguments. Do they both rely equally on reasonable propositions? Does one rely more on an emotional appeal? Explain your answers.
5. Analyze Ehrenreich's use of transitions. Which is most impressive?
6. What kinds of support does the writer use to bolster her minor propositions?
7. Why is the writer's conclusion effective? Explain your answer. How does it help the essay to cohere?

Exploring the Writer's Argument

1. How do you think Jones would react to Ehrenreich's points that Ice-T and his songs are "not even dangerous" (par. 3) and that "young African Americans are not so naive and suggestible that they have to

depend on a compact disc for their sociology lessons" (par. 6)? What is your reaction to those statements?

2. Do you think Ehrenreich's placing Ice-T in the stream of music history in paragraph 4 is effective? Why or why not?

3. Do you find Ehrenreich's arguments in paragraph 9—that (1) rap is no more dangerous than action movies, and (2) there is free speech, so rap artists can say anything they want—compatible? Why or why not?

4. How effective is Ehrenreich's comparison of Ice-T to the "past masters of sedition"? Do you think this is a fair comparison? Is it an effective argumentative technique? Explain your answers.

▶ Ideas for Writing Arguments

Prewriting

What other elements of popular culture might be considered dangerous, and why? What is your position?

Writing a Guided Argument

Choose an activity that many critics agree is dangerous, such as riding motorcycles or skydiving, and write an essay defending the right of people to do it.

1. Begin your essay by explaining your topic and summarizing the main objections on the grounds of its danger.
2. Write your major proposition clearly.
3. Use a tone that is similar to Ehrenreich's.
4. Offer at least three minor propositions to explain why critics of your chosen action are overreacting.
5. Support your ideas with vivid examples and, if possible, statistics.
6. For at least one of your minor propositions, explain that other activities that are not criticized are at least, if not more, dangerous.
7. Pick out one word that the critics would use to describe your chosen action (for example, some might call skydiving "suicidal"), and close your essay as Ehrenreich does, with a long analysis of how that word is not apt in describing the action.

Thinking, Arguing, and Writing Collaboratively

With the class divided into two arbitrary groups, have one group take Jones's position that rap music is dangerous and have the other group argue, as Ehrenreich does, that it is harmless. As a group, think of arguments and facts to add to those already explored by the writer whose position you are taking, and fix weaknesses in his or her argument. You may do research and bring in examples from home or the library. Take notes on your intragroup discussion, and use your notes to prepare for a debate on the issue of rap music. Present your position to the class as a group, with each member of the group presenting a certain aspect of your argument. As a class, discuss which group's argument was stronger, and explain why.

Writing About the Text

Compare Ehrenreich's argument in this essay with her argument in "From Stone Age to Phone Age" in Chapter 1. "Ice-T: The Issue Is Creative Freedom" was written in 1992, whereas "From Stone Age" was written in 1999. What development do you see in Ehrenreich's style? What is the difference in argumentative technique? How does the tone in her essays differ?

More Writing Ideas

1. In a journal entry, write notes about the word *sedition.* All the "past masters of sedition" Ehrenreich lists were seditious long ago. Can you think of any examples of true sedition or anarchy today?
2. In paragraph 3, Ehrenreich makes a point about American rhetoric, saying that arguing against rap music is "posturing and requires no more courage than it takes to stand up in a VFW hall and condemn communism or crack." In a paragraph, explain this quote, and give at least two examples of this kind of posturing and rhetoric that you have seen in the past year.
3. Write an essay in which you analyze an artistic medium other than music, such as movies, television, books, or radio. Explain how, as Ehrenreich notes, "precisely because it is taboo, it sells" (par. 1). How does the medium exploit the public's desire for "outlaw subcultures" or the shocking?

5 College Sports: Should We Seek Equal Rights Between the Sexes?

In 1972, President Richard Nixon signed into law legislation called the Education Amendments. Title IX of that legislation aimed to force equality between men's and women's sports in any school around the country that receives federal funds. The law says, simply: "No person in the United States shall, on the basis of sex, be excluded from participation in, be denied the benefits of, or be subjected to discrimination under any educational program or activity receiving Federal financial assistance." The law had an impact on all public schools in the country and most private schools and colleges, which receive funding through financial aid programs. Any school found in violation of Title IX would lose its federal funding.

By 1979, Title IX still languished without enforcement, so a Department of Education civil rights commission interpreted the law and issued the rule that would cause heated controversy in the years to come: the three-part test. To comply with Title IX, schools had to fulfill at least one of the following conditions: (1) make sure that the number of student athletes of each sex is roughly equivalent to enrollment percentages (the rule that would come to be known as the "proportionality" rule), (2) show a history and continuing practice of promoting women's sports, or (3) demonstrate that the campus fully and effectively accommodated the athletic interests and abilities of women.

In the years after the adoption of the three-part test, the courts have tested Title IX again and again. One such case, in 1996, involved Brown University, which tried to make the case that women shouldn't have an equal share in collegiate sports because they are not as involved in sports. Brown lost the case.

Critics accuse Title IX of supporting reverse discrimination and a form of unnecessary affirmative action. Supporters laud it for increasing equality for women in educational institutions. Most of the controversy has centered on sports, but note that Title IX covers "any educational program or activity." Americans are still debating the landmark law after more than 30 years.

In the following two selections, Billie Jean King, a retired world-class tennis player, and John Irving, a popular novelist, offer their positions on Title IX. King believes that the law does not go far enough; Irving maintains that although the intentions of the law are good, its interpretation, especially the three-part rule, have had unintentional negative side effects.

BILLIE JEAN KING
For All the Good Things It Has Done, Title IX Is Still Plagued by Myths

Tennis player Billie Jean King was born in 1943 in Long Beach, California. She had a long and spectacular career, winning the women's singles tournament at Wimbledon six times. In 1971 she became the first woman athlete to earn $100,000 in a year. In the famed "Battle of the Sexes" match in Texas in 1973, 30-year-old King beat 55-year-old Bobby Riggs in straight sets. King, who was captain of the women's tennis Olympic team in 1996 and 2000, has been an outspoken supporter of women's rights for many years, pushing especially for parity for the prize money that goes to women athletes. In this selection, King defends the Title IX legislation against widely held misconceptions.

▶ Prereading: Thinking About the Essay in Advance

What do you think are the myths King is referring to in the title? What myths can you imagine exist about women's sports? How can those myths harm the future of women's sports?

▶ Words to Watch

pit (par. 2) set up against each other
inception (par. 4) beginning
rhetoric (par. 5) insincere speech
irrefutably (par. 7) immune from criticism
hampered (par. 7) restricted
curtail (par. 7) restrain
proportionality (par. 12) system regulating amounts based on proportions
compliance (par. 12) conforming to requirements

1   When my brother Randy and I were growing up, we supported each other's dreams of being professional athletes. We both loved sports and we were there for each other as we went through the ups and downs

of being athletes; he as a baseball player for the San Francisco Giants and me as an international tennis player.

2   As Title IX turns 30 today, there are those who want us to believe that this is a male-versus-female issue. There are those who want the public to believe that this is a "zero sum" game; that if women get a chance to play, men lose. This is no time for extremism and no time for anyone to pit men versus women or boys against girls. Those days are over. We are in this together—male and female athletes who love sports, and families who want their sons and daughters to play because of the health, confidence, and other benefits they will receive as a result of such participation. That's the bottom line and we had better not forget it. Also, there are a number of negative myths about Title IX that need to be addressed.

3   MYTH: Title IX requires cutting men's teams.

4   FACT: There is nothing in Title IX that requires schools to cut men's teams. Men's sports participation in high school and college has increased since the law's inception 30 years ago. More important, two-thirds of the schools that have added women's sports to comply with Title IX did not eliminate any men's sports.

5   We can afford to maintain all of our exciting football and basketball programs, keep all men's minor sports and add new women's sports if schools exercise fiscal restraint and support each sport with a smaller piece of the budgetary pie. Financial responsibility is what we should be talking about, not weakening civil-rights laws. We simply cannot believe rhetoric claiming football will die if our daughters have an equal chance to play.

6   MYTH: Women are less interested in sports than men.

7   FACT: Development of women's interest in sports since the enactment of Title IX shows irrefutably that interest reflects opportunity. While fewer than 30,000 women participated in college sports before Title IX, today that number exceeds 150,000—five times the pre-Title IX rate. Women's participation continues to be hampered simply by schools not sponsoring teams for them to play on. To accept the notion that women are less interested in sports than men would simply maintain existing discrimination and curtail opportunities at artificially limited levels.

8   Lets's face it, there will always be more kids interested in playing than we have resources to provide them with opportunities. There are more than six million boys and girls playing high school sports today who are vying for fewer than half a million college athletic participation slots. All Title IX says is that if you have sports participation opportunities, you offer equal opportunity to men and women.

9   MYTH: Women are no longer the victims of discrimination in sports.

10   FACT: Despite Title IX's considerable successes, the playing field is far from level. Spending on men's sports continues to vastly exceed spending on women's sports. Male athletes annually receive $133 million more in athletic scholarships than female athletes. Thirty years after Title IX, women still receive 30 percent fewer sports participation opportunities.

Louisiana State's Muna Lee holds the baton after
anchoring LSU's college women's 800 relay team
Saturday, April 26, 2003, at the Penn Relays in
Philadelphia. LSU tied a meet record with four
relay wins. LSU won the 800 in 1:29.78.
(Associated Press/Douglas M. Bovitt)

MYTH: Title IX requires quotas for women.   11

FACT: Title IX requires that women and girls be given equal opportu- 12
nities to participate in athletics. Because Title IX allows sports teams to be
segregated by gender, in essence it allows schools to decide how many
teams they will sponsor and how many slots they will allocate for female,
as compared to male, students. Title IX simply requires that schools allocate these slots in a nondiscriminatory manner. Title IX does not require
"proportionality" or any other mathematical test, as some are alleging.
There are many schools that are conducting athletic programs that are in
compliance with Title IX with athletic program male/female participation
numbers that are not proportional to the percentages of men and women
in their general student bodies. Use of the word quota misleads the public.

Do I feel Title IX has worked in the intended way the law was created 13
30 years ago? I would say, judging by the 847 percent increase in high
school athletic participation by girls, yes. But, Title IX needs stronger

enforcement because girls are still receiving 1.1 million fewer chances to play high school sports than boys. Thirty years after the passage of Title IX, it's estimated that 80 percent of all schools and colleges are still out of compliance with the law.

14   The Bush administration needs to send a clear message that Title IX is valid and legal and women are entitled to full and equal rights to participate in federally funded education programs and activities. The public expects our government to strongly defend equal rights for men and women. Taxpayers expect their sons and daughters to receive equal educational opportunities, whether it's math, science, drama, or athletics. That's the bottom line. Let's go for it!

▶ Building Vocabulary

In her essay, King uses figurative speech, but in most of those cases, her use of such language is clichéd. Look up the definition of cliché and explain why the following are clichés. What could you replace them with to make them more interesting?

1. went through the ups and downs (par. 1)
2. That's the bottom line (par. 2, 14)
3. smaller piece of the pie . . . (par. 5)
4. the playing field is far from level (par. 10)
5. send a clear message (par. 14)

▶ Thinking Critically About the Argument

Understanding the Writer's Argument

1. Why, according to King, should people stop fighting over Title IX?
2. According to King, why does Title IX not mean that men's sports will disappear?
3. How are men's and women's sports still not equal after 30 years of Title IX, in King's view?
4. What is King's answer to opponents of Title IX who accuse the law of forcing quotas on schools?
5. What does King want the government to do now to improve the situation?

Understanding the Writer's Techniques

1. Where does King's introduction end? How do you know? What is her major proposition? What minor propositions does she use to support her major proposition?

2. What is the argumentative effect of using the words MYTH and FACT instead of other words? What is the effect of presenting them in uppercase letters?

3. The four myths that the writer highlights are really objections to Title IX that she rebuts. Make a list of the myths, and outline her rebuttals. Which is her most successful rebuttal? Which is her weakest? Explain your answers.

4. King uses statistics to help her case. How effective do you find them? What do you think is King's strongest piece of evidence?

5. Why does King use the word "segregated" in paragraph 12? What is the effect?

6. Do you think King's closing, including the use of the exclamation point, is persuasive? Why or why not?

Exploring the Writer's Argument

1. Is there any good argumentative reason why King includes her opening about her brother and her? If so, what is it? If not, how would you improve her introduction?

2. Do you find the structure of King's essay to be effective? Why or why not? Does the "MYTH/FACT" list format work for or against her argument?

3. King suggests in paragraph 2 that there are those who want to "pit men versus women," but she doesn't say who those people are. Does her vagueness hurt her argument? Justify your response.

4. King writes that both men's and women's sports have increased their numbers since 1972. She implies that this is because of Title IX. Can you think of any other explanation?

5. At the end of her essay, King implies that athletics are as important as the major subjects in school. Do you agree with her? Why or why not?

▶ Ideas for Writing Arguments

Prewriting

Draft a brief outline arguing against misconceptions about a segment of the population on campus. What are the myths that circulate about them? What is the truth?

Writing a Guided Argument

Write an essay in which you dispel myths about a book, movie, television show, video game, or other technology. Choose something that you know a good deal about.

1. Begin your essay by recounting an anecdote in which you watch, read, or play with your chosen subject.
2. Connect your experience, using transitions, with the idea that there are common myths about your subject.
3. Write your major proposition.
4. Organize your minor propositions, rebuttals to myths, in an effective manner to maintain coherence in your argument.
5. Offer evidence in the form of statistics or facts to support your rebuttals.
6. Close your essay with a call for greater tolerance and understanding, explaining how the truth about your subject will benefit people.

Thinking, Arguing, and Writing Collaboratively

Exchange a draft of your Writing a Guided Argument assignment with a classmate. Review your partner's essay for its success in following the steps. Does the writer express the major proposition as a choice? Is the major proposition reflected in the minor propositions? Is there sufficient evidence to back up the minor propositions? Write a paragraph evaluating the essay and suggesting revisions.

Writing About the Text

Read John Irving's essay on page 165. Write an essay in which you compare and contrast King's and Irving's arguments. In what ways are the two writers in agreement, and where do they differ? Which do you think is the stronger argument? Use either writer's essay as a basis for the structure of your essay.

More Writing Ideas

1. In your journal, freewrite about the concept of a "'zero sum' game" (par. 2). Write for at least 15 minutes without editing your work. Then look over your journal entry and find any candidates for a major proposition.
2. Write two or three paragraphs that take issue with the way King uses statistics in her essay. What is suspect? Why?
3. John Irving writes in his essay that the Women's Sport Foundation and other women's groups are being "vindictive" in their faith in the success of Title IX and "their continuing endorsement of proportionality in collegiate athletics." King is the founder of the Women's Sport Foundation. Examine Irving's exact words, and write an essay in which you argue whether or not you think Irving's accusation of King and her organization is fair and in which you speculate as to how King might respond to Irving's accusation.

JOHN IRVING
Wrestling with Title IX

John Irving was born in Exeter, New Hampshire, in 1942. He was educated at Phillips Exeter Academy, a prep school, where he started to wrestle competitively, and later studied in Vienna, Austria, Pittsburgh, and at the prestigious Writer's Workshop at the University of Iowa. He is the author of several novels, including, Setting Free the Bears *(1968),* The World According to Garp *(1974),* The Cider House Rules *(1985), and* A Prayer for Owen Meany *(1989). He has been awarded many honors for his writing, including an American Book Award and a Guggenheim Fellowship. During the early part of his writing career, Irving supported himself by teaching and coaching wrestling. In this selection, the novelist and former wrestler explores the difference between the Title IX legislation and how it has been enforced over the years.*

▶ Prereading: Thinking About the Essay in Advance

If you were to choose which college sports to abolish, which would you select? Explain your reasoning.

▶ Words to Watch

disparate (par. 3) unfairly different
criteria (par. 4) requirements
proportionality (par. 4) system regulating amounts based on proportion
zealots (par. 6) overly enthusiastic believers
intramural (par. 8) occurring within an institution
equity (par. 12) equality
gulch (par. 16) ravine; small canyon

Title IX, the federal law that prohibits sex discrimination in educational   1
programs receiving federal assistance, may be in for an overhaul. This week a committee appointed by the Bush administration will hold its final meetings before submitting its recommendations for changing the law to Secretary of Education Rod Paige. Since Title IX was enacted in 1972, it has been the subject of debate—much of it misguided—about its application to college athletics. At issue now is how to alter the law—or not—so that, as Secretary Paige has put it, we can find ways of "expanding opportunities to ensure fairness for all college athletes."

I hope the commission will realize that what's wrong with Title IX   2
isn't Title IX. What's wrong is that, in practice, there are two Title IX's. The first Title IX was the one passed by Congress in 1972 to put an end to sex discrimination in schools—good for the original Title IX! The second

Title IX, the one currently enforced, is the product of a policy interpretation in 1979 by the Department of Education's Office for Civil Rights (but never debated or approved by Congress)—and which is functioning as a gender quota law.

3   In its prohibition against sex discrimination, the 1972 law expressly states as "exceptions" any "preferential or disparate treatment because of imbalance in participation" or any "statistical evidence of imbalance." In English, this means that Congress recognized that the intent of Title IX was not to establish gender quotas or require preferential treatment as reparation for past discrimination. Smart thinking—after all, the legislation was intended to prohibit discrimination against either sex.

4   But what happened in 1979—and in subsequent re-evaluations of the law—has invited discrimination against male athletes. The 1979 interpretation required colleges to meet at least one of the following three criteria: that the number of athletes from each sex be roughly equivalent to the number of students enrolled; that colleges demonstrate a commitment to adding women's sports; and that they prove that the athletic interests of female students are effectively accommodated. The problems lie in complying with the first criterion. In order to achieve gender proportionality, men's collegiate sports are being undermined and eliminated. This was never the intention of Title IX.

5   The proportionality rule stipulates that the ratio of male to female athletes be proportionate to the ratio of male to female students at a particular college. On average, females make up about 56 percent of college enrollment, males 44 percent; for most colleges to be in compliance with proportionality, more than half the athletes on team rosters must be women. Can you imagine this rule being applied to all educational programs—classes in science, engineering, accounting, medicine or law? What about dance, drama or music—not to mention women's studies?

6   In 1996, the Department of Education further bolstered the proportionality zealots by requiring colleges to count every name on a team's roster—scholarship and nonscholarship athletes, starters and nonstarters. It is this ruling that has prompted a lawsuit by the National Wrestling Coaches Association, the Committee to Save Bucknell Wrestling, the Marquette Wrestling Club, the Yale Wrestling Association, and the National Coalition for Athletics Equity, all of whom argue that the 1996 rules exceed the Department of Education's statutory authority "by effectively mandating the very discrimination that Title IX prohibits."

7   Why are wrestlers so upset about this? The number of collegiate wrestling programs lost to Title IX compliance is staggering; this is especially alarming because, since 1993, wrestling has been a rapidly growing sport at the high-school level. Data compiled by Gary Abbott, director of special projects at USA Wrestling, indicates that in 2001, there were 244,984 athletes wrestling in high school; only 5,966 got to wrestle in the

National Collegiate Athletic Association. Not to put too fine a point on it: there is only one N.C.A.A., spot for every 41 high-school wrestlers. The numbers have been going downhill for a while. In 1982, there were 363 N.C.A.A. wrestling teams with 7,914 wrestlers competing; in 2001, there were only 229 teams with fewer than 6,000 wrestlers. Yet, in that same period, the number of N.C.A.A. institutions has increased from 787 to 1,049. No wonder wrestlers are unhappy.

As for the virtual elimination of walk-ons (nonscholarship athletes) in many men's sports, and the unrealistic capping of male team rosters—again, to make the number of male athletes proportional to the number of females—the problem is that athletic programs are going to absurd lengths to fill the unfilled rosters for women's teams. But women, statistically, aren't interested in participating in intercollegiate athletics to the degree that men are. J. Robinson, wrestling coach at the University of Minnesota, cites intramural sports, which are wholly interest driven, as an example. In a column about Title IX published in the *Chronicle of Higher Education*, Robinson wrote that "men outnumber women 3–1 or 4–1 on the intramural field."   8

Don't we need to know the exact numbers for how many women are interested in playing college sports now? But the Women's Sports Foundation, an advocacy group that favors maintaining proportionality, opposes conducting surveys of incoming students—that is, expressly to gauge interest in athletics. These surveys, they say, would force "female athletes to prove their interest in sports in order to obtain the right to participate and be treated fairly." But men would fill out the same surveys.   9

One suggestion that the presidential commission is considering is counting the available spots on teams, rather than the actual participants. The Women's Sports Foundation rejects this idea, arguing that it counts "ghost female participants." However, the foundation has no objection to counting interest that isn't there.   10

In fact, those women's groups opposed to tampering with either the 1979 interpretation or the 1996 ruling, which endorses the proportionality arm of Title IX, often argue that there are three ways (at least on paper) for an institution to comply with Title IX—not just proportionality. But only proportionality can be measured concretely. A 1996 clarification letter from the Department of Education refers to the proportionality test as a "safe harbor"—meaning that this simple-to-apply numerical formula can assure an athletic director and a university president that their institution is in compliance and not subject to legal action. In other words, proportionality is not only wrong—it's lazy.   11

Some women's advocates argue that it is not proportionality that forces athletic directors to cut men's teams; they blame the budget excesses of Division I football and men's basketball. But there are countless examples where money was not the issue in the case or the sport   12 that was dropped. Marquette University had a wrestling team that was completely financed by alumni and supporters; yet the sport was dropped in 2001, to comply with gender equity. (Marquette has no football team.)

13   Boston College dropped three sports that had only part-time coaches and offered no scholarships; these sports could easily have been sponsored by fund-raising. Keep in mind, too, that the majority of male college teams dropped in the 1990's were from Division II and Division III programs, which don't have big-time football or men's basketball.

14   Furthermore, many Division I football and basketball programs earn millions of dollars a year, enough to support all the other sports programs—men's and women's. Moreover, most schools with high-profile football programs are schools where women's teams have thrived. (Witness the Big 10, the S.E.C., the Big 12, and other Division I athletic conferences, which have produced both winning football teams as well as great women's teams in other sports.)

15   While eliminating men's sports like wrestling, where the interest in participation is increasing, athletic programs go begging to find women athletes to fill the vacancies on an ever-expanding number of women's teams.

16   One of the most ludicrous examples of this was the attempt by Arizona State University in Tempe—a cactus-studded campus in the middle of the Sonoran Desert—to add a competitive women's rowing team. There's not a lot of water in Arizona. But the school asked the city to create a body of water (by flooding a dry gulch) on which the team could practice. Because of a lack of funds, the school had to drop the plan. This is probably just as well; taxpayer dollars would have financed scholarships either to rowers from out of state or to teach Arizona women (most of whom have never held an oar) how to row. But Arizona State is to be commended. It not only worked to meet the numerical demands of proportionality, it tried to adhere to the original spirit of Title IX by adding opportunities for women, not by cutting opportunities for men.

17   To apply the rule of proportionality to men's and women's collegiate athletics amounts to a feminist form of sex discrimination. And I won't be dismissed by that other argument I've heard (ad nauseam) from those women's advocates unwilling to let proportionality go—namely, that to oppose proportionality, or even the crudest enforcement of Title IX to eliminate men's sports programs, is tantamount to being antifeminist and hostile to women in sports. Don't try to lay that on me.

18   I *am* a women's advocate. I have long been active in the pro-choice movement; my principal political commitment is my longstanding and continuing role as an abortion-rights advocate. But I'm also an advocate of fairness. What is unfair is not Title IX—it is Title IX's enforcement of proportionality, which discriminates against men.

19   In 1992, Brian Picklo, a walk-on, asked the Michigan State Wrestling coach, Tom Minkel, if he could try out for the team. Picklo

had wrestled for only two years in high school and never qualified for state tournaments. Minkel thought Picklo's chances of wrestling in the Big 10 were "slim to none." But Picklo became a two-time Division I All-American, and he won the Big 10 title at 190 pounds. In most wrestling programs across the country today, Brian Picklo wouldn't be allowed to be a walk-on.

Title IX, the original legislation, was conceived as a fairness-for-all law; it has been reinvented as a tool to treat men unfairly. Advocates of proportionality claim that universities that are not "proportional" are breaking the law, but they're not breaking the original law.   20

The Women's Sports Foundation has accused the presidential commission of politicizing Title IX. But Title IX was politicized by the Department of Education in 1979 and 1996—during Democratic administrations. Is it only now political because a Republican administration is taking a closer look at the way Title IX is applied? (I make this criticism, by the way, as a Democrat. I'd have a hard time being an abortion rights advocate in the Bush administration, wouldn't I?)   21

Based on 2001 membership data—raw data from the National Federation of State High Schools, and from the N.C.A.A.—for every single N.C.A.A. sports opportunity for a woman, there are 17 high school athletes available to fill the spot; for a man, there are 18. Isn't that equal enough? In fact, women have more opportunity to compete in college than men do. Yet the attitude represented by the Women's Sports Foundation, and other women's groups, is that women are far from achieving gender equity; by their continuing endorsement of proportionality in collegiate athletics, these women's advocates are being purely vindictive.   22

Years ago, I was playing in a Little League baseball game when an umpire made what I thought was a memorable mistake. Later, in another game, he made it again. I realized it was no mistake at all—he meant to say it. Instead of hollering "Play ball!" at the start of the game, this umpire shouted "Play fair!"   23

Keep Title IX; eliminate proportionality. Play fair.   24

▶ Building Vocabulary

Define the following words and use each in a sentence of your own:

1. policy (par. 2)
2. criterion (par. 4)
3. bolstered (par. 6)
4. mandating (par. 6)
5. absurd (par. 8)
6. clarification (par. 11)
7. tantamount (par. 17)
8. vindictive (par. 22)

▶Thinking Critically About the Argument

Understanding the Writer's Argument

1. What, according to Irving, is the problem with Title IX? What does he mean when he writes that "there are two Title IX's"? (par. 2)
2. Why does Irving point out that the Department of Education's 1979 interpretation of Title IX was "never debated or approved by Congress"? (par. 2)
3. Paraphrase Irving's argument in paragraph 5.
4. What did the Department of Education do in 1996 concerning Title IX? Explain why Irving thinks it was a bad idea.
5. Who are "walk-ons," and why is it significant that they rarely make college teams anymore?
6. Why, according to Irving, would it be valuable to know the number of women who are interested in playing sports in college, and why is it difficult to get that number?
7. Why do colleges use the proportionality rule to comply with Title IX instead of one of the other two criteria?
8. How could money-starved college sports programs be funded, if not by the school, according to Irving?

Understanding the Writer's Techniques

1. How effective is Irving's opening? Explain.
2. What is Irving's major proposition? Make an outline of Irving's many minor propositions. Which is more effective? Which is the weakest? Explain your answers.
3. Why does Irving ask two rhetorical questions at the end of paragraph 5? How do they advance his argument?
4. Why does Irving write that "women, statistically, aren't interested in participating in intercollegiate athletics to the degree that men are"? (par. 8) How does he back up this point? King includes this in her essay as one of the myths of Title IX. How might she respond to Irving's statement?
5. Paraphrase Irving's point in paragraph 11. How effective is this point?
6. Irving shifts tone several times in this essay. Answer the following questions:
   a. Where in the essay does Irving use a tone of authority?
   b. Where in the essay does Irving switch to a sarcastic tone?
   c. Where in the essay does Irving use a sentimental tone?
   d. Can you identify any other tones?
   e. Why does he shift tone so much? How is the multiple shift in tone effective?

7. Paraphrase Irving's argument in paragraph 21. Do you find it to be effective? Why or why not?

8. Do you think that Irving's conclusion is effective? Explain your answer.

Exploring the Writer's Argument

1. Irving was a wrestler for many years and then coached for several years more. Does this give him enough authority to write about Title IX? Why or why not?

2. Do you think that Irving's essay is marred by too narrow a focus on wrestling? How could he widen the discussion? Where in his essay could you imagine he might refer to other men's sports that are less popular than football and basketball?

3. In her essay, King argues, that schools can save men's sports, even minor ones like wrestling, if they "exercise fiscal restraint and support each sport with a smaller piece of the budgetary pie." What would Irving's answer to this be? Do you agree with King? With Irving? Why?

4. Does Irving offer a solution to the problems he explores? If he does, what is it? If not, what do you think the solution is?

▶ Ideas for Writing Arguments

Prewriting

Jot down some notes about other well-intentioned laws or rules that have caused problems. What was their original intention? What were the unintentional side effects? Were there any repercussions for the rule- or lawgiver?

Writing a Guided Argument

Write an essay that argues that colleges could easily comply with Title IX by using one of the criteria other than the proportionality rule. Pretend that you are preparing your paper as a speech to be given at a conference of collegiate athletic directors.

1. Begin your essay by explaining the problem, using quotes from either King's essay (about quotas) or Irving's essay (about the proportionality rule).

2. Acknowledge, in kind words, that most of the athletic directors, by using the proportionality rule, are, as Irving says in paragraph 11, "lazy." Do not use the word *lazy* so that you do not alienate your audience.

3. Shift your tone at some point to one of gentle accusation.

4. Write your major proposition.
5. Offer at least three minor propositions.
6. Support your minor propositions with examples and facts, using effective transitions to aid coherence.
7. Defend your own identity in the essay, making sure your audience has no question about your authority and integrity.
8. Close your essay with an anecdote that illustrates your major proposition.

Thinking, Arguing, and Writing Collaboratively

Break the class into four groups. Two groups will prepare an argument *for* the proportionality rule in Title IX, and the other two groups will prepare an argument *against* it. Both groups on each side should meet to come up with two good grounds to support their position, one for each group. Each group should prepare evidence to support its chosen ground. At the end of the preparation period, the groups should all come together and the four groups should present their argument, alternating between sides.

Writing About the Text

At a few points in Irving's essay, he defends himself personally against perceived objections from his reader. Write an essay analyzing those passages, explaining why you think he felt it necessary to go on the defensive.

More Writing Ideas

1. In your journal, write notes for an essay arguing that tuition money should not be used for college athletics at all.
2. Write an imaginary interview between King and Irving about women's tennis programs.
3. Investigate the way in which your school complies with Title IX (if it does comply), and write an essay on your findings. Explain how you think King and Irving would respond to your school's approach. If your school does not comply with Title IX, write a letter to the school's athletic director demanding the school does comply.

6 Animal Rights: Should They Compromise Human Needs?

I n recent years the idea of *animal* rights has gained many supporters. Animal rights advocates believe that other species should exist without human interference. Modern researchers have argued that animals feel pain and emotions and, in some cases, are capable of reasoning. Organizations such as the People for the Ethical Treatment of Animals (PETA) go so far as to claim that drinking milk is immoral because it causes the cows suffering. Some animal rights advocates are more moderate and abstain from eating meat from big commercial farms or become vegetarians altogether. Some will not wear leather.

Most people, if pressed, will agree that we do not need to eat hamburgers to live, but what happens when it is a question of life and death? For example, what if the suffering of animals can help save the lives of humans who are sick with disease? Many drugs and procedures that humans rely on for health emerged through medical research on animals.

In the selections that follow, written by two writers of vastly different backgrounds and viewpoints, notice how emotional the arguments for or against animal experimentation can be.

JANE MCCABE
Is a Lab Rat's Fate More Poignant than a Child's?

Jane McCabe was a wife and mother living in northern California when she published this essay in Newsweek. *She is not a professional writer, nor is she a public person. Her only qualification for writing is that she believes strongly about animal experimentation and has a stake in the issue. Her daughter has an incurable disease, and hope for a cure lies mostly in the ability of scientists to continue doing experiments on animals. In this selection, McCabe argues passionately that animal experimentation must continue.*

▶ Prereading: Thinking About the Essay in Advance

Think about the question posed in the title. Consider giving an answer to that question. What about the fate of a chimpanzee? A pet dog's fate? A cat's? Where would you personally draw the line and why?

▶ Words to Watch

stark (par. 1) plain, harsh
cystic fibrosis (par. 1) a disease that appears in early childhood affecting the digestive system and the lungs
supplemental (par. 4) making up for something lacking
enzymes (par. 5) molecules that help biological function
antibiotics (par. 5) drugs designed to fight bacterial infection
diabetes (par. 5) a disease caused by a low level of insulin, the hormone in the body that controls the level of sugar in the blood
semblance (par. 6) an outward appearance or likeness
poignant (par. 7) deeply affecting the emotions
eloquent (par. 9) forcefully expressive and persuasive

1   I see the debate about using animals in medical research in stark terms. If you had to choose between saving a very cute dog or my equally cute, blond, brown-eyed daughter, whose life would you choose? It's not a difficult choice, is it? My daughter has cystic fibrosis. Her only hope for a normal life is that researchers, some of them using animals, will find a cure. Don't misunderstand. It's not that I don't love animals, it's just that I love Claire more.

2   Nine years ago I had no idea that I would be joining the fraternity of those who have a vital interest in seeing that medical research continues. I was a very pregnant woman in labor; with my husband beside me I gave birth to a 7-pound 1-ounce daughter. It all seemed so easy. But for the next four months she could not gain weight. She was a textbook case of failure to thrive. Finally a hospital test of the salt content in her sweat led to the diagnosis of cystic fibrosis.

3   The doctor gave us a little reason for hope. "Your daughter will not have a long life, but for most of the time, it will be a good life. Her life expectancy is about 13 years, though it could be longer or shorter. As research continues, we're keeping them alive longer."

4   "As research continues." It's not a lot to rely on but what's our alternative? We haven't waited passively. We learned how to take care of our little girl; her medical problems affect her digestion and lungs. We protected her from colds, learned about supplemental vitamins and antibiotics. We moved to California where the winters aren't so harsh and the

(People for the Ethical Treatment of Animals/AP)

cold and flu season isn't so severe. Our new doctor told us that the children at his center were surviving, on the average, to age 21. So far, our daughter is doing well. She is a fast runner and plays a mean first base. She loves her friends and is, in general, a happy little girl. All things considered, I feel very lucky.

How has research using animals helped those with CF? Three times a   5
day my daughter uses enzymes from the pancreas of pigs to digest her food. She takes antibiotics tested on rats before they are tried on humans. As an adult, she will probably develop diabetes and need insulin—a drug developed by research on dogs and rabbits. If she ever needs a heart-lung transplant, one might be possible because of the cows that surgeons practiced on. There is no animal model to help CF research, but once the CF gene is located, new gene-splicing techniques may create a family of mice afflicted with the disease. Researchers would first learn to cure the mice with drugs, then cautiously try with humans.

There are only about 10,000 people with CF in the United States. But   6
the number of people dependent on research is much larger. Walk with me through the Children's Hospital at Stanford University: here are the youngsters fighting cancer, rare genetic illnesses, immunological diseases.

Amid their laughter and desperate attempts to retain a semblance of childhood, there is suffering.

7   I think the motivation of animal-rights activists is to cut down on the suffering in this world, but I have yet to hear them acknowledge that people—young and old—suffer, too. Why is a laboratory rat's fate more poignant than that of an incurably ill child?

8   There are advocates for animals who only seek to cut down on "unnecessary research." They don't specify how to decide what is unnecessary, but they do create an atmosphere in which doing medical research is seen as distasteful work. I think that's wrong. Researchers should be thanked, not hassled.

9   Every time I see a bumper sticker that says "Lab animals never have a nice day," a fantasy plays in my brain. I get out of my car, tap on the driver's window and ask to talk. In my fantasy, the other driver gets out, we find a coffee shop and I show her photos of my kids. I ask her if she has ever visited Children's Hospital. I am so eloquent that her eyes fill with tears and she promises to think of the children who are wasting away as she considers the whole complicated issue of suffering.

10   I have other fantasies, too, that a cure is found for what ails my daughter, that she marries and gives us some grandchildren, and does great work in her chosen profession, which at this moment appears to be cartooning or computer programming. We can still hope—as long as the research continues.

▶ Building Vocabulary

1. In this essay, the writer uses several medical terms. Find at least five and write definitions for each.
2. Sometimes, writers use idiomatic phrases that they assume their reader will either know or understand from context. Rewrite the following phrases in your own language:
   a. the fraternity of those (par. 2)
   b. a textbook case (par. 2)
   c. plays a mean first base (par. 4)
   d. cut down on (par. 7)
   e. who are wasting away (par. 9)

▶ Thinking Critically About the Argument

Understanding the Writer's Argument

1. Why does McCabe begin her essay by admitting that she sees the issue of animal experimentation "in stark terms"? What does she mean? Why does she see the choice between child and animal as "stark"?

2. Why does McCabe place herself in the "fraternity of those who have a vital interest in seeing that medical research continues"? Why does she use the word "fraternity"? (par. 2)
3. In paragraph 4, McCabe mentions all the things that her husband and she have done for their daughter. What is she implying? In what ways has animal experimentation helped McCabe's daughter?
4. What other diseases can animal experimentation give hope for? Why does McCabe mention only children with diseases in paragraph 6?
5. In paragraph 7, McCabe repeats the title question, but in different words. What is the difference?
6. According to McCabe, what is the result of animal rights advocates making vague claims that research is "unnecessary"?
7. What is McCabe's reason for including her fantasy about confronting the driver? (par. 9)

Understanding the Writer's Techniques

1. What is McCabe's major proposition and where does she place it? Is it effective where it is? Explain.
2. What is the effect of McCabe's "stark" admission in paragraph 1? If this admission is part of the warrant behind her claim, why does she state it? Why can this warrant not remain implied?
3. What other implied or stated warrants affect McCabe's argument?
4. Who is McCabe's audience? How does her audience affect the tone of the essay?
5. Paraphrase McCabe's argument. Write one sentence for each paragraph explaining the function of that paragraph.
6. What examples does McCabe use to back up her major proposition?
7. McCabe's argument is emotional. What emotional appeals does she make?
8. Discuss the conclusion. Is it effective? Why or why not?
9. **(Mixing modes)** How does McCabe use narrative and illustration together? Does she do it successfully? Why or why not?

Exploring the Writer's Argument

1. What is your emotional reaction to the essay? Does she pull your "heart-strings" too much? Look at your list of emotional appeals from question 7, above. Which of McCabe's emotional appeals are unfair appeals?
2. What logical appeals could you think of to help out McCabe's argument?
3. McCabe writes that any criticism of animal experimentation is harmful. What reason does she give for this? What do you think of this argument?

4. McCabe offers examples of her daughter suffering, but never mentions the sufferings of the animals that are experimented upon. Is this a weakness in her argument? Why or why not?

▶ Ideas for Writing Arguments

Prewriting

List the ways in which humans seem superior to animals. Are there ways in which humans are inferior to animals?

Writing a Guided Argument

Write an argument that supports animal experimentation, but assume that you, like McCabe, are a parent, friend, or relative of a seriously ill child who has been helped and perhaps can be cured by furthering animal experimentation.

1. Begin your essay by expressing the rules. What is your warrant, and what is your claim?
2. Address the expectations of the opposition.
3. State your first minor proposition to support your claim.
4. Support your first proposition with evidence.
5. State your second minor proposition.
6. Support your second proposition with evidence from McCabe's essay. Use her own words to prove your point.
7. End your essay by expressing, once again, how surprising your position is. Explain why your point of view lends your position more credibility.

Thinking, Arguing, and Writing Collaboratively

Work in small groups of three or four. List ways in which humans assert their superiority over animals. Which of these ways are acceptable ethically? Report the differences of opinion in your group, including reasons for your various claims.

Writing About the Text

Because McCabe is a parent, it is natural that she is going to argue for the value of her child's life over that of anonymous animals. Does her identity weaken her position because she will always be emotional about the topic? Does she anticipate this question in her essay? If not, how could she anticipate it? If so, could she do better and would doing so strengthen her argument?

More Writing Ideas

1. The most famous animal rights advocate, the contemporary philosopher Peter Singer, argues that the real question is one stated 150 years ago by Jeremy Bentham, a 19th-century English philosopher. Bentham, talking about the rights of animals, said, "The question is not, 'Can they reason?' nor, 'Can they talk?' But rather, 'Can they suffer?'" Do you agree with this view, or are the other questions he mentions worth considering? Write an essay agreeing or disagreeing with Singer and Bentham.

2. Some animals kill each other. Humans are, essentially, just animals with the ability to reason. If animals can kill each other for food, why can't we kill animals to prolong our own lives? Does our ability to reason take away our right to use animals for experimentation, food, or sport?

3. Many people wear leather or eat meat but still believe that animal experimentation is wrong. Write an essay about people wanting to have the issue of animal rights their own way. What is your position on the issue? Do you have a double standard? Justify your position.

4. Working with your list of claims and evidence from your collaborative work, write an essay in which you defend one human use of animals—for example, for food or in fashion. Choose a specific use, as in harvesting caviar or wearing leather belts.

JANE GOODALL

A Question of Ethics

Jane Goodall, born in 1934 in London, England, is best known for her work studying chimpanzees in the wild. In 1960, at the age of 26, with no college degree or formal training, she began to study chimps at the Gombe Stream Reserve in Tanzania in eastern Africa, working as a secretary to fund her work. By watching the chimps closely, she was able to gain their trust. Soon she saw differences between the individual chimps. She was the first scientist to note that chimps are not strictly vegetarian and that the species uses tools, something previously thought to be purely a human trait. Goodall wrote many books about her work, including My Friends the Wild Chimpanzees *(1967),* In the Shadow of Man *(1971),* The Chimpanzees of Gombe: Patterns of Behavior *(1986),* Through a Window: My Thirty Years with the Chimpanzees of Gombe *(1990), and* The Chimpanzee: The Living Link Between Man and Beast *(1992). She has received several awards for her research and for conservation, including the prestigious Albert Schweitzer Award. In this essay, Goodall displays her signature thoughtfulness and humanism.*

▶ Prereading: Thinking About the Essay in Advance

Think about the word *ethics*. Ethics is the branch of philosophy that deals with moral obligations and duties. What is more ethical: protecting the rights and lives of animals or looking for cures for human diseases?

▶ Words to Watch

fuzzy (par. 1) unclear
distinction (par. 1) difference
vaccines (par. 2) medicines that prevent a disease
surly (par. 2) bad tempered
sentient (par. 3) capable of feeling
dilemma (par. 3) problem with two unsatisfactory alternatives
vigorously (par. 4) with great energy
apathy (par. 5) lack of interest

1   David Greybeard first showed me how fuzzy the distinction between animals and humans can be. Forty years ago I befriended David, a chimpanzee, during my first field trip to Gombe in Tanzania. One day I offered him a nut in my open palm. He looked directly into my eyes, took the nut out of my hand and dropped it. At the same moment he very gently squeezed my hand as if to say, I don't want it, but I understand your motives.

2   Since chimpanzees are thought to be physiologically close to humans, researchers use them as test subjects for new drugs and vaccines. In the labs, these very sociable creatures often live isolated from one another in 5-by-5-foot cages, where they grow surly and sometimes violent. Dogs, cats and rats are also kept in poor conditions and subjected to painful procedures. Many people would find it hard to sympathize with rats, but dogs and cats are part of our lives. Ten or 15 years ago, when the use of animals in medical testing was first brought to my attention, I decided to visit the labs myself. Many people working there had forced themselves to believe that animal testing is the only way forward for medical research.

3   Once we accept that animals are sentient beings, is it ethical to use them in research? From the point of view of the animals, it is quite simply wrong. From our standpoint, it seems ridiculous to equate a rat with a human being. If we clearly and honestly believe that using animals in research will, in the end, reduce massive human suffering, it would be difficult to argue that doing so is unethical. How do we find a way out of this dilemma?

4   One thing we can do is change our mind-set. We can begin by questioning the assumption that animals are essential to medical research. Scientists have concluded that chimpanzees are not useful for AIDS research

because, even though their genetic makeup differs from ours by about 1 percent, their immune systems deal much differently with the AIDS virus. Many scientists test drugs and vaccines on animals simply because they are required to by law rather than out of scientific merit. This is a shame, because our medical technology is beginning to provide alternatives. We can perform many tests on cell and tissue cultures without recourse to systemic testing on animals. Computer simulations can also cut down on the number of animal tests we need to run. We aren't exploring these alternatives vigorously enough.

Ten or 15 years ago animal-rights activists resorted to violence   5
against humans in their efforts to break through the public's terrible apathy and lack of imagination on this issue. This extremism is counterproductive. I believe that more and more people are becoming aware that to use animals thoughtlessly, without any anguish or making an effort to find another way, diminishes us as human beings.

▶ Building Vocabulary

For each of the following words, write both a definition and a sentence of your own:

1. fuzzy (par. 1)
2. surly (par. 2)
3. sentient (par. 3)
4. dilemma (par. 3)
5. vigorously (par. 4)
6. apathy (par. 5)
7. counterproductive (par. 5)

▶ Thinking Critically About the Argument

Understanding the Writer's Argument

1. Why does Goodall start her essay with the story of giving the nut to the chimp David Greybeard?
2. According to Goodall, how are lab animals treated, and what does this do to their behavior? What are other physical and emotional effects of experimentation on animals?
3. Why did Goodall visit the labs where animal experimentation was taking place? (par. 2)
4. In paragraph 3, Goodall questions whether it is "ethical" to use animals in medical research. What does she mean here by ethical? In your own words, what is the "dilemma" Goodall refers to in paragraph 3?

5. Goodall thinks that people should change their "mind-set" about animal experimentation. What is the current mind-set of people about the issue?
6. How can people change the way that they think about animal experimentation, according to Goodall?
7. Goodall says that extreme forms of protest are "counterproductive," alluding to violence by activists against people who use animals for medical research. What are *productive* ways of changing people's minds about the issue?

Understanding the Writer's Techniques

1. Which sentence in the essay states Goodall's claim?
2. Goodall is known as a scientist with a heart, a person who cares about all creatures of Earth. How does knowing this information influence how you perceive her argument?
3. What are Goodall's warrants for this essay? Who is her audience, and how does that affect the tone of the essay?
4. Make an outline of Goodall's essay, paraphrasing her argument.
5. What form of reasoning does Goodall use in this essay, deductive or inductive? What kind of evidence does she use?
6. Although this is mostly a reasoned argument, it is about an emotional issue. Can you locate the places where she appeals to her readers' emotions?

Exploring the Writer's Argument

1. Goodall makes many assumptions in her essay. For example, she interprets David Greybeard's behavior as a kindly, understanding response. Is this the only way we can interpret his behavior? What other assumptions does Goodall ask her readers to make?
2. The workers who worked at the labs, according to Goodall, "forced themselves" to believe that what they were doing was okay. Is this good logic? Do you see any logical fallacies here or elsewhere in her essay?
3. Goodall seems to offer solutions to the problem of animal experimentation when, in paragraph 3, she says that "if we clearly and honestly believe that using animals in research will, in the end, reduce massive human suffering, it would be difficult to argue that doing so is unethical." What burden does this place on her argument? Do you think she gives enough evidence for her own side?
4. In paragraph 4, Goodall states that people have to change their mind-set, and then, in the last sentence, she writes that she thinks that people's minds are changing. Are these statements contradictory? Why or why not?

▶Ideas for Writing Arguments

Prewriting

List the moral, or ethical, arguments for and against the use of medical research on animals.

Writing a Guided Argument

In paragraph 3, Goodall poses a dilemma: We want to be ethical, but if animals suffer, how can it be ethical to harm them for any reason? Write a letter to Jane Goodall in which you satisfy Goodall's grounds for her own argument: She says that if we believe that animal experimentation will "reduce massive human suffering, it would be difficult to argue that doing so is unethical." Argue that animal experimentation is ethical because of this reason.

1. Start your essay by quoting Goodall from paragraph 3.
2. Next, state your major proposition, using Goodall's own words against her. Focus on establishing the correct tone in your first paragraph.
3. In the next paragraph, write your first minor proposition using a logical appeal.
4. Offer evidence to support your proposition.
5. Next, write a paragraph in which you offer another minor proposition, but this time use an emotional appeal.
6. Offer evidence to support your proposition.
7. In your concluding paragraph, make it clear to Goodall that you are correct on moral or ethical grounds, again repeating, for rhetorical reasons, her ideas.

Thinking, Arguing, and Writing Collaboratively

In small groups of four or five, discuss the dilemma explored in your Writing a Guided Argument paper. Where is the issue of animal experimentation headed in the future? Will people change their minds? Will protests lead to more violence, as Goodall warns against? Can animal experimentation ever end, realistically?

Writing About the Text

Goodall presents her essay as a reasoned argument, but much of what she writes is an emotional appeal presented as logic. Write an essay in which you explore the question of whether one can write about animal experimentation without an excess of emotion?

More Writing Ideas

1. Many people argue that animals can't understand their own death so their suffering is not as severe as human suffering. Do you agree or disagree? Outline your reasons in a persuasive essay.
2. David Greybeard showed Goodall "how fuzzy the distinction between animals and humans can be." What are other "fuzzy" distinctions between animals and humans? Are there clear distinctions?
3. On the basis of some research, write an essay about the similarities between the struggle for animal rights and other modern struggles for rights, such as the civil rights movement, the fight for gay rights, or the struggle for female suffrage.

7 Immigration: Should We Limit It?

The United States is a country of immigrants. All residents, except for Native American Indians and those descended from slaves, have ancestors who left another country to come to the United States to find a better life. However, immigrants have rarely trod an easy road. The Puritans settled here first, and all future immigrants have almost always been feared and hated. Before the Civil War, immigrants were mostly Protestants from Western Europe and Great Britain. After the war, when Eastern and Southern Europeans (mostly Catholic), along with Asians, came to the United States, they met with great resistance. Could they ever truly be Americans? Would they take jobs from citizens and ruin the society?

Despite the opposition, immigration grew. In the decade between 1900 and 1910, almost 1 million legal immigrants per year flooded the country. And with each new group of immigrants came a new attempt to limit their arrival through immigration laws. In the early 1920s, Congress passed litigation that limited the number of immigrants from Europe and barred immigration from Asia. These laws eventually prevented the entry of many Eastern Europeans who were threatened by Nazism before and during World War II. The laws highlight the ethical question surrounding immigration into the United States, which has always held itself up as a beacon of freedom and refuge, as symbolized by the Statue of Liberty. Since the end of World War II, immigration has steadily risen. In the 1980s and 1990s, more than 700,000 immigrants came to the United States per year. Since 1970, the number of immigrants in the United States has almost tripled. The numbers have changed, and the demographics have shifted—most immigrants today are Hispanic or Asian rather than European—but the problems for the new groups are the same as always: poverty, xenophobia from native-born Americans, unemployment, and overcrowding in the cities. Much immigration today is illegal immigration, which is often dangerous to the immigrants, especially Mexicans trying to escape through the desert into California or Arizona.

Immigration advocates point out the contributions that immigrants historically have made to the nation through hard work and that many immigrant families are interested in home ownership and in starting small businesses, which stimulate the economy. They say that immigrants help to revitalize previously neglected city neighborhoods and that if the United States limits immigration, it is going against the principles of freedom and liberty that America stands for. If people are in need of our help, should we turn them away? Those who think we should limit immigration say that the United States would not be betraying its principles. They point out that the situation today is different from the turn of the last century, when the country was developing. These critics say that there is great overpopulation here already, and immigration compounds those problems. Also, unskilled laborers from other countries take jobs from Americans who need them, and they drain resources from government programs paid with by tax dollars.

The following two selections offer disparate perspectives on the issue of immigration. Richard Rodriguez, a second-generation Mexican-American, explains why immigrants are better for America than native-born Americans. Mortimer B. Zuckerman explores the often dismal future today's immigrants face.

RICHARD RODRIGUEZ
Trouble Is, Native-Born Just Don't Measure Up

Richard Rodriguez was born to Mexican-American immigrants in 1944. He was educated at Stanford University and Columbia University. He won a Fulbright scholarship to England in 1972 when he was a doctoral student at the University of California at Berkeley. He is the author of The Hunger of Memory: The Education of Richard Rodriguez (1982), *in which he discusses his assimilation into American culture. His latest book is* Days of Obligation: An Argument with My Mexican Father. *His essays appear in many magazines and on* NewsHour with Jim Lehrer *on PBS. In this selection, Rodriguez takes to task those Americans who celebrate immigration while complaining about immigrants.*

▶ Prereading: Thinking About the Essay in Advance

What did your ancestors have to do to allow you to be taking this college course?

▶ Words to Watch

moratorium (par. 3) official halt
crucifixes (par. 4) image of Jesus Christ on the cross

sweatshops (par. 5) factories with poor working conditions
gleaned (par. 7) adopted
theological (par. 11) based in religion
mired (par. 14) stuck

"Come to Ellis Island," a friend said. "I will show you my Russian   1
grandfather's name on the wall."

On a gray weekday morning, I went to Ellis Island with little armies   2
of school children, in search of the past. But I was left thinking about the
descendants of immigrants who came through that place.

Polls indicate that a majority of Americans favor a moratorium on   3
immigration. Some even say that we should stop immigration altogether. Americans conclude that we have an immigrant problem. No
one wonders if perhaps America has a native-born problem. Does
America need the native-born?

"We are a nation of immigrants," Americans like to say. We tend,   4
however, to celebrate immigration after the fact. When the pavilions of
Ellis Island were crowded at the turn of the century, most Americans
probably didn't want foreigners, didn't like them—the way they looked,
the way they spoke, their garlic and their crucifixes, their funny clothes.

Idealism prevailed. Pragmatism prevailed. America needed the cheap   5
labor of Yiddish-speaking grandmothers in the sweatshops. We needed
immigrants to build our bridges and carve the Great Plains. Out West, the
Chinese were imported to build the railroads. Once the Chinese had finished, Americans wished they would go back to China.

But idealism also created Ellis Island. Americans in the 19th cen-   6
tury understood the individual's right to flee the past. How could
America resist these newcomers?

Just like immigrants, native-born Americans habitually are on the   7
move—moving from Ohio to Kansas, moving from Dallas to Orlando,
Portland to Boise. Our highways are crowded with the restlessness we
gleaned from our immigrant ancestors.

The trouble is, we never measure up. We, the children of immigrants,   8
are never as bold, never as driven, as our grandparents. That is why we become annoyed sometimes by immigrant ambition. In California—the destination of the majority of today's immigrants—people complain that the immigrants are coming for welfare dollars. The more interesting complaint
one hears these days in California is that the immigrants work too hard.

One hears it particularly about illegal immigrants; they are taking our   9
jobs. Or I remember the parent who told me—after his children failed to
gain entrance into the University of California—that Asians were unfair
because they worked so hard. Because of immigrants, Los Angeles has
become a working town, no longer the golden, blond city of leisure. Immigrants are blamed for the change—the traffic, the bad air. Immigrants
have turned L.A. into Cleveland.

10   The Puritans were America's first immigrants. They came, fleeing intolerance. Puritans ended up intolerant of other immigrants who came after. What the Puritans nonetheless planted on American soil was a Protestant faith: You can be born again.

11   In the 1840s, the Irish were America's major immigrant group. The nativist complaint against the Irish was theological. Today, we talk ethnicity and race. In the 19th century, it wasn't a question of Asians and Hispanics, but whether a Catholic could become a good American. Could a Jew?

12   The irony is that the Jews, the Orthodox Greeks, the Mennonites, the Irish Catholics who came through Ellis Island became the new Puritans, restoring the early Protestant determination, the founders' optimistic individualism.

13   Who doubts it now? The immigrants of Ellis Island created America. We, their children and grandchildren, inherited America. And this is the problem. For the native-born, America is not a destination, it is our address. They tore down the forests; we become environmentalists. They were fiercely set on the new; we remember when it was possible to find a parking space in downtown L.A.

14   Who will say it? Native-born blacks are being outpaced by immigrant blacks from the Caribbean. I worry less about the newly arrived Mexican

kid who is job-hunting today in Phoenix than I worry about the third generation "Chicano" undergraduate at UCLA who is mired in the despair of
American pop culture.

Coming to Ellis Island, I expected the place to be haunted. Instead, I   15
found a freshly painted irony. A few years ago, Ellis Island was restored
by native-born Americans as a monument to the past. For those of us
who are native-born Americans, Ellis Island is a historical landmark. But
for the immigrants who came through this place, Ellis Island was only a
stop on their way to the future. They rushed away. That is why Ellis Island is not haunted.

▶ Building Vocabulary

Identify the following and explain how they relate to the topic of
immigration:

1. Ellis Island (par. 1)
2. Great Plains (par. 5)
3. idealism (par. 5)
4. pragmatism (par. 5)
5. Yiddish (par. 5)
6. Puritans (par. 10)
7. Mennonites (par. 12)

▶ Thinking Critically About the Argument

Understanding the Writer's Argument

1. What, according to the writer, is the public's majority view of
   immigration?
2. What does Rodriguez mean that we "celebrate immigration after the
   fact"? (par. 4) Why is that so?
3. Native-born Americans didn't want immigrants to come to America
   at the turn of the 20th century. Why did they let immigration take
   place, then?
4. How is America's immigrant past reflected in our present-day
   behavior?
5. Why, according to Rodriguez, are Americans today bothered by the
   ambition of immigrants? What are some common complaints against
   immigration, especially illegal immigration?
6. Explain what Rodriguez means when he says that it is ironic that
   Jewish, Irish Catholic, and other immigrants adopted the Puritan's
   work ethic and ambition? Why is this ironic?
7. Explain, in your own words, why the author thinks that native-born
   Americans are more of a problem for America than immigrants.

Understanding the Writer's Techniques

1. What is Rodriguez's major proposition?
2. Why does Rodriguez start his essay with the trip to Ellis Island? How does this connect with his major proposition?
3. How many minor propositions does Rodriguez use to support his major proposition? What are they?
4. Analyze the unusual structure of Rodriguez's essay by making an outline. How effective is the structure?
5. What kind of evidence does Rodriguez use most frequently to support his position? Where does he use sensory detail effectively?
6. How does Rodriguez support his assertion that he worries "less about the newly arrived Mexican kid . . . than I worry about the third generation 'Chicano' undergraduate at UCLA"? (par. 14)
7. How does Rodriguez's conclusion tie the essay together? Does it provide both closure and coherence? Explain your answer.

Exploring the Writer's Argument

1. Is it such a bad thing that "we tend . . . to celebrate immigration after the fact," as Rodriguez implies in paragraph 4? Why or why not?
2. Rodriguez says in paragraph 8 that we are "never as bold, never as driven, as our grandparents." Do you agree with him? Why or why not? Isn't that a vast generalization? What does that say about future generations?
3. In paragraph 13, Rodriguez makes the point that our experiences of American life are diluted. Do you think that's fair? Why or why not?
4. Answer question 6 in the "Understanding the Writer's Techniques" section, and write about why Rodriguez would worry so much about the third-generation undergraduate. What is he so worried about? Do you think his worrying is warranted? Why or why not?

▶ Ideas for Writing Arguments

Prewriting

What was your family's history with immigration? Which generation, in your opinion, worked the hardest? What was the result of all that hard work? Which is the happiest generation?

Writing a Guided Argument

Think of an area of difference between you and a grandparent or someone you know well from you grandparent's generation (for example, consider the differences between your level of education, your experiences with dating or marriage, or your experiences working). Write an essay that outlines the various aspects of this difference, and explain the reasons for the difference.

1. Begin your essay with an experience that caused you to reflect on your chosen subject.
2. In the next section, introduce your grandparent or acquaintance.
3. State your major proposition clearly and directly.
4. Maintain a respectful and even tone throughout your essay.
5. Give two or three aspects of the difference in the form of clearly stated minor propositions.
6. Support your minor propositions with examples and cause analysis.
7. Close your essay with a new perspective on the experience with which you opened your essay.

Thinking, Arguing, and Writing Collaboratively

In small groups of four or five, talk to local longtime residents or merchants in your town. Collect quotes and comments about how the area has changed over the years in their memories and based on stories they have heard. Try to determine how much of this change is due to the influence of new people moving into town. Listen carefully to these people and take notes. Let them talk, and consider their judgment of the changes. Are they pleased, or are there complaints? Write up your findings in several paragraphs, and share your writing with the class.

Writing About the Text

Write an essay on question 3 in Exploring the Writer's Argument. Explain why you think the writer's assessment of native-born Americans is fair or not.

More Writing Ideas

1. In your journal, explore the ways in which you think American culture maintains a "Puritan" characteristic.
2. Write an extended paragraph about the circumstances that would have to exist for you to emigrate to another country from the United States.
3. Choose one immigrant group in America and go to the library to do research on their experiences upon arrival. Write an essay in which you explain how they and their descendents have both succeeded and struggled.

Mortimer B. Zuckerman
Our Rainbow Underclass

Mortimer B. Zuckerman is a graduate of Harvard Law School and used to teach at Harvard Business School. He is now chairman and copublisher of the New York Daily News *and the publisher and editor in chief of* U.S. News & World Report, *for which he frequently writes. In this selection, which appeared in that weekly magazine in 2002, eight years after Rodriguez's article appeared, Zuckerman tackles the issue many people don't want to talk about: the fact that many immigrants are terribly poor and remaining poor because of poor schooling opportunities.*

▶ Prereading: Thinking About the Essay in Advance

Who was the first person in your family to go to college? How did that affect the fortunes of the family?

▶ Words to Watch

linguistic (par. 3) relating to speech and language
infrastructure (par. 4) resources required for an activity
disquieting (par. 5) disturbing
myriad (par. 5) various
incalculable (par. 5) overwhelmingly large
consensus (par. 6) general agreement

1   The roll of honor read at the 9/11 ceremonies was a tapestry of America, of native-born Americans of all ethnic origins and more recent immigrants. Of course, we know too well that some of the assassins and others plotting against America were immigrants who betrayed our ideals, so it is natural that many people feel we should now close the door altogether, beginning with immigrants from Muslim countries. Natural, and wrong. What is long overdue, however, is a sustained national dialogue on immigration.

2   Most politicians fear offending blocs of votes—a cowardice that does not serve the country well. Immigration has been out of control since 1965, when Sen. Edward Kennedy introduced a "reform" bill that ended the historic basis of the American melting pot. It was a bill remarkable for the fact that every single one of the assurances he and others gave proved wildly wrong—not because they wanted to mislead but because the bill unleashed forces they did not foresee. Indeed, the ensuing Immigration Reform Act triggered an immigration explosion, involving millions more than any other period, plus millions of illegals. There was a gross miscalculation of the effect of basing entry on "family reunification"; the crite-

rion of "immediate relatives" was lost in the daisy-chain effect of brothers sponsoring brothers sponsoring cousins. It was said the goal was not to upset "the ethnic mix of this country," but the opposite occurred. Traditional immigrants from northern and western Europe were discriminated against in favor of Third World immigrants.

Schooling is the ticket. What is more disturbing is that the longer these   3 new immigrants stay in the country the worse they do, reversing the history of upward mobility in previous waves of immigration. Why? Traditionally, there were well-paid manufacturing jobs for immigrants, enabling them to join the ranks of blue-collar workers who secured a middle-class lifestyle without much formal education. Those days are gone. Schooling is today's ticket for a better future—with a high school diploma as the minimum. The original European newcomers could also send their children to high-quality urban schools. Assimilation was swift. The immigrants, however numerous, were from many different countries, so they took to English more rapidly: There was no linguistic minority to dominate any large city the way Spanish speakers now dominate Miami and Los Angeles. Today Latino immigrants live in a subnation with their own radio and TV stations, newspapers, films, and magazines, stunting assimilation and diminishing economic opportunity. Mexican-born males, handicapped by low or nonexistent English ability, earn half of what non-Latino whites earn. Although Mexican immigrants are often perceived as highly reliable, disciplined workers, Harvard Prof. Christopher Jencks makes the point that "having the right attitude is often enough to get an $8-an-hour job; it is seldom enough to get one for $16 an hour."

A critical question that is almost never asked: What is the impact on   4 the children, the second generation? Some thrive, but the majority do not. They form a rainbow underclass, caught in a cycle of downward assimilation, poverty combined with racial segregation. Often separated for long periods from their parents, especially their fathers, during the immigration process, they stop doing homework, reject their parents' values, and succumb to the dangers of an overcrowded inner-city culture. They face overwhelmed teachers, limited social service resources, and a decaying infrastructure, and they often adopt the negative behavior pattern of their peer groups, such as academic indifference and substance abuse, leading to dropout rates three times as high as for native-born Americans. Even the stellar performance of Asian children declines—studies show that by the third generation, Chinese students no longer exceed whites in educational success.

There is another disquieting connection, the trifecta effect of rising   5 immigrant fertility rates. Our population is projected to rise to over 500 million by 2050, roughly double what America is today—with post-1965 immigrants and their descendants making up about half. The effect of these numbers on myriad aspects of our environment, from rush-hour traffic to air and water pollution and social tensions, is incalculable.

6   How, then, should we proceed? No matter what, we must find more resources for the schools and other institutions that will support the development of second-generation children. Second, we must rebalance the number of visas provided for extended-family programs and add more to attract immigrants with skills transferable to the information economy. Third, we should slow down the process until we can thoroughly assess how the children of today's immigrants will fare as adults. Only through such measures can a national consensus on these issues begin to be forged.

▶ Building Vocabulary

In this essay, the author uses a number of words and phrases from the world of sociology. Look up the following terms in a dictionary, and write out the definition. Then use each word or phrase in a sentence of your own having to do with immigration:

1. tapestry (par. 1)
2. melting pot (par. 2)
3. Third World (par. 2)
4. upward mobility (par. 3)
5. blue-collar workers (par. 3)
6. assimilation (par. 3)
7. underclass (par. 4)
8. fertility rates (par. 5)
9. visas (par. 6)

▶ Thinking Critically About the Argument

Understanding the Writer's Argument

1. Why does Zuckerman think it's natural for Americans to want to stop immigration? What is his opinion of that viewpoint?
2. What was the intention of the 1965 Immigration Reform Act? What was the unintended result?
3. Why is the success of today's immigrant dependent on different factors than those that affected the immigrant of the early part of the 20th century?
4. Explain why Zuckerman thinks that earlier immigrants seemed to learn English more readily than today's immigrant? Why does he think this is important?
5. What is the effect of today's immigration trends on the first native-born generation, according to Zuckerman?
6. How can proper schooling help immigrants?

Understanding the Writer's Techniques

1. What is the argumentative effect of mentioning 9/11 and the terrorists in the beginning of the essay?
2. What is Zuckerman's major proposition? What does he explain to the reader before he offers his major proposition? Explain why, in your view, he takes this approach.
3. What is the writer's tone? Where does Zuckerman deviate from this tone for effect? Is it, in fact, effective?
4. What are Zuckerman's minor propositions?
5. What kinds of evidence does Zuckerman offer to promote his argument?
6. How does Zuckerman's prediction in paragraph 5 support his position?
7. What is your view of his proposed solutions to the problem in the conclusion? Are they useful suggestions? Why or why not?

Exploring the Writer's Argument

1. Zuckerman seems to believe that assimilation is a purely positive thing. Why does Zuckerman equate "stunting assimilation" with fewer economic opportunities for immigrants in paragraph 3? Do you agree with him? Does he support this idea with enough evidence? Is there anything about this idea that gives you pause? Explain your answer fully.
2. Analyze Zuckerman's use of transitions in this essay. Are they sufficient? Why or why not? How could you improve them to help his argument?
3. In his last paragraph, Zuckerman offers a number of solutions to the problems he addresses. Do you think his solutions are vague? Why or why not? Especially, his last solution seems like a tall order, but does not offer any suggestions for how to achieve this. Why is or why is this not a problem for his argument?

▶ Ideas for Writing Arguments

Prewriting

How does language relate to ethnicity? Do you speak the language of your ancestors? In either case, how does that affect your experience as an American?

Writing a Guided Argument

The United States, unlike most countries, does not have an official language. Write an essay in which you argue that English should or should not be the official language of the United States. Before you write, search the online archives of *The New York Times* or other newspapers and magazines to acquaint yourself with the arguments on both sides.

1. Open your essay with an exploration of the issue, using your research to give some of the background.
2. Write your major proposition.
3. Have at least three minor propositions.
4. Organize your essay so that your most important point comes last.
5. Appeal to your reader's patriotism by making it clear in your argument that you are arguing for the best choice for the United States.
6. Support your minor propositions with examples and predictions for the future.
7. Include at least one opposing point. Rebut this point.
8. Conclude by restating your major proposition in light of the evidence. Use a quote from your research as your final piece of evidence.

Thinking, Arguing, and Writing Collaboratively

Hold a debate in class. Work in two groups. One group should prepare arguments that America is a "melting pot." The other group should argue that instead, America is what Bill Clinton used to call a "salad bowl." After about 20 minutes of preparation, mount a debate in which each side gets ten minutes to make their case, and then the other side gets 5 minutes to rebut their points.

Writing About the Text

How does your reading of Rodriguez's essay inform your reading of Zuckerman's? Write an essay in which you examine how the two arguments are related, and in what ways they disagree.

More Writing Ideas

1. In your journal, freewrite about this topic: assimilation. Do not edit your writing. Write nonstop for at least 15 minutes. When you finish, exchange journal entries with another student in the class. How do your responses compare? contrast?
2. How does the Internet change the lives of today's immigrants? Write a paragraph in which you develop an opinion and value judgment about this topic.
3. Write an essay expanding on Zuckerman's dire predictions in paragraph 5. What are other possible effects of overcrowding in the United States? Consider the question of any positive effects.

8 Affirmative Action: What Role Should It Play in Our Lives?

What does the government and other institutions owe women and minorities for previous years of discrimination?

Women were, in the past, locked out of many careers and did not even get the vote in this country until the 1920s. African Americans were slaves for centuries until the Emancipation Proclamation in 1865. But that did not cure all: True progress in civil rights did not become a reality until the 1960s. The policy of affirmative action is an attempt to make up for these past shortcomings by giving women and minorities special consideration in employment, education, and business decisions.

Proponents of affirmative action say that although the country made great strides in civil rights since the 1960s, the job of ending discrimination is not over, and although racism and sexism are not as overt as in the past, they are still a problem. Minorities and women still are not equally paid nor do they appear in proportionate numbers in high-paying jobs or positions of power. The defenders of affirmative action say that the policy can "level the playing field" until past wrongs are set right. Opponents of affirmative action say that the policy is reverse discrimination, in that it takes jobs away from more qualified candidates just because they happen to be white men. Another important argument from opponents (even opponents among the black community) is that the policy can have a negative effect on minorities and women by lowering their self-respect and respect from others because others see these minority groups as not having earned their positions. For decades, affirmative action has stood at the center of the argument over our "multicultural" society and about how we can advance the careers of future generations of minorities while still being fair and equitable to all.

Linda Chavez writes that affirmative action has a purely negative effect on the fabric of American society, whereas Nathan Glazer (who is a convert to affirmative action) insists that the United States must face up to

197

its responsibility and realize that the time has not yet come to eliminate affirmative action. As you read the following selections, pay attention to how the writers appeal to your sense of fairness.

LINDA CHAVEZ
Affirmative Action Is Driving Us Apart

Linda Chavez was born in 1947 in Albuquerque, New Mexico. She is the author of Out of the Barrio: Toward a New Politics of Hispanic Assimilation *(2001). Since serving in President Ronald Reagan's Commission on Civil Rights, Chavez has worked to end various federal civil rights programs, including affirmative action and the minimum wage. She has promoted English as the official language of the United States. She is founder and president of the Center for Equal Opportunity, an organization that focuses on issues related to race, ethnicity, assimilation, and public policy. In 2000, the Library of Congress honored Chavez as a "Living Legend" for her contributions to America's cultural and historical legacy. In 2001, George W. Bush nominated Chavez to be the Secretary of Labor, but the Senate rejected the nomination because of her conservative views and opposition from organized labor. In this essay, which appeared in* USA Today *in 1996, Chavez argues that affirmative action and other racially and ethnically based programs tend to cause resentment and anger rather than solve problems.*

▶ Prereading: Thinking About the Essay in Advance

Do you think that being identified by your race or ethnicity diminishes you or makes you less of an individual? Or does such identification strengthen you because of your part in a large group? What are the benefits of having a strong racial identity? What are the negative aspects?

▶ Words to Watch

compensatory (par. 5) designed to make up for disadvantage
presumptive (par. 5) based on probability and assumption
morphology (par. 11) study of forms
alleviates (par. 13) reduces
imperative (par. 13) necessity
mores (par. 14) moral standards
linchpin (par. 14) crucial element
inextricable (par. 18) unable to be separated from
imbuing (par. 18) instilling
indoctrination (par. 19) teaching
exogamy (par. 21) marriage outside a specific group
cleavages (par. 28) breaks

I n the name of eliminating discrimination, we continue to pursue poli-   1
cies that define people by color. In schools and universities, at work, at the polling place, even in the courts, race is an important, sometimes deciding, factor in admitting students or devising curricula, hiring or promoting employees, determining political representation, and selecting a jury. It is not only a few white supremacists who promote such policies, but mainstream civil rights advocates as well.

The crux of the complaint against quotas or other forms of racial or   2
ethnic preferences is that they force both benefactors and beneficiaries to elevate race and ethnicity in importance, which is fundamentally incompatible with reducing racism. It is not possible to argue that race or ethnicity alone entitles individuals to special consideration without also accepting that such characteristics are intrinsically significant.

Those who promote preferential affirmative action programs argue   3
that race and ethnicity are important because they are the basis on which individuals have been, and continue to be, discriminated against. Setting employment or college admission quotas, by this reasoning, simply is a way of compensating for the discrimination that blacks, Hispanics, and some other minority groups face on the basis of their skin color.

However, most programs that confer special benefits to racial and   4
ethnic minorities make no effort at all to determine whether the individuals who will receive them ever have been victims of discrimination. Indeed, the government regulations that govern Federal contractors state explicitly: "Individuals who certify that they are members of named groups (Black Americans, Hispanic Americans, Native Americans, Asian-Pacific Americans, Subcontinental Asian Americans) are to be considered socially and economically disadvantaged."

Such programs are not compensatory, but presumptive; they assume   5
that race equals disadvantage. While there are many blacks, Hispanics, and Asians who have been discriminated against on the basis of their race or ethnicity, there are many others who have not, and still others for whom the discrimination either was trivial or, even if more serious, had no lasting consequences.

In 1995, at Indiana University following a debate in which I opposed   6
affirmative action, a group of black and Hispanic students approached me to complain that I was not sensitive enough to the discrimination they said they faced daily on campus. I asked them to give me some examples. Only two spoke. The first, a young black woman, told me her father was a surgeon who makes more than $300,000 a year, but that her economic status doesn't protect her from the prejudice of her teachers. When I asked her to describe how that prejudice manifested itself, she said none of her professors would give above a "B" to any minority student. I pushed her a little further, asking whether that meant that a student who scored 98% on an exam would be given a "B" rather than a deserved "A." At that point, she dropped the issue with a dismissive, "You just don't understand."

7   A second student, a Mexican-American woman, said that she has to deal with discrimination every day. She cited as an example that her Spanish teacher expects her to do better than the other students because she is presumed to know Spanish. I was sympathetic with her frustration, since I am aware that most third-generation Hispanics speak only English—like third-generation Italians, Jews, Germans, and other ethnic groups in the United States. Nevertheless, although being presumed to speak your ancestral language may be annoying, it hardly constitutes pernicious discrimination.

8   In fact, what ethnic or religious minority has not suffered its share of slights and prejudices? Certainly, Jews and Asians have faced significant levels of bigotry at certain points in their history in the United States. Jews often were the victims of private discriminatory actions, and Asians historically were the target of both private and state-sponsored exclusion and bias. The Chinese, for instance, were not allowed to become citizens, own property, or enter certain professions, or even to immigrate at all for certain periods of time. During World War II, Japanese-Americans had their property confiscated and were removed forcibly from their homes and interned in camps in the West. Nonetheless, despite persistent discrimination, these groups, on average, have excelled in this society, and it is difficult to argue that they are entitled to compensatory, preferential affirmative action on the basis of any current disadvantage.

9   It is true that blacks and, to a lesser degree, Hispanics are far more likely to face present disadvantage, some of it (though a declining share) the result of past discrimination. Again, though, many affirmative action programs make little effort to distinguish among potential beneficiaries on the basis of actual disadvantage, preferring instead to rely on race or ethnicity *per se* in awarding benefits.

10   Some of the most prestigious affirmative action slots—such as those at Ivy League universities, Fortune 500 corporations, or Wall Street law firms—go to middle- and upper-class blacks and Hispanics, who suffer no clear disadvantage compared with their white counterparts. For instance, a recent study at the University of California, Berkeley, found that, on average, black, Hispanic, and Asian students admitted through affirmative action guidelines come from families whose median income actually is *higher* than the national average. Affirmative action recipients frequently are the graduates of elite prep schools, universities, and professional schools. Increasingly, advocates of this select type of affirmative action eschew traditional arguments about discrimination or disadvantage, opting to emphasize the presumed benefits of racial and ethnic diversity.

11   What does this diversity imply? The current scientific consensus suggests that race or ethnicity is nothing more than a description of broad morphology of skin, hair, and eye color, bone structure, and hair type—hardly the basis for making moral claims or distinctions. If race and ethnicity, stripped of their power to demand retribution, represent nothing more than a common ancestry and similar physical attributes, culture, on

the other hand, evinces something more controversial and enduring. Not surprisingly, practitioners of the politics of race have seized on culture as their new weapon. Americans—of all races—have grown tired of affirmative action. Many of those who still support racial preferences, such as Yale law professor Stephen Carter, admit that those preferences have been a mixed blessing for the beneficiaries, conferring tangible benefits, but often undermining self-confidence. The politics of race requires a new rationale and a new vocabulary. Multiculturalism supplies both.

Race-conscious policies now permeate not only employment and education, but also the courts and even the democratic process itself. Race or ethnicity often determines political representation and establishes voting procedures. In addition, the list of groups eligible to benefit continues to grow and now embraces even the most recent immigrants to America, who, by definition, have suffered no past discrimination. As the policies and the beneficiaries expand, so has their rationale.   12

The compensatory model has given way to one based on culture, which alleviates the necessity of proving past discrimination or present disadvantage. The demand to redress past or present wrongs evolves into the imperative to enhance and preserve culture. America becomes not simply a multi-racial, multi-ethnic society made up of individuals of different backgrounds—some of whom have suffered discrimination because of their color—but a *multicultural* nation.   13

The distinction is an important one. It implies that Americans differ not only in skin color and origin, but in values, mores, customs, temperament, language—all those attributes that endow culture with meaning. Indeed, multiculturalism questions the very concept of an *American* people. It replaces affirmative action as the linchpin in the politics of race with a much more profound power to shape how all Americans, not just racial and ethnic minorities, think of themselves and conceive the nation.   14

Multiculturalists insist on treating race or ethnicity as if they were synonymous with culture. They presume that skin color or national origin, which are immutable traits, determine values, mores, language, and other cultural attributes, which, of course, are learned. In the multiculturalists' world view, African-Americans, Puerto Ricans, or Chinese-Americans living in New York City, for instance, share more in common with persons of their ancestral group living in Lagos, San Juan, or Hong Kong than they do with other New Yorkers who are white. Culture becomes a fixed entity, transmitted, as it were, in the genes, rather than through experience.   15

Such convictions lead multiculturalists to conclude that, in the words of Molefi Kete Asante, a guru of the multicultural movement, "There is no common American culture." The logic is simple, if wrongheaded. Since Americans (or, more often, their forebears) hail from many different places, each with its own specific culture, the United States must be multicultural. Moreover, they claim, it is becoming more so every day as new immigrants bring their cultures with them when they come to the United States.   16

17   Indeed, multiculturalists hope to ride the immigrant wave to greater power and influence. They certainly have done so in education. The influx of non-English-speaking children into public schools has given added impetus to the multicultural movement. Approximately 2,300,000 youngsters who can not speak English well now attend public school, an increase of 1,000,000 since 1989. The Los Angeles Unified School District alone offers instruction to 160,000 students in Spanish, Armenian, Korean, Cantonese, Tagalog, Russian, and Japanese. In New York, students come from 167 different countries, speaking 120 separate languages. The costs for such programs are astronomical—more than $300,000,000 a year for 126,000 pupils in New York. Multicultural advocates cite the presence of such children to demand bilingual education and other multicultural services. Federal and state governments literally spend billions of dollars on these initiatives, although an exact estimate of total outlay is difficult to obtain since it is allocated across several programs and layers of government.

18   The multiculturalists' emphasis on education, though, undercuts their own argument that culture is inextricable from race or national origin. The multiculturalists are acutely aware of just how fragile cultural identification is. If they were not, they would be less adamant about preserving and reinforcing it. The current emphasis on Afrocentric curricula for black elementary and secondary students, for instance, would be unnecessary if race itself conferred culture. Nor would multiculturalists insist on teaching immigrant children in their native language, instructing them in the history and customs of their native land, and imbuing them with reverence for their ancestral heroes, if ethnicity and national origin alone were antidotes to the appeal of American culture.

19   Multiculturalists haven't lost faith in the power of assimilation. If anything, they seem to believe that, without a heavy dose of multicultural indoctrination, immigrants won't be able to resist assimilation. They are right, though it remains to be seen whether anything, including the multiculturalists' crude methods, ultimately will detour immigrants from the assimilation path.

20   The urge to assimilate traditionally has been overpowering in the United States, especially among the children of immigrants. Only groups that maintain strict rules against intermarriage and other social contact with persons outside the group, such as Orthodox Jews and the Amish, ever have succeeded in preserving distinct, full-blown cultures within American society after one or two generations have been living here. It is interesting to note that religion seems to be a more effective deterrent to full assimilation than the secular elements of culture, including language.

21   Although many Americans worry that Hispanic immigrants, for example, are not learning English and therefore will fail to assimilate into the American mainstream, there is little evidence that this is the case. As already noted, a majority of Hispanics speak only English by the third generation in the United States, and are closer to other Americans on

most measures of social and economic status than they are to Hispanic immigrants. On one of the most rigorous gauges of assimilation—intermarriage—Hispanics rank high. About one-third of young, third-generation Hispanics marry non-Hispanic whites, a pattern similar to that of young Asians. Even for blacks, exogamy rates, which have been quite low historically, are going up. About 3 percent of blacks now marry outside their group, though the rate in the western states is much higher—17 percent among black males marrying for the first time.

The impetus for multiculturalism is not coming from immigrants—   22
even among groups such as Hispanics and Asians—but from their more affluent and (ironically) assimilated native-born counterparts in their ethnic communities. The proponents most often are the elite, best-educated, and most successful members of their respective racial and ethnic groups. Not surprisingly, college campuses are fertile recruiting grounds, where the most radical displays of multiculturalism take place.

In May, 1993, for instance, a group of Mexican-American students at   23
UCLA, frustrated that the university would not elevate the school's 23-year-old Chicano studies program to full department status, stormed the campus faculty center, breaking windows and furniture and causing $500,000 in damage. During the same month, a group of Asian-American students at the University of California, Irvine, went on a hunger strike to pressure administrators into hiring more professors to teach Asian-American studies courses there. These were not immigrants or even, by and large, disadvantaged students, but middle-class beneficiaries of their parents' or grandparents' successful assimilation into the American mainstream.

The protesters' actions had almost nothing to do with any effort to   24
maintain their ethnic identity. For the most part, such students probably never thought of themselves as anything but American before they entered college. According to the Berkeley study cited earlier, most Hispanic and Asian students "discovered" their ethnic identity after they arrived on campus. Speaking of Asian students, the researchers reported: "After being around [the University of California] for one or two years, students who were integrated into predominantly white worlds of friendship and association in high school report a shift towards having predominantly Asian American friends, roommates, or affiliations with an Asian American organization."

The same was true for other groups as well, including blacks. "On arrival   25
on the Berkeley campus, these students are surprised to discover themselves no longer the 'token black person.' . . . These students experience a new kind of pressure: it comes from other African American students on campus, and it is experienced as pressure to make decisions about friends, networks, even who you sit with at lunch, on the basis of race."

Many of these students learn to define themselves as victims as well.   26
As one Mexican-American freshman summed it up, she was "unaware of the things that have been going on with our people, all the injustices

we've suffered, how the world really is. I thought racism didn't exist here, you know, it just comes to light." The researchers went on to note that all "students of color" had difficulty pinpointing exactly what constituted this "subtle form of the new racism." Instead of empirical evidence, "There was much talk of certain facial expressions, or the way people look, and how white students 'take over the class' and speak past you."

27   If terms like racism and discrimination can be applied to such innocuous behavior, what words can be used to describe the real thing? As author George Orwell said in his 1946 essay, "Politics and the English Language," "if thought corrupts language, language can also corrupt thought." Misusing words like racism undermines the very legitimacy of the concept.

28   The re-racialization of American society that is taking place in the name of multiculturalism is not a progressive movement, but a step backward to the America that existed before *Brown* v. *Board of Education* and the passage of the major civil rights laws of the 1960s. We are at a critical juncture in our history. Even if we are not, as the multiculturalists claim, about to become a majority minority nation, racial and ethnic diversity in our population is increasing. If we allow race and ethnicity to determine public policy, we invite the kind of cleavages that will oil one group against another in ways that cannot be good for the groups themselves or the society we all must live in.

29   The more diverse we become, the more crucial it is that we commit ourselves to a shared, civic culture. The distinguishing characteristic of American culture always has been its ability to incorporate so many disparate elements into a new whole. While conservative philosopher Russell Kirk was indisputably right that the United States owes much of its culture to Great Britain—our legal tradition, particularly the concept of the rule of law, our belief in representative government, and certainly our language and literatures—American assimilation always has entailed some give and take. American culture itself has been enriched by what individual groups brought to it.

30   Yet, it is more important that all of us—no matter where we come from or what circumstances brought us or our ancestors here—think of ourselves as Americans if we are to retain the sense that we are one people, not simply a conglomeration of different and competing groups. It is nonsense to think we can do so without being clear about our purposes.

31   We can by acknowledging that it is more important for immigrant children to learn English than to maintain their native language, although the two not necessarily are mutually exclusive. We should make sure that American students have a firm grasp of the history of this nation, the people who helped build it, and the institutions and principles on which the United States was founded. We should be careful not to repeat past errors, when American history courses conveniently excluded facts, but neither should history become simply an exercise in building the self-esteem of those who previously were left out. Finally, we need to get be-

yond the point where race and ethnicity are the most important factors in the way we identify ourselves or form allegiances. The principles and values that unite us remain far more important than our differences in ancestry, a lesson that bears repeating in our schools and universities.

▶ Building Vocabulary

Write definitions and your own sentences for the following words:

1. **devising** (par. 1)
2. **crux** (par. 2)
3. **pernicious** (par. 7)
4. **eschew** (par. 10)
5. **evinces** (par. 11)
6. **redress** (par. 13)
7. **immutable** (par. 15)
8. **adamant** (par. 18)
9. **secular** (par. 20)
10. **innocuous** (par. 27)

▶ Thinking Critically About the Argument

Understanding the Writer's Argument

1. What is the center of the argument against using race to decide preference, according to Chavez?
2. What does it mean that affirmative action programs "are not compensatory, but presumptive"? (par. 5) Why does Chavez think that's a bad idea?
3. Who is receiving the benefits of affirmative action who shouldn't, according to Chavez?
4. What, according to Chavez, does science tell us about race?
5. What is wrong, according to Chavez, with the multiculturalists calling for bilingual education?
6. What is one of the most reliable signs of assimilation?

Understanding the Writer's Techniques

1. What is Chavez's major proposition? Where do you find it in the essay? Is it in an effective location? Why or why not?
2. Outline the paragraphs leading up to the major proposition. What is their argumentative purpose?
3. What minor propositions does Chavez offer to help prove that affirmative action is not a realistic option?

4. How does Chavez support the perspective that multiculturalism threatens the idea of a unified American society? Explain the various ways in which Chavez says this happens.
5. What evidence does Chavez cite to support her claim that much of the call for multiculturalism comes not from immigrants, but from their second and third-generation descendents? Why does she think this is a problem? Is her explanation sufficient?
6. Where does Chavez's conclusion start? Is it effective? Why or why not?

Exploring the Writer's Argument

1. What is wrong with accepting that race and ethnicity are "intrinsically significant"? (par. 2)
2. Chavez says that the programs that offer preference to racial minorities don't determine whether the individuals have been discriminated against. Is she missing the point of affirmative action? Explain your answer.
3. In paragraph 11, Chavez writes that "Americans—of all races—have grown tired of affirmative action." Does she support this idea effectively? Why or why not? Is there another way to formulate this idea?
4. How successful is Chavez's argument in paragraphs 8 and 9 that affirmative action isn't a well made way of distributing money because every ethnic group has suffered discrimination. Is that a fair assessment? Why or why not?

▶ Ideas for Writing Arguments

Prewriting

What evidence of affirmative action policy have you observed in American life? How has affirmative action policy affected you or others you know?

Writing a Guided Argument

Select a job or profession that you think particularly needs affirmative action programs to help minorities achieve equality. Write an essay arguing that affirmative action should apply to hiring or promotion in that profession or career.

1. Begin your essay by mentioning Chavez's essay and briefly summarizing her position on affirmative action.
2. Explain a little bit about the profession you have chosen to write about.
3. Write a major proposition in which you rebut Chavez and assert your own position.

4. Use clear and effective transitions to develop your ideas.
5. Write your minor propositions in the form of rebuttals to Chavez's points.
6. Make sure your argument is focused on your chosen subject.
7. Conclude by widening your argument and explaining how affirmative action, in your view, can help not only minorities in the profession you are writing about, but minorities in all jobs.

Thinking, Arguing, and Writing Collaboratively

Class members should divide into two groups, one of which will argue in favor of the quote by multiculturalist Molefi Kete Asante that Chavez includes in paragraph 16. He says that "There is no common American culture." The other group will argue Chavez's view that this is "wrongheaded." The group that supports the idea in the quote should think of arguments for that position, and the group that opposes the quote should come up with arguments to refute that idea. After debating the issue, come together as a class and discuss it.

Writing About the Text

Analyze Chavez's points in paragraph 10 about the current distribution of affirmative action benefits and argue that this point is either one of the strongest or one of the weakest in her argument.

More Writing Ideas

1. Write notes in your journal for an essay that supports or refutes Chavez's point that affirmative action programs should try to determine whether an individual has been discriminated against before bestowing benefits on that person.
2. Write two or three paragraphs that argue for or against the fact that some students in Los Angeles and other cities are taught their classes in Spanish and languages other than English.
3. Write an essay that explores the implications of the view that affirmative action might undermine self-confidence in minorities who received benefits.

Nathan Glazer
In Defense of Preference

Nathan Glazer was born in 1924, went to City College and the University of Pennsylvania, and earned his Ph.D. in sociology from Columbia University.

For years he taught in the graduate school of education at Harvard University. He is the author of We Are All Multiculturalists Now *and* Beyond the Melting Pot. *He has written extensively on urban policy, education, and minority issues. In the 1970s, Glazer was against affirmative action and actually wrote a book arguing against it,* Affirmative Discrimination *(1975). Since the 1970s, Glazer has changed his mind about affirmative action. "I have definitely come to the conclusion that strict colorblindness is unrealistic and probably inadvisable," he has said. In this selection, Glazer argues that affirmative action is a crucial step in the road toward leveling the playing field for African Americans.*

▶ Prereading: Thinking About the Essay in Advance

Write some notes on the idea of *preference*. What does that word mean to you? How does it relate to affirmative action? Glazer is arguing for preference, but does that word have any negative connotations? What are they?

▶ Words to Watch

equanimity (par. 3) fairness
galvanized (par. 6) strengthened and bonded together
glacially (par. 6) slowly
vetted (par. 6) checked
elided (par. 12) reduced
egalitarian (par. 20) useless
discharged (par. 22) fulfilled
magistrates (par. 25) local official
demographically (par. 28) relating to population trends

1   The battle over affirmative action today is a contest between a clear principle on the one hand and a clear reality an the other. The principle is that ability, qualifications, and merit, independent of race, national origin, or sex, should prevail when one applies for a job or promotion, or for entry into selective institutions for higher education, or when one bids for contracts. The reality is that strict adherence to this principle would result in few African Americans getting jobs, admissions, and contracts. What makes the debate so confused is that the facts that make a compelling case for affirmative action are often obscured by the defenders of affirmative action themselves. They have resisted acknowledging how serious the gaps are between African Americans and others, how deep the preferences reach, how systematic they have become. Considerably more than a mild bend in the direction of diversity now exists, but it exists because painful facts make it necessary if blacks are to participate in more than token numbers in some key institutions of our society. The opponents of affirmative action can also be faulted: they have not fully con-

fronted the consequences that must follow from the implementation of the principle that measured ability, qualification, merit, applied without regard to color, should be our only guide.

I argued for that principle in a 1975 book titled, provocatively, *Affirmative Discrimination*. It seemed obvious that that was what all of us, black and white, were aiming to achieve through the revolutionary civil rights legislation of the 1960s. That book dealt with affirmative action in employment, and with two other kinds of governmentally or judicially imposed "affirmative action," the equalization of the racial proportions in public schools and the integration of residential neighborhoods. I continued to argue and write regularly against governmentally required affirmative action, that is, racial preference, for the next two decades or more: it was against the spirit of the Constitution, the clear language of the civil rights acts, and the interests of all of us in the United States in achieving an integrated and just society.

It is not the unpopularity of this position in the world in which I live, liberal academia, that has led me to change my mind but, rather, developments that were unforeseen and unexpected in the wake of the successful civil rights movement. What was unforeseen and unexpected was that the gap between the educational performance of blacks and whites would persist and, in some respects, deepen despite the civil rights revolution and hugely expanded social and educational programs, that innercity schools would continue to decline, and that the black family would unravel to a remarkable degree, contributing to social conditions for large numbers of black children far worse than those in the 1960s. In the presence of those conditions, an insistence on color-blindness means the effective exclusion today of African Americans from positions of influence, wealth, and power. It is not a prospect that any of us can contemplate with equanimity. We have to rethink affirmative action.

In a sense, it is a surprise that a fierce national debate over affirmative action has not only persisted but intensified during the Clinton years. After twelve years under two Republican presidents, Ronald Reagan and George Bush, who said they opposed affirmative action but did nothing to scale it back, the programs seemed secure. After all, affirmative action rests primarily on a presidential executive order dating back to the presidencies of Lyndon Johnson and Richard Nixon which requires "affirmative action" in employment practices from federal contractors—who include almost every large employer, university, and hospital. The legal basis for most of affirmative action could thus have been swept away, as so many noted at the time, with a "stroke of the pen" by the president. Yet two presidents who claimed to oppose affirmative action never wielded the pen.

Despite the popular majority that grumbles against affirmative action, there was (and is) no major elite constituency strongly opposed to it: neither business nor organized labor, religious leaders nor university

(AP Oakland Tribune.)

presidents, local officials nor serious presidential candidates are to be found in opposition. Big business used to fear that affirmative action would undermine the principle of employment and promotion on the basis of qualifications. It has since become a supporter. Along with mayors and other local officials (and of course the civil rights movement), it played a key role in stopping the Reagan administration from moving against affirmative action. Most city administrations have also made their peace with affirmative action.

6   Two developments outside the arena of presidential politics galvanized both opponents and defenders of affirmative action. The Supreme Court changed glacially after successive Republican appointments—each of which, however, had been vetted by a Democratic Senate—and a number of circuit courts began to chip away at the edifice of affirmative action. But playing the largest role was the politically unsophisticated effort of two California professors to place on the California ballot a proposition that would insert in the California Constitution the simple and clear words, taken from the Civil Rights Act of 1964, which ban discrimination on the basis of race, national origin, or sex. The decision to launch a state constitutional proposition, Proposition 209, suddenly gave opponents the political instrument they needed to tap the majority sentiment that has always existed against preferences.

7   While supporters of affirmative action do not have public opinion on their side, they do have the still-powerful civil rights movement, the major elites in education, religion, philanthropy, government, and the mass

media. And their position is bolstered by a key fact: how far behind African Americans are when judged by the tests and measures that have become the common coin of American meritocracy.

The reality of this enormous gap is cleanest where the tests in use are   8
the most objective, the most reliable, and the best validated, as in the case of the various tests used for admission to selective institutions of higher education, for entry into elite occupations such as law and medicine, or for civil service jobs. These tests have been developed over many years specifically for the purpose of eliminating biases in admissions and appointments. As defenders of affirmative action often point out, paper-and-pencil tests of information, reading comprehension, vocabulary, reasoning, and the like are not perfect indicators of individual ability. But they are the best measures we have for success in college and professional schools, which, after all, require just the skills the tests measure. And the tests can clearly differentiate the literate teacher from the illiterate one or the policeman who can make out a coherent arrest report from one who cannot.

To concentrate on the most hotly contested area of affirmative action—   9
admission to selective institutions of higher education—and on the group in the center of the storm—African Americans: If the Scholastic Assessment Test were used for selection in a color-blind fashion, African Americans, who today make up about 6 percent of the student bodies in selective colleges and universities, would drop to less than 2 percent, according to a 1994 study by the editor of the *Journal of Blacks in Higher Education.*

Why is this so? According to studies summarized in Stephan and   10
Abigail Thernstrom's book, *America in Black and White*, the average combined SAT score for entering freshmen in the nation's top 25 institutions is about 1300. White applicants generally need to score a minimum of 600 on the verbal portion of the test—a score obtained by 8 percent of the test-takers in 1995—and at least 650 on the mathematics section—a score obtained by 7 percent of the test-takers in 1995. In contrast, only 1.7 percent of black students scored over 600 on the verbal section in 1995, and only 2 percent scored over 650 on the math. This represents considerable progress over the last 15 years, but black students still lag distressingly far behind their white counterparts.

There is no way of getting around this reality. Perhaps the tests are ir-   11
relevant to success in college? That cannot be sustained. They have been improved and revised over decades and predict achievement in college better than any alternative. Some of the revisions have been carried out in a near-desperate effort to exclude items which would discriminate against blacks. Some institutions have decided they will not use the tests, not because they are invalid per se, but because they pose a barrier to the increased admission of black students. Nor would emphasizing other admissions criteria, such as high school grades, make a radical difference. In any case, there is considerable value to a uniform national standard, given the enormous differences among high schools.

12   Do qualifications at the time of admission matter? Isn't the important thing what the institutions manage to do with those they admit? If they graduate, are they not qualified? Yes, but many do not graduate. Two or three times as many African American students as white students drop out before graduation. And the tests for admission to graduate schools show the same radical disparities between blacks and others. Are there not also preferences for athletes, children of alumni, students gifted in some particular respect? Yes, but except for athletes, the disparities in academic aptitude that result from such preferences are not nearly as substantial as those which must be elided in order to reach target figures for black students. Can we not substitute for the tests other factors—such as the poverty and other hardships students have overcome to reach the point of applying to college? This might keep up the number of African Americans, but not by much, if the studies are to be believed. A good number of white and Asian applicants would also benefit from such "class-based" affirmative action.

13   (I have focused on the effect of affirmative action—and its possible abolition—on African Americans. But, of course, there are other beneficiaries. Through bureaucratic mindlessness, Asian Americans and Hispanics were also given affirmative action. But Asian Americans scarcely need it. Major groups—not all—of Hispanic Americans trail behind whites but mostly for reasons we understand: problems with the English language and the effect on immigrant children of the poor educational and economic status of their parents. We expect these to improve in time as they always have with immigrants to the United States. And, when it comes to women, there is simply no issue today when it comes to qualifying in equal numbers for selective institutions of higher and professional education.)

14   How, then, should we respond to this undeniable reality? The opponents of affirmative action say, "Let standards prevail whatever the result." So what if black students are reduced to two percent of our selective and elite student bodies? Those who gain entry will know that they are properly qualified for entry, that they have been selected without discrimination, and their classmates will know it too. The result will actually be improved race relations and a continuance of the improvements we have seen in black performance in recent decades. Fifteen years from now, perhaps three or four percent of students in the top schools will be black. Until then, blacks can go to less competitive institutions of higher education, perhaps gaining greater advantage from their education in so doing. And, meanwhile, let us improve elementary and high school education—as we have been trying to do for the last 15 years or more.

15   Yet we cannot be quite so cavalier about the impact on public opinion—black and white—of a radical reduction in the number of black students at the Harvards, the Berkeleys, and the Amhersts. These institutions have become, for better or worse, the gateways to prominence, priv-

ilege, wealth, and power in American society. To admit blacks under affirmative action no doubt undermines the American meritocracy, but to exclude blacks from them by abolishing affirmative action would undermine the legitimacy of American democracy.

My argument is rooted in history. African Americans—and the strug-   16
gle for their full and fair inclusion in U.S. society—have been a part of
American history from the beginning. Our Constitution took special—but
grossly unfair—account of their status, our greatest war was fought over
their status, and our most important constitutional amendments were
adopted because of the need to right past wrongs done to them. And,
amid the civil rights revolution of the 1960s, affirmative action was instituted to compensate for the damage done to black achievement and life
chances by almost 400 years of slavery, followed by state-sanctioned discrimination and massive prejudice.

Yet, today, a vast gulf of difference persists between the educational   17
and occupational status of blacks and whites, a gulf that encompasses statistical measures of wealth, residential segregation, and social relationships with other Americans. Thirty years ago, with the passage of the
great civil rights laws, one could have reasonably expected—as I did—
that all would be set right by now. But today, even after taking account of
substantial progress and change, it is borne upon us how continuous,
rooted, and substantial the differences between African Americans and
other Americans remain.

The judgment of the elites who support affirmative action—the college   18
presidents and trustees, the religious leaders, the corporate executives—
and the judgment even of many of those who oppose it but hesitate to act
against it—the Republican leaders in Congress, for example—is that the
banning of preference would be bad for the country. I agree. Not that
everyone's motives are entirely admirable; many conservative congress-
men, for example, are simply afraid of being portrayed as racists even if
their opposition to affirmative action is based on a sincere desire to support meritocratic principle. The college presidents who support affirmative action, under the fashionable mantra of diversity, also undoubtedly
fear the student demonstrations that would occur if they were to speak
out against preferences.

But there are also good-faith motives in this stand, and there is some-   19
thing behind the argument for diversity. What kind of institutions of
higher education would we have if blacks suddenly dropped from 6 or
7 percent of enrollment to 1 or 2 percent? The presence of blacks, in
classes in social studies and the humanities, immediately introduces another tone, another range of questions (often to the discomfort of black
students who do not want this representational burden placed upon
them). The tone may be one of embarrassment and hesitation and self-
censorship among whites (students and faculty). But must we not all
learn how to face these questions together with our fellow citizens? We

should not be able to escape from this embarrassment by the reduction of black students to minuscule numbers.

20   The weakness in the "diversity" defense is that college presidents are not much worried about the diversity that white working-class kids, or students of Italian or Slavic background, have to offer. Still, there is a reputable reason for that apparent discrepancy. It is that the varied ethnic and racial groups in the United States do not, to the same extent as African Americans, pose a test of the fairness of American institutions. These other groups have not been subjected to the same degree of persecution or exclusion. Their status is not, as the social status of African Americans is, the most enduring reproach to the egalitarian ideals of American society. And these other groups have made progress historically, and make progress today, at a rate that incorporates them into American society quickly compared to blacks.

21   This is the principal flaw in the critique of affirmative action. The critics are defending a vitally important principle, indeed, the one that should be the governing principle of institutions of higher education: academic competence as the sole test for distinguishing among applicants and students. This principle, which was fought for so energetically during the 1940s and 1950s through laws banning discrimination in admission on the basis of race, national origin, or religion, should not be put aside lightly. But, at present, it would mean the near exclusion from our best educational institutions of a group that makes up 12 percent of the population. In time, I am convinced, this preference will not be needed. Our laws and customs and our primary and secondary educational systems will fully incorporate black Americans into American society, as other disadvantaged groups have been incorporated. The positive trends of recent decades will continue. But we are still, though less than in the past, "two nations," and one of the nations cannot be excluded so thoroughly from institutions that confer access to the positions of greatest prestige and power.

22   On what basis can we justify violating the principle that measured criteria of merit should govern admission to selective institutions of higher education today? It is of some significance to begin with that we in the United States have always been looser in this respect than more examination-bound systems of higher education in, say, Western Europe: we have always left room for a large degree of freedom for institutions of higher education, public as well as private, to admit students based on nonacademic criteria. But I believe the main reasons we have to continue racial preferences for blacks are, first, because this country has a special obligation to blacks that has not been fully discharged, and second, because strict application of the principle of qualification would send a message of despair to many blacks, a message that the nation is indifferent to their difficulties and problems.

23   Many, including leading black advocates of eliminating preference, say no: the message would be, "Work harder and you can do it." Well,

now that affirmative action is becoming a thing of the past in the public colleges and universities of California and Texas, we will have a chance to find out. Yet I wonder whether the message of affirmative action to black students today really ever has been, "Don't work hard; it doesn't matter for you because you're black; you will make it into college anyway." Colleges are indeed looking for black students, but they are also looking for some minimal degree of academic effort and accomplishment, and it is a rare ambitious African American student seeking college entry who relaxes because he believes his grades won't matter at all.

One of the chief arguments against racial preference in college and professional school admissions is that more blacks will drop out, the quality of blacks who complete the courses of instruction will be inferior, and they will make poorer lawyers, doctors, or businessmen. Dropping out is common in American higher education and does not necessarily mean that one's attendance was a total loss. Still, the average lower degree of academic performance has, and will continue to have, effects even for the successful: fewer graduating black doctors will go into research; more will go into practice and administration. More blacks in business corporations will be in personnel. Fewer graduating black lawyers will go into corporate law firms; more will work for government. 24

And more will become judges, because of another and less disputed form of affirmative action, politics. Few protest at the high number of black magistrates in cities with large black populations—we do not appoint judges by examination. Nor do we find it odd or objectionable that Democratic presidents will appoint more black lawyers as judges, or that even a Republican president will be sure to appoint one black Supreme Court justice. What is at work here is the principle of participation. It is a more legitimate principle in politics and government than it is for admission to selective institutions of higher education. But these are also gateways to power, and the principle of participation cannot be flatly ruled out for them. 25

Whatever the case one may make in general for affirmative action, many difficult issues remain: What kind, to what extent, how long, imposed by whom, by what decision-making process? It is important to bear in mind that affirmative action in higher education admissions is, for the most part, a policy that has been chosen (albeit sometimes under political pressure) by the institutions themselves. There are racial goals and targets for employment and promotion for all government contractors, including colleges and universities, set by government fiat, but targets on student admissions are not imposed by government, except for a few traditionally black or white institutions in the South. 26

Let us preserve this institutional autonomy. Just as I would resist governmentally imposed requirements that these institutions meet quotas of black admissions, so would I also oppose a judicial or legislative ban on the use of race in making decisions on admission. Ballot measures like 27

Proposition 209 are more understandable given the abuses so common in systems of racial preference. But it is revealing that so many other states appear to have had second thoughts and that the California vote is therefore not likely to be repeated. (A report in the *Chronicle of Higher Education* was headlined "LEGISLATURES SHOW LITTLE ENTHUSIASM FOR MEASURES TO END RACIAL PREFERENCES"; in this respect, the states are not unlike Congress.)

28   We should retain the freedom of institutions of higher and professional education to make these determinations for themselves. As we know, they would almost all make room for a larger percentage of black students than would otherwise qualify. This is what these institutions do today. They defend what they do with the argument that diversity is a good thing. I think what they really mean is that a large segment of the American population, significant not only demographically but historically and politically and morally, cannot be so thoroughly excluded. I agree with them.

29   I have discussed affirmative action only in the context of academic admissions policy. Other areas raise other questions, other problems. And, even in this one area of college and university admissions, affirmative action is not a simple and clear and uncomplicated solution. It can be implemented wisely or foolishly, and it is often done foolishly, as when college presidents make promises to protesting students that they cannot fulfill, or when institutions reach too far below their minimal standards with deleterious results for the academic success of the students they admit, for their grading practices, and for the legitimacy of the degrees they offer. No matter how affirmative action in admissions is dealt with, other issues remain or will emerge. More black students, for example, mean demands for more black faculty and administrators and for more black-oriented courses. Preference is no final answer (just as the elimination of preference is no final answer). It is rather what is necessary to respond to the reality that, for some years to come, yes, we are still two nations, and both nations must participate in the society to some reasonable degree.

30   Fortunately, those two nations, by and large, want to become more united. The United States is not Canada or Bosnia, Lebanon or Malaysia. But, for the foreseeable future, the strict use of certain generally reasonable tests as a benchmark criterion for admissions would mean the de facto exclusion of one of the two nations from a key, institutional system of the society, higher education. Higher education's governing principle is qualification—merit. Should it make room for another and quite different principle, equal participation? The latter should never become dominant. Racial proportional representation would be a disaster. But basically the answer is yes—the principle of equal participation can and should be given some role. This decision has costs. But the alternative is too grim to contemplate.

▶ Building Vocabulary

1. In this essay, Glazer uses a number of words and phrases that have come into the English language from other languages, in most cases with the same spelling and meaning. Look up the following, identify the source language, and write a definition for each:
   a. edifice (par. 6)
   b. philanthropy (par. 7)
   c. cavalier (par. 15)
   d. mantra (par. 18)
   e. albeit (par. 26)
   f. fiat (par. 26)
   g. de facto (par. 30)
2. Write definitions and your own sentences for each of the following:
   a. provocatively (par. 2)
   b. insistence (par. 3)
   c. constituency (par. 5)
   d. bureaucratic (par. 13)
   e. meritocracy (par. 15)
   f. autonomy (par. 27)
   g. deleterious (par. 29)

▶ Thinking Critically About the Argument

Understanding the Writer's Argument

1. What makes the debate over affirmative action so confused, according to Glazer?
2. What made Glazer change his position on affirmative action?
3. If affirmative action was put into place through an executive order, how did the policy manage to survive despite the fact that later on two presidents opposed it?
4. What can the SATs and other tests tell us about the need for affirmative action?
5. What is the "principle flaw in the critique of affirmative action"? (par. 21)
6. How is "institutional autonomy" important for the success of affirmative action, according to Glazer?

Understanding the Writer's Techniques

1. Why does Glazer begin his essay with a summary of the arguments on both sides of the affirmative action debate?
2. What is the argumentative effect of Glazer's admission in paragraph 3 that he has changed sides in the debate?

3. What is Glazer's claim in this essay? Where does he articulate it most clearly?

4. Compare and contrast the kind of support Glazer and Chavez use to make their arguments. Do they both rely equally on logic? Does one make a more emotional appeal? Explain your answers.

5. Compare and contrast the tone Glazer takes in his essay with Chavez's in hers.

6. What evidence does Glazer cite to support his minor proposition that there is little real opposition to affirmative action?

7. How does Glazer support his point that abolishing affirmative action "would undermine the legitimacy of American democracy"? (par. 15)

8. How effective is Glazer's conclusion? Explain.

Exploring the Writer's Argument

1. Glazer acknowledges that one of the central tenets of the civil rights movement is the prohibition of discrimination based on race. How does he make a case for why affirmative action is not in violation of this principle? Explain.

2. What would Chavez say in response to Glazer's point that "the judgment of the elites who support affirmative action—the college presidents and trustees, the religious leaders, the corporate executives—and the judgment even of many of those who oppose it but hesitate to act against it—the Republican leaders in Congress, for example—is that the banning of preference would be bad for the country"? (par. 18)

3. In the course of his essay, Glazer uses the same statistic, the one introduced in paragraph 9, several times. He repeats the idea that if the SAT were used for admissions without looking at race, African Americans would go from 6 percent of students at top colleges to 2 percent. Where else in the essay does he mention this statistic, and what is the effect? What would happen to his argument if he didn't have this statistic?

4. Why do you think Chavez writes about minorities in general in her essay and Glazer, on the other hand, focuses on African Americans?

▶ Ideas for Writing Arguments

Prewriting

In his conclusion, Glazer writes that affirmative action "has costs. But the alternative is too grim to contemplate." List the pros and cons of affirmative action.

Writing a Guided Argument

At the end of the 2003 term, the U.S. Supreme Court handed down two important decisions about affirmative action in Michigan: *Grutter v.*

Bollinger and *Gratz v. Bollinger*. Find the text of the two decisions, read them, and choose one case and one of the justice's opinions (majority or dissenting) on that case. Write an essay that supports that position.

1. Open your essay with a summary of the Supreme Court case and its importance.
2. Explain which position you agree with, and write your major proposition.
3. Offer a minor proposition giving a ground for your position.
4. Support your minor proposition with facts from one of the essays in this chapter.
5. Write another minor proposition, and support it sufficiently.
6. Use strong transitions, and write another minor proposition if needed.
7. Bring your essay to a close by predicting what the consequences of the case will be and whether those consequences will be positive or negative.

Thinking, Arguing, and Writing Collaboratively

Divide into two equal groups, one taking Chavez's position and one taking Glazer's. As a group, think of arguments and facts to add to those already given by the writer whose position you are defending. Try to strengthen weaknesses you see in the original essays. Take notes on your discussion, and prepare an outline for a debate. Debate the issue, and then reconvene as a class and discuss the success of the respective arguments.

Writing About the Text

Write an essay that expands on questions 4 and 5 in the Understanding the Writer's Techniques section.

More Writing Ideas

1. Look up what has happened to Proposition 209 in California. What has been the result and the consequence? Collect notes on your research in your journal.
2. Write a paragraph about the fact that the United States has not fully repaid blacks for years of slavery. What other ways could the United States pay them back?
3. Find out your own college's affirmative action policy. Write an essay in support of or in opposition to the policy.

9 Capital Punishment: Should We Take a Human Life?

D oes the government have the right to put one of its citizens to death for any reason? Does the death penalty violate the "cruel and unusual" punishment clause in the Eighth Amendment?

After World War II, many European and industrialized nations signed the *Universal Declaration of Human Rights* and banned the death penalty within their borders. The United States, however, kept the death penalty. The debate has intensified in this country over the fairness and humaneness of the punishment. One argument focuses on whether it is fair to execute a convict who is mentally ill or retarded. Another highlights the fact that a disproportionate number of people on death row are African Americans. A question here remains: Are blacks punished with execution more frequently than whites, and if so, why, and what does that say about our use of the death penalty? One other objection to capital punishment is that humans administer it and humans make mistakes. Innocent people have gone to their death.

Defenders of the death penalty, however, say that besides being a deterrent to people who might commit capital crimes in the future, execution fulfills a need by society for retribution—the public demands and deserves to see wrongdoers punished severely.

In the selections that follow, George Orwell, writing in the early 1930s, expresses his disgust for executions by showing one to his readers. His vivid and carefully chosen descriptions evoke a feeling of moral decay. David Gelernter, who was almost killed by a mail bomb sent by the Unabomber (a secretive terrorist who sent bombs by mail at the end of the 20th century), argues that we should administer the death penalty as the triumph of rationality over emotion. What do you think about the topic? As you read these two selections, consider why you feel the way you do about the death penalty. Is there a rational way to approach the subject, or are arguments only accessible through the emotions? How does that question affect these essays?

220

GEORGE ORWELL
A Hanging

George Orwell (whose real name was Eric Blair) was born in India in 1903 and died in London at the age of 47. During his short life, he became famous for his political writing, especially his political novels. Orwell's parents were members of the Indian Civil Service, and, after his education at Eton College in England, at the age of 19, Orwell joined the Indian Imperial Police in Burma, which he wrote about in his novel Burmese Days *(1934) and in various essays. One of those essays, "Killing an Elephant," expresses his disillusion with British colonialism. His politics shifted to the left and he became a socialist. He left Burma, traveled around Europe in self-enforced poverty, and wrote his first book about the experience,* Down and Out in Paris and London *(1933). Soon, in the mid-1930s, he joined many writers and intellectuals from all over the Western world in fighting with the Republicans against the Fascists in the Spanish Civil War.* Homage to Catalonia *(1938) tells of his experiences in the war. Orwell was wounded, and, when the Communists attempted to eliminate their allies on the far left, he fought against them and was forced to flee for his life.*

His most famous books, however, are Animal Farm *(1945), a modern fable that attacked the Soviet system of communism by setting the events among animals on a farm; and* 1984 *(1949), a novel about a frightening future.* 1984 *introduced the phrase "Big Brother" into the English language. In the years after his death, Orwell has become renowned for above all things his clarity of writing and his clarity of moral thought. In "A Hanging," written in 1931, Orwell tells of an experience watching an execution in Burma. The essay betrays his feelings about capital punishment, but he remains somewhat ambiguous. Elsewhere, Orwell wrote, "Society, apparently, cannot get along without capital punishment—for there are some people whom it is simply not safe to leave alive—and yet there is no one, when the pinch comes, who feels it right to kill another human being in cold blood."*

▶ Prereading: Thinking About the Essay in Advance

Orwell's quote, that "society . . . cannot get along without capital punishment," has implications for the United States, one of the only industrial nations in the world that still executes prisoners. Why can't the United States get along without capital punishment?

▶ Words to Watch

Dravidian (par. 4) a member of a group of southern Indians
spectacles (par. 4) glasses
magistrates (par. 6) local governmental officials
gambolled (par. 8) moved evasively
incuriously (par. 8) indifferent

timorously (par. 15) timidly
lathis (par. 17) batons
pannikin (par. 17) a small pan or cup
boxwallah (par. 18) peddler
refractory (par. 22) stubborn

1   It was in Burma, a sodden morning of the rains. A sickly light, like yellow tinfoil, was slanting over the high walls into the jail yard. We were waiting outside the condemned cells, a row of sheds fronted with double bars, like small animal cages. Each cell measured about ten feet by ten and was quite bare within except for a plank bed and a pot of drinking water. In some of them brown silent men were squatting at the inner bars, with their blankets draped round them. These were the condemned men, due to be hanged within the next week or two.

2   One prisoner had been brought out of his cell. He was a Hindu, a puny wisp of a man, with a shaven head and vague liquid eyes. He had a thick, sprouting moustache, absurdly too big for his body, rather like the moustache of a comic man on the films. Six tall Indian warders were guarding him and getting him ready for the gallows. Two of them stood by with rifles with fixed bayonets, while the others handcuffed him, passed a chain through his handcuffs and fixed it to their belts, and lashed his arms tight to his sides. They crowded very close about him, with their hands always on him in a careful, caressing grip, as though all the while feeling him to make sure he was there. It was like men handling a fish which is still alive and may jump back into the water. But he stood quite unresisting, yielding his arms limply to the ropes, as though he hardly noticed what was happening.

3   Eight o'clock struck and a bugle call, desolately thin in the wet air, floated from the distant barracks. The superintendent of the jail, who was standing apart from the rest of us, moodily prodding the gravel with his stick, raised his head at the sound. He was an army doctor, with a grey toothbrush moustache and a gruff voice. "For God's sake hurry up, Francis," he said irritably. "The man ought to have been dead by this time. Aren't you ready yet?"

4   Francis, the head jailer, a fat Dravidian in a white drill suit and gold spectacles, waved his black hand. "Yes sir, yes sir," he bubbled. "All iss satisfactorily prepared. The hangman iss waiting. We shall proceed."

5   "Well, quick march, then. The prisoners can't get their breakfast till this job's over."

6   We set out for the gallows. Two warders marched on either side of the prisoner, with their files at the slope; two others marched close against him, gripping him by arm and shoulder, as though at once pushing and supporting him. The rest of us, magistrates and the like, followed behind. Suddenly, when we had gone ten yards, the procession stopped short without any order or warning. A dreadful thing had happened—a dog,

come goodness knows whence, had appeared in the yard. It came bound-
ing among us with a loud volley of barks, and leapt round us wagging its
whole body, wild with glee at finding so many human beings together. It
was a large woolly dog, half Airedale, half pariah. For a moment it
pranced round us, and then, before anyone could stop it, it had made a
dash for the prisoner, and jumping up tried to lick his face. Everyone
stood aghast, too taken aback even to grab at the dog.

"Who let that bloody brute in here?" said the superintendent angrily.   7
"Catch it, someone!"

A warder, detached from the escort, charged clumsily after the dog,   8
but it danced and gambolled just out of his reach, taking everything as
part of the game. A young Eurasian jailer picked up a handful of gravel
and tried to stone the dog away, but it dodged the stones and came after
us again. Its yaps echoed from the jail walls. The prisoner, in the grasp of
the two warders, looked on incuriously, as though this was another for-
mality of the hanging. It was several minutes before someone managed to
catch the dog. Then we put my handkerchief through its collar and
moved off once more, with the dog still straining and whimpering.

It was about forty yards to the gallows. I watched the bare brown back   9
of the prisoner marching in front of me. He walked clumsily with his
bound arms, but quite steadily, with that bobbing gait of the Indian who
never straightens his knees. At each step his muscles slid neatly into place,
the lock of hair on his scalp danced up and down, his feet printed themselves on the wet gravel. And once, in spite of the men who gripped him
by each shoulder, he stepped slightly aside to avoid a puddle on the path.

It is curious, but till that moment I had never realised what it means to   10
destroy a healthy, conscious man. When I saw the prisoner step aside to
avoid the puddle, I saw the mystery, the unspeakable wrongness, of cutting a life short when it is in full tide. This man was not dying, he was alive
just as we were alive. All the organs of his body were working—bowels di-
gesting food, skin renewing itself, nails growing, tissues forming—all toil-
ing away in solemn foolery. His nails would still be growing when he
stood on the drop, when he was falling through the air with a tenth of a
second to live. His eyes saw the yellow gravel and the grey walls, and his
brain still remembered, foresaw, reasoned—reasoned even about puddles.
He and we were a party of men walking together, seeing, hearing, feeling,
understanding the same world; and in two minutes, with a sudden snap,
one of us would be gone—one mind less, one world less.

The gallows stood in a small yard, separate from the main grounds   11
of the prison, and overgrown with tall prickly weeds. It was a brick erec-
tion like three sides of a shed, with planking on top, and above that two
beams and a crossbar with the rope dangling. The hangman, a grey-
haired convict in the white uniform of the prison, was waiting beside his
machine. He greeted us with a servile crouch as we entered. At a word
from Francis the two warders, gripping the prisoner more closely than

ever, half led, half pushed him to the gallows and helped him clumsily up the ladder. Then the hangman climbed up and fixed the rope round the prisoner's neck.

12   We stood waiting, five yards away. The warders had formed in a rough circle round the gallows. And then, when the noose was fixed, the prisoner began crying out on his god. It was a high, reiterated cry of "Ram! Ram! Ram! Ram!", not urgent and fearful like a prayer or a cry for help, but steady, rhythmical, almost like the tolling of a bell. The dog answered the sound with a whine. The hangman, still standing on the gallows, produced a small cotton bag like a flour bag and drew it down over the prisoner's face. But the sound, muffled by the cloth, still persisted, over and over again: "Ram! Ram! Ram! Ram! Ram!"

13   The hangman climbed down and stood ready, holding the lever. Minutes seemed to pass. The steady, muffled crying from the prisoner went on and on, "Ram! Ram! Ram!" never faltering for an instant. The superintendent, his head on his chest, was slowly poking the ground with his stick; perhaps he was counting the cries, allowing the prisoner a fixed number—fifty, perhaps, or a hundred. Everyone had changed colour. The Indians had gone grey like bad coffee, and one or two of the bayonets were wavering. We looked at the lashed, hooded man on the drop, and listened to his cries—each cry another second of life; the same thought was in all our minds; oh, kill him quickly, get it over, stop that abominable noise!

14   Suddenly the superintendent made up his mind. Throwing up his head he made a swift motion with his stick. "Chalo!" he shouted almost fiercely.

15   There was a clanking noise, and then dead silence. The prisoner had vanished, and the rope was twisting on itself. I let go of the dog, and it galloped immediately to the back of the gallows; but when it got there it stopped short, barked, and then retreated into a corner of the yard, where it stood among the weeds, looking timorously out at us. We went round the gallows to inspect the prisoner's body. He was dangling with his toes pointed straight downwards, very slowly revolving, as dead as a stone.

16   The superintendent reached out with his stick and poked the bare body; it oscillated, slightly. "*He's* all right," said the superintendent. He backed out from under the gallows, and blew out a deep breath. The moody look had gone out of his face quite suddenly. He glanced at his wristwatch. "Eight minutes past eight. Well, that's all for this morning, thank God."

17   The warders unfixed bayonets and marched away. The dog, sobered and conscious of having misbehaved itself, slipped after them. We walked out of the gallows yard, past the condemned cells with their waiting prisoners, into the big central yard of the prison. The convicts, under the command of warders armed with lathis, were already receiving their breakfast. They squatted in long rows, each man holding a tin pannikin, while two warders with buckets marched round ladling out rice; it seemed quite a homely, jolly scene, after the hanging. An enormous relief

had come upon us now that the job was done. One felt an impulse to sing, to break into a run, to snigger. All at once everyone began chattering gaily.

The Eurasian boy walking beside me nodded towards the way we   18
had come, with a knowing smile: "Do you know, sir, our friend (he meant the dead man), when he heard his appeal had been dismissed, he pissed on the floor of his cell. From fright—Kindly take one of my cigarettes, sir. Do you not admire my new silver case, sir? From the boxwallah, two rupees eight annas. Classy European style."

Several people laughed—at what, nobody seemed certain.   19

Francis was walking by the superintendent, talking garrulously: 20
"Well, sir, all hass passed off with the utmost satisfactoriness. It wass all finished—flick! like that. It iss not always so—oah, no! I have known cases where the doctor wass obliged to go beneath the gallows and pull the prisoner's legs to ensure decease. Most disagreeable!"

"Wriggling about, eh? That's bad," said the superintendent.   21

"Ach, sir, it iss worse when they become refractory! One man, I recall,   22
clung to the bars of hiss cage when we went to take him out. You will scarcely credit, sir, that it took six warders to dislodge him, three pulling at each leg. We reasoned with him. 'My dear fellow,' we said, 'think of all the pain and trouble you are causing to us!' But no, he would not listen! Ach, he wass very troublesome!"

I found that I was laughing quite loudly. Everyone was laughing.   23
Even the superintendent grinned in a tolerant way. "You'd better all come out and have a drink," he said quite genially. "I've got a bottle of whisky in the car. We could do with it."

We went through the big double gates of the prison, into the road.   24
"Pulling at his legs!" exclaimed a Burmese magistrate suddenly, and burst into a loud chuckling. We all began laughing again. At that moment Francis's anecdote seemed extraordinarily funny. We all had a drink together, native and European alike, quite amicably. The dead man was a hundred yards away.

▶ Building Vocabulary

Find the following words in the essay. Write brief definitions for each without using a dictionary. If the words are unfamiliar, try to figure out their meaning based on the context in which they appear:

1. sodden (par. 1)
2. desolately (par. 3)
3. aghast (par. 6)
4. solemn (par. 10)
5. abominable (par. 13)
6. oscillated (par. 16)
7. snigger (par. 17)

8. garrulously (par. 20)
9. genially (par. 23)
10. amicably (par. 24)

▶Thinking Critically About the Argument

Understanding the Writer's Argument

1. Recount, in outline form, the events in Orwell's essay.
2. How much does Orwell, as the narrator, actually participate in the hanging? Is he neutral or involved? Why do you think Orwell makes that choice for his essay?
3. What makes Orwell start thinking about the nature of the death penalty?
4. What does he mean in paragraph 10 by "solemn foolery"?
5. What is Orwell's speculation as to why the superintendent pokes the ground with his stick in paragraph 13?
6. Why does everyone laugh after the hanging, in your opinion?

Understanding the Writer's Techniques

1. What is Orwell's claim in this essay? Is there an explicit statement in which he states his claim? If not, how does the essay succeed without one?
2. Explain how Orwell's description of the jail and the weather help him to make his point. Give specific examples.
3. In paragraph 10, what is the argumentative effect of the phrase "one world less"? Why it is effective?
4. What is Orwell's tone? Point out his uses of irony in this essay. Explain how irony contributes to his argument.
5. Why does Orwell point out that the hangman is also a prisoner?
6. What is the significance of the dog for Orwell's argument?
7. What is the effect of Orwell's outburst at the end of paragraph 13?

Exploring the Writer's Argument

1. Between paragraphs 9 and 10, Orwell begins thinking about the morality of executing the prisoner. What triggers his thoughts? Is this an effective technique, or is it too abrupt and transparent a transition?
2. How does Orwell's description of the immediate aftermath of the execution affect his argument? Is it acceptable that he describes it so matter-of-factly? Why or why not?
3. How does the fact that Orwell writes this essay as a narrative help or harm his argument? What does his choice of form *not* allow him to do? What are the inherent limitations of this form?
4. What do you think the condemned man did to deserve his punishment?

▶ Ideas for Writing Arguments

Prewriting

What ethical arguments do you see for and against the death penalty?

Writing a Guided Argument

One argument for the death penalty is often that it keeps other people who might be considering murder from doing it. Write an essay in which you argue that the death penalty is or is not a deterrent to future murders. Do some research on the topic, and find articles that address the issue of deterrence specifically before your make your choice. Title your essay "Death Penalty as a Deterrent."

1. Open your essay with a reference to an article that you have found in the course of your research, summarizing the opinion of a writer who agrees with your position.
2. Use a proper and effective transition to move into a well-articulated major proposition.
3. Have at least two reasons of your own to back up your position and express them as minor propositions.
4. Support your ideas with facts taken from your research.
5. Credit the articles you use.
6. In the next section, introduce one point made by the other side.
7. Rebut the opposing view.
8. Close your essay with an appeal to the reader's emotions.

Thinking, Arguing, and Writing Collaboratively

Divide into three equal groups. Each group should prepare for a debate on the use of the death penalty for the mentally retarded. You may conduct research on this issue in the library or on the Web. The aim of the preparation should be to win a debate through persuasion. Stage the debate, with one group arguing in favor of the death penalty and the second group arguing against it. The third group will act as jury (but should also prepare for the debate so the jury is familiar with all the basic arguments surrounding the topic). The jury will then vote on a winner and articulate its reasons to the class.

Writing About the Text

Watch a movie about the death penalty, such as Tim Robbins's *Dead Man Walking* or Clint Eastwood's *True Crime*. Write an essay that compares and contrasts the film's narrative techniques for being persuasive with Orwell's techniques.

More Writing Ideas

1. In your journal, consider how you might or might not change your views on capital punishment if someone in your circle of family and friends were murdered.
2. In the next essay you will read, David Gelernter writes that "Even when we resolve in principle to go ahead [with the death penalty], we have to steel ourselves." (par. 17) What does Gelernter mean, and how does Orwell's
   essay reflect this idea? Write two or three paragraphs answering these questions.
3. Write an essay that argues for or against the death penalty, purely on ethical grounds. If need be, investigate further the idea of ethics before you write.

DAVID GELERNTER
What Do Murderers Deserve?

David Gelernter is a professor of computer science at Yale. In 1991 he published a book, Mirror Worlds, *that some say predicted the Internet. In 1993, he was the victim of a letter bomb, and survived, but had a long rehabilitation period. He is a leading figure in the field of artificial intelligence. He is the author of three other books:* The Muse in the Machine *(1994),* 1939: The Lost World of the Fair *(1995), and* Drawing a Life: Surviving the Unabomber *(1998). His experience of almost getting killed informs this selection, in which he discusses what punishment murderers, including his would-be murderer (who did succeed in taking the lives of three people), deserve.*

▶ Prereading: Thinking About the Essay in Advance

Why does a country have the right to execute one of its citizens? What is the political rational for keeping the death penalty?

▶ Words to Watch

penitent (par. 1) those who ask for forgiveness
defiles (par. 4) morally stains
equivocation (par. 6) lack of commitment
reverting (par. 9) returning
inclination (par. 10) tendency
sanctity (par. 14) holiness
capricious (par. 15) impulsive
faculties (par. 18) abilities
bestiality (par. 22) animal-like behavior
smitten (par. 24) attacked

No civilized nation ever takes the death penalty for granted; two re-   1
cent cases force us to consider it yet again. A Texas woman, Karla
Faye Tucker, murdered two people with a pickaxe, was said to have repented in prison, and was put to death. A Montana man, Theodore
Kaczynski, murdered three people with mail bombs, did not repent, and
struck a bargain with the Justice Department; he pleaded guilty and will
not be executed. (He also attempted to murder others and succeeded in
wounding some, myself included.) Why did we execute the penitent and
spare the impenitent? However we answer this question, we surely have
a duty to ask it.

And we ask it—I do, anyway—with a sinking feeling, because in   2
modern America, moral upside-downness is a specialty of the house.
To eliminate race prejudice we discriminate by race. We promote the
cultural assimilation of immigrant children by denying them schooling
in English. We throw honest citizens in jail for child abuse, relying on
testimony so phony any child could see through it. Orgasm studies are
okay in public high schools but the Ten Commandments are not. We
make a point of admiring manly women and womanly men. None of
which has anything to do with capital punishment directly, but it all
obliges us to approach any question about morality in modern America
in the larger context of this country's desperate confusion about elementary distinctions.

Why execute murderers? To deter? To avenge? Supporters of the   3
death penalty often give the first answer, opponents the second. But neither can be the whole truth. If our main goal were deterring crime, we
would insist on public executions—which are not on the political agenda,
and not an item that many Americans are interested in promoting. If our
main goal were vengeance, we would allow the grieving parties to decide
the murderer's fate; if the victim had no family or friends to feel vengeful
on his behalf, we would call the whole thing off.

In fact, we execute murderers in order to make a communal procla-   4
mation: that murder is intolerable. A deliberate murderer embodies evil
so terrible that it defiles the community. Thus the late social philosopher
Robert Nisbet: "Until a catharsis has been effected through trial, through
the finding of guilt and then punishment, the community is anxious, fearful, apprehensive, and above all, contaminated."

Individual citizens have a right and sometimes a duty to speak. A   5
community has the right, too, and sometimes the duty. The community
certifies births and deaths, creates marriages, educates children, fights
invaders. In laws, deeds, and ceremonies it lays down the boundary
lines of civilized life, lines that are constantly getting scuffed and needing renewal.

When a murder takes place, the community is obliged, whether it   6
feels like it or not, to clear its throat and step up to the microphone.
Every murder demands a communal response. Among possible responses, the death penalty is uniquely powerful because it is permanent

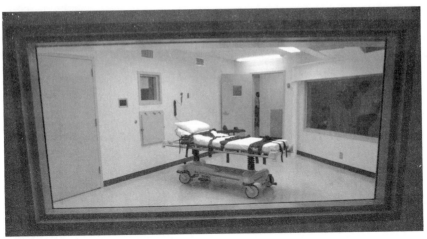

Alabama's lethal injection chamber at Holman Correctional Facility in Atmore, Ala. (Associated Press/Dave Martin)

and can never be retracted or overturned. An execution forces the community to assume forever the burden of moral certainty; it is a form of absolute speech that allows no waffling or equivocation. Deliberate murder, the community announces, is absolutely evil and absolutely intolerable, period.

7   Of course, we could make the same point less emphatically if we wanted to—for example, by locking up murderers for life (as we sometimes do). The question then becomes: is the death penalty overdoing it? Should we make a less forceful proclamation instead?

8   The answer might be yes if we were a community in which murder was a shocking anomaly and thus in effect a solved problem. But we are not. Our big cities are full of murderers at large. "One can guesstimate," writes the criminologist and political scientist John J. DiIulio, Jr., "that we are nearing or may already have passed the day when 500,000 murderers, convicted and undetected, are living in American society."

9   DiIulio's statistics show an approach to murder so casual as to be depraved. We are reverting to a pre-civilized state of nature. Our natural bent in the face of murder is not to avenge the crime but to shrug it off, except in those rare cases when our own near and dear are involved. (And even then, it depends.)

10   This is an old story. Cain murders Abel and is brought in for questioning: where is Abel, your brother? The suspect's response: how should I know? "What am I, my brother's keeper?" It is one of the very first statements attributed to mankind in the Bible; voiced here by an interested party, it nonetheless expresses a powerful and universal inclination. Why mess in other people's problems? And murder is always, in the

most immediate sense, someone else's problem, because the injured party is dead.

Murder in primitive societies called for a private settling of scores. The community as a whole stayed out of it. For murder to count, as it does in the Bible, as a crime not merely against one man but against the whole community and against God—that was a moral triumph that is still basic to our integrity, and that is never to be taken for granted. By executing murderers, the community reaffirms this moral understanding by restating the truth that absolute evil exists and must be punished.   11

Granted (some people say), the death penalty is a communal proclamation; it is nevertheless an incoherent one. If our goal is to affirm that human life is more precious than anything else, how can we make such a declaration by destroying life?   12

But declaring that human life is more precious than anything else is not our goal in imposing the death penalty. Nor is the proposition true. The founding fathers pledged their lives (and fortunes and sacred honor) to the cause of freedom; Americans have traditionally believed that some things are more precious than life. ("Living in a sanitary age, we are getting so we place too high a value on human life—which rightfully must always come second to human ideas." Thus E.B. White in 1938, pondering the Munich pact ensuring "peace in our time" between the Western powers and Hitler.) The point of capital punishment is not to pronounce on life in general but on the crime of murder.   13

Which is not to say that the sanctity of human life does not enter the picture. Taking a life, says the Talmud (in the course of discussing Cain and Abel), is equivalent to destroying a whole world. The rabbis used this statement to make a double point: to tell us why murder is the gravest of crimes, and to warn against false testimony in a murder trial. But to believe in the sanctity of human life does not mean, and the Talmud does not say it means, that capital punishment is ruled out.   14

A newer objection grows out of the seemingly random way in which we apply capital punishment. The death penalty might be a reasonable communal proclamation in principle, some critics say, but it has become so garbled in practice that it has lost all significance and ought to be dropped. DiIulio writes that "the ratio of persons murdered to persons executed for murder from 1977 to 1996 was in the ballpark of 1,000 to 1"; the death penalty has become in his view "arbitrary and capricious," a "state lottery" that is "unjust both as a matter of Judeo-Christian ethics and as a matter of American citizenship."   15

We can grant that, on the whole, we are doing a disgracefully bad job of administering the death penalty. After all, we are divided and confused on the issue. The community at large is strongly in favor of capital punishment; the cultural elite is strongly against it. Our attempts to speak with assurance as a community come out sounding in consequence like a man who is fighting off a choke-hold as he talks. But a community as   16 cavalier about murder as we are has no right to back down. That we are botching things does not entitle us to give up.

17   Opponents of capital punishment tend to describe it as a surrender to our emotions—to grief, rage, fear, blood lust. For most supporters of the death penalty, this is exactly false. Even when we resolve in principle to go ahead, we have to steel ourselves. Many of us would find it hard to kill a dog, much less a man. Endorsing capital punishment means not that we yield to our emotions but that we overcome them. (Immanuel Kant, the great advocate of the death penalty precisely on moral grounds, makes this point in his reply to the anticapital-punishment reformer Cesare Beccaria—accusing Beccaria of being "moved by sympathetic sentimentality and an affectation of humanitarianism.") If we favor executing murderers it is not because we want to but because, however much we do not want to, we consider ourselves obliged to.

18   Many Americans, of course, no longer feel that obligation. The death penalty is hard for us as a community above all because of our moral evasiveness. For at least a generation, we have urged one another to switch off our moral faculties. "Don't be judgmental!" We have said it so many times, we are starting to believe it.

19   The death penalty is a proclamation about absolute evil, but many of us are no longer sure that evil even exists. We define evil out of existence by calling it "illness"—a tendency Aldous Huxley anticipated in his novel *Brave New World* (1932) and Robert Nisbet wrote about in 1982: "America has lost the villain, the evil one, who has now become one of the sick, the disturbed. . . . America has lost the moral value of guilt, lost it to the sickroom."

20   Our refusal to look evil in the face is no casual notion; it is a powerful drive. Thus we have (for example) the terrorist Theodore Kaczynski, who planned and carried out a hugely complex campaign of violence with a clear goal in mind. It was the goal most terrorists have: to get famous and not die. He wanted public attention for his ideas about technology; he figured he could get it by attacking people with bombs.

21   He was right. His plan succeeded. It is hard to imagine a more compelling proof of mental competence than this planning and carrying out over decades of a complex, rational strategy. (Evil, yes; irrational, no; they are different things.) The man himself has said repeatedly that he is perfectly sane, knew what he was doing, and is proud of it.

22   To call such a man insane seems to me like deliberate perversity. But many people do. Some of them insist that his thoughts about technology constitute "delusions," though every terrorist holds strong beliefs that are wrong, and many nonterrorists do, too. Some insist that sending bombs through the mail is ipso facto proof of insanity—as if the 20th century had not taught us that there is no limit to the bestiality of which sane men are capable.

23   Where does this perversity come from? I said earlier that the community at large favors the death penalty, but intellectuals and the cultural elite tend

to oppose it. This is not (I think) because they abhor killing more than other people do, but because the death penalty represents absolute speech from a position of moral certainty, and doubt is the black-lung disease of the intelligentsia—an occupational hazard now inflicted on the culture as a whole.

American intellectuals have long differed from the broader community— particularly on religion, crime and punishment, education, family, the sexes, race relations, American history, taxes and public spending, the size and scope of government, art, the environment, and the military. (Otherwise, I suppose, they and the public have been in perfect accord.) But not until the late 60's and 70's were intellectuals finally in a position to act on their convictions. Whereupon they attacked the community's moral certainties with the enthusiasm of guard dogs leaping at throats.* The result is an American community smitten with the disease of intellectual doubt—or, in this case, self-doubt.

The failure of our schools is a consequence of our self-doubt, of our inability to tell children that learning is not fun and they are required to master certain topics whether they want to or not. The tortured history of modern American race relations grows out of our self-doubt; we passed a civil-rights act in 1964, then lost confidence immediately in our ability to make a race-blind society work; racial preferences codify our refusal to believe in our own good faith. During the late stages of the cold war, many Americans laughed at the idea that the American way was morally superior or the Soviet Union was an "evil empire"; some are still laughing. Within their own community and the American community at large, doubting intellectuals have taken refuge (as doubters often do) in bullying, to the point where many of us are now so uncomfortable at the prospect of confronting evil that we turn away and change the subject.

Returning then to the penitent woman and the impenitent man: the Karla Faye Tucker case is the harder of the two. We are told that she repented of the vicious murders she committed. If that is true, we would still have had no business forgiving her, or forgiving any murderer. As Dennis Prager has written apropos this case, only the victim is entitled to forgive, and the victim is silent. But showing mercy to penitents is part of our religious tradition, and I cannot imagine renouncing it categorically.

Why was Cain not put to death, but condemned instead to wander the earth forever? Among the answers given by the rabbis in the Midrash is that he repented. The moral category of repentance is so important, they said, that it was created before the world itself. I would therefore consider myself morally obligated to think long and hard before executing a penitent. But a true penitent would have to have renounced (as Karla Faye Tucker did) all legal attempts to overturn the original conviction. If every legal avenue has been tried and has failed, the penitence

24

25

26

27

---

*I have written about this before in "How the Intellectuals Took Over (And What to Do About It)," *Commentary*, March 1997.

window is closed. Of course, this still leaves the difficult problem of telling counterfeit penitence from the real thing, but everything associated with capital punishment is difficult.

28   As for Kaczynski, the prosecutors who accepted the murderer's plea-bargain say they got the best outcome they could, under the circumstances, and I believe them. But I also regard this failure to execute a cold-blooded impenitent terrorist murderer as a tragic abdication of moral responsibility. The tragedy lies in what, under our confused system, the prosecutors felt compelled to do. The community was called on to speak unambiguously. It flubbed its lines, shrugged its shoulders, and walked away.

29   Which brings me back to our moral condition as a community. I can describe our plight better in artistic than in philosophical terms. The most vivid illustrations I know of self-doubt and its consequences are the paintings and sculptures of Alberto Giacometti (who died in 1966). Giacometti was an artist of great integrity; he was consumed by intellectual and moral self-doubt, which he set down faithfully. His sculpted figures show elongated, shriveled human beings who seem corroded by acid, eaten-up to the bone, hurt and weakened past fragility nearly to death. They are painful to look at. And they are natural emblems of modem America. We ought to stick one on top of the Capitol and think it over.

30   In executing murderers, we declare that deliberate murder is absolutely evil and absolutely intolerable. This is a painfully difficult proclamation for a self-doubting community to make. But we dare not stop trying. Communities may exist in which capital punishment is no longer the necessary response to deliberate murder. America today is not one of them.

▶ Building Vocabulary

1. In this essay, Gelernter uses several words and phrases that derive from other languages. Look up the following and write a definition for each:
   a. catharsis (par. 4)
   b. anomaly (par. 8)
   c. cavalier (par. 16)
   d. ipso facto (par. 22)
   e. apropos (par. 26)
   f. abdication (par. 28)
2. Identify and define the following:
   a. assimilation (par. 2)
   b. retracted (par. 6)
   c. depraved (par. 9)
   d. integrity (par. 11)
   e. incoherent (par. 12)
   f. evasiveness (par. 18)
   g. abhor (par. 23)
   h. plea-bargain (par. 28)

▶ Thinking Critically About the Argument

Understanding the Writer's Argument

1. Why does the writer choose the Tucker and Kaczynski cases to start his essay? Why does he think that in modern America, "moral up-side-downness is a specialty of the house"? Explain this quote.
2. What is the rationale for executing murderers, according to Gelernter?
3. Why does John DiIulio's statistic in paragraph 8 "show an approach to murder so casual as to be depraved"?
4. How does the writer characterize the progress in crime and punishment from primitive society to today? (par. 11) What does he say to the objection that capital punishment is not administered effectively?
5. What is "bloodlust"? In your own words, summarize Gelernter's answer to the objection that being a supporter of the death penalty is "bloodlust."
6. What is perverse about calling a murderer insane? (par. 22)
7. Why is "self-doubt" such a problem in the United States, according to the writer?
8. What do Giacometti's sculptures have to do with the death penalty?

Understanding the Writer's Techniques

1. What sentence best states Gelernter's major proposition? What is his major argumentative purpose in this essay? Is he trying to convince the reader? Explain.
2. Paraphrase the writer's argument in paragraph 3.
3. What is the writer's overall tone? How and why does he develop this tone? Who is his audience?
4. What is the persuasive effect of the writer's argument in paragraph 9? Does it work? Explain your answer.
5. Analyze the writer's use of quotes from other writers. How well does he succeed in using them to advance his own claim?
6. Do you find effective the writer's argument in paragraph 13, that life isn't always the most precious thing? Explain.
7. Does paragraph 14 find the writer backing off from the earlier argument? Why or why not?
8. How effective is the conclusion?

Exploring the Writer's Argument

1. Analyze Gelernter's argument in paragraph 16. Do you think that his point is valid? Why or why not? What do you think of this statement: "That we are botching things does not entitle us to give up"? Do you think he's right? Explain.

2. Gelernter says that America is morally upside-down. He cites, for one, the fact that we try to right racial discrimination by affirmative action. Isn't calling for the death for murderers just as morally upside-down? Does he address this issue sufficiently? Explain your answers.

3. Gelernter was the victim of attempted murder by the hands of Theodore Kaczynski. To what degree do you think Gelernter's argument is affected by his experience? Explain your answer, addressing specifically the section in paragraphs 20 through 22.

▶ Ideas for Writing Arguments

Prewriting

Freewrite for 15 minutes about the difference between your emotions about the death penalty and your intellectual consideration of the subject. Which do you trust more? Why?

Writing a Guided Argument

The Unabomber, Kaczynski, almost killed Gelernter and succeeded in killing three people. Investigate the Unabomber case and his trial. Why, despite the fact that Kaczynski never repented, did he not get the death penalty for his premeditated crimes? Write an essay in which you argue that it was right that he was spared and got the punishment he deserved, or that he should have been executed. Address Gelernter's statement in paragraph 28 that the community "flubbed its lines, shrugged its shoulders, and walked away."

1. Begin your essay with a summary of the case.
2. State your major proposition clearly.
3. Establish a tone of objectivity throughout your essay, while still being persuasive.
4. Offer at least three well-placed minor propositions to support your major proposition.
5. Support your minor propositions with examples and facts.
6. Refer to Gelernter's essay and argument at least twice.
7. Build up to what you think is your strongest minor proposition.
8. Close your essay with a classical argument for or against the death penalty in general, depending on your position.

Thinking, Arguing, and Writing Collaboratively

In small groups, exchange drafts of the paper you wrote for the Writing a Guided Argument assignment with a fellow student. Write a paragraph of comments to help your peer develop his or her argument. Exchange your paper with another student and compare the feedback. Are they consistent? Why or why not?

Writing About the Text

Write an essay expanding on your consideration of Gelernter's tone and analyzing how his tone affects his argumentative claim. Do you think it helps or hurts his argument? Pay attention, especially, to whether he ever gets cynical. What is his tone in paragraph 24?

More Writing Ideas

1. In your journal, write notes for an essay that examines whether or not you consider life imprisonment a "cruel and unusual" punishment.
2. Write a paragraph in which you argue for this idea: "Penitence doesn't matter—if someone does a crime, they must be punished."
3. Based on Gelernter's arguments on self-doubt and his comments in paragraphs 2 and 25, write an essay in which you argue that Gelernter would be against affirmative action, explaining why you think that is true.

Part Three

Perspectives on
Critical Issues

10 The Internet: What Are the Prospects for Cyberspace?

In the past decade, we have witnessed a huge change in the way we live our lives. When the Internet started in the 1970s and 1980s, only governments and scientists used it in order to exchange information. In the early 1990s, consumer technology advanced and Marc Andreeson developed the extraordinary graphical browser, called Mosaic, which became Netscape Navigator. Soon, the World Wide Web was big news. We forget, but before the Internet, people had to shop in person at stores or through the use of catalogs. People wrote letters to each other. People got their news from the radio or newspapers. Now, because of the new technologies everything has changed, from basic communication between family members and friends to dating to politics. Almost all business done around the world involves the Internet at some point.

With the rise of such a revolutionary technology has come an army of writers trying to understand the change and trying to explain it to their readers. The following four selections suggest the wide range of arguments you will find about the Internet. In "I Surf, Therefore I Am," Judith Levine explores the dangers of students relying on the Internet in doing research. Dave Barry, on the other hand, in "ERROR, ERROR, ERROR," humorously conveys his very real frustration over having to switch to a digital workspace. Humor is a technique Barry and other humorists have shown to be a powerful and quite persuasive tool (in part because of the entertainment value—the reader stays interested). Another effective and stealthy way of being persusive is to give advice. Beth Brophy writes about the variety of online dating problems in "Saturday Night and You're All Alone? Maybe You Need a Cyberdate" and is able to push her own point of view on the topic without being confrontational. Andrew Brown, on the other hand, makes it very clear what his argument is in "The Limits of Freedom," a selection that argues for censorship in some cases.

JUDITH LEVINE
I Surf, Therefore I Am

Author and journalist Judith Levine was born in 1952 in New York City. She is an activist for free speech and sex education, the founder of the feminist group No More Nice Girls, and is active in the National Writers Union. She has published many articles in Ms., Mother Jones, *and* The Village Voice, *among other publications. She is the author of* My Enemy, My Love: Women, Men, and the Dilemmas of Gender *(1992) and, most recently, of* Harmful to Minors: The Perils of Protecting Children from Sex *(1999), a book that rethinks how we approach the topic of sexuality in children and teenagers. The book was quickly denounced by conservatives, who accused Levine of endorsing pedophilia. The following selection, which examines the content of what we read when we surf the Internet, appeared in the online magazine* Salon *in its Mothers Who Think column in 1997.*

▶ Prereading: Thinking About the Essay in Advance

Is reading on the Web the same as reading in the book or magazine or newspaper? Does the information stick with you as long? What kind of reading leaves your head the quickest?

▶ Words to Watch

bestowed (par. 1) donated
scant (par. 4) not sufficient
encumbrance (par. 5) a burden
corral (par. 5) organize
etiology (par. 5) cause, as of a disease
promiscuous (par. 5) casual
gleaned (par. 7) picked up, gathered
think tanks (par. 8) institutions often founded for political research
stratospheric (par. 12) extremely high
relinquishing (par. 12) giving up

1   "Obviously, I'm somebody who believes that personal computers are empowering tools," Bill Gates said after he bestowed a $200 million gift to America's public libraries so they could hook up to the Internet.

2   "People are entitled to disagree," Gates said. "But I would invite them to visit some of these libraries and see the impact on kids using this technology."

3   Well, I have seen the impact, and I disagree. Many of my students—undergraduate media and communications majors at a New York

university—have access to the endless information bubbling through cyberspace, and *it is not* empowering.

Most of the data my students Net is like trash fish—and it is hard for   4
them to tell a dead one-legged crab from a healthy sea bass. Scant on world knowledge and critical thinking skills, they are ill-equipped to interpret or judge the so-called facts, which they insert into their papers confidently but in no discernible order.

Their writing often "clicks" from info-bit to info-bit, their arguments   5
free of that gluey, old-fashioned encumbrance—the transitional sentence. When I try to help them corral their impressions into coherent stories, I keep hearing the same complaint: "I can't concentrate." I've diagnosed this phenomenon as epidemic attention deficit disorder. And I can't help but trace its etiology, at least in part, to the promiscuous pointing and clicking that has come to stand in for intellectual inquiry.

These students surf; therefore, they do not read. They do not read   6
scholarly articles—which can be trusted because they are juried or challenged because they are footnoted. They do not read books—which tell stories and sustain arguments by placing idea and metaphor one on top of the other, so as to hold weight, like a stone wall. Even the journalism students read few magazines and even fewer newspapers, which are edited by people with recognizable and sometimes even admitted cultural and political biases and checked by fact-checkers using other edited sources.

On the Net, nobody knows if any particular "fact" is a dog. One stu-   7
dent handed in a paper about tobacco companies' liability for smokers' health, which she had gleaned almost entirely from the Web pages of the Tobacco Institute. Did she know what the Tobacco Institute is? Apparently not, because she had done her research on the Net, and was deprived of the modifying clause, "a research organization supported by the tobacco industry," obligatory in any edited news article.

Another young woman, writing about teen pregnancy, used data   8
generated by the Family Research Council, which, along with other rightwing Christian think tanks, dominates the links on many subjects related to family and sexuality and offers a decidedly one-sided view.

A teacher at another school told me one of her students had written   9
a paper quoting a person who had a name but no identifying characteristics. "Who's this?" the professor asked. "Someone with a Web page," the young man said.

If there is no context on the Net, neither is there history. My friend   10
who teaches biology told me her students propose research that was completed, and often discredited, 50 years ago. "They go online," she said, "where nothing has been indexed before 1980."

A San Francisco librarian interviewed on National Public Radio worried   11
that, space and resources strained as they are, more computers will inevitably mean fewer books. Another commentator on the Gates gift suggested that the computers would not be very valuable without commensurate human resources—that is, trained workers to help people use them.

12   At New York's gleaming new Science, Industry, & Business Library (SIBL), you can sit in an ergonomically correct chair at one of several hundred lovely color computer terminals and call up, among hundreds of other databases, the powerful journalistic and legal service Nexis/Lexis. But since Nexis/Lexis is in great demand, you have about 45 minutes at the screen, half of which the inexperienced user will blow figuring out the system, because there is only one harassed staff person to assist all the computer-users. Then you'll learn that the library cannot afford the stratospheric fees for downloading the articles. So most users, I imagine, will manage to copy out quotes from a couple of articles before relinquishing the seat to the next person waiting for the cyber-kiosk.

13   Unlike a paper or microfilm version of the same pieces, which could be photocopied or copied at leisure onto a pad or laptop, the zillion articles available on the library's Nexis/Lexis are more or less unavailable— that is, to no avail. Useless.

14   Technology may empower, but how and to what end will that power be used? What else is necessary to use it well and wisely? I'd suggest, for a start, reading books—literature and history, poetry and politics—and listening to people who know what they're talking about. Otherwise, the brains of those kids in Gates' libraries will be glutted with "information" but bereft of ideas, rich in tools but clueless about what to build or how to build it. Like the search engines that retrieve more than 100,000 links or none at all, they will be awkward at discerning meaning, or discerning at all.

▶ Building Vocabulary

Write definitions of the following and use them in sentences of your own:

1. discernible (par. 4)
2. epidemic (par. 5)
3. obligatory (par. 7)
4. ergonomically correct (par. 12)
5. glutted (par. 14)
6. bereft (par. 14)

▶ Thinking Critically About the Argument

Understanding the Writer's Argument

1. What does Levine mean when she says in paragraph 4 that "most of the data my students Net is like trash fish"?
2. What is "the transitional sentence" (par. 5), and why is it important?
3. What is attention deficit disorder?
4. Why, according to Levine, is it important to read books, magazines, and newspapers?

5. Levine's student handed in a paper about tobacco for which she got research only from the Tobacco Institute. Why was Levine less than happy about this?
6. What is the risk, according to Levine, with adding so many computers to libraries?
7. What are the downsides to Lexis/Nexis at the public library?

Understanding the Writer's Techniques

1. What is the argumentative effect in the beginning of Levine's essay, when she openly disagrees with Bill Gates, chairman and founder of Microsoft and an expert of computers?
2. Where does Levine articulate her major proposition most clearly? What minor propositions does Levine offer to support her ideas?
3. Analyze why Levine places her minor propositions in the order she does. Is there a strategy at work? Explain your answer.
4. How would you characterize the tone that Levine uses in this essay? Is it effective in helping her argument?
5. What popular saying about computers does Levine satirizie in the first sentence of paragraph 7?
6. What evidence does Levine use to support her idea that students today are not aware of the source of what they are reading online?
7. How effective is Levine's conclusion? Why does she return her discussion to Bill Gates's libraries?

Exploring the Writer's Argument

1. Levine wrote this article for *Salon* magazine, a publication that is only available on the Web. How can she publish an article criticizing online writing in an online magazine? How does that affect the writing? Explain your answer.
2. Prove Levine wrong. Pretend you are doing a research paper on a topic such as abortion or flag burning. Go to the Internet and print out four articles: two should be "trash fish," as Levine says in paragraph 4, and two should be from a respectable news source.
3. In paragraphs 12 and 13, it seems as if Levine relies too much on one example. What point is she trying to make? What could she do to improve this section? Explain fully.

▶ Ideas for Writing Arguments

Prewriting

In your Web surfing time between classes, pay closer attention to your reading habits online. Write notes later analyzing whether what you read is worth reading.

Writing a Guided Argument

There is a debate among librarians and in communities around the country over the censorship of the Internet in libraries. Free Internet access in libraries is, in some communities, the only way for people to get online. However, through ease of availability everyone has access to pornography and information that could harm others. There are software filters that could stop viewers from visiting some sites, but the filters are imperfect and many find the idea of filters to violate First Amendment rights to free speech. Write an essay in which you argue that Internet access in libraries should or should not be censored. Do some research in the library (not online) to gather evidence for your position.

1. Open your essay by briefly outlining the issue.
2. Write your major proposition clearly and in strong language.
3. Affect a tone similar to Levine's.
4. Explain your minor propositions, offering ample support in the form of fact and examples.
5. Entertain one opposing view with a clear rebuttal.
6. Close your essay by refering in some useful way to the First Amendment.

Thinking, Arguing, and Writing Collaboratively

In small groups, exchange your Writing a Guided Argument papers with another student. Spend at least 15 minutes going through your classmate's paper, commenting on the following categories: (1) strength of basic argument, (2) argumentative effect of support, (3) grammar and quality of the prose, and (4) transitions. Write a short paragraph for your classmate about each of these categories, and give back the paper. Review your peer's comments, and discuss any questions you have.

Writing About the Text

Expand on question 4 in the Understanding the Writer's Techniques section. Levine seems to have a cynical edge to her tone. Write an essay that analyzes the use of cynicism and irony in her article.

More Writing Ideas

1. How has the way you get your news and information changed over the past few years? What do you rely on the Internet for? Answer these questions in a journal entry. Compare your answers with those of a classmate. Are your answers similar? Different? How?
2. Just how real is the threat to books by computers, the Internet, Web sites, e-mail, and so on? Write an extended paragraph to argue your position.

3. Write an essay in the form of a letter from Bill Gates to Judith Levine defending his decision to give $200 million to libraries to hook up to the Internet.

DAVE BARRY
Error Error Error

Humorist Dave Barry was born in Armonk, New York, in 1947 and, as he says, "has been steadily growing older ever since without ever actually reaching maturity." He was educated at Haverford College and worked as a reporter at a local Pennsylvania newspaper. From there he went to work in business, but he soon returned to the world of newspapers at the The Miami Herald. *He won the Pulitzer Prize for commentary in 1988 for his column, which is syndicated in several hundred newspapers. Barry is the author of* Babies and Other Hazards of Sex, Dave Barry Slept Here: A Sort of History of the United States, Dave Barry in Cyberspace, *and* Dave Barry Turns 40. *In this selection from his column, Barry, tongue firmly planted in cheek, explains why computers are far from the time-saving devices we think they are.*

▶ Prereading: Thinking About the Essay in Advance

Do you think the personal computer has increased productivity, or has it just added another level of distraction and complication to our lives?

▶ Words to Watch

wary (par. 6) suspiciously cautious
transmit (par. 8) send
mullet (par. 11) species of fish
pertinent (par. 13) to the point

Without question the most important invention in human history, next 1
to frozen yogurt, is the computer. Without computers, it would be virtually impossible for us to accomploiwur xow;gkc,mf(&(

Hold it, there seems to be a keyboard problem here. Let me just try 2
plugging this cable into . . .

ERROR ERROR ERROR ALL FILES HAVE BEEN DESTROYED YOU 3
STUPID BAZOOTYHEAD

Ha ha! Considering what a wonderful invention computers are, they 4
certainly have a way of making you sometimes feel like pouring coffee into their private parts and listening to them scream. Of course you should not do this. The first rule of data processing is: "Never pour hot beverages into a computer, unless it belongs to somebody else, such as your employer."

5   For many of us, the first "hands-on" experience with computers occurs in the workplace. This was certainly true in the newspaper business. One day we reporters came to work and discovered that our old, slow, horse-drawn typewriters had been replaced by sleek, efficient computers with keys that said mysterious scary things like "BREAK" and "NUM LOCK." Fortunately we were trained by highly skilled professional computer personnel who spoke no English. "Before you macro your ASCII, you have to format your RAM," they would advise us, in a tone of voice clearly suggesting that any member of the vegetable family should know this instinctively.

6   So we reporters were wary at first, but after just 175 weeks of training, we discovered that, instead of writing on clumsy, old-fashioned paper, we could create lengthy stories entirely on the computer screen, and then, simply by pushing a button, send them to the Planet Zembar. Or maybe even farther. We definitely couldn't find them anywhere in the building.

7   "WHERE THE HELL IS MY STORY??" we would say, shaking the computer personnel by their necks. But the lost stories always turned out to be our own fault. We had invariably committed some basic bonehead data-processing error such as—you are going to laugh when I tell you this—failing to modem our ROM BIOS VGA megahertz cache.

8   But gradually we got the hang of it, and today we journalists routinely use highly sophisticated, multimillion-dollar computer systems to perform a function that is vital to the survival of a free society, namely, sending personal messages to each other. Walk into a newspaper office, and you'll see serious-looking journalists clattering away on their keyboards; it looks as though they're writing important stories about the plight of the Kurds, but in fact they're sending each other the joke about what the male giraffe said to the female giraffe in the bar. In the old days, journalists had to transmit jokes manually.

9   Also computers now have "spell-checkers," which enable us to catch and correct common misspellings such as "bazootiehead."

10   Of course there are some problems. You have probably read about computer "viruses," which computers get when they're left uncovered in drafty rooms. This is bad, because if you're working on an infected computer, it will periodically emit electronic sneezes, which unfortunately are not detectable by the naked eye—the word "ACHOO" appears on the screen for less than a millionth of a second—and you'll be showered with billions of tiny invisible pieces of electronic phlegm, called "bytes," which penetrate into your brain and gradually make you stupid.

11   This is definitely happening to me. I'll sit down at my home computer to write a thoughtful column about, say, foreign policy, and I'll type: "In view of the recent dramatic changes in the world geopolitical situation, it's time to play some solitaire." My computer has a solitaire-playing program on it, probably invented by the Japanese in an effort to sabotage the American economy. I used to think solitaire was boring, but now that my brain

is clogged with computer boogers I find it more fascinating than, say, the Sistine Chapel. I spend hours moving the little electronic cards around, staring at the screen with the same facial expression as a mullet, while the computer sneezes on me. None of this was possible just 15 years ago.

The computer is also a great teaching tool for young people. For example, my home computer has an educational program that enables you to control an entire simulated planet—its ecology, its technology, its weather, etc. My 10-year-old son and his friends use this program a lot, and we've all learned some important ecological lessons, the main one being: Never, ever put 10-year-old boys in charge of a planet ("Let's see what happens when you have volcanoes AND nuclear war!").   12

So if you don't already have a home computer, I strongly recommend that you get one. Of course before you buy, you'll want to know the answers to some pertinent questions, especially: What DID the male giraffe say to the female giraffe in the bar? The answer—this'll kill you—is: "The higpowoifj &kjfkjO,dmjd ERROR ERROR ERROR."   13

▶ Building Vocabulary

Although this is a humor essay, Barry uses computer terms because he assumes that his reader knows and understand them. This helps his jokes. Define the following terms and the purpose they serve in a computer:

1. NUM LOCK (par. 5)
2. macro (par. 5)
3. ASCII (par. 5)
4. RAM (par. 5)
5. modem (par. 7)
6. megahertz (par. 7)
7. cache (par. 7)
8. viruses (par. 10)

▶ Thinking Critically About the Argument

Understanding the Writer's Argument

1. Why have newspaper reporters had a difficult time getting to know computers, according to Barry?
2. What, according to Barry, do journalists do with all this high-tech equipment?
3. What point is Barry making with his joke that when he sits down to write a serious article, he ends up playing solitaire? (par. 11)
4. What point does Barry make with his punchline, "None of this was possible just 15 years ago"? (par. 11)

Understanding the Writer's Techniques

1. Does Barry have a major proposition here? If so, what is it? If not, what is his argument about?
2. Barry's essay is obviously a series of jokes, but it has a serious point. How does Barry make his argument? Outline Barry's essay, listing his main points.
3. What is Barry's tone? Point out the instances when you notice him using irony.
4. Explain how jokes such as Barry's require the use of irony.
5. How does the scenario Barry describes in paragraph 11 help his argument?
6. Analyze Barry's closing. Why is it effective? Why is it funny?
7. How effective is the title of this essay? What does it achieve?

Exploring the Writer's Argument

1. Barry is a well-respected humorist, and his columns are always funny, but some say that his humor can be a little uneven. List at least three places where you think Barry has gone too far in his humor and earns a groan from his reader instead of a laugh. Explain your choices.
2. How does Barry's use of language and sentence structure help him achieve his goals?
3. To what degree is Barry's critique of computers fair? Which is the fairest argument? Which is the silliest complaint?

▶ Ideas for Writing Arguments

Prewriting

What is the worst computer-glitch story you know?

Writing a Guided Argument

Write a humorous essay in which you argue that time-and-labor-saving computers have actually made *students'* lives more difficult.

1. Write your essay with a straightforward style. You should play it straight and allow your content to be funny.
2. Open your essay with the statement, "The computer has been the greatest thing to happen to students since . . ." (write your own comparison—for example, the keg).
3. Support your claim with at least three minor propositions.
4. Model your minor propositions on Barry's, as in paragraph 8.
5. Support your minor propositions by starting seriously and ending absurdly.

6. Balance long paragraphs with occasional short paragraphs.
7. Try to close your essay with a reprise of an earlier joke, as Barry reprises the "bazootiehead" joke.

Thinking, Arguing, and Writing Collaboratively

In small groups, share your stories from the Prewriting assignment, and help each other come up with potential subjects for extended paragraphs. Write the paragraphs, arguing for a lesson that you have learned from a computer-glitch horror story. Exchange the paragraphs with classmates, and give each other comments for revision.

Writing About the Text

On the Web or in the library, look up another two essays written by Dave Barry and compare and contrast them with "ERROR ERROR ERROR." What is consistent in his style? Do you see any differences? Write an essay analyzing the Barry style.

More Writing Ideas

1. Write a journal entry about spell-checkers in which you use as many large words and proper nouns as possible. Type your entry into a word-processing program and run a spell-check program. Accept each of the program's suggestions for spellings. Read your journal entry to the class. How has the spell-checker changed your meaning?
2. In a paragraph, describe how you think the future of entertainment will be affected by the Internet.
3. Write an essay in which you argue that trading music online is either morally wrong or morally acceptable. If necessary, do research to gather evidence for your argument.

BETH BROPHY

Saturday Night and You're All Alone?
Maybe You Need a Cyberdate

A Washington, D.C. journalist who has written for Forbes *magazine and* USA Today, *Beth Brophy is the author of* My Ex-Best Friend *(2003), a mystery novel about a suburban mother who solves a friend's murder. In this selection, which appeared in* U.S. News & World Report *in 1997, Brophy demystifies the subject of online dating by giving her take on everything from safety to the question of whether flirting online is actually cheating.*

▶ Prereading: Thinking About the Essay in Advance

Have you tried online dating? Do you know anyone who has? What was your experience or your friend's experience? Was it a positive one? Negative? Why?

▶ Words to Watch

infatuation (par. 3) romantic obsession
dalliance (par. 5) casual romance
clandestine (par. 6) secret
tryst (par. 6) illicit love affair
relented (par. 6) gave up
paradox (par. 7) something seemingly self-contradictory
personas (par. 7) personalities a person puts forth in front of other people

1   *Forget roses, candlelit dinners, pillow talk—or even two people in the same room. And read on for answers to those burning questions.*

2   **How is cyberdating different from meeting at a club?** It's a lot different. Everybody in cyberspace is tall, thin, blond, and rich—at least in theory. Without physical cues to provide a reality check—how someone looks or speaks, or whether he leaves his dirty socks on the floor—the person on the other end can be imagined as the ideal lover. The blank computer screen becomes a projection for hopes and dreams.

3   **I meet lots of people on the Net, but most of my romances last only a day or two. How come?** It's easy to deceive in cyberspace, but it's also easy to fall into premature intimacy. Revealing secrets to a stranger can be intoxicating and, like most stimulants, dangerous. The Internet "seems to be laced with truth serum," says therapist Marshall Jung, co-author of *Romancing the Net.* "All this truth-telling puts enormous pressure on fledgling relationships." So it's no wonder that the cycle of "love, infatuation, and disappointment may take three weeks," says MIT sociology professor Sherry Turkle, author of *Life on the Screen.*

4   Unlike real time, which involves annoying waits in traffic, time in cyberspace is compressed. Sometimes that leads to impulsive actions. Old-fashioned mail, on the other hand, allows time for reflection, for letting a passionate letter sit overnight, or even for tearing it up.

5   **My husband says I spend too much time online. He's worried I'll find somebody else. Is he a control freak, or what?** The relationship gurus of popular culture disagree as to whether extramarital cyber-romance is cheating or not. John Gray, omnipresent author of the bestseller *Men Are From Mars, Women Are From Venus,* gets huffy about online dalliance. "Indulging in sexual arousal is adultery as far as your partner is concerned,"

- ▶ **Search the Ads**
- ▶ **Canadian Ads**
- ▶ **Power Search**
- ▶ **Member's Tools** NEW!
- ▶ **Post Your Ad**
- ▶ Ads of the Month
  - ▶ **Man**
  - ▶ **Woman**
- ▶ **Free Chat**
- ▶ **FBI Truth Test**
- ▶ **Writing Your Ad**
- ▶ **Relationship Advice**
- ▶ **Message Board**
- ▶ **Related Links**
- ▶ **Testimonials**
- ▶ **Christian Singles**
- ▶ **Jewish Personals**
- ▶ **Adult Personals**
- ▶ **Legal Stuff**
- ▶ **Privacy Policy**
- ▶ **Send Feedback**
- ▶ **Add to Favorites**
- ▶ **Webmasters**
- ▶ **Contact Us**

CyberDating ~ Free Dating Services

... The Largest _Totally Free_ Personals site on the Internet.

Totally Free Dating Services

If someone asks for your money ~ It must not be CyberDating.net!
CyberDating is Free! - Always has been... always will be.
We don't ask for your credit card numbers or your phone number so you don't
have to worry about "hidden charges". All we have are totally free dating
services for singles, so there's nothing to subscribe to. You don't even have
to sign up to look at dating personal ads.

Anna

Quick Search our Singles Database!

I am a: [Man seeking a Woman ▾]

State/Prov/Country: [--- Select one --- ▾]

City/Town: [_____]

Must have Pictures: ☐

[Search!] [Reset]

To perform a more detailed Search Click Here.
To perform a Power Search Click Here.

TJ

What's the Catch? Internet Dating can't be Totally Free!

There is no catch. It's a labor of love! Cyberdating is just a hobby and a
venue for us to display our web development talents. The bit of money that
comes from the banner ads simply covers our Internet charges. So enjoy our
free dating services, and if you like our personals, tell your friends to visit
www.CyberDating.net.

Rio

Any Questions about our Free Dating Services?

If you don't find answers to your questions on our FAQ page, please contact
us here.

Suggest CyberDating to a Friend!

Your Friend's Email Address:

[_____]

[Click Here!]

Julie

Dating Success Stories?

You bet! Click Here to read about men and women that have built great
relationships with singles that they met using a Cyber Dating personal ad.

Don't Want to Become a Dating Club Member?

We don't have "memberships"! CyberDating International allows you both,
post your own personal ad, and to browse our database of singles ads
without the hassle of giving us your personal info. And, since many of the
singles that post ads include their email addresses, you can reply to ads
without worrying about a membership of any kind. Remember to read our
News & Notes for the details on how our totally free match maker system
works.

(Web site www.cyberdating.net)

he says. "It's not innocent and harmless; it's a betrayal." Advice columnist Ann Landers is more pragmatic: "It's not adultery; it's just foolishness," she says, "and a little bit on the sick side."

6   Cyber-romance can strain a marriage, sometimes to the breaking point. One woman, an attractive professional in her mid-30s, compares chat rooms to the temptation of drugs. Her husband's clandestine four-month Internet romance with a married woman living in another state nearly wrecked their 10-year marriage. "He wouldn't have gone to a singles bar. A friend or client might have seen him," she says. When she asked him why their monthly bill for using the Net exceeded $200, she says, her husband told her, "I'm in love with the perfect woman and I'm leaving you." His "true love" was planning to leave her husband, but plans changed following an out-of-state tryst. "Each of them thought the other was the greatest—until they actually met," the woman says. Her husband begged to come back. She relented, and they're now in marriage counseling. So ask yourself why you're spending more time online than with your husband.

7   **I met this woman on the Net two months ago. She thinks I'm "Cowboy," a daring Hollywood stuntman. But really I'm just a quiet, skinny accountant. Now she wants a face to face. Help!** Meet her, come clean, and hope she's been lying, too. As Cowboy's dilemma illustrates, cyberspace can lead to a curious paradox: The anonymity of a computer screen makes people bolder and often leads them to try on more daring personas. At the same time, cyberspace allows users to exert tight control over information flow, which can lead to deception and disappointment. "Online is simply a starting point. You don't already have a relationship. You have a cyberflirtation," says Rosalind Resnick, host of the Web site *LoveSearch.com,* a combination dating site, personal data base, and advice column.

8   **I've been e-mailing somebody for three months who lives 60 miles away. I drop hints about a face to face, but he's slow on the uptake. Should I ask him directly?** Sure, but be prepared for rejection. The sad fact is some people are better suited to being behind the screen—they don't want to reveal themselves in person. "True intimacy is not one aspect of the self, it's all aspects," Turkle says. "They may not be up for the lack of fantasy and the challenge of commitment." If that happens, say goodbye and try again.

9   **I've heard there are weirdos on the Net, like the case of that woman who traded fantasies with a guy in an S&M chat room, met him in person and later was found strangled. Is online romance safe?** Yes, there are some strange people online. But there are weirdos everywhere—in cyberspace, in singles bars, at parties, maybe even in

the apartment next door. For some people, the Net offers an opportunity they despair of finding elsewhere. Melinda Stevenson who works for a Washington, D.C., international organization, says between her age and a long commute that left her exhausted at the end of the day, she'd stopped investing energy in dating. "I'm in my 40s," Stevenson says. "I'd given up."

But then she received an e-mail from "Bob," an avid sailor who   10
lived in the Annapolis area. For six weeks, she and Bob e-mailed daily. Finally, Stevenson says, she "tossed out conventional wisdom" and invited him for dinner. He showed up 30 minutes later bearing "flowers, a bottle of wine, no ax—I checked." Their worst fears about each other (that she would be grossly overweight; that he would sport a comb-over hairdo) didn't materialize. Their first date lasted 10 hours—no touching, but "there was an electric sense between us," she says. After a few hours, he politely inquired if they could "share a bracket" (Web talk for hug). Three weeks later he said, "I love you." And five months after that, he proposed. The couple recently returned from their Hawaiian honeymoon.

I hear the Internet is a good place for shy people to meet others. Is it   11
true? Cyberdating, says Frances Maier, general manager of Match.Com, an online personals ad service, "is not about lonely hearts. The Internet is a screener. Generally, the people on it have higher incomes and better jobs." Some shy people find that the Net allows them to meet someone outside their immediate geographic area. For example, attorney Heather Williams and 911 dispatcher Gerald Harrington, both divorced, lived 200 miles away from each other. After meeting in a chat room in December 1995, they e-mailed for two weeks, then talked on the phone. A month later Harrington drove to meet Williams. "I am a shy person who does not interact with people I do not know," he says, but the opportunity to build a relationship online first smoothed the way. "I felt totally at ease after several minutes and knew this was someone I could feel comfortable with." Within a few months, Harrington packed up his belongings and moved to Hollidaysburg, Pa., to be with Williams. He proposed nine months later. They plan to marry in June.

Sound like a Valentine's Day fairy tale? In cyberspace, just as in face-   12
to-face dating, things often don't work out so perfectly. Luckily, the Internet also has a Web site for divorce.

▶ Building Vocabulary

1. Brophy uses phrases in her essay from the world of computers. Often, when a new technology is adopted, terminology from the technology it replaced seeps into its vocabulary. For example, we still say we "dial" the phone when the phone dial, the rotary phone, is long gone. Find

at least three computer phrases in Brophy's essay with origins outside the world of computers, and explain why you think they were adopted.
2. In her essay, Brophy uses figurative language. In the following sentences, replace the italicized phrases with your own words:
   a. without physical cues to *provide a reality check* (par. 2)
   b. Is he *a control freak,* or what? (par. 5)
   c. I *drop hints* about a *face to face,* but he's *slow on the uptake.* (par. 8)
   d. she'd *stopped investing energy* in dating (par. 9)
   e. that he would *sport* a comb-over hairdo (par. 10)
   f. the opportunity to *build a relationship* online first *smoothed the way* (par. 11)

▶Thinking Critically About the Argument

Understanding the Writer's Argument

1. What is cyberdating?
2. Why can every person on a cyberdate be "the ideal lover"? (par. 2)
3. Why can cyberdating often be so intense and accelerated?
4. Does Brophy think that some online flirting is adultery? Explain.
5. Why is it that dating online makes people "bolder and often leads them to try on more daring personas"? (par. 7)
6. Does Brophy give any examples of success stories online? What are they?
7. In what way is the Internet a "screener"?

Understanding the Writer's Techniques

1. What is Brophy's major proposition? Does she have one? Explain.
2. What are the minor propositions in this essay? Make a list of the points Brophy makes.
3. Why do you think Brophy wrote this essay in the form of an advice column? How does the advice column format act as a series of rhetorical questions? Is it an effective way to cover her topic? Why or why not?
4. Who is Brophy's audience? How does that affect her tone?
5. How important is Brophy's use of quotes from experts in this essay? Do they help to convince you?
6. Evaluate Brophy's conclusion. Why does she end on the note she does? Explain.

Exploring the Writer's Argument

1. How good is Brophy's advice? What would you agree with? Disagree with? What would you add to her discussion? What would you like to see her address that she hasn't touched on?

2. Things move quickly on the Internet. Trends change almost weekly, it seems. Brophy's essay was written in 1997, ages ago in Internet years. Are any of her points outdated (so to speak)? Explain.
3. In paragraph 3, Brophy suggests that the Internet encourages people to tell the truth (too much), and in paragraph 7, she suggests that the Internet encourages people to lie about themselves. Is this a contradiction? Does it affect her argument? How? Explain your answers.

▶ Ideas for Writing Arguments

Prewriting

How has e-mail changed the way people communicate?

Writing a Guided Argument

Write an essay that argues that people should write more letters (snail mail) and less e-mail.

1. Open your essay with an anecdote showing that e-mail can be a problem (for example, a misunderstanding or a message sent in anger).
2. Refer to paragraph 4 in Brophy's essay.
3. Move your argument into an articulation of your major proposition.
4. Offer a minor proposition that supports writing letters.
5. Expand on your idea with examples and other support.
6. Write a minor proposition in which you contrast e-mail with snail mail.
7. Repeat steps 4 through 6.
8. Adopt a tone of authority on the subject.
9. Close your essay with a positive anecdote about snail mail to counterbalance the anecdote you told at the beginning. You may refer to your intro if you like.

Thinking, Arguing, and Writing Collaboratively

In two or three paragraphs, write your own online personal ad. How can you persuade someone to answer your ad, purely through your description of yourself. Write your ad without lying about anything. When you are finished, exchange ads with a classmate. Is your classmate's ad persuasive? How are your ads similar? How are they different?

Writing About the Text

Write an essay that expands on this sentence by Brophy: "The blank computer screen becomes a projection for hopes and dreams."

More Writing Ideas

1. Find and print or cut out 10 personal ads, either from a local paper or online. In your journal, analyze the ads. Do you see any similarities? Differences?
2. Find an advice column in your local paper or online. Pick one of the questions and write your own advice to the writer in an extended paragraph.
3. Write an essay in which you argue that cyberdating is pathetic and that people should seek love in other, more social places.

ANDREW BROWN
The Limits of Freedom

Andrew Brown is a freelance journalist who writes for newspapers in his native England, including the Guardian, *the* Independent, *and the* Times, *as well as such American publications as* Vogue, The New York Times Review of Books, *and the online magazine* Salon. *He writes mostly about biology, religion, and technology, although he does not limit himself to those topics. He is the author of* Watching the Detectives *(1988), about the London police department,* The Darwin Wars *(2001), and, most recently,* In the Beginning Was the Worm *(2003), about the 30-year struggle to decode the complete DNA of a nematode worm. In this selection from* New Statesman, *Brown looks at the Internet and concludes that, sometimes, censorship is warranted.*

▶ Prereading: Thinking About the Essay in Advance

Do you think freedom of speech, as protected in the First Amendment to the United States Constitution, is absolute, or are there times when it must be limited?

▶ Words to Watch

libertarian (par. 1) one who believes in absolute liberty
perpetrators (par. 1) ones who committed a crime
mangled (par. 2) bent and broken
foetuses (par. 2) unborn child, also spelled "fetuses"
secular (par. 4) unrelated to religion
provenance (par. 5) origin, source
niggardly (par. 6) without generosity
stultifying (par. 6) causing stupidity
deprave (par. 7) make morally sick
subtle (par. 8) less forceful

There are two general truths about attitudes to *censoring* the Internet.   1
The first is that hardly anyone admits to favouring it in principle. The
second is that whoever you are, and however libertarian, it should never
take more than five minutes at the keyboard to find something you believe should be removed from the net, and its perpetrators locked up in a
criminal lunatic asylum.

Most of the truly disgusting stuff I have come across has been reli-   2
gious in inspiration: the Nuremberg Files website, whose perpetrators
were fined $100 million by an Oregon jury last week, is one example. This
is a site on which pictures of mangled foetuses mingle with photographs
of doctors, usually framed by a line which increasingly drips blood. The
doctors' names and addresses are published, and if they are murdered by
anti-abortion fanatics, then an "X" is placed in front of their photographs.

This sort of thing may not harm children, but it clearly acts to cor-   3
rupt and deprave the adults who take it seriously. The charmingly
named www.godhatesfags.com stops short of incitement to murder,
but it is not much of an advertisement for homo sapiens. There are also
the various Holocaust-denying sites and the aryan churches of Idaho
and western Montana.

Still, my collection of offensive religious sites is probably the result of   4
a sampling error. I have a professional interest in being shocked by believers. A more balanced person could find plenty of secular things to
censor: as well as the fairly obvious child porn there are some truly gut-
wrenchingly awful displays of pornography with adults, too; and once a
month someone with an account at the University of Michigan posts detailed and completely humourless instructions on how to have sexual in-
tercourse with dogs and ponies (there's also something called "scaly sex,"
which I have not read up).

The provenance of these messages shows the first difficulty with   5
censoring the Internet, which is that the First Amendment is held to allow anyone in a university to say anything at all. One might ask why
American laws should apply in this country, or in Germany, and the answer is simple brute force. The only way you can enforce rules about the
content of a website is by physically controlling it. Since it is trivially
easy for anyone with Internet access to rent a website in the USA, it is
American laws and standards that determine what is acceptable around
the world. The result is that you are much more likely to be sent to jail
for having a copy of Windows 98 on your website than a picture of a
woman having sex with a pig. If there were a child involved, you might
get into as much trouble but there wouldn't be nearly as many lawyers
hunting you down.

The paradox in this is that individual American communities are ex-   6
tremely censorious: that is why American network television, which must
appeal to all of them, is so bland, and why American textbooks, which
dare not offend parents, are even worse for children than television is. But

while almost every American community is in favour of censorship, or at least savage sanctions against unpopular speech, they all disapprove of different things. Some want to keep Darwin out of the schoolroom; others would sack people for saying "niggardly." So the choice seems to lie between complete licence and stultifying conformity. Either you offend almost all community standards, or none.

7   If there has to be a choice, I would rather, I suppose, have anarchy than inoffensiveness. I make my living from words, and I would not want this trade threatened by a prison sentence just because I offended someone; and this would be the natural reflex of most of the people who write about the subject. But on reflection, it's less clear that we ought to be so smug. If words could not deprave and corrupt when abused, why would we bother using them in the first place? I'd still rather not suffer for my opinions, but I do hope that they can make my enemies wish I were suffering.

8   The libertarian case relies on a distinction between speech and act which is really quite hard to sustain when you look at it closely. An economist would point out that a journalist actually makes his living delivering readers to advertisers. This is true even when the advertisements are a great deal more subtle than simply crossing out the photographs of murdered doctors. No one who visited the Nuremberg Files site could have been in any doubt about the intention of the pictures and phone numbers there. There are times when censorship is a victory for civilisation: if speech is completely free, it is also valueless.

▶ Building Vocabulary

Use a dictionary to look up any unfamiliar words in the phrases below from Brown's essay. Write a short explanation of each expression.

1. religious in inspiration (par. 2)
2. incitement to murder (par. 3)
3. Holocaust-denying (par. 3)
4. sampling error (par. 4)
5. gut-wrenchingly (par. 4)
6. brute force (par. 5)
7. sack people (par. 6)
8. natural reflex (par. 7)

▶ Thinking Critically About the Argument

Understanding the Writer's Argument

1. What kinds of Web sites does Brown think warrant removal from the Internet?
2. Why does American law seem to dominate Internet law?
3. Why, according to Brown, are American television and textbooks so "bland"?

4. What are the implications of the blandness of American TV for the Internet?

5. Why would Brown rather "have anarchy than inoffensiveness"? (par. 7)

6. What is the "libertarian case" for not censoring the Internet?

Understanding the Writer's Techniques

1. What is Brown's major proposition? Where is it in the essay? Does he place it effectively? Why do you think he places it where he does?

2. What are Brown's minor propositions? Make a list of his points.

3. Analyze Brown's tone. How would you characterize it? Explain.

4. How well does Brown use transitions in his essay? Could you improve them? How?

5. Paraphrase Brown's argument in paragraph 5. Is it easy to understand? Why or why not? Explain.

6. How effective is Brown's conclusion?

Exploring the Writer's Argument

1. In paragraphs 2, 3, and 4, Brown gives examples of "disgusting stuff" on the Internet, both religious and secular. How do the materials he cites compare with each other? In other words, are they all equally disgusting? What is Brown's strategy here? Analyze these paragraphs and decide if, logically, his use of examples is coherent. Explain your answer.

2. Analyze Brown's argument in paragraph 6. Do you agree with his conclusion about American communities being censorious, that "Either you offend almost all community standards, or none"? Explain what he means and why he is right or wrong.

3. What is Brown's standard, finally, for censorship? Does he ever say? Why or why not? What programs on TV or movies or radio programs do you think Brown would want to censor, and why?

4. Brown's conclusion says that "the libertarian case relies on a distinction between speech and act which is really quite hard to sustain when you look at it closely." Do you agree with his assessment of the libertarian case? Does Brown's argument rely on the libertarian case being weak? Explain your answers fully.

▶ Ideas for Writing Arguments

Prewriting

If Brown is right, why are Americans both against censorship and for censorship? Is it something specific in the American character? Is it based in American history? Explain.

Writing a Guided Argument

Write an essay titled "The Limits of . . ." in which you argue that limits should be placed on common elements in American life (for example, television, fast food, or the use of gasoline).

1. Begin your essay with an analysis of Americans' complicated relationship with your topic.
2. Analyze in a cursory way the various negative aspects of your chosen topic.
3. Write your major proposition clearly.
4. Offer at least three minor propositions.
5. Support your minor propositions with examples and narratives that highlight the reason why that product or activity should be curtailed.
6. Suggest a solution for the problem you have analyzed.
7. Write in a tone of cynical disgust.
8. Use effective transitions to build coherence.
9. Close your essay by stating that your solution will help America be more of what it can be.

Thinking, Arguing, and Writing Collaboratively

Write an extended paragraph explaining why Americans are so interested in their right of free speech. There are countries in the world that do not allow their citizens to speak out against the government. Americans have the right to say anything we want against the government. Why are we so concerned with fighting for peoples' rights to post animal pornography? When you are finished with your paragraph, exchange it with someone else in the class and ask for comments on your paper.

Writing About the Text

Brown's argument is filled with an undercurrent of cynicism. Write an essay analyzing Brown's use of cynicism, explaining how that aspect of his essay helps or hurts the force of his argument.

More Writing Ideas

1. Find a widely used textbook in American elementary schools to teach history. Flip through it and write a journal entry about what in the textbook Brown would consider "even worse for children than television is." (par. 6)
2. Web sites devoted to health are popular, but they have been heavily criticized. Investigate the controversy, and write an extended paragraph that argues that online health sites shouldn't have diagnostic information on them.
3. In her essay, Levine writes that much on the Internet is junk. Write an essay that compares and contrasts Brown's argument with Levine's.

11 Work, Money, and Class: Who Benefits?

As economists tell us, the middle class in the United States is shrinking and the gulf that has always existed between the rich and the poor is getting wider. The rich are getting richer, the poor are getting poorer, and everybody is trying to figure out why. Although politicians pass tax cuts or raise and lower interest rates to help the economy, people suffer from poverty in our own country. Meanwhile, while poverty rises, Americans are still working harder. While many Europeans have 35-hour work-weeks and four weeks of vacation a year, Americans are veritable workaholics. Although officially, we have a 40-hour workweek in this country, it is not unusual for people to work 50-, 60-, even 70-hour weeks on a regular basis.

How do our attitudes toward work and working affect our policies and our lives? In "The Case Against Chores," novelist Jane Smiley takes a leisurely look at how one's feelings toward work develop at home. She raises the interesting point that many people don't love what they do because they are taught not to as children. Conservative writer David Brooks takes on a mystery, explaining patiently in "The Triumph of Hope over Self-Interest" why the middle-class and poor don't vote for politicians who might make their lives easier. He argues that we just don't want to believe that we're not rich. If you criticize the wealthy, you criticize us all, this argument goes, because we all want to see ourselves as rich people. Some writers use their pen to try to expose what they see as injustice and inequality. Herbert J. Gans, in "Fitting the Poor into the Economy," doesn't like the attitude of Americans toward the poor. He says we have a notion of the poor as "too lazy or morally deficient to deserve assistance," an attitude, in Gans's opinion, that causes needless suffering. In "Vanishing Jobs," Jeremy Rifkin explores another aspect of the changing economy, the rise of computers as a way of life. He argues that we can't have blind faith in technology and progress, but that people inevitably get left behind. These four writers, all writing on a similar topic, show the range of approaches to the timeless issues of work, money, and class.

JANE SMILEY
The Case Against Chores

Novelist Jane Smiley was born in Los Angeles in 1950 and was reared near St. Louis, Missouri. She was educated at Vassar College and the Writer's Workshop at the University of Iowa. Her novels include The Age of Grief *(1987),* A Thousand Acres *(1991), for which she won the Pulitzer Prize for fiction, and* Horse Heaven *(2000). She has written for many publications, including* The New Yorker, The New York Times Magazine, The Nation, *and, reflecting her interest in horses,* Practical Horseman. *This selection appeared in* Harper's *in 1995 and has an argument that most children would celebrate.*

▶ Prereading: Thinking About the Essay in Advance

How can parents raise their children to appreciate the value of work? Do you know anyone who loves work? Hates work? Which applies to you?

▶ Words to Watch

unrelenting (par. 1) not weakening in force
gleaned (par. 2) found out
pastimes (par. 2) activities
alienated (par. 2) separated from one's true interests
tack (par. 5) put on a horse's saddle and bridle
bales (par. 5) piles
humaneness (par. 5) basic kindness

1   I've lived in the upper Midwest for twenty-one years now, and I'm here to tell you that the pressure to put your children to work is unrelenting. So far I've squirmed out from under it, and my daughters have led a life of almost tropical idleness, much to their benefit. My son, however, may not be so lucky. His father was himself raised in Iowa and put to work at an early age, and you never know when, in spite of all my husband's best intentions, that early training might kick in.

2   Although "chores" are so sacred in my neck of the woods that almost no one ever discusses their purpose, I have over the years gleaned some of the reasons parents give for assigning them. I'm not impressed. Mostly the reasons have to do with developing good work habits or, in the absence of good work habits, at least habits of working. No such thing as a free lunch, any job worth doing is worth doing right, work before play, all of that. According to this reasoning, the world is full of jobs that no one wants to do. If we divide them up and get them over with, then we can go on to pastimes we like. If we do them "right," then we won't have to do them again. Lots of times, though, in a family, that *we* doesn't operate.

The operative word is *you*. The practical result of almost every child-labor scheme that I've witnessed is the child doing the dirty work and the parent getting the fun: Mom cooks and Sis does the dishes; the parents plan and plant the garden, the kids weed it. To me, what this teaches the child is the lesson of alienated labor: not to love the work but to get it over with; not to feel pride in one's contribution but to feel resentment at the waste of one's time.

Another goal of chores: The child contributes to the work of main-   3
taining the family. According to this rationale, the child comes to understand what it takes to have a family, and to feel that he or she is an important, even indispensable member of it. But come on. Would you really want to feel loved primarily because you're the one who gets the floors mopped? Wouldn't you rather feel that your family's love simply exists all around you, no matter what your contribution? And don't the parents love their children anyway, whether the children vacuum or not? Why lie about it just to get the housework done? Let's be frank about the other half of the equation too. In this day and age, it doesn't take much work at all to manage a household, at least in the middle class—maybe four hours a week to clean the house and another four to throw the laundry into the washing machine, move it to the dryer, and fold it. Is it really a good idea to set the sort of example my former neighbors used to set, of mopping the floor every two days, cleaning the toilets every week, vacuuming every day, dusting, dusting, dusting? Didn't they have anything better to do than serve their house?

Let me confess that I wasn't expected to lift a finger when I was grow-   4
ing up. Even when my mother had a full-time job, she cleaned up after me, as did my grandmother. Later there was a housekeeper. I would leave my room in a mess when I headed off for school and find it miraculously neat when I returned. Once in a while I vacuumed, just because I liked the pattern the Hoover made on the carpet. I did learn to run water in my cereal bowl before setting it in the sink.

Where I discovered work was at the stable, and, in fact, there is no   5
housework like horsework. You've got to clean the horses' stalls, feed them, groom them, tack them up, wrap their legs, exercise them, turn them out, and catch them. You've got to clip them and shave them. You have to sweep the aisle, clean your tack and your boots, carry bales of hay and buckets of water. Minimal horsekeeping, rising just to the level of humaneness, requires many more hours than making a few beds, and horsework turned out to be a good preparation for the real work of adulthood, which is rearing children. It was a good preparation not only because it was similar in many ways but also because my desire to do it, and to do a good job of it, grew out of my love of and interest in my horse. I can't say that cleaning out her bucket when she manured in it was an actual joy, but I knew she wasn't going to do it herself. I saw the purpose of my labor, and I wasn't alienated from it.

6   Probably to the surprise of some of those who knew me as a child, I have turned out to be gainfully employed. I remember when I was in seventh grade, one of my teachers said to me, strongly disapproving, "The trouble with you is you do only what you want to do!" That continues to be the trouble with me, except that over the years I have wanted to do more and more.

7   My husband worked hard as a child, out-Iowa-ing the Iowans, if such a thing is possible. His dad had him mixing cement with a stick when he was five, pushing wheelbarrows not long after. It's a long sad tale on the order of two miles to school and both ways uphill. The result is, he's a great worker, much better than I am, but all the while he's doing it he wishes he weren't. He thinks of it as work; he's torn between doing a good job and longing not to be doing it at all. Later, when he's out on the golf course, where he really wants to be, he feels a little guilty, knowing there's work that should have been done before he gave in and took advantage of the beautiful day.

8   Good work is not the work we assign children but the work they want to do, whether it's reading in bed (where would I be today if my parents had rousted me out and put me to scrubbing floors?) or cleaning their rooms or practicing the flute or making roasted potatoes with rosemary and Parmesan for the family dinner. It's good for a teenager to suddenly decide that the bathtub is so disgusting she'd better clean it herself. I admit that for the parent, this can involve years of waiting. But if she doesn't want to wait, she can always spend her time dusting.

▶ Building Vocabulary

Explain these colloquialisms in Smiley's essay:

1. that early training might kick in (par. 1)
2. in my neck of the woods (par. 2)
3. I wasn't expected to lift a finger (par. 4)
4. I have turned out to be gainfully employed (par. 6)
5. he's torn between doing a good job (par. 7)

▶ Thinking Critically About the Argument

Understanding the Writer's Argument

1. Why have Smiley's daughters got away with not doing any work, and why might her son not be so lucky?
2. What are the reasons people give chores to their children?
3. What does Smiley think is the result of giving kids the dirty work in a job?
4. What is "alienated labor"?
5. What is Smiley's answer to the rationale that putting kids to work "contributes to the work of maintaining the family"? (par. 3)

6. What activity kept Smiley from being alienated from work? How did this happen?
7. What was Smiley's husband's childhood like? What has been the result, as it relates to his work habits?

Understanding the Writer's Techniques

1. What is the major proposition of this essay?
2. This essay appeared in *Harper's,* a magazine that attracts a highly educated, relatively wealthy readership. How does that fact affect the writer's tone?
3. How does Smiley attempt to appeal to her readers' emotions in this essay?
4. How does Smiley rebut the arguments in favor of giving chores to children? How effective are her rebuttals?
5. What minor propositions does Smiley offer to support her argument against chores?
6. Which is Smiley's strongest paragraph? Explain your response.
7. Smiley writes about a subject she loves, horses, in paragraph 5. Analyze her use of language in that paragraph. How does she make the paragraph effective?
8. How effective is Smiley's conclusion? Explain.

Exploring the Writer's Argument

1. Smiley admits in paragraph 4 that the very thing she's arguing for is how she was raised. Does that make her argument suspect? Why or why not? If so, how? If not, how does she overcome that limitation in her argument?
2. Smiley writes at the beginning of her essay that her daughters "have led a life of almost tropical idleness." Later, at the end of her essay, she writes that kids should do work that is good for them (i.e., that doesn't alienate them from the work). Are these two statements contradictory? Why or why not?
3. Smiley writes that she lives in the Midwest, and she seems to imply that this is important to her argument. Do you think it is? Explain where she refers to her geographical location and how she makes her essay universal despite this focus.

▶ Ideas for Writing Arguments

Prewriting

Jot some notes on the following questions: What did your parents, grandparents, or other family members do during your upbringing that you don't agree with? What did they do right?

Writing a Guided Argument

In her essay, Smiley is giving parental advice. Write an essay with the title "The Case Against . . ." in which you argue that parents should avoid doing something that you don't agree with. For example, argue against spankings, letting kids go out on bicycle rides by themselves, or attending rap concerts.

1. Begin your essay by explaining your own personal relationship with your chosen subject.
2. In the next section, lay out at least two arguments the opposition might have.
3. Write your major proposition.
4. Rebut the arguments with effective support.
5. Adopt an informal tone, much like Smiley's.
6. About halfway through your argument, write a personal reminiscence that illustrates the correct way to go about things.
7. Offer at least two minor propositions to support your argument.
8. Close your essay with a discussion of how you will approach the rearing of your children in relation to this topic.

Thinking, Arguing, and Writing Collaboratively

In groups of four or five, discuss alternate opposition arguments from those you present in your Writing a Guided Argument essay, and come up with possible rebuttals. Jot down notes and incorporate them into your essay's final draft.

Writing About the Text

Write an essay in which you analyze Smiley's informal style. What is informal here? How does she keep the reader relaxed? How does the fact that Smiley is a novelist come through in the essay?

More Writing Ideas

1. In your journal, freewrite about this topic: fun work. Do not edit your writing. Write for at least 15 minutes. When you are done, read over your unedited writing to see if there are any propositions that could be used as the basis for an essay.
2. What are your feelings about those people who have domestic help, such as maids, butlers, and chauffeurs? Is it really necessary to have that kind of help? Write an extended paragraph on the topic.
3. Write an essay in which you argue that children should stop receiving an allowance at age 14 and work for their own money.

DAVID BROOKS
The Triumph of Hope Over Self-Interest

David Brooks is a senior editor at the conservative magazine The Weekly Standard *and is the author of* Bobos in Paradise: The New Upper Class and How They Got There, *which was published in 2001. He is also a contributing editor at* Newsweek *and the* Atlantic Monthly, *writes for* The New York Times Magazine, *and recently began a twice weekly column in* The New York Times. *He is also a regular commentator on National Public Radio. He was educated at the University of Chicago, and started his career as a newspaper reporter. In this selection, Brooks explains why people don't vote for politicians who support policies that will help them.*

▶ Prereading: Thinking About the Essay in Advance

What are your feelings about those who are more wealthy than you are? Do you envy them? Do you want to be like them? Do you resent them? Why do you react as you do?

▶ Words to Watch

populist (par. 2) appealing to the common people
overdetermined (par. 3) having many reasons
savaged (par. 5) destroyed
appointed (par. 7) furnished
resentment (par. 8) feeling of anger and being injured
sommeliers (par. 10) waiter in a restaurant who helps customers choose wine
eau (par. 10) French for "water"
subsumes (par. 18) overwhelms

Why don't people vote their own self-interest? Every few years the Republicans propose a tax cut, and every few years the Democrats pull out their income distribution charts to show that much of the benefits of the Republican plan go to the richest 1 percent of Americans or thereabouts. And yet every few years a Republican plan wends its way through the legislative process and, with some trims and amendments, passes.   1

The Democrats couldn't even persuade people to oppose the repeal of the estate tax, which is explicitly for the mega-upper class. Al Gore, who ran a populist campaign, couldn't even win the votes of white males who didn't go to college, whose incomes have stagnated over the past decades and who were the explicit targets of his campaign. Why don't more Americans want to distribute more wealth down to people like themselves?   2

3   Well, as the academics would say, it's overdetermined. There are several reasons.

4   **People vote their aspirations.**

5   The most telling polling result from the 2000 election was from a *Time* magazine survey that asked people if they are in the top 1 percent of earners. Nineteen percent of Americans say they are in the richest 1 percent and a further 20 percent expect to be someday. So right away you have 39 percent of Americans who thought that when Mr. Gore savaged a plan that favored the top 1 percent, he was taking a direct shot at them.

6   It's not hard to see why they think this way. Americans live in a culture of abundance. They have always had a sense that great opportunities lie just over the horizon, in the next valley, with the next job or the next big thing. None of us is really poor; we're just pre-rich.

7   Americans read magazines for people more affluent than they are (*W, Cigar Aficionado, The New Yorker, Robb Report, Town and Country*) because they think that someday they could be that guy with the tastefully appointed horse farm. Democratic politicians proposing to take from the rich are just bashing the dreams of our imminent selves.

8   **Income resentment is not a strong emotion in much of America.**

9   If you earn $125,000 a year and live in Manhattan, certainly, you are surrounded by things you cannot afford. You have to walk by those buildings on Central Park West with the 2,500-square-foot apartments that are empty three-quarters of the year because their evil owners are mostly living at their other houses in L.A.

10   But if you are a middle-class person in most of America, you are not brought into incessant contact with things you can't afford. There aren't Lexus dealerships on every corner. There are no snooty restaurants with water sommeliers to help you sort though the bottled eau selections. You can afford most of the things at Wal-Mart or Kohl's and the occasional meal at the Macaroni Grill. Moreover, it would be socially unacceptable for you to pull up to church in a Jaguar or to hire a caterer for your dinner party anyway. So you are not plagued by a nagging feeling of doing without.

11   **Many Americans admire the rich.**

12   They don't see society as a conflict zone between the rich and poor. It's taboo to say in a democratic culture, but do you think a nation that watches Katie Couric in the morning, Tom Hanks in the evening and Michael Jordan on weekends harbors deep animosity toward the affluent?

13   On the contrary. I'm writing this from Nashville, where one of the richest families, the Frists, is hugely admired for its entrepreneurial skill and community service. People don't want to tax the Frists—they want to elect them to the Senate. And they did.

14   Nor are Americans suffering from false consciousness. You go to a town where the factories have closed and people who once earned $14 an hour now work for $8 an hour. They've taken their hits. But odds are you

will find their faith in hard work and self-reliance undiminished, and their suspicion of Washington unchanged.

Americans resent social inequality more than income inequality.   15

As the sociologist Jennifer Lopez has observed: "Don't be fooled by   16
the rocks that I got, I'm just, I'm just Jenny from the block." As long as rich people "stay real," in Ms. Lopez's formulation, they are admired. Meanwhile, middle-class journalists and academics who seem to look down on megachurches, suburbia and hunters are resented. If Americans see the tax debate as being waged between the economic elite, led by President Bush, and the cultural elite, led by Barbra Streisand, they are going to side with Mr. Bush, who could come to any suburban barbershop and fit right in.

Most Americans do not have Marxian categories in their heads.   17

This is the most important reason Americans resist wealth redistribu-   18
tion, the reason that subsumes all others. Americans do not see society as a layer cake, with the rich on top, the middle class beneath them and the working class and underclass at the bottom. They see society as a high school cafeteria, with their community at one table and other communities at other tables. They are pretty sure that their community is the nicest, and filled with the best people, and they have a vague pity for all those poor souls who live in New York City or California and have a lot of money but no true neighbors and no free time.

All of this adds up to a terrain incredibly inhospitable to class-based   19
politics. Every few years a group of millionaire Democratic presidential aspirants pretends to be the people's warriors against the overclass. They look inauthentic, combative rather than unifying. Worst of all, their basic message is not optimistic.

They haven't learned what Franklin and Teddy Roosevelt and even   20
Bill Clinton knew: that you can run against rich people, but only those who have betrayed the ideal of fair competition. You have to be more hopeful and growth-oriented than your opponent, and you cannot imply that we are a nation tragically and permanently divided by income. In the gospel of America, there are no permanent conflicts.

▶ Building Vocabulary

Write out definitions for the following words from Brook's essay, and use them each in a sentence:

1. stagnated (par. 2)
2. abundance (par. 6)
3. affluent (par. 7)
4. imminent (par. 7)
5. incessant (par. 10)
6. taboo (par. 12)

7. animosity (par. 12)
8. aspirants (par. 19)

▶Thinking Critically About the Argument

Understanding the Writer's Argument

1. Why do Republicans want to cut the taxes of the richest 1 percent of Americans?
2. What is the estate tax? Who benefits from it?
3. Why do so many Americans think they're in the richest 1 percent? What does Brooks mean when he says that "none of us is really poor; we're just pre-rich"? (par. 6)
4. Why, according to Brooks, do Americans admire the rich?
5. What does Brooks mean by "Marxian categories"? (par. 17)
6. What, according to Brooks, did Franklin Roosevelt, Teddy Roosevelt, and Bill Clinton know that made them popular politicians?
7. What is the "gospel of America"? (par. 20)

Understanding the Writer's Techniques

1. What is Brooks's major proposition in this essay?
2. Why does Brooks start with a question?
3. Brooks only uses one statistic in his essay, the *Time* poll. Is this single information enough to help his case? Explain.
4. Does Brooks put his minor propositions in any strategic order? Explain.
5. Brooks uses causal analysis. How does he manage to use that rhetorical mode within his argument? Is it effective?
6. What is the argumentative effect of Brooks's section headings? Do they help or hurt his argument?
7. Analyze Brooks's analogies in paragraph 18. Are they effective? Why or why not?
8. How well done is Brooks's conclusion? What is its strongest element?

Exploring the Writer's Argument

1. Brooks is a conservative, yet he seems to work in this essay to give away one of the secrets of the Republican party's success: that often people who should vote Democratic do not. Why would he want to expose this secret?
2. In his essay, Brooks uses many vivid examples. Choose at least three that you find particularly effective and explain your choices.
3. Do you agree with Brooks's argument in paragraph 10 that people in middle-class America outside of New York City do not resent rich people? Why or why not?

▶ Ideas for Writing Arguments

Prewriting

Are there any activities you take part in regularly that you know are counterproductive to your safety or health or to the safety or health of other people? Jot down some ideas for an essay on the topic.

Writing a Guided Argument

Write an essay that attempts to explain why someone might take part in an activity that not everyone would understand. For example, explain why people still smoke although they know it is bad for them or why people live in cities that are often hit with natural disasters.

1. Begin your essay with a rhetorical question.
2. Describe the activity you are going to explain.
3. State your major proposition.
4. Offer at least three reasons why people take part in the activity you've chosen to write about.
5. After each reason, support the idea with evidence in the form of examples.
6. In the next section, offer a solution to the problem: How can one stop doing the activity?
7. Close with a switch to a neutral, detached discussion of the issue.

Thinking, Arguing, and Writing Collaboratively

In groups of four or five, study one of the magazines Brooks mentions in paragraph 7, or find another magazine geared for a luxury readership. Each group should examine a different magazine. What images support Brooks's position that middle-class readers essentially are "wannabes" who see themselves in the places of the rich? Discuss the images, and present your findings to the class.

Writing About the Text

Write an essay that analyzes Brooks's use of irony. Choose at least three passages from Brooks's essay that you find particularly ironic. Explain how what Brooks says and what he means are two different things. How does irony fit into Brooks's overall tone, and how effective is it?

More Writing Ideas

1. In your journal, illustrate at least three times in the past few days when you observed class to be an issue between two or more people.
2. Write a paragraph or two that explores celebrity worship in our culture as the worship of the rich.
3. In an essay, argue that Americans should be more class conscious, and explain how this might come about.

HERBERT J. GANS

Fitting the Poor into the Economy

Herbert J. Gans, a professor of sociology at Columbia University, was born in Germany in 1927. The rise of the Nazis caused his family to flee to England in 1938. Gans came to America in 1940 and subsequently became a U.S. citizen. He went to the University of Chicago and then earned a Ph.D. at the University of Pennsylvania. He has been a professor at Pennsylvania Teachers College and M.I.T. Gans has written a number of books about class and culture in America, including The Levittowners *(1967),* People and Plans *(1968),* Popular Culture and High Culture *(1974),* Deciding What's News *(1979),* The War Against the Poor *(1995), and* Making Sense of America *(1999). In this selection, Gans examines the attitudes Americans have about the poor, especially the way in which people blame the poor for their own poverty.*

▶ Prereading: Thinking About the Essay in Advance

What are the reasons for poverty in a rich country like America? Do people blame the poor for their poverty? Are there any realistic solutions to the problem?

▶ Words to Watch

allocations (par. 1) money given for a specific purpose
affluent (par. 1) wealthy
onus (par. 2) responsibility
scapegoats (par. 2) those falsely blamed for a problem
antidote (par. 4) solution to a problem
inroads (par. 6) progress
paltry (par. 7) small, insignificant
dereliction (par. 8) serious shortcoming
spawned (par. 11) been the source for
utopian (par. 11) unrealistically idealistic

1   The notion of the poor as too lazy or morally deficient to deserve assistance seems to be indestructible. Public policies limit poor people to substandard services and incomes below the subsistence level, and Congress and state legislatures are tightening up even on these miserly allocations—holding those in the "underclass" responsible for their own sorry state. Indeed, labeling the poor as undeserving has lately become politically useful as a justification for the effort to eliminate much of the antipoverty safety net and permit tax cuts for the affluent people who do most of the voting.

Such misplaced blame offers mainstream society a convenient eva-   2
sion of its own responsibility. Blaming poor men and women for not
working, for example, takes the onus off both private enterprise and government for failing to supply employment. It is easier to charge poor unmarried mothers with lacking family values than to make sure that there
are jobs for them and for the young men who are not marriageable because they are unable to support families. Indeed, the poor make excellent scapegoats for a range of social problems, such as street crime and
drug and alcohol addiction. Never mind the reversal of cause and effect
that underlies this point of view—for centuries crime, alcoholism, and
single motherhood have risen whenever there has not been enough work
and income to go around.

The undeserving underclass is also a useful notion for employers as   3
the economy appears to be entering a period of long-term stagnation. Jobs
are disappearing—some displaced by labor-saving technologies, others
exported to newly industrializing, low-wage countries, others lost as
companies "downsize" to face tougher global competition. Indeed, the
true rate of unemployment—which includes involuntary part-time workers and long-term "discouraged" workers who have dropped out of the
job market altogether—has remained in double digits for more than a
generation and no longer seems to drop during times of economic
strength. Labeling poor people as lacking the needed work ethic is a politically simple way of shedding them from a labor market that will most
likely never need them again.

The most efficient antidote to poverty is not welfare but full employ-   4
ment. In the short run, therefore, today's war against the poor should be
replaced with efforts to create jobs for now-surplus workers. New Deal–
style programs of large-scale governmental employment, for example,
can jump-start a slow economy. Besides being the fastest way to put people to work, a public-works program can improve the country's infrastructure, including highways, buildings, parks, and computer databases.

In addition, private enterprise and government should aim to stimu-   5
late the most promising labor-intensive economic activities and stop encouraging new technology that will further destroy jobs—reviving, for
example, the practice of making cars and appliances partly by hand. A
parallel policy would tax companies for their use of labor-saving technology; the revenues from this tax would pay for alternative jobs for people
in occupations that technology renders obsolete. This idea makes good
business as well as social sense: human workers are needed as customers
for the goods that machines now produce.

To distribute the jobs that do exist among more people, employers   6
could shorten the work day, week, or year. Several large manufacturing
companies in Western Europe already use worksharing to create a 35-hour
week. Making significant inroads on U.S. joblessness may require reducing the work week to 30 hours.

7   A more generous welfare system would go a long way toward solving the problems of the remainder: those who cannot work or cannot find jobs. By persisting in the belief that poor people deserve their fate, society can easily justify a paltry and demeaning welfare system that pays recipients only about one-quarter of the median income. A system that paid closer to half the median income, by contrast, would enable those without work to remain full members of society and thus minimize the despair, anger, and various illnesses, as well as premature mortality, distinctive to the poor.

8   For such antipoverty policies to gain acceptance, mainstream America will have to unlearn the stereotype of poor people as immoral. Most of the poor are just as law-abiding as everyone else. (While a minority of poor people cheat on their welfare applications, an even larger minority of affluent people cheat on their tax returns—yet the notion of undeservingness is never applied to the middle or upper classes.) In admitting that the phenomena now explained as moral dereliction are actually traceable to poverty, Americans will force themselves to find solutions, not scapegoats, to the country's problems.

9   Most of the people assigned to today's undeserving underclass are the first victims of what is already being called the future "jobless economy." In the long run, if the cancer of joblessness spreads more widely among the population, large numbers of the present middle class will have to adapt to the reality that eventually most workers may no longer be employed full time. In that case, more drastic job-creation policies will be needed, including a ban on additional job-destroying technology and the establishment of permanent public employment modeled on the kind now associated with military spending. Worksharing would most likely be based on a 24-hour week.

10   At that point, everyone would in fact be working part time by today's standards, and new ways to maintain standards of living would have to be found. One approach, already being discussed in Europe, is a universal, subsistence-level income grant. This "demogrant," a twenty-first-century version of the $1,000-per-person allotment that presidential candidate George McGovern proposed in 1972, would be taxed away from people still working full time. In any case, private and government agencies should begin now to study what policies might be needed to preserve the American way of life when the full-time job will no longer be around to pay for the American Dream.

11   It is possible, of course, that new sources of economic growth will suddenly develop to revive the full employment and prosperity of the post–World War II decades. And some labor-saving technologies may, in the long run, create more jobs than they destroy; that may well be the case for computers, which have spawned a large sector of the economy. Such happy outcomes cannot be counted on to materialize, however, and there remains the danger that the war on the poor will continue as the politically most convenient path. We will undoubtedly find that when the

economy begins to threaten the descendants of today's middle and even affluent classes with becoming poor, and then "undeserving," policies that today seem utopian will be demanded, and quickly.

▶ Building Vocabulary

This selection assumes a general familiarity with basic economic and political terms and concepts. Identify and write definitions for the following:

1. subsistence level (par. 1)
2. safety net (par. 1)
3. private enterprise (par. 2)
4. underclass (par. 3)
5. stagnation (par. 3)
6. downsize (par. 3)
7. work ethic (par. 3)
8. welfare (par. 4)
9. New Deal (par. 4)

▶ Thinking Critically About the Argument

Understanding the Writer's Argument

1. What responsibility does Gans say mainstream society has toward the poor? (par. 2)
2. Why, historically, are crime, alcoholism, and single motherhood common?
3. Why is the idea of an "undeserving underclass" something employers can use to shed responsibility, according to Gans?
4. What does Gans suggest in place of welfare, or does he think welfare is all right?
5. What are people on welfare paid in proportion to the average income? What does Gans think welfare recipients should be paid? Why?
6. How can shortening the 40-hour workweek reduce poverty, according to Gans?
7. What is a "demogrant"? How is it designed to help?

Understanding the Writer's Techniques

1. What is Gans's claim? Where does he express it best?
2. What grounds does Gans offer to support his claim?
3. Outline Gans's argument. How does he structure his points?
4. What is the nature of the switch in Gans's argument from paragraph 3 to paragraph 4?

5. How does Gans's position as a professor of sociology at Columbia University, an Ivy League school, help his essay? Explain.
6. What is the author's tone? Explain your answer fully, showing examples from the essay that led to your answer.
7. Is Gans's closing effective? Why or why not?

Exploring the Writer's Argument

1. Gans objects to society blaming the "underclass" for various social problems. He wants to take the responsibility off the poor. Is that, however, considering poor people as children who can't be held accountable for their actions? Is that what he's saying? Explain your answer fully? Do you agree?
2. In his essay (page 269), David Brooks writes about how people don't always act in their own political best interest. Do you see any arguments, implied or overt, in Brooks's essay that could help the poor with the problems Gans identifies? Explain.
3. Gans makes some radical suggestions to improve life in America. Do you think any of his suggestions are feasible? Why or why not?
4. In paragraph 8, Gans writes that if people change their minds about the poor, that will allow new policies to take shape. Do you agree with his assessment? Explain your answer.

▶ Ideas for Writing Arguments

Prewriting

What are the effects, psychologically, of being unemployed? What are the psychological effects of making too little money in a job? Write notes on your thoughts.

Writing a Guided Argument

Write an essay arguing that a New Deal–style project, such as building a hypothetical high-speed highway from Los Angeles to New York (or some other comparably huge project of your own devising) would improve the economy.

1. Open your essay with a discussion of the problems of unemployment and poverty in our society, as described by Gans.
2. Write your major proposition, proposing your project.
3. Offer at least three minor propositions that explain why this project would benefit the economy.
4. Explain the long-term positive economic effects of full employment.
5. Use effective transitions to move from point to point.

6. Predict a possible objection to the project, and rebut that point.
7. Bring your essay to a close by illustrating how your project would provide a great convenience to everyone.

Thinking, Arguing, and Writing Collaboratively

After dividing into four equal groups, have members of each group read their essays from the Writing a Guided Argument assignment out loud. Select your group's strongest essay, and as a group help the writer to improve any weak points. List the strengths of the essay. Read the four strongest essays to the whole class, and discuss the strengths and weaknesses of each.

Writing About the Text

Write an essay that explores the concept of what it means to be "undeserving," as Gans defines it. Is this a useful concept? Does Gans make good use of it in his essay? What does it mean to "deserve" your economic fate? Do we have any control at all? Is there upward mobility in the United States?

More Writing Ideas

1. In your journal, speculate on what it would be like to live in poverty in a wealthy country like the United States.
2. In a paragraph or two, explore the responsibility you have personally as a citizen of this country to the poor of the country.
3. Write an essay in which you argue that the poor are actually *more* moral than the rich in the United States.

JEREMY RIFKIN
Vanishing Jobs

Jeremy Rifkin has made a career out of wide-ranging activism. He is founder and president of the Foundation on Economic Trends, president of the Greenhouse Crisis Foundation, and head of the Beyond Beef Coalition. During the 1960s and 1970s, he was involved in the peace movement, founding the Citizens Commission, which was established to draw the public's attention to abuses of power in the war in Vietnam. Rifkin has also worked to place controls on biotechnology, including genetic engineering. He is the author of The Age of Access (2002). *In the following selection, Rifkin worries that as technology advances, the economy will leave many people, especially the unskilled poor, behind.*

▶ Prereading: Thinking About the Essay in Advance

How has the advent of high technology and the Internet changed the workforce? What does it mean when the government says that jobs have been created or lost?

▶ Words to Watch

sullen (par. 4) depressed
camp (par. 5) kitschy and ironic
malaise (par. 9) feeling of lack of mental wellness
incessantly (par. 11) without stopping
plethora (par. 14) wide variety
bellwether (par. 17) sign of things to come
progressive (par. 30) marked by a belief that government can cause social improvements
venerable (par. 31) respected because of longevity
discourse (par. 31) exchange of ideas
fledgling (par. 35) new

1
2   "Will there be a job for me in the new Information Age?"
       This is the question that most worries American voters—and the question that American politicians seem most determined to sidestep. President Bill Clinton warns workers that they will have to be retrained six or seven times during their work lives to match the dizzying speed of technological change. Speaker of the House Newt Gingrich talks about the "end of the traditional job" and advises every American worker to become his or her own independent contractor.

3   But does the president really think 124 million Americans can reinvent themselves every five years to keep up with a high-tech marketplace? Does Gingrich honestly believe every American can become a freelance entrepreneur, continually hustling contracts for short-term work assignments?

4   Buffeted by these unrealistic employment expectations, American workers are increasingly sullen and pessimistic. Most Americans have yet to recover from the recovery of 1993–1995, which was essentially a "jobless" recovery. While corporate profits are heading through the roof, average families struggle to keep a roof over their heads. More than one-fifth of the workforce is trapped in temporary assignments or works only part time. Millions of others have slipped quietly out of the economy and into an underclass no longer counted in the permanent employment figures. A staggering 15 percent of the population now lives below the official poverty line.

5   Both Clinton and Gingrich have asked American workers to remain patient. They explain that declining incomes represent only short-term adjustments. Democrats and Republicans alike beseech the faithful to

"I've stopped looking for work, which, I believe,
helps the economic numbers."

place their trust in the high-tech future—to journey with them into cyberspace and become pioneers on the new electronic frontier. Their enthusiasm for technological marvels has an almost camp ring to it. If you didn't know better, you might suspect Mickey and Pluto were taking you on a guided tour through the Epcot Center.

Jittery and genuinely confused over the yawning gap between the official optimism of the politicians and their own personal plight, middle- and working-class American families seem to be holding on to a tiny thread of hope that the vast productivity gains of the high-tech revolution will somehow "trickle down" to them in the form of better jobs, wages, and benefits. That thread is likely to break by election time [November 1996] if, as I anticipate, the economy skids right by the soft landing predicted by the Federal Reserve Board and crashes headlong into a deep recession.   6

The Labor Department reported that payrolls sank by 101,000 workers in May 1995 alone—the largest drop in payrolls since April 1991, when the U.S. economy was deep in a recession. In June 1995, overall unemployment remained virtually unchanged, but manufacturing jobs declined by an additional 40,000. At the same time, inventories are up and consumer spending and confidence are down—sure signs of bad economic times ahead.   7

8   The psychological impact of a serious downturn coming so quickly upon the heels of the last one would be devastating. It is likely to set the framework for a politically wild roller-coaster ride for the rest of the 1990s, opening the door not only to new parties but to extralegal forms of politics.

9   Meanwhile, few politicians and economists are paying attention to the underlying causes of—dare we say it—the new "malaise" gripping the country. Throughout the current [1995] welfare reform debate, for example, members of both parties have trotted onto the House and Senate floors to urge an end to welfare and demand that all able-bodied men and women find jobs. Maverick Sen. Paul Simon (D-Ill.) has been virtually alone in raising the troubling question: "What jobs?"

10   The hard reality is that the global economy is in the midst of a transformation as significant as the Industrial Revolution. We are in the early stages of a shift from "mass labor" to highly skilled "elite labor," accompanied by increasing automation in the production of goods and the delivery of services. Sophisticated computers, robots, telecommunications, and other Information Age technologies are replacing human beings in nearly every sector. Factory workers, secretaries, receptionists, clerical workers, salesclerks, bank tellers, telephone operators, librarians, wholesalers, and middle managers are just a few of the many occupations destined for virtual extinction. In the United States alone, as many as 90 million jobs in a labor force of 124 million are potentially vulnerable to displacement by automation.

11   A few mainstream economists pin their hopes on increasing job opportunities in the knowledge sector. Secretary of Labor Robert Reich, for example, talks incessantly of the need for more highly skilled technicians, computer programmers, engineers, and professional workers. He barnstorms the country urging workers to retrain, retool, and reinvent themselves in time to gain a coveted place on the high-tech express.

12   The secretary ought to know better. Even if the entire workforce could be retrained for very skilled, high-tech jobs—which, of course, it can't—there will never be enough positions in the elite knowledge sector to absorb the millions let go as automation penetrates into every aspect of the production process.

13   It's not as if this is a revelation. For years the Alvin Tofflers and the John Naisbitts of the world have lectured the rest of us that the end of the industrial age also means the end of "mass production" and "mass labor," What they never mention is what "the masses" should do after they become redundant.

14   Laura D'Andrea Tyson, who now heads the National Economic Council, argues that the Information Age will bring a plethora of new technologies and products that we can't as yet even anticipate, and therefore it will create many new kinds of jobs. After a debate with me on CNN, Tyson noted that when the automobile replaced the horse and buggy, some people lost their jobs in the buggy trade but many more

found work on the assembly line. Tyson believes that the same operating rules will govern the information era.

Tyson's argument is compelling. Still, I can't help but think that she   15
may be wrong. Even if thousands of new products come along, they are likely to be manufactured in near-workerless factories and marketed by near-virtual companies requiring ever-smaller, more highly skilled workforces.

This steady decline of mass labor threatens to undermine the very   16
foundations of the modern American state. For nearly 200 years, the heart of the social contract and the measure of individual human worth have centered on the value of each person's labor. How does society even begin to adjust to a new era in which labor is devalued or even rendered worthless?

This is not the first time the issue of devalued human labor has arisen   17
in the history of the United States. The first group of Americans to be marginalized by the automation revolution was black men, more than 40 years ago. Their story is a bellwether.

In the mid-1950s, automation began to take a toll on the nation's fac-   18
tories. Hardest hit were unskilled jobs in the industries where black workers concentrated. Between 1953 and 1962, 1.6 million blue-collar manufacturing jobs were lost. In an essay, "Problems of the Negro Movement," published in 1964, civil rights activist Tom Kahn quipped, "It's as if racism, having put the Negro in his economic place, stepped aside to watch technology destroy that 'place.'"

Millions of African-American workers and their families became part   19
of a perpetually unemployed "underclass" whose unskilled labor was no longer required in the mainstream economy. Vanquished and forgotten, many urban blacks vented their frustration and anger by taking to the streets. The rioting began in Watts in 1965 and spread east to Detroit and other Northern industrial cities.

Today, the same technological and economic forces are beginning to   20
affect large numbers of white male workers. Many of the disaffected white men who make up ultraright-wing organizations are high school or community college graduates with limited skills who are forced to compete for a diminishing number of agricultural, manufacturing, and service jobs. While they blame affirmative action programs, immigrant groups, and illegal aliens for their woes, these men miss the real cause of their plight—technological innovations that devalue their labor. Like African-American men in the 1960s, the new militants view the government and law enforcement agencies as the enemy. They see a grand conspiracy to deny them their basic freedoms and constitutional rights. And they are arming themselves for a revolution.

The Information Age may present difficulties for the captains of in-   21
dustry as well. By replacing more and more workers with machines, employers will eventually come up against the two economic Achilles' heels

of the Information Age. The first is a simple problem of supply and demand: If mass numbers of people are underemployed or unemployed, who's going to buy the flood of products and services being churned out?

22   The second Achilles' heel for business—and one never talked about—is the effect on capital accumulation when vast numbers of employees are let go or hired on a temporary basis so that employers can avoid paying out benefits—especially pension fund benefits. As it turns out, pension funds, now worth more than $5 trillion in the United States alone, keep much of the capitalist system afloat. For nearly 25 years, the pension funds of millions of workers have served as a forced savings pool that has financed capital investments.

23   Pension funds account for 74 percent of net individual savings, more than one-third of all corporate equities, and nearly 40 percent of all corporate bonds. Pension assets exceed the assets of commercial banks and make up nearly one-third of the total financial assets of the U.S. economy. In 1993 alone, pension funds made new investments of between $1 trillion and $1.5 trillion.

24   If too many workers are let go or marginalized into jobs without pension benefits, the capitalist system is likely to collapse slowly in on itself as employers drain it of the workers' funds necessary for new capital investments. In the final analysis, sharing the vast productivity gains of the Information Age is absolutely essential to guarantee the well-being of management, stockholders, labor, and the economy as a whole.

25   Sadly, while our politicians gush over the great technological breakthroughs that lie ahead in cyberspace, not a single elected official, in either political party, is raising the critical question of how we can ensure that the productivity gains of the Information Age are shared equitably.

26   In the past, when new technology increased productivity—such as in the 1920s when oil and electricity replaced coal- and steam-powered plants—American workers organized collectively to demand a shorter workweek and better pay and benefits. Today, employers are shortening not the workweek, but the workforce—effectively preventing millions of American workers from enjoying the benefits of the technology revolution.

27   Organized labor has been weakened by 40 years of automation, a decline in union membership, and a growing temp workforce that is difficult to organize. In meetings with union officials, I have found that they are universally reluctant to deal with the notion that mass labor—the very basis of trade unionism—will continue to decline and may even disappear altogether. Several union leaders confided to me off the record that the labor movement is in survival mode and trying desperately to prevent a rollback of legislation governing basic rights to organize. Union leaders cannot conceive that they may have to rethink their mission in order to accommodate a fundamental change in the nature of work. But the unions' continued reluctance to grapple with a technology revolution that

might eliminate mass labor could spell their own elimination from American life over the next three or four decades.

Working women may hold the key to whether organized labor can   28
reinvent itself in time to survive the Information Age. Women now make up about half of the U.S. workforce, and a majority of employed women provide half or more of their household's income.

In addition to holding down a 40-hour job, working women often   29
manage the household as well. Significantly, nearly 44 percent of all employed women say they would prefer more time with their family to more money.

This is one reason many progressive labor leaders believe the rebirth   30
of the American labor movement hinges on organizing women workers. The call for a 30-hour workweek is a powerful rallying cry that could unite trade unions, women's groups, parenting organizations, churches, and synagogues. Unfortunately, the voice of trade union women is not often heard inside the inner sanctum of the American Federation of Labor and Congress of Industrial Organizations (AFL-CIO) executive council. Of the 83 unions in the AFL-CIO, only one is headed by a woman.

The women's movement, trapped in struggles over abortion, discrim-   31
inatory employment practices, and sexual harassment, has also failed to grasp the enormous opportunity brought on by the Information Age. Betty Friedan, the venerable founder of the modern women's movement and someone always a step or two ahead of the crowd, is convinced that the reduction of work hours offers a way to revitalize the women's movement, and take women's interests to the center of public policy discourse.

Of course, employers will argue that shortening the workweek is too   32
costly and would threaten their ability to compete both domestically and abroad. That need not be so. Companies like Hewlett-Packard in France and BMW in Germany have reduced their workweek while continuing to pay workers at the same weekly rate. In return, the workers have agreed to work shifts. Management executives reason that, if they can operate the new high-tech plants on a 24-hour basis, they can double or triple productivity and thus afford to pay workers the same.

In France, government officials are playing with the idea of forgiving the   33
payroll taxes for employers who voluntarily reduce their workweek. While the government will lose tax revenue, economists argue that fewer people will be on welfare, and the new workers will be taxpayers with purchasing power. Employers, workers, the economy, and the government all benefit.

In this country, generous tax credits could be extended to any com-   34
pany willing both to reduce its workweek voluntarily and implement a profit-sharing plan so that its employees will benefit directly from productivity gains.

The biggest surprise I've encountered in the fledgling debate over re-   35
thinking work has been the response of some business leaders. I have found genuine concern among a small but growing number of business executives

over the critical question of what to do with the millions of people whose labor will be needed less, or not at all, in an increasingly automated age. Many executives have close friends who have been re-engineered out of a job—replaced by the new technologies of the Information Age. Others have had to take part in the painful process of letting employees go in order to optimize the bottom line. Some tell me they worry whether their own children will be able to find a job when they enter the high-tech labor market in a few years.

36   To be sure, I hear moans and groans from some corporate executives when I zero in on possible solutions—although there are also more than a few nods of agreement. But still, they are willing—even eager—to talk about these critical questions. They are hungry for engagement—the kind that has been absent in the public policy arena. Until now, politicians and economists have steadfastly refused to entertain a discussion of how we prepare for a new economic era characterized by the diminishing need for mass human labor. Until we have that conversation, the fear, anger, and frustration of millions of Americans are going to grow in intensity and become manifest through increasingly hostile and extreme social and political venues.

37   We are long overdue for public debate over the future of work and how to share the productivity gains of the Information Age. The 1996 election year offers the ideal time to begin talking with each other—both about our deep misgivings and our guarded hopes—as we journey into a new economic era.

▶ Building Vocabulary

Explain the meaning of the following examples of figurative language. Rewrite the sentence by putting the figures of speech in your own words.

1. Jittery and genuinely confused over the *yawning* gap between the official optimism of the politicians and their own personal plight, middle- and working-class American families seem to be *holding on to a tiny thread of* hope that the vast productivity gains of the high-tech *revolution* will somehow *"trickle down"* to them in the form of better jobs, wages, and benefits. (par. 6)
2. It is likely to set the framework for a politically *wild roller-coaster ride* for the rest of the 1990s, *opening the door* not only to new parties but to extralegal forms of politics. (par. 8)
3. He *barnstorms* the country urging workers to retrain, retool, and reinvent themselves in time to gain a coveted place on the *high-tech express.* (par. 11)
4. By replacing more and more workers with machines, employers will eventually come up against the two economic *Achilles' heels* of the Information Age. (par. 21)
5. If too many workers are *let go* or marginalized into jobs without pension benefits, the capitalist system is likely to *collapse slowly in on itself* as employers *drain it* of the workers' funds necessary for new capital investments. (par. 24)

6. This is one reason many progressive labor leaders believe the rebirth of the American labor movement *hinges on* organizing women workers. (par. 30)

▶ Thinking Critically About the Argument

Understanding the Writer's Argument

1. What was happening in the U.S. economy at the time this essay appeared in 1995? What was the hope for the future of the economy at that time? What did Rifkin think would happen to the economy soon after he published this essay?
2. What effect on jobs does Rifkin say the computer revolution is having?
3. What does Rifkin think about Laura Tyson's optimism as quoted in paragraph 14?
4. How can Americans learn about how technological change affects job markets over history? Who is always hurt the most?
5. Paraphrase Rifkin's argument about the loss of benefits starting in paragraph 22.
6. In the past, as Rifkin points out, unions joined together "to demand a shorter workweek and better pay." (par. 26) What was the status of organized labor when this essay appeared?
7. What are the economic benefits of a shorter workweek, according to Rifkin?
8. What, in Rifkin's view, is the reaction of business leaders when they hear his proposals to help the situation?

Understanding the Writer's Techniques

1. What claim does Rifkin make in this essay?
2. What is the argumentative effect of Rifkin's rhetorical questions in paragraph 3?
3. What is the argumentative function of each section Rifkin has created in the essay?
4. Which argument supporting Rifkin's claim is the strongest? Which is the weakest? Why?
5. Analyze the transitions Rifkin uses in his essay to link his various points.
6. How does Rifkin's concluding few paragraphs support his claim?

Exploring the Writer's Argument

1. This essay was written in 1995. Rifkin predicts that by late 1996, the economy would slide "headlong into a deep recession." (par. 6) However, until 2000 or so, the economy grew at unprecedented levels, in

part because of technology. For you, does this knowledge undermine Rifkin's basic message? Explain.

2. In paragraph 10, Rifkin argues that a number of jobs are "destined for virtual extinction" because of the Information Revolution. Do you agree with him? If so, which jobs do you think will not survive? If you don't agree with his assessment, explain how the jobs he mentions will survive.

3. Are Rifkin's dire predictions about pension funds and benefits in paragraphs 22 to 24 persuasive? If so, how are they persuasive? If not, what is lacking?

▶Ideas for Writing Arguments

Prewriting

What problems do freelancers and most part-time workers have because of their employment status? Make an outline listing as many as you can think of.

Writing a Guided Argument

Write an essay in which you argue that the current trend toward employers using part-time and freelance workers is a dangerous problem for workers, who don't receive overtime or benefits. You might need to do some reading in the library or online to gather evidence and facts, especially statistics, if you can find them.

1. Open your essay with a rhetorical question posing the problem to the reader.
2. In the next paragraph, establish the history of the issue, explaining that this is a new trend in employment.
3. Write your major proposition.
4. Organize your minor propositions so that your strongest point comes last.
5. Support your minor propositions by offering examples from life to illustrate the hardship of this problem.
6. Develop a tone of cynicism that reflects the frustration you think these workers feel.
7. Close your essay by stating that you are a pessimist about the situation or an optimist.

Thinking, Arguing, and Writing Collaboratively

In groups of four or five class members, discuss the possible audience for Rifkin's essay. Come up with at least two passages you think are directed at each of the following audiences: (1) corporate executive and business leaders, (2) organized labor and union workers, (3) liberal intellectuals, (4) government workers. Explain why your group thinks each passage could be persuasive to that audience, then convene as a class and discuss your groups' answers.

Writing About the Text

Write an essay in which you evaluate Rifkin's use of statistics. Which are most impressive? Which are the weakest? What kind of statistics aren't here that you would like to see?

More Writing Ideas

1. Freewrite in your journal for 15 minutes on the subject of finding jobs on the Internet. Do not edit your work. When you are done, show your writing to a classmate and discuss possibilities for future essays.
2. Write one or two paragraphs analyzing how the time Rifkin describes (1995) is similar to and different from today.
3. Do some research on the Industrial Revolution. Which jobs disappeared when machines started to be used extensively? To take a well-known example, when the automobile replaced the horse and buggy, makers of horsewhips went out of business. Write an essay based on your research in which you argue that the Industrial Revolution was responsible for many lost jobs.

12 The Media: Do We Control It, or Does It Control Us?

I n our media-saturated culture, there are hundreds of channels on cable television, from entertainment TV to sports to movies to music videos. How can the media *not* influence us? Almost every movie we want to watch is available at our local video store. Video cameras are getting smaller and cheaper, so that few events can escape taping. Since the early 1900s, when movies started, through the 1950s, when television became a popular medium (and advertisers discovered its power), the images created by Hollywood, the TV industries, and the advertising companies on Madison Avenue have become as familiar to us as our own family members. We watch for entertainment, but we are also aware that the media manipulate us at the same time.

Some would argue that even adults cannot resist the onslaught of images, but what about children? Children learn about the world, in part, by imitating what they see. Parents influence their children by offering themselves as behavioral models. But children today witness things that they normally wouldn't see in real life—on television and in the movies. What, for example, is the effect of video gunfights on children? This is the subject of one of the most bitterly fought debates today. In an age when children have gone to school with guns and shot their teachers and classmates, the question arises: How responsible are the media for these tragedies? And if they are responsible, can we really ask them to stop showing things people want to see? Violence and sex sell, and so that is what shows up on TV and in the movies. But are images of violence and sex enough to make youngsters imitate what they see, or are children media savvy enough today to have sufficient distance from what they view? How can parents protect their children?

Karen Springen, a parent of two girls, explores one response. She explains in "Why We Tuned Out" that she is simply not letting her children watch any TV or movies. To some, this might seem extreme. Gregg Easterbrook, in "Watch and Learn," makes a more scholarly attempt to argue about the influence of violence on youngsters. But talking about causes is one thing. Although she might disagree with Springen, Wendy Kaminer, like Springen, chooses to focus on solutions, with vastly different results. In "Toxic Media," Kaminer examines the danger of government censorship and finds that prospect to be scarier than the scariest slasher film.

KAREN SPRINGEN
Why We Tuned Out

Karen Springen has written for Newsweek *since the 1980s, and focuses on health, social issues, and parenting. She has also written freelance articles for many magazines, including* Vegetarian Times, Working Woman, *and* Elle. *Springen was educated at Stanford University and got her master's degree in journalism from Columbia University, where she teaches journalism. She also teaches a reporting and writing class at Columbia College. Springen is a wife and the mother of two daughters who are the subjects of this selection about her and her husband's decision to keep their children from watching television.*

▶ Prereading: Thinking About the Essay in Advance

Were you allowed to watch television when you were a child? What effect did it have on you, do you think?

▶ Words to Watch

inquisitive (par. 2) asking a lot of questions
cartwheels (par. 2) a gymnastic move in which, arms and legs extended, one turns over sideways like a wheel
puritanical (par. 4) overly moral
outcasts (par. 4) those excluded from a group
cringed (par. 7) reacted out of pain or disgust
crusading (par. 7) acting as if on a mission
ridicule (par. 7) being made fun of, mockery

"What's your favorite TV show?" our girls' beloved ballet instruc-   1
tor asked each pint-size dancer in her class. Our oldest daughter, Jazzy, didn't know how to answer. She shrugged. Her moment of awkwardness results from a decision my husband, Mark, and I made five years ago. We don't allow our kids to watch TV. Period. Not at home, not at friends' houses; and they don't watch videos or movies, either. We want our daughters, Jazzy, now nearly 6, and Gigi, 3, to be as active as

Tuning in. (www.mediawatch.com)

possible, physically and mentally. So when a babysitter asked whether Jazzy, then 1 year old, could watch TV, we thought about it—and said no.

When we look at our inquisitive, energetic daughters, we have no re-2 grets. And our reading of the research makes us feel even better. Nielsen Media Research reports that American children 2 through 11 watch three hours and 16 minutes of television every day. Kids who watch more than 10 hours of TV each week are more likely to be overweight, aggressive and slow to learn in school, according to the American Medical Association. For these reasons, the American Academy of Pediatrics recommends no TV for children younger than 2 and a maximum of two hours a day of "screen time" (TV, computers or videogames) for older kids. We are convinced that without TV, our daughters spend more time than other kids doing cartwheels, listening to stories and asking such interesting questions as "How old is God?" and "What makes my rubber ducks float?" They also aren't haunted by TV images of September 11—because they never saw them.

Going without TV in America has its difficult moments. When I   3
called my sister, Lucy, to make arrangements for Thanksgiving, she warned that her husband was planning to spend the day watching football. We're going anyway. We'll just steer the girls toward the playroom. And some well-meaning friends tell us our girls may be missing out on good educational programming. Maybe. But that's not what most kids are watching. Nielsen Media Research reports that among children 2 through 11, the top-five TV shows in the new fall season were "The Wonderful World of Disney," "Survivor: Thailand," "Yu-Gi-Oh!", "Poké-mon" and "Jackie Chan Adventures."

Will our happy, busy girls suffer because they're not participating in   4
such a big part of the popular culture? Will they feel left out in school when they don't know who won on "Survivor"? "Kids are going to make fun of them," warns my mother-in-law. And a favorite child psychiatrist, Elizabeth Berger, author of "Raising Children With Character," cautions that maintaining a puritanical approach may make our kids into social outcasts. "Part of preparing your children for life is preparing them to be one of the girls," she says. "It's awful to be different from the other kids in fourth grade."

Our relatives all watch TV. So did we. I was born in 1961, the year   5
Newton Minow, then the chairman of the U.S. Federal Communications Commission, called television a "vast wasteland." But I loved it. My sister, Katy, and I shared a first crush on the TV cartoon hero Speed Racer. Watching "Bewitched" and "The Brady Bunch" and, later, soap operas gave us an easy way to bond with our friends. Am I being selfish in not wanting the same for our children?

So far, our daughters don't seem to feel like misfits. We have no prob-   6
lem with the girls enjoying products based on TV characters. The girls wear Elmo pajamas and battle over who can sit on a big Clifford stuffed animal. From books, they also know about Big Bird, the Little Mermaid and Aladdin. And they haven't mentioned missing out on "Yu-Gi-Oh!" cartoon duels. Dr. Miriam Bar-on, who chairs the American Academy of Pediatrics committee on public education, says I'm helping our kids be creative, independent learners and calls our decision "awesome." And Mayo Clinic pediatrician Daniel Broughton, another group member, says that "there's no valid reason" the girls need to view television.

As the girls grow older, we can't completely shield them from TV   7
anyway. We'll probably watch Olympic rhythmic gymnastics; the girls love it. And if Jazzy's favorite baseball team, the Cubs, ever make the World Series, we'll tune in. Last Monday Jazzy's music teacher showed "The Magic School Bus: Inside the Haunted House." Though "Magic School Bus" is a well-regarded Scholastic product, I still cringed, wondering why the kids weren't learning about vibrations and sounds by singing

and banging on drums. But I kept silent; I'd never require my kids to abstain in school. Like Jean Lotus, the Oak Park, Ill., mom who founded the anti-TV group the White Dot and who also reluctantly allows her kids to view TV in school, I'm wary of being seen "as the crusading weirdo." But some public ridicule will be worth it if I help get even a few people to think twice before automatically turning on the tube. Now it's time for me to curl up with the girls and a well-worn copy of "Curious George."

▶ Building Vocabulary

Identify and explain the following references, looking them up in reference works if necessary:

1. Nielsen Media Research (par. 2)
2. American Medical Association (par. 2)
3. *Survivor* (par. 4)
4. Federal Communications Commission (par. 5)
5. Mayo Clinic (par. 6)
6. Scholastic (par. 7)
7. *Curious George* (par. 7)

▶ Thinking Critically About the Argument

Understanding the Writer's Argument

1. What is negative about the statistic that, on average, children watch more than three hours of television a day?
2. Why is it difficult to go without TV in America, according to Springen?
3. Why does Springen list the top five TV shows for children in the fall of 2002?
4. What did Newton Minow mean in 1961 when he called TV a "vast wasteland"?
5. Did Springen watch TV as a kid? What did she watch? How did it affect her?
6. Do Springen's girls know anything about what's on TV?
7. Will Springen always bar her children from watching TV? Explain.

Understanding the Writer's Techniques

1. What is Springen's major proposition? Where does she articulate it best in her essay?
2. What are Springen's minor propositions? List them in the form of an outline.

3. How does Springen use transitions effectively to build coherence in her essay? Analyze her use of transitions. Could you improve them? How?

4. What point is Springen making when she lists the top five TV shows for children ages 2 to 11 in paragraph 3?

5. What is the effect of Springen quoting Elizabeth Berger in paragraph 4? Why does she do this? Does it help or hurt her argument? Explain.

6. What is your reaction to paragraph 6? Do you find it persuasive? Why or why not?

7. Do you find the last paragraph persuasive? Why or why not?

8. What is the effect of the title? What meanings can you suggest for the phrase "tuned out"?

Exploring the Writer's Argument

1. Springen's daughters did not see images of the September 11 attacks. The children were young, and the images are disturbing. But if Springen's no-TV rule remains in place, her children will most likely miss out on the images that help shape American culture. Do you think that the children are missing out or will miss out on becoming involved Americans? Or are they better off without those images? Do we rely on those images today? Explain your answers.

2. Is Springen's essay presumptuous? Is she telling people how to rear their children or is she merely sharing her own experiences? Is she too self-congratulatory or appropriately proud? Explain your view of how Springen's argument is affected by how she presents her subject.

3. What does Springen's point about her children doing cartwheels and asking interesting questions contribute to the argument? Is a lack of TV the only reason they do these things? Explain your response. Do you know any children who are active and imaginative yet also watch TV? Explain your answers.

▶ Ideas for Writing Arguments

Prewriting

What is it about television that you think has a *positive* effect on children? Are there any programs that kids like that are also educational and make them think? Jot down some notes on the topic.

Writing a Guided Argument

Write an essay in which you argue that television is good for children. You might have to do some research by watching television during those hours when children watch—Saturday mornings and weekday afternoons.

1. Begin with a paragraph that introduces your reader to the subject through an anecdote or interesting example.
2. Write your claim clearly.
3. Establish a tone early on of self-importance—make sure your reader understands that you are absolutely sure of your argument.
4. Allow two rhetorical questions that put voice to the opposition's viewpoint—for example, "Doesn't television make kids lazy?"
5. Answer the rhetorical questions with persuasive grounds to back up your claim.
6. Use effective transitions to maintain coherence.
7. Close your essay by asserting that you are going to let your children watch television.

Thinking, Arguing, and Writing Collaboratively

In small groups of three or four, exchange your Writing a Guided Argument papers. Offer suggestions in the form of a paragraph or two to help your classmate develop his or her essay. After revising the essay at home, meet with the same partner to discuss the success of the revisions.

Writing About the Text

Consider the weaknesses in Springen's essay. What are the major problems in her argument? Write an essay in the form of a letter to Springen in which you point out at least three criticisms you have of her essay.

More Writing Ideas

1. Write notes for an essay on the effect advertising has on children.
2. Write a paragraph or two that argues that even if TV isn't great for children, it's great for *parents*.
3. Write an essay that explores the idea of popular culture and its importance. What is popular culture, and what is its effect on our lives?

GREGG EASTERBROOK
Watch and Learn

Journalist and novelist Gregg Easterbrook is a senior editor at The New Republic *and a contributing editor for* Atlantic Monthly *and* Washington Monthly. *He is the author of nonfiction books* A Moment on the Earth *(1996), about environmentalism, and* Beside Still Waters: Searching for Meaning in an Age of Doubt *(1999), about faith in the modern world. He is also author of the novel* The Here and Now *(2002). In this selection, which appeared in* The New Republic *in 1999, Easterbrook calls the media to account for their glorification of violence. How much responsibility do they have?*

▶ Prereading: Thinking About the Essay in Advance

How do you think TV and the movies can influence children?

▶ Words to Watch

wry (par. 1) dryly humorous
provocative (par. 1) meant to elicit a strong response
carnage (par. 3) bloody violence
whimpering (par. 3) softly crying
gratuitously (par. 4) without good reason
dramatizations (par. 5) reenactments for a movie or TV show
psyche (par. 8) psychological term for the mind
calculus (par. 11) way of figuring out
absolve (par. 13) forgive
cohabitation (par. 19) living with someone before marriage

Millions of teens have seen the 1996 movie *Scream*, a box-office and 1
home-rental hit. Critics adored the film. The *Washington Post* declared
that it "deftly mixes irony, self-reference, and social wry commentary." The
Los Angeles Times hailed it as "a bravura, provocative send-up." *Scream* opens
with a scene in which a teenage girl is forced to watch her jock boyfriend tortured and then disemboweled by two fellow students who, it will eventually
be learned, want revenge on anyone from high school who crossed them. After jock boy's stomach is shown cut open and he dies screaming, the killers
stab and torture the girl, then cut her throat and hang her body from a tree so
that Mom can discover it when she drives up. A dozen students and teachers
are graphically butchered in the film, while the characters make running
jokes about murder. At one point, a boy tells a big-breasted friend she'd better be careful because the stacked girls always get it in horror films; in the
next scene, she's grabbed, stabbed through the breasts, and murdered. Some
provocative send-up, huh? The movie builds to a finale in which one of the
killers announces that he and his accomplice started off by murdering
strangers but then realized it was a lot more fun to kill their friends.

Now that two Colorado high schoolers have murdered twelve class- 2
mates and a teacher—often, it appears, first taunting their pleading victims, just like celebrity stars do in the movies!—some commentators
have dismissed the role of violence in the images shown to the young,
pointing out that horrific acts by children existed before celluloid or the
phosphor screen. That is true—the Leopold-Loeb murder of 1924, for example. But mass murders by the young, once phenomenally rare, are

suddenly on the increase. Can it be coincidence that this increase is happening at the same time that Hollywood has begun to market the notion that mass murder is fun?

3   For, in cinema's never-ending quest to up the ante on violence, murder as sport is the latest frontier. Slasher flicks began this trend; most portray carnage from the killer's point of view, showing the victim cowering, begging, screaming as the blade goes in, treating each death as a moment of festivity for the killer. (Many killers seek feelings of power over their victims, criminology finds; by reveling in the pleas of victims, slasher movies promote this base emotion.) The 1994 movie *Natural Born Killers* depicted slaying the helpless not only as a way to have a grand time but also as a way to become a celebrity; several dozen on-screen murders are shown in that film, along with a discussion of how great it makes you feel to just pick people out at random and kill them. The 1994 movie *Pulp Fiction* presented hit men as glamour figures having loads of interesting fun; the actors were mainstream stars like John Travolta. The 1995 movie *Seven,* starring Brad Pitt, portrayed a sort of contest to murder in unusually grotesque ways. (Screenwriters now actually discuss, and critics comment on, which film's killings are most amusing.) The 1995 movie *The Basketball Diaries* contains an extended dream sequence in which the title character, played by teen heartthrob Leonardo DiCaprio, methodically guns down whimpering, pleading classmates at his high school. A rock soundtrack pulses, and the character smiles as he kills.

4   The new Hollywood tack of portraying random murder as a form of recreation does not come from schlock-houses. Disney's Miramax division, the same mainstream studio that produced *Shakespeare in Love,* is responsible for *Scream* and *Pulp Fiction.* Time-Warner is to blame for *Natural Born Killers* and actually ran television ads promoting this film as "delirious, daredevil fun." (After it was criticized for calling murder "fun," Time-Warner tried to justify *Killers* as social commentary; if you believe that, you believe *Godzilla* was really about biodiversity protection.) Praise and publicity for gratuitously violent movies come from the big media conglomerates, including the newspapers and networks that profit from advertising for films that glorify murder. Disney, now one of the leading promoters of violent images in American culture, even feels that what little kids need is more violence. Its Christmas 1998 children's movie *Mighty Foe Young* begins with an eight-year-old girl watching her mother being murdered. By the movie's end, it is 20 years later, and the killer has returned to stalk the grown daughter, pointing a gun in her face and announcing, "Now join your mother in hell." A Disney movie.

5   One reason Hollywood keeps reaching for ever-more-obscene levels of killing is that it must compete with television, which today routinely airs the kind of violence once considered shocking in theaters. According to studies conducted at Temple University, prime-time network (nonnews) shows now average up to five violent acts per hour. In February 1999, NBC

ran in prime time the movie *Eraser,* not editing out an extremely graphic scene in which a killer pulls a gun on a bystander and blasts away. The latest TV movie based on *The Rockford Files,* which aired on CBS the night of the Colorado murders, opened with a scene of an eleven-year-old girl in short-shorts being stalked by a man in a black hood, grabbed, and dragged off, screaming. *The Rockford Files* is a comedy. Combining television and movies, the typical American boy or girl, studies find, will observe a stunning 40,000 dramatizations of killing by age 18.

In the days after the Colorado slaughter, discussion of violent images   6
in American culture was dominated by the canned positions of the anti-Hollywood right and the mammon-is-our-God film lobby. The debate missed three vital points: the distinction between what adults should be allowed to see (anything) and what the inchoate minds of children and adolescents should see; the way in which important liberal battles to win free expression in art and literature have been perverted into an excuse for antisocial video brutality produced by cynical capitalists; and the difference between censorship and voluntary acts of responsibility.

The day after the Colorado shooting, Mike De Luca, an executive of   7
New Line Cinema, maker of *The Basketball Diaries,* told *USA Today* that, when kids kill, "bad home life, bad parenting, having guns in the home" are "more of a factor than what we put out there for entertainment." Setting aside the disclosure that Hollywood now categorizes scenes of movie stars gunning down the innocent as "entertainment," De Luca is correct: studies do show that upbringing is more determinant of violent behavior than any other factor. But research also clearly shows that the viewing of violence can cause aggression and crime. So the question is, in a society already plagued by poor parenting and unlimited gun sales, why does the entertainment industry feel privileged to make violence even more prevalent?

Even when researchers factor out other influences such as parental at-   8
tention, many peer-reviewed studies have found causal links between viewing phony violence and engaging in actual violence. A 1971 surgeon general's report asserted a broad relationship between the two. Studies by Brandon Centerwall, an epidemiologist at the University of Wisconsin, have shown that the postwar murder rise in the United States began roughly a decade after TV viewing became common. Centerwall also found that, in South Africa, where television was not generally available until 1975, national murder rates started rising about a decade later. Violent computer games have not existed long enough to be the subject of many controlled studies, but experts expect it will be shown that playing such games in youth also correlates with destructive behavior. There's an eerie likelihood that violent movies and violent games amplify one another, the film and television images placing thoughts of carnage into the psyche while the games condition the trigger finger to act on those impulses.

Leonard Eron, a psychologist at the University of Michigan, has   9
been tracking video violence and actual violence for almost four

decades. His initial studies, in 1960, found that even the occasional violence depicted in 1950s television—to which every parent would gladly return today—caused increased aggression among eight-year-olds. By the adult years, Eron's studies find, those who watched the most TV and movies in childhood were much more likely to have been arrested for, or convicted of, violent felonies. Eron believes that 10 percent of U.S. violent crime is caused by exposure to images of violence, meaning that 90 percent is not but that a 10 percent national reduction in violence might be achieved merely by moderating the content of television and movies. "Kids learn by observation," Eron says. "If what they observe is violent, that's what they learn." To cite a minor but telling example, the introduction of vulgar language into American public discourse traces, Eron thinks, largely to the point at which stars like Clark Gable began to swear onscreen, and kids then imitated swearing as normative.

10   Defenders of bloodshed in film, television, and writing often argue that depictions of killing don't incite real violence because no one is really affected by what they see or read; it's all just water off a duck's back. At heart, this is an argument against free expression. The whole reason to have a First Amendment is that people are influenced by what they see and hear: words and images do change minds, so there must be free competition among them. If what we say, write, or show has no consequences, why bother to have free speech?

11   Defenders of Hollywood bloodshed also employ the argument that, since millions of people watch screen mayhem and shrug, feigned violence has no causal relation to actual violence. After a horrific 1992 case in which a British gang acted out a scene from the slasher movie *Child's Play 3*, torturing a girl to death as the movie had shown, the novelist Martin Amis wrote dismissively in the *New Yorker* that he had rented *Child's Play 3* and watched the film, and it hadn't made him want to kill anyone, so what was the problem? But Amis isn't homicidal or unbalanced. For those on the psychological borderline, the calculus is different. There have, for example, been at least two instances of real-world shootings in which the guilty imitated scenes in *Natural Born Killers.*

12   Most telling, Amis wasn't affected by watching a slasher movie because Amis is not young. Except for the unbalanced, exposure to violence in video "is not so important for adults; adults can watch anything they want," Eron says. Younger minds are a different story. Children who don't yet understand the difference between illusion and reality may be highly affected by video violence. Between the ages of two and eight, hours of viewing violent TV programs and movies correlates closely to felonies later in life; the child comes to see hitting, stabbing, and shooting as normative acts. The link between watching violence and engaging in violence continues up to about the age of 19, Eron finds, after which most people's characters have been formed, and video mayhem no longer correlates to destructive behavior.

Trends in gun availability do not appear to explain the murder rise   13
that has coincided with television and violent films. Research by John
Lott Jr., of the University of Chicago Law School, shows that the percentage of homes with guns has changed little throughout the postwar era.
What appears to have changed is the willingness of people to fire their
guns at one another. Are adolescents now willing to use guns because violent images make killing seem acceptable or even cool? Following the
Colorado slaughter, the *New York Times* ran a recounting of other postwar
mass murders staged by the young, such as the 1966 Texas tower killings,
and noted that they all happened before the advent of the Internet or
shock rock, which seemed to the *Times* to absolve the modern media. But
all the mass killings by the young occurred after 1950—after it became
common to watch violence on television.

When horrific murders occur, the film and television industries rou-   14
tinely attempt to transfer criticism to the weapons used. Just after the Colorado shootings, for instance, TV talkshow host Rosie O'Donnell called for
a constitutional amendment banning all firearms. How strange that
O'Donnell didn't call instead for a boycott of Sony or its production company, Columbia Tristar—a film studio from which she has received generous paychecks and whose current offerings include *8MM*, which glamorizes the sexual murder of young women, and *The Replacement Killers*,
whose hero is a hit man and which depicts dozens of gun murders. Hand-
guns should be licensed, but that hardly excuses the convenient sanctimony of blaming the crime on the weapon, rather than on what resides in
the human mind.

And, when it comes to promoting adoration of guns, Hollywood might   15
as well be the National Rifle Association's (NRA) marketing arm. An ever-
increasing share of film and television depicts the firearm as something the
virile must have and use, if not an outright sexual aid. Check the theater
section of any newspaper, and you will find an ever-higher percentage of
movie ads in which the stars are prominently holding guns. Keanu Reeves,
Uma Thurman, Laurence Fishburne, Geena Davis, Woody Harrelson, and
Mark Wahlberg are just a few of the hip stars who have posed with guns for
movie advertising. Hollywood endlessly congratulates itself for reducing
the depiction of cigarettes in movies and movie ads. Cigarettes had to go,
the film industry admitted, because glamorizing them gives the wrong
idea to kids. But the glamorization of firearms, which is far more dangerous, continues. Today, even female stars who otherwise consider themselves politically aware will model in sexualized poses with guns. Ads for
the movie *Goodbye Lover* show star Patricia Arquette nearly nude, with very
little between her and the viewer but her handgun.

But doesn't video violence merely depict a stark reality against which   16
the young need to be warned? American society is far too violent, yet the
forms of brutality highlighted in the movies and on television—
prominently "thrill" killings and serial murders—are pure distortion.

Nearly 99 percent of real murders result from robberies, drug deals, and domestic disputes; figures from research affiliated with the FBI's behavioral sciences division show an average of only about 30 serial or "thrill" murders nationally per year. Thirty is plenty horrifying enough, but, at this point, each of the major networks and movie studios alone depicts more "thrill" and serial murders annually than that. By endlessly exploiting the notion of the "thrill" murder, Hollywood and television present to the young an entirely imaginary image of a society in which killing for pleasure is a common event. The publishing industry, including some [*New Republic*] advertisers, also distorts for profit the frequency of "thrill" murders.

17   The profitability of violent cinema is broadly dependent on the "down-rating" of films—movies containing extreme violence being rated only R instead of NC-17 (the new name for X)—and the lax enforcement of age restrictions regarding movies. Teens are the best market segment for Hollywood; when moviemakers claim their violent movies are not meant to appeal to teens, they are simply lying. The millionaire status of actors, directors, and studio heads—and the returns of the mutual funds that invest in movie companies—depends on not restricting teen access to theaters or film rentals. Studios in effect control the movie ratings board and endlessly lobby it not to label extreme violence with an NC-17, the only form of rating that is actually enforced. *Natural Born Killers*, for example, received an R following Time-Warner lobbying, despite its repeated close-up murders and one charming scene in which the stars kidnap a high school girl and argue about whether it would be more fun to kill her before or after raping her. Since its inception, the movie ratings board has put its most restrictive rating on any realistic representation of lovemaking, while sanctioning ever-more-graphic depictions of murder and torture. In economic terms, the board's pro-violence bias gives studios an incentive to present more death and mayhem, confident that ratings officials will smile with approval.

18   When R-and-X battles were first fought, intellectual sentiment regarded the ratings system as a way of blocking the young from seeing films with political content, such as *Easy Rider,* or discouraging depictions of sexuality; ratings were perceived as the rubes' counterattack against cinematic sophistication. But, in the 1960s, murder after murder after murder was not standard cinema fare. The most controversial violent film of that era, *A Clockwork Orange,* depicted a total of one killing, which was heard but not on-camera. (*Clockwork Orange* also had genuine political content, unlike most of today's big-studio movies.) In an era of runaway screen violence, the '60s ideal that the young should be allowed to see what they want has been corrupted. In this, trends in video mirror the misuse of liberal ideals generally.

19   Anti-censorship battles of this century were fought on firm ground, advocating the right of films to tackle social and sexual issues (the 1930s Hays office forbid among other things cinematic mention of cohabitation)

and free access to works of literature such as *Ulysses, Story of O,* and the original version of Norman Mailer's *The Naked and the Dead.* Struggles against censors established that suppression of film or writing is wrong.

But to say that nothing should be censored is very different from saying   20
that everything should be shown. Today, Hollywood and television have twisted the First Amendment concept that occasional repulsive or worthless expression must be protected, so as to guarantee freedom for works of genuine political content or artistic merit, into a new standard in which constitutional freedoms are employed mainly to safeguard works that make no pretense of merit. In the new standard, the bulk of what's being protected is repulsive or worthless, with the meritorious work the rare exception.

Not only is there profit for the performers, producers, management,   21
and shareholders of firms that glorify violence, so, too, is there profit for politicians. Many conservative or Republican politicians who denounce Hollywood eagerly accept its lucre. Bob Dole's 1995 anti-Hollywood speech was not followed up by any anti-Hollywood legislation or campaign-funds strategy. After the Colorado murders. President Clinton declared, "Parents should take this moment to ask what else they can do to shield children from violent images and experiences that warp young perceptions." But Clinton was careful to avoid criticizing Hollywood, one of the top sources of public backing and campaign contributions for him and his would-be successor, Vice President Al Gore. The president had nothing specific to propose on film violence—only that parents should try to figure out what to do.

When television producers say it is the parents' obligation to keep   22
children away from the tube, they reach the self-satire point of warning that their own product is unsuitable for consumption. The situation will improve somewhat beginning in 2000, by which time all new TVs must be sold with the "V chip"—supported by Clinton and Gore—which will allow parents to block violent shows. But it will be at least a decade before the majority of the nation's sets include the chip, and who knows how adept young minds will prove at defeating it? Rather than relying on a technical fix that will take many years to achieve an effect, TV producers could simply stop churning out the gratuitous violence. Television could dramatically reduce its output of scenes of killing and still depict violence in news broadcasts, documentaries, and the occasional show in which the horrible is genuinely relevant. Reduction in violence is not censorship; it is placing social responsibility before profit.

The movie industry could practice the same kind of restraint without   23
sacrificing profitability. In this regard, the big Hollywood studios, including Disney, look craven and exploitative compared to, of all things, the porn-video industry. Repulsive material occurs in underground porn, but, in the products sold by the mainstream triple-X distributors such as Vivid Video (the MGM of the erotica business), violence is never, ever, ever depicted—because that would be irresponsible. Women and men perform every conceivable explicit act in today's mainstream porn,

but what is shown is always consensual and almost sunnily friendly. Scenes of rape or sexual menace never occur, and scenes of sexual murder are an absolute taboo.

24   It is beyond irony that today Sony and Time-Warner eagerly market explicit depictions of women being raped, sexually assaulted, and sexually murdered, while the mainstream porn industry would never dream of doing so. But, if money is all that matters, the point here is that mainstream porn is violence-free and yet risqué and highly profitable. Surely this shows that Hollywood could voluntarily step back from the abyss of glorifying violence and still retain its edge and its income.

25   Following the Colorado massacre, Republican presidential candidate Gary Bauer declared to a campaign audience, "In the America I want, all of these producers and directors, they would not be able to show their faces in public" because fingers "would be pointing at them and saying, 'Shame, shame.'" The statement sent chills through anyone fearing right-wing thought-control. But Bauer's final clause is correct—Hollywood and television do need to hear the words "shame, shame." The cause of the shame should be removed voluntarily, not to stave off censorship, but because it is the responsible thing to do.

26   Put it this way. The day after a teenager guns down the sons and daughters of studio executives in a high school in Bel Air or Westwood, Disney and Time-Warner will stop glamorizing murder. Do we have to wait until that day?

▶ Building Vocabulary

Identify the following words, phrases, and references, and write a definition for each:

1. bravura (par. 1)
2. stacked (par. 1)
3. Leopold/Loeb case (par. 2)
4. slasher flicks (par. 3)
5. dream sequence (par. 3)
6. shlock (par. 4)
7. conglomerates (par. 4)
8. mammon (par. 6)
9. peer-reviewed (par. 8)
10. market segment (par. 17)

▶ Thinking Critically About the Argument

Understanding the Writer's Argument

1. What events do you think prompted Easterbrook's essay?
2. What does the writer think is responsible for the rise in mass murders by young people?

3. What does the phrase "murder as sport is the final frontier" imply? Who, according to the writer, is responsible for movies that have the most violent content? Why do movies keep getting more violent?
4. Why does the writer quote Mike DeLuca of New Line Cinema, in paragraph 7?
5. What do the Wisconsin and Michigan studies show?
6. What, according to the writer, is the difference between the novelist Martin Amis and people who might be influenced to imitate violent acts?
7. What does the writer make of the *Times* report he mentions in paragraph 13?
8. What is the writer's opinion of the current movie ratings system?

Understanding the Writer's Techniques

1. What is the writer's major proposition? Where does it appear?
2. What argumentative function does the opening, describing the movie *Scream,* have?
3. What kinds of authoritative sources does Easterbrook use to support his argument? Which do you think are the most effective?
4. The writer relies heavily on examples. Which do you see as his most persuasive example? How does he make the example stronger by explaining it?
5. What is the writer's tone? Explain and offer examples to support your answer.
6. How do paragraphs 4 to 7 support the writer's major proposition?
7. Is the concluding paragraph effective? Why or why not?

Exploring the Writer's Argument

1. The beginning of Easterbrook's essay summarizes the shocking contents of the popular movie *Scream.* He includes the gory and graphic details, presumably for effect. Should he tone it down for his audience? Is he committing the same offense that he accuses the filmmakers of committing? Explain your answers.
2. Easterbrook uses loaded language in his essay. For example he writes that the movie *8MM* "glamorizes the sexual murder of young women." (paragraph 14) Obviously, the filmmakers do not think their movies were glamorizing murder. Find at least five more places in which Easterbrook uses such language to stack the debate in his favor. Do you think this kind of usage is fair? Explain your answer fully.
3. The argument Easterbrook makes is open to debate, but what about his audience? How persuasive can Easterbrook really be with his essay? Is there any chance that this essay can persuade anyone? Who

has the power to effect the changes he wants, and how could they truly be persuaded to change their minds and actions? Is it possible? Explain.

▶ Ideas for Writing Arguments

Prewriting

Assuming that violence in movies is influential to children, are all images of violence in movies harmful? Write some notes for an essay about this topic.

Writing a Guided Argument

Write an essay arguing that some kinds of violence in the movies can actually have a positive effect on children.

1. Begin your essay with a vivid example of the kind of violence you are going to argue for.
2. Admit that this violence can influence children.
3. Surprise your reader by writing your claim that this kind of violence can have a positive effect on children.
4. Offer at least three kinds of film violence that can be beneficial.
5. Illustrate your points with good examples.
6. Use strong transitions to bind your argument.
7. Address at least one view from the opposition's perspective.
8. Rebut the opposition's argument.
9. Close your essay by reaffirming your claim.

Thinking, Arguing, and Writing Collaboratively

In groups of four or five students, exchange drafts of your Writing a Guided Argument essays with each member of your group, passing them around the group. Each student should read each other student's essay, marking notes directly on the essay and writing a short paragraph commenting on the success of the argument. Then collect your essay and use the comments as the basis for your final draft.

Writing About the Text

In his essay "The Limits of Freedom" in Chapter 10, Andrew Brown argues for occasional censorship of offensive and provocative content on the Internet. Write an essay that compares and contrasts both the content and the effectiveness of Brown's and Easterbrook's arguments.

More Writing Ideas

1. Watch the news on television and write a journal entry about how the TV news can contribute to violence in our society.
2. Write a paragraph or two that explore the implications of Easterbrook's sentence in paragraph 26: "The day after a teenager guns down the sons and daughters of studio executives in a high school in Bel Air or Westwood, Disney and Time-Warner will stop glamorizing murder."
3. Recently, a great deal of controversy has arisen over the violence in video games like Duke Nukem and Grand Theft Auto. Write an essay in which you argue that violent video games are (or are not) much more likely to incite violence than the violence children see in the movies.

WENDY KAMINER
Toxic Media

Lawyer and writer Wendy Kaminer is a contributing editor for The Atlantic Monthly *and is on the board of the libertarian legal organization the American Civil Liberties Union. She is the author of* Sleeping with Extra-Terrestrials: I'm Dysfunctional, You're Dysfunctional *(1992),* It's All the Rage: Crime and Culture *(1995), and* The Rise of Irrationalism and Perils of Piety *(1999). She also writes freelance for* The New York Times, The Wall Street Journal, The Nation, *and* Newsweek. *This essay, which appeared in 2000 in* The American Prospect, *for which she is a senior correspondent, warns against the danger of censorship gone out of control.*

▶ Prereading: Thinking About the Essay in Advance

Is there anything on television you'd like to see censored? What, and why?

▶ Words to Watch

ceasefire (par. 1) a break in fighting
concomitant (par. 2) accompanying
centrist (par. 3) politically between the extremes of liberal and conservative
complemented (par. 3) made complete or matched up with
bipartisan (par. 4) having members from both parties
stringent (par. 8) strict and unbending
abhors (par. 9) hates
hyperbolic (par. 10) wildly exaggerated
dearth (par. 10) a lack of, insufficient amount
de facto (par. 12) in reality, even if not official

1   Like Claude Rains in Casablanca, Al Gore is shocked!, shocked! that the entertainment industry is marketing violent material to minors. Countering Hollywood's macho entertainments with some macho rhetoric of his own, he gave the industry six months to "clean up its act" and declare a "ceasefire" in what he apparently sees as the media's war against America's children.

2   No one should be surprised by the vice president's threat to impose government regulations on the marketing of popular entertainments, which immediately followed the issuance of a new Federal Trade Commission (FTC) report on the subject. As his choice of running mate [Joseph Lieberman] made clear, Gore is positioning himself as the moral voice of the Democratic Party—replete with Godliness and a desire to cleanse the culture. With a concomitant promise to protect ordinary Americans from rapacious corporations, Gore is an early twenty-first-century version of a nineteenth-century female Progressive—a Godloving social purist with a soft spot for working families and, not so incidentally, women's rights.

3   Many Victorian women's rights activists, like Frances Willard of the Women's Christian Temperance Union and Julia Ward Howe, enthusiastically supported the suppression of "impure" or "vicious" literature, which was blamed for corrupting the nation's youth. "Books are feeders for brothels" according to the notorious nineteenth-century antivice crusader Anthony Comstock, for whom the nation's first obscenity law was named. Gun violence is fed by violent media, Al Gore, Joseph Lieberman, and others assert. The new FTC report was commissioned by President Clinton immediately after the 1999 shootings at Columbine High. That was when centrist politicians (and commentators) were touting the new "commonsense" view of youth violence: It was caused by both the availability of firearms and the availability of violent media. Gun control would be complemented by culture control.

4   So in June 1999, two Democratic senators, Lieberman and the usually thoughtful Kent Conrad of North Dakota, joined with [Senators] Trent Lott and John McCain in proposing federal legislation requiring the labeling of violent audio and visual media. These requirements, which were to be enforced by the FTC, were amendments to the cigarette labeling act. (When politicians revisit their bad ideas, critics like me repeat themselves. I discussed this proposed bill and the bipartisan drive to censor in a November 23, 1999, *American Prospect* column, "The Politics of Sanctimony.")

5   Advocates of censorship often charge that media can be "toxic" (as well as "addictive") like tobacco and other drugs. By describing whatever film or CD they disdain as a defective product, they undermine the view of it as speech. (We should regulate pornography the way we regulate exploding Ford Pintos, one feminist antiporn activist used to say; she seemed to consider *Playboy* an incendiary device.) In endorsing Internet filtering programs, Gore has remarked that minors should be protected

from "dangerous places" on the Internet—in other words, "dangerous" speech. Some Web sites should effectively be locked up, just as medicine cabinets are locked up to protect children from poisons, the vice president remarked at a 1997 Internet summit.

Once you define violent or sexually explicit media as toxic products, it is not terribly difficult to justify regulating their advertising, at least, if not their distribution and production. Commercial speech generally enjoys constitutional protection, but as advocates of marketing restrictions assert, the First Amendment does not protect false or misleading advertising or ads promoting illegal activities. That's true but not necessarily relevant here. Campaigns marketing violent entertainment to children may be sleazy, but they don't promote an illegal activity (the sale of violent material to minors is not generally criminal); and they're not deceptive or unfair (many popular entertainments are just as bad as they purport to be). Ratings are not determined or mandated by the government (not yet, anyway), so why should it be a federal offense for industry executives to violate the spirit of their own voluntary codes?

Effective regulation of media marketing campaigns would require new federal legislation that would entangle the government in the production of popular entertainments. What might this legislation entail? Ratings and labeling would be mandatory, supervised by the FTC (or some other federal agency), and any effort to subvert the ratings system would be a federal offense. Testifying before the Senate Commerce Committee on September 12, 2000, Lieberman promised that regulation of the entertainment industry would focus on "how they market, not what they produce," but that promise ignores the effect of marketing considerations on content.

Some may consider the decline of violent entertainments no great loss, imagining perhaps that slasher movies and violent video games will be the primary victims of a new federal labeling regime. But it's not hard to imagine a docudrama about domestic abuse or abortion, or a coming-of-age story about a gay teen, receiving the same restricted rating as a sleazy movie about a serial murderer. In any case, a stringent, federally mandated and monitored rating and labeling system will not enhance parental control; it's a vehicle for bureaucratic control. Federal officials, not parents, will determine what entertainment will be available to children when they devise and enforce the ratings.

Some claim that federal action is justified, nonetheless, by an overriding need to save lives. At the September 12 hearing inspired by the FTC report, several senators and other witnesses vigorously condemned the entertainment industry for "literally making a killing off of marketing to kids," in the words of Kansas Republican Sam Brownback. He called upon the industry to stop producing the entertainments he abhors. Lieberman charged that media violence was "part of a toxic mix that has turned some of our children into killers." Lynne Cheney, former head of the National Endowment for the Humanities, declared that "there is a problem with the product they market, no matter how they market it." Democratic Senator Fritz Hollings proposed giving the Federal Communications Commission the power to impose a partial ban on whatever programming it considers violent and harmful to minors.

10   What all this hyperbolic rhetoric obscured (or ignored) was the dearth of hard evidence that violent media actually turns "children into killers." In fact, the FTC study on which would-be censors rely found no clear causal connection between violent media and violent behavior. "Exposure to violent materials probably is not even the most important factor" in determining whether a child will turn violent, FTC Chairman Robert Pitofsky observed. The most he would say was that exposure to violent media "does seem to correlate with aggressive attitudes, insensitivity toward violence, and an exaggerated view of how much violence occurs in the world."

11   This is not exactly a defense of media violence, but it may present a fairly balanced view of its effects, which do not justify limitations on speech. Living in a free society entails a commitment not to prohibit speech unless it clearly, directly, and intentionally causes violence. If violent entertainment can be regulated by the federal government because it allegedly causes violence, so can inflammatory political rhetoric, like assertions that abortion providers kill babies. Anti-abortion rhetoric probably has even a clearer connection to violence than any violent movie, but both must be protected. If Disney can be brought under the thumb of federal regulators, so can Cardinal Law when he denounces abortion as murder.

12   It's unfortunate and ironic that apparently amoral corporations, like Disney or Time-Warner, stand as champions and beneficiaries of First Amendment rights. As gatekeepers of the culture, they're not exactly committed to maintaining an open, diverse marketplace of ideas. Indeed, the de facto censorship engineered by media conglomerates may threaten public discourse nearly as much as federal regulation. And neither our discourse nor our culture is exactly enriched by gratuitously violent media.

13   But speech doesn't have to provide cultural enrichment to enjoy constitutional protection. We don't need a First Amendment to protect popular, inoffensive speech or speech that a majority of people believe has social value. We need it to protect speech that Lynne Cheney or Joseph Lieberman consider demeaning and degrading. Censorship campaigns often begin with a drive to protect children (or women), but they rarely end there.

▶Building Vocabulary

1. Write out the meanings of the following idioms:
   a. the moral voice (par. 2)
   b. cleanse the culture (par. 2)
   c. a soft spot for working families (par. 2)

  d. entangle the government (par. 7)
  e. making a killing off (par. 9)
  f. under the thumb (par. 11)
  g. marketplace of ideas (par. 12)
2. Identify and define the following references, and explain their significance to American culture:
  a. Federal Trade Commission (par. 2)
  b. Victorian (par. 3)
  c. Ford Pintos (par. 5)
  d. slasher movies (par. 8)
  e. National Endowment for the Humanities (par. 9)
  f. Cardinal Law (par. 11)

▶ Thinking Critically About the Argument

Understanding the Writer's Argument

1. What does it mean that Al Gore is "shocked! shocked!" about the entertainment industry's marketing of violence? What is the writer referring to here? Why is Kaminer not surprised by Gore's threat to the entertainment industry?
2. What is the history of labeling media? According to Kaminer, what are the risks of labeling entertainment?
3. What does the First Amendment not protect when it comes to advertising?
4. What is Kaminer's view of the politicians and their opinions as quoted in paragraph 9? What does Kaminer think is more of a risk to America than media violence?
5. What, according to Kaminer, is the problem with the argument that media violence is a direct cause of the rise in violence?
6. Why does Kaminer think it's odd that large media corporations "stand as champions and beneficiaries of First Amendment rights"? (par. 12)

Understanding the Writer's Techniques

1. What is Kaminer's major proposition? Where does it appear?
2. Why does the writer start her essay with the voices of politicians? How does she portray them? What argumentative effect does her opening have?
3. Why does Kaminer give the history of politicians' attempts to regulate media? What point is she making? Is it effectively done? Why or why not?
4. What tone is the writer taking in this essay? Give examples to explain your answer.
5. How do paragraphs 9 and 10 support Kaminer's position?

6. List two or three of her most effective transitions, and explain why they are effective.
7. Is the conclusion effective? What makes it so, or how could it be improved?

Exploring the Writer's Argument

1. In paragraph 6, Kaminer complains that "once you define violent or sexually explicit media as toxic products, it is not terribly difficult to justify regulating their advertising, at least, if not their distribution and production." Do you agree with her statement? Do you still think it is difficult, no matter what a politician or other public figure might say? Why or why not?
2. Do you think Kaminer's occasionally combative tone strengthens or weakens her argument? Explain your answer.
3. Although this essay was written recently, in 2000—after the shootings at Columbine High School in 1999 and after other school shootings— do you think Kaminer would have any reason today to change her mind about her claim? Why or why not? Can you think of any reason Kaminer would change her mind? Explain your response.

▶Ideas for Writing Arguments

Prewriting

Warning labels now appear on video games and television shows to indicate violence, sexually explicit material, and so on. What is your opinion of those labels? Are they helpful? Why or why not? Write some notes on your feelings and the reasons for your feelings.

Writing a Guided Argument

Write an essay arguing for or against the warning labels on television shows. Do some research online or in the library to determine the origin of the labels. Who made the networks include them, or did the networks put them in on their own?

1. Open your essay with an account of watching television and noticing a label on a show.
2. Link your experience with your major proposition by using a transition.
3. Give the history of the labels and a partial list, for your reader's information, of the labels.
4. Explain in brief why you are for or against the labels.
5. In the next section, offer your minor propositions.

6. Support your minor propositions with examples and facts you gleaned from your research.
7. Address the issue of television as "toxic media."
8. Establish a tone that has some irony and cynicism.
9. Rebut at least one possible objection to your argument.
10. Close your essay with a discussion of how the television industry is doing things the right way, or offer a proposal to address the problem.

Thinking, Arguing, and Writing Collaboratively

Help to divide the class into two equal groups. One group should take Kaminer's position that violence in the media does not warrant censorship, and the other should take Easterbrook's position that violence at least warrants self-censorship. As a group, think of arguments and facts to add to those already given by the writer whose position you are taking and try to remedy weaknesses you might see. Take notes on your group discussion and prepare an outline for a debate. Debate the issue, and afterwards reconvene as a class to discuss the success of the structure of the debate and how effective the arguments your group added were. Discuss what you left out or improved.

Writing About the Text

Write an essay that expands on the following sentence by Kaminer: "Campaigns marketing violent entertainment to children may be sleazy, but they don't promote an illegal activity (the sale of violent material to minors is not generally criminal); and they're not deceptive or unfair (many popular entertainments are just as bad as they purport to be)." (par. 6)

More Writing Ideas

1. In your journal, write an entry about your feelings on the First Amendment.
2. If violent media is one possible risk that we face in an open society, what other risks are there? Write one or two paragraphs outlining the various dangers that arise from living as we do in a free country.
3. Find an item in the media (a song, a clip from a movie, a television show, a radio show, or a newspaper or magazine advertisement, for example) that you find particularly offensive and bad for society, then defend it in an essay. Defend the piece's right to be created, distributed, and marketed, addressing each of these rights in order.

13 ► Education: How Do We Teach and Learn?

As long as there are parents, they will argue about education. How can parents today make sure that their children are brought up with the values that the parents believe in? When children are 5, 4, or even 3 years old (parents are working more and more these days), they go out in the world and become the responsibility of teachers, who act *in loco parentis* (that is, as substitute parents). The future adults of society are molded in school, which is what makes education such a volatile topic. What is the best way to educate our children so that our society heads in the right direction? How do the issues change, if it all, when we're talking about high school and college?

In a wide variety of ways, newspapers, magazines, and books published across the country are answering these questions. Each writer engages the emotional issue with a different level of authority, a different set of credentials, a different point of view. For example, Ellen Goodman writes in "Religion in the Textbooks" about her dissatisfaction with what she sees as a loss of nerve among school officials. Religion is a part of almost everyone's life, yet schools are shying away from the topic and transforming it into something it's not. She calls for a braver approach. In "Their Cheating Hearts," William Raspberry approaches his topic, that of cheating in school, with a bemused interest. What's behind the fact that 80 percent of students have admitted to cheating? Raspberry is merely interested in finding answers, but along the way he manages to make an argument about what he thinks is the source. "The Dangerous Myth of Grade Inflation" by Alfie Kohn and "Curtailing High School: A Radical Proposal" by Leon Botstein are different takes on education, but both offer well-reasoned, forceful suggestions for changes that the authors think can improve schools in America. As you read the selections that follow, think about how these writers try to influence their readers.

ELLEN GOODMAN
Religion in the Textbooks

Pulitzer Prize–winning editor and journalist Ellen Goodman started her ca-
reer as a researcher at Newsweek. *She began reporting for the* Detroit Free
Press *in 1965, and then moved on to* The Boston Globe, *where the column*
she has written for many years has been praised for its lively writing and
strong voice. Goodman was educated at Radcliffe College at Harvard, which is
where she began writing her column. She is the author of Turning Points
(1979) and of several collections of her columns, including Keeping in Touch
(1985), Making Sense *(1989), and* Value Judgments *(1993). In this selec-*
tion, Goodman explores the squeamishness Americans seem to have about
teaching religion in public schools.

▶ Prereading: Thinking About the Essay in Advance

If you attended a public school, did you discuss religion in class? What
were the content and tenor of those discussions? In what other settings
did you discuss religion?

▶ Words to Watch

crockery (par. 1) ceramic dishware
pluralistic (par. 4) theory that there should be many different groups co-
existing
subtexts (par. 6) meanings that lie underneath the main content
masquerading (par. 7) pretending to be
taboo (par. 8) considered unacceptable by social or traditional standards
curriculum (par. 10) what is taught in a school course
incorporate (par. 10) include

There was a time when people who wanted to keep the peace and keep   1
the crockery intact held to a strict dinner-table rule: Never argue
about politics or religion. I don't know how well it worked in American
dining rooms, but it worked pretty well in our schools. We dealt with religion by not arguing about it.

Children who came out of diverse homes might carve up the turf of   2
their neighborhood and turn the playgrounds into a religious battlefield, but
the public classroom was common ground. Intolerance wasn't tolerated.

In place of teaching one religion or another, the schools held to a com-   3
mon denominator of values. It was, in part, the notion of Horace Mann,
the nineteenth-century father of the public-school system. He believed
that the way to avoid religious conflicts was to extract what all religions
agreed upon and allow this "non-religious" belief system into schools.

4   I wonder what Mann would think of that experiment now. Was it naive or sophisticated? Was it a successful or a failed attempt to avoid conflict in a pluralistic society?

5   Today, textbooks are the texts of public-school education and their publishers are, if anything, controversy-phobic. Textbooks are written and edited by publishing committees that follow elaborate guidelines to appease state and local education committees. They must avoid alienating either atheist or fundamentalist. And still these books have become centerpieces, controversial sources of evidence in courtrooms.

6   A judge in Tennessee recently allowed a group of students to "opt out" of reading class because the textbooks violated their religious beliefs. Their parents had managed to read religious subtexts, even witchcraft, into such tales as "Goldilocks," "Cinderella" and "The Three Little Pigs." Nothing was safe enough or bland enough to please them.

7   At the same time, a group of parents in Alabama went to court protesting that textbooks are teaching a state religion masquerading as "secular humanism." Not to teach about God is to teach about no God. The attempt to keep religion out of the textbooks was no guarantee against controversy either.

8   There is still a third argument about religion in the public schools that doesn't come from fanatics but from educators. They maintain that the attempt to avoid conflict has pushed textbook publishers to excise religion altogether, even from history class. It is not just the teaching *of* religion that has become taboo, they claim. It is teaching *about* religion.

Sources as diverse as William Bennett's Department of Education and   9
Norman Lear's People for the American Way have reported in the past
year on the distortions that result. There is a history book that tells about
Joan of Arc without mentioning her religious motives. Others explain
Thanksgiving without discussing the religious beliefs of the Puritans or to
Whom they were giving thanks.

"The result of wanting to avoid controversy is a kind of censorship,"   10
maintains Diane Ravitch of Columbia University. "It becomes too controversial to write about Christianity and Judaism." Ravitch is involved in
creating a new history curriculum for California that would incorporate
teaching about people's belief systems and their impact on society. It may
be tricky, she admits, to teach about religion without teaching religion, but
then all good teaching is risky. So is learning. And that's what is at stake.

The common ground of values, neutral turf in the religious strife,   11
threatens to shrink to the size of a postage stamp. In Tennessee, the court
agreed to protect the religious beliefs of a set of parents whose own beliefs included intolerance of other religions and the importance of binding
a child's imagination. These are ideas that are profoundly hostile to the
American concept of education.

If textbook publishers keep retreating to a shrinking patch of safe   12
ground, they will end up editing chunks out of "The Three Little Pigs."
The task is not to shy away from our diversity, but to teach it to our children, and proudly. The strength of our system, what's worth telling the
young, is not that Americans deny their differences or always resolve
them, but that we have managed, until now, to live with them.

▶ Building Vocabulary

1. In this essay, Goodman uses a number of colloquial phrases. Identify
   them and come up with another way to write each.
   a. religious battlefield (par. 2)
   b. common ground (par. 2)
   c. common denominator (par. 3)
   d. father of the public-school system (par. 3)
   e. threatens to shrink to the size of a postage stamp (par. 11)
   f. the task is not to shy away (par. 12)
2. This essay assumes knowledge of several terms and references having to do with religion. Identify and explain each.
   a. atheist (par. 5)
   b. fundamentalist (par. 5)
   c. secular humanism (par. 7)
   d. William Bennett (par. 9)
   e. People for the American Way (par. 9)
   f. Joan of Arc (par. 9)
   g. Puritans (par. 9)

▶Thinking Critically About the Argument

Understanding the Writer's Argument

1. Why does the writer start with a look into the past?
2. Who was Horace Mann, and what does he have to do with the issue of religion in schools?
3. What was the rationale of the judge who allowed students to leave classes because the textbooks "violated their religious beliefs"? (par. 6) What does the writer think of his decision?
4. What do most educators want to do with religion in textbooks, according to Goodman?
5. What is wrong with teaching about the Puritans without mentioning their religious beliefs?
6. Paraphrase Diane Ravitch's argument in paragraph 10.
7. What does the writer see as the threat of religion being taken out of textbooks?

Understanding the Writer's Techniques

1. What is the writer's major proposition? Where is it located? Is it located in an effective place? Why do you think so?
2. Where does the writer's extended introduction end? What comes after the introduction?
3. Is the writer's structure in this essay effective? Explain.
4. Why does the writer present questions in paragraph 4? Is this technique effective or not?
5. What is the argumentative effect of showing the fighting on both sides of the issue of religion in the classroom? What is the writer trying to do by illustrating this infighting?
6. The word *appease* in paragraph 5 has historical connotations from the years before World War II. What are those connotations, and how do they affect your reading of this paragraph?
7. How effective are the author's transitions? Explain your answer.
8. Is the closing paragraph effective? Why or why not?

Exploring the Writer's Argument

1. Goodman quotes Diane Ravitch in paragraph 10 but never explicitly says whether she agrees with Ravitch. Do you think the writer agrees with Ravitch's sentiment or not? Why do you think that? What is your opinion of Ravitch's argument that "to avoid controversy is a kind of censorship"?
2. One solution to this problem might be to teach only about the history of religion, without mentioning the state of the religions today. Is that

a possible solution? What would William Bennett say to that? What would Norman Lear say? What would Ellen Goodman say?

3. In paragraph 11, Goodman writes about a judge who protected the rights of parents whose children were brought up to be intolerant of other religions. She says that "These are ideas that are profoundly hostile to the American concept of education." Does citing an extreme case weaken her argument here or leave it strong? Explain your answer.

▶ Ideas for Writing Arguments

Prewriting

Jot down some notes about prayer and other religious content in schools.

Writing a Guided Argument

Controversy often surrounds the question of whether religion has any place in public schools at all. Coaches leading prayers before a football game, the Ten Commandments posted in a school hallway, mandated moments of silence for prayer—all are hotly contested. Write an essay in which you argue that either there is no place for religious content in schools or that there are some areas in which religious topics are okay.

1. Open your essay with an illustration of religious activity that you are either going to argue for or against.
2. Take a position on the issue in the form of a major proposition.
3. Give a short history of the issue and give the reader an overview of the main players in the debate.
4. Address possible opposing points and rebut them.
5. Include at least two minor propositions that support your position.
6. Link paragraphs with effective transitions.
7. Establish an even, neutral-sounding tone.
8. Close your essay with a prediction about the future of religion in schools.

Thinking, Arguing, and Writing Collaboratively

Find a section of a textbook designed for public school instruction. In groups of three or four, read a section about religion out loud. Write notes based on your reading. Is the section overly bland? Does it leave out crucial information? Do you see anything that could possibly offend a parent? Convene as a class and discuss your findings.

Writing About the Text

Read Anna Quindlen's essay "One Nation, Indivisible? Wanna Bet?" from Chapter 1. Write an essay arguing that Quindlen's and Goodman's arguments reflect the same tendency in American culture to be confused on the issue of the separation of church and state.

More Writing Ideas

1. Write a journal entry addressing the following question: Which religions do you think would be most difficult to teach to schoolchildren? Which religions would it be most important to teach children in the United States about? Why?
2. Question 3 of "Exploring the Writer's Argument" refers to Goodman's statement that restrictive educational ideas are "profoundly hostile to the American concept of education." Do you think that is true? Write a paragraph or two arguing for one side or the other.
3. Look up the concept and history of "secular humanism." (par. 7) Write an essay in which you argue for or against the "faith" of secular humanism.

WILLIAM RASPBERRY
Their Cheating Hearts

William Raspberry grew up in a small, segregated town in Mississippi. He served in the army and then joined the Washington Post, *where he worked his way up to being an editor and reporter. He now writes a column for the newspaper that is also syndicated in more than 100 newspapers around the country. He has received many honors for his work, including a Capital Press Club's "Journalist of the Year" award, a citation of merit in journalism from Lincoln University in Jefferson City, Missouri. In 1994 he received both the Pulitzer Prize and a Lifetime Achievement Award from the National Association of Black Journalists. Raspberry is also the Knight professor of the practice of communications and journalism at Duke University. In this selection, Raspberry, from his point of view as a teacher, tries to get to the bottom of the growing phenomenon of cheating among young people in America.*

▶ Prereading: Thinking About the Essay in Advance

Have you or someone you know ever cheated on an exam or plagiarized an essay? If so, would you call the act a serious offense? If not, why not?

▶**Words to Watch**

infraction (par. 1) offense against a law or rule
lax (par. 4) not strict
pragmatic (par. 6) concerned with practical results rather than ideas
epiphany (par. 12) sudden realization
ambivalent (par. 12) having mixed feelings

B y the time I arrived for my "Family and Community" class, I still   1
was reeling from the results of a survey I'd just seen. A poll of more
than 3,000 students listed in "Who's Who Among High School
Students"—the cream of our scholastic crop—revealed that 80 percent
had engaged in academic cheating and thought cheating was common-
place. Moreover, most saw cheating as a minor infraction.

Surely this couldn't be correct, I thought.   2

But close to half of my Duke University students (encouragingly less   3
than 80 percent) acknowledged some high school cheating, though all of
them insisted they'd outgrown the practice since they had entered college. I decided to spend the bulk of the period talking about it, and the result was one of the more interesting classes of the semester.

We began with a discussion of honor codes and their enforcement: 4
stiff codes, such as the University of Virginia's, where students are required to report any cheating they observe and name the cheaters on pain
of expulsion; softer codes such as Duke's, which requires students to report infractions but permits them, under some circumstances, to do so
anonymously; or lax codes that amount to a no-cheating policy statement
that says, in effect, don't get caught.

Most of the class—predictably—chose the middle ground. Nearly all   5
said they would have walked away from a stolen answer sheet rather
than use it to boost their college-entry SAT scores. Only a handful said
they would have gone all the way and told school authorities what was
being done and by whom. On the other hand, most said they were likelier
to report cheating that put them at a competitive disadvantage.

The attitude toward reporting—and to a serious degree toward   6
cheating—turned out to be remarkably pragmatic. Do it, or don't do it, because it works—to make life more fair, more comfortable, more predictable.

Then came what was for me the interesting part. The class was after   7
all about community—about understanding and strengthening the institution that, along with family, is the foundation on which our society
rests.

So I asked which sort of community they'd rather live in: one in   8
which nearly everyone adhered to the highest ethical standards or one
that embraced a live-and-let-live attitude. They were almost unanimous
in preferring the high-standard community.

9   "You'd want neighbors with higher ethical standards than your own?" I asked. They would but also thought it likely that they'd raise their own standards to meet the community norm. "And also lower them to meet that norm?" They weren't sure, but fitting in did seem to count for something; isn't that what standards are about?

10   Then I asked them to imagine they had come up with a foolproof way of counterfeiting money. Would they be tempted? Not enough to ruin the economy, of course. Just, say, $100,000 in undetectable counterfeit. You could pay off your college loans, help out the family, get the jalopy fixed . . . and then destroy the plates. After all, you're no career criminal. Who would get hurt? Your family's better off, your debts are paid, the mechanic has a job he wouldn't have had. Maybe the trickle-down effect of your clever counterfeiting improves the local community.

11   And no one would do it. Ethics, they decided, wasn't only about pragmatism and getting along. Personal integrity mattered for its own sake. Who would be hurt? They would, they agreed.

12   I'm not alleging major epiphany in a single afternoon. Many of my students remain ambivalent (and unbelievably honest) about the temptation to lower their ethical standards, particularly in settings where lower standards are the norm. And if 80 percent of the brightest and best own up to cheating, those lower standards are the norm.

13   Nor is this some personal discovery of mine. Donald McCabe, the Princeton professor who conducted the survey that launched our discussion, is the founding president of the Center for Academic Integrity, a consortium of some 200 colleges and universities (including Duke, where the center is based). This group is exploring ways not merely to reverse the rising tide of academic cheating and plagiarism, but, more important, to get students to embrace high ethical standards as a matter of personal integrity.

14   It won't be easy, as McCabe's survey makes clear. But it's hard to think of anything more worth whatever effort it will take.

▶ Building Vocabulary

In his essay, Raspberry uses several idiomatic phrases. For each of the following, rewrite the sentences they come from into your own words without using the idiom:

1. the cream of our scholastic crop (par. 1)
2. insisted they'd outgrown the practice (par. 3)
3. the middle ground (par. 5)
4. nearly everyone adhered to the highest (par. 8)
5. the trickle-down effect (par. 10)
6. reverse the rising tide (par. 13)

▶Thinking Critically About the Argument

Understanding the Writer's Argument

1. In the beginning of his essay, why is Raspberry "reeling"?
2. What is an honor code?
3. What is the spectrum of different honor codes? Which does Duke University have?
4. What opinion do Raspberry's students have on reporting people they know to be cheating?
5. What part of the discussion about cheating does Raspberry find most interesting? Why?
6. What is the point of the hypothetical situation that Raspberry offers his class?
7. What is the purpose of the Center for Academic Integrity?

Understanding the Writer's Techniques

1. What is the author's claim? Where does he state it, if at all?
2. What are the implied warrants in this essay? Are there any explicit ones? Which are they?
3. What is the writer's tone? How does the tone support the author's argument?
4. What is the rhetorical effect of starting the essay with the beginning of Raspberry's "Family and Community" class? How does the first paragraph frame the argument?
5. Why does the writer progress through his ideas in the order that he does?
6. What is the argumentative effect of admitting that his "epiphany" is not a "personal discovery"?
7. How effective is the concluding paragraph? The title? Explain.

Exploring the Writer's Argument

1. In paragraph 7, Raspberry says that the implications of the community are for him "the interesting part." Do you think this is the most interesting part of this discussion? Explain your answer.
2. Is there any aspect of cheating that you think Raspberry fails to explain? What would you have liked him to address?
3. Explore the last sentence in paragraph 9. Is Raspberry being sarcastic here, or is he respectful of his students' answers? Explain your response.
4. Are you persuaded by the author when he says of cheating that "it's hard to think of anything more worth whatever effort it will take" (par. 14) to stop it? Why or why not?

▶ Ideas for Writing Arguments

Prewriting

Make an outline of what you think are the causes of cheating among students.

Writing a Guided Argument

In his essay, Raspberry explores the implications of cheating and addresses the idea of integrity, but he doesn't really dig into the sources of cheating. If even half of Raspberry's students, almost definitely people with integrity, have cheated, then what is the root cause of cheating? Write an essay in which you argue for what you think are the real causes of cheating among students.

1. Open your essay with a moment that led you to think about the origins of cheating (for example, a time when you or someone you know cheated).
2. Continue by writing your major proposition clearly.
3. Explain further what it means to cheat and explain your minor propositions.
4. Cultivate a tone of professorial authority.
5. Support your minor propositions with examples and anecdotes as well as appropriate reasoning.
6. Do not hesitate to appeal to the reader's sense of decency and integrity.
7. Bring your essay to a close with a section that attempts to prescribe a solution to the causes you offered.

Thinking, Arguing, and Writing Collaboratively

In one of four equal groups, invent a hypothetical situation as Raspberry does in paragraph 10. Then, each group should poll the class on its hypothetical situation. Record the results, and talk as a group about what you think the implications are. Report what you think the results are to the class, and discuss them.

Writing About the Text

Raspberry is both a columnist and a professor, but this column feels very scholarly. Write an essay in which you tease out the ways in which Raspberry uses his style and word choice to make this seem like an intellectual enterprise that has a home in academia. How does his voice sound like a professor's voice rather than the voice of a newspaper columnist?

More Writing Ideas

1. Do you think that it is more likely or less likely that cheating occurs on the average test given at your school? Explain your answer in a journal entry.
2. In a paragraph or two, explain why nearly all of the students in Raspberry's class would refrain from cheating on the SATs, whereas half of them would cheat (and have cheated) on other exams.
3. Visit the Web site for the Center for Academic Integrity, or colleges' individual Web sites, and find at least three honor codes, one of which, if possible, is the honor code from your own school. Print them out and read them. Write an essay in which you argue for one honor code over the other two, exploring the issue of what you think is the proper balance between honesty and pragmatism.

ALFIE KOHN
The Dangerous Myth of Grade Inflation

Alfie Kohn is the author of No Contest: The Case Against Competition *(1986),* Punished By Rewards: The Trouble with Gold Stars, Incentive Plans, A's, Praise, and Other Bribes *(1993),* The Schools Our Children Deserve: Moving Beyond Traditional Classrooms and "Tougher Standards" *(1999), and* The Case Against Standardized Testing: Raising the Scores, Ruining the Schools *(2000). He has published articles in* The Nation, Harvard Business Review, *the* Atlantic Monthly, Parents, Psychology Today, The New York Times *and other publications.* Time *has called Kohn "perhaps the country's most outspoken critic of education's fixation on grades [and] test scores." In this selection, Kohn makes his case for why giving grades to students is bad for education.*

▶ Prereading: Thinking About the Essay in Advance

Do you think your grades in school have always matched your effort and skill? Why or why not? Are there any alternatives to giving grades in school? What are they?

▶ Words to Watch

harrumphing (par. 2) making comments of displeasure
indignation (par. 2) anger over unfairness
dubious (par. 4) suspiciously unreliable
lamentations (par. 5) expressions of sorrow
aggregate (par. 9) collected together to make a whole
epistemological (par. 13) having to do with the philosophy of knowledge

constituencies (par. 19) group of people with the same ideas or views
dichotomy (par. 28) separation into two divisions
candor (par. 29) absolute honesty
inducement (par. 36) something that gives someone a reason to do something

Grade inflation got started . . . in the late '60s and early '70s. . . . The grades that faculty members now give . . . deserve to be a scandal.
—Professor Harvey Mansfield, Harvard University, 2001

Grades A and B are sometimes given too readily—Grade A for work of no very high merit, and Grade B for work not far above mediocrity. . . . One of the chief obstacles to raising the standards of the degree is the readiness with which insincere students gain passable grades by sham work.
—Report of the Committee on Raising the Standard, Harvard University, 1894

1 Complaints about grade inflation have been around for a very long time. Every so often a fresh flurry of publicity pushes the issue to the foreground again, the latest example being a series of articles in *The Boston Globe* last year that disclosed—in a tone normally reserved for the discovery of entrenched corruption in state government—that a lot of students at Harvard were receiving A's and being graduated with honors.

2 The fact that people were offering the same complaints more than a century ago puts the latest bout of harrumphing in perspective, not unlike those quotations about the disgraceful values of the younger generation that turn out to be hundreds of years old. The long history of indignation also pretty well derails any attempts to place the blame for higher grades on a residue of bleeding-heart liberal professors hired in the '60s. (Unless, of course, there was a similar countercultural phenomenon in the *1860s*.)

3 Yet on campuses across America today, academe's usual requirements for supporting data and reasoned analysis have been suspended for some reason where this issue is concerned. It is largely accepted on faith that grade inflation—an upward shift in students' grade-point averages without a similar rise in achievement—exists, and that it is a bad thing. Meanwhile, the truly substantive issues surrounding grades and motivation have been obscured or ignored.

4 The fact is that it is hard to substantiate even the simple claim that grades have been rising. Depending on the time period we're talking about, that claim may well be false. In their book *When Hope and Fear Collide* (Jossey-Bass, 1998), Arthur Levine and Jeanette Curteon tell us that more undergraduates in 1993 reported receiving A's (and fewer reported receiving grades of C or below) compared with their counterparts in 1969 and 1976 surveys. Unfortunately, self-reports are notoriously unreliable, and the numbers become even more dubious when only a self-selected, and possibly unrepresentative, segment bothers to return the questionnaires. (One out of three failed to do so in 1993; no information is offered about the return rates in the earlier surveys.)

To get a more accurate picture of whether grades have changed over   5
the years, one needs to look at official student transcripts. Clifford Adel-
man, a senior research analyst with the U.S. Department of Education,
did just that, reviewing transcripts from more than 3,000 institutions and
reporting his results in 1995. His finding: "Contrary to the widespread
lamentations, grades actually declined slightly in the last two decades."
Moreover, a report released just this year by the National Center for Education Statistics revealed that fully 33.5 percent of American undergraduates had a grade-point average of C or below in 1999-2000, a number that
ought to quiet "all the furor over grade inflation," according to a
spokesperson for the Association of American Colleges and Universities.
(A review of other research suggests a comparable lack of support for
claims of grade inflation at the high-school level.)

However, even where grades *are* higher now as compared with   6
then—which may well be true in the most selective institutions—that
does not constitute proof that they are inflated. The burden rests with
critics to demonstrate that those higher grades are undeserved, and one
can cite any number of alternative explanations. Maybe students are
turning in better assignments. Maybe instructors used to be too stingy
with their marks and have become more reasonable. Maybe the concept
of assessment itself has evolved, so that today it is more a means for allowing students to demonstrate what they know rather than for sorting
them or "catching them out." (The real question, then, is why we spent so
many years trying to make good students look bad.) Maybe students
aren't forced to take as many courses outside their primary areas of interest in which they didn't fare as well. Maybe struggling students are now
able to withdraw from a course before a poor grade appears on their
transcripts. (Say what you will about that practice, it challenges the hypothesis that the grades students receive in the courses they complete are
inflated.)

The bottom line: No one has ever demonstrated that students today   7
get A's for the same work that used to receive B's or C's. We simply do not
have the data to support such a claim.

Consider the most recent, determined effort by a serious source to   8
prove that grades are inflated: "Evaluation and the Academy: Are We
Doing the Right Thing?" a report released this year by the American
Academy of Arts and Sciences. Its senior author is Henry Rosovsky, formerly Harvard's dean of the faculty. The first argument offered in support of the proposition that students couldn't possibly deserve higher
grades is that SAT scores have dropped during the same period that
grades are supposed to have risen. But this is a patently inapt comparison, if only because the SAT is deeply flawed. It has never been much
good even at predicting grades during the freshman year in college,
to say nothing of more-important academic outcomes. A four-year
analysis of almost 78,000 University of California students, published
last year by the UC president's office, found that the test predicted only

13.3 percent of variation in freshman grades, a figure roughly consistent with hundreds of previous studies. (I outlined numerous other problems with the test in "Two Cheers for an End to the SAT," *The Chronicle*, March 9, 2001.)

9   Even if one believes that the SAT is a valid and valuable exam, however, the claim that scores are dropping is a poor basis for the assertion that grades are too high. First, it is difficult to argue that a standardized test taken in high school and grades for college course work are measuring the same thing. Second, changes in aggregate SAT scores mostly reflect the proportion of the eligible population that has chosen to take the test. The American Academy's report states that average SAT scores dropped slightly from 1969 to 1993. But over that period, the pool of test takers grew from about one-third to more than two-fifths of high-school graduates—an addition of more than 200,000 students.

10   Third, a decline in overall SAT scores is hardly the right benchmark against which to measure the grades earned at Harvard or other elite institutions. Every bit of evidence I could find—including a review of the SAT scores of entering students at Harvard over the past two decades, at the nation's most selective colleges over three and even four decades, and at all private colleges since 1985—uniformly confirms a virtually linear rise in both verbal and math scores, even after correcting for the renorming of the test in the mid-1990s. To cite just one example, the latest edition of "Trends in College Admissions" reports that the average verbal-SAT score of students enrolled in all private colleges rose from 543 in 1985 to 558 in 1999. Thus, those who regard SAT results as a basis for comparison should *expect* to see higher grades now rather than assume

11   that they are inflated.

The other two arguments made by the authors of the American Academy's report rely on a similar sleight of hand. They note that more college students are now forced to take remedial courses, but offer no reason to think that this is especially true of the relevant student population—namely, those at the most selective colleges who are now receiving A's in-

12   stead of B's.

Finally, they report that more states are adding high-school graduation tests and even standardized exams for admission to public universities. Yet that trend can be explained by political factors and offers no evidence of an objective decline in students' proficiency. For instance, scores on the National Assessment of Educational Progress, known as "the nation's report card" on elementary and secondary schooling, have shown very little change over the past couple of decades, and most of the change that has occurred has been for the better. As David Berliner and Bruce Biddle put it in their tellingly titled book *The Manufactured Crisis* (Addison-Wesley, 1995), the data demonstrate that "today's students are at least as well informed as students in previous generations." The latest round of public-school bashing—and concomitant reliance on high-stakes testing—began with the Reagan administration's "Nation at Risk" report, featuring claims now widely viewed by researchers as exaggerated and misleading.

Beyond the absence of good evidence, the debate over grade inflation brings up knotty epistemological problems. To say that grades are not merely rising but inflated—and that they are consequently "less accurate" now, as the American Academy's report puts it—is to postulate the existence of an objectively correct evaluation of what a student (or an essay) deserves, the true grade that ought to be uncovered and honestly reported. It would be an understatement to say that this reflects a simplistic and outdated view of knowledge and of learning.   13

In fact, what is most remarkable is how rarely learning even figures into the discussion. The dominant disciplinary sensibility in commentaries on this topic is not that of education—an exploration of pedagogy or assessment—but rather of economics. That is clear from the very term "grade inflation," which is, of course, just a metaphor. Our understanding is necessarily limited if we confine ourselves to the vocabulary of inputs and outputs, incentives, resource distribution, and compensation.   14

Suppose, for the sake of the argument, we assumed the very worst—not only that students are getting better grades than did their counterparts of an earlier generation, but that the grades are too high. What does that mean, and why does it upset some people so?   15

To understand grade inflation in its proper context, we must acknowledge a truth that is rarely named: The crusade against it is led by conservative individuals and organizations who regard it as analogous—or even related—to such favorite whipping boys as multicultural education, the alleged radicalism of academe, "political correctness" (a label that permits the denigration of anything one doesn't like without having to offer a reasoned objection), and too much concern about students' self-esteem. Mainstream media outlets and college administrators have allowed themselves to be put on the defensive by accusations about grade inflation, as can be witnessed when deans at Harvard plead nolo contendere and dutifully tighten their grading policies.   16

What are the critics assuming about the nature of students' motivation to learn, about the purpose of evaluation and of education itself? (It is surely revealing when someone reserves time and energy to complain bitterly about how many students are getting A's—as opposed to expressing concern about, say, how many students have been trained to think that the point of going to school is to get A's.)   17

"In a healthy university, it would not be necessary to say what is wrong with grade inflation," Harvey Mansfield asserted in an opinion article last year (*The Chronicle*, April 6, 2001). That, to put it gently, is a novel view of health. It seems reasonable to expect those making an argument to be prepared to defend it, and also valuable to bring their hidden premises to light. Here are the assumptions that seem to underlie the grave warnings about grade inflation: 18

19   **The professor's job is to sort students for employers or graduate schools.** Some are disturbed by grade inflation—or, more accurately, grade compression—because it then becomes harder to spread out students on a continuum, ranking them against one another for the benefit of postcollege constituencies. One professor asks, by way of analogy, "Why would anyone subscribe to *Consumers Digest* if every blender were rated a 'best buy'"?

20   But how appropriate is such a marketplace analogy? Is the professor's job to rate students like blenders for the convenience of corporations, or to offer feedback that will help students learn more skillfully and enthusiastically? (Notice, moreover, that even consumer magazines don't grade on a curve. They report the happy news if it turns out that every blender meets a reasonable set of performance criteria.)

21   Furthermore, the student-as-appliance approach assumes that grades provide useful information to those postcollege constituencies. Yet growing evidence—most recently in the fields of medicine and law, as cited in publications like *The Journal of the American Medical Association* and the *American Educational Research Journal*—suggests that grades and test scores do not in fact predict career success, or much of anything beyond subsequent grades and test scores.

22   **Students should be set against one another in a race for artificially scarce rewards.** "The essence of grading is exclusiveness," Mansfield said in one interview. Students "should have to compete with each other," he said in another.

23   In other words, even when no graduate-school admissions committee pushes for students to be sorted, they ought to be sorted anyway, with grades reflecting relative standing rather than absolute accomplishment. In effect, this means that the game should be rigged so that no matter how well students do, only a few can get A's. The question guiding evaluation in such a classroom is not "How well are they learning?" but "Who's beating whom?" The ultimate purpose of good colleges, this view holds, is not to maximize success, but to ensure that there will always be losers.

24   A bell curve may sometimes—but only sometimes—describe the range of knowledge in a roomful of students at the beginning of a course. When it's over, though, any responsible educator hopes that the results would skew drastically to the right, meaning that most students learned what they hadn't known before. Thus, in their important study, *Making Sense of College Grades* (Jossey-Bass, 1986), Ohmer Milton, Howard Pollio, and James Eison write, "It is not a symbol of rigor to have grades fall into a 'normal' distribution; rather, it is a symbol of failure—failure to teach well, failure to test well, and failure to have any influence at all on the intellectual lives of students." Making sure all students are continually re-sorted, with excellence turned into an artificially scarce commodity, is almost perverse.

25   What does relative success signal about student performance in any case? The number of peers that a student has bested tells us little about

how much she knows and is able to do. Moreover, such grading policies may create a competitive climate that is counter-productive for winners and losers alike, to the extent that it discourages a free exchange of ideas and a sense of community that's conducive to exploration.

Harder is better (or higher grades mean lower standards). Com- 26
pounding the tendency to confuse excellence with victory is a tendency to confuse quality with difficulty—as evidenced in the accountability fad that has elementary and secondary education in its grip just now, with relentless talk of "rigor" and "raising the bar." The same confusion shows up in higher education when professors pride themselves not on the intellectual depth and value of their classes but merely on how much reading they assign, how hard their tests are, how rarely they award good grades, and so on. "You're going to have to *work* in here!" they announce, with more than a hint of machismo and self-congratulation.

Some people might defend that posture on the grounds that students 27
will perform better if A's are harder to come by. In fact, the evidence on this question is decidedly mixed. Stringent grading sometimes has been shown to boost short-term retention as measured by multiple-choice exams— never to improve understanding or promote interest in learning. The most recent analysis, released in 2000 by Julian R. Betts and Jeff Grogger, professors of economics at the University of California at San Diego and at Los Angeles, respectively, found that tougher grading was initially correlated with higher test scores. But the long-term effects were negligible—with the exception of minority students, for whom the effects were negative.

It appears that something more than an empirical hypothesis is behind 28
the "harder is better" credo, particularly when it is set up as a painfully false dichotomy: Those easy-grading professors are too lazy to care, or too worried about how students will evaluate them, or overly concerned about their students' self-esteem, whereas *we* are the last defenders of what used to matter in the good old days. High standards! Intellectual honesty! No free lunch!

The American Academy's report laments an absence of "candor" 29
about this issue. Let us be candid, then. Those who grumble about undeserved grades sometimes exude a cranky impatience with—or even contempt for—the late adolescents and young adults who sit in their classrooms. Many people teaching in higher education, after all, see themselves primarily as researchers and regard teaching as an occupational hazard, something they're not very good at, were never trained for, and would rather avoid. It would be interesting to examine the correlation between one's view of teaching (or of students) and the intensity of one's feelings about grade inflation. Someone also might want to examine the personality profiles of those who become infuriated over the possibility that someone, somewhere, got an A without having earned it.

Grades motivate. With the exception of orthodox behaviorists, psychol- 30
ogists have come to realize that people can exhibit qualitatively different kinds of motivation: intrinsic, in which the task itself is seen as valuable, and

extrinsic, in which the task is just a means to the end of gaining a reward or escaping a punishment. The two are not only distinct but often inversely related. Scores of studies have demonstrated, for example, that the more people are rewarded, the more they come to lose interest in whatever had to be done in order to get the reward. (That conclusion is essentially reaffirmed by the latest major meta-analysis on the topic: a review of 128 studies, published in 1999 by Edward L. Deci, Richard Koestner, and Richard Ryan.)

31   Those unfamiliar with that basic distinction, let alone the supporting research, may be forgiven for pondering how to "motivate" students, then concluding that grades are often a good way of doing so, and consequently worrying about the impact of inflated grades. But the reality is that it doesn't matter how motivated students are; what matters is *how* students are motivated. A focus on grades creates, or at least perpetuates, an extrinsic orientation that is likely to undermine the love of learning we are presumably seeking to promote.

32   Three robust findings emerge from the empirical literature on the subject: Students who are given grades, or for whom grades are made particularly salient, tend to display less interest in what they are doing, fare worse on meaningful measures of learning, and avoid more-challenging tasks when given the opportunity—as compared with those in a nongraded comparison group. College instructors cannot help noticing, and presumably being disturbed by, such consequences, but they may lapse into blaming students ("grade grubbers") rather than understanding the systemic sources of the problem. A focus on whether too many students are getting A's suggests a tacit endorsement of grades that predictably produces just such a mind-set in students.

33   These fundamental questions are almost completely absent from discussions of grade inflation. The American Academy's report takes exactly one sentence—with no citations—to dismiss the argument that "lowering the anxiety over grades leads to better learning," ignoring the fact that much more is involved than anxiety. It is a matter of why a student learns, not only how much stress he feels. Nor is the point just that low grades hurt some students' feelings, but that grades, per se, hurt all students' engagement with learning. The meaningful contrast is not between an A and a B or C, but between an extrinsic and an intrinsic focus.

34   Precisely because that is true, a reconsideration of grade inflation leads us to explore alternatives to our (often unreflective) use of grades. Narrative comments and other ways by which faculty members can communicate their evaluations can be far more informative than letter or number grades, and much less destructive. Indeed, some colleges—for example, Hampshire, Evergreen State, Alverno, and New College of Florida—have eliminated grades entirely, as a critical step toward raising intellectual standards. Even the American Academy's report acknowledges that "relatively undifferentiated course grading has been a traditional practice in

many graduate schools for a very long time." Has that policy produced lower-quality teaching and learning? Quite the contrary: Many people say they didn't begin to explore ideas deeply and passionately until graduate school began and the importance of grades diminished significantly.

If the continued use of grades rests on nothing more than tradition   35 ("We've always done it that way"), a faulty understanding of motivation, or excessive deference to graduate-school admissions committees, then it may be time to balance those factors against the demonstrated harms of getting students to chase A's. Ohmer Milton and his colleagues discovered—and others have confirmed—that a "grade orientation" and a "learning orientation" on the part of students tend to be inversely related. That raises the disturbing possibility that some colleges are institutions of higher learning in name only, because the paramount question for students is not "What does this mean?" but "Do we have to know this?"

A grade-oriented student body is an invitation for the administration   36 and faculty to ask hard questions: What unexamined assumptions keep traditional grading in place? What forms of assessment might be less destructive? How can professors minimize the salience of grades in their classrooms, so long as grades must still be given? And: If the artificial inducement of grades disappeared, what sort of teaching strategies might elicit authentic interest in a course?

To engage in this sort of inquiry, to observe real classrooms, and to re-   37 view the relevant research is to arrive at one overriding conclusion: The real threat to excellence isn't grade inflation at all; it's grades.

▶ Building Vocabulary

1. This essay assumes knowledge of a number of terms that you might find unfamiliar. For each of the following terms, define it and use it in a sentence of your own:
   a. bleeding-heart liberal (par. 2)
   b. countercultural (par. 2)
   c. high-stakes testing (par. 12)
   d. whipping boys (par. 16)
   e. radicalism (par. 16)
   f. political correctness (par. 16)
   g. nolo contendere (par. 16)
   h. bell curve (par. 24)
   i. behaviorists (par. 30)
   j. meta-analysis (par. 30)
2. Write a definition for each of the following words:
   a. hypothesis (par. 6)
   b. inapt (par. 8)
   c. benchmark (par. 10)
   d. linear (par. 10)

e. continuum (par. 19)
f. scarce (par. 22)
g. machismo (par. 26)
h. stringent (par. 27)
i. credo (par. 28)

▶ Thinking Critically About the Argument

Understanding the Writer's Argument

1. What is grade inflation? Why is the beginning of this essay concerned with Harvard University?
2. Why can we not blame grade inflation on political changes in the 1960s?
3. What makes Kohn doubt that grades have been inflated? What evidence does he show that says the opposite?
4. According to Kohn, what is the problem with the SAT?
5. What does Kohn mean when he writes that without "good evidence, the debate over grade inflation brings up knotty epistemological problems"? (par. 13)
6. What are the reasons Kohn outlines for why grades seem so important to everyone? What are the institutional barriers to dropping grades entirely?
7. What is Kohn's opinion of competition over grades in school?
8. What is the relationship between difficult classes and the quality of the education?
9. Does Kohn believe that grades motivate students to learn more? Explain. What does it mean that grades and the level of learning "tend to be inversely related"? (par. 35)

Understanding the Writer's Techniques

1. What is Kohn's claim in this essay? Where is it located? Does he state it in just one sentence? Explain.
2. What is the argumentative effect of starting his essay with epigraphs, the quotes that appear before the essay proper? Why do they both have to do with Harvard?
3. What is Kohn's tone in this essay? Offer examples to show why you answered as you did.
4. The writer divides the argument into sections. Make a list of the sections and the rhetorical strategy used in each section.
5. How much of Kohn's argument depends on the debunking of grade inflation in the first part of his essay? Explain.
6. Which point that Kohn makes in this essay do you find the most surprising? Why?

7. What point is Kohn making in paragraph 9 about the SAT as it relates to grades?
8. How effective is Kohn's conclusion? Explain your answer.

Exploring the Writer's Argument

1. Kohn tries to show that grade inflation cannot be proven. Does his argument convince you? Why or why not? What are the strengths and weaknesses of the argument?
2. Analyze Kohn's parenthetical comment in paragraph 17. Do you think he's right? His point is crucial to his argument. Why does he put it in parentheses? Does that weaken his argument? Explain your answers.
3. Kohn rebuts the arguments of various reports and professors. What is your opinion of his rebuttals? Are they effective? Which is the most effective rebuttal? Which is the weakest? Why?
4. Attempt to find an answer to Kohn's question in paragraph 36, "How can professors minimize the salience of grades in their classrooms, so long as grades must still be given?"
5. How does the fact that Kohn doesn't give any real solutions to the problem he exposes affect the essay's quality?

▶ Ideas for Writing Arguments

Prewriting

How can seemingly innocent language, language we don't even think about being persuasive, be used to make a point? For example, the phrase "pro-life" seems innocent enough, but it implies that the other side might be considered "pro-death." List as many of these terms as you can.

Writing a Guided Argument

Kohn says in paragraph 16 that the term "political correctness" permits us to condemn anything we don't like without having to offer a reasoned objection. Public discourse in our day, it seems, contains phrases that allow us to condemn without having to offer a reasoned objection. Write an essay in which you explain the use and abuse of at least three of those phrases.

1. Begin your essay with an explanation of Kohn's point about the term "political correctness." Explain the term and its meaning.
2. Introduce your claim that other terms are used similarly.
3. Tell your reader the terms.
4. In the next section, explain where these terms are used most often (for example, television talk shows or politicians' speeches) and how.

5. Next, make your case for your first term or phrase.

6. Support your point with examples from your experience and from your reading.

7. Do the same with the other two phrases.

8. In your concluding section, argue that discourse is only hurt by phrases such as the ones explored in your essay.

Thinking, Arguing, and Writing Collaboratively

Divide the class into two groups. One group should adopt the position that grades are good for education and the other the position that they have a negative effect. Each group should amplify or refute the writer's main points.

Writing About the Text

Kohn's essay appeared in a weekly publication directed at college and university teachers and administrators. How does his language and sentence structure reflect an understanding of his audience?

More Writing Ideas

1. In your journal, consider the question of what alternatives there might be to giving grades in college. Would you like to eliminate grades? Why or why not?

2. Kohn raises the question of why students even go to college in the first place. In one or two paragraphs, explore the idea of what you believe is the most important reason to go to college, and determine if you are living up to that standard.

3. Some colleges have done away with grades. Do some research to determine which colleges have done this. Write an essay to evaluate the success of those schools. Are the students learning?

Leon Botstein
Curtailing High School: A Radical Proposal

The president of Bard College in upstate New York, Botstein is also the music director of the American Symphony Orchestra and is a well-respected conductor for most of the orchestra's concerts. He also is the music director and conductor of the Jerusalem Symphony Orchestra. He has traveled the world as a guest conductor and is a classically trained violinist, a scholar of music history, and an editor and a writer. He is also an education theorist and the author of Jefferson's Children: Education and the Promise of American Culture *(1997), which makes several suggestions about the future of public schools. This selection argues for one of those ideas, that high school should not last as long as it does today.*

▶ Prereading: Thinking About the Essay in Advance

Why do you think American society keeps children in school until age 18? Is there some reason for that age, or is it arbitrary?

▶ Words to Watch

pressing (par. 1) urgently important
evenhandedly (par. 1) fairly
immunization (par. 2) act of giving medicine to prevent disease
presumptions (par. 3) beliefs
aspire (par. 4) seek a higher goal
infantilize (par. 6) treat like a child

The most pressing concern for the future of the American high school is   1
correcting the fatal flaw in the way we educate adolescents, revealed through its inability to deliver excellence evenhandedly over the past 40 years. It is that failure from which we must learn. The high school has outlived its usefulness to the point of catastrophe, not only with respect to those least privileged who live in the inner cities and poor rural districts of America. It has also let down the children of families with sufficient incomes to move to suburbia in hopes of finding superior public education there.

The primary cause for the inadequacy of high school rests with irre-   2
versible changes in adolescent development. The current system of public education was designed when the onset of puberty was three years later than it is today. Over the past century, the age of physical maturation has steadily dropped as a result of immunization and nutritional standards. Before World War II, 18, the traditional age of high school graduation, was two or three years after maturation. That age also coincided with the onset of adult sexual activity. In the beginning of the 21st century, 16-year-old Americans are, in development and behavior, comparable to the 18-year-olds of a century ago. High school was designed to deal with large children. It is now faced with young adults whose adult behavior has already begun.

Neither the personnel, the buildings, the schedule nor the curriculum   3
of high school can satisfy the presumptions of adulthood that today's high school age adolescents legitimately bring with them. The issue is not whether today's adolescents are more mature because of earlier development. The fact is they are *able* to act as adults whether they do so responsibly or not. They are treated by our consumer society as adults; the fashion industry and Hollywood recognize their role as consumers. Modern transportation and communication have given adolescents the freedom of movement we associate with adulthood. Neither community nor home effectively limits their freedom of movement.

4   Plans to extend the high school education to five years, or to expand its degree-granting range, fly in the face of social and biological facts. The freedom in learning, the dignity of serious study and the access to the deep command of subject matter that adulthood and higher education require are not available in the American high school today, nor can they be created within the current high school framework. The Advanced Placement courses that are taught, for example, are largely substandard and inferior to what is available in most colleges. The definition of what constitutes the Advanced Placement curriculum is dictated not by the teacher, but by a private testing agency. No university or college of standing permits such a system to define its standards. The professional preparation, autonomy and academic freedom characteristic of the faculty in American higher education do not exist and cannot flourish within the walls of the American high school. Yet these qualities are essential to the high standards in science, mathematics, history and all other subjects to which adolescents can aspire.

5   The future of the American high school rests with shifting its existing curriculum and practices to younger students and reforming these practices as the shift takes place. In other words, during the next decade, we should rationalize our education system into a two-part elementary and secondary system that ends at age 16. Already it is estimated that more than 1 million young Americans complete their high school education outside the walls of the high school. The majority of college-bound seniors admit that their final year of high school is a waste of time. Increasingly, that criticism is being leveled at the last two years. The high school should, therefore, replace the junior high school and refocus its energies on a younger population, from the ages of 13 to 16.

6   In place of a high school that ends at age 18, the education system should offer multiple options for those between 16 and 19. With a high school diploma, a 16-year-old could choose to attend a community college, to enter a four-year college, or to engage in work, internships or other alternatives to formal school, as well as perhaps national service. We must maintain the democratic pattern of the American educational system by allowing individuals to start college at any time, not necessarily immediately after completing high school. The most important gain from shifting high school graduation to age 16 would be that we would no longer "infantilize" older adolescents and retard their intellectual development.

▶ Building Vocabulary

This essay uses several words and terms from the world of education. Define the following:

1. curriculum (par. 3)
2. Advanced Placement (par. 4)
3. elementary (par. 5)

4. secondary (par. 5)
5. internships (par. 6)

▶Thinking Critically About the Argument

Understanding the Writer's Argument

1. What does Botstein think is the way that the inadequacy of the high school system in America reveals itself?
2. Has the system only been insufficient for a certain segment of the population? Explain.
3. What is the main reason high school has been inadequate, according to Botstein?
4. Other than physically, what other ways are teenagers today different from their predecessors?
5. What is the problem with Advanced Placement tests, according to Botstein?
6. What is Botstein's suggestion to reform the high school system?
7. What does Botstein say we can gain by adopting his suggestions?

Understanding the Writer's Techniques

1. What is Botstein's major proposition in this essay? Where does he state it?
2. Do you find the introductory paragraph to be effective? Why or why not?
3. How does Botstein support his major proposition? Write an outline that reflects the structure of his essay.
4. What evidence does Botstein offer to prove that teenagers have changed over the years?
5. Do you find the structure of his essay to be effective? Why or why not?
6. How does paragraph 3 help to support the writer's position?
7. Has the writer made his case about the Advanced Placement test? Explain your answer.
8. What is the writer's tone? Do you think it helps his argument? Explain.
9. How effective is the conclusion? Explain your answer.

Exploring the Writer's Argument

1. Botstein includes some scientific information about the onset of puberty today compared to before World War II. Are you convinced by his presentation of this evidence and his explanation of it? Why or why not?
2. Does Botstein persuade you that his suggestion for ending high school early is a good one? Does he persuade you that it is a feasible

suggestion? What is the difference between these two questions? Explain your answers.

3. In paragraph 5, Botstein writes that high school seniors don't think much of the last two years of high school. From this, he concludes that educators need to focus on earlier years in their education. Are you convinced by this reasoning? Why or why not?

4. Do you think the end of Botstein's essay is satisfactory, bringing his argument to a natural close, or do you think it is too abrupt? Explain your answer fully.

▶ Ideas for Writing Arguments

Prewriting

Botstein's essay might be easy to accept in the abstract, but how would you feel if your family was affected by his ideas? Jot some notes down about your feelings on the matter.

Writing a Guided Argument

Imagine that you are the parent of a 16-year-old child who has just read Botstein's essay and agrees with him. Your child now wants to quit school, get a GED, and travel and read for two years before college. Your child has articulated his or her views on the subject and has argued from Botstein's position. Write a letter to your child in response.

1. Begin by acknowledging your child's decision.
2. Explain your views on the subject and why you hold them.
3. Write your major proposition, either agreeing with your child or disagreeing.
4. Adopt a tone of patience and authority.
5. Present minor propositions to support your position.
6. Support your minor propositions by offering evidence from your own life and from Botstein's essay.
7. Close your essay with a pledge that your child can do whatever it is he or she wants to do, and that you either agree or disagree with the decision.

Thinking, Arguing, and Writing Collaboratively

Working in small groups, share with a classmate your paper that grew out of the Guided Argument assignment. On your classmate's paper, write a paragraph or two about the effectiveness of the student's argument. Are you convinced? Why or why not? Return your classmate's paper and discuss your classmate's comments with him or her.

Writing About the Text

In this essay, Botstein writes in an extremely clear, lucid style. Write an essay in which you analyze Botstein's style, explaining how he resists overwriting and instead uses prose that does not rely on unnecessary words or ideas.

More Writing Ideas

1. In your journal, freewrite on the idea of extending high school to a fifth year. Write for at least 15 minutes, and do not edit your writing until the time is up. Afterward, read your work and see if there is anything in what you have written that might be the basis for an argument.
2. In an extended paragraph, explore the implications of what Botstein writes in paragraph 1 of his essay, that what he is concerned about is high school's "inability to deliver excellence evenhandedly over the past 40 years."
3. Write an essay in which you argue for what is right about the present-day high school system. What does the public school system do well? How does it help students achieve their goals?

14 The Environment: How Can We Preserve It?

Will we leave any resources for our children and our children's children? That's the urgent question from the environmentalist movement. Humankind is the only species able to alter the climate artificially and pollute the land, water, and air, and we certainly have done that. The Industrial Revolution marked a move away from an agricultural economy to one dominated by machines and factories. Trains, running on coal fuel, belched out black smoke and fouled the atmosphere. Factories dumped chemicals into rivers and harbors. Not until relatively recently did scientists understand the extent to which 200 years of industrialization was damaging the world we live in.

Nature writers helped bring to light the diversity of plants and animals and moved readers to try to protect this diversity. Many writers mobilized to persuade people (especially legislators and politicians) to sit up and take notice and to understand that how they act affects the rest of the world. "Think globally, act locally" became one of the slogans of environmentalism. Much of the recent conversation has focused on global warming and trying to reduce greenhouse gases, which result from the burning of coal or gasoline. The gases warm the atmosphere and have upset Earth's climate. Scientists warn that if humanity doesn't stop global warming, many species will become extinct.

New York Times columnist Bob Herbert, in "No Margin for Error," attempts to frighten his readers into caring about the future of the coral reefs. Verlyn Klinkenborg, in "Out of the Wild," uses a different and more genteel strategy to underline the wonder of the natural world, telling the story of surprising a sick fox in the writer's barn. Barry Lopez in "Apologia" takes this sense of wonder to an extreme in his account of a road trip. Feeling guilty for all the animals he sees dead on the road, he takes his time to pay tribute to them. Fiction writer Wendell Berry, in "In Distrust of Movements," agrees with these writers, but he has no patience for the environmentalist movement or any other movement. In his essay, he circles his subject until arriving at a prescription—have respect for the Earth, and everything will be okay.

Bob Herbert
No Margin for Error

Bob Herbert was born in Brooklyn in 1945 and started his career as a reporter for The Star-Ledger, *a Newark, New Jersey, newspaper. He worked in television news for NBC before returning to newspaper writing in 1993 as a columnist for* The New York Times *op-ed page. He has won numerous awards, including the American Society of Newspaper Editors award for distinguished newspaper writing. He has taught journalism at Brooklyn College and the Columbia University Graduate School of Journalism. Herbert is known for having a strong moral compass in his columns, and in this selection, he takes a look at global warming and its effects on the world's coral reefs.*

▶ Prereading: Thinking About the Essay in Advance

What do you think is the greatest threat to Earth as a result of global warming? What effects have we felt already as a result?

▶ Words to Watch

disintegrate (par. 1) fall apart
emissions (par. 5) things released or given off
phenomena (par. 7) things that occur
indisputable (par. 9) impossible to doubt
catastrophic (par. 12) causing terrible damage
epochs (par. 14) long period of time

G lobal warming is already attacking the world's coral reefs and, if noth- 1
ing is done soon, could begin a long-term assault on the vast West
Antarctic Ice Sheet. If the ice sheet begins to disintegrate, the worldwide
consequences over the next several centuries could well be disastrous.

Coral reefs are sometimes called the rain forests of the oceans because 2
of the tremendous variety of animal and plant life that they support.

"They're the richest ocean ecosystem, and if they are destroyed or se- 3
verely damaged, a lot of the biological diversity simply goes away," said
Dr. Michael Oppenheimer, a professor of geosciences and international
affairs at Princeton who is an expert on climate change.

Dr. Oppenheimer and Brian C. O'Neill, a professor at Brown, have 4
an article in the current issue of *Science* magazine that addresses some of
the long-term dangers that could result if nothing is done about global
warming.

One of the things that is not widely understood about the greenhouse 5
gases that are contributing to the warming of the planet is that once they
are spewed into the atmosphere, they stay there for centuries, and in

some cases, millenniums. So a delay of even a decade or so in reducing those emissions can make it much more difficult—and costly—to slow the momentum of the warming and avert the more extreme consequences.

6   In their article, Dr. Oppenheimer and Dr. O'Neill suggest that public officials and others trying to determine what levels of global warming would actually be dangerous could use the destruction of the world's coral reefs as one of their guides.

7   Coral reefs, which are breathtakingly beautiful natural phenomena, tend to thrive in water temperatures that are only slightly below the maximum temperature at which they can survive. There is not much margin for error. Even allowing for some genetic adaptation, a sustained increase in water temperatures of as little as a couple of degrees Fahrenheit can result in widespread coral reef destruction in just a few years.

(www.ClimateStar.org)

A number of factors are already contributing to the destruction of coral reefs, and global warming is one of them. As the earth's temperature continues to rise, global warming will most likely become the chief enemy of what Dr. Oppenheimer calls "these wonderful sources of biological diversity." 8

The threat to coral reefs is clear and indisputable. Much less clear is the danger that global warming presents to the West Antarctic Ice Sheet. 9

"We really don't know with any level of certainty what amount of warming would destroy the ice sheet or how quickly that would happen," said Dr. Oppenheimer. He and Dr. O'Neill wrote, "In general, the probability is thought to be low during this century, increasing gradually thereafter." 10

There is not even agreement among scientists on the amount of warming necessary to begin the destruction. But what is clear is that if the ice sheet were to disintegrate, the consequences would be profound. So you don't want to play around with this. You want to make sure it doesn't happen. 11

"We know," said Dr. Oppenheimer, "that if the ice sheet were destroyed, sea levels would rise about five meters, which would be catastrophic for coastal regions. That would submerge much of Manhattan below Greenwich Village, for instance. It would drown the southern third of Florida, an area inhabited by about four million people." 12

Five meters is approximately 16 feet. Tremendous amounts of housing, wetlands and farming areas around the world would vanish. Large portions of a country like Bangladesh, on the Bay of Bengal, would disappear. 13

So what could actually set this potential catastrophe in motion? Dr. Oppenheimer has looked back at past geological epochs. "There is some evidence," he said, "that when the global temperature was warmer by about four degrees Fahrenheit than it is today the ice sheet disintegrated." 14

It is now estimated that if we do nothing to stem the rise of global warming, the increase in the earth's temperature over the course of this century will be between 3 and 10.5 degrees Fahrenheit. That is a level of warming that could initiate the disintegration of the ice sheet. And stopping that disintegration, once the planet gets warm, may be impossible. 15

▶ Building Vocabulary

In this essay, Herbert uses several terms from the world of ecology and earth science. Identify and write definitions for the following:

1. global warming (par. 1)
2. rain forests (par. 2)
3. ecosystem (par. 3)
4. geosciences (par. 3)
5. climate change (par. 3)
6. greenhouse gases (par. 5)
7. wetlands (par. 13)

▶Thinking Critically About the Argument

Understanding the Writer's Argument

1. What are coral reefs? Why are they so special?
2. Why is time of the essence when dealing with issues of global warming?
3. How are coral reefs a good gauge of the destruction wrought by global warming?
4. What is the West Antarctic Ice Sheet, and why should we care what happens to it?
5. What is the main cause of global warming?

Understanding the Writer's Techniques

1. What is Herbert's major proposition? Where does he express it most clearly?
2. Why does Herbert begin his essay with such a confrontational paragraph? Explain how it affects his argument.
3. This essay lists the effects of global warming. Identify these effects in the order that Herbert presents them. Which is most surprising or powerful? Why?
4. Why does Herbert present his argument in the order that he does?
5. Why does Herbert pause in his argument to explain how many feet five meters is, after he has already mentioned much of the destruction that might occur if the ice sheet melts?
6. How does the concluding paragraph help to wrap up Herbert's argument?

Exploring the Writer's Argument

1. There are a few places in this short essay when Herbert repeats information. Why does he repeat himself? Is the strategy effective or it is a weakness in the essay?
2. Herbert doesn't spend much time explaining what his readers could do to help the coral reefs or the ice sheet. Is this a weakness in his essay? Explain your answer.
3. Herbert praises the coral reefs and explains why it would be terrible if they were lost, but at the end of his essay he doesn't mention them again. Why? Does this omission weaken his essay? Why or why not?

▶Ideas for Writing Arguments

Prewriting

Herbert says that people are the problem. What can you do yourself to help stop global warming, if it is such a problem?

Writing a Guided Argument

One of the sayings in the environmental movement is "think globally, act locally." Activists say that if many people do little things to conserve resources, then we will see the benefits worldwide. Write an essay in the form of an open letter to the other students in your college arguing that they can act locally to help the environment. (You might have to do a little bit of research to gather evidence.)

1. Open your essay with an explanation of the problem and why it is urgent that we protect the environment.
2. Write your major proposition, and explain how students can play a role in this effort.
3. Next, show how students can be wasteful and act in ways that harm the environment.
4. Offer your minor propositions in the next section, showing exactly what students can do to help protect the environment.
5. Support your minor propositions with facts and process analysis, giving your reader a "how-to" for each.
6. Affect a tone that reflects the seriousness and urgency of the topic.
7. Explain to your reader that students are important because they are the future leaders of the world.
8. Bring your essay to a close on an ominous note, explaining what might happen if students don't take a role.

Thinking, Arguing, and Writing Collaboratively

In groups of four or five, discuss the ideas presented in your Writing a Guided Argument assignment. Jot down notes, and incorporate your peers' opinions—making sure they suit your essay—in your final draft.

Writing About the Text

In this essay, Herbert depends for his evidence almost entirely on the single article in *Science* magazine by Drs. Michael Oppenheimer and Brian C. O'Neill. Where in Herbert's essay do you, as the reader, desire more varied evidence? Or do you not need more? Write an essay in which you analyze how Herbert's essay is either strengthened or weakened by having only one source?

More Writing Ideas

1. In your journal, write an entry assessing your own activities when it comes to saving or wasting natural resources.
2. Some people, despite all scientific evidence for global warming, have denied that it's happening at all. Do some research and in several

paragraphs, summarize the arguments of those who don't believe in global warming.

3. Many countries have tried to reduce the effects of global warming. One of those efforts, the Kyoto Conference, was an international meeting brokered under the power of the United Nations. The conference drafted the Kyoto Protocol, which called for countries to reduce emissions and other greenhouse gases. Most industrial nations agreed to adhere to Kyoto, but the United States, which causes most of the emissions in the world, refused to agree. Do some research on the topic, and write an essay that argues either for or against the United States' agreeing to the Kyoto Protocol.

VERLYN KLINKENBORG
Out of the Wild

Verlyn Klinkenborg lives on a small farm in upstate New York, from which he writes his popular "The Rural Life" column on the editorial page of The New York Times. *He published a collection of the columns in 2003. Klinkenborg comes from a family of Iowa farmers. His unique vision as someone from the country who lived in the city and then returned to the country makes his essays poignant and touching. He is also the author of* Making Hay *(1986). A member of the editorial board of* The New York Times, *he has written for* The New Yorker, Harper's, Esquire, National Geographic, Mother Jones, *and* The New York Times Magazine, *among others. In this essay Klinkenborg narrates his face-to-face meeting with a wild animal and is forced to rethink his preconceptions.*

▶ Prereading: Thinking About the Essay in Advance

Have you or someone you know ever encountered a wild animal? What was the reaction—fear, awe, surprise, respect, or some other emotion?

▶ Words to Watch

bale (par. 1) pile bound together
transgression (par. 1) act of crossing a forbidden boundary
frigid (par. 3) bitterly cold
platonic (par. 4) perfect and idealistic in form
vertebrae (par. 5) backbones

1   The other morning I lifted a bale of hay from a loose pile of bales on the barn floor, and a fox jumped out from under it. The fox ran to the back of the barn and turned to watch me. It paced a few steps, uncertain,

and then scurried under the door and out into the cold rain. It was a moment of pure transgression. All the old story lines broke apart—the ones about farmers and foxes and chickens—and just when the old story had been going so well. The fox had stolen a couple of our chickens. I had chased it off several times. It would lope up the hill in the middle pasture and sit on the ridge looking back at me, waiting for my next move. We hated to lose the chickens, and we hated the fox for taking them, but it was a conventional hatred, a part we knew we were supposed to play.

But there are no stories in which the fox sleeps overnight in the barn   2
on a bed of hay only a few feet from three horses in a run-in shed and a big, campaigning dog in his kennel. In all the traditional tales the fox keeps its distance, a playful distance perhaps, always respecting the invisible boundary between wildness and not-wildness. But the other morning that fox ignored the boundary completely.

The reason was obvious. It was dying from a terrible case of sarcop-   3
tic mange, an all-too-common disease caused by mites that infest the skin and cause severe inflammation and hair loss. Foxes with mange die of malnutrition or they freeze to death. The night had been frigid, with a blowing, soaking rainfall. Even the driest den would have been insufferable, and so the fox took refuge in a burrow among hay bales in a dry barn.

My wife and I have been seeing foxes ever since we moved to this   4
place. They skirted the far edge of the pasture at a businesslike trot, keeping watch as if they knew that someday we'd give in and get chickens. But because they always kept their distance, they were platonic foxes, storybook foxes with sharp muzzles and thick red fur and bushy tails and the gloss of wild health. They looked the way they were supposed to look, the way you imagine a fox looks. The binoculars only confirmed what we knew we'd find, the very idea of Vulpes vulpes. Every now and then a fox would get hit by a car on the nearby highway, and one of us would wonder aloud if it was our fox and we would miss it in advance. And yet there was always another fox crossing the pasture.

But seeing this nearly hairless fox shivering at the barn door, its tail   5
a pitiful file of vertebrae under bare flesh, I couldn't help thinking what a thin concept of wildness I had been living with. The wild I imagined was where the archetypes lived, negotiating their survival. Each animal in the wild embodied its species, which means that it lived up to its portrait in "The Sibley Guide to Birds" or "Walker's Mammals of the World." And though I had a rough idea of how creatures died in the wild, I had never come across an animal driven out of the wild— across that taboo boundary and into my barn—by its suffering. The fox and I looked at each other, only a few feet apart. If it had been a dog I could have helped it. But even the pity in my eyes reminded it that it had come too close.

▶ Building Vocabulary

Define and write a sentence of your own using each of the following words:

1. scurried (par. 1)
2. lope (par. 1)
3. businesslike (par. 4)
4. archetypes (par. 5)
5. embodied (par. 5)
6. taboo (par. 5)

▶ Thinking Critically About the Argument

Understanding the Writer's Argument

1. What does the writer have against the fox at the beginning of his essay?
2. Why does Klinkenborg think it unusual that the fox was taking refuge in his barn?
3. Why *was* the fox in the barn?
4. What is the normal behavior of foxes around the writer's farm?
5. What is the writer's usual view of "wildness"? How has it changed after his run-in with the fox?

Understanding the Writer's Techniques

1. What is Klinkenborg's major proposition? Is it a clear statement? If so, what is it? If not, what do you think it is?
2. The essay is essentially a narrative and attempts to move its readers emotionally. How does the writer build an emotional appeal to his readers?
3. Analyze the use of transitions. How do they move the essay along?
4. This essay aims for an urban readership, and the writer must educate his readers about the rural life. How does Klinkenborg get this information into his essay?
5. What are the warrants in this essay? Are they implied or explicit?
6. Most of the writer's explicit argument is in the final paragraph. How effective is his conclusion?

Exploring the Writer's Argument

1. Klinkenborg writes that if the fox had been a dog, he "could have helped it." Do you think that makes him seem heartless? Or is he merely being realistic? Could he have helped the fox, do you think? Should he have?

2. The writer speaks as a gentleman-farmer, an observer of nature who is educated. Do you believe he is a real farmer? Is his voice authentic? Defend your answers.
3. What relation does the essay imply between humans and animals? Why might you agree or disagree with the relation as Klinkenborg suggests it?

▶ Ideas for Writing Arguments

Prewriting

What did people have to do to domesticate animals like dogs, cats, pigs, and cows? Why did they do it? What do humans gain from domesticating animals?

Writing a Guided Argument

Many of us have pets for companionship and safety, and they are reliable and veritable members of the family. Every once in a while, however, we get a glimpse of just how much they are still animals. Write an essay in which you argue that a pet such as a dog or cat remains, in part, wild, no matter how domesticated it is.

1. Open your essay with a short narrative about a time when you saw the wild animal inside of a pet come through.
2. Next, write a major proposition that argues that pets are, in part, wild.
3. State at least two or three minor propositions to support your position.
4. Show examples to illustrate your minor propositions.
5. Establish a tone that shows how you are amused by the idea of pets being wild.
6. Somewhere near the end, break the normal tone of your essay to express that although it is amusing that pets can be wild, there is something a bit frightening about the fact.
7. Close your essay by reestablishing the normal tone.

Thinking, Arguing, and Writing Collaboratively

In groups of four or five students, share your papers that grew out of the Guided Argument assignment. Discuss the success of the opening narrative and the examples offered to support the minor propositions. Can the passages be improved by omission or rewriting? Can the argument be improved by altering the facts?

Writing About the Text

Write an essay in which you analyze Klinkenborg's style in "Out of the Wild." How does the writer succeed in creating an argument out of a situation he encounters on his farm? He is writing for a newspaper for the biggest city in the United States. How does his rural, laid-back style work?

More Writing Ideas

1. In your journal, freewrite on the topic of boundaries between humans and animals. Write for at least 15 minutes, but do not edit your work as you go. After the time is up, look at what you wrote, and take notes on anything that might be the basis for an essay.
2. Write a paragraph or two in which you explore how nature asserts itself in a city.
3. Write an essay in which you defend or challenge people's efforts to assist animals in the wild—a beached whale or an injured bird, for example. Should humankind help beasts in the wild, or should we leave them to the fate to which nature has led them?

BARRY LOPEZ
Apologia

Barry Lopez was born in 1945 in rural California and now lives in Oregon. He is a short story and nonfiction writer best known for his nature writing, especially Arctic Dreams *(1986), which won the National Book Award for nonfiction. He is also the author of* Crow and Weasel *(1990) and* Field Notes *(1994), among other books. In this selection, Lopez tells the story of a road trip turned deadly—for animals in the wild.*

▶ Prereading: Thinking About the Essay in Advance

Have you ever run over an animal or seen one run over? What did you feel, if anything? Do you ever feel grief at seeing a dead animal on the road?

▶ Words to Watch

maniacally (par. 1) in a crazy way
cornea (par. 2) the membrane that covers the eye
seers (par. 5) people who can see the future
carcass (par. 9) dead body of an animal
tawny (par. 11) of an orange-brown color
gunnysack (par. 11) a bag made from a rough material
cloister (par. 12) place in a monastery where monks live; considered secluded

macadam (par. 14) road surface made of asphalt mixed with rocks
fractious (par. 15) irritable and complaining
beryl (par. 16) a hard mineral consisting of many colors
mandibular (par. 18) relating to the jaw
limpid (par. 21) clear and calm
exculpation (par. 23) to free someone from blame
lavabo (par. 25) a ceremony in a Catholic mass in which a congregant ritually washes his hands

A few miles east of home in the Cascades I slow down and pull over 1
for two raccoons, sprawled still as stones in the road. I carry them
to the side and lay them in sun-shot windblown grass in the barrow pit.
In eastern Oregon along U.S. 20, black-tailed jackrabbits lie like welts of
sod—three, four, then a fifth. By the bridge over Jordan Creek, just shy
of the Idaho border in the drainage of the Owyhee River, a crumpled
adolescent porcupine leers up almost maniacally over its blood-flecked
teeth. I carry each one away from the pavement into a cover of grass or
brush out of decency, I think. And worry. Who are these animals, their
lights gone out? What journeys have fallen apart here?

I do not stop to remove each dark blister from the road. I wince before 2
the recently dead, feel my lips tighten, see something else, a fence post, in
the spontaneous aversion of my eyes, and pull over. I imagine white silk
threads of life still vibrating inside them, even if the body's husk is
stretched out for yards, stuck like oiled muslin to the road. The energy
that once held them erect leaves like a bullet, but the memory of that energy fades slowly from the wrinkled cornea, the bloodless fur.

The raccoons and, later, a red fox carry like sacks of wet gravel and 3
sand. Each animal is like a solitary child's shoe in the road.

Once a man asked, Why do you bother? 4

You never know, I said. The ones you give some semblance of burial, 5
to whom you offer an apology, may have been like seers in a parallel culture. It is an act of respect, a technique of awareness.

In Idaho I hit a young sage sparrow—thwack against the right fender 6
in the very split second I see it. Its companion rises from the same spot
but a foot higher, slow as smoke, and sails off clean into the desert. I rest
the walloped bird in my left hand, my right thumb pressed to its chest. I
feel for the wail of the heart. Its eyes glisten like rain on crystal. Nothing
but warmth. I shut the tiny eyelids and lay it beside a clump of bunch-
grass. Beyond a barbed-wire fence the overgrazed range is littered with
cow flops. The road curves away to the south. I nod before I go, a ridiculous gesture, out of simple grief.

I pass four spotted skunks. The swirling air is acrid with the rup- 7
ture of each life.

Darkness rises in the valleys of Idaho. East of Grand View, south of 8
the Snake River, nighthawks swoop the roads for gnats, silent on the

wing as owls. On a descending curve I see two of them lying soft as clouds in the road. I turn around and come back. The sudden slowing down and my K-turn at the bottom of the hill draw the attention of a man who steps away from a tractor, a dozen yards from where the birds lie. I can tell by his step, the suspicious tilt of his head, that he is wary, vaguely proprietary. Offended, or irritated, he may throw the birds back into the road when I leave. So I wait, subdued like a penitent, a body in each hand.

9   He speaks first, a low voice, a deep murmur weighted with awe. He has been watching these flocks feeding just above the road for several evenings. He calls them whippoorwills. He gestures for a carcass. How odd, yes, the way they concentrate their hunting right on the road, I say. He runs a finger down the smooth arc of the belly and remarks on the small whiskered bill. He pulls one long wing out straight, but not roughly. He marvels. He glances at my car, baffled by this out-of-state courtesy. Two dozen nighthawks career past, back and forth at arm's length, feeding at our height and lower. He asks if I would mind—as though I owned it—if he took the bird up to the house to show his wife. "She's never seen anything like this" He's fascinated. "Not close."

10   I trust, later, he will put it in the fields, not throw the body in the trash, a whirligig.

11   North of Pinedale in western Wyoming on U.S. 189, below the Gros Ventre Range, I see a big doe from a great distance, the low rays of first light gleaming in her tawny reddish hair. She rests askew, like a crushed tree. I drag her to the shoulder, then down a long slope by the petals of her ears. A gunnysack of plaster mud, ears cold as rain gutters. All of her doesn't come. I climb back up for the missing leg. The stain of her is darker than the black asphalt. The stains go north and off to the south as far as I can see.

12   On an afternoon trafficless, quiet as a cloister, headed across South Pass in the Wind River Range, I swerve violently but hit a bird, and then try to wrestle the gravel-spewing skid in a straight line along the lip of an embankment. I know even as I struggle for control the irony of this: I could easily pitch off here to my own death. The bird is dead somewhere in the road behind me. Only a few seconds and I am safely back on the road, nauseated, light-headed.

13   It is hard to distinguish among younger gulls. I turn this one around slowly in my hands. It could be a western gull, a mew gull, a California gull. I do not remember well enough the bill markings, the color of the legs. I have no doubt about the vertebrae shattered beneath the seamless white of its ropy neck.

14   East of Lusk, Wyoming, in Nebraska, I stop for a badger. I squat on the macadam to admire the long claws, the perfect set of its teeth in the broken jaw, the ramulose shading of its fur—how it differs slightly, as does every badger's, from the drawings and pictures in the field guides. A car drifts toward us over the prairie, coming on in the other lane, a white 1962 Chevro-

let station wagon. The driver slows to pass. In the bright sunlight I can't see his face, only an arm and the gesture of his thick left hand. It opens in a kind of shrug, hangs briefly in limp sadness, then extends itself in supplication. Gone past, it curls into itself against the car door and is still.

Farther on in western Nebraska I pick up the small bodies of mice   15
and birds. While I wait to retrieve these creatures I do not meet the eyes of passing drivers. Whoever they are, I feel anger toward them, in spite of the sparrow and the gull I myself have killed. We treat the attrition of lives on the road like the attrition of lives in war: horrifying, unavoidable, justified. Accepting the slaughter leaves people momentarily fractious, embarrassed. South of Broken Bow, at dawn, I cannot avoid an immature barn swallow. It hangs by its head, motionless in the slats of the grille.

I stop for a rabbit on Nebraska 806 and find, only a few feet away, a   16
garter snake. What else have I missed, too small, too narrow? What has gone under or past me while I stared at mountains, hay meadows, fencerows, the beryl surface of rivers? In Wyoming I could not help but see pronghorn antelope swollen big as barrels by the side of the road, their legs splayed rigidly aloft. For animals so large, people will stop. But how many have this habit of clearing the road of smaller creatures, people who would remove the ones I miss? I do not imagine I am alone. As much sorrow as the man's hand conveyed in Nebraska, it meant gratitude too for burying the dead.

Still, I do not wish to meet anyone's eyes.   17

In Southwestern Iowa, outside Clarinda, I haul a deer into high   18
grass out of sight of the road and begin to examine it. It is still whole, but the destruction is breathtaking. The skull, I soon discover, is fractured in four places; the jaw, hanging by shreds of mandibular muscle, is broken at the symphysis, beneath the incisors. The pelvis is crushed, the left hind leg unsocketed. All but two ribs are dislocated along the vertebral column, which is complexly fractured. The intestines have been driven forward into the chest. The heart and lungs have ruptured the chest wall at the base of the neck. The signature of a tractor-trailer truck: 80,000 pounds at 65 mph.

In front of a motel room in Ottumwa I finger-scrape the dry, stiff car-   19
casses of bumblebees, wasps, and butterflies from the grille and headlight mountings, and I scrub with a wet cloth to soften and wipe away the nap of crumbles, the insects, the aerial plankton of spiders and mites. I am uneasy cleaning so many of the dead. The carnage is so obvious.

In Illinois, west of Kankakee, two raccoons as young as the ones in Ore-   20
gon. In Indiana another raccoon, a gray squirrel. When I make the left turn into the driveway at the house of a friend outside South Bend, it is evening, hot and muggy. I can hear cicadas in a lone elm. I'm glad to be here.

From the driveway entrance I look back down Indiana 23, toward In-   21
diana 8, remembering the farm roads of Illinois and Iowa. I remember how beautiful it was in the limpid air to drive Nebraska 2 through the sand hills, to see how far at dusk the land was etched east and west of

Wyoming 28. I remember the imposition of the Wind River Range in a hard, blue sky beneath white ranks of buttonhook clouds, windy hay fields on the Snake River plain, the welcome of Russian olive trees and willows in western creek bottoms. The transformation of the heart such beauty engenders is not enough tonight to let me shed the heavier memory, a catalog too morbid to write out, too vivid to ignore.

22   I stand in the driveway now, listening to the cicadas whirring in the dark tree. My hands grip the sill of the open window at the driver's side, and I lean down as if to speak to someone still sitting there. The weight I wish to fall I cannot fathom, a sorrow over the world's dark hunger.

23   A light comes on over the porch. I hear a deadbolt thrown, the shiver of a door pulled free. The words of atonement I pronounce are too inept to offer me release. Or forgiveness. My friend is floating across the tree-shadowed lawn. What is to be done with the desire for exculpation?

24   "Later than we thought you'd be," he says.

25   I do not want the lavabo. I wish to make amends.

26   "I made more stops than I thought I would," I answer. "Well, bring in your things. And whatever I can take," he offers.

27   I anticipate, in the powerful antidote of our conversation, the reassurance of a human enterprise, the forgiving embrace of the rational. It waits within, beyond the slow tail-wagging of two dogs standing at the screen door.

▶ Building Vocabulary

1. Go through this essay again and list at least ten of the animals mentioned. Write a short description of each, using reference works, if necessary.
2. For each of the following words, write a definition:
   a. leers (par. 1)
   b. wince (par. 2)
   c. semblance (par. 5)
   d. walloped (par. 6)
   e. acrid (par. 7)
   f. penitent (par. 8)
   g. supplication (par. 14)
   h. atonement (par. 23)

▶ Thinking Critically About the Argument

Understanding the Writer's Argument

1. What are the Cascades? Why is Lopez driving east through them? Where is he going?
2. Why does Lopez carry the bodies of dead animals to the side of the road? What does Lopez mean by "What journeys have fallen apart here?" (par. 1) How do you know?

3. List the different encounters Lopez has with people along his trip, and explain the nature of each encounter.
4. What does Lopez mean in paragraph 5 that offering a "semblance of burial" to a dead animal on the road is "a technique of awareness"? Where does this phrase come from?
5. Why does Lopez write that his nod to the bird in paragraph 6 is a "ridiculous gesture"?
6. Why doesn't Lopez tell his friend what he had been thinking at the end of his essay?
7. Paraphrase the following sentence: "I anticipate, in the powerful antidote of our conversation, the reassurance of a human enterprise, the forgiving embrace of the rational." (par. 27)

Understanding the Writer's Techniques

1. This essay's argument is complicated. It is not as simple as it seems at first glance. What is Lopez's claim, and where does he state it? If he doesn't state it, why not?
2. Comment on Lopez's use of transitions. How do they contribute to the coherence of the essay and his portrayal of the passage of time?
3. Why does Lopez write about the man who asks him "Why do you bother?" in paragraph 4?
4. What tense does the writer use for the verbs is this essay? Why do you think Lopez uses this tense? Is it effective? Why or why not?
5. What is the effect of the transition between paragraphs 12 and 13? At first, the reader thinks Lopez has driven away from his near-accident, and then the reader realizes that Lopez has turned around. How does he explain this?
6. What three descriptions in Lopez's essay do you think help his position the most?
7. Why does Lopez describe the driver of the Chevrolet driving past him in paragraph 14?
8. Why does Lopez make paragraph 17 one sentence? Is it effective? If so, how, and if not, why not?
9. What is the rhetorical effect of the last section of the essay, after Lopez has pulled into his friend's driveway?
10. What is your opinion of the last paragraph? Is it effective? How does it contribute to the essay's message?

Exploring the Writer's Argument

1. Lopez describes carefully the dead animals he finds. What is your reaction to his descriptions? Do you find the descriptions beautiful? Repulsive? Attractive? Why would he make them so? Explain your answers.

2. The language that Lopez uses in this essay is lyrical, but some readers also might consider it unnecessarily flowery and overwritten. Which do you think it is? Do you think the language in this essay is appropriate? Why or why not?

3. Do you agree with Lopez's statement in paragraph 15 that "we treat the attrition of lives on the road like the attrition of lives in war: horrifying, unavoidable, justified." Is this an apt simile? Why or why not?

▶ Ideas for Writing Arguments

Prewriting

What kind of purely legal and natural behavior do people engage in as a matter of course that we would have to apologize for or defend?

Writing a Guided Argument

Write a narrative argumentative essay also called "Apologia," in which you apologize for or defend some frequent action you take, or action you believe requires apology or defense. For example, you might apologize for last-minute, all-night vigils before a major test; for deciding to break off a relationship with someone you liked; or for refusing to give money to a homeless person begging for help.

1. Begin your narrative at the moment when you first start doing something that needs explaining. Do not start before this.
2. After you establish your story, fill in the back story, explaining anything your reader needs to know.
3. Attempt a lyrical style and tone in your essay, adding descriptions where appropriate.
4. Continue your story, breaking it up into episodes.
5. Offer your reader part of your argument after each episode.
6. Use effective transitions to move your essay along chronologically.
7. Close your essay with a section that ends the narrative and widens the discussion of the lesson you have learned (and which your reader can presumably learn) from your narrative.

Thinking, Arguing, and Writing Collaboratively

In groups of four or five, share experiences that you have had in nature when you felt either superior as humans (perhaps crushing a line of ants) or small as humans (perhaps watching a major storm). Make a list of the kinds of experiences that can make us feel one way or the other.

Writing About the Text

In this essay, Lopez uses many similes, such as in paragraph 11 when describing the dead deer: "She rests askew, like a crushed tree." Write an essay analyzing Lopez's use of figurative language, such as similes and metaphors, and how it helps his argument.

More Writing Ideas

1. In your journal, write a beautiful description of something not ordinarily seen as beautiful—such as withered trees, a sick old dog or cat, or a beaten-up automobile, for example.
2. Write a couple of paragraphs about a trip you took that led you to think about something you hadn't thought about before.
3. *Merriam-Webster Collegiate Dictionary* defines *apologia* as "a defense especially of one's opinions, position, or actions" but also lists it as a synonym of "apology." Does the definition surprise you? Do you think this essay is a defense at all, or an apology? Write an essay in which you analyze the extent to which this essay is an apologia as Webster's defines it, and to what extent it is an apology. What would Lopez be apologizing for? What would he be defending?

WENDELL BERRY
In Distrust of Movements

Prolific Kentucky writer Wendell Berry was born in 1934. He was educated at the University of Kentucky. He is the author of 32 books of essays, poetry, and fiction. His collections of poetry include There Is Singing Around Me *(1976)* Traveling at Home *(1989), and* Entries: Poems *(1994). His novels include* Remembering *(1988) and* A World Lost *(1996). He is also the author of essay collections* A Continuous Harmony *(1972),* Standing on Earth: Selected Essays *(1991),* Sex, Economy, Freedom, & Community *(1993), and* Another Turn of the Crank *(1995). He has taught English at New York University and his alma mater, University of Kentucky. Berry lives on a farm in Port Royal, Kentucky. In this selection, originally published in 1999, Berry expresses his impatience with organized environmental efforts and offers an alternative way to make a difference.*

▶ Prereading: Thinking About the Essay in Advance

Have you ever given money to a cause? Why or why not? What do you think are the most respectable nonprofit organizations? Why?

▶**Words to Watch**

preemption (par. 3) action that comes before something else can happen
advocates (par. 3) people who support something
appropriate (par. 3) claim or use something as one's own
irradiation (par. 8) treating food with radiation to kill germs
reconciled (par. 4) have accepted that something is going to happen
erosion (par. 14) a wearing-away from water or air
watersheds (par. 4) area of land that drains into a body of water
husbandry (par. 10) science and art of farming
constituency (par. 11) group of possible voters
profound (par. 12) very great
timber (par. 13) wood to be used as lumber
reductionist (par. 16) oversimplified
hubris (par. 24) excessive arrogance and pride

1   I must burden my readers as I have burdened myself with the knowledge that I speak from a local, some might say a provincial, point of view. When I try to identify myself to myself I realize that, in my most immediate reasons and affections, I am less than an American, less than a Kentuckian, less even than a Henry Countian, but am a man most involved with and concerned about my family, my neighbors, and the land that is daily under my feet. It is this involvement that defines my citizenship in the larger entities. And so I will remember, and I ask you to remember, that I am not trying to say what is thinkable everywhere, but rather what it is possible to think on the westward bank of the lower Kentucky River in the summer of 1998.

2   Over the last twenty-five or thirty years I have been making and remaking different versions of the same argument. It is not "my" argument, really, but rather one that I inherited from a long line of familial, neighborly, literary, and scientific ancestors. We could call it "the agrarian argument." This argument can be summed up in as many ways as it can be made. One way to sum it up is to say that we humans can escape neither our dependence on nature nor our responsibility to nature—and that, precisely because of this condition of dependence *and* responsibility, we are also dependent upon and responsible for human culture.

3   Food, as I have argued at length, is both a natural (which is to say a divine) gift and a cultural product. Because we must *use* land and water and plants and animals to produce food, we are at once dependent on and responsible to what we use. We must know both how to use and how to care for what we use. This knowledge is the basis of human culture. If we do not know how to adapt our desires, our methods, and our technology to the nature of the places in which we are working, so as to make them productive *and to keep them so,* that is a cultural failure of the gross-

est and most dangerous kind. Poverty and starvation also can be cultural products—if the culture is wrong.

Though this argument, in my keeping, has lengthened and acquired   4
branches, in its main assumptions it has stayed the same. What has changed—and I say this with a good deal of wonder and with much thankfulness—is the audience. Perhaps the audience will always include people who are not listening, or people who think the agrarian argument is merely an anachronism, a form of entertainment, or a nuisance to be waved away. But increasingly the audience also includes people who take this argument seriously, because they are involved in one or more of the tasks of agrarianism. They are trying to maintain a practical foothold on the earth for themselves or their families or their communities. They are trying to preserve and develop local land-based economies. They are trying to preserve or restore the health of local communities and ecosystems and watersheds. They are opposing the attempt of the great corporations to own and control all of Creation.

In short, the agrarian argument now has a significant number of   5
friends. As the political and ecological abuses of the so-called global economy become more noticeable and more threatening, the agrarian argument is going to have more friends than it has now. This being so, maybe the advocate's task needs to change. Maybe now, instead of merely propounding (and repeating) the agrarian argument, the advocate must also try to see that this argument does not win friends too easily. I think, myself, that this is the case. The tasks of agrarianism that we have undertaken are not going to be finished for a long time. To preserve the remnants of agrarian life, to oppose the abuses of industrial land use and finally correct them, and to develop the locally adapted economies and cultures that are necessary to our survival will require many lifetimes of dedicated work. This work does not need friends with illusions. And so I would like to speak—in a friendly way, of course—out of my distrust of "movements."

I have had with my friend Wes Jackson a number of useful conversa-   6
tions about the necessity of getting out of movements—even movements that have seemed necessary and dear to us—when they have lapsed into self-righteousness and self-betrayal, as movements seem almost invariably to do. People in movements too readily learn to deny to others the rights and privileges they demand for themselves. They too easily become unable to mean their own language, as when a "peace movement" becomes violent. They often become too specialized, as if they cannot help taking refuge in the pinhole vision of the industrial intellectuals. They almost always fail to be radical enough, dealing finally in effects rather than causes. Or they deal with single issues or single solutions, as if to assure themselves that they will not be radical enough.

And so I must declare my dissatisfaction with movements to pro-   7
mote soil conservation or clean water or clean air or wilderness preservation or sustainable agriculture or community health or the welfare of

children. Worthy as these and other goals may be, they cannot be achieved alone. They cannot be responsibly advocated alone. I am dissatisfied with such efforts because they are too specialized, they are not comprehensive enough, they are not radical enough, they virtually predict their own failure by implying that we can remedy or control effects while leaving the causes in place, Ultimately, I think, they are insincere; they propose that the trouble is caused by *other* people; they would like to change policy but not behavior.

8   The worst danger may be that a movement will lose its language either to its own confusion about meaning and practice, or to preemption by its enemies. I remember, for example, my naive confusion at learning that it was possible for advocates of organic agriculture to look upon the "organic method" as an end in itself. To me, organic farming was attractive both as a way of conserving nature and as a strategy of survival for small farmers. Imagine my surprise in discovering that there could be huge "organic" monocultures. And so I was somewhat prepared for the recent attempt of the United States Department of Agriculture to appropriate the "organic" label for food irradiation, genetic engineering, and other desecrations by the corporate food economy. Once we allow our language to mean anything that anybody wants it to mean, it becomes impossible to mean what we say. When "homemade" ceases to mean neither more nor less than "made at home," then it means anything, which is to say that it means nothing. The same decay is at work on words such as "conservation," "sustainable," "safe," "natural," "healthful," "sanitary," and "organic." The use of such words now requires the most exacting control of context and the use immediately of illustrative examples.

9   Real organic gardeners and farmers who market their produce locally are finding that, to a lot of people, "organic" means something like "trustworthy." And so, for a while, it will be useful for us to talk about the meaning and the economic usefulness of trust and trustworthiness. But we must be careful. Sooner or later, Trust Us Global Foods, Inc., will be upon us, advertising safe, sanitary, natural food irradiation. And then we must be prepared to raise another standard and move on.

10   As you see, I have good reasons for declining to name the movement I think I am a part of. I call it The Nameless Movement for Better Ways of Doing—which I hope is too long and uncute to be used as a bumper sticker. I know that movements tend to die with their names and slogans, and I believe that this Nameless Movement needs to live on and on. I am reconciled to the likelihood that from time to time it will name itself and have slogans, but I am not going to use its slogans or call it by any of its names. After this, I intend to stop calling it The Nameless Movement for Better Ways of Doing, for fear it will become the NMBWD and acquire a headquarters and a budget and an inventory of T-shirts covered with language that in a few years will be mere spelling.

Let us suppose, then, that we have a Nameless Movement for Better   11
Land Use and that we know we must try to keep it active, responsive, and
intelligent for a long time. What must we do?

What we must do above all, I think, is try to see the problem in its full   12
size and difficulty. If we are concerned about land abuse, then we must see
that this is an economic problem. Every economy is, by definition, a land-
using economy. If we are using our land wrong, then something is wrong
with our economy. This is difficult. It becomes more difficult when we recognize that, in modern times, every one of us is a member of the economy
of everybody else. Every one of us has given many proxies to the economy
to use the land (and the air, the water, and other natural gifts) on our behalf. Adequately supervising those proxies is at present impossible; with-
drawing them is for virtually all of us, as things now stand, unthinkable.

But if we are concerned about land abuse, we have begun an extensive   13
work of economic criticism. Study of the history of land use (and any local
history will do) informs us that we have had for a long time an economy
that thrives by undermining its own foundations. Industrialism, which is
the name of our economy, and which is now virtually the only economy of
the world, has been from its beginnings in a state of riot. It is based
squarely upon the principle of violence toward everything on which it depends, and it has not mattered whether the form of industrialism was
communist or capitalist, the violence toward nature, human communities,
traditional agricultures, and local economies has been constant. The bad
news is coming in from all over the world. Can such an economy somehow be fixed without being radically changed? I don't think it can.

The Captains of Industry have always counseled the rest of us to "be   14
realistic." Let us, therefore, be realistic. Is it realistic to assume that the
present economy would be just fine if only it would stop poisoning the
earth, air, and water, or if only it would stop soil erosion, or if only it
would stop degrading watersheds and forest ecosystems, or if only it
would stop seducing children, or if only it would quit buying politicians,
or if only it would give women and favored minorities an equitable share
of the loot? Realism, I think, is a very limited program, but it informs us at
least that we should not look for bird eggs in a cuckoo clock.

Or we can show the hopelessness of single-issue causes and single-   15
issue movements by following a line of thought such as this: We need a
continuous supply of uncontaminated water. Therefore, we need (among
other things) soil-and-water-conserving ways of agriculture and forestry
that are not dependent on monoculture, toxic chemicals, or the indifference and violence that always accompany big-scale industrial enterprises
on the land. Therefore, we need diversified, small-scale land economies
that are dependent on people. Therefore, we need people with the
knowledge, skills, motives, and attitudes required by diversified, small-
scale land economies. And all this is clear and comfortable enough, until
we recognize the question we have come to: *Where are the people?*

16   Well, all of us who live in the suffering rural landscapes of the United States know that most people are available to those landscapes only recreationally. We see them bicycling or boating or hiking or camping or hunting or fishing or driving along and looking around. They do not, in Mary Austin's phrase, "summer and winter with the land." They are unacquainted with the land's human and natural economies. Though people have not progressed beyond the need to eat food and drink water and wear clothes and live in houses, most people have progressed beyond the domestic arts—the husbandry and wifery of the world—by which those needful things are produced and conserved. In fact, the comparative few who still practice that necessary husbandry and wifery often are inclined to apologize for doing so, having been carefully taught in our education system that those arts are degrading and unworthy of people's talents. Educated minds, in the modern era, are unlikely to know anything about food and drink or clothing and shelter. In merely taking these things for granted, the modern educated mind reveals itself also to be as superstitious a mind as ever has existed in the world. What could be more superstitious than the idea that money brings forth food?

17   I am not suggesting, of course, that everybody ought to be a farmer or a forester. Heaven forbid! I *am* suggesting that most people now are living on the far side of a broken connection, and that this is potentially catastrophic. Most people are now fed, clothed, and sheltered from sources, in nature and in the work of other people, toward which they feel no gratitude and exercise no responsibility.

18   We are involved now in a profound failure of imagination. Most of us cannot imagine the wheat beyond the bread, or the farmer beyond the wheat, or the farm beyond the farmer, or the history (human or natural) beyond the farm. Most people cannot imagine the forest and the forest economy that produced their houses and furniture and paper; or the landscapes, the streams, and the weather that fill their pitchers and bathtubs and swimming pools with water. Most people appear to assume that when they have paid their money for these things they have entirely met their obligations. And that is, in fact, the conventional economic assumption. The problem is that it is possible to starve under the rule of the conventional economic assumption; some people are starving now under the rule of that assumption.

19   Money does not being forth food. Neither does the technology of the food system. Food comes from nature and from the work of people. If the supply of food is to be continuous for a long time, then people must work in harmony with nature. That means that people must find the right answers to a lot of questions. The same rules apply to forestry and the possibility of a continuous supply of forest products.

20   People grow the food that people eat. People produce the lumber that people use. People care properly or improperly for the forests and the farms that are the sources of those goods. People are necessarily at

both ends of the process. The economy, always obsessed with its need to sell products, thinks obsessively and exclusively of the consumer. It mostly takes for granted or ignores those who do the damaging or the restorative and preserving work of agriculture and forestry. The economy pays poorly for this work, with the unsurprising result that the work is mostly done poorly. But here we must ask a very realistic economic question: Can we afford to have this work done poorly? Those of us who know something about land stewardship know that we cannot afford to pay poorly for it, because that means simply that we will not get it. And we know that we cannot afford land use without land stewardship.

21 One way we could describe the task ahead of us is by saying that we need to enlarge the consciousness and the conscience of the economy. Our economy needs to know—and care—what it is doing. This is revolutionary, of course, if you have a taste for revolution, but it is also merely a matter of common sense. How could anybody seriously object to the possibility that the economy might eventually come to know what it is doing?

22 Undoubtedly some people will want to start a movement to bring this about. They probably will call it the Movement to Teach the Economy What It Is Doing—the MTEWIID, Despite my very considerable uneasiness, I will agree to participate, but on three conditions.

23 My first condition is that this movement should begin by giving up all hope and belief in piecemeal, one-shot solutions. The present scientific quest for odorless hog manure should give us sufficient proof that the specialist is no longer with us. Even now, after centuries of reductionist propaganda, the world is still intricate and vast, as dark as it is light, a place of mystery, where we cannot do one thing without doing many things, or put two things together without putting many things together. Water quality, for example, cannot be improved without improving farming and forestry, but farming and forestry cannot be improved without improving the education of consumers—and so on.

24 The proper business of a human economy is to make one whole thing of ourselves and this world. To make ourselves into a practical wholeness with the land under our feet is maybe not altogether possible—how would *we* know?—but, as a goal, it at least carries us beyond *hubris,* beyond the utterly groundless assumption that we can subdivide our present great failure into a thousand separate problems that can be fixed by a thousand task forces of academic and bureaucratic specialists. That program has been given more than a fair chance to prove itself, and we ought to know by now that it won't work.

25 My second condition is that the people in this movement (the MTEWIID) should take full responsibility for themselves as members of the economy. If we are going to teach the economy what it is doing, then we need to learn what *we* are doing. This is going to have to be a private movement as well as a public one. If it is unrealistic to expect wasteful industries

to be conservers, then obviously we must lead in part the public life of complainers, petitioners, protesters, advocates and supporters of stricter regulations and saner policies. But that is not enough. If it is unrealistic to expect a bad economy to try to become a good one, then we must go to work to build a good economy. It is appropriate that this duty should fall to us, for good economic behavior is more possible for us than it is for the great corporations with their miseducated managers and their greedy and oblivious stockholders. Because it is possible for us, we must try in every way we can to make good economic sense in our own lives, in our households, and in our communities. We must do more for ourselves and our neighbors. We must learn to spend our money with our friends and not with our enemies. But to do this, it is necessary to renew local economics, and revive the domestic arts. In seeking to change our economic use of the world, we are seeking inescapably to change our lives. The outward harmony that we desire between our economy and the world depends finally upon an inward harmony between our own hearts and the creative spirit that is the life of all creatures, a spirit as near us as our flesh and yet forever beyond the measures of this obsessively measuring age. We can grow good wheat and make good bread only if we understand that we do not live by bread alone.

26   My third condition is that this movement should content itself to be poor. We need to find cheap solutions, solutions within the reach of everybody, and the availability of a lot of money prevents the discovery of cheap solutions. The solutions of modern medicine and modern agriculture are all staggeringly expensive, and this is caused in part, and maybe altogether, by the availability of huge sums of money for medical and agricultural research.

27   Too much money, moreover, attracts administrators and experts as sugar attracts ants—look at what is happening in our universities. We should not envy rich movements that are organized and led by an alternative bureaucracy living on the problems it is supposed to solve. We want a movement that is a movement because it is advanced by all its members in their daily lives.

28   Now, having completed this very formidable list of the problems and difficulties, fears and fearful hopes that lie ahead of us, I am relieved to see that I have been preparing myself all along to end by saying something cheerful. What I have been talking about is the possibility of renewing human respect for this earth and all the good, useful, and beautiful things that come from it. I have made it clear, I hope, that I don't think this respect can be adequately enacted or conveyed by tipping our hats to nature or by representing natural loveliness in art or by prayers of thanksgiving or by preserving tracts of wilderness—though I recommend all those things. The respect I mean can be given only by using well the world's goods that are given to us. This good use, which renews respect—which is the only currency, so to speak, of respect—also renews our pleasure. The callings and disciplines that I have spoken of as the domestic

arts are stationed all along the way from the farm to the prepared dinner, from the forest to the dinner table, from stewardship of the land to hospitality to friends and strangers. These arts are as demanding and gratifying, as instructive and as pleasing as the so-called fine arts. To learn them, to practice them, to honor, and reward them is, I believe, our profoundest calling. Our reward is that they will enrich our lives and make us glad.

▶ Building Vocabulary

Write out a definition for each of the following words, then write a sentence using it:

1. invariably (par. 1)
2. naive (par. 3)
3. undermining (par. 7)
4. degrading (par. 10)
5. formidable (par. 11)
6. oblivious (par. 18)

▶ Thinking Critically About the Argument

Understanding the Writer's Argument

1. Wes Jackson is the founder of the Land Institute, which does research on agriculture. Why does Berry mention Jackson at the beginning of his essay? How does this help you to understand the Nameless Movement for Better Land Use in paragraph 10?
2. What kinds of movements is Berry talking about in the title? What does he see as the main problems with movements? What does he say is the worst problem, and how does it have larger implications for society?
3. Who are the "Captains of Industry"? (par. 14) Why are they important to Berry's argument?
4. What does Berry mean when he writes that "we should not look for bird eggs in a cuckoo clock"?
5. Paraphrase Berry's crucial argument in paragraph 15.
6. Berry lives in the country. What cues does Berry give you to express that information?
7. What point is Berry making when he writes that "we are involved now in a profound failure of imagination"? (par. 18)
8. What is the Movement to Teach the Economy What It Is Doing? What does he demand from the movement?
9. What are the "domestic arts"? What do they have to do with Berry's argument?
10. Berry says in paragraph 28 that he has been preparing to say "something cheerful." What is that cheerful thing?

Understanding the Writer's Techniques

1. What is Berry's claim? In what sentence does he express it most clearly?
2. Berry organizes this essay in three sections. Make an outline in which you paraphrase the essential argument in each section, and then analyze how the argument moves from one to the other. How does he develop his claim?
3. Make a shorter outline in which you analyze the second section in Berry's essay. How does Berry move from identifying a problem in paragraph 15 to his demand for conditions starting in paragraph 22?
4. What is Berry's tone? Point out the uses of irony in the essay. How does irony contribute to Berry's intent?
5. Why doesn't Berry use the real names of movements? What is the effect of making up names for hypothetical movements?
6. What is the argumentative purpose of Berry's accusations regarding the "Captains of Industry"? Is it effective? How is it effective or how is it not?
7. Who is Berry's audience for this essay? What assumption about the audience does he imply in his conclusion?
8. Evaluate the success of Berry's concluding paragraph. Does he tie his essay together? If so, how? If not, why not?

Exploring the Writer's Argument

1. Berry's introduction lists "dealing . . . in effects rather than causes" (par. 6) as one of his grievances against movements. In what way does Berry take his own advice here and concentrate on causes rather than effects? In what way does he *not* take his own advice?
2. Why doesn't Berry argue against nonprofit organizations, which are the organizations working for these "single causes"? Instead, he targets "movements." What are the implications of the choice for his argument and for how you understand the essay?
3. How effective are Berry's arguments in support of his statement in paragraph 16, that in taking modern conveniences for granted "the modern educated mind reveals itself also to be as superstitious a mind as ever has existed in the world"?
4. Write a response to Berry's accusation that because people don't think of wheat when they eat bread, "we are involved now in a profound failure of imagination." (par. 18)

▶ Ideas for Writing Arguments

Prewriting

How do you pay your respects to nature, or do you at all? What do you do that Berry states in his conclusion everyone should do?

Writing a Guided Argument

Write an essay that attempts to prove that you, a modern educated mind, are not alienated from the everyday items and activities that you consume or are engaged in and that you do what Berry asks in his conclusion, that you use "well the world's goods that are given to us."

1. Begin by explaining to your reader why you are writing this essay—to defend yourself against Wendell Berry's accusations.
2. Continue with a brief personal story in which you illustrate your lack of alienation from nature.
3. Link your illustration with a major proposition.
4. Support your main point with a number of minor propositions.
5. Expand each minor proposition with details and examples that explain your grounds for believing yourself to understand and live in accordance with Berry's demands.
6. End your essay with a paragraph that extends your use of goods to a larger philosophy of living.

Thinking, Arguing, and Writing Collaboratively

In small groups, share your papers that grew out of the Writing a Guided Argument assignment. Discuss possible weak examples of your respectful use of nature and possible objections that a reader might have. Brainstorm in your groups about how you might address these objections or weaknesses in your essay. Take notes, and incorporate your notes into your final draft.

Writing About the Text

All of the essays in this book are arguments of some sort. Some argue for simple policy changes, whereas Berry's essay is qualitatively different. He is calling for his readers to change their belief systems, to look at the world in a whole new way. Find another essay in this book that calls for the same kind of radical shift in thinking, and compare and contrast Berry's essay with that selection. How are the arguments similar? Different? Which is more successful, and why?

More Writing Ideas

1. In your journal, list the causes identified in paragraph 2 of this essay, and do some research to find which nonprofit organizations are the leaders of those movements. Which are you drawn to? Why?
2. In an extended paragraph, explore Berry's idea from paragraph 6 that "every one of us is a member of the economy of everybody else."
3. Write an essay in which you argue that even in private life, Berry's statement in paragraph 19 is true: "the availability of a lot of money prevents the discovery of cheap solutions."

15 Human Rights: Why Does Society Need Them?

I n 1948, the United Nations adopted the Universal Declaration of Human Rights, a document meant to assert the natural rights of humankind. For example, Article 3 of the declaration says, "Everyone has the right to life, liberty and security of person." The remaining 29 articles outline other basic rights.

After World War II, the great colonial powers collapsed, freeing billions of people from oppression and giving hope. The declaration set a standard for all countries to refer to and instructed them on how they are to treat their citizens. But why do we need a document like the Universal Declaration? Governments believe that they cannot control their people if their people have all the rights, so many countries simply don't grant their citizens these rights. Organizations and movements rose up to try to shame countries into ensuring their people these basic freedoms, and writers have used their voices to raise consciences and explain the necessity of human rights standards and basic respect for human life.

The essential message behind human rights is simple, but as with other topics, writers choose to tackle their subject in many different ways. In this chapter, you will read former President Jimmy Carter's argument in "A World Criminal Court Is Urgently Needed." In a straightforward way, he offers his view as an elder statesman lending his authority to a cause. In "Let It Be," Jonathan Rauch, on the other hand, projects a wry cynicism to highlight what he sees as a way to remove a hindrance to human rights, religious fervency. Israeli writer Amos Oz, in "Two Stubborn Men, Many Dead," chooses to argue in highly emotional terms, in speaking of slain children and in calling for the end of the Israeli-Palestinian war. Terry Tempest Williams, in "The Clan of the One-Breasted Women," also uses emotional appeals to expose the plight of the victims of U.S. atomic testing the desert in the 1950s. Each of these writers has a position to defend, but each uses a vastly different technique.

JIMMY CARTER
A World Criminal Court Is Urgently Needed

The 39th president of the United States of America, James Earl Carter was born in 1924 in Plains, Georgia, which has remained his home to this day. A devout Baptist, Carter spent seven years in the navy, serving on a nuclear submarine, before returning to Plains to take over the family business, peanut farming. After a successful business career, he turned to politics. He was elected the governor of Georgia in 1962 and was elected president in 1976 over Republican incumbent Gerald Ford. His administration struggled with the terrible inflation and unemployment that affected the country in the late 1970s. Carter worked to improve domestic affairs, including race relations and government efficiency. He worked toward peace in the Middle East and brokered the Camp David agreement of 1978 that marked an end of aggression between Israel and Egypt. A crisis overshadowed the end of his administration, however, when Iran took as hostages 52 members of the U.S. embassy in Tehran. Carter paid the price, and he was defeated by Ronald Reagan in the 1980 election. (Iran released the hostages on Carter's last day in office.)

Carter's career did not end with his presidency, however. He and his wife, Rosalyn, went back to Plains and started the Carter Center in 1982, which "seeks to prevent and resolve conflicts, enhance freedom and democracy, and improve health." The center acts as a neutral observer of elections around the world and works to eradicate diseases in Third World countries (they were successful in Africa with Guinea worm disease). Since the 1980s, Carter has been involved with Habitat for Humanity, a nonprofit organization that builds houses for people in need. Carter is the author of The Blood of Abraham *(1985), about the Middle East peace process,* An Outdoor Journal *(1988), and* An Hour Before Daylight *(2001). In 2002 he received the Nobel Peace Prize for "his decades of untiring efforts to find peaceful solutions to international conflict." In this selection, published in the* Los Angeles Times *in 1996, Carter lends his moral authority to what he sees as the need for a permanent international criminal court.*

▶ Prereading: Thinking About the Essay in Advance

What possible arguments can you think of for not supporting a criminal court subject to international law?

▶ Words to Watch

avert (par. 1) prevent
compliance (par. 1) agreement to do something
convene (par. 3) come together for an official reason
marred (par. 5) spoiled or took away from
acute (par. 8) very serious
undermine (par. 11) weaken

arbiter (par. 11) someone who has the power to decide
panacea (par. 12) cure-all for all problems
expeditiously (par. 13) quickly

1   Out of the horrors of World War II, world leaders collectively agreed that genocide and crimes against humanity represented a threat to international peace and security, above and beyond the populations directly affected. To avert future occurrences, mechanisms were devised, such as the Geneva and Genocide conventions, which place obligations on states engaged in warfare and the international community at large. Unfortunately, these have been inadequate in their ability to enforce state compliance. Genocide has been perpetrated twice within the last few years, in the former Yugoslavia and Rwanda.

2   Political efforts to address these crises failed for far too long. World leaders have been largely divided about what could have been done to prevent them, given the absence of enforceable protection procedures. One response to this concern has been the creation of special tribunals to prosecute the architects of genocidal policies and practices in the two countries.

3   Simultaneously, negotiations have been under way within the United Nations to create an International Criminal Court. This would be a permanent court for prosecuting suspected perpetrators of crimes against humanity when national courts are not able to do so, eliminating the need for special tribunals. In November 1996, these negotiations resulted in a landmark agreement to convene a diplomatic conference in 1998, during which a treaty establishing the court would be concluded.

4   These developments offer hope in the struggle to protect human rights, but will require greater care and attention in the coming years.

5   Since the creation of the two special tribunals, they have been marred with difficulties that provide lessons for the permanent court. Early on, financial resources were scarce. While this lack seems to have been solved for the time being, other matters threaten the tribunals' effectiveness.

6   After initial missteps, the Bosnia Tribunal has gradually addressed many of these issues, including performing more effective investigations of crimes of sexual violence against women. This required proper definitions of crimes in international law, adequate specialized training and arrangements for collection of evidence and testimonies as well as witness protection.

7   However, more general problems, such as failure to arrest and extradite the vast majority of those indicted by the tribunal, could undermine its prospects for successful prosecutions.

8   The Rwanda Tribunal suffers from more acute problems, including shortages of qualified personnel, limited training, faulty methodology and weak investigative procedures. The matter of investigating crimes of

sexual violence against women has not been handled well and needs dedicated resources and expertise. In addition to indictments having been slow in emerging, as of December 1996 only three of the 21 of those indicted are in the custody of the Tribunal.

The responsibility falls upon the international community to ensure   9
the effective functioning of the tribunals by investing in them resources and political will that until now, have fallen short of what is needed. One place to start is for all nations to enact laws that enable them to extradite indicted war criminals to The Hague.

The permanent court is needed so that any future cases can be   10
brought forward quickly without waiting years for procedures and structures to be built, as has been the case with the special tribunals. Now that a date has been set for the court's establishment, the U.S. government should play a leadership role in ensuring that it will be constituted in a way that enables it to work independently from political pressures. We should reflect on our own experience which shows that a judicial process must not be vulnerable to politics or personal preferences. It must be guided by the law alone.

In that light, a U.S. proposal to grant the Security Council control   11
over prosecutions in the court would undermine its very purpose. Such a move rightly would be seen by many nations as a means for serving only the interests of the permanent members of the Security Council rather than as an independent arbiter of justice.

The court will not be a panacea. As we have found in our own society,   12
a criminal justice system does not ensure the absence of violence, but we would never consider eliminating it as a key ingredient in any strategy to protect civil rights and public safety in general.

The International Criminal Court will be good for America, and it   13
will be good for the world. Meanwhile, all nations should consider it their duty to ensure that the existing tribunals overcome current difficulties and complete their work as expeditiously and effectively as possible.

▶ Building Vocabulary

In this essay, Carter uses several words from the legal profession and the world surrounding it. Define the following words (looking them up in reference works, if necessary), and offer an example of each from outside the realm of the World Criminal Court:

1. genocide (par. 1)
2. perpetrated (par. 1)
3. tribunals (par. 2)
4. extradite (par. 7)
5. indicted (par. 8)

▶Thinking Critically About the Argument

Understanding the Writer's Argument

1. Which "horrors of World War II" is Carter referring to in paragraph 1?
2. What does Carter think we can do to help prevent genocide around the world?
3. What is the International Criminal Court?
4. What are the "two special tribunals" to which Carter refers in paragraph 5? What problems have they faced?
5. What does Carter mean when he writes that "The court will not be a panacea"? (par. 12)

Understanding the Writer's Techniques

1. What is Carter's major proposition? In which sentence does it appear?
2. What minor propositions does Carter present to show why a permanent international criminal court is needed? What details does he offer to back up those minor propositions?
3. In what order has Carter chosen to present his argument? Why do you think he chooses that order? Is it effective? Why do you think so?
4. Carter's style is extremely straightforward. Why does he choose this style? Is it appropriate? Explain.
5. Analyze how Carter maintains coherence in this essay. What techniques does he use?
6. Who do you think is Carter's audience for this essay? Why?
7. How effective is Carter's conclusion? Why does he close by mentioning the temporary courts if his essay is about the need for a permanent court?

Exploring the Writer's Argument

1. Do you agree with Carter that developing criminal courts to prosecute those accused of genocide "offer hope in the struggle to protect human rights"? Why or why not?
2. One of Carter's points is that temporary tribunals, for individual conflicts, do not work, and a permanent court is needed to do a good job. Does he convince you of this need, or are you still not sure if temporary courts would do a fine enough job?
3. Do you think it is appropriate for an ex-president of this country to be criticizing a U.S. proposal to the United Nations, as Carter does in paragraph 11? Why or why not?

▶ Ideas for Writing Arguments

Prewriting

Can you think of any reasons why a country would not want to agree to the establishment of the International Criminal Court? List as many objections as you can come up with.

Writing a Guided Argument

Two years after Carter wrote this essay in 1996, a convention was held in Rome, Italy, officially beginning the process to establish the court Carter calls for in this essay. Then-President Bill Clinton agreed to adhere to the convention. His successor, President George W. Bush, has said that he would not allow the United States to be a party to the International Criminal Court. Do some research to learn the arguments of the Bush administration, and write an essay in which you argue that the United States will or will not eventually sign on to the court.

1. Open your essay with an update about the International Criminal Court since Carter's essay was published in December 1996.
2. Next, include a reference to the controversy over the court's founding, paying attention to the United States' recent arguments against it.
3. Assert your claim that the United States will or will not join on eventually.
4. Present the grounds for your claim in separate paragraphs.
5. Support the grounds for your position with evidence from your research and your own opinions.
6. Make reference to other international treaties the United States does not want to be a part of, or has left, and link this idea with the court.
7. Conclude with a summary of your own opinion about the International Criminal Court, and what you think the United States *should* do, based on your research.

Thinking, Arguing, and Writing Collaboratively

In groups of four or five, discuss what a proper punishment is for war crimes. Is it better to execute war criminals convicted of genocide, or is it better to keep them alive as an example? Your group might want to do some research to see what temporary tribunals have done with war criminals over the years.

Writing About the Text

During his presidency, Carter was caricatured as always having a huge grin and being too soft-spoken for the job. Carter's calm voice comes through in this essay. Write an essay in which you argue either that his flatness of style lacks the impact needed to influence anyone or that his voice is exactly the one that is needed in an argument of this type.

More Writing Ideas

1. Will humans ever succeed in ending genocide, or will there always be madmen with the means to achieve their goals? In your journal record your responses to this question.
2. Write a paragraph that explores the idea of human rights and how an International Criminal Court can advance the cause of human rights throughout the world.
3. Wendell Berry argues in his essay "In Distrust of Movements" that often people who act to help the world lose their way and don't help much at all. Read Berry's essay, and ascertain what he thinks can be done to help movements stay on track. Do some research on Jimmy Carter's Carter Center, and write an essay in which you argue that the Carter Center is (or is not) faithful to Berry's prescriptions.

JONATHAN RAUCH
Let It Be

Born in Phoenix, Arizona, in 1960, Jonathan Rauch attended Yale University before starting his career as a reporter and writer at the Winston-Salem Journal *in North Carolina. Rauch moved to Washington in 1984 for a stint as a staff writer for the* National Journal. *Since then he has written freelance for many magazines and newspapers on political and cultural issues, and since 1991 he has also written as an openly gay writer about gay rights. He is the author of* The Outnation *(1992),* Kindly Inquisitors *(1993),* Demosclerosis *(1994), and* Government's End: Why Washington Stopped Working *(1999). He currently writes a biweekly column for the* National Journal. *In this selection published in the* Atlantic Monthly *in 2002, Rauch argues in favor of an attitude toward religion that he calls "apatheism."*

▶ Prereading: Thinking About the Essay in Advance

What religion were you brought up with? Do you still practice? Do you think organized religion makes the world a better place? Why or why not?

▶ Words to Watch

induced (par. 1) caused by
disinclination (par. 2) reluctance to do something
ostensibly (par. 2) seeming to be true, but perhaps not
pious (par. 2) devoutly religious

quaint (par. 3) charmingly old-fashioned
unrepentantly (par. 7) in a way as not to apologize for something
divisive (par. 8) causing disagreements
volatile (par. 8) unstable
pragmatic (par. 9) concerned with practical results rather than ideas
snicker (par. 11) laugh condescendingly

It came to me recently in a blinding vision that I am an apatheist. Well, "blinding vision" may be an overstatement. "Wine-induced haze" might be more strictly accurate. This was after a couple of glasses of Merlot, when someone asked me about my religion. "Atheist," I was about to say, but I stopped myself. "I used to call myself an atheist," I said, "and I still don't believe in God, but the larger truth is that it has been years since I really cared one way or another. I'm"—that was when it hit me—"an . . . apatheist!"   1

That got a chuckle, but the point was serious. Apatheism—a disinclination to care all that much about one's own religion, and an even stronger disinclination to care about other people's—may or may not be something new in the world, but its modern flowering, particularly in ostensibly pious America, is worth getting excited about.   2

Apatheism concerns not what you believe but how. In that respect it differs from the standard concepts used to describe religious views and people. Atheism, for instance, is not at all like apatheism; the hot-blooded atheist cares as much about religion as does the evangelical Christian, but in the opposite direction. "Secularism" can refer to a simple absence of devoutness, but it more accurately refers to an ACLU-style disapproval of any profession of religion in public life—a disapproval that seems puritanical and quaint to apatheists. Tolerance is a magnificent concept, John Locke's inestimable gift to all mankind; but it assumes, as Locke did, that everyone brims with religious passions that everyone else must work hard to put up with.   3

And agnostics? True, most of them are apatheists, but most apatheists are not agnostics. Because—and this is an essential point—many apatheists are believers.   4

In America, as Thomas Byrne Edsall reported in these pages recently, the proportion of people who say they never go to church or synagogue has tripled since 1972, to 33 percent in 2000. Most of these people believe in God (professed atheists are very rare in the United States); they just don't care much about him. They do care a bit; but apatheism is an attitude, not a belief system, and the over-riding fact is that these people are relaxed about religion.   5

Even regular churchgoers can, and often do, rank quite high on the apatheism scale. There are a lot of reasons to attend religious services: to connect with a culture or a community, to socialize, to expose children to religion, to find the warming comfort of familiar ritual. The softer   6 denominations in America are packed with apatheists. The apatheism of Reform Jews is so well known as to be a staple of synagogue humor. (Orthodox rabbi to Reform rabbi: "One of my congregants says his son wants a Harley for his bar mitzvah. What's a Harley?" Reform rabbi to Orthodox rabbi: "A Harley is a motor-cycle. What's a bar mitzvah?")

7   Finally, and this may seem strangest of all, even true-believing godliness today often has an apatheistic flavor. I have Christian friends who organize their lives around an intense and personal relationship with God, but who betray no sign of caring that I am an unrepentantly atheistic Jewish homosexual. They are exponents, at least, of the second, more important part of apatheism: the part that doesn't mind what *other* people think about God.

8   I believe that the rise of apatheism is to be celebrated as nothing less than a major civilizational advance. Religion, as the events of September 11 and after have so brutally underscored, remains the most divisive and volatile of social forces. To be in the grip of religious zeal is the natural state of human beings, or at least of a great many human beings; that is how much of the species seems to be wired. Apatheism, therefore, should not be assumed to represent a lazy recumbency, like my collapse into a soft chair after a long day. Just the opposite: it is the product of a determined cultural effort to discipline the religious mindset, and often of an equally determined personal effort to master the spiritual passions. It is not a lapse. It is an achievement.

9   "A world of pragmatic atheists," the philosopher Richard Rorty once wrote, "would be a better, happier world than our present one." Perhaps. But best of all would be a world generously leavened with apatheists: people who feel at ease with religion even if they are irreligious; people who may themselves be members of religious communities, but who are neither controlled by godly passions nor concerned about the (nonviolent, noncoercive) religious beliefs of others. In my lifetime America has taken great strides in this direction and its example will be a source of strength, not weakness, in a world still beset by fanatical religiosity (al Qaeda) and tyrannical secularism (China).

10   Ronald Reagan used to insist that he was religious even though, as President, he hardly ever entered a church. It turns out he was in good company. Those Americans who tell pollsters they worship faithfully? Many of them are lying. John G. Stackhouse Jr., a professor of theology and culture, wrote recently in *American Outlook* magazine, "Beginning in the 1990s, a series of sociological studies has shown that many more Americans tell pollsters that they attend church regularly than can be found in church when teams actually count." In fact, he says, actual churchgoing may be at little more than half the professed rate. A great many Americans, like their fortieth President, apparently care about religion enough to say they are religious but not enough to go to church.

11   You can snicker at Reagan and the millions of others like him; you can call them hypocrites if you like. I say, God bless them, every one.

▶ Building Vocabulary

1. Identify the following:
   a. ACLU (par. 3)
   b. John Locke (par. 3)
   c. The difference between Orthodox and Reform Judaism (par. 6)
   d. Richard Rorty (par. 9)
   e. pollsters (par. 10)
2. This essay explores different approaches to various aspects of religion. Identify and define the following religious terms:
   a. atheist (par. 1)
   b. evangelical Christian (par. 3)
   c. secularism (par. 3)
   d. puritanical (par. 3)
   e. agnostics (par. 4)
   f. denominations (par. 6)
   g. religious zeal (par. 8)

▶ Thinking Critically About the Argument

Understanding the Writer's Argument

1. What is an *apatheist*? What two words does Rauch combine to get this word?
2. In paragraph 2, Rauch explains why apatheism is different from other ways people can be indifferent to religion. In your own words, explain the difference.
3. What are the "softer denominations" among the religions in America? (par. 6) List at least three.
4. In paragraph 7, Rauch describes himself as an "atheistic Jewish homosexual." How can he be atheistic and Jewish at the same time?
5. What does Rauch mean in paragraph 9 when he says that if there were many apatheists, the world would be "leavened"? Do you recognize the joke here? What is it?
6. Rauch quotes John G. Stackhouse as saying that perhaps half of the people who tell pollsters they go to church actually go. Why do you think people would lie to people taking polls?
7. Why does Rauch like Reagan's approach to religion?

Understanding the Writer's Techniques

1. What is Rauch's claim? In which paragraph does it appear?
2. What is the effect of Rauch in saying that he was mildly drunk when he came up with his idea?
3. What grounds does Rauch offer to back up his claim?

4. In what order does Rauch present his points? Why do you think he chose that order? Is it effective?

5. What is the effect of Rauch's joke in paragraph 6? Do you think it is appropriate? Why or why not? Does it help his essay? Explain.

6. How has Rauch used the strategy of definition here? What other rhetorical modes can you identify in this essay?

7. Do you like Rauch's conclusion? Do you think it's funny? Does it help his argument? If so, how? If not, why not?

Exploring the Writer's Argument

1. Some people suggest that with the loss of interest in religion comes the loss of something noble and exalted in the human mind. Do you think Rauch properly addresses this objection to his argument? Explain your answer.

2. In paragraph 7, Rauch makes the point that one aspect of apatheism is the fact that some people don't mind "what *other* people think about God." Do you think he fully explains why this is the "more important part of apatheism"? Explain your answer fully.

3. Do you agree with Rauch that apatheism is "the product of a determined cultural effort to discipline the religious mindset," (par. 8) or do you think it is just laziness? Why?

▶ Ideas for Writing Arguments

Prewriting

Look up the word *neologism* in the dictionary. Brainstorm to come up with as many neologisms as you can, in the style of Rauch's *apatheism*.

Writing a Guided Argument

Write an essay in which you combine two words to create a new word, and then defend that word and its idea as a new, important concept that sheds light on a recent controversy. (For example, you might call people who illegally download music on the Internet but also buy music in stores "KaZumers," combining the popular program KaZaa and the word "consumers.")

1. Begin with a paragraph that dramatizes your discovery of the new word, modeled on Rauch's discovery of *apatheism*.

2. Explain how you were at first amused by your discovery but that in reality, your idea has serious implications.

3. In the body of your essay, explore at least three major implications of your new word.

4. Indicate your own beliefs about the issue that you are illustrating.

5. Link your paragraphs with appropriate transitions.

6. Write an appropriate conclusion, a quick jab of a paragraph that closes on a witty statement.

Thinking, Arguing, and Writing Collaboratively

In small groups, talk about what this essay has to do with human rights, and expand on how Rauch's idea can actually improve human rights around the United States and the world. On the basis of your discussion, write notes for an outline of possible minor propositions supporting this idea.

Writing About the Text

Concentrating on the fact that the message behind all religions is peace, and contrasting this with Rauch's judgments about the problems religion has caused, write an essay that takes issue with Rauch and defends religion against his charges.

More Writing Ideas

1. In paragraph 8, Rauch writes that "to be in the grip of religious zeal is the natural state of human beings." Write a journal entry explaining why you think that is.

2. Write a paragraph explaining why the title of Rauch's essay is ironic.

3. Turn the notes from your Thinking, Arguing, and Writing Collaboratively activity into an essay.

AMOS OZ
Two Stubborn Men, Many Dead

Israeli writer and novelist Amos Oz was born in 1939 in Jerusalem. He studied literature at the Hebrew University in Jerusalem and has taught at Oxford University and Ben Gurion University of the Negev. He has published 18 books in Hebrew, including the novels My Michael *(1968),* Touch the Water, Touch the Wind *(1973),* Black Box *(1987), and* To Know a Woman *(1989), and collections of essays and fiction. Many of his works have been translated extensively. He has also published many essays in international magazines and newspapers. During the Six Day War in 1967 and in the 1973 Yom Kippur War, Oz fought for the Israeli Army as a soldier in a tank unit. He is involved in the movement for peace in the Middle East and writes often about the topic, supporting the idea of a Palestinian state in the West Bank and Gaza. In this selection, published as an op-ed piece in* The New York Times *in 2002, Oz takes the leaders of both Israel and Palestine to task for delaying the peace process while people die.*

▶ Prereading: Thinking About the Essay in Advance

What keeps leaders of countries from making peace? Why do war and conflict between two countries often go on for years?

▶ Words to Watch

accordance (par. 2) such a way as to conform
demographic (par. 2) having to do with patterns of populations
persona (par. 4) public personality
sovereign (par. 5) independent and self-governing
credentials (par. 7) official papers that show a person's position

1   On Saturday night a 9-month old baby girl, an Israeli, was murdered in Netanya by a group of Palestinian gunmen. A few days earlier another baby girl, a Palestinian, was blown up by an Israeli bomb. Innocent civilians are dying, killed on both sides nearly every day. They are dying not because there is no way of resolving the crisis, but, on the contrary, they are dying precisely because a way exists and is known very well by all.

2   Every Israeli in the street knows what the solution is, just as every Palestinian knows it. Even Ariel Sharon and Yasir Arafat know the solution: peace between two states, established by the partition of the land roughly in accordance with demographic realities based on Israel's pre-1967 borders.

3   During this period of long sleepless nights, I sometimes wish I could believe in ghosts. I turn and toss in bed and imagine being able to send the ghosts of all the dead children, Israeli and Palestinian, to haunt Mr. Sharon and Mr. Arafat. I imagine that I am able to assemble these innocents around the beds of the two leaders; two men, both more than 70 years old, each a prisoner of the other, each at the mercy of the other. Each ready to act every day exactly as the enemy foresees, to throw more fuel on the flames, to spill yet more blood.

4   Sometimes during these nights I see these two men fused into the persona of an ancient warrior, a wicked Nero, amusing himself by playing with fire, laughing savagely while stoking the flames. During the same troubled nights, I find myself hoping for the opposite, too—that Mr. Sharon and Mr. Arafat will not be haunted by the ghosts of the dead children, but will instead be sent away to sleep for weeks and months, to be awakened only after the signing of a peace treaty.

A child holds up a sign at the "Women on the Move" March
Thursday, Dec. 10, 1998 in New Delhi, India during International
Human Rights Day. (Associated Press/John McConnico)

History will never forget their offenses, because the solution is   5
here, visible, manifestly clear before us all. Every Israeli and every
Palestinian knows that this land will be divided into two sovereign nations and become like a semi-detached two-family house. Even those
who loathe this future already know, deep in their hearts, that all this is
inevitable.

I suspect that even the Siamese twins, Mr. Sharon and Mr. Arafat—I   6
now call them "Mr. Sharafat"—know this. But fear and stagnation stifle
them both. They are living under the dominion of a bloodstained past.
They are hostages to one another, so much so that the entire historical dynamic of the conflict of the Middle East has become captive to their fears,
their immobility.

7   One day when the peace treaty is achieved, and the Palestinian ambassador presents his credentials to the president of Israel in the Western section of Jerusalem, while the Israeli ambassador presents his to the Palestinian president in East Jerusalem, we shall all have to laugh at the stupidities of our past. Even as we laugh, we shall have to answer for the spilling of so much innocent blood. But the mothers and fathers of the dead will not be laughing.

▶ Building Vocabulary

For each of the following words, write a definition that shows how Oz uses the word in his essay, and write an original sentence:

1. innocents (par. 3)
2. loathe (par. 5)
3. stagnation (par. 6)
4. dynamic (par. 6)
5. immobility (par. 6)

▶ Thinking Critically About the Argument

Understanding the Writer's Argument

1. Why does Oz start his essay by referring to the two children who were killed?
2. What is the solution Oz refers to in the first paragraph?
3. Who are Sharon and Arafat?
4. Who was Nero, and why is Oz's image of Sharon and Arafat as Nero appropriate?
5. What does Oz mean when he says that Sharon and Arafat are "living under the dominion of a bloodstained past"?

Understanding the Writer's Techniques

1. What is Oz's claim? Where is it stated most clearly?
2. What warrants does Oz imply in this essay?
3. Outline the essay by paragraph, summarizing the purpose of each.
4. How does the portrait of Sharon and Arafat as being haunted help to focus the essay? More important, how does each succeeding image of the two men build on the last?
5. What is the argumentative effect of Oz's statement that "history will never forget their offences"? Explain.
6. Oz punctuates his essay with phrases and words intended to lend his argument emotional force, such as "laughing savagely" in paragraph 4. List three more examples of such words and phrases, and explain how they add to (or weaken) Oz's argument.

7. What do you think of Oz's conclusion? Is it effective? Why or why not?

Exploring the Writer's Argument

1. Does Oz do a good enough job of convincing you, the reader, that splitting the land into two separate countries is "inevitable"? Explain your answers.
2. What is Oz's aim in this essay? Is he trying to convince anyone in particular of anything? If so, who and what? Who is his audience? If he isn't trying to convince, then why does he bother to write? Explain.
3. Oz claims that Sharon and Arafat are afraid and that the peace process is stifled, as he says, by the fear of these two men. Does Oz explain what they are afraid of? Does he suggest anything? Explain.

▶ Ideas for Writing Arguments

Prewriting

Write some notes on what effect the ongoing war in Israel is likely to have on future generations of Israeli and Palestinian children.

Writing a Guided Argument

In many ways, the Mideast peace process is like a bitter divorce. The two sides know they must split up, but they are fighting to the end to gain as much advantage as possible before the split is complete. Write an essay in which you write a letter to divorcing parents of two children, arguing that their fight is really hurting the children.

1. Begin your essay with an invocation of the children in the marriage and how the divorce is hurting them.
2. Explain that the divorce is inevitable, and that the parents must end it quickly to save their children.
3. In the next section, explain the effects the divorce is likely to have on the children. Feel free to invent details about the hypothetical children.
4. Organize the various effects on the children in a separate paragraph, taking your time to develop each one.
5. Use charged language to deepen the emotional appeal to the parents.
6. Establish a slightly cynical tone in your essay, while remaining objective and not placing the blame on either parent.
7. If you have them, use statistics to back up your points about the effects divorce has on children.
8. Close your essay with an unabashedly emotional plea to the parents to put aside their differences and think of their children.

Thinking, Arguing, and Writing Collaboratively

With the class divided into three groups, one group will represent the Israelis, one group will represent the Palestinians, and one group will represent the United States and European peacemakers. Each group should go to the library to do research on the positions each side holds. What do the Israelis want from the peace process? What do the Palestinians want? Then reconvene as a class and hold a mock peace conference in which you make proposals and concessions and draw up a plan that will lead to peace. What points are hardest to resolve?

Writing About the Text

Oz has a simple but powerful point to make in this essay. He must be rational to get his point across, but, as he writes, everyone knows what the solution is. So he depends on an emotional appeal to promote his position about peace. Write an essay in which you consider how Oz mixes the basic rational argument for peace with rhetorical emotional arguments. How do his emotional passages help or hurt his rational argument?

More Writing Ideas

1. In your journal, freewrite on the idea of innocents in war. Do not edit your work. Just write for at least 15 minutes. When you are finished, show your work to a classmate.
2. Arafat, of course, has been the leader of the Palestinians since there was a Palestinian movement, but he will eventually be replaced or die; Sharon is an elected official. Still, the peace process has been going on for a long time, without real peace, there has been no progess by these men since Oz wrote, militant groups seem to be in charge, and peace is elusive. Do some reading on the topic, and write an extended paragraph on how you think things could change if one or both of the men leave their positions of power.
3. In the past couple of years, a new plan has been drawn up for peace in Israel, a plan called the "roadmap" that mandates several deadlines for specific accomplishments along the way to peace. Do some research on the roadmap, and write an essay arguing that it is or is not the best hope for the region.

TERRY TEMPEST WILLIAMS
The Clan of the One-Breasted Women

Terry Tempest Williams grew up in Salt Lake City, Utah, and has worked to protect the natural landscape of that state. She was inducted into the Rachel

Carson Honor Roll and has received the National Wildlife Federation's Conservation Award for Special Achievement. Williams is the author of several books, including Pieces of White Shell: A Journey to Navajoland *(1984),* Coyote's Canyon *(1989),* Red: Patience and Passion in the Desert *(2001), and* Refuge: An Unnatural History of Family and Place *(1991), about the Great Salt Lake and the surrounding areas. She has published widely, in such magazines as* The New Yorker, The Nation, *and* The New England Review. *This selection, which is the epilogue from* Refuge, *deals with Williams's mother's cancer, believed to be caused by radioactive fallout from the nuclear tests in the Nevada desert in the 1950s and 1960s.*

▶ Prereading: Thinking About the Essay in Advance

What is a citizen's responsibility to act when the government is not acting in its people's best interests?

▶ Words to Watch

stoic (par. 6) showing patience and calmness in the face of problems
permeated (par. 13) spread throughout
deceit (par. 19) act of misleading
midwife (par. 32) literally, someone who helps to deliver babies
wax (par. 39) grow
wane (par. 39) shrink
mesa (par. 47) mostly flat elevated area that is usually found in the Southwest

I belong to a Clan of One-Breasted Women. My mother, my grandmothers, and six aunts have all had mastectomies. Seven are dead. The two who survive have just completed rounds of chemotherapy and radiation. 1

I've had my own problems: two biopsies for breast cancer and a small tumor between my ribs diagnosed as a "borderline malignancy." 2

This is my family history. 3

Most statistics tell us breast cancer is genetic, hereditary, with rising percentages attached to fatty diets, childlessness, or becoming pregnant after thirty. What they don't say is living in Utah may be the greatest hazard of all. 4

We are a Mormon family with roots in Utah since 1847. The "word of wisdom" in my family aligned us with good foods—no coffee, no tea, tobacco, or alcohol. For the most part, our women were finished having their babies by the time they were thirty. And only one faced breast cancer prior to 1960. Traditionally, as a group of people, Mormons have a low rate of cancer. 5

6   Is our family a cultural anomaly? The truth is, we didn't think about it. Those who did, usually the men, simply said, "bad genes." The women's attitude was stoic. Cancer was part of life. On February 16, 1971, the eve of my mother's surgery, I accidentally picked up the telephone and overheard her ask my grandmother what she could expect.

7   "Diane, it is one of the most spiritual experiences you will ever encounter."

8   I quietly put down the receiver.

9   Two days later, my father took my brothers and me to the hospital to visit her. She met us in the lobby in a wheelchair. No bandages were visible. I'll never forget her radiance, the way she held herself in a purple velvet robe, and how she gathered us around her.

10   "Children, I am fine. I want you to know I felt the arms of God around me."

11   We believed her. My father cried. Our mother, his wife, was thirty-eight years old.

12   A little over a year after Mother's death, Dad and I were having dinner together. He had just returned from St. George, where the Tempest Company was completing the gas lines that would service southern Utah. He spoke of his love for the country, the sandstoned landscape, bare-boned and beautiful. He had just finished hiking the Kolob trail in Zion National Park. We got caught up in reminiscing, recalling with fondness our walk up Angel's Landing on his fiftieth birthday and the years our family had vacationed there.

13   Over dessert, I shared a recurring dream of mine. I told my father that for years, as long as I could remember, I saw this flash of light in the night in the desert—that this image had so permeated my being that I could not venture south without seeing it again, on the horizon, illuminating buttes and mesas.

14   "You did see it," he said.

15   "Saw what?"

16   "The bomb. The cloud. We were driving home from Riverside, California. You were sitting on Diane's lap. She was pregnant. In fact, I remember the day, September 7, 1957. We had just gotten out of the Service. We were driving north, past Las Vegas. It was an hour or so before dawn, when this explosion went off. We not only heard it, but felt it. I thought the oil tanker in front of us had blown up. We pulled over and suddenly, rising from the desert floor, we saw it, clearly, this golden-stemmed cloud, the mushroom. The sky seemed to vibrate with an eerie pink glow. Within a few minutes, a light ash was raining on the car."

17   I stared at my father.

18   "I thought you knew that," he said. "It was a common occurrence in the fifties."

19   It was at this moment that I realized the deceit I had been living under. Children growing up in the American Southwest, drinking contam-

inated milk from contaminated cows, even from the contaminated breasts of their mothers, my mother—members, years later, of the Clan of One-Breasted Women.

It is a well-known story in the Desert West, "The Day We Bombed   20
Utah," or more accurately, the years we bombed Utah: above ground atomic testing in Nevada took place from January 27, 1951, through July 11, 1962. Not only were the winds blowing north covering "low-use segments of the population" with fallout and leaving sheep dead in their tracks, but the climate was right. The United States of the 1950s was red, white, and blue. The Korean War was raging. McCarthyism was rampant. Ike was it, and the cold war was hot. If you were against nuclear testing, you were for a communist regime.

Much has been written about this "American nuclear tragedy." Public   21
health was secondary to national security. The Atomic Energy Commissioner, Thomas Murray, said, "Gentlemen, we must not let anything interfere with this series of tests, nothing."

Again and again, the American public was told by its government, in   22
spite of burns, blisters, and nausea, "It has been found that the tests may be conducted with adequate assurance of safety under conditions prevailing at the bombing reservations." Assuaging public fears was simply a matter of public relations. "Your best action," an Atomic Energy Commission booklet read, "is not to be worried about fallout." A news release typical of the times stated, "We find no basis for concluding that harm to any individual has resulted from radioactive fallout."

On August 30, 1979, during Jimmy Carter's presidency, a suit was   23
filed, *Irene Allen* v. *The United States of America*. Mrs. Allen's case was the first on an alphabetical list of twenty-four test cases, representative of nearly twelve hundred plaintiffs seeking compensation from the United States government for cancers caused by nuclear testing in Nevada.

Irene Allen lived in Hurricane, Utah. She was the mother of five chil-   24
dren and had been widowed twice. Her first husband, with their two oldest boys, had watched the tests from the roof of the local high school. He died of leukemia in 1956. Her second husband died of pancreatic cancer in 1978.

In a town meeting conducted by Utah Senator Orrin Hatch, shortly   25
before the suit was filed, Mrs. Allen said, "I am not blaming the government, I want you to know that, Senator Hatch. But I thought if my testimony could help in any way so this wouldn't happen again to any of the generations coming up after us . . . I am happy to be here this day to bear testimony of this."

God-fearing people. This is just one story in an anthology of thousands.   26

On May 10, 1984, Judge Bruce S. Jenkins handed down his opinion.   27
Ten of the plaintiffs were awarded damages. It was the first time a federal court had determined that nuclear tests had been the cause of cancers. For

the remaining fourteen test cases, the proof of causation was not sufficient. In spite of the split decision, it was considered a landmark ruling. It was not to remain so for long.

28   In April 1987, the Tenth Circuit Court of Appeals overturned Judge Jenkins's ruling on the ground that the United States was protected from suit by the legal doctrine of sovereign immunity, a centuries-old idea from England in the days of absolute monarchs.

29   In January 1988, the Supreme Court refused to review the Appeals Court decision. To our court system it does not matter whether the United States government was irresponsible, whether it lied to its citizens, or even that citizens died from the fallout of nuclear testing. What matters is that our government is immune: "The King can do no wrong."

30   In Mormon culture, authority is respected, obedience is revered, and independent thinking is not. I was taught as a young girl not to "make waves" or "rock the boat."

31   "Just let it go," Mother would say. "You know how you feel, that's what counts."

32   For many years, I have done just that—listened, observed and quietly formed my own opinions, in a culture that rarely asks questions because it has all the answers. But one by one, I have watched the women in my family die common, heroic deaths. We sat in waiting rooms hoping for good news, but always receiving the bad. I cared for them, bathed their scarred bodies, and kept their secrets. I watched beautiful women become bald as Cytoxan, Cisplatin, and Adriamycin were injected into their veins. I held their foreheads as they vomited green-black bile, and I shot them with morphine when the pain became inhuman. In the end, I witnessed their last peaceful breaths, becoming a midwife to the rebirth of their souls.

33   The price of obedience has become too high.

34   The fear and inability to question authority that ultimately killed rural communities in Utah during atmospheric testing of atomic weapons is the same fear I saw in my mother's body. Sheep. Dead sheep. The evidence is buried.

35   I cannot prove that my mother, Diane Dixon Tempest, or my grandmothers, Lettie Romney Dixon and Kathryn Blackett Tempest, along with my aunts developed cancer from nuclear fallout in Utah. But I can't prove they didn't.

36   My father's memory was correct. The September blast we drove through in 1957 was part of Operation Plumbbob, one of the most intensive series of bomb tests to be initiated. The flash of light in the night in the desert, which I had always thought was a dream, developed into a family nightmare. It took fourteen years, from 1957 to 1971, for cancer to manifest in my mother—the same time, Howard L. Andrews, an authority in radioactive fallout at the National Institutes of Health, says radiation cancer requires to become evident. The more I learn about what it means to be a "downwinder," the more questions I drown in.

What I do know, however, is that as a Mormon woman of the fifth   37
generation of Latter-day Saints, I must question everything, even if it
means losing my faith, even if it means becoming a member of a border
tribe among my own people. Tolerating blind obedience in the name of
patriotism or religion ultimately takes our lives.

When the Atomic Energy Commission described the country north of   38
the Nevada Test Site as "virtually uninhabited desert terrain," my family
and the birds at Great Salt Lake were some of the "virtual uninhabitants."

One night, I dreamed women from all over the world circled a blaz-   39
ing fire in the desert. They spoke of change, how they hold the moon in
their bellies and wax and wane with its phases. They mocked the presumption of even-tempered beings and made promises that they would
never fear the witch inside themselves. The women danced wildly as
sparks broke away from the flames and entered the night sky as stars.

And they sang a song given to them by Shoshone grandmothers: 40

Ah ne nah, nah	Consider the rabbits
nin nah nah—	How gently they walk on the earth—
ah ne nah, nah	Consider the rabbits
nin nah nah—	How gently they walk on the earth—
Nyaga mutzi	We remember them
oh ne nay—	We can walk gently also—
Nyaga mutzi	We remember them
oh ne nay—	We can walk gently also—

The women danced and drummed and sang for weeks, preparing them-   41
selves for what was to come. They would reclaim the desert for the sake
of their children, for the sake of the land.

A few miles downwind from the fire circle, bombs were being   42
tested. Rabbits felt the tremors. Their soft leather pads on paws and feet
recognized the shaking sands, while the roots of mesquite and sage were
smoldering. Rocks were hot from the inside out and dust devils
hummed unnaturally. And each time there was another nuclear test,
ravens watched the desert heave. Stretch marks appeared. The land was
losing its muscle.   43

The women couldn't bear it any longer. They were mothers. They had
suffered labor pains but always under the promise of birth. The red hot
pains beneath the desert promised death only as each bomb became a
stillborn. A contract had been made and broken between human beings
and the land. A new contract was being drawn by the women, who understood the fate of the earth as their own.

Under the cover of darkness, ten women slipped under a barbed-   44
wire fence and entered the contaminated country. They were trespassing.
They walked toward the town of Mercury, in moonlight, taking their
cues from coyote, kit fox, antelope squirrel, and quail. They moved

quietly and deliberately through the maze of Joshua trees. When a hint of daylight appeared they rested, drinking tea and sharing their rations of food. The women closed their eyes. The time had come to protest with the heart that to deny one's genealogy with the earth was to commit treason against one's soul.

45   At dawn, the women draped themselves in mylar, wrapping long streamers of silver plastic around their arms to blow in the breeze. They wore clear masks, that became the faces of humanity. And when they arrived at the edge of Mercury, they carried all the butterflies of a summer day in their wombs. They paused to allow their courage to settle.

46   The town that forbids pregnant women and children to enter because of radiation risks was asleep. The women moved through the streets as winged messengers, twirling around each other in slow motion, peeking inside homes and watching the easy sleep of men and women. They were astonished by such stillness and periodically would utter a shrill note or low cry just to verify life.

47   The residents finally awoke to these strange apparitions. Some simply stared. Others called authorities, and in time, the women were apprehended by wary soldiers dressed in desert fatigues. They were taken to a white, square building on the other edge of Mercury. When asked who they were and why they were there, the women replied, "We are mothers and we have come to reclaim the desert for our children."

48   The soldiers arrested them. As the ten women were blindfolded and handcuffed, they began singing:

> *You can't forbid us everything*
> *You can't forbid us to think—*
> *You can't forbid our tears to flow*
> *And you can't stop the songs that we sing.*

49   The women continued to sing louder and louder, until they heard the voices of their sisters moving across the mesa:

> *Ah ne nah, nah*
> *nin nah nah—*
> *Ah ne nah, nah*
> *nin nah nah—*
> *Nyaga mutzi*
> *oh ne nay—*
> *Nyaga mutzi*
> *oh ne nay—*

"Call for reinforcements," one soldier said.

50   "We have," interrupted one woman, "we have—and you have no idea of our numbers."

51   I crossed the line at the Nevada Test Site and was arrested with nine other Utahans for trespassing on military lands. They are still conducting nuclear tests in the desert. Ours was an act of civil disobedience. But as I

walked toward the town of Mercury, it was more than a gesture of peace. It was a gesture on behalf of the Clan of One-Breasted Women.

As one officer cinched the handcuffs around my wrists, another frisked my body. She found a pen and a pad of paper tucked inside my left boot.   52

"And these?" she asked sternly.   53

"Weapons," I replied.   54

Our eyes met. I smiled. She pulled the leg of my trousers back over my boot.   55

"Step forward, please," she said as she took my arm.   56

We were booked under an afternoon sun and bused to Tonopah, Nevada. It was a two-hour ride. This was familiar country. The Joshua trees standing their ground had been named by my ancestors, who believed they looked like prophets pointing west to the Promised Land. These were the same trees that bloomed each spring, flowers appearing like white flames in the Mojave. And I recalled a full moon in May, when Mother and I had walked among them, flushing out mourning doves and owls.   57

The bus stopped short of town. We were released.   58

The officials thought it was a cruel joke to leave us stranded in the desert with no way to get home. What they didn't realize was that we were home, soul-centered and strong, women who recognized the sweet smell of sage as fuel for our spirits.   59

▶ Building Vocabulary

1. Williams uses several medical terms in this essay. Write out a definition for each. Try to figure out what each is from the context of the essay, and if you cannot identify it, use a reference book.
   a. mastectomies (par. 1)
   b. chemotherapy (par. 1)
   c. hereditary (par. 4)
   d. leukemia (par. 24)
   e. bile (par. 32)
   f. stillborn (par. 42)
2. This essay tells the story of government actions and their consequences. Explain at least five of the following terms from government and American history:
   a. McCarthyism (par. 20)
   b. cold war (par. 20)
   c. national security (par. 21)
   d. Atomic Energy Commission (par. 22)
   e. sovereign immunity (par. 28)
   f. Shoshone (par. 40)
   g. desert fatigues (par. 46)
   h. Promised Land (par. 55)

▶ Thinking Critically About the Argument

Understanding the Writer's Argument

1. What does Williams mean by the "Clan of One-Breasted Women"?
2. Why is Williams sure that the people in her family didn't get sick from an unhealthy lifestyle?
3. What is Williams's sudden realization when she has dinner with her father as she describes in paragraphs 12 to 18?
4. What is Williams's double meaning in paragraph 20 when she uses the word "climate"?
5. Why did the U.S. Court of Appeals for the Tenth Circuit overturn Judge Jenkins's decision? How did the people involved respond?
6. Where in the essay does Williams indicate that she had decided not to sit quietly anymore about the government's atomic testing?
7. How does Williams's family's Mormon faith prevent them from fighting for their rights?
8. Why do the women in Williams's dream speak in a Native American language?
9. How does Williams connect her dream with her actual protest experience?
10. What is Williams's double meaning when she replies "Weapons" when asked by the police officer what her pen and pad are?

Understanding the Writer's Techniques

1. What is Williams's major proposition? Where is it located?
2. This essay is structured into three main sections. What happens in each one? How does the structure help Williams argument?
3. What is the effect of Williams's withholding a clear statement that her mother died soon after surgery?
4. Certainly Williams has much to be cynical about, but do you think this shows up in her tone? If not, why not? If so, offer at least three examples where you think Williams is being cynical.
5. How does Williams connect rhetorically the fact that the Tenth Circuit overturned the Allen case with her family members dying of cancer?
6. Paraphrase Williams's argument in paragraph 34. What is the argumentative effect of including her mother's and grandmothers' names in paragraph 35?
7. Analyze Williams's dream. How is it persuasive here? What themes does she illustrate that previously she had only talked about in the abstract?
8. Do you think the conclusion of this essay is effective? Why or why not? What is your view of the title?

Exploring the Writer's Argument

1. What does Williams mean by the sentences in paragraph 42: "A contract had been made and broken between human beings and the land. A new contract was being drawn by the women who understood the fate of the earth as their own"?
2. Find information online or in the library about depleted uranium, which is a radioactive material used in bombs and ammunition by the U.S. military. What does depleted uranium have to do with the plight of the "downwinders" like Williams's family?
3. This essay's title focuses on women, and Williams mentions only women in her family who got sick. She describes women as being protectors of the land. But what about men, who got sick as well and protested against the government's atmospheric tests? Is she able to get men on her side? If so, how? If not, why not?

▶ Ideas for Writing Arguments

Prewriting

Prepare a list of what you think are the most pressing issues in human rights. What can be done about each?

Writing a Guided Argument

Do some research on how people fight for human rights. Write an essay about human rights in which you argue for one country as the worst offender against human rights. Visit the Web site or read the annual report of a human rights group such as Human Rights Watch, and investigate what kinds of problems it focuses on. Which countries are the worst offenders? Is the United States an offender? How does the organization you looked at fight for human rights? Do you agree?

1. Open your essay with an illustration of an abuse of human rights drawn from your research.
2. Write a short summary of the extent of your research.
3. Offer your major proposition, that you have concluded that a particular country is the world's worst offender against human rights.
4. Establish a serious tone in the beginning that carries moral weight.
5. In separate paragraphs, write the minor propositions that will build your case against the country you are focusing on.
6. In the next section, explain what the hope is for ending the human rights abuses.
7. Conclude your essay with a section that examines in brief the United States's current problems with human rights? Are there any serious issues?
8. Finish with an emotional plea for human rights.

Thinking, Arguing, and Writing Collaboratively

In groups of four or five, explore Williams's use of imagery in this essay. In your group, make a list of at least five powerful images that she uses to help her argument, along with an explanation of why each is powerful. Choose the best two, and present them with your group to the class. As a class, discuss how this kind of imagery can advance an argument based on emotion and ethics.

Writing About the Text

Williams is writing about a very emotional topic, so she must not let her reader become too comfortable. She does rely on emotional situations, and she does have grotesque images, but she also uses her skills as a writer to do the job a bit more subtly. For example, in paragraph 1, her sentence, "Seven are dead" hits the reader hard, as does her statement that "living in Utah may be the greatest hazard of all" in paragraph 4. Write an essay about how Williams uses surprises and double meanings in her prose to keep her readers unsettled.

More Writing Ideas

1. In your journal act as devil's advocate and argue that the atmospheric tests might have harmed people in the desert, but they saved many more lives by helping the United States win the Cold War.
2. Read the Universal Declaration of Human Rights, which was adopted by the United Nations in 1948. Write a paragraph exploring the implications of having a document like that. What can it possibly do to help matters?
3. In part because of the efforts of Senator Hatch (par. 25), in 1990, the U.S. Congress passed and George H. W. Bush signed the Radiation Exposure Compensation Act. This law has led to monetary awards of more than $300 million to the people who lived downwind from the tests. Any "downwinder" who contracts a serious disease gets $50,000 from the government. The government also has apologized officially to the participants. Write an essay in which you argue that this is fair or that the government could have done (or can do) more.

16 ▶ Terrorism: How Should We Meet the Challenge?

The planes crash into the World Trade Center and the Pentagon on September 11, 2001, shocking what many saw as a complacent nation. All of a sudden, Americans are vulnerable to sneak attack. The country went into mourning. For whom? For what? For the dead, yes, the more than 2,700 murdered. It seemed that most of us had some direct or indirect connection to someone who died that day. But Americans have also mourned their innocence, their lost way of life. The world since 9/11 has grown darkly complex. Two wars later, we are trying to deal with many issues raised by the attacks: What is the nature of patriotism? How can we balance our open society and our civil liberties with national security? Is it possible to defend ourselves against terrorism at all? And if not, then how can we prepare for the next attacks? How do we heal? The questions go on and on, and there seem to be few answers.

There are viewpoints, though. Columnist Thomas L. Friedman in "Globalization, Alive and Well" argues that we have no choice but to go forward with the international economy, as it is inevitable—something he thinks is obvious since 9/11. Reshma Memon Yaqub, a Muslim-American writer expresses her fear of being blamed for terrorism in "You People Did This." She counsels education to counter the ignorance that leads to violence. In "Words Fail, Memory Blurs, Life Wins," novelist Joyce Carol Oates offers a humanist-reading of our response to terrorism. We'll all be okay, she says, if we trust life. Finally, Jeffrey Rosen in "Bad Luck," cautions us against exaggerating the terrorist threat. Sometimes argumentative essays can make hopeful claims!

THOMAS L. FRIEDMAN
Globalization, Alive and Well

Thomas L. Friedman has written for The New York Times *since 1981. He has reported for the paper from Beirut in Lebanon, Jerusalem in Israel, New*

397

York, and Washington, D.C. Since 1995 he has served as the paper's foreign-affairs columnist. In all he has won three Pulitzer Prizes. He is the author of From Beirut to Jerusalem *(1989), which won the National Book Award for nonfiction, and* The Lexus and the Olive Tree: Understanding Globalization *(2000). Friedman was born in Minneapolis in 1953 and went to Brandeis University and Oxford University. In January 1989, Friedman took up a new assignment in Washington as the* Times' *chief diplomatic correspondent. His sobering and intelligent columns on all topics touching American foreign policy and events around the world are read widely and are influential. In this column, published just after a year after the September 11 attacks, Friedman scoffs at those who said that 9/11 would end the process of globalization.*

▶ Prereading: Thinking About the Essay in Advance

What is globalization? Do you see its effects in your life? What does globalization have to do with terrorism?

▶ Words to Watch

integration (par. 1) act of combining
pampered (par. 3) comfortable financially
abject (par. 3) hopeless, complete
subsidies (par. 3) money given from a government to a company to help it function
ideology (par. 4) system of beliefs

1   If one were having a contest for the most wrongheaded prediction about the world after 9/11, the winner would be the declaration by the noted London School of Economics professor John Gray that 9/11 heralded the end of the era of globalization. Not only will Sept. 11 not be remembered for ending the process of global financial, trade and technological integration, but it may well be remembered for bringing some sobriety to the antiglobalization movement.

2   If one thing stands out from 9/11, it's the fact that the terrorists originated from the least globalized, least open, least integrated corners of the world: namely, Saudi Arabia, Yemen, Afghanistan and northwest Pakistan. Countries that don't trade in goods and services also tend not to trade in ideas, pluralism or tolerance.

3   But maybe the most important reason why globalization is alive and well post-9/11 is that while pampered college students and academics in the West continue to debate about whether countries should globalize, the two biggest countries in the world, India and China—who represent one-third of humanity—have long moved beyond that question. They have decided that opening their economies to trade in goods and services is the best way to lift their people out of abject poverty and are now focused sim-

ply on how to globalize in the most stable manner. Some prefer to go faster, and some prefer to phase out currency controls and subsidies gradually, but the debate about the direction they need to go is over.

"Globalization fatigue is still very much in evidence in Europe and   4
America, while in places like China and India, you find a great desire for participation in the economic expansion processes," said Jairam Ramesh, the Indian Congress Party's top economic adviser. ". . . Even those who are suspicious now want to find a way to participate, but in a way that manages the risks and the pace. So we're finding ways to 'glocalize,' to do it our own way. It may mean a little slower growth to manage the social stability, but so be it. . . . I just spent a week in Germany and had to listen to all these people there telling me how globalization is destroying India and adding to poverty, and I just said to them, 'Look, if you want to argue about ideology, we can do that, but on the level of facts, you're just wrong.'"

That truth is most striking in Bangalore, India's Silicon Valley, where   5
hundreds of thousands of young Indians, most from lower-middle-class families, suddenly have social mobility, motor scooters and apartments after going to technical colleges and joining the Indian software and engineering firms providing back-room support and research for the world's biggest firms—thanks to globalization. Bangalore officials say each tech job produces 6.5 support jobs, in construction and services.

"Information technology has made millionaires out of ordinary peo-   6
ple [in India] because of their brainpower alone—not caste, not land, not heredity," said Sanjay Baru, editor of India's Financial Express. "India is just beginning to realize that this process of globalization is one where we have an inherent advantage."

Taking advantage of globalization to develop the Indian I.T. industry   7
has been "a huge win in terms of foreign exchange [and in] self-confidence," added Nandan Nilekani, chief executive of Infosys, the Indian software giant. "So many Indians come and say to me that 'when I walk through immigration at J.F.K. or Heathrow, the immigration guys look at me with respect now.' The image of India changed from a third-world country of snake charmers and rope tricks to the software brainy guys."

Do a majority of Indians still live in poor villages? Of course. Do we   8
still need to make globalization more fair by compelling the rich Western countries to open their markets more to those things that the poor countries are best able to sell: food and textiles? You bet.

But the point is this: The debate about globalization before 9/11 got   9
really stupid. Two simple truths got lost: One, globalization has its upsides and downsides, but countries that come at it with the right institutions and governance can get the best out of it and cushion the worst. Two, countries that are globalizing sensibly but steadily are also the ones that are becoming politically more open, with more opportunities for their people, and with a young generation more interested in joining the world system than blowing it up.

▶ Building Vocabulary

Friedman uses some common expressions in his essay to make his prose feel familiar. Use each of the following terms in a sentence of your own based on how they are used in the essay:

1. alive and well (par. 3)
2. pampered (par. 3)
3. abject poverty (par. 3)
4. phase out (par. 3)
5. in evidence (par. 4)
6. social mobility (par. 5)
7. back-room support (par. 5)
8. third-world country (par. 7)
9. simple truths (par. 9)

▶ Thinking Critically About the Argument

Understanding the Writer's Argument

1. What is globalization in your own words?
2. Who is John Gray? What was his prediction after 9/11, and why is he wrong, according to Friedman?
3. Where were the 9/11 terrorists from? Why is that significant to Friedman?
4. What does Friedman mean when he says that China and India have moved past the question of whether globalization is alive and well?
5. What does Jairam Ramesh mean by the word "glocalize" (par. 4), and why is this desirable?
6. In Friedman's view, what effect is globalization having on India?
7. What effect does globalization have on how Indians are viewed around the world, according to Friedman? Explain.
8. What two truths about globalization were forgotten before 9/11, according to Friedman?

Understanding the Writer's Techniques

1. What is Friedman's major proposition?
2. How does Friedman structure his essay? Make an outline that reflects the flow of his argument.
3. What kinds of evidence does Friedman offer to back up his position?
4. Paraphrase Friedman's argument in paragraph 3. Is it effective?
5. What is the effect of the quotes Friedman offers? Are they persuasive? Why or why not?
6. Which quote is the most effective? Which is the least effective? Why?

7. What is Friedman's tone in this essay? How do you know?
8. How do paragraphs 8 and 9 work together to make up a complete conclusion? Explain.

Exploring the Writer's Argument

1. Friedman depends in this essay on India as a test country for his claim. Is this convincing enough? Why doesn't he include examples from other countries? Explain your answers.
2. What aspects (if any) of Friedman's argument cause you to have confidence in his conclusions? What aspects of his argument cause you to distrust him (if any)?
3. Friedman does not include in his argument the idea that there are many people in developing countries who do not want globalization because they resent the influence of more developed countries, like the United States. Why, do you think, does Friedman not discuss this point?

▶ Ideas for Writing Arguments

Prewriting

What causes young men and women to resort to terrorism as a means of making their point?

Writing a Guided Argument

Write an essay in which you argue that the root causes of terrorism are mainly economic. Refer to Friedman's argument at least once in your essay.

1. Open your essay with a discussion of a hypothetical person who might turn to terrorism because of his or her economic situation.
2. Offer your claim in a clear statement.
3. Back up your claim with at least strong grounds for why economic problems might cause terrorism.
4. Use examples to demonstrate the grounds for your claim.
5. Link your paragraphs with strong transitions to improve the coherence of the essay.
6. End by restating your claim in other words.

Thinking, Arguing, and Writing Collaboratively

In groups of four or five, discuss how globalization has already deeply affected our lives and has for many years. List the ways in which this has happened, and choose the three most important ones to present to the class. As a class, discuss the future of globalization and how it will affect the United States.

Writing About the Text

Write an essay in which you explore the positive aspects of globalization as Friedman sees it. What are the "upsides," as he puts it? What are the main factors that will promote these upsides? How can the common person promote upsides? How does religion play a role?

More Writing Ideas

1. In your journal, freewrite about social mobility. Do not edit your writing. Write nonstop for at least 15 minutes. When you are done, exchange journal entries with another student in your class. How do your responses compare? Contrast?
2. Write a two- or three-paragraph letter in which you, as a "pampered college student," take issue with Friedman's statement that we shouldn't "debate about whether countries should globalize."
3. Antiglobalization groups have protested around the world, most famously in Seattle in 1999, when protesters smashed the facades of Starbucks stores. Read about the antiglobalization forces, and write an essay in which you argue that they are either justified in their protests or wrong and being unrealistic.

RESHMA MEMON YAQUB
You People Did This

Reshma Memon Yaqub is a writer living in Maryland who, after the attacks on America on September 11, found herself faced with a familiar prejudice. As a Muslim-American, she knew immediately that she would have to deal with people's misconceptions. Yaqub, a graduate of the University of Pennsylvania, is a writer for Worth *magazine and has written for the* St. Louis Post-Dispatch, *the* Washington Post, Parents, Men's Health, *and* Reader's Digest, *among other publications. She currently writes a monthly consumer-help column for* Good Housekeeping. *This selection, which contain her thoughts soon after the attacks, was published in* Rolling Stone.

▶ Prereading: Thinking About the Essay in Advance

How much do you know about Islam? What were the different reactions to Muslims in the United States after the events of 9/11?

▶ Words to Watch

miscarry (par. 4) lose a fetus, which is expelled dead
travesty (par. 5) a grotesque, twisted version of something
epithets (par. 6) abusive, insulting words

assailant (par. 6) attacker
decry (par. 8) express strong disapproval

A s I ran through my neighborhood on the morning of September 11th,   1
in search of my son, who had gone to the park with his baby sitter, I
wasn't just afraid of another hijacked plane crashing into us. I was also
afraid that someone else would get to my son first, someone wanting revenge against anyone who looks like they're from "that part of the
world." Even if he is just one and a half years old.

I know I wasn't just afraid that the building where my husband works,   2
a D.C. landmark, might fall on him. I was also afraid that another American might stop him on the street and harass him, or hurt him, demanding
to know why "you people" did this. As soon as we heard the news, 7 million American Muslims wondered in terror, "Will America blame me?"

When our country is terrorized, American Muslims are victimized   3
twice. First, as Americans, by the madmen who strike at our nation, at our
physical, mental and emotional core. Then we're victimized again, as Muslims, by those Americans who believe that all Muslims are somehow accountable for the acts of some madmen, that our faith—that our God, the
same peace-loving God worshipped by Jews and Christians—sanctions it.

It didn't matter when the federal building in Oklahoma City blew up   4
that a Muslim didn't do it. That a Christian man was responsible for the
devastation in Oklahoma City certainly didn't matter to the thugs who
terrorized a Muslim woman there, nearly seven months pregnant, by attacking her home, breaking her windows, screaming religious slurs. It
didn't matter to them that Sahar Al-Muwsawi, 26, would, as a result, miscarry her baby. That she would bury him in the cold ground, alongside
other victims of the Oklahoma City bombing, after naming him Salaam,
the Arabic word for "peace."

But that travesty and hundreds like it certainly were on my mind   5
that Tuesday morning. And they were reinforced every time a friend
called to check on my family and to sadly remind me, "It's over for us.
Muslims are done for."

Even as we buckled under the same grief that every American was   6
feeling that day, American Muslims had to endure the additional burden
of worrying for our own safety, in our own hometowns, far from hijackers
and skyscrapers. Shots would be fired into the Islamic Center of Irving,
Texas; an Islamic bookstore in Virginia would have bricks thrown
through its windows; a bag of pig's blood would be left on the doorstep
of an Islamic community center in San Francisco; a mosque near Chicago
would be marched on by 300 people shouting racist epithets. A Muslim of
Pakistani origin would be gunned down in Dallas; a Sikh man would be
shot and killed in Mesa, Arizona (possibly by the same assailant who
would go on to spray bullets into the home of a local Afghani family).

7   And those were just the cases that were reported. I know I didn't report it when a ten-year-old neighborhood boy walked by and muttered, "Terrorist," as I got into my car. My neurosurgeon friend didn't report that a nurse at the prominent Washington hospital where they both work had announced in front of him that all Muslims and Arabs should be rounded up and put into camps, as Japanese were in World War II. My family didn't report that we're sick with worry about my mother-in-law, another sister-in-law and my niece, who are visiting Pakistan, with their return uncertain.

8   In the days to come, in the midst of the darkness, there is some light. A neighbor stops by to tell me that he doesn't think Muslims are responsible for the acts of madmen. Strangers in Starbucks are unusually friendly to me and my son, reaching out as if to say, "We know it's not your fault." The head of a church told me his congregation wants to come and put its arms around us, and to help in any way possible—by cleaning graffiti off a mosque, by hosting our Friday prayers, whatever we needed. President Bush warns Americans not to scapegoat Muslims and Arabs. He even visits a mosque, in a show of solidarity. Congress swiftly passes a resolution to uphold the civil rights of Muslims and Arabs, urging Americans to remain united. Jewish and Christian leaders publicly decry the violence against Muslims. At a mosque in Seattle, Muslim worshippers are greeted by members of other faiths bringing them flowers.

9   There's something America needs to understand about Islam. Like Judaism, like Christianity, Islam doesn't condone terrorism. It doesn't allow it. It doesn't accept it. Yet, somehow, the labels *jihad, holy war* and *suicide martyrs* are still thrown around. In fact, jihad doesn't even mean holy war. It's an Arabic word that means "struggle"—struggle to please God. And suicide itself is a forbidden act in Islam. How could anyone believe that Muslims consider it martyrdom when practiced in combination with killing thousands of innocents? Anyone who claims to commit a politically motivated violent act in the name of Islam has committed a hate crime against the world's 1.2 billion Muslims.

10   It is not jihad to hijack a plane and fly it into a building. But in fact there was jihad done that Tuesday. It was jihad when firemen ran into imploding buildings to rescue people they didn't know. It was jihad when Americans lined up and waited to donate the blood of their own bodies. It was jihad when strangers held and comforted one another in the streets. It was jihad when rescue workers struggled to put America back together, piece by piece.

11   Yes, there were martyrs made that Tuesday. But there were no terrorists among them. There were only Americans, of every race and religion, who, that Tuesday, took death for us.

▶ Building Vocabulary

Define and use each of the following words in a sentence of your own, making sure that you use the word as Yaqub uses it in her essay.

1. core (par. 3)
2. sanctions (par. 3)
3. slurs (par. 4)
4. buckled (par. 6)
5. scapegoat (par. 8)
6. condone (par. 9)

▶ Thinking Critically About the Argument

Understanding the Writer's Argument

1. In the beginning of her essay, why does Yaqub run to find her son on the morning of September 11, 2001? Why is she afraid for her husband?
2. Why and how do people harass Muslims in America when terrorism strikes America? What examples does Yaqub give of Muslims being harassed? Why aren't all incidents of harassment reported?
3. How does Yaqub show that not all people she comes into contact with harass her?
4. What do most people think *jihad* is? What is it, in fact?
5. What does Yaqub mean when she says that anybody who commits an act of terrorism "in the name of Islam has committed a hate crime" against all Muslims?

Understanding the Writer's Techniques

1. What is Yaqub's major proposition? Where in the essay does she state it?
2. Why does Yaqub mention that there are 7 million Muslims in the United States? She also states that there are 1.2 billion in the world. Is she setting up a deliberate comparison? Explain your answer.
3. Which examples that Yaqub gives of Muslims being harassed are the most effective? How does her title project the sense of harassment?
4. What is the emotional impact of Yaqub quoting her friend as saying, "It's over for us. Muslims are done for"?
5. How does Yaqub use transitions to maintain coherence in her essay? Are there any places you think need stronger transitions? Where?
6. In paragraph 10, Yaqub uses the word *jihad* over and over. What is the argumentative effect of this technique?
7. How effective is Yaqub's conclusion? Why?

Exploring the Writer's Argument

1. In what way does Yaqub's description convince you of her fears? Do you think they are warranted based on her essay? In what ways does she build your trust? Or do you distrust her? If so, why?
2. In paragraph 8, Yaqub mentions actions by the president and Congress to make sure that Americans show tolerance of Islam and Muslims. In what ways are their actions useful? Do you think that after 9/11, President George W. Bush's visits helped matters? Why or why not?
3. How do Yaqub's examples of *jihad* in paragraph 10 support her definition of the word?

▶ Ideas for Writing Arguments

Prewriting

During and after the 9/11 attacks, men and women across the country took the opportunity to perform both great and completely rotten acts. Draw a line down the middle of the page and make two lists headed NOBLE and IGNOBLE. Fill in each column as best you can.

Writing a Guided Argument

Write an essay in which you argue that although times of adversity and crisis lead to displays of both the best humankind has to offer and the worst, one of these always dominates. Feel free to be as optimistic or pessimistic as you'd like.

1. Open your essay with a summary of the events of 9/11.
2. After this, give one example of a noble act and one example of an ignoble act.
3. Write your claim that one tendency is the dominant one.
4. Build your case by giving grounds for your claim.
5. Analyze what it is about human nature that led you to make your claim.
6. Offer examples to back up your case.
7. Link paragraphs with appropriate transitions.
8. In your conclusion, offer a suggestion for how to tilt people's behavior in the direction of nobility.

Thinking, Arguing, and Writing Collaboratively

Exchange draft versions of your Guided Argument assignment with a classmate. Review your partner's essay for its success in following the guidelines and how well it succeeds on its own. What are the paper's greatest strengths? Weaknesses? Write one or two paragraphs that will help your partner take the paper to the next draft.

Writing About the Text

In "Let It Be," Jonathan Rauch argues for a kind of attitude toward religion called apatheism. Read Rauch's essay and argue that he's right—that the kind of problems Yaqub faces here would be a thing of the past if apatheism were more widely practiced.

More Writing Ideas

1. Write in your journal about why you think the Department of Homeland Security's color coding terror alert system does more harm than good or more good than harm. Pick your side.
2. In a paragraph or two, explore the notion of how America's reaction to terrorism is bound to change if it becomes more common.
3. Read some accounts of how Germans and Japanese people in the United States were treated during World War II, how the Japanese were put into internment camps in California, and how, during the Vietnam and Korean wars, Asian Americans were treated. Compare any of those episodes in American history with the most recent episode of the treatment of Muslim Americans after 9/11.

JOYCE CAROL OATES
Words Fail, Memory Blurs, Life Wins

Novelist, short story writer, essayist, poet, and teacher Joyce Carol Oates was born in 1938 in Lockport in upstate New York. She has been writing novels since the age of 14, and she hasn't stopped since. She went to Syracuse University where she won the coveted Mademoiselle *fiction contest. She graduated at the top of her class at Syracuse and went to graduate school at the University of Wisconsin. During her career, she has published more than 75 books. To comments that she is a "workaholic," she has responded, "I am not conscious of working especially hard, or of 'working' at all. Writing and teaching have always been, for me, so richly rewarding that I don't think of them as work in the usual sense of the word." Her novels, which are noted for their unflinching eye on the noble as well as the profane aspects of human life, include* Them *(1969),* Bellefleur *(1980),* Solstice *(1984),* Black Water *(1992), and* Blonde *(2000), among many others. In this essay, from* The New York Times *on New Year's Eve 2001, Oates argues that terrorism cannot destroy basic human hope.*

▶ Prereading: Thinking About the Essay in Advance

After September 11, 2001, people in the United States were nervous and on edge. How long did people's nerves remain raw? Are they still? How long does the grieving process take in the wake of such an event?

▶ Words to Watch

demonized (par. 1) caused someone or something to seem evil
palliative (par. 2) soothing and alleviating pain
invests (par. 4) to give someone or something a characteristic
visceral (par. 6) directly from the emotions rather than from rational thought
aphorisms (par. 6) short statements representing a larger truth
crevices (par. 9) small openings in something
amnesia (par. 9) state of forgetfulness

1   Since Sept. 11, what might be called the secondary wave of the terrorist attacks has been nearly as traumatic to some of us as the attacks themselves: our discovery that we have been demonized and that because we are Americans, we are hated; because we are Americans, we are seen to be deserving of death. "Words fail us" was the predominant cliché in the days immediately after the attacks, but for some, even intellectuals in other secular democracies, words have been too easily and cheaply produced; they matter-of-factly declared, "The United States had it coming."

2   The closest I've knowingly come to a "senseless" violent death was during an airline flight from New Orleans to Newark when turbulence so rocked, shook, rattled the plane that it seemed the plane could not endure and would break into pieces. White-faced attendants were strapped into their seats, and the rest of us, wordless, very still except for the careenings and lurchings of the plane, sat with eyes fixed forward and hands clenched into fists. In the earlier, less alarming stages of the turbulence, the passenger beside me had remarked that turbulence "per se" rarely caused plane crashes, that crashes were caused by "mechanical failure" or bad takeoffs or landings. But now he was silent, for we'd passed beyond even the palliative value of words.

3   If I survive this, I vowed, I will never fly again. No doubt every passenger on the flight was making a similar vow. *If—survive!—never again.*

4   The utterly physical—visceral—adrenaline-charged—sensation that you may be about to die is so powerful that it invests the present tense with an extraordinary lucidity and significance. To imagine the next stage as it has been experienced by countless fellow human beings—when the plane actually disintegrates, or begins to fall, or, in the case of hijacked planes, nears the targets chosen by "martyrs" in the holy war—is to re-experience symptoms of anxiety that culminate in the mind simply blanking out: as words fail us in extremis, so do coherent sensations fail us.

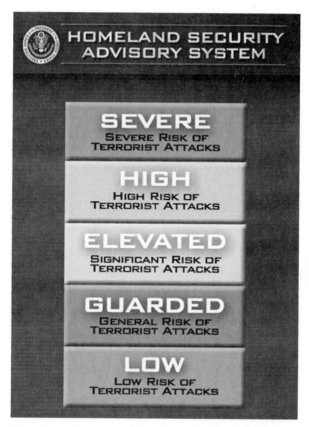

The color-coded terrorism warning system is shown
Tuesday, March 12, 2002, in Washington. The five-level
system is a response to public complaints that broad terror
alerts issued by the government since the Sept. 11, 2001
attacks raised alarm without providing useful guidance.
(AP Photo/Joe Marquette)

We flew through the turbulence. If there was a narrative developing   5
here it was not to be a narrative of tragedy or even melodrama but one
that lends itself to a familiar American subgenre, the anecdote.

As soon as such an experience—whether anecdotal or tragic—is over,   6
we begin the inevitable process of "healing": that is, forgetting. We extract
from the helpless visceral sensation some measure of intellectual summary or control. We lie to ourselves: we revise experience to make it light-
hearted and amusing to others. For in what other way is terror to be
tamed, except recycled as anecdotes or aphorisms, a sugary coating to
hide the bitter pellet of truth within?

How many airplane flights I've taken since that day I vowed I would   7
never fly again, I can't begin to estimate. Dozens, certainly. Perhaps more
than 100. The promise I'd made to myself in extremis was quickly

broken, though it was a reasonable promise and perhaps my terror-stricken mind was functioning more practically than my ordinary mind, uncharged by adrenaline.

8   Yet the fact is: Words fail us. There is the overwhelming wish to "sum up"—"summarize"—"put into perspective." As if typed-out words possessed such magic and could not, instead, lead to such glib summations as "The United States had it coming."

9   Admittedly, having survived that rocky airplane flight, I could not long retain its significance in my mind, still less in my emotions. Amnesia seeps into the crevices of our brains, and amnesia heals. The present tense is a needle's eye through which we thread ourselves—or are threaded—and what's past is irremediably past, to be recollected only in fragments. So, too, the collective American experience of the trauma of Sept. 11 has begun already to fade and will continue to fade, like previous collective traumas: the shock of Pearl Harbor, the shock of President John F. Kennedy's assassination.

10   The great narrative of our planet isn't human history but the history of evolving life. Environments alter, and only those species and individuals that alter with them can survive.

11   "Hope springs eternal in the human breast" may be a cliché, but it is also a profound insight. Perhaps unfairly, the future doesn't belong to those who only mourn, but to those who celebrate.

12   The future is ever-young, ever forgetting the gravest truths of the past.

13   Ideally we should retain the intellectual knowledge that such traumas as the terrorist attacks have given us, while assimilating and moving beyond the rawness of the emotional experience. In this season of unease, as ruins continue to smolder, we celebrate the fact of our existence, which pity, terror and visceral horror have made more precious, at least in our American eyes.

▶ Building Vocabulary

1. Write a paragraph describing a car or train trip in which you use at least five words that help bring the events to life.
2. For each of the following words, write a definition and a sentence of your own:
   a. turbulence (par. 2)
   b. lucidity (par. 4)
   c. melodrama (par. 5)
   d. cliché (par. 11)
   e. gravest (par. 13)

▶ **Thinking Critically About the Argument**

Understanding the Writer's Argument

1. What does Oates mean by the "secondary wave of the terrorist attacks"? (par. 1)
2. Who, after the 9/11 attacks, said that America "had it coming"? Why doesn't Oates mention any of them?
3. How does Oates describe the feeling of impending death? What happens, in her opinion?
4. What does "in extremis" mean? How does Oates use it here?
5. According to Oates, what is the natural way people deal with harrowing situations?
6. What does Oates mean when she writes in paragraph 9 that "The present tense is a needle's eye through which we thread ourselves"? What does this have to do with 9/11?
7. How does hope come out of forgetfulness, according to Oates?

Understanding the Writer's Techniques

1. What is Oates's major proposition? Where does she state it most clearly?
2. Is her major proposition in an effective place? Why or why not?
3. What is Oates's rhetorical intent in this essay? Is she trying to convince her reader of something? If so, of what? If not, what is she trying to do?
4. How well does Oates's title reflect the argument in her essay?
5. How does Oates connect paragraph 1 with paragraph 2? There doesn't seem to be any transition. How does this affect her argument?
6. How does Oates's repetition of the phrase "words fail us" help to hold the essay together?
7. Analyze Oates's concluding paragraph. Is it effective? Why or why not?

Exploring the Writer's Argument

1. Do you agree with Oates that one can call the idea that Americans are to blame for terrorism "the secondary wave of the terrorist attacks"? Explain.
2. Oates says that the "future is ever-young," and that we forget quickly, thus gaining hope. Do you think that is always true with tragedies? Is that true for everyone? Explain your answers.
3. Do our minds always blur when we are in situations "in extremis"? How can we change that?

4. Do you think Oates's conclusion is too analytical for such an emotional topic, or do you think she gets the emotion across properly? Explain your answer.

▶ Ideas for Writing Arguments

Prewriting

What did the United States do, if anything, to deserve the attacks on the World Trade Center and the Pentagon on 9/11? Write some notes on the subject.

Writing a Guided Argument

Write a letter in the form of an argumentative essay in which you take issue with those people who say about 9/11, "The United States had it coming."

1. Open your essay by summarizing the argument that the United States had it coming. Give at least three arguments that can be made for this position.
2. Write that you can understand why the opposition feels as it does, but that you disagree.
3. Write your major proposition.
4. For each of the opposition arguments, write a paragraph in rebuttal.
5. Explain how the opposition's idea can be dangerous.
6. In the next section, explain how the United States can change the minds of people around the world.
7. In your conclusion, restate your major proposition and assess how successful the United States is being in convincing the world that it is not responsible for being attacked.

Thinking, Arguing, and Writing Collaboratively

In groups of four or five, exchange drafts of the essays that grew out of your Writing a Guided Argument assignment. After making general comments about the success of your partner's paper, write a paragraph or two about the effectiveness of the conclusion. How well has your partner succeeded in tying the paper together? Is the conclusion appropriate?

Writing About the Text

How does Oates, as a novelist, use her gifts of description and narration (and her powers of imagination) to help her argument? Write an essay in which you analyze both (1) how Oates is led to her conclusion because she is a fiction writer and (2) how her fiction writing leads her to write this essay as it is written.

More Writing Ideas

1. In your journal, write about a "senseless violent death" that you may have witnessed or heard about.
2. Write a paragraph or two in which you explore the implications of Oates's assertion that "the future doesn't belong to those who only mourn, but to those who celebrate."
3. People who suffer tragedies and crises deal with lingering effects for years, or perhaps for their entire lives. In an essay, argue that, contrary to what Oates says, people never completely get over tragedies.

Jeffrey Rosen

Bad Luck: Why Americans Exaggerate the Terrorist Threat

A teacher at George Washington Law School in Washington, D.C., Jeffrey Rosen holds degrees from Harvard, Balliol, and Oxford Universities. He is a staff writer for the New Republic, *in which this essay first appeared in November of 2001. He is the author of* The Unwanted Gaze: The Destruction of Privacy in America *(2000), in which he draws on a broad historical perspective to examine the right of privacy in a variety of cultures. In this essay, Rosen examines the response to terrorism in America. As you can see from the title, he finds our fears overblown.*

▶ **Prereading: Thinking About the Essay in Advance**

What does the phrase "bad luck" suggest to you? What connections can you make between the notion of misfortune and terrorism?

▶ **Words to Watch**

vulnerability (par. 3) weakness, helplessness
assaulted (par. 6) attacked
scenarios (par. 7) outlines of a plan of likely events
melodramatically (par. 7) in an exaggerated or over-emotional manner
arbitrary (par. 8) determined by chance or whim, not logic or reason
calamities (par.8) disasters; catastrophes
egregious (par. 9) extremely bad; shocking
inegalitarian (par. 11) not supporting equal political, economic, and legal rights for all human beings

The terrorist threat is all too real, but newspapers and TV stations   1
around the globe are still managing to exaggerate it. As new cases of anthrax infection continue to emerge, the World Health Organization is begging people not to panic. But tabloid headlines like this one from *The Mirror* in London send a different message: "panic." A Time/CNN poll

found that nearly half of all Americans say they are "very" or "somewhat" concerned that they or their families will be exposed to anthrax, even though only a handful of politicians and journalists have been targeted so far.

2   This isn't surprising. Terrorism is unfamiliar, it strikes largely at random, and it can't be easily avoided by individual precautions. Criminologists tell us that crimes with these features are the most likely to create hysteria. If America's ability to win the psychological war against terrorism depends upon our ability to remain calm in the face of random violence, our reaction to similar threats in the past is not entirely reassuring.

3   In the academic literature about crime, scholars have identified a paradox: "Most surveys discover that people apparently fear most being a victim of precisely those crimes they are least likely to be victims of," writes Jason Ditton of the University of Sheffield. "Little old ladies apparently worry excessively about being mugged, but they are the least likely to be mugging victims." Women worry most about violent crime, though they have the lowest risk of being victims, while young men worry the least, though they have the highest risk. And because of their physical vulnerability, women tend to worry more about violence in general, even when the risk of experiencing a particular attack is evenly distributed. In a Gallup poll at the end of September, 62 percent of women said they were "very worried" that their families might be victimized by terrorist attacks. Only 35 percent of the men were similarly concerned.

4   Why are people most afraid of the crimes they are least likely to experience? According to Wesley Skogan of Northwestern University, "it may be the things we feel we can't control or influence, those uncontrollable risks, are the ones that make people most fearful." It's why people fear flying more than they fear being hit by a car. We think we can protect ourselves against cars by looking before crossing the street—and therefore underestimate the risk, even though it is actually higher than being killed in a plane crash.

5   People also overestimate the risk of crimes they have never experienced. The elderly are no more fearful than anyone else when asked how safe they feel when they go out at night. That's because many senior citizens don't go out at night, or they take precautions when they do. But when surveys ask how safe they would feel if they did go out at night more often, old people say they would be very afraid, since they have less experience to give them context. Instead they tend to assess risk based on media hype and rumors. "To be able to estimate the probability of an event occurring, you first have to know the underlying distribution of those events, and second the trend of those events—but when it comes to crime, people usually get both hugely wrong," writes Ditton.

6   The media is partly to blame. A survey by George Gerbner, former dean of the Annenberg School at the University of Pennsylvania, found that people who watch a lot of television are more likely than occasional

viewers to overestimate their chances of being a victim of violence, to believe their neighborhood is unsafe, to say fear of crime is a very serious problem, to assume that crime is rising, and to buy locks, watchdogs, and guns. And this distortion isn't limited to television. Jason Ditton notes that 45 percent of crimes reported in the newspaper involve sex or violence, even though they only represent 3 percent of crimes overall. When interviewed about how many crimes involve sex or violence, people tend to overestimate it by a factor of three or four. People believe they are more likely to be assaulted or raped than robbed, even though the robbery rate is much higher.

Will sensationalistic reports of worst-case terrorist scenarios exaggerate people's fear of being caught in an attack? There's every reason to believe that they will because of the media's tendency to exaggerate the scope and probability of remote risks. In a book called *Random Violence,* Joel Best, then of Southern Illinois University, examined the "moral panics" about a series of new crimes that seized public attention in the 1980s and '90s: freeway violence in 1987, wilding in 1989, stalking around 1990, kids and guns in 1991, and so forth. In each case, Best writes, television seized on two or three incidents of a dramatic crime, such as freeway shooting, and then claimed it was part of a broader trend. By taking the worst and most infrequent examples of criminal violence and melodramatically claiming they were typical, television created the false impression that everyone was equally at risk, thereby increasing its audience.   7

The risk of terrorism is more randomly distributed than the crimes the media has hyped in the past. This makes it even more frightening because it is hard to avoid through precautions. (The anthrax envelopes were more narrowly targeted than the World Trade Center attack, of course, but they still infected postal workers.) Contemporary Americans, in particular, are not well equipped to deal with arbitrary threats because, in so many realms of life, we refuse to accept the role of chance. In his nineteenth-century novel *The Gilded Age,* Mark Twain described a steamship accident that killed 22 people. The investigator's verdict: "nobody to blame." This attitude was reflected in nineteenth-century legal doctrines such as assumption of risk, which refused to compensate victims who behaved carelessly. In the twentieth century, by contrast, the United States developed what the legal historian Lawrence Friedman has called an expectation of "total justice"—namely, "the general expectation that somebody will pay for any and all calamities that happen to a person, provided only that it is not the victim's 'fault,' or at least not solely his fault."   8

This effort to guarantee total justice is reflected throughout American society—from the regulation of product safety to the elimination of legal doctrines like assumption of risk. Since September 11 the most egregious display of this total justice mentality has been the threat by various personal injury lawyers to sue the airlines, security officials, and the architects of the World Trade Center on behalf of the victims'   9 families. One of their claims: Flaws in the design of the twin towers may have impeded escape.

10   Given America's difficulty in calculating and accepting unfamiliar risk, what can be done, after September 11, to minimize panic? Rather than self-censoring only when it comes to the ravings of Osama bin Laden, the broadcast media might try to curb its usual focus on worst-case scenarios. Wesley Skogan found that when people were accurately informed about the real risk, they adjusted their fears accordingly. Politicians also need to be careful about passing on unspecified but terrifying threats of future attacks. In the middle of October the Justice Department warned that a terrorist attack might be imminent, but didn't say what the attack might be, or where it might strike. The vagueness of the warning only increased public fear and caused people to cancel travel plans. But it didn't make anyone more secure.

11   While Americans learn to take sensible precautions, we need to also learn that there is no insurance against every calamity or compensation for every misfortune. There is something inegalitarian about risk: It singles out some people from the crowd for no good reason and treats them worse than everybody else. But even in the United States, there is no such thing as perfect equality or total justice. If the first foreign attack on U.S. soil helps teach Americans how to live with risk, then perhaps we can emerge from this ordeal a stronger society as well as a stronger nation.

▶ Building Vocabulary

Determine the meanings of the familiar words that follow by using your knowledge of prefixes, roots, and suffixes and your understanding of compound words—that is, two words put together to form a new word. Define each word in the list; then explain how the parts of the word contribute to the definition. Check your definitions in a dictionary.

1. criminologists (par. 2)
2. uncontrollable (par. 2)
3. underestimate (par. 2)
4. precautions (par. 5)
5. watchdogs (par. 6)
6. freeway (par. 7)
7. steamship (par, 8)
8. self-censoring (par. 10)
9. worst-case (par. 10)
10. misfortune (par 11)

▶ Thinking Critically About the Argument

Understanding the Writer's Argument

1. Who, according to Rosen, is to blame for America's anxiety about different kinds of threats?
2. What paradox does Rosen identify in paragraph 3?
3. According to the writer, why are people afraid of the crimes they are least likely to experience? Why do they overestimate the risk of crimes that they never have experienced?
4. Why does the writer feel that "sensationalist reports of worst-case terrorist scenarios" will exaggerate people's fear of being caught in an attack?
5. Why are contemporary Americans not equipped to deal with arbitrary threats, according to Rosen?
6. What, according to the writer, can we do to minimize panic, given our difficulty to calculate and accept unfamiliar risk?

Understanding the Writer's Techniques

1. What is Rosen's major proposition? Which sentence or two do you think best sums it up? How would you state the proposition in your own words?
2. Why does the writer use the words "Bad Luck" as the opening of his title? How does the statement after the colon in the title help establish the writer's purpose in the essay?
3. How has Rosen used cause-and-effect strategies in this essay? In what way does the title establish the audience's expectations of a cause-and-effect analysis?
4. Rosen uses many external sources for expert testimony to support his argument. What is the effect of the statistical reports he cites? What is the effect of the quotes from scholars, writers, and university professors? What is the effect of the quotation drawn from Mark Twain in paragraph 8? In what ways do you find the evidence he presents convincing?
5. Rosen has considerable legal training. How does his knowledge of the law and legal issues contribute to the way he builds his case in this essay?
6. In what ways does the last paragraph serve as an effective conclusion to the essay? How does the last paragraph relate to the introductory paragraph?
7. How does Rosen maintain a tone of calm and logic despite the frightening topic of terrorism?

Exploring the Writer's Argument

1. Why might you agree or disagree with the idea that the media are exaggerating the terrorist threat? In what ways do the newspapers you read or the television news programs you watch contribute to your fears of terrorism? Or do you think that the media respond appropriately to terrorist threats?
2. How do you think that people can learn to remain calm in the face of random violence?
3. How effective is Rosen's point about why people fear flying more than they fear automobiles?
4. Why do you think Americans refuse to accept the role of chance? In what ways do you think our expectation of total justice is a good thing? A bad thing? How much should we support the 19th-century idea of "nobody to blame" when it comes to accidents?
5. Rosen complains about personal injury lawyers who try to sue airlines, security officials, and World Trade center architects on behalf of the 9/11 victims. Why might you agree or disagree with his position? How has the "total justice" belief affected recent controversies at fast-food restaurants like McDonald's? Accidental injuries or deaths in doctors' offices or hospitals? Automobile accidents?

▶ Ideas for Writing Arguments

Prewriting

In what ways do you think that we have to take terrorist threats seriously, even when they are ambiguous?

Writing a Guided Argument

Terrorist threats have reached new highs across the world, and whereas nobody supports panic in response to them, many people—government authorities included—believe that we have to take these threats seriously, both as a society and as individuals. Write an essay in which you argue that we should take terrorist threats seriously—that is, write an essay opposing Rosen's proposition.

1. Open your essay with an introduction to the notion of terrorist threats, and cite one or two of the most recent examples.
2. Introduce and deal with the *opposing* argument—that most of the threats *are* exaggerated and that we should not panic when we hear about imminent threats.
3. State your major proposition about how the threats are not exaggerated and that we must take them seriously.

4. Offer at least two minor propositions to back up your major proposition. Draw on recent threats you know of that require more than "sensible precautions"—Rosen's point in the last paragraph. Offer suggestions about how we should respond in the light of threats and subsequent government warnings.
5. Present statistics, quotations, or cases to reinforce your argument.
6. Establish a calm tone that uses logic as opposed to emotional appeal.
7. Use appropriate transitions to link your points.

Thinking, Arguing, and Writing Collaboratively

In small groups, discuss the possibilities inherent in Rosen's tenth paragraph: that the broadcast media can and should "curb its usual focus on worst-case scenarios." In what ways might this idea, if acted upon, keep people calm? In what ways does the suggestion fringe on censorship on potentially misinforming the public?

Writing About the Text

Write a brief essay in which you analyze Rosen's use of expert testimony. How do the quotes, paraphrases, and survey data strengthen the piece? What shortfalls do you see in drawing on expert testimony in the way that Rosen has?

More Writing Ideas

1. Write a journal entry about your own response to a recent terrorist threat.
2. In an extended paragraph, define "random violence" as you understand the use of the term today.
3. Write an essay called "The Responsibilities of the Media" in which you argue that newspapers, radio, and television have important responsibilities in providing information to American citizens. Include your views on how well the media are meeting those responsibilities.

Part Four

Five Classic Arguments

PLATO
The Allegory of the Cave

Plato (c. 427–347 B.C.) was born into a wealthy family in Athens, Greece. He turned early to philosophy, studying under the famous philosopher Socrates, who had the reputation of a "gadfly," a person who challenged the traditional ideas of society. His pestering of the powerful men in Athens led to Socrates' conviction on trumped-up charges of corrupting the youth of Athens. He was executed in 399 B.C. Soon after, Plato founded the Academy, a school of philosophy, and began writing his famous works, inquiries into philosophical topics in the form of conversations starring Socrates. Plato portrays his mentor as interrogating members of Athenian society, breaking down their assumptions and leading to an abstract discussion about a philosophical subject such as virtue or love. Some of these dialogues are the Phaedo, Symposium, Crito, *and* Meno.*

Plato's most famous dialogue is the Republic, *perhaps the most influential work in all of world philosophy. The* Republic *inquires into what it means to live the good life, especially as it pertains to government's role in that endeavor. "The Allegory of the Cave" is perhaps the most influential passage in that influential work. Plato introduces his idea of Forms or Ideas, the idea that there is a "real" world outside of the one the everyday person experiences, and the ones who can discover that world are philosophers. As you read, consider how Socrates attempts to persuade Glaucon of his position.*

1   And now, I said, let me show in a figure how far our nature is enlightened or unenlightened: Behold! human beings living in an underground den, which has a mouth open towards the light and reaching all along the den; here they have been from their childhood, and have their legs and necks chained so that they cannot move, and can only see before them, being prevented by the chains from turning round their heads. Above and behind them a fire is blazing at a distance, and between the fire and the prisoners there is a raised way; and you will see, if you look, a low wall built along the way, like the screen which marionette players have in front of them, over which they show the puppets.

2   I see.

3   And do you see, I said, men passing along the wall carrying all sorts of vessels, and statues and figures of animals made of wood and stone and various materials, which appear over the wall? Some of them are talking, others silent.

4   You have shown me a strange image, and they are strange prisoners.

5   Like ourselves, I replied; and they see only their own shadows, or the shadows of one another, which the fire throws on the opposite wall of the cave.

6   True, he said; how could they see anything but the shadows if they were never allowed to move their heads?

And of the objects which are being carried in like manner they would 7
only see the shadows?

Yes, he said.   8

And if they were able to converse with one another, would they not 9
suppose that they were naming what was actually before them?

Very true.   10

And suppose further that the prison had an echo which came from 11
the other side, would they not be sure to fancy when one of the passersby
spoke that the voice which they heard came from the passing shadow?

No question, he replied.   12

To them, I said, the truth would be literally nothing but the shad- 13
ows of the images.

That is certain.   14

And now look again, and see what will naturally follow if the prison- 15
ers are released and disabused of their error. At first, when any of them is
liberated and compelled suddenly to stand up and turn his neck round
and walk and look towards the light, he will suffer sharp pains; the glare
will distress him and he will be unable to see the realities of which in his
former state he had seen the shadows; and then conceive some one saying
to him, that what he saw before was an illusion, but that now, when he is
approaching nearer to being and his eye is turned towards more real existence, he has a clearer vision—what will be his reply? And you may further imagine that his instructor is pointing to the objects as they pass and
requiring him to name them—will he not be perplexed? Will he not fancy
that the shadows which he formerly saw are truer than the objects which
are now shown to him?

Far truer.   16

And if he is compelled to look straight at the light, will he not have a 17
pain in his eyes which will make him turn away to take refuge in the objects of vision which he can see, and which he will conceive to be in reality clearer than the things which are now being shown to him?

True, he said.   18

And suppose once more, that he is reluctantly dragged up a steep 19
and rugged ascent, and held fast until he is forced into the presence of the
sun himself, is he not likely to be pained and irritated? When he approaches the light his eyes will be dazzled and he will not be able to see
anything at all of what are now called realities.

Not all in a moment, he said.   20

He will require to grow accustomed to the sight of the upper world. 21
And first he will see the shadows best, next the reflections of men and
other objects in the water, and then the objects themselves; then he will
gaze upon the light of the moon and the stars and the spangled heaven;
and he will see the sky and the stars by night better than the sun or the
light of the sun by day?

Certainly.   22

23   Last of all he will be able to see the sun, and not mere reflections of him in the water, but he will see him in his own proper place, and not in another; and he will contemplate him as he is.

24   Certainly.

25   He will then proceed to argue that this is he who gives the season and the years, and is the guardian of all that is in the visible world, and in a certain way the cause of all things which he and his fellows have been accustomed to behold?

26   Clearly, he said, he would first see the sun and then reason about him.

27   And when he remembered his old habitation, and the wisdom of the den and his fellow-prisoners, do you not suppose that he would felicitate himself on the change, and pity them?

28   Certainly, he would.

29   And if they were in the habit of conferring honors among themselves on those who were quickest to observe the passing shadows and to remark which of them went before, and which followed after, and which were together; and who were therefore best able to draw conclusions as to the future, do you think that he would care for such honors and glories, or envy the possessors of them? Would he not say with Homer, Better to be the poor servant of a poor master, and to endure anything, rather than think as they do and live after their manner?

30   Yes, he said, I think that he would rather suffer anything than entertain these false notions and live in this miserable manner.

31   Imagine once more, I said, such an one coming suddenly out of the sun to be replaced in his old situation; would he not be certain to have his eyes full of darkness?

32   To be sure, he said.

33   And if there were a contest, and he had to compete in measuring the shadows with the prisoners who had never moved out of the den, while his sight was still weak, and before his eyes had become steady (and the time which would be needed to acquire this new habit of sight might be very considerable) would he not be ridiculous? Men would say of him that up he went and down he came without his eyes; and that it was better not even to think of ascending; and if any one tried to loose another and lead him up to the light, let them only catch the offender, and they would put him to death.

34   No question, he said.

35   This entire allegory, I said, you may now append, dear Glaucon, to the previous argument; the prison-house is the world of sight, the light of fire is the sun, and you will not misapprehend me if you interpret the journey upwards to be the ascent of the soul into the intellectual world according to my poor belief, which, at your desire, I have expressed—whether rightly or wrongly God knows. But, whether true or false, my opinion is that in the world of knowledge the idea of good appears last of all, and is seen only with an effort; and, when seen, is also inferred to be the univer-

sal author of all things beautiful and right, parent of light and of the lord of light in this visible world, and the immediate source of reason and truth in the intellectual; and that this is the power upon which he who would act rationally either in public or private life must have his eye fixed.

I agree, he said, as far as I am able to understand you.   36

Moreover, I said, you must not wonder that those who attain to this   37
beautiful vision are unwilling to descend to human affairs; for their souls are ever hastening into the upper world where they desire to dwell; which desire of theirs is very natural, if our allegory may be trusted.

Yes, very natural.   38

And is there anything surprising in one who passes from divine con-   39
templations to the evil state of man, misbehaving himself in a ridiculous manner; if, while his eyes are blinking and before he has become accustomed to the surrounding darkness, he is compelled to fight in courts of law, or in other places, about the images or the shadows of images of justice, and is endeavouring to meet the conceptions of those who have never yet seen absolute justice?

Anything but surprising, he replied.   40

Any one who has common sense will remember that the bewilder-   41
ments of the eyes are of two kinds, and arise from two causes, either from coming out of the light or from going into the light, which is true of the mind's eye, quite as much as of the bodily eye; and he who remembers this when he sees any one whose vision is perplexed and weak, will not be too ready to laugh; he will first ask whether that soul of man has come out of the brighter light, and is unable to see because unaccustomed to the dark, or having turned from darkness to the day is dazzled by excess of light. And he will count the one happy in his condition and state of being, and he will pity the other; or, if he have a mind to laugh at the soul which comes from below into the light, there will be more reason in this than in the laugh which greets him who returns from above out of the light into the den.

That, he said, is a very just distinction.   42

Responding to the Essay

1. What is Plato's argument? What is an allegory, and why does he use the form to make his claim rather than just stating it right away? Explain.
2. Is the dialogue format effective here? Is Glaucon a real part of the conversation with Socrates? Defend your answers.
3. In many Platonic dialogues, Socrates appears as a combative and a tough debater. Do you see any evidence of that in this selection? Explain.
4. Analyze Plato's use of syllogistic argument in this selection. Trace his reasoning, especially throughout the first section.

5. How does Plato contrast the people who live in the world of shadows with the ones who have seen the light? What is he saying about himself, do you think?

Responding in Writing

1. How are Plato's ideas in this essay relevant to modern life? Write an essay in which you argue that the influence of this selection is apparent in your experience.
2. Do some research on Plato on the Internet, and write a short history of his ideas, focusing on how the *Republic*'s political philosophy influenced Western political science.
3. Write your own allegory that brings to life a belief you have about college.

JONATHAN SWIFT
A Modest Proposal

Satirist and poet Jonathan Swift (1667–1745), one of the greatest prose writers in the history of English literature, was born in Dublin in Ireland, where he is still a national hero. After studying in Ireland, he was forced for political reasons to emigrate to England, where he read widely and went into the Anglican Church as a clergyman. He worked for the Church his entire life, but soon realized his gift for writing. Swift composed poems and prose satires, including A Tale of a Tub *(1704), which makes a target of the corruption he saw among the religious and educational leaders of his time. Again, because of a change in the political winds, he returned to Dublin as dean of St. Patrick's Cathedral and lived in the city for the rest of his life. In 1726 Swift published* Gulliver's Travels, *which was a wide-ranging satire that took aim at all 18th-Century society as he saw it. Swift always fought for the rights of Ireland against what he saw as English oppression, publishing many articles for the cause, including the series of letters written as "M.B. Drapier" that helped to foil English plans that might have hurt the Irish economy.*

In this selection, which he wrote in 1729, Swift uses all his powers of satire to propose, tongue in cheek, that Ireland could solve its problems of poverty if the Irish ate their own children. Pay close attention as you read to see how his argument works through the device of irony.

1   It is a melancholy object to those who walk through this great town or travel in the country, when they see the streets, the roads, and cabin doors, crowded with beggars of the female-sex, followed by three, four, or six children, all in rags and importuning every passenger for an alms. These mothers, instead of being able to work for their honest livelihood,

are forced to employ all their time in strolling to beg sustenance for their helpless infants, who, as they grow up, either turn thieves for want of work, or leave their dear native country to fight for the Pretender in Spain, or sell themselves to the Barbadoes.

I think it is agreed by all parties that this prodigious number of children in the arms, or on the backs, or at the heels of their mothers, and frequently of their fathers, is in the present deplorable state of the kingdom a very great additional grievance; and therefore whoever could find out a fair, cheap, and easy method of making these children sound, useful members of the commonwealth would deserve so well of the public as to have his statue set up for a preserver of the nation.   2

But my intention is very far from being confined to provide only for the children of professed beggars; it is of a much greater extent, and shall take in the whole number of infants at a certain age who are born of parents in effect as little able to support them as those who demand our charity in the streets.   3

As to my own part, having turned my thoughts for many years upon this important subject, and maturely weighted the several schemes of other projectors, I have always found them grossly mistaken in their computation. It is true, a child just dropped from its dam may be supported by her milk for a solar year, with little other nourishment; at most not above the value of two shillings, which the mother may certainly get, or the value in scraps, by her lawful occupation of begging; and it is exactly at one year old that I propose to provide for them in such a manner as instead of being a charge upon their parents or the parish, or wanting food and raiment for the rest of their lives, they shall on the contrary contribute to the feeding, and partly to the clothing, of many thousands.   4

There is likewise another great advantage in my scheme, that it will prevent those voluntary abortions, and that horrid practice of women murdering their bastard children, alas, too frequent among us, sacrificing the poor innocent babes, I doubt, more to avoid the expense than the shame, which would move tears and pity in the most savage and inhuman breast.   5

The number of souls in this kingdom being usually reckoned one million and a half, of these I calculate there may be about two hundred thousand couples whose wives are breeders; from which number I subtract thirty thousand couples who are able to maintain their own children, although I apprehend there cannot be so many under the present distresses of the kingdom; but this being granted, there will remain an hundred and seventy thousand breeders. I again subtract fifty thousand for those women who miscarry, or whose children die by accident or disease within the year. There only remain an hundred and twenty thousand children of poor parents annually born. The question therefore is, how this number shall be reared and provided for, which, as I have already said, under the present situation of affairs, is utterly impossible by all the methods hitherto proposed. For we can neither employ them in handicraft or agriculture; we neither build houses (I mean in the country) nor   6 cultivate land. They can very seldom pick up a livelihood by stealing till they arrive at six years old, except where they are of towardly parts; although I confess they learn the rudiments much earlier, during which time they can however be looked upon only as probationers, as I have been informed by a principal gentleman in the county of Cavan, who protested to me that he never knew above one or two instances under the age of six, even in a part of the kingdom so renowned for the quickest proficiency in that art.

7   I am assured by our merchants that a boy or girl before twelve years old is no salable commodity; and even when they come to this age they will not yield above three pounds, or three pounds and half a crown at most on the Exchange; which cannot turn to account either to the parents or the kingdom, the charge of nutriment and rags having been at least four times that value.

8   I shall now therefore humbly propose my own thoughts, which I hope will not be liable to the least objection.

9   I have been assured by a very knowing American of my acquaintance in London, that a young healthy child well nursed is at a year old a most delicious, nourishing, and wholesome food, whether stewed, roasted, baked or boiled; and I make no doubt that it will equally serve in a fricassee or a ragout.

10   I do therefore humbly offer it to public consideration that of the hundred and twenty thousand children, already computed, twenty thousand may be reserved for breed, whereof only one fourth part to be males, which is more than we allow to sheep, black cattle, or swine; and my reason is that these children are seldom the fruits of marriage, a circumstance not much regarded by our savages, therefore one male will be sufficient to serve four females. That the remaining hundred thousand may at a year old be offered in sale to the persons of quality and fortune through the kingdom, always advising the mother to let them suck plentifully in the last month, so as to render them plump and fat for a good table. A child will make two dishes at an entertainment for friends; and when the family dines alone, the fore or hind quarter will make a reasonable dish, and seasoned with a little pepper or salt will be very good boiled on the fourth day, especially in winter.

11   I have reckoned upon a medium that a child just born will weigh twelve pounds, and in a solar year if tolerably nursed increaseth to twenty-eight pounds.

12   I grant this food will be somewhat dear, and therefore very proper for landlords, who, as they have already devoured most of the parents, seem to have the best title to the children.

13   Infant's flesh will be in season throughout the year, but more plentiful in March, and a little before and after. For we are told by a grave author, an eminent French physician, that fish being a prolific diet, there are more children born in Roman Catholic countries about nine months after Lent than at any other season: therefore, reckoning a year after Lent, the mar-

kets will be more glutted than usual, because the number of popish infants is at least three to one in this kingdom; and therefore it will have one other collateral advantage, by lessening the number of Papists among us.

I have already computed the charge of nursing a beggar's child (in   14 which list I reckon all cottagers, laborers, and four fifths of the farmers) to be about two shillings per annum, rags included: and I believe no gentleman would repine to give ten shillings for the carcass of a good fat child, which, as I have said, will make four dishes of excellent nutritive meat, when he hath only some particular friend or his own family to dine with him. Thus the squire will learn to be a good landlord, and grow popular among the tenants; the mother will have eight shillings net profit, and be fit for work till she produces another child.

Those who are more thrifty (as I must confess the times require) may   15 flay the carcass; the skin of which artificially dressed will make admirable gloves for ladies, and summer boots for fine gentlemen.

As to our city of Dublin, shambles may be appointed for this purpose   16 in the most convenient parts of it, and butchers we may be assured will not be wanting; although I rather recommend buying the children alive, and dressing them hot from the knife as we do roasting pigs.

A very worthy person, a true lover of his country, and whose virtues I   17 highly esteem, was lately pleased in discoursing on this matter to offer a refinement upon my scheme. He said that many gentlemen of this kingdom, having of late destroyed their deer, he conceived that the want of venison might be well supplied by the bodies of young lads and maidens, not exceeding fourteen years of age nor under twelve, so great a number of both sexes in every county being now ready to starve for want of work and service; and these to be disposed of by their parents, if alive, or otherwise by their nearest relations. But with due deference to so excellent a friend and so deserving a patriot, I cannot be altogether in his sentiments; for as to the males, my American acquaintance assured me from frequent experience that their flesh was generally tough and lean, like that of our schoolboys, by continual exercise, and their taste disagreeable; and to fatten them would not answer the charge. Then as to the females, it would, I think with humble submission, be a loss to the public, because they soon would become breeders themselves: and besides, it is not improbable that some scrupulous people might be apt to censure such a practice (although indeed very unjustly) as a little bordering upon cruelty; which, I confess, hath always been with me the strongest objection against any project, how well so ever intended.

But in order to justify my friend, he confessed that this expedient was   18 put into his head by the famous Psalmanazar, a native of the island Formosa, who came from thence to London above twenty years ago, and in conversation told my friend that in his country when any young person happened to be put to death, the executioner sold the carcass to persons of quality as a prime dainty; and that in his time the body of a plump girl of fifteen, who was crucified for an attempt to poison the emperor, was sold to his Imperial Majesty's prime minister of state, and other great mandarins of the court, in joints from the gibbet, at four hundred crowns. Neither indeed can I deny that if the same use were made of several plump young girls in this town, who without one single groat to their fortunes cannot stir abroad without a chair, and appear at the playhouse and assemblies in foreign fineries which they never will pay for, the kingdom would not be the worse.

19   Some persons of a desponding spirit are in great concern about that vast number of poor people who are aged, diseased, or maimed, and I have been desired to employ my thoughts what course may be taken to ease the nation of so grievous an encumbrance. But I am not in the least pain upon that matter, because it is very well known that they are every day dying and rotting by cold and famine, and filth and vermin, as fast as can be reasonably expected. And as to the younger laborers, they are now in almost as hopeful a condition. They cannot get work, and consequently pine away for want of nourishment to a degree that if at any time they are accidentally hired to common labor, they have not strength to perform it; and thus the country and themselves are happily delivered from the evils to come.

20   I have too long digressed, and therefore shall return to my subject. I think the advantages by the proposal which I have made are obvious and many, as well as of the highest importance.

21   For first, as I have already observed, it would greatly lessen the number of Papists, with whom we are yearly overrun, being the principal breeders of the nation as well as our most dangerous enemies; and who stay at home on purpose to deliver the kingdom to the Pretender, hoping to take their advantage by the absence of so many good Protestants, who have chosen rather to leave their country than to stay at home and pay tithes against their conscience to an Episcopal curate.

22   Secondly, the poorer tenants will have something valuable of their own, which by law may be made liable to distress, and help to pay their landlord's rent, their corn and cattle being already seized and money a thing unknown.

23   Thirdly, whereas the maintenance of an hundred thousand children, from two years old and upwards, cannot be computed at less than ten shillings a piece per annum, the nation's stock will be thereby increased fifty thousand pounds per annum, besides the profit of a new dish introduced to the tables of all gentlemen of fortune in the kingdom who have any refinement in taste. And the money will circulate among ourselves, the goods being entirely of our own growth and manufacture.

24   Fourthly, the constant breeders, besides the gain of eight shillings sterling per annum by the sale of their children, will be rid of the charge of maintaining them after the first year.

Fifthly, this food would likewise bring great custom to taverns, 25
where the vintners will certainly be so prudent as to procure the best
receipts for dressing it to perfection, and consequently have their
houses frequented by all the fine gentlemen, who justly value themselves upon their knowledge in good eating; and a skillful cook, who
understands how to oblige his guests, will contrive to make it as expensive as they please.

Sixthly, this would be a great inducement to marriage, which all wise 26
nations have either encouraged by rewards or enforced by laws and
penalties. It would increase the care and tenderness of mothers toward
their children, when they were sure of a settlement for life to the poor
babes, provided in some sort by the public, to their annual profit instead
of expense. We should see an honest emulation among the married
women, which of them could bring the fattest child to the market. Men
would become as fond of their wives during the time of their pregnancy
as they are now of their mares in foal, their cows in calf, or sows when
they are ready to farrow; nor offer to beat or kick them (as is too frequent
a practice) for fear of a miscarriage.

Many other advantages might be enumerated. For instance, the ad- 27
dition of some thousand carcasses in our exportation of barreled beef,
the propagation of swine's flesh, and improvement in the art of making
good bacon, so much wanted among us by the great destruction of
pigs, too frequent at our tables, which are no way comparable in taste
or magnificence to a well-grown, fat yearling child, which roasted
whole will make a considerable figure at a lord mayor's feast or any
other public entertainment. But this and many others I omit, being stu-
dious of brevity.

Supposing that one thousand families in this city would be constant 28
customers for infants' flesh, besides others who might have it at merry
meetings, particularly weddings and christenings, I compute that Dublin
would take off annually about twenty thousand carcasses, and the rest of
the kingdom (where probably they will be sold somewhat cheaper) the
remaining eighty thousand.

I can think of no one objection that will possibly be raised against 29
this proposal, unless it should be urged that the number of people will be
thereby much lessened in the kingdom. This I freely own, and it was indeed one principal design in offering it to the world. I desire the reader
will observe, that I calculate my remedy for this one individual kingdom
of Ireland and for no other that ever was, is, or I think ever can be upon
earth. Therefore let no man talk to me of other expedients: of taxing our
absentees at five shillings a pound: of using neither clothes nor household furniture except what is of our own growth and manufacture: of utterly rejecting the materials and instruments that promote foreign luxury: of curing the expensiveness of pride, vanity, idleness, and gaming in

our women: of introducing a vein of parsimony, prudence, and temperance: of learning to love our country, in the want of which we differ even from Laplanders and the inhabitants of Topinamboo: of quitting our animosities and factions, nor acting any longer like the Jews, who were murdering one another at the very moment their city was taken: of being a little cautious not to sell our country and conscience for nothing: of teaching landlords to have at least one degree of mercy toward their tenants: lastly, of putting a spirit of honesty, industry, and skill into our shopkeepers; who, if a resolution could be now taken to buy only our native goods, would immediately unite to cheat and exact upon us in the price, the measure and the goodness, nor could ever yet be brought to make one fair proposal of just dealing, though often and earnestly invited to it.

30   Therefore I repeat, let no man talk to me of these and the like expedients, till he hath at least some glimpse of hope that there will ever be some hearty and sincere attempt to put them in practice.

31   But as to myself, having been wearied out for many years with offering vain, idle, visionary thoughts, and at length utterly despairing of success, I fortunately fell upon this proposal, which, as it is wholly new, so it hath something solid and real, of no expense and little trouble, full in our own power, and whereby we can incur no danger in disobliging England. For this kind of commodity will not bear exportation, the flesh being of too tender a consistence to admit a long continuance in salt, although perhaps I could name a country which would be glad to eat up our whole nation without it.

32   After all, I am not so violently bent upon my own opinion as to reject any offer proposed by wise men, which shall be found equally innocent, cheap, easy, and effectual. But before something of that kind shall be advanced in contradiction to my scheme, and offering a better, I desire the author or authors will be pleased maturely to consider two points. First, as things now stand, how they will be able to find food and raiment for an hundred thousand useless mouths and backs. And secondly, there being a round million of creatures in human figure throughout this kingdom, whose sole subsistence put into a common stock would leave them in debt two millions of pounds sterling, adding those who are beggars by profession to the bulk of farmers, cottagers, and laborers, with their wives and children who are beggars in effect; I desire those politicians who dislike my overture, and may perhaps be so bold to attempt an answer, that they will first ask the parents of these mortals whether they would not at this day think it a great happiness to have been sold for food at a year old in the manner I prescribe, and thereby have avoided such a perpetual scene of misfortunes as they have since gone through by the oppression of landlords, the impossibility of paying rent without money or trade, the want of common sustenance, with neither house nor clothes to cover them from the inclemencies of the weather, and the most inevitable prospect of entailing the like or greater miseries upon their breed forever.

I profess, in the sincerity of my heart, that I have not the least per-   33
sonal interest in endeavoring to promote this necessary work, having
no other motive than the public good of my country, by advancing our
trade, providing for infants, relieving the poor, and giving some pleasure to the rich. I have no children by which I can propose to get a
single penny; the youngest being nine years old, and my wife past
childbearing.

Responding to the Essay

1. What is Swift's major proposition? What is the true nature of his argument? Explain.
2. Where in the essay does Swift come closest to criticizing openly the
   English and especially the rich? Is he ever openly critical to the poor
   Irish Catholics? Offer evidence for your answers.
3. Analyze the structure of Swift's essay. How does he build this argument slowly? Make an outline in which you trace his reasoning.
4. Discuss the title of the essay. Why use the word *modest*? What is modest about his argument? Is there irony in the title too? How does it
   play out in his essay? Defend your answers.

Responding in Writing

1. Write a modest proposal of your own on a social problem of your
   choosing. For example, perhaps propose an ironic solution for the
   War on Terrorism.
2. Research the life of Jonathan Swift, focusing on his political beliefs.
   How did he fight for them during his life, and how does he reveal
   them in "A Modest Proposal"?
3. In small groups, make a list of two columns: In one column, list
   Swift's minor propositions in this essay. In the other column, list the
   corresponding serious arguments hiding behind the propositions.
   Present your list to the class.

Virginia Woolf
Professions for Women

*Virginia Woolf (1882–1941) was born Virginia Stephen in London into a
wealthy and influential family. As an adult she moved with her brother to
the Bloomsbury area of the city, where they became friends with many leading lights of their generation, including writers, painters, scholars, and critics. She met her husband, Leonard Woolf, in this group, and later they*

founded Hogarth Press, which published many important works including her own books. Mrs. Dalloway *(1925),* To the Lighthouse *(1927), and* The Waves *(1931) are among the most famous of Woolf's novels, which she wrote in the modernist technique called "stream of consciousness." Her fiction depicted the flow of her characters' thoughts. Woolf also published many essays and works of criticism, some of which were collected in* The Common Reader *(1925). After a lifelong struggle with depression, Woolf committed suicide by filling her pockets with rocks and walking into the Thames River.*

Woolf was always concerned with the situation of women in society, especially women who had a desire for independence, as she did. Her writing on the topic is well known, especially the long essays A Room of One's Own *(1929) and* Three Guineas *(1938). In 1931, Woolf gave a lecture on feminism, which she shortened and published later the same year as "Professions for Women." In this selection, Woolf picked up on the idea of the Angel in the House, which she took from a famous Victorian poem, and described how women must fight against preconceptions about their abilities and feelings and against how men try to suppress them.*

1   When your secretary invited me to come here, she told me that your Society is concerned with the employment of women and she suggested that I might tell you something about my own professional experiences. It is true I am a woman; it is true I am employed; but what professional experiences have I had? It is difficult to say. My profession is literature; and in that profession there are fewer experiences for women than in any other, with the exception of the stage—fewer, I mean, that are peculiar to women. For the road was cut many years ago—by Fanny Burney, by Aphra Behn, by Harriet Martineau, by Jane Austen, by George Eliot—many famous women, and many more unknown and forgotten, have been before me, making the path smooth, and regulating my steps. Thus, when I came to write, there were very few material obstacles in my way. Writing was a reputable and harmless occupation. The family peace was not broken by the scratching of a pen. No demand was made upon the family purse. For ten and sixpence one can buy paper enough to write all the plays of Shakespeare—if one has a mind that way. Pianos and models, Paris, Vienna and Berlin, masters and mistresses, are not needed by a writer. The cheapness of writing paper is, of course, the reason why women have succeeded as writers before they have succeeded in the other professions.

2   But to tell you my story—it is a simple one. You have only got to figure to yourselves a girl in a bedroom with a pen in her hand. She had only to move that pen from left to right—from ten o'clock to one. Then it occurred to her to do what is simple and cheap enough after all—to slip a few of those pages into an envelope, fix a penny stamp in the corner, and drop the envelope into the red box at the corner. It was thus that I became a journal-

ist; and my effort was rewarded on the first day of the following month—a very glorious day it was for me—by a letter from an editor containing a cheque for one pound ten shillings and sixpence. But to show you how little I deserve to be called a professional woman, how little I know of the struggles and difficulties of such lives, I have to admit that instead of spending that sum upon bread and butter, rent, shoes and stockings, or butcher's bills, I went out and bought a cat—a beautiful cat, a Persian cat, which very soon involved me in bitter disputes with my neighbors.

What could be easier than to write articles and to buy Persian cats   3 with the profits? But wait a moment. Articles have to be about something. Mine, I seem to remember, was about a novel by a famous man. And while I was writing this review, I discovered that if I were going to review books I should need to do battle with a certain phantom. And the phantom was a woman, and when I came to know her better I called her after the heroine of a famous poem, The Angel in the House. It was she who used to come between me and my paper when I was writing reviews. It was she who bothered me and wasted my time and so tormented me that at last I killed her. You who come of a younger and happier generation may not have heard of her—you may not know what I mean by the Angel in the House. I will describe her as shortly as I can. She was intensely sympathetic. She was immensely charming. She was utterly unselfish. She excelled in the difficult arts of family life. She sacrificed herself daily. If there was a chicken, she took the leg; if there was a draught she sat in it—in short she was so constituted that she never had a mind or a wish of her own, but preferred to sympathize always with the minds and wishes of others. Above all—I need not say it—she was pure. Her purity was supposed to be her chief beauty—her blushes, her great grace. In those days—the last of Queen Victoria—every house had its Angel. And when I came to write I encountered her with the very first words. The shadow of her wings fell on my page; I heard the rustling of her skirts in the room. Directly, that is to say, I took my pen in hand to review that novel by a famous man, she slipped behind me and whispered: "My dear, you are a young woman. You are writing about a book that has been written by a man. Be sympathetic; be tender; flatter; deceive; use all the arts and wiles of our sex. Never let anybody guess that you have a mind of your own. Above all, be pure." And she made as if to guide my pen. I now record the one act for which I take some credit to myself, though the credit rightly belongs to some excellent ancestors of mine who left me a certain sum of money—shall we say five hundred pounds a year—so that it was not necessary for me to depend solely on charm for my living. I turned upon her and caught her by the throat. I did my best to kill her. My excuse, if I were to be had up in a court of law, would be that I acted in self-defense. Had I not killed her she would have killed me. She would have plucked the heart out of my writing. For, as I found, directly I put pen to paper, you cannot review even a novel without having a mind of your own, without expressing what you think to be the truth about human relations, morality, sex. And all these questions, according to the Angel in the House, cannot be dealt with freely and openly by women; they must charm, they must conciliate, they must—to put it bluntly—tell lies if they are to succeed. Thus, whenever I felt the shadow of her wing or the radiance of her halo upon my page, I took up the inkpot and flung it at her. She died hard. Her fictitious nature was of great assistance to her. It is far harder to kill a phantom than a reality. She was always creeping back when I thought I had dispatched her. Though I flatter myself that I killed her in the end, the struggle was severe; it took much time that had better have been spent upon learning Greek grammar; or in roaming the world in search of adventures. But it was a real experience; it was an experience that was bound to befall all women writers at that time. Killing the Angel in the House was part of the occupation of a woman writer.

4   But to continue my story. The Angel was dead; what then remained? You may say that what remained was a simple and common object—a young woman in a bedroom with an inkpot. In other words, now that she had rid herself of falsehood, that young woman had only to be herself. Ah, but what is "herself"? I mean, what is a woman? I assure you, I do not know. I do not believe that you know. I do not believe that anybody can know until she has expressed herself in all the arts and professions open to human skill. That indeed is one of the reasons why I have come here— out of respect for you, who are in process of showing us by your experiments what a woman is, who are in process of providing us, by your failures and successes, with that extremely important piece of information.

5   But to continue the story of my professional experiences. I made one pound ten and six by my first review; and I bought a Persian cat with the proceeds. Then I grew ambitious. A Persian cat is all very well, I said; but a Persian cat is not enough. I must have a motor car. And it was thus that I became a novelist—for it is a very strange thing that people will give you a motor car if you will tell them a story. It is a still stranger thing that there is nothing so delightful in the world as telling stories. It is far pleasanter than writing reviews of famous novels. And yet, if I am to obey your secretary and tell you my professional experiences as a novelist, I must tell you about a very strange experience that befell me as a novelist. And to understand it you must try first to imagine a novelist's state of mind. I hope I am not giving away professional secrets if I say that a novelist's chief desire is to be as unconscious as possible. He has to induce in himself a state of perpetual lethargy. He wants life to proceed with the utmost quiet and regularity. He wants to see the same faces, to read the same books, to do the same things day after day, month after month, while he is writing, so that nothing may break the illusion in which he is living—so that nothing may disturb or disquiet the mysterious nosings about, feelings round, darts, dashes and sudden discoveries of that very shy and illusive spirit, the imagination. I suspect that this state is the

same both for men and women. Be that as it may, I want you to imagine me writing a novel in a state of trance. I want you to figure to yourselves a girl sitting with a pen in her hand, which for minutes, and indeed for hours, she never dips into the inkpot. The image that comes to my mind when I think of this girl is the image of a fisherman lying sunk in dreams on the verge of a deep lake with a rod held out over the water. She was letting her imagination sweep unchecked round every rock and cranny of the world that lies submerged in the depths of our unconscious being. Now came the experience, the experience that I believe to be far commoner with women writers than with men. The line raced through the girl's fingers. Her imagination had rushed away. It had sought the pools, the depths, the dark places where the largest fish slumber. And then there was a smash. There was an explosion. There was foam and confusion. The imagination had dashed itself against something hard. The girl was roused from her dream. She was indeed in a state of the most acute and difficult distress. To speak without figure she had thought of something, something about the body, about the passions which it was unfitting for her as a woman to say. Men, her reason told her, would be shocked. The consciousness of what men will say of a woman who speaks the truth about her passions had roused her from her artist's state of unconsciousness. She could write no more. The trance was over. Her imagination could work no longer. This I believe to be a very common experience with women writers—they are impeded by the extreme conventionality of the other sex. For though men sensibly allow themselves great freedom in these respects, I doubt that they realize or can control the extreme severity with which they condemn such freedom in women.

These then were two very genuine experiences of my own. These were   6
two of the adventures of my professional life. The first—killing the Angel in the House—I think I solved. She died. But the second, telling the truth about my own experiences as a body, I do not think I solved. I doubt that any woman has solved it yet. The obstacles against her are still immensely powerful—and yet they are very difficult to define. Outwardly, what is simpler than to write books? Outwardly, what obstacles are there for a woman rather than for a man? Inwardly, I think, the case is very different; she has still many ghosts to fight, many prejudices to overcome. Indeed it will be a long time still, I think, before a woman can sit down to write a book without finding a phantom to be slain, a rock to be dashed against. And if this is so in literature, the freest of all professions for women, how is it in the new professions which you are now for the first time entering?

Those are the questions that I should like, had I time, to ask you. And   7
indeed, if I have laid stress upon these professional experiences of mine, it is because I believe that they are, though in different forms, yours also. Even when the path is nominally open—when there is nothing to prevent a woman from being a doctor, a lawyer, a civil servant—there are many phantoms and obstacles, as I believe, looming in her way. To discuss and

define them is I think of great value and importance; for thus only can the labour be shared, the difficulties be solved. But besides this, it is necessary also to discuss the ends and the aims for which we are fighting, for which we are doing battle with these formidable obstacles. Those aims cannot be taken for granted; they must be perpetually questioned and examined. The whole position, as I see it—here in this hall surrounded by women practising for the first time in history I know not how many different professions—is one of extraordinary interest and importance. You have won rooms of your own in the house hitherto exclusively owned by men. You are able, though not without great labour and effort, to pay the rent. You are earning your five hundred pounds a year. But this freedom is only a beginning; the room is your own, but it is still bare. It has to be furnished; it has to be decorated; it has to be shared. How are you going to furnish it, how are you going to decorate it? With whom are you going to share it, and upon what terms? These, I think, are questions of the utmost importance and interest. For the first time in history you are able to ask for them; for the first time you are able to decide for yourselves what the answers should be. Willingly would I stay and discuss those questions and answers—but not tonight. My time is up; and I must cease.

Responding to the Essay

1. Woolf originally gave as a speech what is now this essay. Why did Woolf keep the trappings of the speech when she published the essay? Why not recast it as a straight essay? How does making it a speech help the argument?
2. What is the Angel in the House? Why is she an "Angel"? How does Woolf use description of the Angel to advance her argument?
3. How does Woolf use a humble tone in this essay? Is her humbleness honest, or is she being ironic? Explain your answer.
4. How does Woolf use contrast analysis in this essay to highlight the different stages of women's freedom?

Responding in Writing

1. Identify the women writers Woolf mentions in paragraph 1 and explain how each of them struggled (if they did) against their own Angels in the House.
2. In groups, discuss the idea that men today face certain obstacles in their work life and in their own head that are unique to their gender. What do you think Woolf would say to your speculations? Make a list of these obstacles and how they manifest themselves. Compare your group's work with the rest of the class.
3. Write an essay in which you bring Woolf's problems up to date. Does a woman, even after all the advances of more than 70 years, still have "phantoms and obstacles . . . looming in her way"? (par. 7)

RACHEL CARSON
The Obligation to Endure

*Writer and scientist Rachel Carson (1907–1964) helped make modern envi-
ronmentalism a popular cause. After getting her master's degree in zoology
from Johns Hopkins University in 1932, she went to work for the U.S. government as a scientist and writer, eventually working her way up to the position
of editor in chief of all publications for the U.S. Fish and Wildlife Service.
During her career in government, Carson wrote freelance works, becoming
well known for her ability to move her readers on topics such as nature and
conservation. From 1952, when she resigned from her job, she wrote full time,
producing such books as* The Sea Around Us *(1952) and* The Edge of the
Sea *(1955).*

*The wide use of pesticides (especially the insecticide DDT) to improve
agricultural production without a thought to the cost in wildlife alarmed Carson, and she wrote* Silent Spring *(1962) to warn against the practice. The
book and her articles helped convince President John F. Kennedy to order an
investigation, for which Carson testified before Congress. Her appearance
gave rise to legislation that limited the industrial and agricultural use of
harmful chemicals and led eventually to the founding of the Environmental
Protection Agency.*

In this selection, an excerpt from Silent Spring, *Carson lays out her case
against DDT and other chemicals, arguing that humans need to be more responsible with the lives of their fellow animals.*

The history of life on earth has been a history of interaction between   1
living things and their surroundings. To a large extent, the physical
form and the habits of the earth's vegetation and its animal life have been
molded by the environment. Considering the whole span of earthly time,
the opposite effect, in which life actually modifies its surroundings, has
been relatively slight. Only within the moment of time represented by the
present century has one species—man—acquired significant power to alter the nature of his world.

During the past quarter century this power has not only increased to   2
one of disturbing magnitude but it has changed in character. The most
alarming of all man's assaults upon the environment is the contamination
of air, earth, rivers, and sea with dangerous and even lethal materials.
This pollution is for the most part irrecoverable; the chain of evil it initi-
ates not only in the world that must support life but in living tissues is for
the most part irreversible. In this now universal contamination of the environment, chemicals are the sinister and little recognized partners of radiation in changing the very nature of the world—the very nature of this
life. Strontium 90, released through nuclear explosions into the air, comes
to earth in rain or drifts down as fallout, lodges in soil, enters into the
grass or corn or wheat grown there, and in time takes up its abode in the

bones of a human being, there to remain until his death. Similarly, chemicals sprayed on croplands or forests or gardens lie long in soil, entering into living organisms, passing from one to another in a chain of poisoning and death. Or they pass mysteriously by underground streams until they emerge and, through the alchemy of air and sunlight, combine into new forms that kill vegetation, sicken cattle, and work unknown harm on those who drink from once-pure wells. As Albert Schweitzer has said, "Man can hardly even recognize the devils of his own creation."

3   It took hundreds of millions of years to produce the life that now inhabits the earth—eons of time in which developing and evolving the diversifying life reached a state of adjustment and balance with its surroundings. The environment, rigorously shaping and directing the life it supported, contained elements that were hostile as well as supporting. Certain rocks gave out dangerous radiation: even within the light of the sun, from which all life draws its energy, there were short-wave radiations with power to injure. Given time—time not in years but in millennia—life adjusts, and a balance has been reached. For time is the essential ingredient; but in the modern world there is no time.

4   The rapidity of change and the speed with which new situations are created follow the impetuous and heedless pace of man rather than the deliberate pace of nature. Radiation is no longer merely the background radiation of rocks, the bombardment of cosmic rays, the ultraviolet of the sun that have existed before there was any life on earth; radiation is now the unnatural creation of man's tampering with the atom. The chemicals to which life is asked to make its adjustment are no longer merely the calcium and silica and copper and all the rest of the minerals washed out of the rocks and carried in rivers to the sea; they are the synthetic creations of man's inventive mind, brewed in his laboratories, and having no counterparts in nature.

5   To adjust to these chemicals would require time on the scale that is nature's; it would require not merely the years of a man's life but the life of generations. And even this, were it by some miracle possible, would be futile, for the new chemicals come from our laboratories in an endless stream; almost five hundred annually find their way into actual use in the United States alone. The figure is staggering and its implications are not easily grasped—500 new chemicals to which the bodies of men and animals are required somehow to adapt each year, chemicals totally outside the limits of biologic experience.

6   Among them are many that are used in man's war against nature. Since the mid-1940's over 200 basic chemicals have been created for use in killing insects, weeds, rodents, and other organisms described in the modern vernacular as "pests"; and they are sold under several thousand different brand names.

7   These sprays, dusts, and aerosols are now applied almost universally to farms, gardens, forests, and homes—nonselective chemicals that have

the power to kill every insect, the "good" and the "bad," to still the song of birds and the leaping of fish in the streams, to coat the leaves with a deadly film, and to linger on in soil—all this though the intended target may be only a few weeds or insects. Can anyone believe it is possible to lay down such a barrage of poisons on the surface of the earth without making it unfit for all life? They should not be called "insecticides," but "biocides."

The whole process of spraying seems caught up in an endless spiral.   8
Since DDT was released for civilian use, a process of escalation has been going on in which ever more toxic materials must be found. This has happened because insects, in a triumphant vindication of Darwin's principle of the survival of the fittest, have evolved super races immune to the particular insecticide used, hence a deadlier one has always to be developed—and then a deadlier one than that. It has happened also because, for reasons to be described later, destructive insects often undergo a "flareback," or resurgence, after spraying, in numbers greater than before. Thus the chemical war is never won, and all life is caught in its violent crossfire.

Along with the possibility of the extinction of mankind by nuclear   9
war, the central problem of our age has therefore become the contamination of man's total environment with such substances of incredible potential for harm—substances that accumulate in the tissues of plants and animals and even penetrate the germ cells to shatter or alter the very material of heredity upon which the shape of the future depends.

Some would-be architects of our future look toward a time when it   10
will be possible to alter the human germ plasm by design. But we may easily be doing so now by inadvertence, for many chemicals, like radiation, bring about gene mutations. It is ironic to think that man might determine his own future by something so seemingly trivial as the choice of an insect spray.

All this has been risked—for what? Future historians may well be   11
amazed by our distorted sense of proportion. How could intelligent beings seek to control a few unwanted species by a method that contaminated the entire environment and brought the threat of disease and death even to their own kind? Yet this is precisely what we have done. We have done it, moreover, for reasons that collapse the moment we examine them. We are told that the enormous and expanding use of pesticides is necessary to maintain farm production. Yet is our real problem not one of *overproduction*? Our farms, despite measures to remove acreages from production and to pay farmers *not* to produce, have yielded such a staggering excess of crops that the American taxpayer in 1962 is paying out more than one billion dollars a year as the total carrying cost of the surplus-food storage program. And is the situation helped when one branch of the Agriculture Department tries to reduce production while another states, as it did in 1958, "It is believed generally that reduction of crop acreages under provisions of the Soil Bank will stimulate interest in use of chemicals to obtain maximum production on the land retained in crops."

12   All this is not to say there is no insect problem and no need of control. I was saying, rather, that control must be geared to realities, not to mythical situations, and that the methods employed must be such that they do not destroy us along with the insects.

Responding to the Essay

1. What is Carson's major proposition? What minor propositions does she offer to support her main one?
2. In what order does Carson present her minor propositions? Why does she put them in that order?
3. How does Carson use emotional language to help her claim?
4. How does Carson deftly connect man's invention and use of chemicals with the threat of the atomic bomb? How was this notion radical in 1962?
5. Do you find Carson's conclusion convincing? Why or why not?

Responding in Writing

1. Look at Bob Herbert's essay "No Margin for Error." How are Herbert's and Carson's arguments different? Similar? Explain your answer.
2. In groups of four or five students, investigate the levels of chemicals that are present in your drinking water. This information is readily available on the Internet. Then split up and do research into the danger of each chemical on humans and on the environment. Present your findings to the class.
3. Write an essay in which you argue that not all of the changes made by modern society have caused disastrous effects on the environment but that some might, in fact, have helped the environment.

MARTIN LUTHER KING JR.
I Have a Dream

The Reverend Martin Luther King Jr., civil rights leader and Nobel Peace Prize winner, was born in 1929 in Atlanta, Georgia. He went to traditionally black Morehouse College, where both his father and grandfather had studied. He then attended Crozer Theological Seminary and Boston University, from which he earned his doctorate. King then became a pastor in Montgomery, Alabama, and a member of the National Association for the Advancement of Colored People. He began organizing for the civil rights movement. King believed in nonviolent protest, the technique for civil disobedience he took from Gandhi. He organized major protests all over the South as president of the Southern Christian Leadership Conference, a civil rights group.

King was arrested and assaulted and his house was bombed, but he continued to speak, write, and lead. In the summer of 1963, he directed the March on Washington, in which 250,000 people participated. The emotional and rhetorical culmination of the march was King's "I Have a Dream" speech, printed here, which was immediately recognized as one of the major speeches in American history. King's work ended in 1968, when he was assassinated in Memphis, Tennessee, but the legacy of this speech—which blends brilliantly the emotional rhythms of religious oratory and allusions to American guarantees of freedom—stands as one of his greatest achievements. As you read, pay close attention to how King is able to manipulate his audience emotionally with a strong rational argument.

I am happy to join with you today in what will go down in history as   1
the greatest demonstration for freedom in the history of our nation.

Fivescore years ago, a great American, in whose symbolic shadow we   2
stand today, signed the Emancipation Proclamation. This momentous decree came as a great beacon light of hope to millions of Negro slaves who had been seared in the flames of withering injustice. It came as a joyous daybreak to end the long night of their captivity.

But one hundred years later, the Negro still is not free; one hundred   3
years later, the life of the Negro is still sadly crippled by the manacles of segregation and the chains of discrimination; one hundred years later, the Negro lives on a lonely island of poverty in the midst of a vast ocean of material prosperity; one hundred years later, the Negro is still languishing in the corners of American society and finds himself in exile in his own land.

So we've come here today to dramatize a shameful condition. In a sense we've come to our nation's capital to cash a check. When the archi-   4
tects of our republic wrote the magnificent words of the Constitution and the Declaration of Independence, they were signing a promissory note to which every American was to fall heir. This note was the promise that all men, yes, black men as well as white men, would be guaranteed the unalienable rights of life, liberty, and the pursuit of happiness.

It is obvious today that America has defaulted on this promissory   5
note in so far as her citizens of color are concerned. Instead of honoring this sacred obligation, America has given the Negro people a bad check; a check which has come back marked "insufficient funds." We refuse to believe that there are insufficient funds in the great vaults of opportunity of this nation. And so we've come to cash this check, a check that will give us upon demand the riches of freedom and the security of justice.

We have also come to this hallowed spot to remind America of the   6
fierce urgency of now. This is no time to engage in the luxury of cooling off or to take the tranquilizing drug of gradualism. Now is the time to make real the promises of democracy; now is the time to rise from the dark and desolate valley of segregation to the sunlit path of racial justice; now is the time to lift our nation from the quicksands of racial injustice to the solid

rock of brotherhood; now is the time to make justice a reality for all God's children. It would be fatal for the nation to overlook the urgency of the moment. This sweltering summer of the Negro's legitimate discontent will not pass until there is an invigorating autumn of freedom and equality.

7   Nineteen sixty-three is not an end, but a beginning. And those who hope that the Negro needed to blow off steam and will now be content, will have a rude awakening if the nation returns to business as usual.

8   There will be neither rest nor tranquility in America until the Negro is granted his citizenship rights. The whirlwinds of revolt will continue to shake the foundations of our nation until the bright day of justice emerges.

9   But there is something that I must say to my people who stand on the warm threshold which leads into the palace of justice. In the process of gaining our rightful place we must not be guilty of wrongful deeds.

10   Let us not seek to satisfy our thirst for freedom by drinking from the cup of bitterness and hatred. We must forever conduct our struggle on the high plane of dignity and discipline. We must not allow our creative protest to degenerate into physical violence. Again and again we must rise to the majestic heights of meeting physical force with soul force.

11   The marvelous new militancy which has engulfed the Negro community must not lead us to a distrust of all white people, for many of our white brothers, as evidenced by their presence here today, have come to realize that their destiny is tied up with our destiny and they have come to realize that their freedom is inextricably bound to our freedom. This offense we share mounted to storm the battlements of injustice must be carried forth by a biracial army. We cannot walk alone.

12   And as we walk, we must make the pledge that we shall always march ahead. We cannot turn back. There are those who are asking the devotees of civil rights, "When will you be satisfied?" We can never be satisfied as long as the Negro is the victim of the unspeakable horrors of police brutality.

13   We can never be satisfied as long as our bodies, heavy with fatigue of travel, cannot gain lodging in the motels of the highways and the hotels of the cities. We cannot be satisfied as long as the Negro's basic mobility is from a smaller ghetto to a larger one.

14   We can never be satisfied as long as our children are stripped of their self-hood and robbed of their dignity by signs stating "for whites only." We cannot be satisfied as long as a Negro in Mississippi cannot vote and a Negro in New York believes he has nothing for which to vote. No, we are not satisfied, and we will not be satisfied until justice rolls down like waters and righteousness like a mighty stream.

15   I am not unmindful that some of you have come here out of excessive trials and tribulation. Some of you have come fresh from narrow jail cells. Some of you have come from areas where your quest for freedom left you battered by the storms of persecution and staggered by the winds of police brutality. You have been the veterans of creative suffering. Continue to work with the faith that unearned suffering is redemptive.

Go back to Mississippi; go back to Alabama; go back to South Car-   16
olina; go back to Georgia; go back to Louisiana; go back to the slums and
ghettos of the northern cities, knowing that somehow this situation can,
and will be changed. Let us not wallow in the valley of despair.

So I say to you, my friends, that even though we must face the diffi-   17
culties of today and tomorrow, I still have a dream. It is a dream deeply
rooted in the American dream that one day this nation will rise up and
live out the true meaning of its creed—we hold these truths to be self-
evident, that all men are created equal.

I have a dream that one day on the red hills of Georgia, sons of former   18
slaves and sons of former slave-owners will be able to sit down together
at the table of brotherhood.

I have a dream that one day, even the state of Mississippi, a state   19
sweltering with the heat of injustice, sweltering with the heat of oppression, will be transformed into an oasis of freedom and justice.

I have a dream my four little children will one day live in a nation   20
where they will not be judged by the color of their skin but by the content
of their character. I have a dream today!

I have a dream that one day, down in Alabama, with its vicious   21
racists, with its governor having his lips dripping with the words of inter-
position and nullification, that one day, right there in Alabama, little black
boys and black girls will be able to join hands with little white boys and
white girls as sisters and brothers. I have a dream today!

I have a dream that one day every valley shall be exalted, every hill   22
and mountain shall be made low, the rough places shall be made plain,
and the crooked places shall be made straight and the glory of the Lord
will be revealed and all flesh shall see it together.

This is our hope. This is the faith that I go back to the South with.   23

With this faith we will be able to hear out of the mountain of despair   24
a stone of hope. With this faith we will be able to transform the jangling
discords of our nation into a beautiful symphony of brotherhood.

With this faith we will be able to work together, to pray together, to   25
struggle together, to go to jail together, to stand up for freedom together,
knowing that we will be free one day. This will be the day when all of
God's children will be able to sing with new meaning—"my country 'tis
of thee; sweet land of liberty; of thee I sing; land where my fathers died,
land of the pilgrims' pride; from every mountain side, let freedom
ring"—and if America is to be a great nation, this must become true.

So let freedom ring from the prodigious hilltops of New Hampshire.   26
Let freedom ring from the mighty mountains of New York.   27
Let freedom ring from the heightening Alleghenies of Pennsylvania.   28
Let freedom ring from the snow-capped Rockies of Colorado.   29
Let freedom ring from the curvaceous slopes of California.   30
But not only that.   31
Let freedom ring from Stone Mountain of Georgia.   32
Let freedom ring from Lookout Mountain of Tennessee.   33

34   Let freedom ring from every hill and molehill of Mississippi, from every mountainside, let freedom ring.

35   And when we allow freedom to ring, when we let it ring from every village and hamlet, from every state and city, we will be able to speed up that day when all of God's children—black men and white men, Jews and Gentiles, Catholics and Protestants—will be able to join hands and to sing in the words of the old Negro spiritual, "Free at last, free at last; thank God Almighty, we are free at last."

Responding to the Essay

1. In his introduction, King echoes another great speech, Lincoln's Gettysburg Address. Compare and contrast the arguments in those two speeches.
2. King uses many different metaphors and similes. Which are the strongest? The weakest? Do you think he has too many different ones, or does his strategy work? Defend your answers.
3. King's essay makes use of religious and biblical speech. How does his speech actually use references and phrases from the Bible, and where does his speech just carry the cadences and rhythms of biblical rhetoric? How does repetition figure in his technique?
4. How effective is King's ending? Why does he end on a quote from an old Negro spiritual?
5. King subscribed to the protest technique of nonviolence, and he spent considerable time convincing people to remain nonviolent in the face of great abuse. How can we reconcile his ideas of nonviolence with his language in paragraph 5? Explain.

Responding in Writing

1. Do some research to discover what led King, in his life, to the point at which he came to make a speech before 200,000 people on the Mall in Washington, D.C.
2. More than 40 years have passed since King delivered his speech at the March on Washington. In groups, discuss whether King's hopes and his dream have been fulfilled. Write your answers down, and compare them with the answers of the other groups.
3. The King family holds the copyright to the "I Have a Dream" speech. Investigate the various battles they have waged with people and companies they thought were infringing on the copyright. Write an essay in which you either defend the King family's action or in which you argue that the speech is the property of the entire country, as it was delivered during a massive public event.
4. Seek out an audio file or video of King delivering the "I Have a Dream" speech. Write an essay that contrasts experiencing the speech visually or aurally and reading it.

Part Five

A Casebook of Arguments on Americans' Eating Habits: Are We What We Eat?

People today work more hours than ever before. They rush from school to work to home to school again. Families used to eat together at home, but today there frequently is nobody to stay at home to cook wholesome, nutritious, and healthy meals. Instead, we grab whatever we can on the run and eat on our way to school or work, on the street, or in our cars.

What is more convenient than fast food? As we get busier, McDonald's, Burger King, and other fast-food chains get busier and busier too. But these restaurants aren't serving carrot and celery sticks. They serve red meat and fried food—high-calorie, high-carbohydrate, high-fat meals that taste good.

Americans face a public health crisis. Heart disease is the number one cause of death in the country, and a disturbing percentage of Americans are morbidly obese. Obviously there is some connection between fast-food restaurants and Americans' unhealthy eating habits—but who is at fault? Obese customers have filed lawsuits against the fast-food companies, which, they feel, are responsible for their health problems. Are companies so adept at marketing and making their food so attractive that Americans cannot resist? Is it the lack of time available and the lack of quick, healthful food? Or are the overweight to blame for their own actions? And, of course, in the media, everyone is slim, and glamorous. How does that situation affect how we eat?

The selections in this casebook provide multiple perspectives on these issues. Shannon Brownlee, in "We're Fatter but Not Smarter," sees the problem in growing portion sizes (as opposed to the portion sizes eaten by the relatively thin French, who eat fatty foods in small amounts). David Zinczenko, in "Don't Blame the Eater" also blames the companies, arguing that children are particularly susceptible to their misrepresentations. Adam Cohen in "The McNugget of Truth in the Lawsuits Against Fast-Food Restaurants" argues that restaurants ignore these lawsuits at their own peril. Sometimes writers use satire to get their point across. Jonathan Rauch, in "The Fat Tax," proposes that the government penalize overweight people for every pound they gain. Michele Ingrassia wonders why it seems that black girls are more comfortable with their bodies than white girls in "The Body of the Beholder." Jay Walljasper in "The Joy of Eating" takes a more leisurely journey through the problems of how Americans are alienated from their food and sees some hope in the organic arm of the environmentalist movement. Ellen Goodman in "The Culture of Thin Bites Fiji" and Dawn Mackeen in "Waifs on the Web" take more journalistic looks at two phenomena: an island nation formally obsessed with gaining weight and a subculture of young girls in America who are obsessed with losing weight at any cost. As you read these essays, pay attention to how the writers use their reported facts to make their points.

SHANNON BROWNLEE
We're Fatter but Not Smarter

Science journalist Shannon Brownlee has written about genetics, cancer research, and public health policy for many publications, including Discover *magazine,* U.S. News & World Report, Time, The New York Times, *and* The New Republic. *She is a senior fellow at the New America Foundation. In this selection, which appeared in* The Washington Post, *Brownlee takes a look at what many scientists think is the key to the epidemic of obesity in America—out-of-control portion sizes.*

I t was probably inevitable that one day people would start suing McDonald's for making them fat. That day came last summer, when New York lawyer Samuel Hirsch filed several lawsuits against McDonald's, as well as four other fast-food companies, on the grounds that they had failed to adequately disclose the bad health effects of their menus. One of the suits involves a Bronx teenager who tips the scale at 400 pounds and whose mother, in papers filed in U.S. District Court in Manhattan, said, "I always believed McDonald's food was healthy for my son."   1

Uh-huh. And the tooth fairy really put that dollar under his pillow. But once you've stopped sniggering at our litigious society, remember that it once seemed equally ludicrous that smokers could successfully sue tobacco companies for their addiction to cigarettes. And while nobody is   2

claiming that Big Macs are addictive—at least not yet—the restaurant industry and food packagers have clearly helped give many Americans the roly-poly shape they have today. This is not to say that the folks in the food industry want us to be fat. But make no mistake: When they do well economically, we gain weight.

3   It wasn't always thus. Readers of a certain age can remember a time when a trip to McDonald's seemed like a treat and when a small bag of French fries, a plain burger and a 12-ounce Coke seemed like a full meal. Fast food wasn't any healthier back then; we simply ate a lot less of it.

4   How did today's oversized appetites become the norm? It didn't happen by accident or some inevitable evolutionary process. It was to a large degree the result of consumer manipulation. Fast food's marketing strategies, which make perfect sense from a business perspective, succeed only when they induce a substantial number of us to overeat. To see how this all came about, let's go back to 1983, when John Martin became CEO of the ailing Taco Bell franchise and met a young marketing whiz named Elliott Bloom.

5   Using so-called "smart research," a then-new kind of in-depth consumer survey, Bloom had figured out that fast-food franchises were sustained largely by a core group of "heavy users," mostly young, single males, who ate at such restaurants as often as 20 times a month. In fact, 30 percent of Taco Bell's customers accounted for 70 percent of its sales. Through his surveys, Bloom learned what might seem obvious now but wasn't at all clear 20 years ago—these guys ate at fast-food joints because they had absolutely no interest in cooking for themselves and didn't give a rip about the nutritional quality of the food. They didn't even care much about the taste. All that mattered was that it was fast and cheap. Martin figured Taco Bell could capture a bigger share of these hard-core customers by streamlining the food production and pricing main menu items at 49, 59 and 69 cents—well below its competitors.

6   It worked. Taco Bell saw a dramatic increase in patrons, with no drop in revenue per customer. As Martin told Greg Critser, author of "Fat Land: How Americans Became the Fattest People in the World," when Taco Bell ran a test of its new pricing in Texas, "within seven days of initiating the test, the average check was right back to where it was before—it was just four instead of three items." In other words, cheap food induced people to eat more. Taco Bell's rising sales figures—up 14 percent by 1989 and 12 percent more the next year—forced other fast-food franchises to wake up and smell the burritos. By the late '80s, everybody from Burger King to Wendy's was cutting prices and seeing an increase in customers—including bargain-seeking Americans who weren't part of that original hardcore group.

7   If the marketing strategy had stopped there, we might not be the nation of fatties that we are today. But the imperatives of the marketplace are growth and rising profits, and once everybody had slashed prices to the bone, the franchises had to look for a new way to satisfy investors.

And what they found was . . . super-sizing.   8

Portion sizes had already been creeping upward. As early as 1972, for   9
example, McDonald's introduced its large-size fries (large being a relative
term, since at 3.5 ounces the '72 "large" was smaller than a medium serving today). But McDonald's increased portions only reluctantly, because
the company's founder, Ray Kroc, didn't like the image of lowbrow, cheap
food. If people wanted more French fries, he would say, "they can buy two
bags." But price competition had grown so fierce that the only way to keep
profits up was to offer bigger and bigger portions. By 1988, McDonald's
had introduced a 32-ounce "super size" soda and "super size" fries.

The deal with all these enhanced portions is that the customer gets a   10
lot more food for a relatively small increase in price. So just how does that
translate into bigger profits? Because the actual food in a fast-food meal is
incredibly cheap. For every dollar a quick-service franchiser spends to
produce a food item, only 20 cents, on average, goes toward food. The
rest is eaten up by expenses such as salaries, packaging, electric bills, insurance and, of course, the ubiquitous advertising that got you in the
door or to the drive-through lane in the first place.

Here's how it works. Let's say a $1.25 bag of french fries costs $1 to   11
produce. The potatoes, oil and salt account for only 20 cents of the cost.
The other 80 cents goes toward all the other expenses. If you add half
again as many French fries to the bag and sell it for $1.50, the non-food
expenses stay pretty much constant, while the extra food costs the franchise only 10 more pennies. The fast-food joint makes an extra 15 cents in
pure profit, and the customer thinks he's getting a good deal. And he
would be, if he actually needed the extra food, which he doesn't because
the nation is awash in excess calories.

That 20 percent rule, by the way, applies to all food products, whether   12
it's a bag of potato chips, the 2,178-calorie mountain of fried seafood at
Red Lobster or the 710-calorie slab of dessert at the Cheesecake Factory.
Some foods are even less expensive to make. The flakes of your kid's
breakfast cereal, for example, account for only 5 percent of the total
amount Nabisco or General Mills spent to make and sell them. Soda costs
less to produce than any drink except tap water (which nobody seems to
drink anymore), thanks to a 1970s invention that cut the expense of making high-fructose corn syrup. There used to be real sugar in Coke; when
Coca-Cola and other bottlers switched to high-fructose corn syrup in
1984, they slashed sweetener costs by 20 percent. That's why 7-Eleven can
sell the 64-ounce Double Gulp—half a gallon of soda and nearly
600 calories—for only 37 cents more than the 16-ounce, 89-cent regular
Gulp. You'd feel ripped off if you bought the smaller size. Who wouldn't?

The final step in the fattening of America was the "upsell," a stroke of   13
genius whose origins are buried somewhere in the annals of marketing.
You're already at the counter, you've ordered a cheeseburger value meal
for $3.74, and your server says, "Would you like to super-size that for

only $4.47?" Such a deal. The chain extracts an extra 73 cents from the customer, and the customer gets an extra 400 calories—bringing the total calorie count to 1,550, more than half the recommended intake for an adult man for an entire day.

14   When confronted with their contribution to America's expanding waistline, restaurateurs and food packagers reply that eating less is a matter of individual responsibility. But that's not how the human stomach works. If you put more food in front of people, they eat more, as studies have consistently shown over the last decade. My personal favorite: The researcher gave moviegoers either a half-gallon or a gallon bucket of popcorn before the show (it was "Payback," with Mel Gibson) and then measured how much they ate when they returned what was left in the containers afterward. Nobody could polish off the entire thing, but subjects ate 44 percent more when given the bigger bucket.

15   The downside, of course, is that 20 years of Big Food has trained us to think that oceanic drinks and gargantuan portions are normal. Indeed, once fast food discovered that big meals meant big profits, everybody from Heineken to Olive Garden to Frito Lay followed suit. Today, says Lisa Young, a nutritionist at New York University, super-sizing has pervaded every segment of the food industry. For her PhD, Young documented the changes in portion sizes for dozens of foods over the past several decades. M&M/Mars, for example, has increased the size of candy bars such as Milky Way and Snickers four times since 1970. Starbucks introduced the 20-ounce "venti" size in 1999 and discontinued its "short" 8-ounce cup. When 22-ounce Heinekens were introduced, Young reported, the company sold 24 million of them the first year, and attributed the sales to the "big-bottle gimmick." Even Lean Cuisine and Weight Watchers now advertise "Hearty Portions" of their diet meals. Everything from plates and muffin tins to restaurant chairs and the cut of our Levi's has expanded to match our growing appetites, and the wonder of it all is not that 60 percent of Americans are overweight or obese, but rather that 40 percent of us are not.

16   Where does it end? Marketers and restaurateurs may scoff at lawsuits like the ones brought this summer against fast-food companies, and they have a point: Adults are ultimately responsible for what they put in their own mouths. But maybe there's hope for us yet, because it looks as if fast-food companies have marketed themselves into a corner. "Omnipresence"—the McDonald's strategy of beating out competitors by opening new stores, sometimes as many as 1,000 a year—"has proved costly and self-cannibalizing," says author Critser. With 13,000 McDonald's units alone, most of America is so saturated with fast food there's practically no place left to put a drive-through lane. Now, fast-food companies are killing each other in a new price war they can't possibly sustain, and McDonald's just suffered its first quarterly loss since the company went public 47 years ago.

The obvious direction to go is down, toward what nutritional policy-   17
makers are calling "smart-sizing." Or at least it should be obvious, if food
purveyors cared as much about helping Americans slim down as they
would have us believe. Instead of urging Americans to "Get Active, Stay
Active"—Pepsi Cola's new criticism-deflecting slogan—how about bringing back the 6.5-ounce sodas of the '40s and '50s? Or, imagine, as Critser
does, the day when McDonald's advertises Le Petit Mac, made with high-
grade beef, a delicious whole-grain bun and hawked by, say, Serena
Williams. One way or another, as Americans wake up to the fact that obesity is killing nearly as many citizens as cigarettes are, jumbo burgers and
super-size fries will seem like less of a bargain.

Responding to the Essay

1. What is Brownlee's claim? Where is it stated? Is it placed effectively?
   Why or why not?
2. Analyze Brownlee's use of statistics. Do you find the ones that she
   chose to be persuasive? Which are most persuasive? Which are the
   weakest? Defend your answers.
3. Presumably, some of Brownlee's readers are going to be fast-food customers. How does Brownlee make her claim and still ensure that she
   doesn't make her reader feel bad?
4. Write about Brownlee's use of verbs. How does she use exciting or action verbs to help her argument?
5. What do you think of Brownlee's conclusion and her suggestions for
   solving the problems she has outlined? Are they sufficient, or do you
   find yourself hungry for more ideas? Explain.

Responding in Writing

1. In what other areas of business do you see this tendency toward a
   philosophy of bigger is better? In groups of four or five students, discuss where else in American culture you see this idea spreading.
   Make an outline for an essay along the lines of "We're Fatter but Not
   Smarter."
2. Write an essay in which you write a letter to the CEO of a fast-food
   chain explaining why he or she is singly responsible for the obesity
   epidemic in the United States and trying to convince him or her to
   lower portion sizes. Maintain a cordial tone even as you make your
   accusations.
3. In paragraph 4, Brownlee introduces the idea that the marketing of
   fast food, even though it causes people to overeat, still makes sense
   from a business point of view. Write an essay in which you argue that
   other kinds of marketing and advertising from other industries cause
   social problems such as obesity.

DAVID ZINCZENKO
Don't Blame the Eater

David Zinczenko, who admits that he was an overweight child, became the editor in chief of Men's Health *at the age of 30. In this essay from* The New York Times *in 2002, Zinczenko takes a harsh look at the responsibility that fast-food chains have in adding to the public health crisis of obesity among children.*

1   If ever there were a newspaper headline custom-made for Jay Leno's monologue, this was it. Kids taking on McDonald's this week, suing the company for making them fat. Isn't that like middle-aged men suing Porsche for making them get speeding tickets? Whatever happened to personal responsibility?

2   I tend to sympathize with these portly fast-food patrons, though. Maybe that's because I used to be one of them.

3   I grew up as a typical mid-1980s latchkey kid. My parents were split up, my dad off trying to rebuild his life, my mom working long hours to make the monthly bills. Lunch and dinner, for me, was a daily choice between McDonald's, Taco Bell, Kentucky Fried Chicken or Pizza Hut. Then as now, these were the only available options for an American kid to get an affordable meal. By age 15, I had packed 212 pounds of torpid teenage tallow on my once lanky 5-foot-10 frame.

4   Then I got lucky. I went to college, joined the Navy Reserves and got involved with a health magazine. I learned how to manage my diet. But most of the teenagers who live, as I once did, on a fast-food diet won't turn their lives around: They've crossed under the golden arches to a likely fate of lifetime obesity. And the problem isn't just theirs—it's all of ours.

5   Before 1994, diabetes in children was generally caused by a genetic disorder—only about 5 percent of childhood cases were obesity-related, or Type 2, diabetes. Today, according to the National Institutes of Health, Type 2 diabetes accounts for at least 30 percent of all new childhood cases of diabetes in this country.

6   Not surprisingly, money spent to treat diabetes has skyrocketed, too. The Centers for Disease Control and Prevention estimate that diabetes accounted for $2.6 billion in health care costs in 1969. Today's number is an unbelievable $100 billion a year.

7   Shouldn't we know better than to eat two meals a day in fast-food restaurants? That's one argument. But where, exactly, are consumers—particularly teenagers—supposed to find alternatives? Drive down any thoroughfare in America, and I guarantee you'll see one of our country's more than 13,000 McDonald's restaurants. Now, drive back up the block and try to find someplace to buy a grapefruit.

Complicating the lack of alternatives is the lack of information about   8
what, exactly, we're consuming. There are no calorie information charts
on fast-food packaging, the way there are on grocery items. Advertisements don't carry warning labels the way tobacco ads do. Prepared foods
aren't covered under Food and Drug Administration labeling laws. Some
fast-food purveyors will provide calorie information on request, but even
that can be hard to understand.

For example, one company's Web site lists its chicken salad as con-   9
taining 150 calories; the almonds and noodles that come with it (an additional 190 calories) are listed separately. Add a serving of the
280-calorie dressing, and you've got a healthy lunch alternative that
comes in at 620 calories. But that's not all. Read the small print on the
back of the dressing packet and you'll realize it actually contains
2.5 servings. If you pour what you've been served, you're suddenly up
around 1,040 calories, which is half of the government's recommended
daily calorie intake. And that doesn't take into account that 450-calorie
super-size Coke.

Make fun if you will of these kids launching lawsuits against the fast-   10
food industry, but don't be surprised if you're the next plaintiff. As with
the tobacco industry, it may be only a matter of time before state governments begin to see a direct line between the $1 billion that McDonald's
and Burger King spend each year on advertising and their own swelling
health care costs.

And I'd say the industry is vulnerable. Fast-food companies are mar-   11
keting to children a product with proven health hazards and no warning
labels. They would do well to protect themselves, and their customers, by
providing the nutrition information people need to make informed
choices about their products. Without such warnings, we'll see more sick,
obese children and more angry, litigious parents. I say, let the deep-fried
chips fall where they may.

Responding to the Essay

1. What is the author's claim? What minor propositions does he offer to
   back up his claim, and why does he put them in the order he does?
2. What is your opinion of the author's mini-memoir in paragraphs 2
   to 4? Do you find it to be an effective way to link the introduction to
   the rest of the essay? Why or why not?
3. In paragraph 4, the author writes that he "learned to manage my
   diet." He is arguing, as his title says, not to "blame the eater." Are
   these two statements contradictory? If not, explain. If so, does he reconcile the statements in the rest of his argument?
4. Analyze the author's conclusion. Is it effective? Why or why not?
   How well does it wrap up his argument?

Responding in Writing

1. Write an essay called "Don't Blame the . . . ," in which you argue that the responsibility for a problem is not with the actor but with an authority figure. For example, you might write an essay titled "Don't Blame the Downloader" that argues that the fault for people stealing music lies with the music companies.

2. One thing Zinczenko calls for is proper labeling. Do some research about the fight for labeling in this country. Write an essay explaining the history of the present labeling laws and how experts think they have changed how people eat.

3. Divide the class in three groups, and prepare a mock trial. One group will take the side of the defendants, the fast-food companies; one group will take the side of the plaintiffs, the families who are suing the companies; and the last group will act as the jury. The plaintiffs' side should prepare a case against the companies, and the defense should prepare to rebut the arguments they think the plaintiffs will make. The jury should attempt to anticipate both sides' arguments. Your teacher will act as judge. At the end of the trial, the jury will decide the case and, if necessary, award damages.

CAST-A-WAY

Instructions for Stress Diet

There are numerous Internet sites and cable channels dedicated to the funny bone, providing new and old programming designed to make viewers laugh. You can still catch some classic episodes of the naughty cartoon series South Park *if your cable provider offers the channel. And Comedy Central produces a Web site with a number of links to other comedic spots. One excellent site is Cast-a-Way, which offers a joke archive.*

"Instructions for Stress Diet" is a typical selection. How does it provide a humorous sidebar to our problems with weight gain and tantalizing food?

Responding to the Visual Text

1. Explain the assumptions implicit in the presentation of this "diet." What claim or major proposition does this diet present?
2. Where and how does the tone of this text change?
3. How do process analysis and classification bolster the argument?
4. What design elements does the artist use to present this diet?
5. What does the "rules" section of this text contribute to the overall effect?

Instructions for Stress Diet

BREAKFAST:
- 1/2 grapefruit
- 1 slice whole wheat toast
- 8 oz. skim milk

LUNCH:
- 4 oz. lean broiled chicken breast
- 1 cup steamed spinach
- 1 cup herb tea
- 1 Oreo cookie

MID-AFTERNOON SNACK:
- The rest of Oreos in the package
- 2 pints Rocky Road ice cream nuts, cherries, and whipped cream
- 1 jar hot fudge sauce

DINNER:
- 2 loaves garlic bread
- 4 cans or 1 large pitcher Coke
- 1 large sausage, mushroom, and cheese pizza
- 3 Snickers bars

LATE EVENING NEWS:
- Entire frozen Sara Lee cheesecake (eaten directly from freezer)

RULES FOR THIS DIET:
1. If you eat something and no one sees you eat it, it has no calories.
2. If you drink a diet soda with a candy bar, the calories in the candy bar are canceled out by the diet soda.
3. When you eat with someone else, calories don't count if you do not eat more than they do.
4. Foods used for medicinal purposes NEVER count, such as hot chocolate, brandy, toast, and Sara Lee Cheesecake.
5. If you fatten up everyone else around you, then you look thinner.
6. Movie-related foods do not have additional calories because they are part of the entertainment package and not part of one's personal fuel. (Examples: Milk Duds, buttered popcorn, Junior Mints, Red Hots, and Tootsie Rolls.)
7. Cookie pieces contain no calories. (The process of breaking causes calorie leakage.)
8. Things licked off knives and spoons have no calories if you are in the process of preparing something.
9. Foods that have the same color have the same number of calories. (Examples are: spinach and pistachio ice cream; mushrooms and mashed potatoes.)
10. Chocolate is a universal color and may be substituted for any other food color.
11. Anything consumed while standing has no calories. This is due to gravity and the density of the caloric mass.
12. Anything consumed from someone else's plate has no calories since the calories rightfully belong to the other person and will cling to his/her plate. (We ALL know how calories like to cling!)

Remember, "stressed" spelled backwards is "desserts."

This is a joke, folks!

(www.cast.co.za)

Responding in Writing

1. In a paragraph or two, analyze the elements that make this text provocative and appealing.
2. Imitate the elements in this visual text and compose your own "Diet for . . ." Aim for a comic effect.

ADAM COHEN

The McNugget of Truth in the Lawsuits Against Fast-Food Restaurants

Adam Cohen is a senior writer for Time, *for which he covers law and politics. He has also written for* Chicago Magazine, Chicago Tribune, *and* The Harvard Law Review. *He lives in New York. In this* New York Times *editorial, Cohen explores the lawsuits recently being aimed at the fast-food industry and makes some suggestions to the largest of all the chains, McDonald's.*

1   When McDonald's first rolled out the Chicken McNugget in the 1980's, comedians could always get a laugh by asking, with a leer, just what part of the chicken the McNugget was supposed to be. But thanks to a recent federal court ruling, the composition of the McNugget is no laughing matter.

2   The Chicken McNugget, a lab experiment of an entree, larded with ingredients like TBHQ, a flavorless "stabilizer," and Dimethylpolysiloxane, an "anti-foaming agent," is Exhibit A in a lawsuit that could transform the fast-food industry. And it is the McNugget's artificiality—the judge labeled it a "McFrankenstein creation"—that is putting McDonald's on the legal defensive.

3   The showdown over the Chicken McNugget comes in a lawsuit by Ashley Pelman and Jazlyn Bradley, two New York girls who say that McDonald's is to blame for their obesity and health problems. Plaintiffs' lawyers have high hopes. Just as Big Tobacco has been held liable for cancer, they say, Big Food should pay for hypertension, diabetes, and heart disease. With obesity costing Americans an estimated $117 billion in 2000—and on its way, according to the surgeon general, to causing as much preventable disease and death as cigarettes—the damage awards could be enormous.

4   Critics of the suit call it litigation run amok. The Center for Consumer Freedom, a food and beverage trade group, has taken out ads showing a man with a paunch and the caption: "Did you hear the one about the fat guy suing the restaurants? It's no joke." An industry spokesman has thrown the blame right back on customers, saying that "anyone with an I.Q. higher than room temperature will understand that excessive consumption of food served in fast-food restaurants will lead to weight gain." And the media have largely joined in the skepticism, coining a new word along the way—McScapegoat.

Fast-food litigation has been greeted coolly so far because it appears   5
to run up against a core American value: personal responsibility. Judge
Robert Sweet, who is hearing the Pelman suit, dismissed it earlier this
month for just this reason. If customers know the risks, he held, "they
cannot blame McDonald's if they, nonetheless, choose to satiate their appetite with a surfeit of supersized McDonald's products."

If Judge Sweet had stopped there, it would have been a happy day in   6
McDonaldland. But the reason Pelman v. McDonald's Corp. may yet be a
problem is that the judge went on to explain how the plaintiffs could fix
their suit, and gave them time to do it. The key, he said, is to focus on the
fact that customers may not have a reasonable chance to learn what they
are getting into when they eat at McDonald's.

Judge Sweet didn't absolve fast-food customers of the need for self-   7
restraint. Instead, he grounded the case in a basic doctrine of tort law: that
certain products may be unreasonably dangerous because they contain
items that are "outside the reasonable contemplation of the consuming
public." In other words, it is O.K. to sell unhealthy food. But when an
item is substantially less healthy than it appears, a seller may be held liable for the resulting harm.

Judge Sweet offered up, by way of example, Chicken McNuggets.   8
"Rather than being merely chicken fried in a pan," he wrote, they are "a
McFrankenstein creation of various elements not utilized by the home
cook." His decision listed 30 or 40 ingredients other than chicken, and
noted that although chicken is regarded as healthier than beef, Chicken
McNuggets are actually far fattier. "It is at least a question of fact," he
held, whether a reasonable consumer would know that a McNugget
"contained so many ingredients other than chicken and provided twice
the fat of a hamburger."

The Pelman plaintiffs may be able to find other, similarly misleading   9
products. McDonald's suffered a legal setback last year when it paid
$10 million to settle a class action by Hindus and vegetarians who sued
because McDonald's had failed to disclose that even after its widely pub-
licized switch to vegetable oil, it was still using beef in its fries.

Fully understanding McDonald's food can be difficult even with   10
more straightforward items. Consumers who go to the McDonald's Web
site might be confused to find that its "nutrition facts" chart for beverages
contains the calories only for small beverages, a size rarely encountered
in real life. (A downloadable "nutrient card" elsewhere on the site contains more complete data.)

McDonald's argues that the plaintiffs have only themselves to blame,   11
since everyone knows that the highly processed food they serve is less
healthy than normal food. And its Congressional allies are introducing a
bill to insulate fast-food restaurants from suits of this kind.

But the company's stance bucks two key trends in American life—   12
healthy eating and corporate transparency. McDonald's would position itself better in the fast-food market if it communicated more

openly with its customers about what they were getting. A good start would be to listen to consumer advocates and post calorie content on menu boards.

13   Better still, McDonald's should ramp up its fitful efforts to make its food more nutritious. The Pelman plaintiffs have plainly identified a problem. With obesity at epidemic levels—more than 60 percent of adults are now overweight or obese—McDonald's is doing real harm by promoting '"extra value meals" that contain three-quarters of the calories an adult needs for a full day.

14   The news that it could be legally liable could hardly have come at a worse time for the company, which has just suffered the first quarterly loss in its history. If the McFrankenstein lawsuits start to win, McDonald's may find that it truly has created a monster.

Responding to the Essay

1. Analyze how Cohen uses the Chicken McNugget to lead into his essay. Does he do this successfully? Explain your answer.
2. How does Cohen use syllogistic reasoning in this essay? Trace his argument from the end of his introductory section to his conclusion.
3. Cohen offers surprising facts to his reader to help make his case. Analyze how he does this? Which facts are most surprising? Explain.
4. Does Cohen successfully prepare the reader for his claim? Explain your answer fully.

Responding in Writing

1. Find some advertisements for fast-food restaurants in a magazine or newspaper, or watch some on television. Write a description of at least three different advertisements, and bring them to class. In small groups, discuss and contrast how the ads represent (or misrepresent) their products.
2. On the Internet, get the nutritional information for popular meals from two separate fast-food restaurants. Write an essay in which you compare and analyze the nutritional content of the meals. How are they contributing to obesity? (Cohen mentions that accessibility to this information is a crucial part of a possible lawsuit against the companies. As a part of your essay, describe how easy or difficult it was to find the information.)
3. Write an essay in which you compare and contrast Cohen's argument with Brownlee's. What is similar about their arguments? What is different?

GREASE

Food sales depend to a large degree on advertising and on brand recognition, and the fast-food industry regularly places ads and coupons for discounts in daily and weekly periodicals and flyers. McDonald's, the fast-food giant, has an advantage over competitors because it has a familiar "spokesperson," the happy, smiling, clown Ronald McDonald. Of course, not everyone is happy with McDonald's products. The following spoof advertisement, which appears in the Web site adbusters.org., takes a satirical look at Ronald McDonald and the products he promotes.

Responding to the Visual Text

1. If you had to state a proposition that suggests the argument of this spoof ad, what would it be?
2. How does the illustration question the wisdom of consuming any McDonald's product?

3. How does the illustration rely on popular brand recognition to achieve its effect?

4. Advertisements often contain language designed to reinforce the visual impact of the images they present. Why is language (aside from the one word taped over Ronald McDonald's mouth) unnecessary in this ad? Why does this one word sum up the ad's claim?

5. How might this ad contribute, or not contribute, to what a lawsuit against McDonald's—as explained in the essay by Adam Cohen on page 458—alleges as the company's blame for obesity and other health problems of those who buy the company's products? How might Ronald McDonald be perceived as a "McFrankenstein creation," as the judge in the McDonald's lawsuit dubbed Chicken McNuggets?

6. Consider one product that Ronald McDonald promotes—the breakfast sandwich of eggs, cheese, and meat known as "McGriddles." A sausage, egg, and cheese McGriddles contains 450 calories, 270 calories of which come from fat; 30 grams of fat in total, which is 40 percent of the daily value of fat; and 20 mg of cholesterol. (This information appears on the McDonald's Web site, www.mcdonalds.com.) What does this information tell you about the value and attraction of the product? Why doesn't McDonald's print this information in its advertisements?

Responding in Writing

1. In your journal, write your own spoof advertisement for a particular food product, in which you use enticing but satirical language to get people to buy it. You may use a product currently on the market or invent one.

2. Write a letter to junior high school students advising them either to buy or not buy a particular fast-food product. State the proposition clearly enough for your audience to understand, and back up your proposition with appropriate supporting details. You can research many of these products on their Web sites.

3. Write an essay in which you argue that the fast-food industry either is or is not to blame in part for the current high rate of obesity in America.

JONATHAN RAUCH
The Fat Tax: A Modest Proposal

Jonathan Rauch was born in Phoenix, Arizona, in 1960. He attended Yale University before starting his career as a reporter and writer at the Winston-Salem Journal *in North Carolina. Rauch moved to Washington in 1984 for a stint as a staff writer for* National Journal. *He has written freelance for many magazines and newspapers on political and cultural issues, and since 1991 he has worked as an openly gay writer discussing gay issues. He is the author of* The Outnation *(1992),* Kindly Inquisitors *(1993),* Demosclerosis *(1994), and* Government's End: Why Washington Stopped Working *(1999). He currently writes a biweekly column for* National Journal. *In this selection, which appeared in the* Atlantic Monthly *in 2002, Rauch proposes—seriously or not?—that the government should levy a tax on fatty food.*

I n September, McDonald's announced plans to cook its fries in health- 1
ier oil. And not a moment too soon. Just a few days later the Centers
for Disease Control and Prevention announced that in 2000 (the latest year
for which final figures are available) the death rate in America, adjusted
for the fact that the population is aging, reached an all-time low. Not only
that, but life expectancy reached an all-time high, of about seventy-seven
years. Obviously, those numbers can mean only one thing: America is in
the grip of a gigantic public-health crisis. To wit—an obesity epidemic!

That America is marching fatward seems not to be in doubt. Obesity has
risen substantially, in recent years, to 31 percent of adults, according to the 2
most recent data from the National Center for Health Statistics. Soft-drink
cups are bigger, restaurant portions are larger, and health campaigns con-
demning fatty foods have persuaded people, wrongly, that they can eat
twice as much bread as before, provided that they cut down on the butter.
Also not in doubt is that other things being equal, being blubbery is not
good. Still, one cannot help scratching one's head. If Americans are living
longer, and if they are dying less (so to speak), and if, as the CDC reports, the
proportion rating their own health as excellent or very good has remained at
a solid 69 percent for the past five years, what exactly is the problem?

Call me oversensitive, but I think I detect a hint of snobbery in the national anti-fat drive. More than occasionally I read things like a recent arti- 3
cle from the online *Bully Magazine,* which was headlined "AMERICA:
LAND OF THE FAT, DRUNKEN SLOBS." The author, one Ken Wohlrob,
writes, "We're quickly becoming a society of sloths who spend their free
hours driving around in SUVs and staring at televisions or computer mon-
itors . . . Goddamn, as if we need more fat, bloated people in America."
Do I sniff a trace of condescension here? In the September issue of *The Atlantic* a letter writer named Ken Weiss pointedly (and wrongly) mentioned
that "more than 50 percent of our population is obese" amid a list of ways
in which America is inferior to Europe, beginning with our shorter vaca-
tions, continuing through our lack of a national health plan, and ending,
inevitably, with our "polluting SUVs." It's not just that Americans are fat,
apparently. It's that Americans are the kind of people who *would* be fat, in
the kind of country that would encourage their piggishness.

4   What is to be done? The letters pages of magazines are often good places to preview the great bad ideas of tomorrow, and recently three letters in *The New Republic* offered a peek. The first, co-signed by the executive director of the Center for Science in the Public Interest and an academic nutritionist, said that the government should "slap small taxes on junk foods like soft drinks" to generate money for public-health campaigns. The next letter, from someone with the Center for the Advancement of Public Health, in Washington, D.C., said, "No one is suggesting the creation of a refrigerator police, but so long as the government is spending $360 billion per year at the federal level on health through Medicare, Medicaid, and the Children's Health Insurance Program, the government's interest in trying to prevent needless illness and death from obesity is kind of simple." The third letter came from a professor of public-interest law who wrote that he had helped to sue McDonald's for "failing to disclose the fat content of its French fries." He warned that more such suits could be on the way. "As with smoking," he wrote, "health advocates may increasingly be forced"—forced?—"to turn to the courts if legislatures continue to do little or nothing about the problem."

5   If obesity really is such a big crisis, I want to suggest a different approach, because the ones above seem deficient. For one thing, snack taxes that pay for public-health campaigns, and lawsuits against food companies, seem pretty likely to fatten the wallets of the people advocating them—public-health activists and lawyers—without necessarily making anyone any thinner. Besides, most people snack sensibly, so why should they pay to harangue lazy gluttons? And I know of no conclusive evidence that people are fat because food companies fail to disclose that fries and bacon cheeseburgers are fattening.

6   It seems to me that the only honest and effective way to confront this issue is to tax not fattening foods or fattening companies but fat people. It is they, after all, who drive up the government's health-care costs, so it is they who should pay. What I propose, then, is to tax people by the pound.

7   This needn't be very complicated. Fat-tax rates would be set by a National Avoirdupois Governing System (NAGS). To hit the worst offenders the hardest, the tax could be graduated. People would pay one per-pound rate above the "overweight" threshold, and a stiffer rate above the "obese" threshold. Fat people might not like this tax, but of course they could avoid it by becoming thinner.

8   In fact, I might go further. Carrots often work even better than sticks, so I propose a skinny subsidy to complement the fat tax. People who maintain trim, firm physiques should be rewarded for their public-spiritedness with large tax credits—funded, of course, by the fat tax.

9   My plan would address the nation's fat epidemic equitably and efficiently. It would make Americans put their money where their mouths are. And did I mention that I weigh 135 pounds?

Responding to the Essay

1. Analyze Rauch's introduction. How does it use irony to introduce the reader to the essay's rhetorical strategy? Is he successful in this or not? Explain.
2. The subtitle for Rauch's essay is "A Modest Proposal." How does this essay relate to Swift's essay of the same name? How is Rauch's argument similar to Swift's? How is it different?
3. Does Rauch's essay have coherence? Outline his essay, and explain how he uses transitions to move from one minor proposition to the next. Does his argument work? Explain your answer.
4. Does Rauch take too long getting to his "modest proposal"? Why or why not?

Responding in Writing

1. Rauch writes in paragraph 4 that "the letters pages of magazines are often good places to preview the great bad ideas of tomorrow." Look at the letters page of a major political magazine or newspaper, and read the letters about a controversial topic. Is Rauch right? What did you find? Write up your findings in several paragraphs.
2. Write a modest proposal essay in which you ironically argue for a ridiculous solution to a serious problem.
3. Rauch is being ironic about a fat tax, but the government does place taxes on things, and gives tax breaks on other things, in order to influence behavior in a way it thinks is good for the country. In small groups, investigate how the government tries to manipulate the populace through the use of creative taxation.

ROZ CHAST
Trick or Treat

New Yorker *is perhaps the last bastion among national magazine publishers in its dedication to wry, sophisticated cartoons, usually with an unmistakable urban cast. Each week, in addition to the urbane essays, stories, and sumptuous advertisements that are regular features of the publication, readers await the many pen-and-ink drawings by commentators who provide a slightly perverse mirror to human foibles. Roz Chast is one of* New Yorker's *most popular and most frequent contributors to this visual medium. In "Trick or Treat" she implies the grand contrast between expectation and fulfillment as Halloween urchins make their neighborhood visits. In addition, she offers an ironic view of America's eating habits.*

(The *New Yorker*/www.cartoonbank.com)

Responding to the Visual Text

1. Who are the characters in the cartoon? Describe them. What familiar American occasion does the cartoon mark?

2. What assumptions does Chast build on here? What major proposition does the cartoon imply?

3. Why are the neighbors offering the children broccoli and lentil salad? What's wrong with this contribution to the trick-or-treaters?

4. What do you think the children expected when they rang the doorbell? How do you think the children feel when they receive their goodies? Why does Chast not show the children's faces? If she did, what expressions do you think they would wear?

5. What is the basic argument that Chast seems to be making here? What assumptions does she build on? What major proposition does the image imply? What warrants does Chast build on?

6. How does the cartoon help explain the success of fast-food outlets like McDonald's, Baskin and Robbins, and Pizza Hut?

Responding in Writing

1. Write a paragraph or two about the relationship between the foods kids crave and the foods that are good for them.
2. Write an essay about trick-or-treating in which you either support it or condemn it. State your major proposition clearly, and provide substantive support for your argument.

MICHELE INGRASSIA
The Body of the Beholder

Michele Ingrassia has been a reporter for the local New York newspapers the Daily News *and* Newsday. *In this selection, which appeared in* Newsweek, *Ingrassia argues, based on a university study that while white girls seem to be dissatisfied with their bodies, black girls seem to like theirs.*

When you're a teenage girl, there's no place to hide. Certainly not in   1
gym class, where the shorts are short, the T shirts revealing and the adolescent critics eager to dissect every flaw. Yet out on the hardwood gym floors at Morgan Park High, a largely African-American school on Chicago's Southwest Side, the girls aren't talking about how bad their bodies are, but how good. Sure, all of them compete to see how many sit-ups they can do—Janet Jackson's washboard stomach is their model. But ask Diane Howard about weight, and the African-American senior, who carries 133 pounds on her 5-foot 7½-inch frame, says she'd happily add 15 pounds—if she could ensure they'd land on her hips. Or La'Taria Stokes, a stoutly built junior who takes it as high praise when boys remark, "Your hips are screaming for twins!" "I know I'm fat," La'Taria says. "I don't care."

In a society that worships at the altar of supermodels like Claudia,   2
Christy and Kate, white teenagers are obsessed with staying thin. But there's growing evidence that black and white girls view their bodies in dramatically different ways. The latest findings come in a study to be published in the journal *Human Organization* this spring by a team of black and white researchers at the University of Arizona. While 90 percent of the white junior-high and high-school girls studied voiced dissatisfaction with their weight, 70 percent of African-American teens were satisfied with their bodies.

In fact, even significantly overweight black teens described them-   3
selves as happy. That confidence may not carry over to other areas of

black teens' lives, but the study suggests that, at least here, it's a life-long source of pride. Asked to describe women as they age, two thirds of the black teens said they get more beautiful, and many cited their mothers as examples. White girls responded that their mothers may have been beautiful—back in their youth. Says anthropologist Mimi Nichter, one of the study's coauthors, "In white culture, the window of beauty is so small."

4   What is beauty? White teens defined perfection as 5 feet 7 and 100 to 110 pounds—superwaif Kate Moss's vital stats. African-American girls described the perfect size in more attainable terms—full hips, thick thighs, the sort of proportions about which Hammer ("Pumps and a Bump") and Sir Mix-Alot ("Baby Got Back") rap poetic. But they said that true beauty—"looking good"—is about more than size. Almost two thirds of the black teens defined beauty as "the right attitude."

5   The disparity in body images isn't just in kids' heads. It's reflected in fashion magazines, in ads, and it's out there, on TV, every Thursday night. On NBC, the sitcom "Friends" stars Courteney Cox, Jennifer Aniston and Lisa Kudrow, all of them white and twentysomething, classically beautiful and reed thin. Meanwhile, Fox Television's "Living Single," aimed at an African-American audience, projects a less Hollywood ideal—its stars are four twentysomething black women whose bodies are, well, *real*. Especially the big-boned, bronze-haired rapper Queen Latifah, whose size only adds to her magnetism. During a break at the Lite Nites program at the Harlem YMCA, over the squeal of sneakers on the basketball court, Brandy Wood, 14, describes Queen Latifah's appeal: "What I like about her is the way she wears her hair and the color in it and the clothes she wears."

6   Underlying the beauty gap are 200 years of cultural differences. "In white, middle-class America, part of the great American Dream of making it is to be able to make yourself over," says Nichter. "In the black community, there is the reality that you might not move up the ladder as easily. As one girl put it, you have to be realistic—if you think negatively about yourself, you won't get anywhere." It's no accident that Barbie has long embodied a white-adolescent ideal—in the early days, she came with her own scale (set at 110) and her own diet guide ("How to Lose Weight: Don't Eat"). Even in this postfeminist era, Barbie's tight-is-right message is stronger than ever. Before kindergarten, researchers say, white girls know that Daddy eats and Mommy diets. By high school, many have split the world into physical haves and have-nots, rivals across the beauty line. "It's not that you hate them [perfect girls]," says Sarah Immel, a junior at Evanston Township High School north of Chicago. "It's that you're kind of jealous that they have it so easy, that they're so perfect-looking."

7   In the black community, size isn't debated, it's taken for granted—a sign, some say, that after decades of preaching black-is-beautiful, black parents and educators have gotten across the message of self-respect. In-

deed, black teens grow up equating a full figure with health and fertility. Black women's magazines tend to tout NOT TRYING TO BE SIZE 8, not TEN TIPS FOR THIN THIGHS. And even girls who fit the white ideal aren't necessarily comfortable there. Supermodel Tyra Banks recalls how, in high school in Los Angeles, she was the envy of her white girlfriends. "They would tell me, 'Oh, Tyra, you look so good'," says Banks. "But I was like, 'I want a booty and thighs like my black girl-friends'."

Men send some of the strongest signals. What's fat? "You got to be   8
real fat for me to notice," says Muhammad Latif, a Harlem 15-year-old. White girls follow what they *think* guys want, whether guys want it or not. Sprawled across the well-worn sofas and hard-back chairs of the student lounge, boys at Evanston High scoff at the girls' idealization of Kate Moss. "Sickly," they say, "gross." Sixteen-year-old Trevis Milton, a blond swimmer, has no interest in dating Kate wanna-bes. "I don't want to feel like I'm going to break them." Here, perfection is a hardbody, like Linda Hamilton in "Terminator II." "It's not so much about eating broccoli and water as running," says senior Kevin Mack.

And if hardbodies are hot, girls often need to diet to achieve them,   9
too. According to the Arizona study, which was funded by the National Institute of Child Health and Human Development, 62 percent of the white girls reported dieting at least once in the past year. Even those who say they'd rather be fit than thin get caught up. Sarah Martin, 16, a junior at Evanston, confesses she's tried forcing herself to throw up but couldn't. She's still frustrated: "I have a big appetite, and I feel so guilty when I eat."

Black teens don't usually go to such extremes. Anorexia and bulimia   10
are relatively minor problems among African-American girls. And though 51 percent of the black teens in the study said they'd dieted in the last year, follow-up interviews showed that far fewer were on sustained weight-and-exercise programs. Indeed, 64 percent of the black girls thought it was better to be "a little" overweight than underweight. And while they agreed that "very overweight" girls should diet, they defined that as someone who "takes up two seats on the bus."

The black image of beauty may seem saner, but it's not necessarily   11
healthy. Black women don't obsess on size, but they do worry about other white cultural ideals that black men value. "We look at Heather Locklear and see the long hair and the fair, pure skin," says *Essence* magazine senior editor Pamela Johnson. More troubling, the acceptance of fat means many girls ignore the real dangers of obesity. Dieting costs money—even if it's not a fancy commercial program; fruits, vegetables and lean meats are pricier than high-fat foods. Exercise? Only one state—Illinois—requires daily physical education for every kid. Anyway, as black teenagers complain, exercise can ruin your hair—and, if you're plunking down $35 a week at the hairdresser, you don't want to sweat out your 'do in the gym. "I don't think we should obsess about

weight and fitness, but there is a middle ground," says the well-toned black actress Jada Pinkett. Maybe that's where Queen Latifah meets Kate Moss.

Responding to the Essay

1. Who is Ingrassia's audience, in your opinion? What is her tone, and how does her audience affect the tone? Explain your answers.
2. Analyze how Ingrassia uses contrast analysis to make her argument. Is she successful? Explain.
3. Do you agree with Ingrassia's conclusions? If so, what is the one element that makes her argument so persuasive? If not, what keeps you from agreeing with her?
4. Does Ingrassia end her essay on a satisfying note? Why or why not?

Responding in Writing

1. In groups, listen to the song "Baby Got Back" by Sir Mix-A-Lot, and read along with the lyrics, which you can find on the Internet. Discuss the lyrics as an illustration of what Ingrassia argues for in her essay. How do the lyrics contribute to a healthy body image, and how do they hurt? When you are finished, reconvene as a class and discuss your responses.
2. Write an essay in which you argue that it is not a good thing to be satisfied with a body image that allows young people to be overweight.
3. Write an essay in which you explore the body images of two other classes of people. Instead of black and white girls, what about black and white boys, or men? How do Japanese women feel about their bodies as opposed to Chinese women? Do West Indian women feel differently from African-American women?

Jay Walljasper
The Joy of Eating

This selection appeared in the 2002 issue of the Utne Reader, *where Walljasper is the editor at large. In it he explores the paradox that being responsible and paying attention to food can take the fun out of eating, but he argues that it doesn't have to be the case.*

1   One of the great joys for my wife, Julie, and me is watching our 7-year-old eat. He approaches a plate of food with something like awe. A smile breaks across his face and questions fly across the kitchen: What's this called? How do you cook that? Why are those potatoes yellow and

not brown? If he senses we're not looking, he will surreptitiously grab a handful of vegetables or noodles to explore their texture and temperature.

Soren happily chows down with no thought of calories, carcinogens,   2
grocery bills, fat grams, E. coli, or genetically modified ingredients. His only real concerns at the dinner table are that something may be too spicy or, even more tragically, that we might have forgotten dessert.

Dining with Soren offers a glimpse of Eden, remembrance of a time   3
when we assumed that everything on our fork was wholesome. This has always been childhood's state of grace, and it was shared by most American adults until sometime in the 1970s. It may have been cyclamates, a carcinogen lurking in every can of diet cola until the FDA banned it. Or the publication of Frances Moore Lappe's Diet for a Small Planet, which indicted meat-eating as a waste of valuable food resources that heightens world hunger. Or maybe it was just our collective belly expanding a little more every year. But over the past three decades, Americans have become ever more wary of what they eat. Now we talk about cheesecake and pork chops in hushed tones once reserved for oral sex and hashish.

The simple act of breaking bread has become a complicated matter of   4
personal health, humanitarian concern, political commitment, and public safety. That's one reason it's so much fun to watch Soren eat. For him, food is about tasting good and filling up, not a thrice-daily symposium on medical and moral issues. It's not surprising that many Americans are sick and tired of thinking about everything they put in their mouths. "Damn the tofu and oatmeal and skim milk," they declare, "I'm going to enjoy a double bacon cheeseburger with extra mayo, a supersize order of fries, and a bucket of Coke." Burp!

And we can see the results all around us—in rural landscapes over-   5
run by factory farms, in food and water laced with chemicals, in the cardiac unit and cancer ward of a hospital near you.

Like it or not, what we eat has consequences for us and for the world.   6
Dinner is not something that just magically appears on our plates. In ordering a burger or making a salad, we are inextricably linked to the land, cycles of rain and sunshine, farmers and farmworkers, compost or chemicals, processing facilities and slaughterhouses, truck drivers and miles of highway, co-ops or corporations, and a whole web of ecological and human activity.

"You are what you eat. We all know that old motto," notes Mark   7
Ritchie, a longtime food activist who is president of the Minneapolis-based Institute for Agriculture and Trade Policy. "But now we know that what you eat dramatically affects the well-being of many others—human, animal and otherwise."

The system that delivers food to our table is far different from the   8
days when Farmer Brown trucked his sweet corn, pears, and eggs to town. It's changed radically over the past 25 years as family farms have been displaced by huge operations that depend on intensive chemical

use, minimum-wage workers, and industrial facilities such as animal confinement buildings. This same period has also seen the rise of the natural food business, offering us healthier and more environmentally sustainable alternatives to practically everything in the supermarket aisles.

9   "Eating is the most intimate relationship we have with the environment," explains Andrew Kimbrell, executive director of the Washington-based Center for Food Safety, which coordinates the Organic & Beyond campaign, and the editor of a compelling new book, *Fatal Harvest: The Tragedy of Industrial Agriculture* (Island Press, 2002). "Three times a day, it's how we can re-create the world. We can shape a different future for our children, for farmworkers, the landscape, wildlife, villages around the world, and genetic diversity."

10   "We all want to do the responsible thing," Kimbrell continues. "Who wants to be cruel to animals and poison the soil? But what's great is that being responsible also means better health and better-tasting food you can enjoy with a greater sense of joy."

11   The joy of eating! That's what everyone seeks at mealtime. Soren exudes it every time he tears into a a platter of pancakes. Joy is the much-advertised promise hawked by fast food chains and frozen dinner manufacturers. And it's the point of the obligatory picnic scene in almost every foreign movie and food magazine: a long table under a canopy of trees, laden with fresh-from-the-garden delights and plentiful wine, surrounded by several generations of smiling people engaged in robust conversation.

12   Cooking and eating good food are the cornerstones of human civilization, our daily reward for all the hard work and innumerable difficulties of life. I have a favorite story that I've heard quoted numerous times. There was once an extensive study of National Merit Scholars to find the common denominator in these bright kids' upbringing. Turns out it wasn't household income, private schools, parents' educational levels, or wealthy neighborhoods. It was families who ate their meals together.

13   Just as the American farm has been transformed in recent years, so has dinnertime. Joy is out of the picture in many (if not most) households, where time-pressed people wolf down microwaved dinners or swing through drive-up windows. Breaking bread has become refueling, and it's often a solitary activity since everyone around the house is ruled by a hectic schedule. No wonder we cherish movies like Chocolat, Babette's Feast, and Like Water for Chocolate, and that corporations pour millions into ads artistically trying to convince us that Velveeta and Kentucky Fried Chicken are pure, unadulterated fun. The joy of eating has, in many ways, become a vicarious thrill.

14   That's the real reason—not warnings from killjoy nutritionists and activists—that mealtime now feels unsatisfying to so many of us. Though we're loading up on calories, we are starved for ritual and leisure and pleasure. Thinking too much about what we eat is not what robs us of

happy meals, but rather putting too little thought into the important role that food plays in our lives and in the wider world.

Don't despair (or head to Taco Bell to drown your sorrows in baja   15
sauce), there's also good news from food's frontlines. In the same way the natural food business sprouted as an alternative to industrialized agriculture and junk food, a new movement has arisen to put the joy back into eating. Beginning with Alice Waters' Chez Panisse restaurant in Berkeley, which, inspired by peasant food traditions around the world, put a premium on fresh, local ingredients, there's been a growing appreciation for authentic, healthy food. The newfound popularity of regional cuisine, the growth of farmers' markets and community-supported agriculture (CSAs), and the happy emergence (or in some cases re-emergence) of microbrew beers, artisan cheeses, traditional breads, all-natural meats, and heirloom fruits and vegetables amount to a culinary revolution.

While the quest for tastier food is what drives these trends, they   16
square with most environmental and ethical concerns. Fresh organic produce from local farmers not only improves a meal, it prevents pollution, saves fuel, and boosts your local economy. Dairy and meat from free-ranging animals that have not been force-fed antibiotics are both tastier and healthier. (There is no ethical consensus, however, on using animals for food. Vegetarians and vegans argue that killing animals is cruel no matter how humanely they were raised, while meat eaters note that carnivorism is a fact of nature and that manure from livestock is essential in most methods of organic farming.)

The organic label has now become familiar to us, but Jim Slama, pres-   17
ident of Sustain, a Chicago-based environmental advocacy organization, says that's just the beginning. Slama envisions a time when you will be able to know the story of what happened to food on its way to your plate. Beyond the organic label ensuring that your food was raised without chemicals, irradiation, genetically modified ingredients, or toxic sludge, a "fair trade" label will certify that the people producing it were treated and paid well, and a "regional" label will let you know where it comes from. Sustain has launched an organic local foods initiative in Chicago. This is also the theme of the Organic & Beyond campaign (www.organic andbeyond.org), a coalition of grassroots groups that includes Sustain.

While some folks might view such a project as more reasons to feel   18
guilty over lunch, it actually offers the chance for a richer connection with our food, a way to put meaning back into our meals. Sure, you probably don't want to know the story behind a serving of factory farm meat: an animal stuffed into a tiny cage, living in its own excrement (which is then flushed into a stream), pumped with antibiotics, slaughtered by a poorly paid worker in a factory notorious for on-the-job injuries, doused in a chemical bath, and then shipped to a faraway supermarket or fast-food joint. Maybe you don't want to know about all this, but it will affect your health, your environment, and the social fabric of your country.

19   But what if that animal was raised on a farm in your region, perhaps by Farmer Brown's great-granddaughter, and you could see it from the highway grazing in a pasture instead of the ugly confinement buildings that now dot the countryside? And what if your milk and butter came from a small organic co-op, and a lot of your vegetables from the backyard or an old gardener named Tony (or Rosita or Mr. Nguyen), with whom you talk about baseball and the weather every Saturday at the Farmers' Market? Would you feel different cooking it and eating it? Would you mind paying a little more for it, knowing that it was good for you and good for other people too?

20   Soren remains the joy-of-eating authority around our house. Although he doesn't labor over the ethical dimension of every bite he takes (the direct link between the cute piglets he plays with at his cousin Leah's farm and the beloved corn dogs he orders at his favorite neighborhood grill is still hazy for him), he does like to know the story behind his food. We found this out last year when we joined a new CSA run by friends, Don and Joni. Every week all summer we'd get a heaping box of greens, herbs, peppers, and vegetables along with organic eggs Don and Joni brought from one of their country neighbors. On Labor Day, we drove out to the farm to help with the harvest. Julie and I volunteered to weed the tomato patch while Soren was pressed into service picking vegetables. After a while, he ran over dragging a heavy pail. "Mommy, Daddy, look at these cucumbers," he sang, holding one above his head as if it were a championship trophy. "I picked them myself!"

21   And for the next week, Soren jubilantly ate cucumbers at every meal, including breakfast.

Responding to the Essay

1. What is Walljasper's major proposition in this essay? Where is it located? Is it in an effective place? Why or why not? Why does Walljasper place his major proposition where he does?

2. What is the rhetorical effect of Walljasper's discussion of his son Soren? Is it a strength of the paper or a weakness? Explain your answer.

3. Take a look at the transitions in this paper. Find instances where the transitions are weak. Where are they, and how would you change them?

4. Analyze Walljasper's argument in paragraphs 18 and 19. Do you think it is effective or not? Explain.

5. Do you think Walljasper's essay is realistic, or is he being overly sentimental and idealistic? Defend your answer.

Responding in Writing

1. Read a chapter from Eric Schlosser's book *Fast Food Nation*. Write about how your chosen selection from Schlosser's book illustrates Walljasper's claims.
2. How easy is it to find socially responsible ways of eating in your neighborhood? Are they difficult to find? In groups, answer these questions, and come up with ways to tip the balance in favor of the socially responsible.
3. Write an essay called "The Joy of . . ." Argue for a different point of view of a common activity, such as sleeping or travel.

Weight Loss Guide

The Internet has innumerable sites dedicated to dietary programs and ways to take off weight rapidly though a variety of methods, including food plans, exercise regimens, and diet supplements. This Web site (see the following pages) is one example of the options made available to the American public eager to address the struggle with weight gain that is so much a part of the national obsession with food, calories, diets, and obesity.

Responding to the Visual Text

1. How do you "read" this advertisement? What details hold your attention? How do written and visual texts combine to create the persuasive appeal of this Internet ad?
2. Explain the ways in which this ad touches on people's values, attitudes, fears, and aspirations. What social and cultural codes of meaning underlie the design?
3. What is the effect of including multiple links to other sites in this advertisement?
4. Why does Emma Classen personalize the message? How effective is this strategy, and why?

Responding in Writing

1. Write a complete analysis of this Internet advertisement. Explain how the various details and visual elements create a message that might appeal to a viewer who, after all, is a prospective buyer.
2. Search online for other diet advertisements. Download your favorite ad, and attach it to an essay explaining why you find it effective.

Hi! I'm Emma Classen. Over the years I've helped thousands of people just like you lose thousands of unwanted pounds—and keep them off...including many who felt it was utterly impossible. I want to be YOUR Guide...to show you how you too can get that smashing, sexy, new body you envision - without risk to your health. Please read my story

Your Guide - Emma Classen

read my story

The Multi-Purpose Metabolic Marvel

Eat Less - Burn More Fat - Lose Weight - Automatically!

The guiding principle behind weight reduction is for everyone to reduce their caloric intake and do a little exercise. Right? Well, why as a society we're not all thin and perfectly shaped? Because we can't keep our appetites in check. No matter how hard we try we just can't stop eating.

It is this key factor that is most responsible for the growing popularity and phenomenal success of the new "fat-melting pill" that works better than risky prescription drugs to subdue your appetite, invigorate your mind-body-and-spirit, and transform your mood from crappy to happy.

MeltRx 24 Ultra™—It's not magic, it's Science

This smart, ephedra-free, "fast-slimming pill" that achieves remarkable feats without use of caffeine or harmful stimulants is called MeltRx 24 Ultra™. With its special blend of natural herbs formulated in an expensive and exacting procedure it has accomplished the unthinkable. Worried about living without your favorite foods? Don't. Imagine MeltRx 24 Ultra™ as the brakes on your car you need to prevent unwanted mishaps.

When you take MeltRx 24 Ultra™ it literally flips your hunger switch on demand so you feel turned off by food and just don't want to eat. You reduce calories and you slim down automatically. Besides, MeltRx 24 Ultra™ creates a separate afterburner-like effect that fires-up your fat-burning engine causing significant, undeniable weight loss! The result -- you liberate yourself from obsessing over food, you supercharge and prolong your body's natural fat burning capabilities, and you lose weight without dieting or counting calories. What's more, the vast majority of users not only lose weight, but report they look younger, have improved drive and concentration, and become free of stress and anxiety. Don't believe it? Well... published scientific studies don't lie.

Groundbreaking Studies Prove The Phenomenal Success

Results never before seen in the diet supplement industry. In several recent double-blind studies (the only proof accepted by the established scientific community) several MeltRx 24 Ultra™ key ingredients were put to the test. People who took each and every one of the key ingredients in MeltRx 24 Ultra™ lost significant weight. Those who didn't lost absolutely nothing. The primary difference between losing weight and staying fat were the new cutting-edge ingredients in MeltRx 24 Ultra™. What's more, those who continued taking them kept the weight off for more than 12 months with no bounce-back rebound weight gain and no effort. This means, No more guessing! No more wasting your valuable time!

How Does MeltRx 24 Ultra™ Work? (Incredible energy • Fast weight loss • No ephedrine • No caffeine)

While still not entirely clear, researchers say the behavior-controlling chemicals governing appetite, mood and weight loss interact in complex patterns of stimulation and inhibition sometimes leading to discomfort, craving, anxiety and impaired fat burning capability. However, if you ask the thousands upon thousands of overweight men and women who have already used MeltRx 24 Ultra, you get a crystal-clear, straight-forward answer. "Take MeltRx 24 Ultra™ twice daily and you lose weight because you automatically eat less, burn fat, and marshal incredible energy throughout the entire day." It's that simple.

✓ **Risk-Free, Introductory Offer**

By reading my Newsletter and accepting me as your Guide you've shown that you trust me. And believe me, I take that trust very seriously. Above all, I want the products and supplements I recommend to work for you. But the only way I can be sure you'll try them and discover their benefits is if there is absolutely no risk to you. That's what my "Ultimate Guarantee" is all about: Your 100% satisfaction. Think of it as a contract, a handshake between us that binds my reputation as a Guide to your weight loss success. It's just my way of saying: "I'm sure this product is safe and effective, and that it will help you.

So order new MeltRx 24 Ultra™ fat-melting pills today and take advantage of my risk-free, introductory offer. Simply stated, if you use MeltRx 24 Ultra™ fat-melting pills and do not experience the same fast, significant, effortless weight loss experienced by thousands of delighted users, just return the empty bottle within 30 days for a full, prompt, no-questions-asked refund.

Remember, MeltRx 24 Ultra™ is guaranteed to work for you or it costs you absolutely nothing! Finally, it's your chance to get everything you ever wanted out of a diet pill -- fast reliable weight loss, incredible energy, a blissful contented mood, a lean ultra-firm body, and the magnetic self-confidence you've always wanted. Get fast acting MeltRx 24 Ultra™ "Super Pills" today. You will not be disappointed - I guarantee it.

All the best,

Emma Classen -- Guide & Editor
Weight Loss Guide.Com

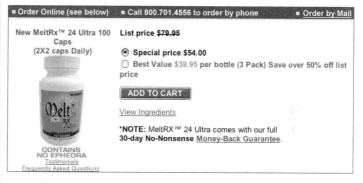

P.S. Benefits of MeltRx 24 Ultra (3 in 1) fat burner: appetite suppressant • energizer • mood enhancer •

- Puts you in the driver's seat -- New MeltRx 24 Ultra™ flips your hunger switch on demand so you just don't want to eat. Result - caloric intake is reduced... fat disappears automatically.
- Fires-up your fat-burning engine (without ephedra) causing significant, undeniable weight loss!
- Accomplishes the unthinkable -- burn fat, subdue appetite & alleviate stress all at once!
- Made in America according to strict FDA guidelines
- Gives you incredible energy. Transforms your mood from crappy to happy!

■ Order Online (see below) ■ Call 800.701.4556 to order by phone ■ Order by Mail

New MeltRx™ 24 Ultra 100 Caps
(2X2 caps Daily)

CONTAINS
NO EPHEDRA
Testimonials
Frequently Asked Questions

List price $79.95

◉ **Special price $54.00**
○ **Best Value $39.95 per bottle (3 Pack) Save over 50% off list price**

ADD TO CART

View Ingredients

*NOTE: MeltRX™ 24 Ultra comes with our full **30-day No-Nonsense** Money-Back Guarantee.

consider this -
The best way to get something done...is to begin!

ELLEN GOODMAN
The Culture of Thin Bites Fiji

Ellen Goodman is a Pulitzer Prize–winning editor and journalist who started out as a researcher at Newsweek. *She has written a column at* The Boston Globe *for many years. She is the author of* Turning Points *(1979) and of several collections of her columns, including* Keeping in Touch *(1985),* Making Sense *(1989), and* Value Judgments *(1993). In this selection from her column, Goodman argues that "going thin" is a cultural phenomenon.*

1   First of all, imagine a place women greet one another at the market with open arms, loving smiles, and a cheerful exchange of ritual compliments:

2   "You look wonderful! You've put on weight!"

3   Does that sound like dialogue from Fat Fantasyland? Or a skit from fat-is-a-feminist-issue satire? Well, this Western fantasy was a South Pacific fact of life. In Fiji, before 1995, big was beautiful and bigger was more beautiful—and people really did flatter one another with exclamations about weight gain.

4   In this island paradise, food was not only love, it was a cultural imperative. Eating and overeating were rites of mutual hospitality. Everyone worried about losing weight—but not the way we do. "Going thin" was considered to be a sign of some social problem, a worrisome indication the person wasn't getting enough to eat.

5   The Fijians were, to be sure, a bit obsessed with food; they prescribed herbs to stimulate the appetite. They were a reverse image of our culture. And that turns out to be the point.

6   Something happened in 1995. A Western mirror was shoved into the face of the Fijians. Television came to the island. Suddenly, the girls of rural coastal villages were watching the girls of "Melrose Place" and "Beverly Hills 90210," not to mention "Seinfeld" and "E.R."

7   Within 38 months, the number of teenagers at risk for eating disorders more than doubled to 29 percent. The number of high school girls who vomited for weight control went up five times to 15 percent. Worse yet, 74 percent of the Fiji teens in the study said they felt "too big or fat" at least some of the time and 62 percent said they had dieted in the past month.

8   This before-and-after television portrait of a body image takeover was drawn by Anne Becker, an anthropologist and psychiatrist who directs research at the Harvard Eating Disorders Center. She presented her research at the American Psychiatric Association last week with all the usual caveats. No, you cannot prove a direct causal link between television and eating disorders. Heather Locklear doesn't cause anorexia. Nor does Tori Spelling cause bulimia.

Calista Flockhart at the Screen Actors Guild
Awards, Boston Globe.

Fiji is not just a Fat Paradise Lost. It's an economy in transition from   9
subsistence agriculture to tourism and its entry into the global economy
has threatened many old values.

Nevertheless, you don't get a much better lab experiment than this. 10
In just 38 months, and with only one channel, a television-free culture
that defined a fat person as robust has become a television culture that
sees robust as, well, repulsive.

All that and these islanders didn't even get "Ally McBeal."   11

"Going thin" is no longer a social disease but the perceived requirement 12
for getting a good job, nice clothes, and fancy cars. As Becker says carefully,
"The acute and constant bombardment of certain images in the media are
apparently quite influential in how teens experience their bodies."

Speaking of Fiji teenagers in a way that sounds all-too familiar, she 13
adds, "We have a set of vulnerable teens consuming television. There's a
huge disparity between what they see on television and what they look
like themselves—that goes not only to clothing, hairstyles, and skin color,
but size of bodies."

14 In short, the sum of Western culture, the big success story of our entertainment industry, is our ability to export insecurity: We can make any woman anywhere feel perfectly rotten about her shape. At this rate, we owe the islanders at least one year of the ample lawyer Camryn Manheim in "The Practice" for free.

15 I'm not surprised by research showing that eating disorders are a cultural byproduct. We've watched the female image shrink down to Calista Flockhart at the same time we've seen eating problems grow. But Hollywood hasn't been exactly eager to acknowledge the connection between image and illness.

16 Over the past few weeks since the Columbine High massacre, we've broken through some denial about violence as a teaching tool. It's pretty clear that boys are literally learning how to hate and harm others.

17 Maybe we ought to worry a little more about what girls learn: To hate and harm themselves.

Responding to the Essay

1. Do you think Goodman's title matches this essay? Why or why not? Think of two alternate titles.
2. How does Goodman use contrast analysis in her essay, and is it effectively done? Explain your answers.
3. Trace Goodman's reasoning throughout the essay? How does she build toward the end?
4. Why does Goodman include paragraph 9? What purpose does it serve in the argument?
5. What is the rhetorical effect of Goodman's mention of the Columbine massacre? Do you see it as a weakness or a strength in her argument? Explain.

Responding in Writing

1. Write an essay in which you take issue with Goodman's conclusions, arguing that it's a good thing that Fijians are concerned about their weight.
2. Find some women's magazines from 1999 (the year this essay was published) in the library and some from today. What conclusions can you draw about how the image of women has changed in such a short time?
3. In small groups, discuss what social problems other than teenage violence and obesity one could blame on the influence of television. Write down notes on your discussion, and present your conclusions to the class.

Dawn Mackeen
Waifs on the Web

Dawn Mackeen has been an editor at online magazine Salon, *an on-air re-porter for a television station in Madison, Wisconsin, a guidebook writer for* Fodor's/The Berkeley Guides, *and is now a staff writer for Long Island, New York, newspaper* Newsday. *She was a Pew International Journalism Fellow in 2002. In this selection from* Teen People, *Mackeen writes about an online subculture of young women with dangerous eating disorders.*

For three days last December, Abbey, 18, subsisted mostly on water. When hunger pangs began to plague her, she simply gulped a little more liquid. Although the 5'6", 115-pound college freshman from Plano, Texas, was achieving her goal—to lose weight as quickly as possible—her body was clearly suffering. On the third day, Abbey (who didn't want her full name used) lay awake in the middle of the night panting uncontrollably, her heart racing. Concerned about what was happening to her, she turned to an online support group. Maybe what she was feeling was normal. This was, after all, the first time she had ever tried starving herself.

"I can't see straight, I can't really hear well, and worst of all, I can't catch my breath," she posted on the Pro-Eating Disorder Society's Web site at around midnight. "Has anyone ever experienced these effects, and will they go away?"

The response came hours later. "Yeah, I get that sometimes when I've been fasting," wrote someone seemingly well-versed in hunger. "The best thing to do is eat an apple, drink a glass of water and go to sleep. Your body is a little exhausted, that's all." Reassured, Abbey never sought medical attention, nor did she tell anyone else about her scare. "The apple comment made me feel like someone had an answer," she says.

What Abbey didn't know is that her body was more than just "a little exhausted." In someone who is fasting, a speeding heart can be a sign of real danger: Severe fasting and dehydration can cause abnormal heart patterns and even cardiac arrest, a condition responsible for many of the anorexia-related deaths each year. Abbey's body was telling her it was in trouble, but her online cheerleaders were telling her she was doing fine—and that's who Abbey believed.

It's this dynamic that has eating-disorder experts worried about the recent popularity of secretive, girl-run "thinspirational" Web sites and e-groups with names like Voice of Anorexia, Anorexic Nation and the Pro-Eating Disorder Society. Catering to "Anas" (after America's estimated 8 million who suffer from anorexia and other eating disorders), the sites are havens where girls cybergather to hash out their problems or listen in on discussions about body obsessions and the best ways to avoid prying family members. "What I do to hide it . . . is complain about my teeth being too sore [because of my braces]," writes Sally The Veggie Stick when asked how she disguises the disease from her mother. "Hi, I'm new to the list," chimes in one participant in the e-group Never Thin Enough. "I am almost 5'10" and I weigh 115. Of course . . . my goal is to weigh around 88."

6   From there, it's on to discussions of how well laxatives and over-the-counter weight-loss supplements work, sign-ups for group fasts, advice on how to curb hunger (one poster recommends looking at photos of dead, bloody animals) and tips such as eating cotton sprinkled with salt instead of food. In one posting a girl details her exercise schedule for the day—aerobics at 9 A.M., Pilates at 10 A.M. and running in the evening—and urges others to work as hard. Many sites also post something called the Anorexic Creed: ". . . I believe in calorie counters as the inspired word of God and memorize them accordingly. I believe in bathroom scales as an indicator of my daily successes and failures . . ."

7   "With the pro-anorexia sites, you don't feel like people are going to be judging you," says Liz, a high school senior from Oak Park, Ill. "There are people who just want to lose weight, and there are people who want to be underweight. But everyone is supported in reaching their goal." Liz admits she used to frequent anorexia-recovery sites but left because she felt pressured to, well, recover.

8   It's no wonder, then, that therapists, doctors and activists are worried, and some suspect that these sites are increasing the incidence of eating disorders. (Abbey, for example, had never fasted before, but after hearing about the dangers of such sites on *The Oprah Winfrey Show*, she went searching for them. Now she logs on every day and wants to shed 15 pounds to get down to 100.) As a result, after media reports and the National Association of Anorexia Nervosa and Associated Disorders (ANAD) outed the sites last summer, ANAD asked Yahoo to review them. According to a Yahoo spokesman, many of the sites violated the company's online rules of conduct and were removed.

9   More determined than ever to protect their private communities, the Anas responded by going underground, hiding their discussions under headings such as "duct tape" or "allergy" and deleting the word "Ana" from their site descriptions so that search engines cannot easily find them. To weed out curious interlopers, some sites now use entry questionnaires, cherry-picking members who are serious about starvation. Any visitors to the sites who disagree with the Ana philosophy aren't welcome. "Everyone deserves a place where they can feel safe and accepted," wrote a 14-year-old on the Yahoo e-group Anabeauty. "We do not want you ruining what is for many of us the only place we can feel comfortable. This is a sanctuary. Would you go into a church and speak against God? Get the hell out of our place of worship."

"[The sites] make me feel pretty helpless," admits Daniel le Grange, 10
Ph.D., director of the University of Chicago's Eating Disorders Program,
adding that their covert nature "just reinforces the secretive tendency of
anorexics," leaving therapists and doctors at a loss to help patients they
can't even find, let alone talk to.

Consequently, the burden of spreading the scary truth has fallen to 11
recovering anorexics like Ashley Jaros, 17, who has made it her mission
to alert the pro-Anas to the dangers of the disease. "It makes me so furious," says the Redding, Calif., native. "If people try fasting, they will
get sucked in. I was never fat to begin with. It was, 'I'll just lose a little
weight.' Then I kept going down." At the depths of her illness, Ashley,
who is 5′9″, weighed just 93 pounds. She stopped menstruating, became
suicidal and was hospitalized for a month. Ashley is thankful she didn't
know about the sites when she was anorexic—everything she did to
lose weight she thought of on her own—and wonders if access to more
dangerous diet tricks would have kept her from recovering, or even led
to her death. "With anorexia, your everyday life is taken away from
you," she says.

Abbey in Texas knows that anorexia is taking over her life and that she's 12
on the verge of a serious illness. Unfortunately, knowing that doesn't necessarily mean stopping the behavior. She still turns to the Anas for advice, but
unlike others on the sites who chat like old friends, she makes no pretense
about the kinds of relationships she is forming there. "I've met some nice
girls, but they're not my friends," Abbey says. "These people are helping
me starve. I was talking to this one girl and I said something like, 'It's weird
that we're basically helping each other starve'. She was like, 'Yeah, I know.'
They call it fasting and they use all these PC terms, but it's really starving."

Responding to the Essay

1. What is Mackeen's major proposition? Does she explicitly state it?
   Why or why not, and how does your answer have to do with Mackeen's projected audience?
2. How does Mackeen use quotes to help her argument? Explain your
   answer fully.
3. Explain how Mackeen uses shocking facts and images. Does this help
   or harm her argument? Explain.
4. What is the rhetorical effect of Mackeen's conclusion? How does it
   achieve that effect?

Responding in Writing

1. Parents used to tell their children who did not want to eat a particular
   food that they were lucky to have enough to eat because there were

children starving elsewhere. Write an essay in the form of an open letter to the users of pro-anorexia Web sites. Argue against them strictly from an ethical standpoint.

2. Why are boys not mentioned at all in this essay? Are they susceptible to anorexia? Why or why not? Do you think that is liable to change? Write several paragraphs on these questions.

3. In groups of four or five classmates, go online and find one of the pro-anorexia Web sites or e-groups. Make a list of disturbing details you did not find in Mackeen's essay, and present them to your class.

Ideas for Writing

These suggestions may help you write an argumentative essay about America's eating habits. Feel free to draw on any of the selections in the casebook to back up your propositions, claims, and warrants. Also, examine the research paper at the end of the appendix to see how one student integrated essential research strategies into an argumentative paper on eating habits.

1. Write an essay in which you argue from one side or the other about the fast-food impact on American society. In other words, do you think that the fast-food industry does more good than bad or more bad than good?

2. Write an argumentative essay about weight-loss programs. Research some of the current popular plans. Then identify what's wrong with many of them, and support a plan that you think makes most sense.

3. Write an essay on how the media is responsible for the contrast between America's eating habits and the way we feel about how we look as a result of our eating habits.

4. Defend or challenge the assumption underlying some of the essays in the casebook—that many eating disorders are "cultural byproducts."

5. Argue for or against the claim made by Brownlee, Cohen, and Zinczenko that fast-food outlets deliberately encourage consumers to buy and eat more, thereby contributing to the obesity and poor health of Americans.

6. Examine Jay Walljasper's argument that there was an Edenic time when "the joy of eating" permeated American culture. Do we still engage in the joy of eating, or is this joy lost to us in our fixation on the unlikely combination of quick meals, snacking, exercise, and weight loss? Is the joy of eating a valuable asset in American life? Write an argumentative essay in which you address some of these points and questions.

7. Overeating has spread from the people in our society to their pets. Do some research on the Internet and in your library, and write an argumentative essay about the way we feed domestic animals and its implications on the weight and health of the pets in our care.

8. Obesity and the struggle to combat it have stimulated a number of radical measures designed to help the seriously overweight to shed pounds. Some of these measures have dubious value (and are downright dangerous), whereas others offer hope and results. Write an argumentative essay about one or several of these extreme measures, and explain the value or dangers inherent in their use. Take a stand on whether radical measures are called for.

9. Very thin people have a reverse problem: they often cannot gain enough weight to sustain good health or good appearance. Write an essay in which you argue about the problems facing the underweight. Do they have real problems? Are their problems serious? How can really thin people address their health needs and their appearance?

10. Do research on societies in which being thin is not valued. Write an argumentative essay to support or challenge cultures that do not revere thinness as an essential goal of good looks and good health.

Part Six

Constructing a Brief Argumentative Research Paper

USING RESEARCH AND DOCUMENTATION TO SUPPORT YOUR ARGUMENT

A good argument uses compelling factual evidence and emotional appeals to convince readers to take a course of action, to modify their existing opinions, or to consider an alternate point of view. Finding that evidence—and ensuring its accuracy and relevance—is the work of *research*. Researching an issue provides you with the evidence and appeals you need to support your claim. The *research process* will also lead you to different points of view about your claim—either outright opposition, which you will need to address in your rebuttal, or alternate ideas about your issue that might lead you to revise your claim.

A *research paper* is an essay that draws on authoritative *sources* to support and illustrate its thesis. In the case of an *argumentative research paper*, your *claim* is your "thesis," and the sources you consult and *cite* (through quotation, paraphrase, or summary) provide the facts, evidence, and appeals you need to convince your reader of the validity of your claim. All research papers provide documentation of the sources of those facts, evidence, and appeals. *Documentation* is the proper attribution of ideas, facts, anecdotes, illustrations, and other material to the original source. Documentation allows your reader to consult the same sources and authors that you did, to retrace the steps of your argument and pursue your claim further. More important, proper documentation and citation protects you, as a writer, from charges of *plagiarism.*

THE RESEARCH PROCESS

The research process has five key stages:

- *Stage One.* Choosing an *issue:* browsing for ideas and limiting your issue.
- *Stage Two.* Establishing your claim: determining your audience and purpose.
- *Stage Three.* Gathering and organizing evidence: facts and expert opinions. Developing a working bibliography, assessing the credibility of sources, taking notes, and constructing an outline. Strategies for avoiding plagiarism.
- *Stage Four.* Writing the paper: drafting, revising, and editing your essay.
- *Stage Five.* Documenting your sources: preparing your final Works Cited page.

Stage One: Choosing an Issue

An *issue* for an argument is debatable and controversial. An issue is *debatable* when there are at least two perfectly reasonable but opposed opinions about it, making debate—that is, informed and civil conversation—possible. "A steady diet of junk food contributes to childhood obesity" is not debatable; no reasonable person would recommend raising a child on Ding-Dongs and Cheetos. However, "To combat childhood obesity, fast-food companies and manufacturers of junk food should be held legally liable for irresponsibly marketing to children" *is* debatable. Parents, pediatricians, lawyers, and, of course, fast-food corporations are all likely to have opposing viewpoints on that specific issue—and even when they are in basic agreement, they are likely to differ on points of strategy. This issue is also *controversial*, in that there is no one clear or obvious solution to the issue, and at least two opinions on the issue are in direct opposition to each other. Even were you to construct an argument supporting the viewpoint of a consumer group pursuing legal action against a snack-food company for marketing to children, you would have to acknowledge that other people—shareholders in that snack-food company, for example—have profound reasons for opposing your viewpoint. Controversial issues are relevant, ongoing, and sometimes insoluble. That's what makes them great topics for argumentation research papers. To determine if a subject that interests you is debatable and controversial, you'll want to begin browsing in the library and online.

Browsing

As you explore an area of general interest, you begin reading and consulting a wide range of sources of information about your general issue. As you browse, remember that you are also beginning to search for knowledgeable, reliable sources to cite in your research paper. Begin your search where you are most likely to find sources appropriate for an academic paper: in the library.

- The library's *reference section* provides both print and online sources of general information, such as encyclopedias, almanacs, maps, dictionaries, bibliographies, and directories. There are many specialized dictionaries and encyclopedias for specific subject areas. Although these general sources should not become primary sources for your argument research paper, they can give you a clearer perspective on your issue and help you begin to determine where the controversy lies.
- The *library catalog* at your campus library probably exists both on paper, in a card catalog, and online. Although it's certainly convenient to access the online catalog from your home or dorm computer, browsing the card catalog can lead to serendipitous discoveries. Card catalogs often contain annotations and corrections by generations of librarians and researchers; much like books on a shelf, they also suggest new ways of thinking about an issue simply through the happy accident of one card bumping up against another. Both a

card catalog and an online catalog will list information by author, title, subject, and key word; you can get a sense of how much material
is available on your issue and how much has been written recently.
If you haven't already taken advantage of your campus library's
orientation programs, now would be a good time to sign up.

- The *stacks* in your library can also provide you with serendipitous
browsing material. Books are organized in the stacks (the shelves)
by *call number;* books on the same or very similar subject are
shelved together. If you notice that many of the books you found in
the card or computer catalog share a similar call number, go to that
shelf in the library and browse through the books. Books with the
most recent publication dates will be your best primary sources of
information, but even older books can give you a sense of how a
debate or controversy came into being.

   Check the following key items as you browse:
   - Publication date. Recent is best.
   - Table of contents. Do any chapter titles sound similar to your
issue?
   - Index. Look up key words and concepts related to your issue.
Will there be enough material and information?
   - Bibliography (a good source for additional material).

- The reference section of your library also holds *periodical indexes,*
which are alphabetical lists of authors, titles, and subjects in most
major newspapers and magazines. These indexes are published annually and will direct you toward specific articles. Your library
probably also subscribes to online databases or CD-ROMs, which
provide access to a tremendous range of publications. You can
search these computerized indexes by subject area or key word.
Ask your reference librarian to direct you to periodical indexes and
databases for your specific topic area. If your library provides access to such powerful databases as ProQuest or LEXIS-NEXIS, it is
to your advantage to learn to use them.

- Although you may be tempted to begin your preliminary research
by typing a few key words into a search engine like Yahoo! or
Google, this is actually the *least* efficient way to begin gathering
ideas and material for an academic research paper. The search pa-
rameter *"obesity* and *children* and *fast food"* in a recent Google search
called up nearly 2,900 Web pages! Because the Web is open to anyone, the information posted there may not be reliable, well written,
correctly sourced, or even true. In general, a good guideline for
Web research is to pay attention to a site's creator, writer, and sponsor. If the site's sponsor is a well-reputed organization or media
outlet, the information you gather there is probably substantive
enough for your research purposes. For example, the Web site of

the Office of the Surgeon General at www.surgeongeneral.gov includes a great deal of information on childhood and adolescent obesity as well as the benefits of physical exercise and nutrition education. Its information is reliable, well sourced, and accurate. On the other hand, a commercial Web page that promises large legal settlements for people willing to participate in a class-action lawsuit against a fast-food chain might have some shock value, but it's not a good source for your academic research paper because it is likely to be biased. If you have questions about information that you find on a Web site, print out the first page and show it to the reference librarian or to your instructor.

Freewriting, Conversation, and Chatting Online

One good test of an issue's controversy is to begin sounding out your friends and your community for their opinions on the issue. Begin by establishing your own beliefs, opinions, and biases. Freewriting can tap in to what you already know—or think you know—about an issue, opening up areas for further exploration and questions for further pursuit. Begin a freewrite—on your computer or in your journal—by writing your issue on the top of the page. Then, for 20 minutes (set a timer!) write down everything your issue makes you think about. What do you already know? Who do you think would disagree with your opinion, and why? How did you come to have this opinion or belief in the first place?

If you and your friends instant-message (IM) each other, find a time when you can post your issue in the form of a question—for instance, "Should parents sue a fast-food restaurant if their child, who eats there frequently, is severely overweight?" In the casual, relatively anonymous world of instant messaging, you'll see a dialogue—or, if you're lucky, an argument!—beginning to take shape.

Many organization Web sites, especially those of academic research centers or government agencies, include a "contact us" button that allows you to e-mail specific questions or concerns to experts in the field. Establishing direct contact with someone involved with your issue can provide you with additional ideas for fieldwork, interviewing, and an immediate perspective.

If you choose to post a query about your issue to a newsgroup or usenet bulletin board, be sure to read the frequently asked questions (FAQ) section of the site to familiarize yourself with the site's etiquette. You should also first browse the site's archives to see if your issue has already been discussed.

Once you have determined the parameters of your issue, you can begin to establish a claim. A claim is your opinion about an issue, which you will defend using well-chosen sources and a carefully organized argument.

Moving from a General Topic to an Issue to a Claim

Broad Topic	General Issue	Specific Claim
Childhood obesity	Junk food marketed to kids	Manufacturers of junk food should not be allowed to market specifically to children.
Kids and physical education	School district cutbacks on physical education programs	Physical education should be mandatory for all school-age children to combat childhood obesity.

Stage Two: Establishing Your Claim

Once you have chosen an issue for your argumentation research paper, you narrow your focus by establishing a claim. (For more on a claim, see p. 5.) Because your claim is a statement that you will support and defend in your argument, you will need to determine the *audience* for your argument as well as your *purpose* in arguing. Are you writing to persuade a hostile audience to consider your viewpoint? Are you arguing for a general audience to move toward your point of view? Or are you arguing for a friendly audience to take a specific course of action? Consider these categories using the example of combating childhood obesity through lawsuits against fast-food and snack-food companies:

> HOSTILE AUDIENCE: Researching the topic, you quickly realize that fast-food and snack-food manufacturers tend to lose a great deal of revenue—and, perhaps, are forced to cut jobs—if lawsuits against them are successfully filed and won. Were you to write for this audience, your purpose would not be to argue that they should stop using cartoon characters and tie-ins to popular kids' movies to promote their food—you already know that your audience is firmly opposed to that idea. Instead, your claim might be that marketing directly to parents by promoting the place snack foods can have in an all-around balanced diet can offset any revenue that is lost when commercials no longer target children. Your research would lead you to sources that focus on what some companies might already be doing to create goodwill among consumers or to promote their products as part of an all-around healthy lifestyle.
>
> GENERAL AUDIENCE: Here you would assume that your audience has no strong opinion about suing fast-food companies for marketing directly to children and contributing to the rise in childhood obesity. Your purpose in arguing for a different ap-

proach to combating childhood obesity would be to educate a general audience and establish their interest and support in your proposed alternatives. In this case, your claim might be that instilling healthy habits, like regular exercise, in young people is more beneficial and cost-effective in the long run than lawsuits. Your research would lead you to sources that address the healthful benefits of exercise to children and adolescents, and how some communities and school districts have managed to maintain physical education programs despite budget cuts (by enlisting the corporate sponsorship of local fast-food franchises, for example).

FRIENDLY AUDIENCE: Perhaps your purpose in writing is to argue for a specific course of action for promoting physical activity in local schools. Your audience might be the readers of a community newspaper or the members of the local school board. Your claim might be that even though the school district has a limited budget, adding more gym classes or sponsoring after-school physical education programs will have long-term beneficial effects for the entire community. Your research would show that children who exercise have greater self-esteem and miss fewer days of school, and it might give examples of communities where local organizations and businesses pitched in to help fund physical education programs.

Remember that your claim, like the working thesis statement of any other research paper, is flexible. As you read more widely and share drafts of your research paper with other readers, you will find additional information and viewpoints that may change the way you phrase your claim.

Having established your claim, you now return to your preliminary browsings and freewritings and begin to gather and organize the evidence (facts, expert opinions, and appeals) that you will need to support that claim.

Stage Three: Gathering and Organizing Evidence

Develop a Working Bibliography

A working bibliography is a list of sources that you consult as you construct your argumentative research paper. It helps you to keep track of where you found information, and in the final stages of drafting your paper it will provide the foundation of your Works Cited page (see p. 503). Your working bibliography provides accurate and complete information about each source that you consult. Because you will rearrange your working bibliography as you find new sources (keeping it in alphabetical order, for example) most researchers keep the working bibliography either on their computer or on index cards. The advantage of index cards, of course, is their portability; you can jot down the information that you need as you browse in the library stacks. A working bibliography on your computer saves time in the later stages of drafting as you finalize your Works Cited page. Whichever method you prefer, you will need to include standard information for each source in your working bibliography:

Working Bibliography: Book Information
Include the following information for each book you consult:

- Author name (or names)
- Complete book title, underlined
- Place of publication
- Publisher's name
- Year of publication
- Call number or location in library

Periodical Information

- Author name (or names)
- Title of article, in quotation marks
- Title of periodical or magazine, underlined
- Volume or issue number
- Publication date
- Page numbers on which article appears
- Call number or location in library

Web Site Information

- Complete site URL
- Date of access

How Much Evidence Do I Need?

Keep your audience and purpose in mind as you do your research and assemble a working bibliography. The evidence (facts, expert opinions, and appeals) you gather should support your purpose in arguing and should provide the kind of information and background that your intended audience will need in order to follow your line of reasoning. Finally, remember that a solid argument includes consideration and rebuttal of opposing viewpoints. Your research should include opposing points of view as well as the necessary evidence on which those viewpoints are based.

Assessing the Credibility of Sources

Your argument will rest on two basic kinds of evidence: facts and expert opinions. *Facts* are generally accepted, irrefutable concepts, ideas, and observations. Paris is the capital of France; diet and exercise are fundamental to good health; seat belts help to save lives—these are all facts. You can assume that your audience will not need the additional support of an expert opinion when you make a statement of fact.

Other evidence you gather to support your claim will come from *expert opinions*. If you are arguing for mandatory physical education in your local school district, you might turn to the opinions of experts in nutrition, pediatrics, child psychology, and education. Your argument would cite the opinions and findings of these experts to support your own claim. But how can you tell if someone is, indeed, an expert? Especially in the age of the Internet, when anyone can publish anything online, it is important to evaluate the reliability and credibility of the sources of evidence.

Here are some general guidelines for assessing the credibility and expertise of the evidence you gather as you research your topic:

Credibility of Print Sources

- How current is the publication date of a book, periodical, or journal? In general, the most recent information is likely to be the most up-to-date and reliable.
- What are the author's own credentials? Turn to the book jacket, or see what information is available on the author in a periodical. Does the author hold an advanced academic degree in the subject? Has the author published other books and articles on this topic?
- What is the source of the publication? Is it a major news media source, a commercial publishing house, or an academic press? In general, the books and print sources you find in your college library have been carefully chosen by library staff. If you aren't sure about the publisher of a book, magazine, or periodical, ask a librarian or your instructor.

Credibility of Online Sources

- Who is the author of the site? Who is the site sponsor? Web sites that are published by major information and media providers, such as sites connected with newspapers, magazines, and television news networks, meet the same standard of reliability and credibility as their print and televised broadcasts.
- Does the site identify its sponsor? Often, a Web site can serve as a political platform or commercial advertisement for a corporation or special-interest group. Be aware of the possible biases in such sites; although they might provide some basic information, they might not give you the whole picture.
- How well designed and maintained is a site? Are links current, or "broken"? A site that does not "work" well might not have been updated for some time.

- Is there information on the site on how to contact the site's authors and sponsors?

Field Research

At this stage of your research, you may wish to bolster your library and online inquiries with research in the real world. *Interviews* with experts on your campus and in your community, *observations* you make of particular phenomena, and informal *surveys* of people can all lend additional perspective and unique insights to your paper. Your browsing of sources and any freewriting may have given you an idea of the kinds of questions you would like to ask an expert. For an interview, contact your subject well in advance of your assignment due date. Arrange a meeting (or phone interview), making your purpose for the conversation clear. Prepare your questions in advance. Although you will want to take notes during your interview, you might also find a small tape or digital recorder to be helpful.

For observations, do a little advance planning to find a place where you know you will observe phenomena that will support your claim. Be sure you can work undisturbed at this location. Take notes or use a digital camera or sound recorder—any technology that will help you gather evidence.

For a survey, keep questions brief and specific, and be sure that your survey sample includes a demographic appropriate to your topic. (For example, if your research paper is on preventing campus binge drinking, your demographic should include mostly people who attend college or live on or near a college campus.)

Taking Notes

Once you have gathered your sources, begin reading more closely for the specific information you will need to support your claim. Taking notes accurately and completely will make drafting your paper, as well as assembling your final Works Cited page, much easier. Index cards might be low-tech, but they are still the most efficient way to take and collect notes on your research. There are three strategies for taking notes: *summary, paraphrase,* and *direct quotation.* Use a new index card for each summary, paraphrase, or direct quotation.

- *Summary* is the best strategy for recording specific facts, summing up general perspectives, and reminding yourself later of what's included in a particular source.
- *Paraphrase* is the recasting of source material in your own words. Rather than copying out a long idea or opinion word for word, you summarize its main points in your own language. However, you still need to provide the correct citation information for a paraphrase; a paraphrase might be in your words, but its idea belongs to someone else, and that original author needs to be properly credited. Para-

phrase is a valuable note-taking strategy, but it's also one area where students and professional writers alike can accidentally plagiarize.

- *Direct quotations* are most useful when the exact words of an expert source or author are the best way of expressing that expert's opinion, idea, or observation. Direct quotations should be concise and clear. *Always* place quotation marks around *any* words you quote directly from another author or source.

Taking Notes on Your Topic

- At the top of each card, write a brief subtopic. Keep a working list of these subtopics, which will help you later as you draft a working outline for your paper.
- On each index card, write the author's name, the book or article title, and the page number. Be sure that you also have an entry for this source in your working bibliography.

The following note cards demonstrate each note-taking strategy:

A. **Sample note card: Summary**

Subtopic	*Benefits of physical activity for adolescents*
Author/title	*Williamson,* "Study: Crime, lack of PE, recreation programs lead U.S. adolescents to couch-potato status"
Page	(Web site)
Summary	Adolescents who do not have access to physical education programs at school do not develop healthy exercise or eating habits for later in life. The problem is especially severe in communities where adolescents lack access to safe environments.

B. **Sample note card: Paraphrase**

Subtopic	*Benefits of physical activity for adolescents*
Author/title	*Williamson:* "Study: Crime, lack of PE, recreation programs lead U.S. adolescents to couch-potato status"
Page	(Web site)
Paraphrase	Adolescents who live in high-crime areas are more likely to stay indoors watching television and playing video games than exercise outside. Adolescents from higher-income families tend to get more exercise.

C. **Sample note card: Direct quotation**

Subtopic	*Benefits of physical activity for adolescents*

Author/title   *Williamson:* "Study: Crime, lack of PE, recreation
                       programs lead U.S. adolescents to couch-potato
                       status"
Page   (Web site)
Direct quotation   "Adolescents from poor families fared ever
                       worse, since high crime rates, low income and
                       less education among mothers reduced vigor-
                       ous physical activity and increased TV, video,
                       and computer/video game use." Dr. Barry M.
                       Popkin

Organizing Your Notes and Developing a Working Outline

Review the basic structure of an argument. This structure—issue, claim,
evidence, and rebuttal—will help to determine the organization of your
working outline. Your instructor may have asked you to use a more specific argumentation strategy (induction/deduction, etc.) for your argumentative research paper; be sure that you understand the parameters of
your assignment as you begin assembling your outline. A working outline is not the fixed, final version of your argument. Instead, a working
outline specifies the order of your main points and the placement of evidence to support those points. As you begin to draft your paper and revisit your notes and sources, you will make some changes in the ordering
of your main points and evidence.

Organizing Your Notes

- Print out your list of subtopics. Organize your index cards according to those subtopics. Really large piles of cards might need to be
  further subdivided into more specific topics; piles of only one or
  two cards might need to be absorbed into a related subtopic.
- Be sure that all of your index cards include source information
  and that all of those sources are included in your working
  bibliography.
- Set aside any index cards that duplicate information, even if
  they are from different source material. However, do not throw
  away any index cards yet.
- Within each subtopic, organize your index cards from most important to least important idea, fact, or opinion.

Use the index cards to assemble a working outline. Your instructor may
have given you a specific outline structure to follow. If not, a general
working outline could look like this:

I. INTRODUCTION. Describe your issue. What is specifically debatable
   and controversial about the issue?

II. CLAIM. A concise and clear statement of your opinion or position on the issue.
   A. FIRST MAIN POINT THAT SUPPORTS YOUR CLAIM
      1. Evidence (fact or expert opinion)
      2. Another piece of evidence
      3. Still more evidence
   B. SECOND MAIN POINT THAT SUPPORTS YOUR CLAIM
      1. Evidence
      2. Another piece of evidence
      3. Still more evidence
   C. OPPOSING POINT OF VIEW
      1. Summary of viewpoint opposed to your claim
         a. Evidence opposition would cite to support their viewpoint
         b. Additional evidence from opposing side
   D. REBUTTAL
      1. Evidence that refutes, disproves, or calls into question your opposition's viewpoint
   E. CONCLUSION

Stage Four: Writing the Paper

As you begin to synthesize your evidence into a coherent argument, remember that your final essay is more than just a collection of data. In an argumentative research paper, you are taking a clear stand on an issue and supporting that stand with well-chosen evidence. The flow between your ideas and the support provided by other writers and experts should be seamless; the connections between each separate piece of evidence and your overall claim should be absolutely clear.

Drafting

Perhaps the most difficult way to begin drafting a paper is to sit in front of a blank computer screen. Instead, copy your outline into a new computer file. Then, with your index cards handy, begin filling in your outline. Refer to your index cards for summary, paraphrase, and direct quotations as necessary, being sure to include citation information (or, at this early stage, the number of the index card so you can find it later).

As you write, remember that your research paper is not a simple repetition or listing of the data you have accumulated. Keep your claim in mind, and in your own words explain how each piece of evidence supports that claim. Your own ideas, insights, and opinions are key to your argumentative research paper; at the same time, keep your audience and purpose in mind. Is your diction appropriate to your essay's audience? Will the organization of your evidence achieve your purpose?

Your outline is flexible, as is the arrangement of your evidence. As you draft, you might rearrange or even set aside some of your index cards. You might rephrase your claim as you begin to see connections between different pieces of evidence. And you might discover that there are gaps in your evidence, questions that arise as you become more engaged with your subject. Begin a separate document where you jot down these questions. If the answers to those questions aren't in the sources you have already consulted, bring your questions back to the library and do some additional research.

Incorporating Sources

Your skill at interweaving the ideas and direct quotations of other sources with your own opinions will determine the success of your argument. Moving from your own voice to that of a summarized, paraphrased, or directly quoted author or source needs to be clear enough so that your reader can distinguish between "voices," between your point and the evidence you are citing to support that point. At the same time, you want those transitions to be graceful enough that your reader has a consistent sense of just whose argument this is.

Moving from your own voice to information from another source is most easily accomplished by using a transition such as the following:

- Overweight adolescent Jazlyn Bradley *confesses* that . . .
- A McDonald's spokesman *acknowledges* that . . .
- Dr. Barry Popkin *describes the issue* as . . .
- Lawyer John Banzhaf III *argues* that . . .
- John Doyle, cofounder of the Center for Consumer Freedom, *suggests* a comparison between . . .
- In the following examples, the Office of the Surgeon General *notes* that . . .

Revising and Polishing

The drafting process organized your argument, arranging appropriate evidence to support each of your points while acknowledging and rebutting your opposition. Your instructor may ask you to share your "rough draft," during a peer review session in class; you should also consider making an appointment with your instructor or with your campus writing center to review your rough draft. As you review your rough draft, ask yourself (and ask peer reviewers to consider): Is my evidence convincing? Have I provided enough evidence to support my claim? Have I avoided logical fallacies (see p. 56)? What was my original purpose for this argument, and will my audience respond in the way I intended? Is it clear where I have incorporated the words and ideas of outside sources, and do I have enough information to correctly document those sources?

Polishing the Final Manuscript

- Does my title accurately describe the content and direction of my argument?
- Do I state my claim clearly in the first paragraph?
- Does each body paragraph include a key piece of evidence to support my claim? Is the link between the evidence and my claim logical?
- Do I incorporate summaries, paraphrases, and quotations accurately and gracefully?
- Have I cross-referenced all of my in-text citations with my Works Cited page?
- Have I fairly and truthfully represented opposing viewpoints?
- Is my diction appropriate for my audience and purpose? Is my grammar correct? Have I read through carefully, without depending on a spell-checking program, to catch any accidental errors?

Before you hand in your paper, check the original assignment one last time to be sure that your paper is formatted and presented exactly as your instructor requested.

Stage Five: Documenting Sources

When you make your research public—either by posting it to a Web site, sharing it with a student group, or handing it in to your instructor—you become part of a larger academic conversation. The ongoing creativity and integrity of that conversation depends on each participant's acknowledgement of the work that has come before. The documentation of sources in your paper grants to everyone in your audience the courtesy of being able to follow up on your sources for themselves, should they be intrigued by your argument and wish to learn more. You also extend professional courtesy to those whose ideas, research, and observations support your own claim when you correctly cite them in your paper and on your Works Cited page.

Plagiarism and Academic Honesty

Careful and accurate paraphrase, summary, and quotation, along with the proper documentation of these citations, is the best defense you have against charges of *plagiarism*. In recent years, charges of plagiarism have embarrassed—and led to the demotion or dismissal—of professionals in leading positions in journalism and the academy. Deliberate plagiarism is the theft of another writer's work; it is no more defensible than stealing another's physical property. The Internet makes it extraordinarily easy to reach around the globe for an enormous range of source material. But that same Internet allows a diligent editor—or a savvy instructor—to easily track and catch a plagiarist in the act. You may have already been apprised of your college's policy toward deliberate plagiarism; penalties range from failing the course to expulsion from school. *Don't do it.*

Materials That Require Documentation

- Anything you wrote on an index card: summaries, paraphrases, and quotations.
- Any illustration you incorporate into your paper (cartoons, photographs, charts, etc.).
- Any information that is not common factual knowledge (see p. 494).
- Any interesting expression or turn of phrase (from a song lyric, a poem, a character in a movie, etc.).
- Any line of reasoning or opinion; especially in an argumentative paper, you must distinguish between your own argument and the ways in which other writers have connected similar evidence to similar claims.

Some instances of plagiarism are perfectly obvious: buying a paper from an online service, handing in something that a friend wrote for a similar course, handing in a paper that you yourself already wrote and handed in for another course. But as you learn to incorporate the ideas of other writers and researchers into your own argument, you will have honest questions about where the line between borrowing and plagiarism falls. Be on the safe side. Any time you have a question about plagiarism, ask your instructor or take your draft to your campus writing center.

There are two ways of indicating the source of material in your paper: *in-text citations,* where you indicate the author and/or source of an idea or fact right as you present it in your essay, and the *Works Cited list,* your final bibliography.

In-Text Citations

Using in-text citations is one of the smoothest ways of making a transition from your own words and ideas to those of an outside source. An in-text citation ("in" the "text" of your paper, as opposed to the Works Cited list) indicates to your reader that you are introducing evidence to support your claim.

In-Text Citations

- Provide enough information so that a reader can easily find the source on your Works Cited page.
- In MLA style, provide the page number—and the author's name, unless you already clearly state that in your text—in

parentheses placed where the source material appears in your text.

- Double-check the sentence in which you incorporate source material and the citation information to be sure it reads smoothly and correctly.

The following examples demonstrate in-text citations in MLA style.

- Eric Schlosser notes that the "American School Food Service Association estimates that about 30 percent of the public high schools in the United States offer branded fast food" (56). *The author's name is mentioned within the body of the text, so his last name does not need to reappear in the parentheses with the page number.*
- Although the lawsuit was dismissed in 2003, the fast food industry—and other American food companies, such as Kraft—are beginning to take the threat of legal action seriously (Barboza 3:1). *The in-text citation gives both the author's last name and the page number where this information is found—in this case, the section and page of a newspaper.*

Works Cited List

If you have been keeping a working bibliography on your computer, you can use that same document to build your final Works Cited page. Have all of your index cards handy, and be sure to cross-reference each entry on your Works Cited page with a reference in your paper.

You do not need to include sources on your Works Cited page that you looked at in your preliminary browsing or that appear on an index card you made during your note taking if you do not use those sources in the final draft of your paper.

- Center the words "Works Cited" on top of a new page. Do not underline or italicize these words.
- Double-space every line. Indent everything in each entry (after the first line) by one stroke of the Tab key (about five spaces).
- Paginate your Works Cited page continuously with your entire research paper.
- List your sources alphabetically by author last name. If the source has no named author, list it alphabetically according to the title of the work (ignoring the words *the, an,* or *a*).
- If you use more than one work by the same author, list them alphabetically by title under the first entry for the author's name.
- Book, newspaper, magazine, and journal titles are always underlined; short story and article titles always appear in quotation marks (not underlined).

Book by One Author

Woodward, Christopher. *In Ruins.* New York: Pantheon Books, 2001.

Several Books by One Author

Tannen, Deborah. *That's Not What I Meant! How Conversational Style Makes or Breaks Your Relations with Others.* New York: Morrow, 1986.
———. *The Argument Culture: Moving from Debate to Dialogue.* New York: Random House, 1998.

Book with Two or Three Authors or Editors

List the names of the authors in the order in which they appear on the book's cover or title page. Begin with the last name of the first author; list the subsequent authors by first and last name.

Bloom, Lynn Z., Donald A. Daiker, and Edward M. White, eds. *Composition in the Twenty-First Century: Crisis and Change.* Carbondale and Edwardsville: Southern Illinois University Press, 1996.

Work with More Than Three Authors or Editors

Use the names of all the authors, or use just the first author listed on the title page followed by the abbreviation *et al.*

Anderson, Lorraine, et al. *Literature and the Environment: A Reader on Nature and Culture.* New York: Longman, 1999.

Work with Group or Organization as Author

Reader's Digest. *Fix-It-Yourself Manual.* Pleasantville: Reader's Digest, 1977.

Work Without an Author

List the work alphabetically according to the first word (other than *a, an,* or *the*) of its title.

Illustrated Atlas of the World. Chicago: Rand McNally, 1995.

Work in a Collection of Pieces All by the Same Author

Dalrymple, Theodore. "Uncouth Chic." *Life at the Bottom: The Worldview That Makes the Underclass.* Chicago: Ivan R. Dee, 2001.

Work in an Anthology

Auerbach, Erich. "Odysseus' Scar." *20th Century Literary Criticism: A Reader.* Ed. David Lodge. London: Longman, 1972.

Work Translated from Another Language

Sebald, W. G. *Austerlitz.* Trans. Anthea Bell. New York: Random House, 2001.

New Edition of an Older Book

Beerbohm, Max. *The Illustrated Zuleika Dobson.* 1911. New Haven and London: Yale University Press, 1985.

Entry from a Reference Volume

Specialized reference books are treated like other books (beginning with the author's last name). Familiar, basic references like dictionaries and encyclopedias need only the edition and date. (If the reference work is organized alphabetically, no page numbers are needed.)

Burchfield, Robert W. "Functional Literacy." *The Oxford Companion to the English Language.* Ed. Tom McArthur. Oxford and New York: Oxford University Press, 1992.

Fox, Luke. *Encylopedia Americana: International Edition.* 1996 ed.

Article in a Weekly or Biweekly Periodical

Dougherty, Carter. "Bunia Dispatch: Talk Is Cheap." *The New Republic* 21 July 2003: 10-11.

Article in a Monthly or Bimonthly Periodical

Hylton, Wil S. "Sick on the Inside: Correctional HMOs and the Coming Prison Plague." *Harper's* August 2003: 43–54.

Article in a Daily Newspaper

Barboza, David. "If You Pitch It, They Will Eat: Barrage of Food Ads Takes Aim at Young Children." *The New York Times* 3 August 2003, sec. 3:1+.

Article with No Author

"Iguanas Cruise the Caribbean." *New Scientist* 10 Oct. 1998: 25.

Editorial in a Newspaper or Periodical

Signed, in a magazine:

Carter, Graydon. "The Phony War." *Vanity Fair* August 2003: 46.

Unsigned, in a newspaper:

"An Important Human Rights Tool." *New York Times* 8 August 2003, sec. A: 16.

Letter to the Editor of a Newspaper or Periodical

Bronstone, Adam. Letter. *Vanity Fair* August 2003: 56.

Article in a Journal with Pagination Continuing Through Each Volume

Root, Robert L., Jr. "Naming Nonfiction (a Polyptych)." *College English* 65 (2003): 242–256.

Article in a Journal with Pagination Continuing Only through Each Issue

Koqen, Myra. "The Conventions of Expository Writing." *Journal of Basic Writing.* 5.1 (1986): 24–37.

Film, Video, DVD

Testament of Orpheus. Dir. Jean Cocteau. Videocassette. Janus Films, 1960.

Radio or Television Program

Radio program:

"Is Hip-Hop Today's Civil Rights Movement?" Narr. Scott Simon. *Weekend Edition Saturday.* Natl. Public Radio. WNYC, New York. 1 March 2003.

Television:

"The Post-It Always Rings Twice." *Sex and the City.* Dir. Alan Taylor. HBO. 1 August 2003.

CD or Other Recording

For an entire album:

Kamakawiwo'ole, Israel. *n Dis Life.* Big Boy Record Company, 1996.

To cite a specific song, place the title in quotation marks.

Evora, Cesaria. "Vida tem um so vida." *The Very Best of Cesaria Evora.* BMG, 2002.

Advertisement

Give the product name, followed by the word *Advertisement* and then the place and date where you saw the ad (for a television program) or the publication date (for an ad in a newspaper or magazine).

McDonald's Dollar Menu. Advertisement. NBC. 21 April 2003.

Personal Interview

Sanderson, Profesor Eleanor. Telephone interview. 13 Dec. 2003.

Online Book, Article, or Other Source

Darwin, Charles. *The Origin of Species.* New York: P. F. Collier & Son Company, 1909-14. *Bartleby.com: Great Books Online.* Ed. Steven van Leeuwen. 2001. 3 July 2003 <http://bartleby .com/11/>.

Entire Internet Site

Arts and Literature Daily. Ed. Denis Dutton. 2003. Chronicle of Higher Education. 30 July 2003 <http://aldaily.com>.

Magazine Article Available Online

When the URLs for specific articles are too long, or if a site requires payment or registration to see an article, abbreviate the URL to give just enough information so that someone could locate the article in a free archive. After the date of original print publication, include the date that you accessed the electronic version, followed by the URL.

Oppenheimer, Todd. "The Computer Delusion." *Atlantic Online* July 1997. 13 July 2003 <http://www.theatlantic.com/issues/ 97jul/computer.htm>.

Newspaper Article Available Online

Santora, Marc. "Teenagers' Suit Says McDonald's Made Them Obese." *The New York Times* 21 November 2002. 11 May 2004 <http://www.nytimes.com/2002/11/21/region>.

Article from an Electronic Journal

Schwarzer, David, Alexia Hayood, and Charla Lorenzen. "Fostering Multiliteracy in a Linguistically Diverse Classroom." *Language Arts* 80:6 (July 2003): 453-462. 8 August 2003 <http:// www.ncte.org/pdfs/subscribers-only/la/0806-july03/LA0806 Fostering.pdf>.

Electronic Posting to a Group

A posting to a discussion group hosted by a Web site:

M. E. Cowan. Online posting. 30 October 2001. "News Media 'Discover' Women of Afghanistan." 8 August 2003 <http://tabletalk .salon.com/webx? 14@239.0bghaUqZFcQ.5@.eec6c38/0>.

A posting to an academic listserv:

Cook, Janice. "Re: What New Day Is Dawning?" 19 June 1997. Online posting. Alliance for Computers and writing listserv. 4 Feb 1998 <acw-1@ttacs6.Hu.edu>.

A posting to a Usenet group:

IrishMom. "Re: Spain Will Send Troops to Aid U.S." Online posting. 2 Nov. 2001. <Ireland_list-og@email.rutgers.edu>.

SAMPLE STUDENT RESEARCH PAPER

Rivera 1

Nelson Rivera

Professor Odomsky

Expository Writing 2

May 26, 2004

Combating Childhood Obesity:

Why Can't Johnny Touch His Toes?

1   The headlines at first seemed like a joke from a late-night talk show: overweight people were filing lawsuits against fast-food restaurants, claiming that the restaurants conspired to hide information about the dangers of eating fast food and contributed to their obesity and other health problems. In New York City in 2002, two teenage girls filed suit against McDonald's. One of the girls, 19-year-old Jazlyn Bradley, weighed 270 pounds; 14-year-old Ashley Pelman weighed 170 pounds (Santora). Although the lawsuit was dismissed in 2003, the fast-food industry—and other American food companies, such as Kraft—are beginning to take the threat of legal action seriously (Barboza 3:1). But unlike successful class-action lawsuits against tobacco companies, where a scientifically proven link between the product and catastrophic health consequences as well as proven coverups by the tobacco companies themselves have given a sound basis for legal action, lawsuits against fast-food companies will do nothing to address the problem of childhood obesity. To productively, creatively, and

The title of Nelson's paper clearly indicates his broad topic: childhood obesity. The last sentence of the paragraph establishes Nelson's claim.

Rivera 2

compassionately help overweight children develop lifelong healthy habits, it is far more beneficial for school systems, parents, and private organizations to promote physical fitness and sports for young people.

2   There is no doubt that American children and adolescents are getting heavier every year. According to the Surgeon General's office, 14 percent of adolescents (aged 12 to 19) in the United States were overweight in 1999—a percentage that has tripled since the 1970s (surgeongeneral.gov). In addition, fewer kids have access to physical education programs in financially strapped school districts, and at home kids are more likely to spend time in front of the computer or television than playing outside. A recent study at the University of North Carolina at Chapel Hill showed that only 21.3 percent of adolescents had at least one day of physical education during the school week (Williamson). Dr. Barry M. Popkin, professor of nutrition and project principal investigator, took note of an even more disturbing finding. "Adolescents from poor families fared even worse, since high crime rates, low income and less education among mothers reduced vigorous physical activity and increased TV, video and computer/video game use," he reported (Williamson).

3   According to the Surgeon General's office, the average American child should get at least 60 minutes of "moderate

Nelson cites established authorities to back up his claim that childhood obesity is on the rise. The Surgeon General of the United States and a medical study conducted by a university are credible sources.

In this transitional paragraph, Nelson moves from supporting his broad topic (American children are becoming obese) to his specific claim (regular physical exercise is the best way to combat childhood obesity).

Rivera 3

physical activity most days of the week." The Surgeon
General's office goes on to note that even higher amounts of
exercise are necessary for children who need to lose weight,
while acknowledging that for many families access to a "safe
environment" for physical activity is an issue
(surgeongeneral.gov).

4   But an hour of safe, supervised physical activity might
not have been possible for the two New York girls who filed
suit against McDonald's. According to an investigation by
The New York Times in 1999, only 12 percent of New York
City high school students participated in team sports—
among the lowest rates of participation in American cities. In
addition, more than half of 1,500 high school students
randomly tested in the New York City public schools showed
elevated risk factors for heart disease, including obesity and
lack of physical activity (Take the Field; Johnson).

5   It's ironic that at the same time Jazlyn Bradley and Ashley
Pelman were claiming that McDonald's made them fat, two of
the greatest African-American female athletes ever signed
an endorsement deal with McDonald's. Tennis superstars
Venus and Serena Williams began appearing in a series of
commercials promoting McDonald's new "Dollar Menu." That
menu includes not only fries and ice cream sundaes, but also
side salads and "snack size Fruit 'n' Yogurt," which are
certainly healthy choices. The message would seem to be

Nelson did
some more
research to
find out more
about the
lives of his
first main
illustration,
the two girls
from New
York who
tried to sue
McDonald's.

Nelson's
observations
of the mass
media—even
commercials
—gives him
an interesting
perspective
on his topic.
Notice how
he uses
quotations
from a
newspaper
interview
with one of
the teenage
girls to prove
his own point.

Rivera 4

that for teenagers who spend their recreation time exercising—as opposed to playing video games, watching TV, or instant-messaging each other—McDonald's can be a reasonable choice for snacks and meals. Jazlyn Bradley, however, wasn't going for the salads and yogurt when she went to McDonald's. By her own admission, "a McMuffin in the morning and the Big Mac meal with an apple pie in the evening was standard operating procedure" (Santora). Apparently no one in Jazlyn's home, nor any health teacher in her school, advised her about making choices between Big Macs and "Fruit 'n' Yogurt."

Here, Nelson considers an opposing viewpoint: that school systems and private citizens can fight childhood obesity through lawsuits.

6   Some school systems are combating student obesity, not by increasing physical education opportunities but by pursuing lawsuits against food-industry giants seeking access to student consumers. The Seattle School Board recently took up the issue of Coca-Cola's five-year contract with the school system, which allowed Coke products to be sold on school grounds. The contract brought in about $400,000 to the school system annually (Bach). Pursuing the lawsuit was a Washington, D.C., lawyer named John Banzhaf III, who had successfully sued tobacco companies and was now taking up obesity issues. He argued that access to Coca-Cola in the Seattle schools made kids fat. Not all school board members agreed. "Obesity and health problems in America have so many different factors, and we are not going to save

Rivera 5

the world by banning Coke," said one board member. "We need to look at nutrition. Our school lunches are much more to blame" (Bach). The issue of physical education opportunities for Seattle schoolchildren was not part of the debate. Nor was the issue of health education. John Doyle, cofounder of the Center for Consumer Freedom, notes that "you make choices in the food you want to purchase, and if you make the wrong choices relentlessly and perpetually, you're going to have health consequences" (Fox). Indeed, in the pursuit of legal action against major food corporations, immediate benefits to students—such as nutrition education and sports opportunities—seem to have been left out of the conversation altogether.

7   While some school systems caught up in budget crunches and tempted to solve problems through lawsuits, others collaborate with fast-food corporations to bring in much-needed revenues. Eric Schlosser notes that the "American School Food Service Association estimates that about 30 percent of the public high schools in the United States offer branded fast food" (56). It's not clear if the revenues provided by fast-food sales on school grounds actually help provide students with "extras"—such as sports programs, music and arts opportunities, and so forth—or if it's just another way to contract out food service that the schools must provide in any case.

Nelson goes on to illustrate that fast-food companies do indeed have an influence on the lives of American schoolchildren, even in the students' own classrooms.

Rivera 6

8   To address these issues, some private individuals and foundations are exploring other ways to give kids opportunities to exercise safely and learn lifelong healthy habits. In New York, the group Take the Field has been renovating and rebuilding abandoned public school gym facilities and playing fields through private donations. As Dr. Penny Gordon-Larsen, an author of the UNC study, pointed out, "School is really the perfect place to start" introducing healthy habits such as exercise. "If we can get schools to provide safe and accessible places for kids to be active, then there's a huge potential to reach a great number of kids. If the schools can't or won't do that, then community recreation centers can make a big difference also."

9   Kids and teenagers are always going to prefer potato chips to carrot sticks and would rather have pizza than salad for dinner. Rather than wasting time and resources in high-profile lawsuits against major food companies, it is demonstrably more productive in the long run to give children opportunities to develop lifelong healthy habits, such as getting enough exercise and participating in team sports. If the Seattle School Board thought about it, that $400,000 annual revenue from its Coca-Cola contract could go toward hiring new gym teachers, developing new sports teams, and eventually producing more Williams sisters rather than a generation of Jazlyns and Ashleys.

After having discussed the opposition, Nelson begins his rebuttal with the example of a private group that is working to bring physical education and sports to public school-children.

Nelson's conclusion sums up his main points and clearly states why his claim (that physical education, rather than lawsuits, are the best way to combat childhood obesity) should be accepted.

Rivera 7

Works Cited

Bach, Deborah. "Legal Threat Bubbling Beneath School Soda
    Contract." Seattle Post-Intelligencer Reporter 17 July
    2003. 12 May 2004 <http://seattlepi.nwsource.com>.

Barboza, David. "If You Pitch It, They Will Eat: Barrage of Food
    Ads Takes Aim at Young Children." The New York Times
    3 August 2003, sec. 3:1+.

Fox News Channel. "Fat Teens Sue McDonald's."
    21 September 2002. 10 May 2004
    <http://www.foxnews.com>.

Johnson, Kirk. "Dropping the Ball: The Decline of School
    Sports; Finding the Middle Ground for Couch Potato and
    Athlete." The New York Times 15 January 1999. 10 May
    2004 <http://query.nytimes.com/search/>.

McDonald's USA. "Tennis Superstars Venus Williams and
    Serena Williams Score with Introduction of McDonald's
    National Dollar Menu." Press release. 10 May 2004
    <http://www.mcdonalds.com/countries/usa/whats
    new/pressrelease/2002/10312002/>.

Office of the Surgeon General. "The Surgeon General's Call
    to Action to Prevent and Decrease Overweight and
    Obesity." 12 May 2004
    <http://www.surgeongeneral.gov/topics/obesity/
    calltoaction/fact_adolescents.htm>.

Rivera 8

Santora, Marc. "Teenagers' Suit Says McDonald's Made Them

Obese." The New York Times 21 November 2002.

11 May 2004

<http://www.nytimes.com/2002/11/21/nyregion>.

Schlosser, Eric. Fast Food Nation: The Dark Side of the All-

American Meal. New York: Perennial/HarperCollins, 2002.

Take the Field. "About Us." 10 May 2004

<http://takethefield.org/aboutus.php>.

Williamson, David. "Study: Crime, Lack of PE, Recreation

Programs Lead U.S. Adolescents to Couch-Potato

Lifestyles." University of North Carolina-Chapel

Hill News Services. 15 May 2004

<http://www.unc.edu/news/>.

Credits

Text Credits

Albacete, Lorenzo. "The Struggle with Celibacy." *The New York Times Magazine* 31 March 2002.

Barry, Dave. "Error, Error, Error." *Miami Herald* 1991. Copyright © 1991 Knight Ridder Tribune.

Berry, Wendell. "In Distrust of Movements." *Citizenship Papers.* Shoemaker & Hoard, Publishers, 2003.

Botstein, Leon. "Curtailing High School: A Radical Proposal." *The Presidency* winter, 2002.

Brady, Judy. "I Want a Wife." *Ms.* December 1971.

Brooks, David. "The Triumph of Hope Over Self-Interest." *The New York Times* 12 January 2003, op-ed edition.

Brown, Andrew. "The Limits of Freedom." *New Statesman* 2 December 1999.

Brownlee, Shannon. "We're Fatter But Not Smarter." *The Washington Post National Weekly Edition* 6 January 2003.

Brophy, Beth. "Saturday Night and You're All Alone? Maybe You Need a Cyberdate." *U.S. News & World Report* 17 February 1997.

Carson, Rachel. "The Obligation to Endure" *Silent Spring* Houghton Mifflin Company, 1962.

Carter, Jimmy. "A World Criminal Court is Urgently Needed." *Los Angeles Times* 10 December 1996.

Cast-A-Way Jokes logo from http://www.cast.co.za/

Chavez, Linda. "Multiculturalism Is Driving Us Apart." *USA Today Magazine* May 1996.

Cohen, Adam. "The McNugget of Truth in Lawsuits Against Fast Food Restaurants." *The New York Times* 3 February 2003.

CyberDating.net homepage, http://www.cyberdating.net/

Didion, Joan. "Marrying Absurd" in *Slouching Towards Bethlehem* Farrar, Straus and Giroux, LLC., 1966, 1968, 1996.

Easterbrook, Gregg. "Watch and Learn." *The New Republic* 17 May 1999.

Ehrenreich, Barbara. "From Stone Age to Phone Age." *The Progressive* September 1999.

Ehrenreich, Barbara. "Ice T: The Issue Is Creative Freedom." *Time* 20 July 1992.

Friedman, Thomas. "Globalization, Alive and Well." *The New York Times* 22 September 2002, op ed edition.

Gans, Herbert J. "Fitting the Poor Into the Economy." *Technology Review* October 1995.

Gelernter, David. "What Do Murderers Deserve?" *Commentary* April 1998.

Glazer, Nathan. "In Defense of Preference." *The New Republic* 6 April 1998.

Goodall, Jane. "A Question of Ethics." *Newsweek International* 7 May 2001.

Goodman, Ellen. "The Culture of Thin Bites Fiji." *Boston Globe* 27 May 1999.

Goodman, Ellen. "Religion in Textbooks." *The Washington Post* 1986.

Herbert, Bob. "No Margin for Error." *The New York Times* 20 June 2002.

Hochswender, Woody. "Did My Car Join Al Qaeda?" *The New York Times* 16 February 2003, op ed edition.

Ingrassia, Michelle. "The Body of the Beholder." *Newsweek* 24 April 1995.

Irving, John. "Wrestling with Title IX." *The New York Times* 28 January 2003, op-ed edition.

Jefferson, Thomas. "The Declaration of Independence." 1776.

Jones, Greg. "Rap Fans Desire a More Positive Product." *The Daily Cougar* University Wire, 29 August 2002.

Kaminer, Wendy. "Toxic Media." *The American Prospect* 11. 22 (2000).

Kantrowitz, Barbara. "Unmarried, With Children." *Newsweek* 28 May 2001.

King, Billie Jean. "For All the Good Things It Has Done, Title IX Is Still Plagued by Myths." *The New York Times* 23 June 2002.

King, Martin Luther, Jr., "I Have a Dream." 1963.

Klinkenborg, Verlyn. "The Rural Life: Out of the Wild." *The New York Times* 29 May 2002.

Kohn, Alfie. "The Dangerous Myth of Grade Inflation." *The Chronicle of Higher Education* 8 November 2002. For more information, please see http://www.alfiekohn.org/

Kristof, Nicholas. "Love and Race." *The New York Times* 6 December 2002, op-ed edition.

Krugman, Paul. "A Failed Mission." *The New York Times* 4 February 2003, op-ed edition.

Levine, Judith. "I Surf, Therefore I Am." *Salon.com* 29 July 1997.

Lopez, Barry. "Apologia" *About This Life*. Sterling Lord Literistic, Inc., 1998.

Mackeen, Dawn. "Waifs on the Web." *Teen People* 1 April 2002.

Marable, Manning. "An Idea Whose Time Has Come." *Newsweek* 27 August 2001.

McCabe, Jane. "Is a Lab Rat's Fate More Poignant Than a Child's?" *Newsweek* 26 December 1988.

Media Watch homepage and banner, http://www.mediawatch.com/

Ng, Fae Yyenne. "False Gold." *The New Republic* 19–26 July 1993.

Oates, Joyce Carol. "Words Fail, Memory Blurs, Life Wins." *The New York Times* 31 December 2001, op-ed edition.

Orwell, George. "A Hanging." *Shooting an Elephant and Other Essays* Harcourt, Inc., 1979.

Oz, Amos. "Two Stubborn Men, and Many Dead." *The New York Times* 12 March 2002, op-ed edition.

Patchet, Ann. "Kissing Cousins." *The New York Times Magazine* 28 April 2002.

Plato. (c. 427-347 B.C.), "The Allegory of the Cave."

Quindlen, Anna. "One Nation, Indivisible? Wanna Bet?" *Newsweek* 15 July 2002.

Raspberry, William. "Their Cheating Hearts." *The Washington Post* 22 November 1999.

Rauch, Jonathan. "The Fat Tax: A Modest Proposal." *The Atlantic Monthly* December 2002.

Rauch, Jonathan. "Let It Be." *The Atlantic Monthly* May 2002.

Rifkin, Jeremy. "Vanishing Jobs." *Mother Jones* September/October 1995.

Rodriguez, Richard. "Trouble Is, Native-Born Just Don't Measure Up." *The National Catholic Reporter* 1994.

Rosen, Jeffrey. "Bad Luck: Why Americans Exaggerate the Terrorist Threat." *The New Republic* 5 November 2001.

Sen, Amartya. "A World Not Neatly Divided." *The New York Times* 23 November 2001, op-ed edition.

Smiley, Jane. "The Case Against Chores." *Harper's Magazine* June 1995.

Springen, Karen. "Why We Tuned Out." *Newsweek* 11 November 2002.

Stalker, Douglas. "How to Duck Out of Teaching." *The Chronicle of Higher Education* 26 April 2002.

Sullivan, Andrew. "Let Gays Marry." *Newsweek* 3 June 1996.

Swift, Jonathan. "A Modest Proposal." 1729.

Takaki, Ronald. "The Harmful Myth of Asian Superiority." *The New York Times* 16 June 1990, op-ed edition.

Tannen, Deborah. "And Rarely the Twain Shall Meet." *Talking from 9 to 5*.

Traub, James. "All Go Down Together." *The New York Times Magazine* 2 March 2003.

Walljasper, Jay. "The Joy of Eating." *Utne Reader* May/June 2002.

WeightLoss Guide Web page, http://www.weightlossguide.com/

Williams, Terry Tempest. *Refuge: An Unnatural History of Family and Place* Random House, Inc., 1991.

Woolf, Virginia. "Professions for Women" *The Death of the Moth and Other Essays* Harcourt, Inc., 1942, 1970.

Yaqub, Reshma Memon. "You People Did This." *Rolling Stone* 25 October 2002.

Zinczenko, David. "Don't Blame the Eater." *The New York Times* 23 November 2002, op-ed edition.

Zuckerman, Mortimer B. "Our Rainbow Underclass." *U.S. News & World Report* 23 December 2002.

Photo Credits

Index